# Practical Quantitative Finance with R

Solving Real-World Problems with R
for Quant Analysts and Individual Traders

# Practical Quantitative Finance with R

Solving Real-World Problems with R
for Quant Analysts and Individual Traders

*Jack Xu, PhD*

**UniCAD Publishing**

**Practical Quantitative Finance with R**


Printed and bound in the United States of America 9 8 7 6 5 4 3 2 1UC

Editor: Tyler Xu



Contact:
jxu@dxudotnet.com
Visit us on the website: www.drxudotnet.com

Published by UniCAD Publishing.
New York, USA
ISBN-13: 978-0-9793725-7-5
ISBN-10: 0-9793725-7-7

**Publisher's Cataloging-in-Publication Data**

Xu, Jack
Practical Quantitative Finance with R – Solving Real-World Problems with R for Quant Analysts and Individual Traders/ Jack Xu
– 1st ed.
p.cm.
ISBN 978-0-9793725-7-5

1. R Programming. 2. Finance. 3. Quant. 4. Time Series. 5. Quant Developer. 6. Quant Analyst. 7. Stock Trading. 8. Algorithmic Trading. 9. Data Analysis. 10. Pricing Engines. 11. Portfolio Optimization
I. Title. II. Title. III Title: Practical Quantitative Finance with R

*For my wonderful family*

# Contents

# Introduction

## Overview

Welcome to *Practical Quantitative Finance with R*. R is not only a general-purpose statistical computing language, but also an excellent choice for fast prototyping quant models and backtesting trading strategies in quantitative finance. This book focuses on introducing R as the scripting environment choice for quantitative finance application development. It will provide the basic R programming, quantitative analysis, and mathematical tools you need to develop real-world financial applications. All the techniques described in this book can be directly used to solve those problems that many quants face every day. I hope this book will be useful for quant developers/analysts, individual traders, and students of all skill levels.

In recent years, quantitative finance has been an attractive field due to the intellectual challenge and high remuneration. Many scientists, engineers, and students wish to change their careers to become a quant developer/analyst in investment banks and hedge fund firms. Most of them have solid background in mathematics, statistical analysis, physics modeling, and programming, but lack knowledge and experience in quantitative finance. A question that they constantly ask is "what do I need to prepare myself to become a quant developer or analyst?" This book will provide answer to this question and prepare you for careers in quantitative analysis and development.

On the other hand, more and more individuals want to become independent ("retail") quantitative traders who are looking to start their own quantitative or algorithmic trading business. The most common issue they are facing is what kind of background do they need in order to be successful in quantitative trading? Most of those individuals received their advanced degrees in physics, mathematics, engineering, or computer science. This kind of training in hard sciences will give them an edge in quantitative analysis and pricing complex derivative instruments. However, the capability to quickly convert trading ideas into trading strategies and the programming skill in implementing the automatic trading system are equally important. This book will prepare you with all the necessary analysis and programming techniques to become a well-equipped individual quant trader.

So what programming languages are most commonly used in quantitative finance? No doubt about it, C++ is traditionally associated with finance applications for pricing complex derivative securities; and much of the older financial infrastructure is also based on C++. In general, C++, C#, and Java tend to be used for application and infrastructure development. In my previous book, *Practical C# and WPF for*

*Financial Markets*, I have chosen C# and WPF as the programming framework in developing various business applications in financial markets. The reason for using C# in that book is that C# is relatively easy to learn in comparison to C++. You can learn C# and use it to develop financial applications quickly. People with a background in VBA, R, or Java will find the transition to C# much easier than the transition to C++. Furthermore, in many cases developers' productivity levels are much higher than those achieved with C++. It is also possible to create interoperable .NET applications that contain different technologies such as C++, VBA, Matlab, and R legacy code.

In addition to create business applications and infrastructure, we also need a script-programming environment that allows for rapid prototyping of an idea, provides us instant feedback, and enables the data and result visualization in an efficient manner. In this regard, R, Python, and Matlab provide the scripting environment and can be used to prototype quant models. All of these three are high-level languages with capabilities such as time series analysis, linear/matrix/vectorization computation, and fast prototyping for trading strategies. They all have strong communities developing code for numerical analysis and quantitative finance. R is especially strong in the finance community. In my work as a quant, I have used all of these three script languages extensively for prototyping quant models and strategy backtesting. You can use any one of them as long as you are comfortable with it. In this book, I will choose R as our scripting environment, mainly because R is a free open-source language, and has strong packages in quantitative finance, as well as efficient data visualization power.

The main advantage of R is that it is free, extremely flexible and extensible. R is not only free, but also open source. You can see the source code, and change it as per your own requirements. People across different disciplines around world reviewed the core of the R system and contributed to make it better. You can use R to perform data processing and analysis and to produce a variety of graphics. R has a substantial collection of packages, which are written by experts in quantitative finance. That is why, whether you are a quant analyst/developer, or individual trader, you should find a set of functions that serve your purpose. The graphic system in R is one of the most powerful tools in this era, and you have full control over every part of graphics produced in R. R is now becoming one of the platforms to implement and prototype the research work, quant models, and trading strategies. You should be able to find an R package suitable for the most recent developments in quantitative finance.

I write this book with the intention of providing a complete and comprehensive explanation of R programming and usage of the relevant R packages in quantitative finance. The book pays special attention to creating various business applications and reusable R libraries that can be directly used in real-world finance applications. Much of this book contains original work based on my own programming experience when I was prototyping quant models, pricing framework, and trading strategies in quantitative financial field.

*Practical Quantitative Finance with R* provides everything you need to create your own advanced applications and reusable packages in quantitative finance using R. It shows you how to use R and relevant R packages to create a variety of financial applications that range from simple market data collection, data visualization, and quantitative analysis to pricing equity options and complex fixed income instruments, machine learning, trading strategy development, and portfolio optimization. I will try my best to introduce you to R programming in quantitative finance in a simple way – simple enough to be easily followed by a quant or individual trader who has basic prior experience in developing business applications using R.

# What this Book Includes

This book and its sample code listings, which are available for download at my website at www.drxudotnet.com, provide you with:

- A complete, in-depth instruction on practical quantitative finance programming with R. After reading this book and running the example programs, you will be able to create various sophisticated business applications in quantitative finance.
- Ready-to-run example programs that allow you to explore the quantitative finance programming techniques described in the book. You can use these examples to understand how the algorithms in finance work. You can modify the code examples or add new features to them to form the basis of your own projects. Some of the example code listings provided in this book are already sophisticated programming packages in quantitative finance that you can use directly in your own real-world business applications.
- Many R functions in the sample code listings that you will find useful in your quant development. These functions include charting libraries, various quantitative analysis models, pricing engines for options and fixed income instruments, machine learning for trading strategy development and backtesting, and the other useful utility functions. You can extract these functions and plug them into your own business applications.

# Is This Book for You?

You do not have to be an experienced quant developer/analyst or R programmer to use this book. I designed this book to be useful to people of all levels of R programming experience and financial background. In fact, I believe that if you have some prior experience with the quantitative analysis and development, programming language such as C++, Java, VBA, C#, Matlab, or Python, you will be able to sit down in front of your computer, startup RStudio, follow the examples provided in this book, and quickly become proficient with quantitative application development using R. For those of you who are already experienced quant analysts/developers or R users, I believe this book has much to offer as well. A great deal of the information in this book about R programming in quantitative finance is not available in other tutorial and reference books. In addition, you can use most of the example programs in this book directly in your own real-world application development. This book will provide you with a level of detail, explanation, instruction, and sample program code that will enable you to do just about anything related to quantitative finance application development using R.

Perhaps you are a scientist, an engineer, a mathematician, or a student, rather than a professional quant developer/analyst; nevertheless, this book is still a good bet for you. In fact, my own background is in theoretical physics, a field involving extensive physical modeling, numerical calculations, and graphical representations of calculated data. I devoted my effort to this field for many years, starting from undergraduate up to PhD. My first computer experience was with FORTRAN. Later on, I had programming experience with Basic, C, C++, MATLAB, VBA, C#, WPF, Python, and R. I always tried to find an ideal development tool that would allow me not only to prototype my research work easily but also to represent data graphically. The R development environment made it possible to develop such integrated applications. I have been able to use R successfully to prototype quant models and trading strategies quickly for quantitative analysis when I have worked on Wall Street.

Quant analysts/developers and individual quant traders can use the majority of the example programs in this book routinely. Throughout the book, I will emphasize the usefulness of R programming to real-world quantitative finance applications. If you follow the instructions presented in this book closely, you will easily be able to develop various practical business applications in quantitative finance from linear analysis, machine learning to pricing engines, trading strategy development, asset allocation, and portfolio optimization. At the same time, I will not spend too much time discussing programming style, execution speed, and code vectorization/optimization, because a plethora of books and tutorial information out there already deal with these topics. Most of the example programs you will find in this book omit error handlings. This makes the code easier to understand by focusing only on the key concepts and practical applications.

# What Do You Need to Use This Book?

You will need no special equipment to make the best use of this book and understand the algorithms. To run and modify the sample programs, you will need to install R and RStudio on your computer. R and RStudio are both free, open-source software, available for all commonly used operating systems, including Windows, Mac OS X, and Linux systems. You can find the installation instructions for different systems at http://cran.r-project.org (for R itself) and http://www.rstudio.com (for RStudio). The RStudio is an R IDE for an integrated editor, execution, and graphical environment. The example code provided with this book was developed and tested on Windows 10 operating system with R version 3.2.3 and RStudio version 0.99.891.

# How the Book Is Organized

This book is organized into eleven chapters, each of which covers a different topic about quantitative finance applications using R. The following summaries of each chapter should give you an overview of the book's content:

Chapter 1, *Introduction to R*

This chapter introduces the basics of R and reviews some of the general aspects of R programming, including the built-in functions, math operations, data frame, data table, and user-defined functions.

Chapter 2, *Market Data*

This chapter contains instructions on how to use R to interact with market data providers' API. It demonstrates how to retrieve the free market data from online data sources, including the end of the day (EOD) stock data, real-time intraday data, interest rate data, foreign exchange rate data, and option-chain data.

Chapter 3, *Plots and Graphics in R*

Data visualization plays a critical role in quantitative finance and trading. Quant analysts and traders need to monitor the real-time changes in market and trading signals visually on their screen. This chapter demonstrates how to use the R built-in plotting capability as well as the other powerful charting and graphic packages, including *ggplot2*, *plot3D*, *rgl*, etc.

Chapter 4, *Stock Charts and Technical Indicators*

This chapter discusses various stock charts and technical indicators. We often use stock charts (line, bar, candlestick) and indicators in quantitative analysis. A technical indicator is just a mathematical calculation based on historic market data including price and volume, which is used to predict market direction. It demonstrates how to use the common indicators from the *TTR* package and extract the output results from the indicators.

Chapter 5, *Options Pricing*

This chapter covers the Black-Scholes formula used for options pricing. It shows several different implementations for calculating the price and Greeks of the European and American options. It also demonstrates how to use the open source quant libraries to price various exotic options, including barrier options.

Chapter 6, *Pricing Fixed-Income Instruments*

This chapter discusses pricing for the fixed-income instruments, including interest rates, bonds, and credit default swaps, as well as various related topics, such as cash flows, term structures, yield curves, discount factors, and zero-coupon bonds. It also presents the detailed procedures on how to use *QuantLib* to price these complex financial instruments.

Chapter 7, *Linear Analysis*

This chapter represents the most fundamental analysis approach in quantitative finance based on linear analysis. It demonstrates how to develop different business applications using the linear regression, principal component analysis (PCA), and correlation.

Chapter 8, *Time Series Analysis*

This chapter introduces some common modeling techniques for time series analysis, including the autoregressive moving average (ARMA), the autoregressive integrated moving average (ARIMA), and the volatility modeling generalized autoregressive conditional heteroscedasticity (GARCH). It also examines the stationarity of a time series using different approaches, such as augmented Dickey-Fuller (ADF) unit root test and Johansen test.

Chapter 9, *Machine Learning*

This chapter discusses the advanced quantitative analysis techniques: machine learning. Machine-learning technique has become one of the most promising fields in quantitative finance. It is widely used in quantitative finance for predicting the future stock prices. This chapter concentrates on the supervised learning and covers several commonly used machine-learning algorithms in finance, including the K-nearest neighbors, random forest, support vector machines, and neural networks.

Chapter 10, *Trading Strategies and Backtesting*

This chapter presents several trading strategies using the simple quantitative analysis techniques, including the moving average and linear regression, as well as the commonly used technical indicators. It also discusses a long-short based backtesting framework and a useful backtesting package named *quantstrat*, which allow us to examine the historical performance of trading strategies for single stock trading, stock pairs trading, and trading for multi-asset portfolios.

Chapter 11, *Portfolio Optimization*

This chapter presents introduction to portfolio optimization. Expected return and risk are the most important parameters with regard to optimal portfolios. The goal of portfolio optimization is to find the best asset allocation strategy that maximizes portfolio's return and minimizes its risk. This chapter discusses portfolio optimization using several different techniques, including, Markowitz's classical mean-variance method, mean-CVaR (conditional risk at risk), and the *portfolioAnalytics* package.

# Using Code Examples

You may use the code in this book in your own applications and documentation. You do not need to contact the author for permission unless you are reproducing a significant portion of the code. For example, writing a program that uses several chunks of code from this book does not require permission. Selling or distributing the example code listings does require permission. Incorporating a significant amount of example code from this book into your applications and documentation also requires permission. Integrating the example code from this book into commercial products is not allowed without written permission of the author.

# Customer Support

I am always interested in hearing from readers, and enjoy learning of your thoughts on this book. You can send me comments by e-mail to jxu@DrXuDotNet.com. I also provide updates, bug fixes, and ongoing support via my website:

```
www.DrXuDotNet.com
```

You can also obtain the complete source code for all of examples in this book from the foregoing website.

# Chapter 1
# Introduction to R

Although R is primarily a language and environment for statistical computing and graphics, it goes well beyond that primary purpose, as it is a very flexible and extendable system. It has a worldwide repository system, the Comprehensive R Archive Network (CRAN) – http://cran.r-project.org – for user-contributed packages to supplement the R base distribution. Currently, there are almost 8000 such packages hosted on CRAN and numerous more on other sites. R has functionality to address an enormous range of problems and still has room to grow. With R, we can perform data processing, write functions, create graphics, perform complex data analysis, and produce our own packages to solve specific problems. In fact, in the quantitative finance field, R has been routinely used by quant analysts and developers to prototype the quant models and backtest trading strategies, mainly because we can easily find all the necessary functions for the analysis of financial instruments from a large number of finance packages contributed by experts in the field.

R is designed around its core scripting language but also allows integration with compiled code written in C, C++, C#, FORTRAN, Java, etc., for computationally intensive tasks or for leveraging tools provided for other languages. In this section, I will give you a brief introduction to R programming under the RStudio environment. R is a functional programming language, not particularly object oriented, but it supports for programming in an object-oriented style. RStudio is an integrated development environment (IDE) for using and programming R, which brings many powerful coding tools together into an intuitive, easy-to-use interface.

## Getting Started with R

R, like other programming languages, is extended through user-written functions. RStudio is designed to facilitate such work. In addition, like Matlab, a typical user interacts with R primarily through the command line console. Therefore, RStudio must include a means for issuing command interactively. I suppose you have already installed both R and RStudio on your computer. RStudio allows you to run R in a more user-friendly environment. Figure 1.1 shows a typical RStudio screen, running under Windows operating system. We see three main components: a *Console*, which should look familiar to any R user, an *Environment* browser, and a *Files* interface. The latter two are part of notebooks that contain other components. The *Source* component, or code editor, is not open in the screenshot in Figure 1-1, as no files are open for editing or viewing.

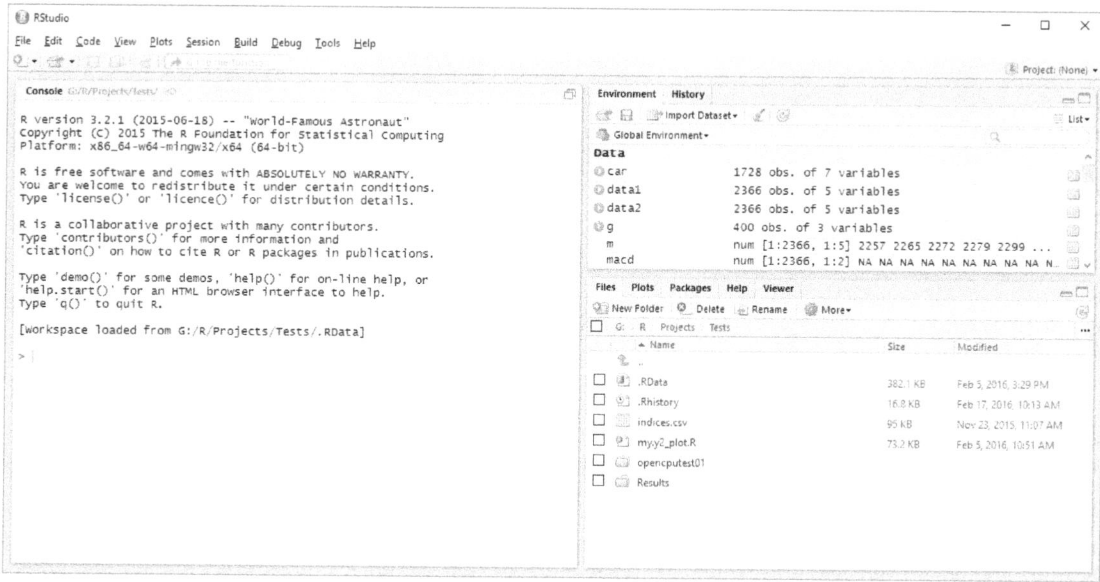


*Figure 1.1 RStudio on initial startup.*

In the command console, we can use R interactively. At the prompt ">", any R command or expression can be entered, and R will respond immediately with the result.

# Variables and Assignment

We use the variable to store the value in an R session, or in a project. One easy way to create a variable is to use an assignment statement. The format of an assignment statement is

```
variablename <- expression
```

The variable is always on the left, followed by the <– symbol (we can also use the = symbol, but the <– symbol is preferred), which is the assignment operator, followed by an expression. The expression is evaluated and then that value is stored in the variable. For example, this is the way it would appear in the console:

```
> mynum <- 2 + 3
> mynum
[1] 5
```

Here, we type "*mynum* <– 2 + 3" at the prompt, and R stores the result 5 in the variable named *mynum*. When we type the variable *mynum* again, R displays the result on the console. The [1] before 5 means that this is the first element of a vector. To change a variable, another assignment statement can be used, which assigns the value of a different expression to it. Consider, for example, the following sequence of statements:

```
> mynum = 2 + 4
> mynum
[1] 6
> mynum = mynum + 2
> mynum
[1] 8
```

In the first assignment statement, the expression 2 + 4 or 6 is assigned to the variable *mynum*. In the next statement, *mynum* is changed to the result of the expression *mynum* + 2. Since at that time *mynum* has the value 6, the value of the expression was 6 + 2, or 8.

Please note that in R, the expressions are case sensitive. The variable *mynum* is not the same as *myNum*. Spaces or special characters are not allowed within variable names, but the dot . operator is an exception. It is valid to have a variable name with a dot (i.e., *.mynum* or *my.num* is a valid variable). Variable names are not allowed to start with numeric characters. In addition, variables in R do not have to be declared as *int*, *double*, or *string* as in other languages. R can dynamically figure out what the type of the variable is during runtime. You can check the type of a variable using the typeof:

```
> typeof(mynum)
[1] "double"
```

The expressions in R can be created using values, variables that have already been created, operators, and functions. For example:

```
> x = 30
> y = 1.5 * log(x)
> y
[1] 5.101796
```

# Operators

There are in general two kinds of operators: unary operators, which operate on a single value, and binary operators, which operate on two values. The symbol "–", for example, is both the unary operator for negation and the binary operator for subtraction.

Here are some of the arithmetic operators in R, which perform arithmetic on numeric or complex vectors (*x* and *y*):

```
+x       # unary operator.
-x       # unary operator.
x + y    # addition
x - y    # subtraction
x * y    # multiplication
x / y    # division
x ^ y    # exponentiation (e.g., 4^2 is 16)
x %% y   # remainder part (modulo)(e.g., 7.5%%3 is 1.5)
x %/% y  # integer part of the quotient (e.g., 7.5%/%3 is 2)
```

In addition to displaying numbers with decimal points, we can also represent numbers using scientific or exponential notation. This uses *e* for the exponent of 10 raised to a power. For example, 3* 10^3 could be written two ways in R:

```
> 3 * 10^3
[1] 3000
> 3e3
[1] 3000
```

R also contains a few common logical operators that perform comparisons on things and return the Boolean values of TRUE or FALSE, depending on the outcome. Here I list some of logical operators in R for your reference:

```
<            # less than
<=           # less than or equal to
```

```
>             # greater than
>=            # greater than or equal to
==            # exactly equal to
!=            # not equal to
!x            # not x
x | y         # x or y
x & y         # x and y
isTRUE(x)     # test if x is TRUE
```

# Built-in Functions

R has many built-in functions, which include the standard math functions, probability functions, statistical functions, and character functions. Here, I list some of these built-in functions for your reference:

***Basic Math numeric Functions***

| Function | Description |
|---|---|
| abs(*x*) | absolute value |
| sqrt(*x*) | square root |
| ceiling(*x*) | ceiling(3.475) is 4 |
| floor(*x*) | floor(3.475) is 3 |
| trunc(*x*) | trunc(5.99) is 5 |
| round(*x*, digits=*n*) | round(3.475, digits=2) is 3.48 |
| signif(*x*, digits=*n*) | signif(3.475, digits=2) is 3.5 |
| cos(*x*), sin(*x*), tan(*x*) | also acos(*x*), cosh(*x*), acosh(*x*), etc. |
| log(*x*) | natural logarithm |
| log10(*x*) | common logarithm |
| exp(*x*) | e^*x* |

***Statistical Probability Functions***

| Function | Description |
|---|---|
| dnorm(*x*) | normal density function (by default m=0 sd=1) |
| pnorm(*q*) | cumulative normal probability for q |
| qnorm(*p*) | normal quantile. Value at the p percentile of normal distribution |
| rnorm(*n*, m=0,sd=1) | n random normal deviates with mean m and standard deviation sd. |
| dbinom(*x*, *size*, *prob*)<br>pbinom(q, size, prob)<br>qbinom(p, size, prob)<br>rbinom(n, size, prob) | binomial distribution where size is the sample size and prob is the probability of a heads (pi) |
| dpois(*x*, *lamda*)<br>rpois(n, lamda)<br>qpois(p, lamda)<br>ppois(q, lamda) | poisson distribution with m=std=lamda |
| dunif(*x*, min=0, max=1)<br>runif(n, min=0, max=1)<br>qunif(p, min=0, max=1)<br>punif(q, min=0, max=1) | uniform distribution, follows the same pattern as the normal distribution above. |

### *Other statistical Functions*

| Function | Description |
|---|---|
| mean(*x*, trim=0, na.rm=FALSE) | mean of object x. # trimmed mean, removing any missing values and # 5 percent of highest and lowest scores. mx <- mean(x,trim=.05,na.rm=TRUE) |
| sd(*x*) | standard deviation of object(x). also look at var(x) for variance and mad(x) for median absolute deviation. |
| median(*x*) | median |
| quantile(*x*, *probs*) | quantiles where x is the numeric vector whose quantiles are desired and probs is a numeric vector with probabilities in [0,1]. |
| range(*x*) | range |
| sum(*x*) | sum |
| diff(*x*, lag=*1*) | lagged differences, with lag indicating which lag to use |
| min(*x*) | minimum |
| max(*x*) | maximum |
| scale(*x*, center=TRUE, scale=TRUE) | column center or standardize a matrix. |

### *Character and String Functions*

| Function | Description |
|---|---|
| substr(*x*, start=*n1*, stop=*n2*) | Extract or replace substrings in a character vector. |
| grep(*pattern*, *x*, ignore.case=FALSE, fixed=FALSE) | Search for pattern in x. If fixed =FALSE then pattern is a regular expression. If fixed=TRUE then pattern is a text string. Returns matching indices. |
| sub(*pattern*, *replacement*, *x*, ignore.case =FALSE, fixed=FALSE) | Find pattern in x and replace with replacement text. If fixed=FALSE then pattern is a regular expression. If fixed = T then pattern is a text string. |
| strsplit(*x*, *split*) | Split the elements of character vector x at split. |
| paste(..., sep="") | Concatenate strings after using *sep* string to seperate them. |
| toupper(*x*) | Uppercase. |
| tolower(*x*) | Lowercase. |

We can apply many of built-in functions not only to individual variables, but also to vectors and matrices. In order to call a function in R, the name of the function is given followed by the argument(s) that are passed to the function in parentheses. Most functions then return value(s). For example, to find the absolute value of $-10$, the following expression would be entered:

```
> abs(-10)
[1] 10
```

which calls the *abs* function. The number in the parentheses, $-10$, is the argument. The value 10 would then be returned as a result. Another function is *sign*, which is not included in the list of math functions. It returns 1 if argument is positive, 0 if it is 0, and $-1$ if it is negative. For example,

```
> sign(-3)
[1] -1
> sign(0)
[1] 0
> sign(3)
[1] 1
```

We use variables to store values that might change, or for which the values are not known ahead of time. Most languages also have the capacity to store constants, which are values that are known ahead of time, and cannot possibly change. An example of a constant value would be *pi*, or $\pi$, which is 3.1415926.... R has a small number of built-in constants, as shown in the following list:

***Built-in Constants***

| Constant | Description |
|---|---|
| LETTERS | 26 upper-case letters |
| letters | 26 lower-case letters |
| month.abb | three-letter abbreviation for month names |
| month.name | names for the months of the year |
| pi | the ratio of the circumference of a circle to its diameter |

## Random Numbers

When a program is being written to work with data whereas the data are not yet available, it is often useful to test the program first by initializing the data variables to random numbers. R has a comprehensive library of functions for generating random numbers from various statistical distributions. Here, I just want to focus on the simplest case: how to generate a random number.

If we want to generate a decimal number where any value between a started minimum and maximum is equally likely, we can use the *runif* function. This function generates values from the uniform distribution. Here is how to generate one random number between 0 and 1:

```
> r1 <- runif(1, 0, 1)
> r1
[1] 0.329183
```

Of course, when we run this again, we may get a different number, but it will definitely be between 0 and 1. However, if we want to reproduce the random number generated, we can call the *set.seed* function. The argument of *set.seed* has to be an integer:

```
> set.seed(1)
> r1 <- runif(1, 0, 1)
> r1
[1] 0.2655087
> set.seed(1)
> r2 <- runif(1, 0, 1)
> r2
[1] 0.2655087
```

We can use the *sample* function to generate a random integer. For example, the following code snippet will generate a random integer between 1 and 100:

```
> sample(1:100, 1)
[1] 91
```

Here, the first argument is a vector of valid numbers (from 1 to 100) to generate, and the second argument indicates one number should be returned.

# Vectors and Matrices

Vectors and matrices are used to store sets of values, all of which are the same type. A vector can be either a row vector or a column vector. A matrix can be visualized as a table of values. The dimensions of a matrix are $m \times n$, where $m$ is the number of rows and $n$ is the number of columns. If a vector has $n$ elements, a row vector would have the dimensions $1 \times n$, and a column vector would have the dimensions $n \times 1$. A scalar (one value) has the dimensions $1 \times 1$. Therefore, vectors and scalars are simply the special cases of matrices.

## Vectors

In R, it is possible to combine objects of different types using the *c* function. In this case, R will find a common type that can accommodate all the objects, resulting in the type of some of the objects changing. Let us look at the following example, which creates three vectors of type numeric and character:

```
> v1 <- c(1, 1.5, 2, 2.5, 3)
> v1
[1] 1.0 1.5 2.0 2.5 3.0
> v2 <- c("Tyler", "Jack", "Hello", "World" )
> v2
[1] "Tyler" "Jack"  "Hello" "World"
> v3 <- c("a", "b", 1, 2, 3)
> v3
[1] "a" "b" "1" "2" "3"
```

We use the concatenation operator *c* to create a vector of numbers, characters, or Booleans. The *v3* vector mixes numbers with characters, in which the numbers have been changed to characters because they are now displayed surrounded by quotes. They will no longer behave like numbers:

```
> v3[3] + v3[4]
Error in v3[3] + v3[4] : non-numeric argument to binary operator
```

All of the vectors we created in the preceding example are row vectors. We can create column vectors using the *cbind* function. For example,

```
> v4 <- cbind(c(1, 2, 3, 4, 5))
> v4
     [,1]
[1,]    1
[2,]    2
[3,]    3
[4,]    4
[5,]    5
```

We can also create a vector with values being regularly spaced, the *seq* function can be used to iterate through these values with a step value:

```
> v6 <- seq(from = 1, to = 9, by = 2)
> v6
[1] 1 3 5 7 9
```

In addition to *by*, we can also have other options such as *length*. For example, we can use the following statement to create a vector with 10 equally spaced values from 0 to 1:

```
> seq(0, 1, length = 10)
```

```
 [1] 0.0000000 0.1111111 0.2222222 0.3333333 0.4444444 0.5555556 0.6666667
 [8] 0.7777778 0.8888889 1.0000000
```

Vector variables can also be created using existing variables. For example, a new vector is created here consisting first of all values from *v*1 followed by all values from *v*6:

```
> newvec <- c(v1, v6)
> newvec
 [1] 1.0 1.5 2.0 2.5 3.0 1.0 3.0 5.0 7.0 9.0
```

Putting two vectors together like this to create a new one is called concatenating the vectors.

The following examples address another important concept – vectorization. Instead of performing operations on one element at a time, vectorization allows us to perform the same operation on all the elements at the same time, which means that we can treat a vector of numbers as a single number. For example:

```
> x <- seq(from = 5, to = 20, by = 5)
> x
[1]  5 10 15 20
> x2 = x - 2
> x2
[1]  3  8 13 18
> x3 <- 2 * x
> x3
[1] 10 20 30 40
> x4 <- x * x
> x4
[1]  25 100 225 400
> x5 <- x/x2
> x5
[1] 1.666667 1.250000 1.153846 1.111111
```

Vectorization allows us to avoid looping through all the elements of the vector.

# Matrices

Creating a matrix variable is simply a generalization of creating row and column vector variables. The following code defines a matrix with two rows and three columns:

```
> m1 <- matrix(c(4, 3, 1, 2, 5, 6), nrow = 2, ncol = 3)
> m1
     [,1] [,2] [,3]
[1,]    4    1    5
[2,]    3    2    6
```

The default *matrix* command assumes that the input data will be arranged in columnar format by default. In order to arrange the data in row format, we need to modify our preceding example slightly:

```
> m2 <- matrix(c(4, 3, 1, 2, 5, 6), nrow = 2, ncol = 3, byrow = T)
> m2
     [,1] [,2] [,3]
[1,]    4    3    1
[2,]    2    5    6
```

Unlike other languages, R allows a matrix object to have a character vector of names for the rows and another character vector of names for the columns. We can put these two vectors into a *list* object and pass an argument to the *dimnames* function:

```
> dimnames(m1) <- list(c("row1", "row2"), c("col1", "col2", "col3"))
> m1
     col1 col2 col3
row1    4    1    5
row2    3    2    6
```

We can then query the matrix *m1* for its attributes:

```
> attributes(m1)
$dim
[1] 2 3

$dimnames
$dimnames[[1]]
[1] "row1" "row2"

$dimnames[[2]]
[1] "col1" "col2" "col3"
```

## *Matrix Elements*

Now, we can access the elements of *m1* using either the index or row/column names. R, like Matlab, uses a 1-based indexing scheme (i.e., the first element of a vector or matrix has an index of 1). This is different from other languages such as C++, C#, Java, etc., in which the first element has an index of 0. To access the element located in row 2 and column 3, we can use the following statements:

```
> m1[2,3]
[1] 6
> m1["row2","col3"]
[1] 6
```

We can also access the entire column or row by issuing the following commands:

```
> # Access column 3 using indexing:
> m1[, 3]
row1 row2
   5    6
> # Access column 3 using column name:
> m1[, "col3"]
row1 row2
   5    6
> # Access row 2 using indexing:
> m1[2, ]
col1 col2 col3
   3    2    6
> # Access row 2 using row name:
> m1["row2", ]
col1 col2 col3
   3    2    6
```

It is also possible to refer to a subset of a matrix. For example, this refers to the first and second rows, second and third columns:

```
> m1[1:2, 2:3]
     col2 col3
row1    1    5
row2    2    6
```

## *Special Matrices*

R also allow us to create special matrices. For example, the *diag* function creates an identity matrix, which is a diagonal matrix with all diagonal elements equal to one. We can also easily create a matrix of all zeros, or a matrix of all ones.

```
> # 4x4 identity matrix:
> diag(4)
     [,1] [,2] [,3] [,4]
[1,]    1    0    0    0
[2,]    0    1    0    0
[3,]    0    0    1    0
[4,]    0    0    0    1

> # 4x4 zeros matrix:
> matrix(0,4,4)
     [,1] [,2] [,3] [,4]
[1,]    0    0    0    0
[2,]    0    0    0    0
[3,]    0    0    0    0
[4,]    0    0    0    0

> # 4x4 ones matrix:
> matrix(1,4,4)
     [,1] [,2] [,3] [,4]
[1,]    1    1    1    1
[2,]    1    1    1    1
[3,]    1    1    1    1
[4,]    1    1    1    1

> # 4x4 matrix with any number filled (i.e., 9)
> matrix(9, 4, 4)
     [,1] [,2] [,3] [,4]
[1,]    9    9    9    9
[2,]    9    9    9    9
[3,]    9    9    9    9
[4,]    9    9    9    9

> # 4x4 diagonal matrix with the diagonal elements filled with a vector:
> diag(c(1, 4, 6, 5))
     [,1] [,2] [,3] [,4]
[1,]    1    0    0    0
[2,]    0    4    0    0
[3,]    0    0    6    0
[4,]    0    0    0    5
```

## *Matrix Operations*

There are several common operations on matrices. These include matrix transpose, matrix inverse, and array operations.

A matrix transpose interchanges the rows and columns of a matrix. For a matrix *m*, we call its transpose matrix *mt*. For example, if

```
> m <- matrix(c(1,2,3,4,5,6), nrow = 2, ncol = 3, byrow = T)
> m
     [,1] [,2] [,3]
[1,]    1    2    3
[2,]    4    5    6
```

We can then use the *t* function to obtain the transpose *mt* from *m*:

```
> mt <- t(m)
> mt
     [,1] [,2]
[1,]    1    4
[2,]    2    5
[3,]    3    6
```

If the result of multiplying a matrix *m* by another matrix is the identity matrix, the second matrix is the inverse of matrix *m*. Calculating the inverse of a matrix by hand is not so easy. R, however, has a function *solve* to compute a matrix inverse. For example, here, a matrix is created, its inverse is found, and then it is multiplied by the original matrix to verify that the product is in fact the identity matrix:

```
> m <- matrix(c(1,2,2,2), nrow = 2, ncol = 2, byrow = T)
> m
     [,1] [,2]
[1,]    1    2
[2,]    2    2
> m1<- solve(m)
> m1
     [,1] [,2]
[1,]   -1  1.0
[2,]    1 -0.5
> m%*%m1
     [,1] [,2]
[1,]    1    0
[2,]    0    1
```

Please note that we use the % * % operator to perform the matrix multiplication, while the operator * is used to perform the element-wise multiplication. Here, I list the basic matrix operations in R for your reference. In this list, we assume that *A* and *B* are matrices, *x* and *b* are vectors.

**Basic Matrix Operations in R**

| Operator or Function | Description |
|---|---|
| A * B | Element-wise multiplication |
| A %*% B | Matrix multiplication |
| A %o% B | Outer product of A and B |
| crossprod(A,B)<br>crossprod(A) | Returns a matrix cross-product of A and B or A and A. |

| | |
|---|---|
| **tcrossprod(A,B)**<br>**tcrossprod(A)** | Take the cross-product of the transpose of a matrix. tcrossprod(A) is faster than A%*%t(A). tcrossprod(A,B) can replace A%*%t(B) |
| **t(A)** | Transpose |
| **diag(x)** | Creates diagonal matrix with elements of **x** in the principal diagonal |
| **diag(A)** | Returns a vector containing the elements of the principal diagonal |
| **diag(k)** | If k is a scalar, this creates a k x k identity matrix. |
| **solve(A, b)** | Returns vector **x** in the equation **b** = **Ax** (i.e., $\mathbf{A}^{-1}\mathbf{b}$) |
| **solve(A)** | Inverse of **A** where **A** is a square matrix. |
| **ginv(A)** | Moore-Penrose Generalized Inverse of **A**.<br>ginv(A) requires loading the **MASS** package. |
| **y <- eigen(A)** | **y$val** are the eigenvalues of **A**<br>**y$vec** are the eigenvectors of **A** |
| **y <- svd(A)** | Single value decomposition of **A**.<br>**y$d** = vector containing the singular values of **A**<br>**y$u** = matrix with columns contain the left singular vectors of **A**<br>**y$v** = matrix with columns contain the right singular vectors of **A** |
| **R <- chol(A)** | Choleski factorization of **A**. Returns the upper triangular factor, such that **R'R** = **A**. |
| **y <- qr(A)** | QR decomposition of **A**.<br>**y$qr** has an upper triangle that contains the decomposition and a lower triangle<br>**y$rank** is the rank of A.<br>**y$qraux** a vector which contains additional information on Q.<br>**y$pivot** contains information on the pivoting strategy used. |
| **cbind(A,B,...)** | Combine matrices(vectors) horizontally. Returns a matrix. |
| **rbind(A,B,...)** | Combine matrices(vectors) vertically. Returns a matrix. |
| **rowMeans(A)** | Returns vector of row means. |
| **rowSums(A)** | Returns vector of row sums. |
| **colMeans(A)** | Returns vector of column means. |
| **colSums(A)** | Returns vector of column sums. |

We see from the above list that we can easily perform various operations on vectors and matrices in R.

# Arrays and List

An *array* is a multiply subscribed data entry that allows the storing of vectors or matrices of different types. In R, matrices are of two dimensions only, but an array can be of any number of dimensions. Sometimes, we need to store multiple matrices into a single object; in this case, we can use arrays to store this data. For example, we can use a single array object to store two matrices of order 2 × 3:

```
> m1 <- matrix(c(1, 2, 3, 4, 5, 6), nrow = 2, ncol = 3, byrow = T)
> m1
     [,1] [,2] [,3]
[1,]    1    2    3
[2,]    4    5    6
> m2 <- matrix(c(6, 5, 4, 3, 2, 1),nrow = 2, ncol = 3, byrow = T)
> m2
     [,1] [,2] [,3]
[1,]    6    5    4
```

```
[2,]    3    2    1
> a1 <- array(dim = c(2, 3, 2))
> a1[,,1] <- m1
> a1[,,2] <- m2
> a1
, , 1

     [,1] [,2] [,3]
[1,]    1    2    3
[2,]    4    5    6

, , 2

     [,1] [,2] [,3]
[1,]    6    5    4
[2,]    3    2    1
```

We can also create an array directly using the array function, where we give the data as the first argument and a vector with the sizes of the dimensions as the second argument. The number of dimension sizes in that argument gives us the number of dimensions. For example, we can create an array with four columns, three rows, and two matrices like this:

```
> a2 <- array(1:24, dim = c(3,4,2))
> a2
, , 1

     [,1] [,2] [,3] [,4]
[1,]    1    4    7   10
[2,]    2    5    8   11
[3,]    3    6    9   12

, , 2

     [,1] [,2] [,3] [,4]
[1,]   13   16   19   22
[2,]   14   17   20   23
[3,]   15   18   21   24
```

A *list* object is a generic R object that can store other objects of any type. In a *list* object, we can store single constants, vectors of numeric values, matrices, and even arrays. For example, we can put two vectors, one matrix, and one array into a single *list* object using the following command:

```
> v1 <- c(1, 1.5, 2, 2.5, 3)
> v2 <- c("Tyler", "Jack", "Hello", "World" )
> m1 <- matrix(c(1, 2, 3, 4, 5, 6), nrow = 2, ncol = 3, byrow = T)
> a1 <- array(1:12, dim = c(2, 3, 2))
> my.list <- list(entry1 = v1, entry2 = v2, entry3 = m1, entry4 = a1)
> my.list
$entry1
[1] 1.0 1.5 2.0 2.5 3.0

$entry2
[1] "Tyler" "Jack"  "Hello" "World"

$entry3
     [,1] [,2] [,3]
```

```
[1,]    1    2    3
[2,]    4    5    6

$entry4
, , 1

     [,1] [,2] [,3]
[1,]    1    3    5
[2,]    2    4    6

, , 2

     [,1] [,2] [,3]
[1,]    7    9   11
[2,]    8   10   12
```

To access individual elements from a *list* object, we can use the name of that element or use double square brackets with the index of those elements. For example, we can use *my.list*[[1]] or *my.list$entry*1 to access the first element of the *my.list* object:

```
> my.list[[1]]
[1] 1.0 1.5 2.0 2.5 3.0
> my.list$entry1
[1] 1.0 1.5 2.0 2.5 3.0
```

# Factors

A *factor* is another important data type in R, which is used for fields that takes only predefined, finite number of values (categorical data). For example, a data field such as marital status may contain only values from single, married, separated, divorced, or widowed. In this case, we know the possible values beforehand and can consider these predefined, distinct values as levels. The following is an example of *factor* in R:

```
> f1 <- factor(c("single", "married", "married", "single", "divorced"))
> f1
[1] single   married  married  single   divorced
Levels: divorced married single
```

Here, we can see that the *f1* factor has five elements and three levels. We can check if a variable is a *factor* or not using class function. Similarly, we can examine the levels of a *factor* using the levels function.

```
> class(f1)
[1] "factor"
> levels(f1)
[1] "divorced" "married"  "single"
```

We create a factor using the *factor* function. Levels of a factor are inferred from the data if not provided. For example:

```
> d1 <- c(10, 20, 20, 50, 10, 20, 10, 50, 20)
> f2 <- factor(d1); f2
[1] 10 20 20 50 10 20 10 50 20
Levels: 10 20 50
> f3 <- factor(d1, levels = c(10, 20, 50)); f3
```

```
[1] 10 20 20 50 10 20 10 50 20
Levels: 10 20 50
```

We see from the preceding example that the levels may be predefined even if not used. Factors are closely related with vectors. In fact, factors are stored as integer vectors. This can be clearly seen from its structure:

```
> f1 <- factor(c("single", "married", "married", "single", "divorced"))
> str(f1)
 Factor w/ 3 levels "divorced","married",..: 3 2 2 3 1
```

Accessing components of a factor is very much similar to that of vectors. For example:

```
> f1[2]          # access 2nd element
[1] married
Levels: divorced married single
> f1[c(2, 4)]    # access 2nd and 4th elements
[1] married single
Levels: divorced married single
> f1[-3]         # access all but 3rd elements
[1] single   married  single   divorced
Levels: divorced married single
```

# Data Frame

A data frame is a two-dimensional data structure in R, which consists of rows and columns of vectors and/or factors, more like a spreadsheet in Microsoft Excel. It is a special case of a list object with each component of equal length. The columns represent variables in the data, and the rows represent records. Each column represents only one type of data: numeric, character, or logical. Each row represents case information across all columns. In an R data frame, we can store different types of variables, such as numeric, logical, factor, and character. To create a data frame, we can use the *data.frame* command. For example:

```
> my.df <- data.frame("SN" = c(123456789, 987654321), "Age" = c(21, 15),
                      "Name" = c("John", "Joe"))
> my.df
         SN Age Name
1 123456789  21 John
2 987654321  15  Joe
> str(my.df)
'data.frame':  2 obs. of  3 variables:
 $ SN  : num  1.23e+08 9.88e+08
 $ Age : num  21 15
 $ Name: Factor w/ 2 levels "Joe","John": 2 1
```

Note that the third column, *Name* is of type factor, instead of a character vector. By default, *data.frame* function converts character vector into factor. To suppress this behavior, we can pass argument *stringAsFactor* = *F* (or *FALSE*):

```
> my.df <- data.frame("SN" = c(123456789,987654321), "Age" = c(21, 15),
                      "Name"=c("John", "Joe"), stringsAsFactors = F)
> str(my.df)
'data.frame':  2 obs. of  3 variables:
 $ SN  : num  1.23e+08 9.88e+08
 $ Age : num  21 15
```

```
 $ Name: chr  "John" "Joe"
```

You can see now that the *Name* column becomes the character type.

We can access components of a data frame like a list or like a matrix. We can use either [, [[ or $ operator to access columns of a data frame:

```
> my.df["Name"]
  Name
1 John
2  Joe
> my.df$Name
[1] "John" "Joe"
> my.df[["Name"]]
[1] "John" "Joe"
> my.df[[3]]
[1] "John" "Joe"
```

Accessing with [[ or $ is similar. However, it differs for [ in that, indexing with [ will return a data frame but the other two will reduce it into a vector.

Data frames can also be accessed like a matrix by providing index for row and column. To demonstrate this, we will use datasets already available in R. We can check available datasets in R by issuing the command:

```
> library(help = "datasets")
```

We will use the *iris* dataset, which can be examined using functions like *str* and *head*:

```
> str(iris)
'data.frame':	150 obs. of  5 variables:
 $ Sepal.Length: num  5.1 4.9 4.7 4.6 5 5.4 4.6 5 4.4 4.9 ...
 $ Sepal.Width : num  3.5 3 3.2 3.1 3.6 3.9 3.4 3.4 2.9 3.1 ...
 $ Petal.Length: num  1.4 1.4 1.3 1.5 1.4 1.7 1.4 1.5 1.4 1.5 ...
 $ Petal.Width : num  0.2 0.2 0.2 0.2 0.2 0.4 0.3 0.2 0.2 0.1 ...
 $ Species     : Factor w/ 3 levels "setosa","versicolor",..: 1 1 1 1 1 1 1 1 1
  1 ...
> head(iris)
  Sepal.Length Sepal.Width Petal.Length Petal.Width Species
1          5.1         3.5          1.4         0.2  setosa
2          4.9         3.0          1.4         0.2  setosa
3          4.7         3.2          1.3         0.2  setosa
4          4.6         3.1          1.5         0.2  setosa
5          5.0         3.6          1.4         0.2  setosa
6          5.4         3.9          1.7         0.4  setosa
```

We see that the *iris* dataset is a data frame with 150 rows and 5 columns. We also display the first 6 rows of the dataset. Now, we proceed to access the dataset like a matrix.

```
> iris[3:6, ]    # select 3rd to 6th rows
  Sepal.Length Sepal.Width Petal.Length Petal.Width Species
3          4.7         3.2          1.3         0.2  setosa
4          4.6         3.1          1.5         0.2  setosa
5          5.0         3.6          1.4         0.2  setosa
6          5.4         3.9          1.7         0.4  setosa
> iris[iris$Sepal.Length > 7.5, ]  # select rows with Sepal.Length > 7.5
    Sepal.Length Sepal.Width Petal.Length Petal.Width   Species
106          7.6         3.0          6.6         2.1 virginica
```

```
118          7.7         3.8         6.7         2.2 virginica
119          7.7         2.6         6.9         2.3 virginica
123          7.7         2.8         6.7         2.0 virginica
132          7.9         3.8         6.4         2.0 virginica
136          7.7         3.0         6.1         2.3 virginica
> iris[2:5, 3]
[1] 1.4 1.3 1.5 1.4
```

We see in the last case that the returned type is a vector since we extracted data from a single column. This behavior can be avoided by passing the argument *drop* = *FALSE* as follows:

```
> iris[2:5,3, drop = F]
  Petal.Length
2          1.4
3          1.3
4          1.5
5          1.4
```

Now, the result returned is a data frame object.

We can add new rows to a data frame using the *rbind* function:

```
> my.df <- data.frame("SN" = c(123456789,987654321), "Age" = c(21, 15),
                      "Name"=c("John", "Joe"), stringsAsFactors = F); my.df
         SN Age Name
1 123456789  21 John
2 987654321  15  Joe
> rbind(my.df, list(121212121,30, "Tom"));
         SN Age Name
1 123456789  21 John
2 987654321  15  Joe
3 121212121  30  Tom
```

Similarly, we can add columns using the *cbind* function:

```
> my.df1 <- cbind(my.df, State = c("AZ", "NY")); my.df1
         SN Age Name State
1 123456789  21 John    AZ
2 987654321  15  Joe    NY
```

We can delete a data frame column by assigning *NULL* to it:

```
> my.df1$Name <- NULL; my.df1
         SN Age State
1 123456789  21    AZ
2 987654321  15    NY
```

Similarly, we can delete a data frame row through reassignments:

```
> my.df1 <- my.df1[-2, ]; my.df1
         SN Age State
1 123456789  21    AZ
```

Note that in R, both the matrix and data frame are two-dimensional data structures. Therefore, we may ask when we should use the data frame or matrix. If the data variables (columns) have different types (numeric, character, logical, etc.), we should use the data frame because the data frame objects can handle data with different data types.

However, if we have data of the same type, the choice between matrix and data frame becomes problematic. The answer depends on what we want to do with the data. Data frames are usually more convenient if we frequently refer to its columns by name. They are also better for reporting tabular information as we can apply formatting to each column separately. On the other hand, we need to use matrices if we want to perform any linear algebra-type of operations. Matrices are also more memory efficient. For example:

```
> m <- matrix(1:9,3,3)
> d <- as.data.frame(m)
> object.size(m)
248 bytes
> object.size(d)
944 bytes
```

# Data Table

The data table inherits from the base R data frame and is an enhanced version of data frame. It allows us to perform much faster data manipulations than the data frame. Since a data table is in fact a data frame, it is compliant with all R functions and packages that accept data frame as object. The big advantage of a data table over a data frame is that it uses the tables as if they are tables in a database, with a high speed of data access.

The goal of the data table is to reduce both the programming time and computation time. This is achieved by fewer function calls, less variable name repetition, fast aggregation, and update by reference. Data table uses binary search instead of vector scan to perform its operations and thus is scalable. The data table is often used in quantitative finance and genomics. It is especially useful when we are working with large data sets, such as 1GB to 100GB in RAM.

In order to use data table in R, we need to install the *data.table* package:

```
> install.packages("data.table")
> library(data.table)
```

## DT[i, j, by] Command

The basic command *DT*[*i*, *j*, *by*] is the core to the data table package. The *DT*[*i*, *j*, *by*] command has three parts: *i*, *j*, and *by*. If we think in SQL terminology, the *i* part corresponds to where, *j* to select, and *by* to group by. Let us look at a simple example using the *iris* dataset:

```
> DT <- data.table(iris)
> head(DT, 3)
   Sepal.Length Sepal.Width Petal.Length Petal.Width Species
1:          5.1         3.5          1.4         0.2  setosa
2:          4.9         3.0          1.4         0.2  setosa
3:          4.7         3.2          1.3         0.2  setosa
> DT[Sepal.Length >= 5, mean(Sepal.Width), by = Species]
      Species       V1
1:     setosa 3.620000
2: versicolor 2.777551
3:  virginica 2.983673
```

Here, we subset the data table to keep only the rows of *Sepal.Length* >= 5, calculate the average of *Sepal.Width*, and then group the results by the *Species*. We see from this example that the *versicolor* species has a smallest average *Sepal.Width* as compared to the *setosa* species. You may notice that the R base functions can be used in the *j* part.

The *i* part is used for subsetting on rows, just like in a data frame. For example:

```
> DT[5:8]
   Sepal.Length Sepal.Width Petal.Length Petal.Width Species
1:          5.0         3.6          1.4         0.2  setosa
2:          5.4         3.9          1.7         0.4  setosa
3:          4.6         3.4          1.4         0.3  setosa
4:          5.0         3.4          1.5         0.2  setosa
```

We can also use column names, as they are evaluated in the scope of *DT*:

```
> DT[Species == "setosa"]
   Sepal.Length Sepal.Width Petal.Length Petal.Width Species
1:          5.1         3.5          1.4         0.2  setosa
2:          4.9         3.0          1.4         0.2  setosa
3:          4.7         3.2          1.3         0.2  setosa
4:          4.6         3.1          1.5         0.2  setosa
......
```

Note that we do not have to use a comma for subsetting rows in a data table. In a data frame doing this gives all the rows of the 5th to 8th column. Instead, we have to specify *DF*[5:8, ] in a data frame.

We use the *j* part to select columns and do something with them. The something here can be really mean anything. All kinds of R base functions can be used, which is a strong point of the data table package. For example:

```
> DT[, mean(Sepal.Length)]
[1] 5.843333
```

Notice that the *i* part is left blank, and the first thing in the brackets is a comma. This simply means that we did not subset on any rows, so all rows are selected. In the *j* part, the average *Sepal.Length* of all species is calculated.

When selecting several columns and doing something with them in the *j* part, we need to use the ".()" notation. This notation is actually just an alias to "*list*()":

```
> DT[, .(mean(Sepal.Length), mean(Sepal.Width), mean(Petal.Length),
      mean(Petal.Width))]
         V1       V2    V3       V4
1: 5.843333 3.057333 3.758 1.199333
```

Another useful feature that requires the ".()" notation allows us to rename columns inside the *DT*[…] command:

```
> DT[, .(avg_Sepal.Length = mean(Sepal.Length),
     avg_Sepal.Width = mean(Sepal.Width))]
   avg_Sepal.Length avg_Sepal.Width
1:         5.843333        3.057333
```

The following example combines the *i* and *j* parts:

```
> DT[Species == "virginica", .(avg_Sepal.Length = mean(Sepal.Length),
     avg_Sepal.Width = mean(Sepal.Width))]
   avg_Sepal.Length avg_Sepal.Width
1:            6.588           2.974
```

Here, we take *DT*, select all rows where the species is *virginica* in the *i* part, calculate the average *Sepal.Length* and *Sepal.Width* in the *j* part. Note that the *j* part is used to perform calculations on columns specified in that part. We can consider the columns of a data table as variables and evaluate the *j* part as expression. Thus, anything can be done in the *j* part, which significantly reduces our programming time.

The *by* part is used when we want to calculate the *j* part grouped by a specific variable. You will see that the *j* expression is repeated for each *by* group. The *by* part is very easy to use: we just need to specify the column that we want to group by in the "*by*" argument:

```
> DT[, .(avg_Sepal.Length = mean(Sepal.Length),
     avg_Sepal.Width = mean(Sepal.Width)), by = Species]
      Species avg_Sepal.Length avg_Sepal.Width
1:     setosa            5.006           3.428
2: versicolor            5.936           2.770
3:  virginica            6.588           2.974
```

Here, we calculate the average *Sepal.Length* and *Sepal.Width*, but grouped by *Species*. It seems that the *setosa* species has smallest average *Sepal.Length*, while the *versicolor* species has the smallest average *Sepal.Width*.

Just like with the *j* part, we can do a lot of stuff in the *by* part. The R functions can also be used in the *by* part, so that the results of the operations done in the *j* part are grouped by something we specified in the *DT*[…] command. Using functions inside *DT*[…] makes that one line very powerful. Likewise, the ".()" notation needs to be used when using several columns in the *by* part. Putting it all together, a typical *DT*[*i*, *j*, *by*] command looks like the following:

```
> DT[Petal.Length >= 3, .(avg_Sepal.Length = mean(Sepal.Length),
     avg_Sepal.Width = mean(Sepal.Width)), by = .(Species, Petal.Width <= 1.5)]
      Species Petal.Width avg_Sepal.Length avg_Sepal.Width
1: versicolor        TRUE         5.908889        2.731111
2: versicolor       FALSE         6.180000        3.120000
3:  virginica       FALSE         6.617021        3.002128
4:  virginica        TRUE         6.133333        2.533333
```

Here, the subset of rows with *Petal.Length* >= 3 (selected in the *i* part, which filters out the *setosa* species because its maximum *Petal.Length* = 1.9) is grouped by their species and by *Petal.Width* (in the *by* part). We also calculated the average *Sepal.Length* and *Sepal.Width* in the *j* part.

## Data Join

The *setkey* command sorts a data table and marks it as sorted. The sorted columns are the *key*. The table is changed by reference and is therefore very memory efficient. The *setkey* is required for joining tables, while it is not absolutely required for the aggregation. However, if we are dealing with the big data, *setkey* can speed up operations.

We can perform various SQL-like data joins in R using data table. First, we create two tables, *symbols* and *prices*, as follows

```
> symbols <- data.table(id = c(1,2,3,4), ticker = c("AMAT", "IBM", "INTC", "MSFT"));
> symbols
   id ticker
1:  1   AMAT
2:  2    IBM
3:  3   INTC
4:  4   MSFT
```

```
> prices
    id       date  price
 1:  1 2016-01-04  18.47
 2:  1 2016-01-05  18.49
 3:  1 2016-01-06  17.73
 4:  2 2016-01-04 135.95
 5:  2 2016-01-05 135.85
 6:  2 2016-01-06 135.17
 7:  3 2016-01-04  33.99
 8:  3 2016-01-05  33.83
 9:  3 2016-01-06  33.08
10:  5 2016-01-04  54.80
11:  5 2016-01-05  55.05
12:  5 2016-01-06  54.05
> setkey(symbols, id)
> setkey(prices, id)
```

Here, the *symbols* consists of four stock tickers with corresponding *id*, and the *prices* table contains the 3-day close price for these stocks. We also set the stock *id* as the *key* for both tables. Now, we can perform the inner join and eliminate not matched rows from right using the following command:

```
> res <- symbols[prices,nomatch = 0]; res
   id ticker       date  price
1:  1   AMAT 2016-01-04  18.47
2:  1   AMAT 2016-01-05  18.49
3:  1   AMAT 2016-01-06  17.73
4:  2    IBM 2016-01-04 135.95
5:  2    IBM 2016-01-05 135.85
6:  2    IBM 2016-01-06 135.17
7:  3   INTC 2016-01-04  33.99
8:  3   INTC 2016-01-05  33.83
9:  3   INTC 2016-01-06  33.08
```

Note that the results for MSFT are not returned because the stock *id* does not match in these two tables. The output of the above statement is equivalent to the inner join in SQL.

We can also perform left join:

```
> res <- merge(symbols, prices, all.x = T); res
    id ticker       date  price
 1:  1   AMAT 2016-01-04  18.47
 2:  1   AMAT 2016-01-05  18.49
 3:  1   AMAT 2016-01-06  17.73
 4:  2    IBM 2016-01-04 135.95
 5:  2    IBM 2016-01-05 135.85
 6:  2    IBM 2016-01-06 135.17
 7:  3   INTC 2016-01-04  33.99
 8:  3   INTC 2016-01-05  33.83
 9:  3   INTC 2016-01-06  33.08
10:  4   MSFT         NA     NA
```

The left join returns all the rows from the left table, filling in matched columns (or *NA*) from the right table. In this case, MSFT is returned *NA* for the fields of the date and price.

Similarly, we can also perform the right join:

```
> res <- symbols[prices]; res
```

```
    id ticker       date  price
 1:  1   AMAT 2016-01-04  18.47
 2:  1   AMAT 2016-01-05  18.49
 3:  1   AMAT 2016-01-06  17.73
 4:  2    IBM 2016-01-04 135.95
 5:  2    IBM 2016-01-05 135.85
 6:  2    IBM 2016-01-06 135.17
 7:  3   INTC 2016-01-04  33.99
 8:  3   INTC 2016-01-05  33.83
 9:  3   INTC 2016-01-06  33.08
10:  5     NA 2016-01-04  54.80
11:  5     NA 2016-01-05  55.05
12:  5     NA 2016-01-06  54.05
```

In this case, the right join returns all the rows from the right table, filling in matched columns (or *NA*) from the left table.

We can also perform the full outer join:

```
> res <- merge(symbols, prices, all = T); res
id ticker       date  price
 1:  1   AMAT 2016-01-04  18.47
 2:  1   AMAT 2016-01-05  18.49
 3:  1   AMAT 2016-01-06  17.73
 4:  2    IBM 2016-01-04 135.95
 5:  2    IBM 2016-01-05 135.85
 6:  2    IBM 2016-01-06 135.17
 7:  3   INTC 2016-01-04  33.99
 8:  3   INTC 2016-01-05  33.83
 9:  3   INTC 2016-01-06  33.08
10:  4   MSFT         NA     NA
11:  5     NA 2016-01-04  54.80
12:  5     NA 2016-01-05  55.05
13:  5     NA 2016-01-06  54.05
```

The results include all rows from both tables, filling in matched columns (or *NA*).

# Functions in R

R comes with many functions that we can use to perform various computations and data manipulations. For example, we can round a number with the *round* function, or calculate its factorial with the *factorial* function. Using a function is pretty simple – simply write the name of the function and then the data we want the function to operate on in parentheses:

```
> round(pi, 2)
[1] 3.14
```

The input data that we pass into the function is called the argument, which can be raw data, an R object, or even the results of another R function.

One of the great strengths in R is that it allows the user to add functions. In fact, many of the functions in R are actually functions of functions. The structure of a function is very simple:

```
functionname <- function(arg1, arg2, ...){
  statements
  return(object)
```

```
}
```

An R function usually consists of three parts: a name, a body of code, and a set of arguments. To make our own function, we need to replicate these parts and store them in an R object, which we can do with the *function* key word. *function* will build a function out of whatever R code we place between the braces. For example, we can create a square function:

```
> my.square <- function(x){
    return(x * x)
  }
```

We can then use our function by typing in the function name with proper input arguments:

```
> my.square(10)
[1] 100
> my.square(1:5)
[1]  1  4  9 16 25
```

Note that the function *my.square* can take either a single value or a vector of values as input. When taking a vector as input, the function manipulates each value in the vector at the same time, instead of using a *for* loop.

We can write an R function in many different ways, but the fast R code will usually take advantage of three things: logical tests, subsetting, and element-wise execution. To see what vectorized code looks like, we can compare the following two examples of an absolute value function. Each takes a vector of numbers and transforms it into a vector of absolute values. The first example is not vectorized, *abs.loop* uses a *for* loop to manipulate each element of the vector one at a time:

```
abs.loop <- function(x){
  for(i in seq_along(x)){
     if(x[i] < 0){
         x[i] <- - x[i]
     }
  }
  return(x)
}
```

The second example, *abs.vec*, is a vectorized version of *abs.loop*. It uses logical subsetting to manipulate every negative number in the vector at the same time:

```
abs.vec <- function(x){
    negs <- x <0
    x[negs] <- -x[negs]
    return(x)
}
```

The *abs.vec* function is much faster than the *abs.loop* function because it based on operations that R does quickly: logical tests, subsetting, and element-wise execution.

We can use the *system.time* function to check how fast *abs.vec* is. The *system.time* function takes an R expression, runs it, and then displays how much time elapsed while the expression ran. To compare *abs.loop* and *abs.vec*, we first make a long vector of positive and negative numbers:

```
x <- rep(c(1,-1), 10000000)
```

We can then use the *system.time* function to measure how much time it takes each function to evaluate the long vector *x*:

```
> system.time(abs.loop(x))
   user  system elapsed
  18.05    0.22   18.30
> system.time(abs.vec(x))
   user  system elapsed
   0.29    0.23    0.53
```

The first two columns of the output of *system.time* report how many seconds our computer spent executing the call on the user side and system side of our process, which will vary depending on your computer operating system. The last column displays how many seconds elapsed when R ran the expression. The results show that *abs.vec* calculated the absolute value 34.5 times faster than *abs.loop* when applied to a vector of 10 million numbers.

Many R built-in functions are already vectorized and have been optimized to perform quickly. We can make our code faster by using these functions whenever possible. For example, R comes with a built-in absolute value function, *abs*. We can measure the speed of *abs* with *system.time*:

```
system.time(abs(x))
 user  system elapsed
 0.03    0.00    0.03
```

We see that it takes *abs* a lightning-fast of 0.03 seconds to calculate the absolute values of 10 million numbers. This is 17.6 times faster than *abs.vec* and nearly 610 times faster than *abs.loop*.

Writing vectorized code in R is easy because most R functions are already vectorized. Code based on these functions can easily be made vectorized and therefore fast. To create vectorized code, we need to use vectorized functions to complete the sequential steps in our program. We also need to use logical subsetting to handle parallel cases. Try to manipulate every element in a case at once.

# Chapter 2
# Market Data

Market data in finance is the most important part of any successful trading business. Regardless if you are a quant analyst, a quant developer, a trader, or an independent investor, you always deal with market data. Market data is price, volume, and trade-related information for a financial instrument reported by a trading venue such as a stock exchange. Market data allows us to know the latest price and see historical trends for instruments such as equities, fixed-income products, derivatives, and currencies. There are a number of market data vendors, which specialize in collecting, cleaning, collating, and distributing market data. This has become the most common way that we get access to market data.

Delivery of price data from exchanges to users is highly time-sensitive. Specialized technologies designed to handle collection and throughput of massive data streams are used to distribute the information to traders and investors. The speed that market data is distributed can become critical when trading systems are based on analyzing the data before others are able to, such as in high frequency trading.

In this chapter, I will show you how to obtain market data from some popular free online data sources, including Yahoo Finance, Google Finance, Oanda, etc. I will also present some useful R packages, such as *quantmod* and *Quandl*, which provide the user-friendly API and allow you to access market data easily. We will utilize the market data from these free data sources heavily in this book. These data sources usually provide the end-of-day (EOD) market data for stocks, options, currencies, and fixed-income instruments. I will also demonstrate how to access the 15-minute delayed stock quotes and historical intraday bar data from Yahoo; and how to obtain the real-time stock quotes and intraday minute bar data from Google.

## Market Data from Yahoo

Yahoo Finance has a popular API that allows us to download daily market data and 15-minute delayed quotes for stocks and exchange-traded funds (ETFs) from its library. In this section, I will show you how to get the market data from Yahoo directly and how to load the market data into R.

# EOD Stock Data

I will first demonstrate how to get historical EOD stock data from Yahoo Finance. The historical data from Yahoo provide us with the open, high, low, close, adjusted close prices, as well as trade volume data. We can load Yahoo Finance data in several ways into R workspace. However, the simplest and the most stable approach is to download the data into a CSV file and upload the CSV file into R. You can also implement an R function or script to download Yahoo Finance data without the needs of additional R packages. Alternatively, we can use an R package such as *quantmod* or *Quandl* to retrieve the data directly into R. However, this second method may be unusable when Yahoo Finance changes some specifications of the data. In this case, only after a patch is created does the package work again. You can avoid such an issue if you download Finance data directly or use your own R functions.

## *Import CSV File*

Download market data directly from Yahoo Finance is easy. The following steps show you how to retrieve a CSV file of the historical data for SPY. Depending on the browser you are using, the steps that appear on your screen may be slightly different:

- Enter the following website: http://finance.yahoo.com.
- Enter the ticker symbol SPY in the *Enter Symbol* box. This will take us to the page of the latest SPY price quote.
- Click the *Historical Prices* link on the left pane.
- On the *Historical Prices* page, we can set the date range for the data we want to download. For example, we enter the date range from Jan. 1, 2010 to Jan. 1, 2016.
- Click the *Daily* radio button to make sure we download the daily market data.
- Right click the *Download to Spreadsheet* link at the bottom of the page and choose the option to *Save Link As* … onto the subdirectory "[*R working directory*]*/inst/extdata/*" with the file name SPYyahoo.csv. To identify what the *R working directory* is, type the *getwd*() command in the R console. You can place the downloaded market data into any directory as you like. Here, we will put the data into the subdirectory "*/inst/extdata/*"

Now, we have downloaded SPY market data from Yahoo Finance and saved it into a CSV file. To load this CSV file into R, we can use either the base R function *read.csv* or the *fread* function from the *data.table* package. Here, we will use the *fread* function because it is faster than the base *read.csv* command and offers certain advantages like auto-detection of separators etc.:

```
>install.packages("data.table")
>library(data.table)
> spy <- fread("./inst/extdata/SPYyahoo.csv")
> head(spy, 3)
         Date   Open   High    Low  Close    Volume Adj Close
1: 2015-12-31 205.13 205.89 203.87 203.87 114877900    203.87
2: 2015-12-30 207.11 207.21 205.76 205.93  63317700    205.93
3: 2015-12-29 206.51 207.79 206.47 207.40  92640700    207.40
> tail(spy, 3)
         Date   Open   High    Low  Close    Volume Adj Close
1: 2010-01-06 113.52 113.99 113.43 113.71 116074400  100.6598
2: 2010-01-05 113.26 113.68 112.85 113.63 111579900  100.5890
3: 2010-01-04 112.37 113.39 111.51 113.33 118944600  100.3234
```

Here, *spy* is a *data.table* object. When we import data, we should always make sure the data is uploaded correctly. Although the *Date* field from the output above looks like a date, R is not treating it as a date. Instead, R treats that field as a character. Using the class command, we can show how R treats the *Date* variable.

```
> class(spy[,Date])
[1] "character"
```

Since we are not using Date as a character variable, we need to convert it to a variable with class *Date* using the *as.Date* function.

```
> spy[, "Date"] <- as.Date(spy[, Date], format = "%Y-%m-%d")
> class(spy[, Date])
[1] "Date"
```

As we can see, the *Date* variable is now of class *Date*.

The row data imported from the CSV file appears in reverse chronological order. Now, we can use the *setkey* command for the *Date* column. The *setkey* command sorts a data table in the chronological order and marks it as sorted.

```
setkey(spy, Date)
> head(spy, 3)
         Date   Open   High    Low  Close    Volume Adj Close
1: 2010-01-04 112.37 113.39 111.51 113.33 118944600  100.3234
2: 2010-01-05 113.26 113.68 112.85 113.63 111579900  100.5890
3: 2010-01-06 113.52 113.99 113.43 113.71 116074400  100.6598
```

Data table or data frame (a data table is a data frame) is a flexible data structure, and we can perform some of data analyses when an object is a data table. However, since we are mainly dealing with financial time series, it is sometimes more convenient to use the data that is of *xts* type. *xts* stands for eXtensible Time Series and allows us to perform many manipulations and operations on time series data easily. To convert a data table into an *xts* object, we need to use the *xts* package:

```
> install_packages("xts")
> library(xts)
```

Once the *xts* package has been loaded, we can use the *xts* command to convert *spy* into an *xts* object. The *xts* command takes on two arguments that denote which are the data columns, which are columns 2-7, and which is the index column. The index column is simply the date column that is used as an index in a time series, which is in Column one. The index column is preceded by the argument *order.by*, which means we want the order of the data to follow the date column.

```
xts.spy <- xts(spy[,2:7, with = F], order.by = spy[,Date])
> head(xts.spy, 3)
             Open   High    Low  Close    Volume Adj Close
2010-01-04 112.37 113.39 111.51 113.33 118944600  100.3234
2010-01-05 113.26 113.68 112.85 113.63 111579900  100.5890
2010-01-06 113.52 113.99 113.43 113.71 116074400  100.6598
> class(xts.spy)
[1] "xts" "zoo"
```

Note that *xts.spy* is now an *xts* object, and also a *zoo* object. An *xts* object is a variant of a *zoo* object, so *xts* and *zoo* share many of the same characteristics.

## *Using R Function*

In the preceding subsection, we download Yahoo Finance data directly from Yahoo website and save the data into a CSV file. This process involves many manual steps. We can create an R function to do this automatically. The following R function, *yahooHist*, can be used to download historical daily market data:

```
yahooHist <- function(ticker, from, to) {
  library(xts)
  sfrom <- unlist(strsplit(from,"-"))
  sto <- unlist(strsplit(to, "-"))
  url <- paste0("http://ichart.finance.yahoo.com/table.csv?s=",ticker,
               "&a=", as.numeric(sfrom[2]) - 1,"&b=", sfrom[3], "&c=", sfrom[1],
               "&d=", as.numeric(sto[2]) - 1, "&e=", sto[3], "&f=", sto[1],
               "&g=d&ignore=.csv")
  dat <- read.table(url, header = T, sep = ",")
  dat$Date <- as.Date(as.character(dat$Date))
  xts.dat <- xts(dat[, 2:7], order.by = dat[, 1])
  return(xts.dat)
}
```

This function takes the stock ticker and the date range (*from* and *to*) as the input arguments. The key for accessing the Yahoo Finance data is to construct the *url* address with a suitable template. Note that Yahoo Finance API uses a month number 1 less than actual month number (e.g., January = "0"), which is why we need to subtract one from the month number in creating *url*. This function use the base R function and the *xts* package. It returns an *xts* object that holds the stock data. I have saved this function into the subdirectory "[*R working directory*]/*R*/" with a file name of *marketdata.R*.

To use this function in R, we need to source in this function:

```
> source("./R/marketdata.R")
> ibm <- yahoohist("IBM","2015-1-01","2016-1-01")
head(ibm)
             Open   High    Low  Close  Volume Adj.Close
2015-01-02 161.31 163.31 161.00 162.06 5525500  155.3485
2015-01-05 161.27 161.27 159.19 159.51 4880400  152.9041
2015-01-06 159.67 159.96 155.17 156.07 6146700  149.6065
2015-01-07 157.20 157.20 154.03 155.05 4701800  148.6288
2015-01-08 156.24 159.04 155.55 158.42 4236800  151.8592
2015-01-09 158.42 160.34 157.25 159.11 4484800  152.5206
> class(ibm)
[1] "xts" "zoo"
```

You can see how easy it is to load the Yahoo Finance data into R using the *yahoohist* function with just one single line code.

## *Using quantmod Package*

The *quantmod* package provides various functions for downloading financial data from different data sources, including Yahoo Finance. First, we need to install and load the package into R:

```
> install_packages("quantmod")
> library(quantmod)
```

Note that during the installation process, *quantmod* automatically loads all the dependencies that it needs. We can then use the *getSymbols* function in *quantmod* to load Yahoo Finance data into R. For example, to retrieve the IBM data for the period 1/1/2015 to 1/1/2016 from Yahoo Finance, we can use the following code snippet:

```
> getSymbols("IBM",from ="2015-01-01",to ="2016-01-01")
> head(IBM)
           IBM.Open IBM.High IBM.Low IBM.Close IBM.Volume IBM.Adjusted
2015-01-02   161.31   163.31  161.00    162.06    5525500     155.3485
2015-01-05   161.27   161.27  159.19    159.51    4880400     152.9041
2015-01-06   159.67   159.96  155.17    156.07    6146700     149.6065
2015-01-07   157.20   157.20  154.03    155.05    4701800     148.6288
2015-01-08   156.24   159.04  155.55    158.42    4236800     151.8592
2015-01-09   158.42   160.34  157.25    159.11    4484800     152.5206
> class(IBM)
[1] "xts" "zoo"
```

The class command verifies that the class of the data object is *xts* and *zoo*. The output for IBM is identical to that we obtained using our own function.

The *quantmod* package also allows us to download market data for a set of stock symbols at once. For example:

```
> getSymbols(c("SPY", "IWM", "QQQ", "DIA"), from = "2015-01-01", to = "2016-01-01")
```

Now, the market data for all of our four stocks, SPY, IWM, QQQ, and DIA, are available. We can examine the data, i.e. for QQQ:

```
> head(QQQ)
           QQQ.Open QQQ.High QQQ.Low QQQ.Close QQQ.Volume QQQ.Adjusted
2015-01-02   103.76   104.20  102.44    102.94   31314600    101.33688
2015-01-05   102.50   102.61  101.14    101.43   36521300     99.85039
2015-01-06   101.58   101.75   99.62    100.07   66205500     98.51157
2015-01-07   100.74   101.60  100.49    101.36   37577400     99.78148
2015-01-08   102.22   103.50  102.11    103.30   40212600    101.69127
2015-01-09   103.61   103.65  102.02    102.62   41410100    101.02186
```

The *quantmod* package contains many options that allow us to process the market data easily. From the preceding data for QQQ, you may notice that the adjusted close price (the *QQQ.Adjusted* column) is different from the close price (the *QQQ.Close* column). This is because the adjusted close price takes into account of the stock split and dividend. However, Yahoo Finance only provides adjusted data for the close price. For trading strategy backtesting, you may want to have the adjusted data for the open, high, and low prices as well. *quantmod* allows us to convert the OHLC prices into the split- and dividend-adjusted OHLC prices by simply issuing the following statements:

```
> QQQ.ad <- adjustOHLC(QQQ, use.Adjusted = T)
> head(QQQ.ad)
            QQQ.Open QQQ.High   QQQ.Low QQQ.Close QQQ.Volume QQQ.Adjusted
2015-01-02 102.14411 102.5773 100.84466 101.33688   31314600    101.33688
2015-01-05 100.90373 101.0120  99.56491  99.85039   36521300     99.85039
2015-01-06  99.99806 100.1654  98.06858  98.51157   66205500     98.51157
2015-01-07  99.17114 100.0177  98.92503  99.78148   37577400     99.78148
2015-01-08 100.62809 101.8882 100.51980 101.69127   40212600    101.69127
2015-01-09 101.99644 102.0358 100.43120 101.02186   41410100    101.02186
```

Note that the close price in the *QQQ.Close* column is now identical to that in the *QQQ.Adjusted* column, indicating that all of the prices become adjusted data. Unlike the original OHLC prices that are fixed, the adjusted price data may have different values from what we list here because the adjusted historical price data will change whenever the new stock split or dividend information becomes available.

## Stock Quotes

We can also access the 15-minute delayed stock quotes from Yahoo Finance. Here, I will show you how to obtain the stock quotes from Yahoo Finance with two approaches: using our own R function or the *quantmod* package.

### *Using R Function*

We will use Yahoo Finance API with YQL (Yahoo Query Language) to access the stock quotes. YQL is an expressive SQL-like language that allows us to query, filter, and combine data across the web through a single interface. A typical YQL statement looks like this:

```
select * from yahoo.finance.quotes where symbol="IBM"
```

This query is very similar to the standard SQL statement and it will get delayed quotes for IBM. YQL works through a REST API. We pass the YQL query and other optional parameters to the REST API to return our query in XML or JSON format. Thus, a typical URL should look like this:

```
http://query.yahooapis.com/v1/public/yql?q=select%20*%20
  from%20yahoo.finance.quotes%20where%20
  symbol%20in%20({0})&env=store%3A%2F%2Fdatatables.org%2Falltableswithkeys
```

Note that the YQL query is passed in the URL as the query string "*q*" and it is HTML encoded. XML is the default format, but you could add "*&format=json*" to get JSON data if you prefer JSON to XML.

You may notice that the preceding URL contains several "%" signs. As you probably know, URLs can only be sent over the internet using the ASCII character set. Since URLs often contain characters outside the ASCII set, we need to convert them into a valid ASCII format. URL encoding just replaces unsafe ASCII characters with a "%" followed by two hexadecimal digits. For example, URLs cannot contain spaces and URL encoding needs to replace a space with "%20". So, in our preceding URL, "%3A" replaces ":" and "%2F" replaces "/".

Now, we will create an R function named *yahooquote*, which is included in the *marketdata.R* file. Here is the code for this function:

```
yahooQuote <- function(tickers){
  library(XML)
  tk1 <- paste0(tickers[1:length(tickers)-1], sep = "%22%2C%22")
  tk2 <- do.call(paste0, c(as.list(tk1), sep=""))
  tk3 <- paste0("%22",tk2, tickers[length(tickers)],"%22", sep="")
  url<- paste0("http://query.yahooapis.com/v1/public/yql?q=select%20*%20from%20yahoo
              .finance.quotes%20where%20symbol%20in%20(", tk3,")&env=
              store%3A%2F%2Fdatatables.org%2Falltableswithkeys", sep="")
  xmlfile <- xmlParse(url)
  x1 <- xmlRoot(xmlfile)
  x2 <- data.frame(xmlToDataFrame(x1[[1]]), stringsAsFactors = F)
  x2$LastUpdate <- rep(format(Sys.time(),format = "%H:%M:%S %p"),nrow(x2))
  x3 <- x2[c("Symbol", "LastUpdate", "LastTradeTime", "Ask", "Bid",
           "LastTradePriceOnly", "Open","Volume", "StockExchange", "DaysHigh",
           "DaysLow", "Change", "PercentChange", "YearHigh", "YearLow")]
  return(x3)
```

```
}
```

Here, we first load the *xml* package, which is needed for process the XML file. Pay special attention to the URL definition that we want to get stock quotes using YQL query and community Open Data Tables. Open Data Tables are XML files that can be integrated into the YQL platform. These files describe how the YQL query can be mapped onto any web service or source on internet. Once mapped, we can then use these data sources in many ways in YQL.

Here, we use YQL to query the stock quotes from *yahoo.finance.quotes*. We download stock quotes directly using the *xmlParse* function and then convert the XML result into a data frame. Finally, we extract the useful stock quote information from the raw data and store this information into another data frame. This function takes an array (or vector) of stock tickers as input argument, and returns the stock quote information for all tickers we specify in the input.

Here, I will use an example to illustrate how to use this function to get stock quotes from Yahoo Finance. First, we create an array of tickers:

```
> source("./R/marketdata.R")
> tickers <- c("%5EIXIC", "%5EGSPC", "MSFT", "INTC", "IBM", "AMZN", "BIDU", "SINA",
               "NVDA", "AMD", "WMT", "GS", "JPM", "MCD")
```

Note that the tickers array consists of fourteen equity instruments with two indices, NASDAQ Composite (^IXIC) and S&P 500 (^GSPC). Since these two indices contains the special character "^", we need to replace it with a valid ASCII format of "%5E". Now, we can get the stock quotes by calling our function, *yahooQuote*:

```
> quotes <- yahooQuote(tickers); quotes
```

| | Symbol | LastUpdate | LastTradeTime | Ask | Bid | LastTradePriceOnly | Open | Volume | StockExchange | DaysHigh | DaysLow | Change | PercentChange | YearHigh | YearLow |
|---|---|---|---|---|---|---|---|---|---|---|---|---|---|---|---|
| 1 | ^IXIC | 2016-02-24 09:53 | 9:53am | | | 4428.35 | 4453.93 | 0 | NIM | 4455.04 | 4428.21 | -73.24 | -1.67% | 5231.94 | 4209.76 |
| 2 | ^GSPC | 2016-02-24 09:53 | 9:53am | 1894.42 | 1893.20 | 1893.79 | 1917.56 | 81874213 | SNP | 1917.56 | 1893.41 | -27.48 | -1.43% | 2134.72 | 1810.10 |
| 3 | MSFT | 2016-02-24 09:53 | 9:38am | 50.51 | 50.50 | 50.50 | 50.69 | 1307230 | NMS | 50.72 | 50.47 | -0.68 | -1.33% | 56.85 | 39.72 |
| 4 | INTC | 2016-02-24 09:53 | 9:38am | 28.49 | 28.48 | 28.49 | 28.52 | 1050513 | NMS | 28.58 | 28.41 | -0.31 | -1.08% | 35.59 | 24.87 |
| 5 | IBM | 2016-02-24 09:53 | 9:38am | 130.88 | 130.78 | 130.54 | 131.55 | 160252 | NYQ | 131.65 | 130.45 | -1.86 | -1.40% | 176.30 | 116.90 |
| 6 | AMZN | 2016-02-24 09:53 | 9:38am | 544.30 | 543.61 | 543.63 | 545.00 | 307649 | NMS | 545.77 | 543.07 | -9.31 | -1.68% | 696.44 | 365.65 |
| 7 | BIDU | 2016-02-24 09:53 | 9:38am | 157.28 | 157.03 | 157.15 | 159.00 | 348525 | NMS | 159.15 | 156.01 | -3.87 | -2.40% | 223.95 | 100.00 |
| 8 | SINA | 2016-02-24 09:53 | 9:38am | 42.75 | 42.67 | 42.67 | 43.09 | 10692 | NMS | 43.13 | 42.60 | -0.87 | -2.00% | 61.25 | 31.92 |
| 9 | NVDA | 2016-02-24 09:53 | 9:38am | 31.08 | 31.07 | 31.08 | 31.15 | 558104 | NMS | 31.47 | 30.86 | -0.52 | -1.65% | 33.94 | 19.09 |
| 10 | AMD | 2016-02-24 09:53 | 9:38am | 1.97 | 1.96 | 1.97 | 1.98 | 836002 | NCM | 1.99 | 1.93 | +0.00 | +0.00% | 3.23 | 1.61 |
| 11 | WMT | 2016-02-24 09:53 | 9:38am | 66.16 | 66.15 | 66.14 | 66.15 | 500231 | NYQ | 66.30 | 66.08 | -0.34 | -0.51% | 84.72 | 56.30 |
| 12 | GS | 2016-02-24 09:53 | 9:38am | 143.6000 | 143.0200 | 142.0531 | 143.0800 | 278858 | NYQ | 143.2000 | 141.6700 | -2.8569 | -1.9715% | 218.7700 | 139.0500 |
| 13 | JPM | 2016-02-24 09:53 | 9:38am | 54.79 | 54.77 | 54.77 | 55.12 | 2029071 | NYQ | 55.28 | 54.70 | -1.35 | -2.41% | 70.61 | 50.07 |
| 14 | MCD | 2016-02-24 09:53 | 9:38am | 116.71 | 116.67 | 116.72 | 116.32 | 218721 | NYQ | 116.77 | 116.22 | -0.18 | -0.15% | 124.83 | 87.50 |

You can see from the above results that we can get real-time quotes for indices such as NASDAQ composite and S&P 500 (the last update time is almost the same as the last trade time); while we can only get the 15-minute delayed quotes for individual stocks (please check the time field in the *LastUpdate* and *LastTradeTime* columns).

## *Using quantmod Package*

We can also use the *quantmod* package to get the stock quotes. Using the same tickers array we just used in the preceding example, we obtain:

```
> qs <- getQuote(tickers); qs
                 Trade Time      Last    Change % Change    Open    High     Low    Volume
%5EIXIC  2016-02-24 10:05:00 4435.2000 -68.3800   -1.52% 4453.93 4455.04 4427.28         0
%5EGSPC  2016-02-24 10:05:00 1894.6900 -26.5800   -1.38% 1917.56 1917.56 1892.02 103619602
MSFT     2016-02-24 09:50:00   50.3600  -0.8200   -1.60%   50.69   50.73   50.35   2346359
INTC     2016-02-24 09:50:00   28.4150  -0.3850  -1.337%   28.52   28.58   28.41   1641492
IBM      2016-02-24 09:50:00  130.0100  -2.3900   -1.81%  131.55  131.65  130.00    345459
AMZN     2016-02-24 09:50:00  535.1428 -17.7972 -3.2186%  545.00  545.77  535.00    892329
BIDU     2016-02-24 09:50:00  156.4100  -4.6100   -2.86%  159.00  159.15  155.33    545650
SINA     2016-02-24 09:49:00   42.3100  -1.2300   -2.82%   43.09   43.13   42.27     21197
```

```
NVDA     2016-02-24 09:50:00   31.0100  -0.5900    -1.87%   31.15   31.47   30.86   868793
AMD      2016-02-24 09:50:00    1.9500  -0.0200    -1.02%    1.98    1.99    1.93  1158879
WMT      2016-02-24 09:50:00   65.8331  -0.6469  -0.9731%   66.15   66.30   65.83  1100778
GS       2016-02-24 09:50:00  141.2700  -3.6400    -2.51%  143.08  143.20  141.01   535943
JPM      2016-02-24 09:50:00   54.7300  -1.3900    -2.48%   55.12   55.28   54.70  3174800
MCD      2016-02-24 09:50:00  116.1200  -0.7800    -0.67%  116.32  116.86  116.09   477007
```

This gives the standard output. If we want to retrieve other fields, we can use the *what* argument, which allows us to get specific data. The value of the *what* argument in the *getQuote* function with Yahoo as data source should be a *quoteFormat* object with Yahoo's formatting string. For example:

```
> qs <- getQuote(tickers, what = yahooQF(c("Ask", "Bid",
        "Last Trade (Price Only)","Open", "Volume", "Stock Exchange", "Days High",
        "Days Low", "Change", "Change in Percent", "52-week High", "52-week Low")))
> qs
                 Trade Time       Ask       Bid      Last    Open    Volume Stock Exchange    High       Low    Change % Change 52-week High 52-week Low
%5EIXIC 2016-02-24 10:27:00       N/A       N/A 4432.4800 4453.93         0            NIM 4455.04 4427.2800 -71.1000    -1.58%      5231.94     4209.76
%5EGSPC 2016-02-24 10:27:00   1894.48   1893.45 1893.8700 1917.56 140752934            SNP 1917.56 1892.0200 -27.4000    -1.43%      2134.72     1810.10
MSFT    2016-02-24 10:12:00    50.280    50.270   50.2790   50.69   3890737            NMS   50.73   50.2200  -0.9010  -1.760%        56.85       39.72
INTC    2016-02-24 10:12:00     28.48     28.47   28.4700   28.52   2678158            NMS   28.58   28.3800  -0.3300    -1.15%        35.59       24.87
IBM     2016-02-24 10:12:00    130.10    130.08  130.4500  131.55    699390            NYQ  131.65  129.6800  -1.9500    -1.47%       176.30      116.90
AMZN    2016-02-24 10:12:00  536.1300  535.7500  536.0035  545.00   1414971            NMS  545.77  533.1501 -16.9365 -3.0630%       696.44      365.65
BIDU    2016-02-24 10:12:00    155.65    155.51  155.8800  159.00    833103            NMS  159.15  154.8000  -5.1400    -3.19%       223.95      100.00
SINA    2016-02-24 10:11:00     42.47     42.40   42.4000   43.09     39076            NMS   43.13   42.2700  -1.1400    -2.62%        61.25       31.92
NVDA    2016-02-24 10:12:00     30.86     30.85   30.8600   31.15   1644259            NMS   31.47   30.6000  -0.7400    -2.34%        33.94       19.09
AMD     2016-02-24 10:12:00     1.940     1.930    1.9350    1.98   1554528            NCM    1.99    1.9300  -0.0350  -1.777%         3.23        1.61
WMT     2016-02-24 10:12:00     65.97     65.96   66.0200   66.15   1738856            NYQ   66.30   65.7200  -0.4600    -0.69%        84.72       56.30
GS      2016-02-24 10:12:00    140.56    140.55  141.2300  143.08    909073            NYQ  143.20  140.2600  -3.6800    -2.54%       218.77      139.05
JPM     2016-02-24 10:12:00     54.60     54.59   54.5800   55.12   5923383            NYQ   55.28   54.3300  -1.5400    -2.74%        70.61       50.07
MCD     2016-02-24 10:12:00    116.21    116.18  116.2200  116.32    866566            NYQ  116.86  115.9600  -0.6800    -0.58%       124.83       87.50
```

This output is similar to that we just obtained using our own function.

# Option Chain Data

We can also access the option chain data from Yahoo Finance API. Here, I will illustrate how to obtain the option data from Yahoo Finance with two approaches, using our own R function or the *quantmod* package.

## *Using R Function*

If we want to obtain the option chain data for the front month from Yahoo Finance, we can use the following R function:

```
yahooOption <- function(ticker){
  url <- paste0("http://finance.yahoo.com/q/op?s=", ticker, sep="")
  dat <- readHTMLTable(url, stringsAsFactors = F)
  dat1 <- dat[[2]]
  dat1$Type <- rep("Call", nrow(dat1))
  dat2 <- dat[[3]]
  dat2$Type <- rep("Put", nrow(dat2))
  res <- rbind(dat1, dat2)
  colnames(res) <- c("Strike", "Contract Name", "Last", "Bid", "Ask","Change",
      "Percent Change", "Volume", "Open Interest", "Implied Vol", "Option Type")
  return(res)
}
```

Here, we retrieve the option data by directly reading the HTML webpage using the *readHTMLTable* function. We simply figure out the call and put option data by manual inspection. If the data location changes across the webpages we are parsing, we might need to define the position programmatically using either the length of table or some other text criteria. This function is also included in the *marketdata.R* file.

Now, we can use this function to retrieve the option chain data. For example:

```
> source("./R/marketdata.R")
> option <- yahooOption("IBM"); option
   Strike      Contract Name  Last   Bid   Ask Change Percent Change Volume Open Interest Implied Vol Option Type
1  100.00 IBM160226C00100000 26.10 29.90 33.45   0.00          0.00%      1             1     247.36%        Call
2  115.00 IBM160226C00115000 16.78 14.85 17.50   0.00          0.00%     10            10     104.49%        Call
3  118.00 IBM160226C00118000 13.67 12.15 14.40   0.00          0.00%      1            55      82.81%        Call
4  119.00 IBM160226C00119000 12.75 13.05 13.40  -1.20         -8.60%      2           181      63.09%        Call
5  120.00 IBM160226C00120000 11.75 12.05 12.25   5.28         81.61%      2           183      61.52%        Call
6  121.00 IBM160226C00121000 11.15 11.05 11.75   0.00          0.00%      1           738      68.07%        Call
7  122.00 IBM160226C00122000 10.14 10.05 10.30   0.00          0.00%      3           205      56.64%        Call
8  123.00 IBM160226C00123000  8.60  9.00  9.25  -1.55        -15.27%     20           179      48.34%        Call
9  124.00 IBM160226C00124000  7.62  8.05  8.30  -1.05        -12.11%    115           286      47.46%        Call
10 125.00 IBM160226C00125000  6.35  7.05  7.35  -1.26        -16.56%     21          1001      45.51%        Call
11 126.00 IBM160226C00126000  5.75  5.70  6.35  -0.86        -13.01%    556          1191      40.53%        Call
12 127.00 IBM160226C00127000  3.60  5.10  5.40  -2.85        -44.19%     71           627      37.70%        Call
13 128.00 IBM160226C00128000  3.90  4.00  4.50  -1.38        -26.14%     32           255      35.94%        Call
14 129.00 IBM160226C00129000  2.42  3.25  3.65  -2.28        -48.51%     60           172      34.47%        Call
15 130.00 IBM160226C00130000  2.23  2.42  2.84  -0.53        -19.20%   1394           415      32.67%        Call
16 131.00 IBM160226C00131000  1.68  1.75  2.11  -0.76        -31.15%    343           100      31.06%        Call
17 132.00 IBM160226C00132000  1.30  1.31  1.57  -0.43        -24.86%    858           817      31.49%        Call
18 133.00 IBM160226C00133000  0.85  0.89  1.06  -0.33        -27.97%   1759           612      30.32%        Call
19 134.00 IBM160226C00134000  0.56  0.51  0.70  -0.21        -27.27%    539          1421      30.08%        Call
20 135.00 IBM160226C00135000  0.36  0.28  0.41  -0.12        -25.00%   2616          6331      29.00%        Call

……

53 124.00 IBM160226P00124000  0.10  0.05  0.11   0.01         11.11%    105           322      43.16%         Put
54 125.00 IBM160226P00125000  0.12  0.08  0.14   0.02         20.00%    123           822      40.82%         Put
55 126.00 IBM160226P00126000  0.19  0.12  0.19   0.05         35.71%    250           783      39.06%         Put
56 127.00 IBM160226P00127000  0.19  0.18  0.23   0.02         11.76%     68           467      35.94%         Put
57 128.00 IBM160226P00128000  0.49  0.27  0.39   0.20         68.97%     63           391      36.62%         Put
58 129.00 IBM160226P00129000  0.47  0.41  0.54   0.02          4.44%    136           280      35.06%         Put
59 130.00 IBM160226P00130000  0.79  0.62  0.74   0.17         27.42%   5217          3786      33.40%         Put
60 131.00 IBM160226P00131000  1.00  0.90  1.04   0.15         17.65%    221           501      32.37%         Put
61 132.00 IBM160226P00132000  1.38  1.32  1.45   0.09          6.98%    957          2867      31.69%         Put
62 133.00 IBM160226P00133000  1.92  1.87  1.96   0.02          1.05%    379          1399      30.96%         Put
63 134.00 IBM160226P00134000  4.00  2.50  2.83   1.79         81.00%      1           516      36.08%         Put
64 135.00 IBM160226P00135000  3.85  3.20  3.80   1.06         37.99%     19           109      42.53%         Put
65 136.00 IBM160226P00136000  3.30  4.05  6.45   0.00          0.00%     20            21      60.16%         Put
66 137.00 IBM160226P00137000  4.10  4.80  6.00   0.00          0.00%     30            34      60.55%         Put
67 138.00 IBM160226P00138000  5.00  5.85  8.20   0.00          0.00%      9             5      67.38%         Put
68 139.00 IBM160226P00139000 18.43  6.80  9.10   0.00          0.00%      3             6      71.24%         Put
69 140.00 IBM160226P00140000  7.30  7.80  9.75   0.00          0.00%      4             4      71.73%         Put
70 142.00 IBM160226P00142000 17.10  9.55 12.15   0.00          0.00%      1             1      84.57%         Put
71 143.00 IBM160226P00143000 19.39 10.55 13.15   0.00          0.00%      3             0      89.65%         Put
72 145.00 IBM160226P00145000 16.82 12.55 15.15   0.00          0.00%      3             1      99.46%         Put
```

If we know the exact expiration date of an option, we can then retrieve the option chain data for that particular expiration date using the following function:

```
yahooOption1 <- function(ticker, expirDate){
  days <- as.Date(expirDate,format="%Y-%m-%d") -
          as.Date("1970-01-01",format="%Y-%m-%d")
  num <- as.numeric(days) * 86400
  url <- paste0("http://finance.yahoo.com/q/op?s=", ticker,"&date=", num, sep="")
  dat <- readHTMLTable(url, stringsAsFactors = F)
  if(length(dat) < 3)
    return(yahoooption(ticker))
  dat1 <- dat[[2]]
  dat1$Type <- rep("Call", nrow(dat1))
  dat2 <- dat[[3]]
  dat2$Type <- rep("Put", nrow(dat2))
  res <- rbind(dat1, dat2)
  colnames(res) <- c("Strike", "Contract Name", "Last", "Bid", "Ask", "Change",
    "Percent Change", "Volume", "Open Interest", "Implied Vol", "Option Type")
```

```
    return(res)
}
```

Note that Yahoo Finance API uses a special format for the expiration date: it uses the seconds cumulated starting from 1/1/1970 as the date units. To obtain the option data using this function, we must enter the exact expiration date. Otherwise, the option data for the front month will be returned. Here are some valid option expiration dates for IBM option chain:

```
2/16/2016    3/4/2016     3/11/2016    3/18/2016    3/24/2016
4/1/2016     4/15/2016    7/15/2016    1/20/2017    1/19/2017
```

We need to check the option expiration calendars for different securities.

For example, we can retrieve the option data for IBM with an expiration date of 1/20/2017:

```
> source("./R/marketdata.R")
> option <- yahooOption1("IBM", "2017-01-20"); option
```

| | Strike | Contract Name | Last | Bid | Ask | Change | Percent Change | Volume | Open Interest | Implied Vol | Option Type |
|---|---|---|---|---|---|---|---|---|---|---|---|
| 1 | 60.00 | IBM170120C00060000 | 74.00 | 69.80 | 74.50 | 0.00 | 0.00% | 20 | 20 | 57.02% | Call |
| 2 | 80.00 | IBM170120C00080000 | 53.69 | 50.05 | 55.00 | 0.00 | 0.00% | 4 | 30 | 42.13% | Call |
| 3 | 85.00 | IBM170120C00085000 | 47.78 | 45.35 | 50.00 | 0.00 | 0.00% | 2 | 12 | 38.08% | Call |
| 4 | 90.00 | IBM170120C00090000 | 45.16 | 40.55 | 45.40 | 0.00 | 0.00% | 5 | 5 | 36.16% | Call |
| 5 | 95.00 | IBM170120C00095000 | 28.34 | 35.85 | 40.50 | 0.00 | 0.00% | 23 | 24 | 32.76% | Call |
| 6 | 100.00 | IBM170120C00100000 | 33.85 | 31.15 | 36.00 | 0.00 | 0.00% | 1 | 417 | 30.95% | Call |
| 7 | 105.00 | IBM170120C00105000 | 28.57 | 26.70 | 31.50 | -2.03 | -6.63% | 1 | 149 | 28.86% | Call |
| 8 | 110.00 | IBM170120C00110000 | 26.30 | 24.55 | 25.20 | 0.00 | 0.00% | 5 | 251 | 20.94% | Call |
| 9 | 115.00 | IBM170120C00115000 | 20.80 | 20.75 | 21.05 | -1.45 | -6.52% | 4 | 557 | 20.08% | Call |
| 10 | 120.00 | IBM170120C00120000 | 16.69 | 17.30 | 18.00 | -1.66 | -9.05% | 20 | 1004 | 21.27% | Call |
| 11 | 125.00 | IBM170120C00125000 | 13.59 | 14.15 | 14.50 | -1.02 | -6.98% | 20 | 1789 | 20.40% | Call |
| 12 | 130.00 | IBM170120C00130000 | 11.25 | 11.30 | 11.60 | -0.35 | -3.02% | 9 | 1807 | 20.08% | Call |

......

From the contract name field, we can see that expiration date is 170120, that is, 1/20/2017.

## *Using quantmod Package*

We can also use the *getOptionChain* function in the *quantmod* package to retrieve the option chain data from Yahoo Finance. For example:

```
> ibm <- getOptionChain("IBM")
> head(ibm$calls)
                   Strike  Last  Chg   Bid   Ask Vol  OI
IBM160226C00100000    100 26.10 0.00 31.25 35.00   1   1
IBM160226C00115000    115 16.78 0.00 16.35 19.80  10  10
IBM160226C00118000    118 13.67 0.00 13.65 15.85   1  55
IBM160226C00119000    119 13.95 0.00 13.90 14.90   6 181
IBM160226C00120000    120 11.75 5.28 12.85 13.55   2 183
IBM160226C00121000    121 11.15 0.00 11.75 12.95   1 738
> head(ibm$puts)
                   Strike Last Chg Bid  Ask Vol  OI
IBM160226P00095000     95 0.03   0   0 0.06   1   4
IBM160226P00100000    100 0.06   0   0 0.06   4  24
IBM160226P00105000    105 0.04   0   0 0.06  10  53
IBM160226P00108000    108 0.24   0   0 0.06  13  13
IBM160226P00110000    110 0.01   0   0 0.04   2 118
IBM160226P00112000    112 0.08   0   0 0.06   2   3
```

This returns the front-month option chain data for IBM. We can also obtain the option data for specified expiration date:

```
> ibm <- getOptionChain("IBM","2017-01-20")
> head(ibm$calls)
                   Strike  Last Chg  Bid  Ask Vol  OI
IBM170120C00060000     60 74.00   0 70.7 75.5  20  20
IBM170120C00080000     80 53.69   0 51.0 55.9   4  30
IBM170120C00085000     85 47.78   0 46.1 51.0   2  12
IBM170120C00090000     90 45.16   0 41.3 46.0   5   5
IBM170120C00095000     95 28.34   0 36.8 41.2  23  24
IBM170120C00100000    100 33.85   0 32.2 36.6   1 417
> head(ibm$puts)
                   Strike Last  Chg  Bid  Ask Vol   OI
IBM170120P00060000     60 0.50 0.00 0.40 0.56   2  216
IBM170120P00065000     65 0.69 0.00 0.55 0.69  10  191
IBM170120P00070000     70 0.82 0.00 0.73 0.89  35  344
IBM170120P00075000     75 1.01 0.06 0.94 1.12  27 1582
IBM170120P00080000     80 1.35 0.10 1.18 1.36  10 1706
IBM170120P00085000     85 1.60 0.00 1.51 1.70   3 1581
```

If we provide the wrong expiration date, the *getOptionChain* function returns the following message with the available expiration dates:

```
> ibm <- getOptionChain("IBM","2017-01-02")
Error in getOptionChain.yahoo(Symbols = "IBM", Exp = "2017-01-02") :
  Provided expiry date(s) not found. Available dates are: 2016-02-26, 2016-03-04,
2016-03-11, 2016-03-18, 2016-03-24, 2016-04-01, 2016-04-15, 2016-07-15, 2017-01-20,
2018-01-19
```

If setting the expiry date to NULL, we will obtain the option chain data for all expirations.

```
> ibm <- getOptionChain("IBM", NULL)
> class(ibm)
[1] "list"
> names(ibm)
 [1] "Feb.26.2016" "Mar.04.2016" "Mar.11.2016" "Mar.18.2016" "Mar.24.2016"
     "Apr.01.2016" "Apr.15.2016" "Jul.15.2016" "Jan.20.2017" "Jan.19.2018"
```

In this case, the output is a list object, which contains the option data for all expiration dates. We can access the data using the following command:

```
> head(ibm$Jul.15.2016$calls)
                   Strike  Last   Chg   Bid   Ask Vol   OI
IBM160715C00100000    100 33.89  0.00 31.60 35.70   1    5
IBM160715C00105000    105 22.80  0.00 27.20 29.75   1    3
IBM160715C00110000    110 22.62 10.05 22.55 25.00   5   52
IBM160715C00115000    115 20.10  0.00 18.15 20.70   4   34
IBM160715C00120000    120 15.60 -0.20 14.35 16.90   3 1486
IBM160715C00125000    125 10.90 -1.45 11.70 12.60  10 1068
```

# Market Data from Google

In the preceding section, I demonstrated how to get market data from Yahoo Finance. We can also obtain the market data from Google. Google started finance service in 2006 in its website *http://www.google.com/finance*. It provides market data for stocks, currencies, and options. However, Google Finance API has been officially deprecated since 2012. In fact, we can still access some of their

API features, including historical EOD data, minute bar data, real-time (without delay) stock quotes, and option chain data. In this section, I will show you how to access these market data from Google.

## EOD and Minute-Bar Data

Using Google finance API, we can access the historical market data.

### *Using R Functions*

We can easily implement a simple R function to retrieve the EOD (daily) stock data. Here is the code for this function named *googleHist*:

```
googleHist <- function(ticker, from, to){
  library(xts)
  url <- paste0("http://www.google.com/finance/historical?q=", ticker,
      "&histperiod=daily&startdate=", from, "&enddate=", to, "&output=csv")
  dat <- read.table(url, header = T, sep=",")
  colnames(dat)[1] <- "Date"
  dat$Date <- as.Date(as.character(dat$Date), format="%d-%b-%y")
  xts.dat <- xts(dat[, 2:6], order.by = dat[, 1])
  return(xts.dat)
}
```

This function takes the stock ticker and the date range (*from* and *to*) as the input arguments. The key for accessing the Google Finance data is to construct the *url* address with a suitable template. It then loads the CSV file from Google into a data frame object. This function also use the *xts* package and converts the data frame into an *xts* object. I also include this function in the *marketdata.R* file.

We can now use this function to retrieve the market data from Google using the following command:

```
> ibm <- googleHist("IBM", "2015-01-01", "2016-01-01"); head(ibm)
             Open   High    Low  Close  Volume
2015-01-02 161.31 163.31 161.00 162.06 5525466
2015-01-05 161.27 161.27 159.19 159.51 4880389
2015-01-06 159.67 159.96 155.17 156.07 6146712
2015-01-07 157.20 157.20 154.03 155.05 4701839
2015-01-08 156.24 159.04 155.55 158.42 4241113
2015-01-09 158.42 160.34 157.25 159.11 4488347
```

You can see that this function returns the standard stock data with the Open, High, Low, and Close prices as well as the Volume data.

In fact, Google Finance has another special API that allows us to download not only the daily stock (EOD) data but also various intraday bar data from its library. This is the undocumented API, which provides EOD data, intraday data for the past 10 days, and bar data going back for years. This is a very powerful tool for collecting the market data. For example, we can use the following URL to pull the historical EOD data for IBM:

```
http://www.google.com/finance/getprices?q=IBM&i=86400&p=2Y&f=d,c,h,l,o,v
```

Note that to retrieve the market data, we need to provide several parameters:

- *q* – Stock ticker.
- *i* – Interval size in seconds (86400 = 1 day intervals).

- *p* – Period (A number followed by a "*d*" for days, "*M*" for months, or "*Y*" for years. i.e., $2Y = 2$ years, meaning that we want to get most recent two-year data).

The following shows the raw data format for IBM EOD stock data from Google:

```
EXCHANGE%3DNYSE
MARKET_OPEN_MINUTE=570
MARKET_CLOSE_MINUTE=960
INTERVAL=86400
COLUMNS=DATE,CLOSE,HIGH,LOW,OPEN,VOLUME
DATA=
TIMEZONE_OFFSET=-240
a1445284800,149.22,149.97,148.38,149.85,7954684
1,140.64,142.88,140.27,142.49,16025591
2,140.92,142.66,139.3,140.25,7134948
3,144.09,145.07,141.62,141.74,5583167
4,144.68,145.49,143.7,144.61,5370439
7,143.66,145,143.21,144.75,3489428
8,137.86,143.83,137.33,143.51,15008527
9,140.83,141.23,137.5,137.92,8511376
10,140.55,140.82,139.0201,140.36,3710445
11,140.08,141.33,139.9,140.44,3983990
......
```

You can see that the raw data consists of two parts, a header and data. It ends with the *TIMEZONE_OFFSET* entry. The *COLUMNS* entry defines the fields of the data and the *INTERVAL* shows the number of seconds that every line of data represents. Each line of the data part includes six fields, Date, Close, High, Low, Open, and Volume, for a period of length specified by *INTERVAL* parameter. Google's raw data represents date in two parts: absolute and relative. The absolute part starts with "*a*" followed by number of seconds elapsed since 1/1/1997 (the beginning of the UNIX era). In the preceding raw data, only the first line of data uses it (*a*1445284800). The relative part just provides the number of intervals elapsed since the last absolute date. The key step here is how to convert the above raw data into a data structure in R, which we can use easily for our financial analysis.

To achieve this goal, I implement an R function named *googleHist1*. Here is the code for this function:

```
googleHist1 <- function(ticker, period, bartype =
               c("EOD", "1Min", "5Mins", "10Mins", "30Mins", "60Mins")){
  barsize <- function(it = c("EOD", "1Min", "5Mins", "10Mins", "30Mins", "60Mins")){
    match.arg(it)
  }
  interval <- barsize(bartype)
  bars <- 0
  if(interval=="EOD"){
    bars <- 86400
  } else if (interval =="1Min"){
    bars <- 60
  } else if(interval == "5Mins"){
    bars <- 300
  } else if(interval == "10Mins"){
    bars <- 600
  } else if(interval == "30Mins"){
    bars <- 1800
  } else if(interval == "60Mins"){
    bars <- 3600
  } else {
```

```
    return(NULL)
  }
  url <- paste0("http://www.google.com/finance/getprices?q=", ticker, "&i=", bars,
                "&p=", period, "&f=d,c,h,l,o,v")
  dat <- readLines(url)
  dat1 <- googleHistProcess(ticker, bars, dat)
  return(dat1)
}
```

Note that this function takes ticker, data range, and *bartype* as input arguments. The *bartype* parameter has six options, including EOD, 1-, 5-, 10-, 30-, and 60-minute bar data. We construct the URL-address from variables inside the function, so that it changes for each value of the stock ticker, the bar type, and the date range required.

Inside the *googleHist1* function, we define another helper function named *barsize*. This function is used to check if the *bartype* parameter is included in our six bar types we predefined. After constructing the URL, we use the *readLines* function to download the raw data and store it into the *dat* object. We then process the raw data using another method called *googleHistProcess*:

```
googleHistProcess <- function(ticker, bars, dat){
  dtlast <- 0
  dtprev <- 0
  df <- data.frame(Date = character(0), Open = numeric(0), High = numeric(0),
                   Low = numeric(0), Close = numeric(0), Volume = numeric(0),
                   stringsAsFactors = F)
  for(i in 7:length(dat)){
    items <- unlist(strsplit(dat[i],","))
    if(length(items) < 6){
      next()
    }
    dt <- 0
    if(grepl("a", items[1])){
      items <- as.numeric(substring(items, 2, nchar(items)))
      dtlast <- as.POSIXct(items[1], origin = "1970-01-01")
      dt <- dtlast
    } else {
      items <- as.numeric(items)
      dt = dtlast + items[1] * bars
    }
    if(as.POSIXct(as.character(as.Date(dt))) == dtprev){
      next()
    }
    df[nrow(df)+1, ] <- c(as.character(dt),items[5], items[3],
                          items[4], items[2], items[6])
    dtprev = dt
  }
  df[,c(2:6)] <- sapply(df[,c(2:6)], as.numeric)
  xts.dat <- xts(df[, -1], order.by = as.POSIXct(df[, 1]))
  return(xts.dat)
}
```

Here, we use a for-loop to process the timestamps just for demonstration purpose. You may optimize or vectorize the above function to speed up the process.

I will use an example to illustrate how to use the *googleHist1* function to retrieve the historical stock bar data from Google:

```
> source("./R/marketdata.R")
> ibm <- googleHist1("IBM","2Y", "1Min")
> head(ibm)
                      Open     High    Low   Close Volume
2016-02-05 09:30:00  27.22  27.2200  27.22  27.220      0
2016-02-05 09:31:00 127.16 127.6300 127.16 127.630  61909
2016-02-05 09:32:00 127.63 127.7899 127.43 127.515  11399
2016-02-05 09:33:00 127.52 127.5299 127.30 127.440   6444
2016-02-05 09:34:00 127.45 127.5000 127.17 127.235  17782
2016-02-05 09:35:00 127.25 127.2900 127.17 127.190  10110
> tail(ibm)
                       Open   High    Low   Close Volume
2016-02-25 15:55:00 134.250 134.30 134.24 134.290  17513
2016-02-25 15:56:00 134.300 134.31 134.24 134.260  16779
2016-02-25 15:57:00 134.270 134.37 134.25 134.320  35791
2016-02-25 15:58:00 134.325 134.37 134.31 134.345  28479
2016-02-25 15:59:00 134.340 134.41 134.32 134.385  45856
2016-02-25 16:00:00 134.380 134.51 134.37 134.510 103206
```

For historical bar data, Google Finance API sets some limits for the date range. For example, we can only access 15-workday minute-bar data, 75-workday 5-minute bar data, 150-workday 10-minute bar data, and so on. From the above output, even though we specify a period of "2*Y*" (2 years) in the *googleHist1* function for the minute-bar (*bartype* = "1*Min*") data, we can only retrieve 15-workday data. We can retrieve the 10-minute bar data using the following command:

```
> ibm <- googleHist1("IBM","2Y", "10Mins")
> head(ibm)
                       Open   High    Low    Close Volume
2015-08-03 09:40:00  61.700  61.85  60.40  60.4586  91886
2015-08-03 09:50:00 160.500 160.50 159.38 159.7500 165145
2015-08-03 10:00:00 159.750 159.94 159.70 159.7760 130040
2015-08-03 10:10:00 159.755 160.50 159.70 159.8550 154471
2015-08-03 10:20:00 159.890 160.55 159.85 160.0000 194927
2015-08-03 10:30:00 160.040 160.06 159.40 159.5000  70602
> tail(ibm)
                       Open   High      Low  Close Volume
2016-02-25 15:10:00 133.630 133.83 133.6000 133.78  61776
2016-02-25 15:20:00 133.770 133.84 133.7000 133.71 104057
2016-02-25 15:30:00 133.715 133.75 133.3500 133.38 100462
2016-02-25 15:40:00 133.390 133.82 133.3600 133.82 109628
2016-02-25 15:50:00 133.760 134.28 133.7005 134.25 247067
2016-02-25 16:00:00 134.250 134.51 134.2300 134.51 379846
```

The output shows that we can indeed retrieve the 10-minute bar data from Google going back to about 150 workdays.

There is no period limitation for the EOD stock data. I should also point out here that you could access the historical market data from Google not only for stocks, but also for other securities, such as forex. For example, we can use the following command to access the USDEUR exchange rate data:

```
> eur <- googleHist1("USDEUR","2Y", "EOD")
> head(eur)
                    Open High Low     Close Volume
2014-02-26 18:58:00    0    0   0 0.7307217     NA
2014-02-27 18:58:00    0    0   0 0.7294212      0
2014-02-28 18:58:00    0    0   0 0.7244960      0
```

```
2014-03-01 18:58:00    0    0    0 0.7244855      0
2014-03-02 18:58:00    0    0    0 0.7260134      0
2014-03-03 18:58:00    0    0    0 0.7279742      0
> tail(eur)
                    Open High Low      Close Volume
2016-02-20 18:58:00    0    0    0 0.8982709      0
2016-02-21 18:58:00    0    0    0 0.8982709      0
2016-02-22 18:58:00    0    0    0 0.9069472      0
2016-02-23 18:58:00    0    0    0 0.9069472      0
2016-02-24 18:58:00    0    0    0 0.9080178      0
2016-02-25 18:58:00    0    0    0 0.9071118      0
```

Here, we want to retrieve the 2-year EOD date for USDEUR. Note that for currency rate, only the *Close* price are available.

### *Using quantmod Package*

We can also use the *quantmod* package to retrieve the historical EOD market data from Google. This is achieved by call the *getSymbols* function by setting the input argument *src* = "*google*". For example:

```
> ibm <- getSymbols("IBM", from = "2015-01-01", to = "2016-01-01",
                    src = "google", auto.assign = F)
> head(ibm)
           IBM.Open IBM.High IBM.Low IBM.Close IBM.Volume
2015-01-02   161.31   163.31  161.00    162.06    5525466
2015-01-05   161.27   161.27  159.19    159.51    4880389
2015-01-06   159.67   159.96  155.17    156.07    6146712
2015-01-07   157.20   157.20  154.03    155.05    4701839
2015-01-08   156.24   159.04  155.55    158.42    4241113
2015-01-09   158.42   160.34  157.25    159.11    4488347
```

The output gives the OHLC and volume data for IBM. Note that if we do not specify the *src* argument, the *getSymbols* function will return the market data from Yahoo Finance (the default *src*). However, the *quantmod* package does not provide functions that allow us to retrieve the historical stock bar data. If we need the recent bar (for example the minute-bar) data, we need to implement our own functions to download the data, like the *googlHist1* function we created in the preceding subsection.

## Real-Time Stock Quotes

Unlike Yahoo Finance API where you can only access the 15-minute delayed stock quotes, Google Finance allows you to access the real-time quotes for most of the US stocks. Note that currently, the *getQuote* function in the *quantmod* package only handles source quotes from Yahoo Finance, which provides 15-minute delayed quotes for most US stocks. Here, I will show you how to implement the *googleQuote* function, which allows you to retrieve the real-time stock quotes from Google Finance.

We can use Google Finance API to access the real-time stock quotes using the URL something like *http://www.google.com/finance/info?infotype=infoquoteall&q=IBM*, which will give us the live quotes for IBM in the JSON format. In order to use the live quotes easily in our financial analysis, we need to convert JSON into a data structure in R, such as the data frame. Add the *googleQuote* function to the *marketdata.R* file. Here is the code snippet for this function:

```
googleQuote <- function(tickers){
  library(RJSONIO)
```

```
  library(RCurl)
  tk1 <- paste0(tickers[1:length(tickers)-1], sep = ",")
  tk2 <- do.call(paste0, c(as.list(tk1)))
  tk3 <- paste0(tk2, tickers[length(tickers)])
  url <- paste0("http://www.google.com/finance/info?infotype=infoquoteall&q=", tk3)
  dat <- getURL(url)
  dat1 <- gsub("//", "", dat)
  dat2 <- fromJSON(dat1)
  dat3 <- as.data.frame(do.call(rbind, dat2))
  dat3$LastUpdate <- rep(format(Sys.time(),format = "%H:%M:%S %p"),nrow(dat3))
  dat4 <- dat3[c("t", "LastUpdate", "lt_dts", "l", "l_cur", "op", "pcls_fix",
                 "e", "hi", "lo", "c", "cp", "hi52", "lo52")]
  colnames(dat4) <- c("Symbol", "LastUpdate", "LastTradeTime", "QuotePrice",
                      "TradePrice", "Open", "PreviousClose", "Exchange", "DayHigh",
                      "DayLow", "Change", "PercentChange", "YearHigh", "YearLow")
  return(dat4)
}
```

Here, to download and process the JSON data, we need to install and load the packages, *RJSONIO* and *RCurl*. Next, we construct URL in a suitable format and use the *getURL* function to retrieve the stock quote data. If we examine this data carefully, we will find this data is not in a pure JSON format. We need to remove the extra "//" character. Next, we convert the JSON data into a data frame and extract the useful information from the raw data. Finally, we use the meaningful names to rename the columns of the data frame. This function takes an array (or vector) of stock tickers as input argument, and returns the stock quote information for all tickers you specify in the input.

Here, I will use an example to demonstrate how to use this function to obtain real-time stock quotes from Google Finance. First, we create an array of tickers:

```
> source("./R/marketdata.R")
> tickers <- c(".DJI", ".IXIC", ".INX", "MSFT", "INTC", "IBM", "AMZN", "BIDU",
               "SINA", "NVDA", "AMD", "WMT", "GS", "JPM", "MCD")
```

Note that the tickers array consists of fifteen equity instruments with three indices, Dow Jones Industrial (.DJI), NASDAQ Composite (.IXIC), and S&P 500 (.INX). Now, we can retrieve the real-time stock quotes by calling our function, *googleQuote*:

```
> q <- googleQuote(tickers); q
```

| | Symbol | LastUpdate | LastTradeTime | QuotePrice | TradePrice | Open | PreviousClose | Exchange | DayHigh | DayLow | Change | PercentChange | YearHigh | YearLow |
|---|---|---|---|---|---|---|---|---|---|---|---|---|---|---|
| 1 | .DJI | 10:45:02 AM | 2016-02-26T10:45:01Z | 16,741.16 | 16,741.16 | 16,712.70 | 16697.289 | INDEXDJX | 16,795.98 | 16.684.36 | +43.87 | 0.26 | 18,351.36 | 15,370.33 |
| 2 | .IXIC | 10:45:02 AM | 2016-02-26T10:45:02Z | 4,603.36 | 4,603.36 | 4,615.14 | 4582.2051 | INDEXNASDAQ | 4,618.85 | 4,588.12 | +21.15 | 0.46 | 5,231.94 | 4,209.76 |
| 3 | .INX | 10:45:02 AM | 2016-02-26T10:45:01Z | 1,958.80 | 1,958.80 | 1,954.95 | 1951.7 | INDEXSP | 1,962.96 | 1,951.70 | +7.10 | 0.36 | 2,134.72 | 1,810.10 |
| 4 | MSFT | 10:45:02 AM | 2016-02-26T10:45:01Z | 51.77 | 51.77 | 52.60 | 52.1 | NASDAQ | 52.68 | 51.70 | -0.33 | -0.63 | 56.85 | 39.72 |
| 5 | INTC | 10:45:02 AM | 2016-02-26T10:45:01Z | 29.93 | 29.93 | 29.88 | 29.62 | NASDAQ | 29.96 | 29.70 | +0.31 | 1.05 | 35.59 | 24.87 |
| 6 | IBM | 10:45:02 AM | 2016-02-26T10:45:00Z | 133.34 | 133.34 | 134.51 | 134.5 | NYSE | 134.92 | 132.31 | -1.16 | -0.86 | 176.30 | 116.90 |
| 7 | AMZN | 10:45:02 AM | 2016-02-26T10:44:58Z | 560.56 | 560.56 | 560.12 | 555.15 | NASDAQ | 562.50 | 557.00 | +5.41 | 0.98 | 696.44 | 365.65 |
| 8 | BIDU | 10:45:02 AM | 2016-02-26T10:45:01Z | 173.26 | 173.26 | 175.24 | 158.22 | NASDAQ | 176.81 | 172.20 | +15.04 | 9.51 | 223.95 | 100.00 |
| 9 | SINA | 10:45:02 AM | 2016-02-26T10:44:19Z | 43.25 | 43.25 | 43.61 | 42.75 | NASDAQ | 43.98 | 43.12 | +0.50 | 1.17 | 61.25 | 31.92 |
| 10 | NVDA | 10:45:02 AM | 2016-02-26T10:45:01Z | 31.50 | 31.50 | 32.04 | 31.89 | NASDAQ | 32.12 | 31.36 | -0.39 | -1.24 | 33.94 | 19.09 |
| 11 | AMD | 10:45:02 AM | 2016-02-26T10:44:42Z | 2.06 | 2.06 | 2.04 | 2.03 | NASDAQ | 2.07 | 2.03 | +0.03 | 1.48 | 3.23 | 1.61 |
| 12 | WMT | 10:45:02 AM | 2016-02-26T10:45:01Z | 67.04 | 67.04 | 68.08 | 68.04 | NYSE | 68.20 | 66.76 | -1.00 | -1.47 | 84.16 | 56.30 |
| 13 | GS | 10:45:02 AM | 2016-02-26T10:45:01Z | 150.61 | 150.61 | 149.72 | 148.25 | NYSE | 150.81 | 149.01 | +2.36 | 1.59 | 218.77 | 139.05 |
| 14 | JPM | 10:45:02 AM | 2016-02-26T10:45:02Z | 57.53 | 57.53 | 57.64 | 57.01 | NYSE | 57.71 | 57.14 | +0.52 | 0.91 | 70.61 | 50.07 |
| 15 | MCD | 10:45:02 AM | 2016-02-26T10:44:40Z | 116.98 | 116.98 | 117.98 | 117.48 | NYSE | 118.27 | 116.81 | -0.50 | -0.43 | 124.83 | 87.50 |

You can see that we can indeed get the real-time quotes from Google without any delay (please check the *LastUpdate* and *TradeTimeDetail* fields), which may be important if you are doing intraday trading.

## Option Chain Data

Google publishes stock chain options on their finance website. We can also access these data in a JSON format from Google Finance API using the following URL:

```
http://www.google.com/finance/option_chain?q=GOOG&output=json
```

This URL returns the option data including the next expiry date, a list of all the available expiry dates for GOOG, a list of all the calls and puts, and the stock price of GOOG. I should point out that the preceding URL only works for the latest expiry and all the options returned will be for that expiry only. We can specify a different expiry using the following modified URL:

```
http://www.google.com/finance/option_chain?
      q=GOOG&expd=20&expm=1&expy=2017&output=json
```

Here, we specify an expiry using its year, month, and day strings. We can get all the available option chain data from Google in a two-step process: calling the previous URL to get the list of valid expiry dates, and then using the above URL to get all the option data by loop-through all the expiry dates.

Here, we implement an R function named *googleOption*, which can be used to retrieve option chain data from Google. Here is the code list for this function:

```
googleOption <- function(ticker, expiry = NULL, allOptions = NULL){
  library(jsonlite)
  library(RCurl)
  dat <- NULL
  url <- NULL
  if(is.null(expiry) && is.null(allOptions)){
    url <- paste0("http://www.google.com/finance/option_chain?q=",
                  ticker, "&output=json")
    dat <- fromJSON(fixJSON(getURL(url)))
    dat <- getOptionNames(dat)
  } else if(is.null(allOptions) && !is.null(expiry)){
    ss <- unlist(strsplit(expiry,"-"))
    url <- paste0("http://www.google.com/finance/option_chain?q=", ticker, "&expd=",
                  strtoi(ss[3]), "&expm=", strtoi(ss[2]), "&expy=",
                  strtoi(ss[1]), "&output=json")
    dat <- fromJSON(fixJSON(getURL(url)))
    dat <- getOptionNames(dat)
  } else if(!is.null(allOptions) && is.null(expiry)) {
    url <- paste0("http://www.google.com/finance/option_chain?q=",
                  ticker, "&output=json")
    dat1 <- fromJSON(fixJSON(getURL(url)))
    expiries <- dim(dat1$expirations)[1]
    dat <- list()
    for(i in 1:expiries){
      y <- dat1$expirations[i,]$y
      m <- dat1$expirations[i,]$m
      d <- dat1$expirations[i,]$d
      exps <- paste(y,m,d,sep = "-")
      if(i > 1){
        url = paste0("http://www.google.com/finance/option_chain?q=", ticker,
        "&expd=", d, "&expm=", m, "&expy=", y,"&output=json")
        dat1 <- fromJSON(fixJSON(getURL(url)))
      }
      dat1 <- getOptionNames(dat1)
      dat[[paste(exps,"calls", sep="-")]] <- dat1$calls
      dat[[paste(exps,"puts", sep="-")]] <- dat1$puts
    }
  }
  return(dat)
```

```
}
```

We need install and load two packages, *RCurl* and *jsonlite*, which are used to download and process the option data in JSON format. This function includes three choices: we can get current available option chain data for the font month if we ignore the input arguments *expiry* and *allOptions* or set them to NULL. We can retrieve the option data for a specified expiration date by setting the expiry argument. We can also obtain the option chain data for all available expiration dates if we set *allOptions* to TRUE.

Inside this function, we construct the URL and download the option data in JSON format. We need to clean it up by replacing some non-JSON strings using another helper function named *fixJSON*:

```
fixJSON() <- function(jsonstr){
  ss <- c("cid","cp","s","cs","vol","expiry","underlying_id","underlying_price",
          "p","c","oi","e","b","strike","a","name","puts","calls","expirations",
          "y","m","d")
  for(i in 1:length(ss)){
    s1 = paste0(',"', ss[i], '":')
    s2 = paste0('\\{"', ss[i], '":')
    sa = paste0(',', ss[i], ':')
    sb = paste0('\\{', ss[i], ':')
    jsonstr = gsub(sa, s1, jsonstr)
    jsonstr = gsub(sb, s2, jsonstr)
  }
  return(jsonstr)
}
```

We also use another helper function named *getOptionNames* to extract useful information from the raw data and rename the columns with more meaningful names. To retrieve the current available IBM option chain data for the front month, we can issue the following command:

```
> source("./R/marketdata.R")
> op <- googleOption("IBM")
```

We can check the current expiration date:

```
> op$expiry
$y
[1] 2016

$m
[1] 2

$d
[1] 26
```

It returns year, month, and day for the expiration, i.e., 2/26/2016. We can also obtain all available expiry dates and the underlying IBM stock price from the *op* object:

```
> op$expirations
     y  m  d
1  2016  2 26
2  2016  3  4
3  2016  3 11
4  2016  3 18
5  2016  3 24
6  2016  4  1
7  2016  4  8
```

```
8  2016  4 15
9  2016  5 20
10 2016  7 15
11 2016 10 21
12 2017  1 20
13 2018  1 19
> op$underlying_price
[1] 132
```

Of course, we can also get the call and put option chain data:

```
> op$calls[30:40,]
        Option Symbol Exchange Strike Price  Bid   Ask Volume Open Interest
30 IBM160226C00122000     OPRA 122.00 11.20 9.60 10.70      8           206
31 IBM160226C00123000     OPRA 123.00  8.73 8.55  9.75      -           179
32 IBM160226C00124000     OPRA 124.00  8.21 7.60  8.90      4           232
33 IBM160226C00125000     OPRA 125.00  7.25 6.80  7.85    188           973
34 IBM160226C00126000     OPRA 126.00  6.40 5.80  6.70     82           738
35 IBM160226C00127000     OPRA 127.00  5.10 4.80  5.40     28           502
36 IBM160226C00128000     OPRA 128.00  4.20 3.85  4.15     24           258
37 IBM160226C00129000     OPRA 129.00  3.22 2.82  3.45     58           200
38 IBM160226C00130000     OPRA 130.00  2.12 1.86  2.13    101          1251
39 IBM160226C00131000     OPRA 131.00  1.08 0.83  2.09      8           396
40 IBM160226C00132000     OPRA 132.00  0.08 0.01  0.15    294          1039
> op$puts[30:40,]
        Option Symbol Exchange Strike Price  Bid  Ask Volume Open Interest
30 IBM160226P00122000     OPRA 122.00 0.03    - 0.50      -           327
31 IBM160226P00123000     OPRA 123.00 0.02    - 0.10      -           252
32 IBM160226P00124000     OPRA 124.00 0.07    - 0.13      -           523
33 IBM160226P00125000     OPRA 125.00 0.01    - 0.11      1          1514
34 IBM160226P00126000     OPRA 126.00 0.01 0.01 0.03     11           943
35 IBM160226P00127000     OPRA 127.00 0.01 0.01 0.12     42           591
36 IBM160226P00128000     OPRA 128.00 0.02 0.01 0.03     41           582
37 IBM160226P00129000     OPRA 129.00 0.01 0.01 0.04     17           388
38 IBM160226P00130000     OPRA 130.00 0.02 0.01 0.04    855          9064
39 IBM160226P00131000     OPRA 131.00 0.01 0.01 0.07    594           724
40 IBM160226P00132000     OPRA 132.00 0.03 0.01 0.03   4564          4685
```

Here, we just display the call and put option data from rows 30 to 40, where the options have the higher trade volume and open interest.

Now, all available expiration dates are available, we can then retrieve option chain data for a specified expiration. For example, for expiration = 1/20/2017, we can issue the following command:

```
> op1 <- googleOption("IBM","2017-01-20")
> op1$calls[10:20,]
        Option Symbol Exchange Strike Price   Bid   Ask Volume Open Interest
10 IBM170120C00105000     OPRA 105.00 28.57 28.65 30.15      -           150
11 IBM170120C00110000     OPRA 110.00 25.97 24.65 25.20    101           251
12 IBM170120C00115000     OPRA 115.00 20.80 19.45 21.50      -           557
13 IBM170120C00120000     OPRA 120.00 18.37 17.25 17.75    124          1024
14 IBM170120C00125000     OPRA 125.00 14.50 14.05 14.45     16          1763
15 IBM170120C00130000     OPRA 130.00 11.40 11.25 11.50     77          2826
16 IBM170120C00135000     OPRA 135.00  9.05  8.85  9.10     27          2443
17 IBM170120C00140000     OPRA 140.00  7.09  6.75  7.00    145          4309
18 IBM170120C00145000     OPRA 145.00  5.40  5.10  5.30      4          1564
19 IBM170120C00150000     OPRA 150.00  3.80  3.75  3.95     13          7087
```

```
20 IBM170120C00155000     OPRA 155.00  2.89  2.70  2.85      2          3433
> op1$puts[10:20,]
        Option Symbol Exchange Strike Price   Bid   Ask Volume Open Interest
10 IBM170120P00105000     OPRA 105.00  4.05  3.95  4.15      3          2463
11 IBM170120P00110000     OPRA 110.00  5.10  5.00  5.20      3          3349
12 IBM170120P00115000     OPRA 115.00  6.20  6.40  6.50     25          2659
13 IBM170120P00120000     OPRA 120.00  8.00  7.95  8.10     18          2923
14 IBM170120P00125000     OPRA 125.00  9.55  9.85 10.05     14          1940
15 IBM170120P00130000     OPRA 130.00 12.05 12.10 12.30     20          4148
16 IBM170120P00135000     OPRA 135.00 14.55 14.65 14.95     19          3515
17 IBM170120P00140000     OPRA 140.00 17.15 17.65 17.95      5          6538
18 IBM170120P00145000     OPRA 145.00 20.50 20.95 21.25      3          1994
19 IBM170120P00150000     OPRA 150.00 25.70 24.60 25.00      -          3413
20 IBM170120P00155000     OPRA 155.00 29.50 28.15 28.95      -          1331
```

If we want to get the option chain data for all expiration dates, we can use the command:

```
op2 <- googleOption("IBM", allOptions = TRUE)
```

In this case, the output is a list object, which holds the option chain data for all expirations. For example, we can access the call option data for expiration = 1/19/2018 by the following command:

```
> head(op2$`2018-1-19-calls`)
       Option Symbol Exchange Strike Price   Bid   Ask Volume Open Interest
1 IBM180119C00060000     OPRA  60.00     - 70.00 75.00      -             0
2 IBM180119C00065000     OPRA  65.00 59.67 65.10 70.00      -             2
3 IBM180119C00070000     OPRA  70.00 48.40 60.05 65.00      -             6
4 IBM180119C00075000     OPRA  75.00 57.63 55.10 60.00      -             9
5 IBM180119C00080000     OPRA  80.00 54.19 50.20 55.00      -            12
6 IBM180119C00085000     OPRA  85.00     - 45.55 50.50      -             0
```

The option chain data will become very useful when you trade stocks and options. It is a bonus when you can get free option data from Google. The option chain data provide valuable information about the security today and where it might be going in the future. However, you can only access the option chain data for currently tradable options from Google API, you cannot access the historical option data for the expired options in the past.

# Market Data from Quandl

*Quandl* is another open source website for financial data and their mission is "to make all the numerical data in the world available". *Quandl* now brings together over 20 million financial and economic datasets from over 500 sources on a single easy-to-use platform, which allows their users (free account registration is required for some datasets) to access data either directly through their site, or by downloading data from the other sources via their API. You can access various financial data using a standard API, regardless of who originally published the data or in what format. If you have not ever heard of *Quandl*, have a look around their site.

## Quandl API

The *Quandl* API provides a uniform, simple, RESTful interface to access all data on their website. You can get the market data in different formats, including CSV, JSON, and XML. Quandl API supports R, Python, Excel, Ruby, and other community supported language libraries such as Java, MATLAB and .NET.

To access *Quandl* market data in R, you need to install and load the *Quandl* package:

```
install_packages("Quandl")
library(Quandl)
```

The *Quandl* R package is free. However, to make more than 50 calls a day, you will need to register for a free Quandl account and provide your API key, like this:

```
Quandl.api_key("Your_API_KEY_HERE")
```

You can obtain an API key from your Quandl account. On your Quandl account home page, click the ME dropdown menu (located at the top right corner) and select the ACCOUNT SETTINGS. Then click the API KEY link on the left pane and your API key will be displayed on the page.

## Adjusted Stock EOD Data

The *Quandl*'s free database for stocks named WiKi EOD Stock Prices is probably the most reliable data source of this kind. It covers over 3000 stock names and includes dividends, splits, and adjustment in a single database. The stock EOD data from Yahoo Finance also includes a field called Adj_Close, but it does not include the adjusted fields for Open, High, Low and Volume. However, I find that *Quandl* EOD stock prices database has all adjusted fields for Open, High, Low, Close, and Volume, which is very impressive and is very useful for back-testing trading strategies.

Here, I will use an example to show you how to access Quandl's EOD stock prices database.

```
> ibm <- Quandl("WIKI/IBM", type="xts")
> dim(ibm)
[1] 13621    12
```

Here, we set type = "*xts*", i.e. the output is an *xts* object. We can set it to other types as we like, such as *raw*, *ts*, and *zoo*. The default output type is a data frame object. The output gives all market data up to today for IBM, which includes over 13600 rows (or workdays) and 12 columns. Here are sample data for top and bottom rows:

```
> head(ibm)
```

```
            Open  High Low  Close   Volume Ex-Dividend Split Ratio Adj. Open Adj. High Adj. Low Adj. Close Adj. Volume
1962-01-02 578.5 578.5 572 572.00 5162.667           0           1  5.074172  5.074172 5.017159   5.017159      387200
1962-01-03 572.0 577.0 572 577.00 3840.000           0           1  5.017159  5.061015 5.017159   5.061015      288000
1962-01-04 577.0 577.0 571 571.25 3413.333           0           1  5.061015  5.061015 5.008387   5.010580      256000
1962-01-05 570.5 570.5 559 560.00 4842.667           0           1  5.004002  5.004002 4.903132   4.911904      363200
1962-01-08 559.5 559.5 545 549.50 7253.333           0           1  4.907518  4.907518 4.780335   4.819805      544000
1962-01-09 552.0 563.0 552 556.00 6549.333           0           1  4.841734  4.938217 4.841734   4.876819      491200
```

```
> tail(ibm)
```

```
             Open   High    Low  Close  Volume Ex-Dividend Split Ratio Adj. Open Adj. High Adj. Low Adj. Close Adj. Volume
2016-02-19 132.36 133.65 130.84 133.08 5108515           0           1    132.36    133.65   130.84     133.08     5108515
2016-02-22 133.84 134.31 132.41 133.77 4440520           0           1    133.84    134.31   132.41     133.77     4440520
2016-02-23 133.14 133.41 132.01 132.40 3366827           0           1    133.14    133.41   132.01     132.40     3366827
2016-02-24 131.55 133.49 129.68 132.80 4079826           0           1    131.55    133.49   129.68     132.80     4079826
2016-02-25 133.29 134.51 130.88 134.50 4353576           0           1    133.29    134.51   130.88     134.50     4353576
2016-02-26 134.51 134.92 131.95 132.03 4382899           0           1    134.51    134.92   131.95     132.03     4382899
```

You can see that the data started from 1/2/1962, and it includes the adjusted values for OHLC EOD prices and volume. If we do not need all the data, we can specify a time period:

```
> ibm <- Quandl("WIKI/IBM", start_date = "2015-01-01", end_date = "2016-01-01",
                 type = "xts")
> head(ibm, 3)
```

```
             Open   High    Low  Close  Volume Ex-Dividend Split Ratio Adj. Open Adj. High Adj. Low Adj. Close Adj. Volume
2015-01-02 161.30 163.31 161.00 162.06 5518469           0           1  156.8734  158.8282 156.5816   157.6125     5518469
2015-01-05 161.02 161.27 159.19 159.51 4862471           0           1  156.6011  156.8442 154.8213   155.1325     4862471
2015-01-06 159.68 159.96 155.17 156.07 6119315           0           1  155.2978  155.5702 150.9116   151.7869     6119315
```

```
> tail(ibm, 3)
```

```
             Open   High    Low  Close  Volume Ex-Dividend Split Ratio Adj. Open Adj. High Adj. Low Adj. Close Adj. Volume
2015-12-29 138.25 140.06 138.20 139.78 3918726           0           1  136.8490  138.6406 136.7995   138.3635     3918726
2015-12-30 139.58 140.44 139.22 139.34 2985559           0           1  138.1655  139.0168 137.8091   137.9279     2985559
2015-12-31 139.07 139.10 137.57 137.62 3443345           0           1  137.6607  137.6903 136.1759   136.2253     3443345
```

We can also change the sampling frequency from daily to weekly, monthly, quarterly, or annually. For example, we can get the monthly data using the following command:

```
> ibm <- Quandl("WIKI/IBM", start_date = "2015-01-01", type = "xts",
                collapse = "monthly")
> head(ibm, 3)
```

```
           Open   High    Low  Close  Volume Ex-Dividend Split Ratio Adj. Open Adj. High Adj. Low Adj. Close Adj. Volume
Jan 2015 153.93 155.24 153.04 153.31 6557778           0           1  149.7056  150.9797 148.8401   149.1027     6557778
Feb 2015 161.05 162.29 160.16 161.94 4403866           0           1  156.6302  157.8362 155.7647   157.4958     4403866
Mar 2015 161.08 162.33 160.40 160.50 4217308           0           1  156.6594  157.8751 155.9981   156.0953     4217308
```

```
> tail(ibm, 3)
```

```
           Open   High    Low  Close  Volume Ex-Dividend Split Ratio Adj. Open Adj. High Adj. Low Adj. Close Adj. Volume
Dec 2015 139.07 139.10 137.57 137.62 3443345           0           1  137.6607  137.6903 136.1759   136.2253     3443345
Jan 2016 123.28 124.79 122.96 124.79 8185576           0           1  122.0307  123.5254 121.7139   123.5254     8185576
Feb 2016 134.51 134.92 131.95 132.03 4382899           0           1  134.5100  134.9200 131.9500   132.0300     4382899
```

*Quandl* allows us to not only retrieve the price data but also perform some elementary calculations on the data prior to downloading it. We can use the transform (available parameters: *diff*, *rdiff*, *rdiff_from*, *cumul*, *normalize*) argument to get different outputs. The following is a list of the available transformations:

| Parameter | Transformation | Effect | Description |
|---|---|---|---|
| diff | Row-on-row change | y'[t] = y[t] - y[t-1] | Transform the data to show the difference between days. |
| rdiff | Row-on-row % change | y'[t] = (y[t] - y[t-1])/y[t-1] | Transform the data to show the difference between days divided by the previous day. |
| rdiff_from | Row-on-row % change from latest value | y'[t] = (y[n] - y[t])/y[t] | Transform the data to show the percentage difference between the latest value and all subsequent values (where y[n] is the latest observation). |
| cumul | Cumulative sum | y'[t] = y[t] + y[t-1] +... + y[0] | Calculate the sum of all preceding data returned. |
| normalize | Start at 100 | y'[t] = (y[t]/y[0])*100 | Normalize the data to the oldest datapoint returned. |

In the above list, *y*[*t*] denotes a data point for time *t* and *y'*[*t*] denotes the transformed data. For example, we can retrieve the percentage changes directly using the following command:

```
> ibm <- Quandl("WIKI/IBM", start_date = "2015-01-01", transform = "rdiff")
> head(ibm)
```

```
        Date         Open         High          Low        Close       Volume Ex-Dividend Split Ratio    Adj. Open    Adj. High     Adj. Low   Adj. Close  Adj. Volume
1 2016-02-26  0.009152975  0.0030481005  0.008175428 -0.018364312  0.006735383          NA           0  0.009152975  0.0030481005  0.008175428 -0.018364312  0.006735383
2 2016-02-25  0.013226910  0.0076410218  0.009253547  0.012801205  0.067098450          NA           0  0.013226910  0.0076410218  0.009253547  0.012801205  0.067098450
3 2016-02-24 -0.011942316  0.0005996552 -0.017650178  0.003021148  0.211771796          NA           0 -0.011942316  0.0005996552 -0.017650178  0.003021148  0.211771796
4 2016-02-23 -0.005230126 -0.0067009158 -0.003020920 -0.010241459 -0.241794429          NA           0 -0.005230126 -0.0067009158 -0.003020920 -0.010241459 -0.241794429
5 2016-02-22  0.011181626  0.0049382716  0.011999389  0.005184851 -0.130761092          NA           0  0.011181626  0.0049382716  0.011999389  0.005184851 -0.130761092
6 2016-02-19  0.018153846 -0.0026119403  0.008400771  0.004756512 -0.485282405          NA           0  0.018153846 -0.0026119403  0.008400771  0.004756512 -0.485282405
```

You may notice that here, we use the "WIKI/IBM" to download market data for IBM from the WIKI data source. The data source field comes from the "Quandl code". You need to know the "Quandl code" of each dataset you want to download. In the example where we want to access the stock prices for IBM, the code will be "WIKI/IBM". You can find the "Quandl code" for different datasets from their website.

## Other Market Data

As mentioned previously, we can use the same *Quandl* API to access not only the stock data, but also other type of the market data, such as bonds, currencies, treasuries, etc. For example, we can access the treasury net marketable borrowing data (published quarterly) using the following command:

```
> tmbor <- Quandl("USTREASURY/TMBOR", start_date = "2010-01-01", type = "xts")
> head(tmbor)
          Bills 2 to Under 5 Years 5-10 Years Over 10 Years 5 - 10 Years TIPS Over 10 Years TIPS Buybacks Totals
2010 Q1 -199.03             160.53     246.81         38.13             14.03              0.00        0 260.47
2010 Q2   50.01             156.53     228.42         44.46             -4.16              8.00        0 483.25
2010 Q3  -60.95             132.18     240.14         44.42            -12.21              0.00        0 343.58
2010 Q4    5.93             112.46     205.04         43.10             22.11              7.17        0 395.82
2011 Q1  -15.92              91.65     224.22         42.73             20.27              0.00        0 362.90
2011 Q2  -74.03              80.89     195.24         42.65             10.93              9.49        0 265.20
> tail(tmbor)
              Bills 2 to Under 5 Years 5-10 Years Over 10 Years 5 - 10 Years TIPS Over 10 Years TIPS Buybacks     Totals
2014 Q2   60.00000           -18.30000    129.500      42.00000           1.48000            9.03000    0.000 264.70000
2014 Q3 -264.00000           -23.90000    120.300      42.00000          14.10000            7.00000    0.000 -63.50000
2014 Q4   22.99000           -33.97000    112.440      42.00000          20.07000            0.00000    0.000 204.50000
2015 Q1   47.00000           -43.00000    104.000      42.00000          29.00000            7.00000   -0.020 227.30000
2015 Q2   20.01000           -59.39000     94.640      31.48000           4.43000            9.00000    0.000 141.20000
2015 Q3  -82.90808           -60.44372    101.415      42.36172           8.11706            6.99999   -0.025  56.57163
```

Here, the data source is the *USTREASURY* and the *TMBOR* is the ticker that represents the treasury net marketable borrowing data.

Similarly, we can access the forex rate data by issuing the following statement:

```
> jpy <- Quandl("CURRFX/USDJPY", start_date = "2015-01-01", type = "xts")
> head(jpy)
              Rate High (est) Low (est)
2015-01-01 119.772     121.22    118.34
2015-01-02 120.150     121.51    118.80
2015-01-05 120.206       0.00      0.00
2015-01-06 119.429     120.80    118.07
2015-01-07 119.048     120.41    117.70
2015-01-08 119.420     120.77    118.09
> tail(jpy)
              Rate High (est) Low (est)
2016-02-19 113.229     114.64    111.83
2016-02-22 112.931     114.18    111.69
2016-02-23 112.546       0.00      0.00
2016-02-24 111.965     113.33    110.62
2016-02-25 112.156       0.00      0.00
2016-02-26 112.878     114.20    111.57
```

Here, "*USDJPY*" is the forex rate ticker and "*CURRFX*" denotes the data source.

We can also access global market data using Google or Yahoo Finance through the *Quandl* API. For example, if we want to download the EOD stock data for General Packer Co., LTD listed in Tokyo stock exchange as ticker = 6267, we can enter "TYO_6267" in the ticker field and "GOOG" in the data source field:

```
> tyo <- Quandl("GOOG/TYO_6267", start_date = "2015-01-01", type = "xts")
> head(tyo)
           Open High Low Close Volume
2015-01-05  280  282 280   282   2000
```

```
2015-01-06  282  282 280   280   5000
2015-01-09  282  282 274   274   2000
2015-01-13  270  270 267   267   2000
2015-01-14  267  268 267   268   2000
2015-01-16  265  265 265   265   2000
> tail(tyo)
           Open High  Low Close Volume
2016-02-12 1325 1325 1220  1220    300
2016-02-15 1245 1245 1245  1245    100
2016-02-22 1255 1255 1255  1255    600
2016-02-23 1266 1323 1266  1282   2600
2016-02-24 1310 1310 1310  1310    100
2016-02-25 1348 1348 1312  1320   1000
```

The standard *Quandl* API allows easily access market data from different data sources. However, the *Quandl* API can only access the EOD data currently; it does not provide intraday data service yet.

# ISDA Rates from Markit

If you are working on the credit or fixed income instruments, you should be familiar with Markit Ltd. Markit provides independent pricing of CDS (credit default swap) single names, indices, and tranches to support price discovery, risk management, and valuations. The interest rates play an important role in pricing fixed-income instruments such as bonds and CDS. In particular, ISDA (International Swaps and Derivatives Association) has set up a standard CDS model, which is managed and maintained by Markit. In order to price the CDS contract consistently, we need to use standardized inputs into the ISDA CDS model. Markit has published the standard interest rates daily for major global currencies in the XML format, including USD, JPY, EUR, etc.

Let us take USD interest rate as an example. The body of the XML includes the interest rates from the indicated sources for the following maturities, as shown in Figure 2-1.

| Maturity | USD Source | Dat Count/Accrual Convention |
|---|---|---|
| 1MO | LIBOR | ACT/360 |
| 2MO | LIBOR | ACT/361 |
| 3MO | LIBOR | ACT/362 |
| 6MO | LIBOR | ACT/363 |
| 1Y | LIBOR | ACT/364 |
| 2Y | SWAP RATE | 30/360 Semi-Annual |
| 3Y | SWAP RATE | 30/360 Semi-Annual |
| 4Y | SWAP RATE | 30/360 Semi-Annual |
| 5Y | SWAP RATE | 30/360 Semi-Annual |
| 6Y | SWAP RATE | 30/360 Semi-Annual |
| 7Y | SWAP RATE | 30/360 Semi-Annual |
| 8Y | SWAP RATE | 30/360 Semi-Annual |
| 9Y | SWAP RATE | 30/360 Semi-Annual |
| 10Y | SWAP RATE | 30/360 Semi-Annual |
| 12Y | SWAP RATE | 30/360 Semi-Annual |
| 15Y | SWAP RATE | 30/360 Semi-Annual |
| 20Y | SWAP RATE | 30/360 Semi-Annual |
| 25Y | SWAP RATE | 30/360 Semi-Annual |
| 30Y | SWAP RATE | 30/360 Semi-Annual |

*Figure 2-1. ISDA standard interest rate format for USD.*

In fact, Markit provides the interest rates in a ZIP file. We need to first extract the ZIP file and then process the XML data. In the following, I will show you how to implement an R function to download the ISDA interest rate from Markit.

Add a new R function named *isdaRate* to the *marketdata.R* file. Here is the code for this function:

```
isdaRate <- function(ccy, rateDate){
  library(XML)
  ss <- unlist(strsplit(rateDate,"-"))
  dstr <- paste0(ss[1], ss[2], ss[3])
  url <- paste0("https://www.markit.com/news/InterestRates_",
                ccy, "_", dstr, ".zip")
  temp <- tempfile()
  download.file(url, temp, mode = "wb")
  dat <- xmlRoot(xmlTreeParse(unzip(temp)[2], useInternalNodes = T))
  unlink(temp)
  asof <- xmlToDataFrame(getNodeSet(dat, "//effectiveasof"),
    stringsAsFactors = F)[1, 1]
  depdayConvention <- (xmlToDataFrame(getNodeSet(dat, "//deposits"),
    stringsAsFactors = F))[, "daycountconvention"]
  deposits <- xmlToDataFrame(getNodeSet(dat, "//deposits/curvepoint"),
    stringsAsFactors = F)
  swdayConvention <- swdayConvention <- xmlToDataFrame(getNodeSet(dat, "//swaps"),
    stringsAsFactors = F)[, "fixeddaycountconvention"]
  swaps <- xmlToDataFrame(getNodeSet(dat, "//swaps/curvepoint"),
    stringsAsFactors = F)
  deposits$Currency <- rep(ccy, nrow(deposits))
  deposits$EffectiveAsOf <- rep(asof, nrow(deposits))
  deposits$DayCount <- rep(depdayConvention, nrow(deposits))
  deposits$RateType <- rep("Deposit", nrow(deposits))
  swaps$Currency <- rep(ccy, nrow(swaps))
  swaps$EffectiveAsOf <- rep(asof, nrow(swaps))
  swaps$DayCount <- rep(swdayConvention, nrow(swaps))
  swaps$RateType <- rep("Swap", nrow(swaps))
  df <- rbind(deposits, swaps)
  colnames(df) <- c("Tenor", "Maturity", "Rate", "Currency",
                    "EffectiveAsOf", "DayCount", "RateType")
  df <- df[, c("Currency","EffectiveAsOf", "RateType", "DayCount",
               "Maturity", "Tenor", "Rate")]
  return(df)
}
```

Here, we first construct the URL, which points to the right location of the ISDA rate data at the Markit website. We then create a temporary file that holds the zip file downloaded from Markit. Next, we unzip this zip file and redirect the unzipped XML file into a *dat* object and delete the temporary file using the *unlink* function. Finally, we process this XML file to extract the useful information and convert the results into a data frame object. This function takes the currency (*ccy*) and the date as the input arguments. Currently, the ISDA rates are available for most of the major currencies, including USD, EUR, JPY, GBP, CAD, AUD, etc.

Now, we can easily use the *isdaRate* function to retrieve the ISDA interest rate data. For example, we can use the following command to get the USD rates:

```
> usd <- isdaRate("USD", "2016-02-23"); usd
   Currency EffectiveAsOf RateType DayCount   Maturity Tenor     Rate
1       USD    2016-02-24  Deposit  ACT/360 2016-03-28    1M 0.004358
```

```
2       USD    2016-02-24  Deposit  ACT/360 2016-04-26    2M 0.005213
3       USD    2016-02-24  Deposit  ACT/360 2016-05-26    3M 0.006291
4       USD    2016-02-24  Deposit  ACT/360 2016-08-26    6M 0.008811
5       USD    2016-02-24  Deposit  ACT/360 2017-02-27    1Y  0.01157
6       USD    2016-02-24     Swap   30/360 2018-02-26    2Y 0.008055
7       USD    2016-02-24     Swap   30/360 2019-02-26    3Y  0.00903
8       USD    2016-02-24     Swap   30/360 2020-02-26    4Y  0.01021
9       USD    2016-02-24     Swap   30/360 2021-02-26    5Y  0.01121
10      USD    2016-02-24     Swap   30/360 2022-02-26    6Y 0.012335
11      USD    2016-02-24     Swap   30/360 2023-02-26    7Y  0.01337
12      USD    2016-02-24     Swap   30/360 2024-02-26    8Y 0.014295
13      USD    2016-02-24     Swap   30/360 2025-02-26    9Y 0.015135
14      USD    2016-02-24     Swap   30/360 2026-02-26   10Y 0.015875
15      USD    2016-02-24     Swap   30/360 2028-02-26   12Y 0.017275
16      USD    2016-02-24     Swap   30/360 2031-02-26   15Y 0.018635
17      USD    2016-02-24     Swap   30/360 2036-02-26   20Y 0.019985
18      USD    2016-02-24     Swap   30/360 2041-02-26   25Y  0.02064
19      USD    2016-02-24     Swap   30/360 2046-02-26   30Y  0.02094
```

Note that the ISDA rate data includes both the cash deposit (1M to 1Y) and fixed swap (2Y to 30Y) rates. Similarly, we can use this function to retrieve the ISDA rates for EUR and JPY:

```
> eur <- isdaRate("EUR", "2016-02-23"); eur
   Currency EffectiveAsOf RateType DayCount   Maturity Tenor     Rate
1       EUR    2016-02-24  Deposit  ACT/360 2016-03-28    1M -0.00261
2       EUR    2016-02-24  Deposit  ACT/360 2016-04-26    2M -0.00232
3       EUR    2016-02-24  Deposit  ACT/360 2016-05-26    3M  -0.0020
4       EUR    2016-02-24  Deposit  ACT/360 2016-08-26    6M -0.00125
5       EUR    2016-02-24  Deposit  ACT/360 2016-11-28    9M -0.00071
6       EUR    2016-02-24  Deposit  ACT/360 2017-02-27    1Y -0.00016
7       EUR    2016-02-24     Swap   30/360 2018-02-26    2Y -0.00167
8       EUR    2016-02-24     Swap   30/360 2019-02-26    3Y -0.00121
9       EUR    2016-02-24     Swap   30/360 2020-02-26    4Y -0.00041
10      EUR    2016-02-24     Swap   30/360 2021-02-26    5Y  0.00055
11      EUR    2016-02-24     Swap   30/360 2022-02-26    6Y  0.00161
12      EUR    2016-02-24     Swap   30/360 2023-02-26    7Y  0.00273
13      EUR    2016-02-24     Swap   30/360 2024-02-26    8Y  0.00385
14      EUR    2016-02-24     Swap   30/360 2025-02-26    9Y  0.00491
15      EUR    2016-02-24     Swap   30/360 2026-02-26   10Y  0.00585
16      EUR    2016-02-24     Swap   30/360 2028-02-26   12Y  0.00742
17      EUR    2016-02-24     Swap   30/360 2031-02-26   15Y  0.00903
18      EUR    2016-02-24     Swap   30/360 2036-02-26   20Y   0.0102
19      EUR    2016-02-24     Swap   30/360 2046-02-26   30Y  0.01049
> jpy <- isdaRate("JPY", "2016-02-23"); jpy
   Currency EffectiveAsOf RateType DayCount   Maturity Tenor       Rate
1       JPY    2016-02-24  Deposit  ACT/360 2016-03-28    1M  -0.000433
2       JPY    2016-02-24  Deposit  ACT/360 2016-04-26    2M  -0.000263
3       JPY    2016-02-24  Deposit  ACT/360 2016-05-26    3M  -0.000080
4       JPY    2016-02-24  Deposit  ACT/360 2016-08-26    6M -0.0000030
5       JPY    2016-02-24  Deposit  ACT/360 2017-02-27    1Y    0.00081
6       JPY    2016-02-24     Swap  ACT/365 2018-02-26    2Y  -0.001413
7       JPY    2016-02-24     Swap  ACT/365 2019-02-26    3Y  -0.001613
8       JPY    2016-02-24     Swap  ACT/365 2020-02-26    4Y   -0.00145
9       JPY    2016-02-24     Swap  ACT/365 2021-02-26    5Y  -0.001088
10      JPY    2016-02-24     Swap  ACT/365 2022-02-26    6Y   -0.00065
11      JPY    2016-02-24     Swap  ACT/365 2023-02-26    7Y  -0.000175
```

```
12        JPY     2016-02-24       Swap  ACT/365 2024-02-26    8Y    0.000325
13        JPY     2016-02-24       Swap  ACT/365 2025-02-26    9Y    0.000825
14        JPY     2016-02-24       Swap  ACT/365 2026-02-26   10Y    0.001375
15        JPY     2016-02-24       Swap  ACT/365 2028-02-26   12Y     0.00255
16        JPY     2016-02-24       Swap  ACT/365 2031-02-26   15Y    0.004463
17        JPY     2016-02-24       Swap  ACT/365 2036-02-26   20Y      0.0070
18        JPY     2016-02-24       Swap  ACT/365 2046-02-26   30Y     0.00905
```

We see from the above results that the short-term interest rates in Eurozone and Japan become negative! The negative interest rate policy (NIRP) is an unconventional monetary policy tool whereby target interest rates are set with a negative value, below the theoretical lower bound of zero percent. NIRP means that the central bank and perhaps private banks will charge negative interest: instead of receiving money on deposits, depositors must pay a fee regularly to keep their money with the bank. This intends to incentivize banks to lend money more freely and to encourage businesses/individuals to invest and spend money rather than pay a fee to keep it safe.

In this chapter, we discussed several approaches to access various market data from different free data sources. You can use some R packages, such as *quantmod* and *Quandl*, to retrieve financial time series data from internet data sources. The *quantmod* package has ability of downloading stock and index EOD prices from Yahoo and Google Finance and contains plotting and charting functionality. The *Quandl* package is a bit different in that it is tied in with the *Quandl* website, a source of financial data itself, as well as a portal to economic and social science data.

These available R packages are convenient and powerful tool for accessing free financial data; however, these packages have some limitations. For example, you cannot use these packages to access some special market data, such as the real-time stock quotes. In this chapter, I also presented a variety of approaches that allow you to implement your own R functions to access the special market data, including the real-time stock and option quotes, historical minutes-bar data, and ISDA interest rate data. I hope that the information provided in this chapter would be useful for quant analysts, individual investors, or students who do not have access to a Bloomberg terminal but want to have market data available to experiment with financial models.

# Chapter 3
# Plots and Graphics in R

A picture is worth a thousand words. Plots and graphics play a very important role in every business application. They make data easier to understand and interest to reports, and have wide applications in our daily life. With the use of advanced data visualization tools in finance, we can translate broad and deep sets of data into easily digested, actionable intelligence for our trading business.

In the finance industry, we deal with data all over the place: in databases, in spreadsheets, in reports from various systems. However, if we can see the data on charts rather than looking at endless rows and columns of numbers, we begin to comprehend what is going on much faster.

Creating plots and graphics for quantitative financial analysis in R is relatively simple within the base R graphics system, which contains functionality for many types of plots and graphics. The base R graphics can produce many plots with extremely fine graphics in many specialized instances. However, we may run into trouble with the R base graphics system if we want to create graphics with complex layouts, more interactivity, and high output quality. In this case, we may need to use some powerful add-on graphics packages, such as *grid*, *lattice*, *ggplot2*, *ggvis*, *rCharts*, and *rgl*. The CRAN graphics task view (https://cran.r-project.org/web/views/Graphics.html) provides a comprehensive listing of functionality to create various graphics.

## Base R Graphics

Within the base R graphic system, we can easily create a variety of graphics using a single command. Usually, we build up plots element by element. In a typical interactive R session, we build a graph one statement at a time, adding features until we have what we want.

### Simple 2D Plots

The most basic and useful type of plot we can create in R is a simple 2D plot of numerical data. Even the most elementary 2D plot consists of several basic elements, including lines, markers, axes, tick marks, labels, a title, and a legend. The X-Y chart uses two values to represent each data point. This type of chart is very useful for describing relationships between data and is often involved in the statistical analysis of data, with wide application in quantitative finance and other fields.

It is easy to create a 2D X-Y plot in R. Consider the following command:

```
> y <- sin(1:70/(2*pi))
> plot(y, type = "l")
```

which produces the scatter plot with default settings shown in Figure 3-1

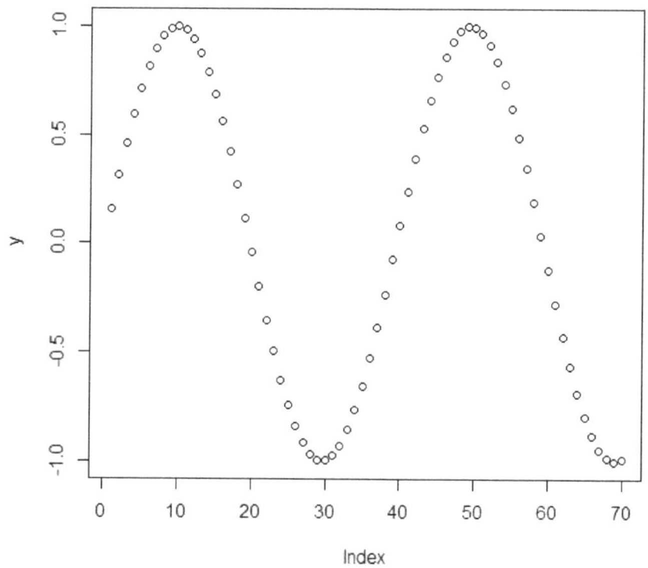


*Figure 3-1. A simple 2D plot in R*

Note that the X-axis labels are just the index numbers of the vector *y*. R automatically plots the data versus the index number when only one *y* argument is passed to the plot function. Although plots with index number as its X-axis are useful in some instances, in many cases plots display the value of the input values along the X-axis will be more informative. In order to achieve this for our previous example, we can use the following commands:

```
> x <- 1:70/(2*pi)
> y <- sin(x)
> plot(x, y)
```

This generates the output shown in Figure 3-2.

Now, we can add a title to make the graph more informative, a line to connect the points, line color, and a grid to assist in estimating values from the line in the graph:

```
> x <- 1:70/(2*pi)
> y <- sin(x)
> plot(x, y, type = "o", col = "blue")
> title("Sine function plot")
> grid()
```

Figure 3-3 shows the results of applying the preceding commands.

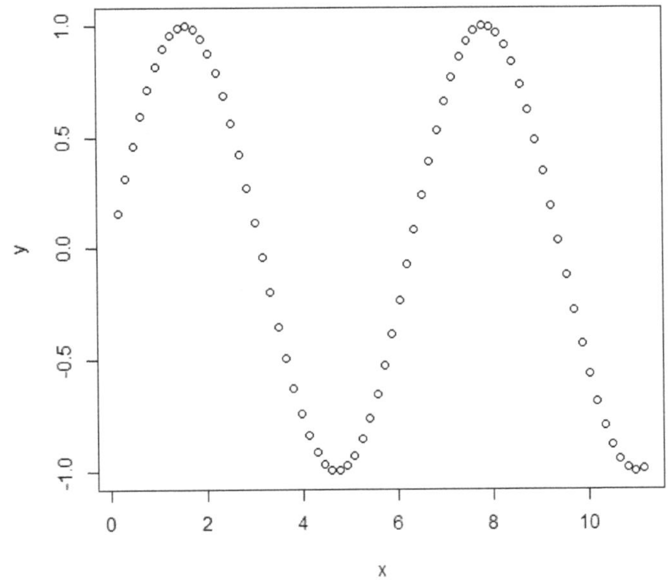


*Figure 3-2. A simple X-Y plot in R*

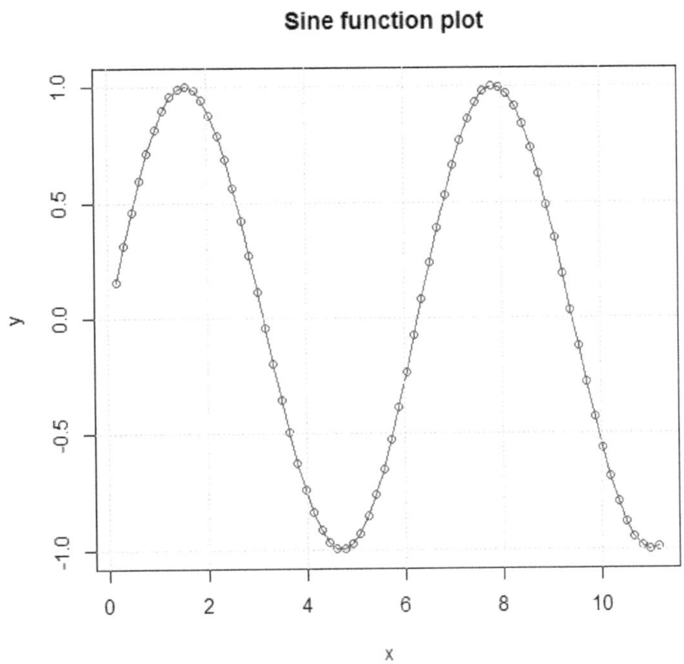


*Figure 3-3. A simple plot with a title and a grid.*

Note that we use the *col* argument to specify the line color and the *type* argument to specify the line type. The *type* argument can take the following values:

| type | Description |
|---|---|
| p | Points |
| l | Lines |
| o | Overplotted points and lines |
| b, c | Points (empty if "c") joined by lines |
| s, S | Stair steps |
| h | Histogram-like vertical lines |
| n | Does not produce any points or lines |

We can also use the *pch* argument to specify symbols to use when plotting points. For symbols 21 through 25, we can also specify the border color (*col*) and fill color (*bg*). Figure 3-4 shows the possible parameters for the *pch* argument:

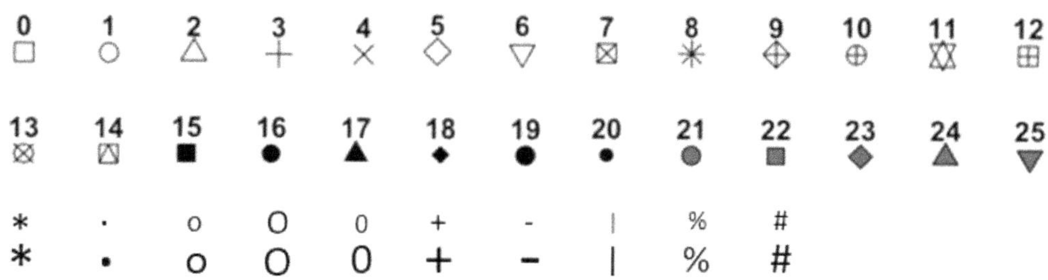


*Figure 3-4. A parameter list for the pch argument.*

We can change the line dashed types using the *lty* argument. This is particularly useful for reference lines, axes, and fit lines. The following list shows the possible parameters for the *lty* argument:

| lty | Description | Example |
|---|---|---|
| 0 | blank | |
| 1 | solid | |
| 2 | dashed | |
| 3 | dotted | |
| 4 | dotdash | |
| 5 | longdash | |
| 6 | twodash | |

We can also use the *lwd* argument to specify the line width relative to the default (default *lwd* = 1).

We can then create a graph with multiple lines using the following commands:

```
> x <- 1:70/(2*pi)
> y <- sin(x)
> y2 = cos(x)
> y3 <- sin(x)*cos(x)
```

```
> plot(x, y, type = "o", pch = 0, lty = 1, col = "blue")
> lines(x, y2, type = "o", pch = 1, lty = 2, col = "green")
> lines(x, y3, type = "o", pch = 2, lty = 3, col = "red")
> legend("topright",legend = c("y", "y2", "y3"), pch = c(0, 1, 2), lty = c(1, 2, 3),
         Col = c("blue", "green", "red"))
> grid()
```

This produces the output shown in Figure 3-5.

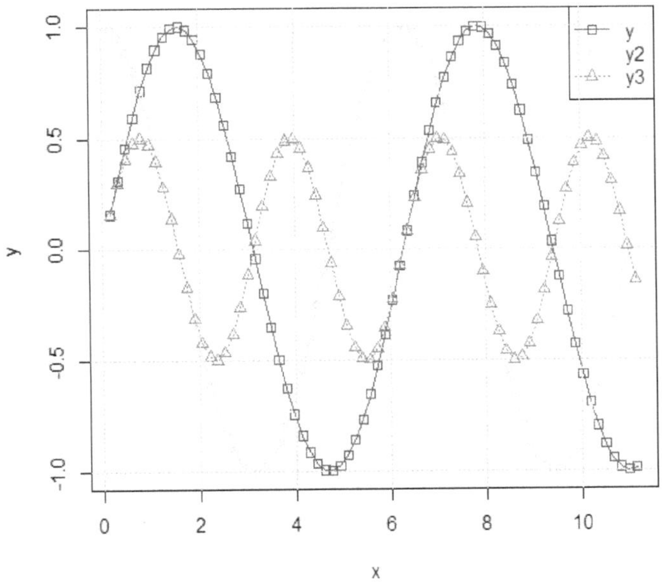


*Figure 3-5. A 2D plot with multiple lines.*

Alternatively, We can use the *matplot* function to create multiple-line graphs much more easily:

```
> matplot(x, cbind(y,y2,y3), type = "o", pch = c(0, 1, 2),
          col = c("blue", "green", "red"))
```

which should produce the same graph shown in Figure 3-5.

## Plots with Two Y Axes

In some instances, we may have multiple data sets we would like to display on the same graph. However, the Y-axis data values for each data set are not within the same range. For example:

```
> x <-1:30
> y <- -100 + 20 * x
> y2 <- x * cos(x)
> plot(x, y, type = "l", lwd = 2)
> lines(x, y2, type = "l", lwd = 2, lty = 2 )
> legend("topleft", legend = c("-100+20*x", "x*cos(x)"), lty = c(1, 2))
```

The above commands produce the output shown in Figure 3-6.

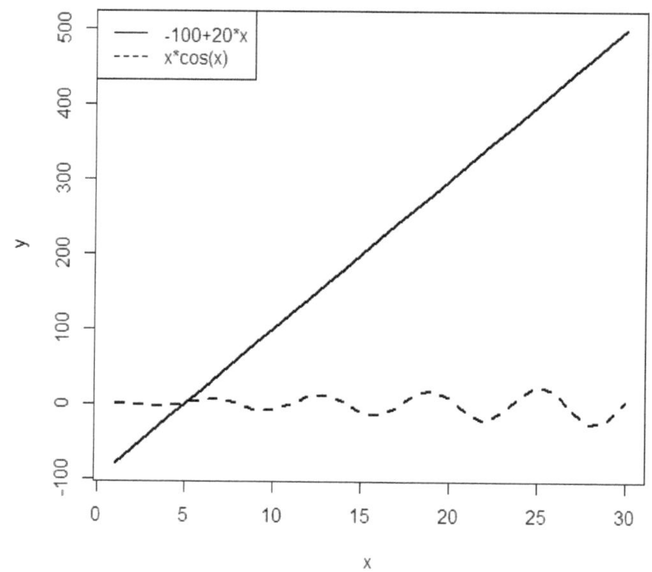


*Figure 3-6. A line plot for y and y2, whose data values fall in different ranges.*

From Figure 3-6, we see how difficult it is to view the values of the *x**cos(*x*) function because the Y-axis limits have been defined to display all of the data points on the same chart; however, the values of these two functions have very different data ranges. We can solve this problem by adding another Y2 axis to the graph using the following statements:

```
> x <-1:30
> y <- -100 + 20 * x
> y2 <- x * cos(x)
> par(mar = c(5, 4, 4, 5) + .1)
> plot(x, y, type = "l", lwd = 2)
> par(new = T)
> plot(x, y2, type = "l", lwd = 2, lty=2, xaxt = "n",yaxt = "n",xlab = "",ylab = "")
> axis(4)
> mtext("y2", side = 4, line = 3)
> legend("topleft", lty = c(1,2), legend = c("y", "y2"))
> grid()
```

You can see that we just create the first plot as usual and then set *par*(*new* = *T*) to prevent R from clearing the graphics device. Next, we create the second plot without axis labels, and use *axis*(4) to add a new axis on the right-hand side of the graph and *mtext*(…, side = 4) to add an axis label on the right-hand side. Finally, we add a legend and a grid to the graph. This produces output shown in Figure 3-7. You can see from the figure that both sets of data are clearly displayed, even though they have dramatically different data ranges.

Now, we can use the above approach to display the market data of some indices on the graph. First, we need to load the data from a CSV file into R:

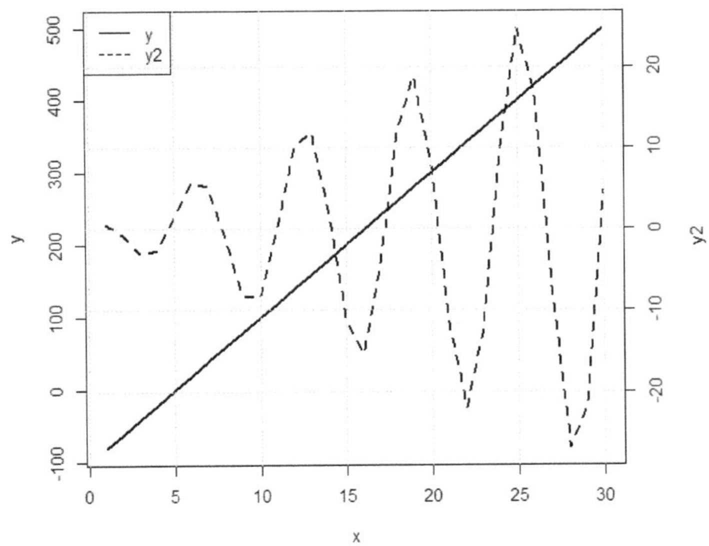


*Figure 3-7. A 2D graph with the second Y axis.*

```
dat <- read.table("./inst/extdata/indices.csv", header = T, sep = ",")
> head(dat, 3)
       Date IGSpread HYSpread     SPX   VIX
1 9/21/2004    53.93    363.0 1129.30 13.66
2 9/22/2004    55.18    367.5 1113.56 14.74
3 9/23/2004    54.69    371.2 1108.36 14.80
> tail(dat, 3)
          Date IGSpread HYSpread     SPX   VIX
2364 5/13/2014 62.48443 337.2766 1897.45 12.13
2365 5/14/2014 63.24887 338.1122 1888.53 12.17
2366 5/15/2014 65.21263 346.5009 1870.85 13.17
```

Here, we first load the CSV file that contains the daily data for some indices, including IGSpread (investment grade CDX spread), HYSpread (high yield CDX spread), SPX (S&P 500), and VIX (Volatility S&P 500). Now, we want to plot the HY and SPX as a function of date on the same graph. You can see that these two data columns have very different data ranges, we need to create a plot with a second Y-axis. First, we need to examine the data type of the *Date* column:

```
> class(dat$Date)
[1] "factor"
```

We need convert it into a date type:

```
> dat$Date <- as.Date(dat$Date, format = "%m/%d/%Y")
> class(dat$Date)
[1] "Date"
```

We can then use the same technique as the previous example to create a time series plot:

```
> par(mar = c(5, 4, 4, 5) + .1)
> plot(dat$Date, dat$HYSpread, type = "l", lwd = 2, col = "blue")
> par(new=T)
> plot(dat$Date, dat$SPX, type = "l", lwd = 2, col = "red", xaxt = "n",
```

```
       yaxt = "n", xlab = "", ylab = "")
> axis(4)
> mtext("dat$SPX", side = 4, line = 3)
> legend("topleft", lty = 1, lwd = 2, col = c("blue","red"), legend = c("HY","SPY"))
> title("HY and SPX time series")
```

This generates the plot shown in Figure 3-8.

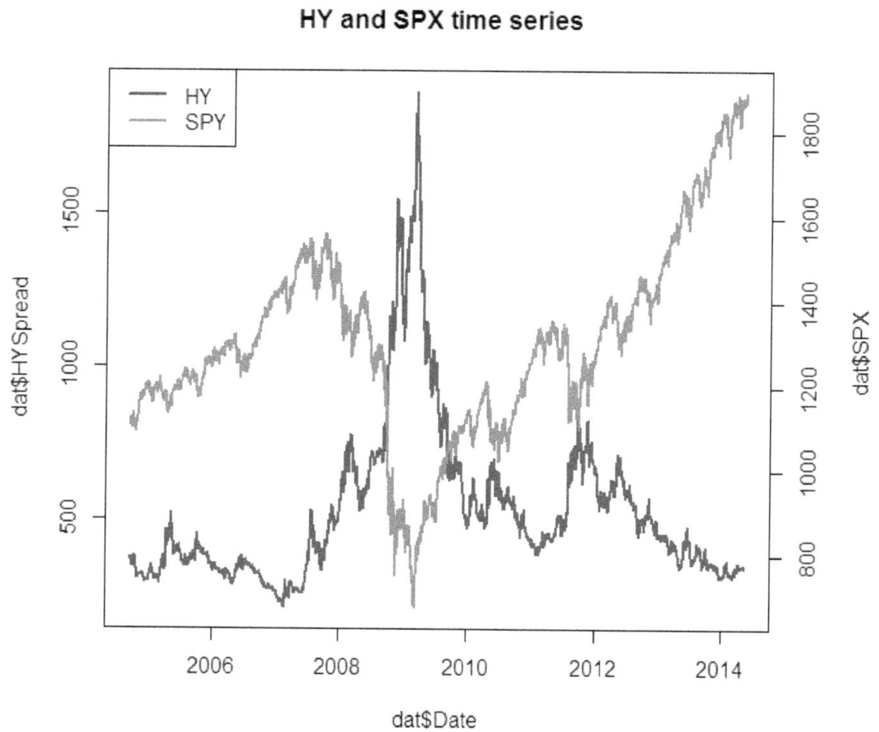


*Figure 3-8. A 2D plot of HY and SPY as a function of date.*

You may notice that to create plots with a second Y-axis, we need to type the same code repeatedly. We can simplify this procedure by implementing a plot helper function. Add a new *plotHelper.R* file and save it into the "[Working directory]/R/" directory. Add the following function named *y2Plot* to this file:

```
y2Plot <- function(x, y, y2, title = NULL, xLabel = NULL, yLable = NULL,
                   y2Label = NULL, isGrid = F){
  if(is.null(xLabel)) xLabel = "X"
  if(is.null(yLable)) yLable = "Y"
  if(is.null(y2Label)) y2Label = "Y2"
  par(mar = c(5, 5, 4, 5) + 0.1)
  plot(x, y, type = "l", col = "blue", main = title, xlab = xLabel, ylab = yLable)
  par(new = T)
  plot(x, y2,type = "l", col = "red", xaxt = "n", yaxt = "n", xlab = "", ylab = "")
  axis(4)
  mtext(y2Label, side = 4, line = 3)
  legend("topleft", col = c("blue", "red"), lty = 1, legend = c(yLable, y2Label))
  if(isGrid) grid()
}
```

Now, we can use the *y2Plot* function to create the graph with two-Y axes just as we do for creating a plot with a single Y-axis. For example, we can use the *dat* object created in the preceding example to plot the SPX and its volatility VIX:

```
> y2Plot(dat$Date, dat$SPX, dat$VIX, xLabel = "Date", yLable = "SPX",
         y2Label = "VIX", title = "SPX and VIX time series")
```

The above single command creates the plot with two Y-axes, as shown in Figure 3-9.

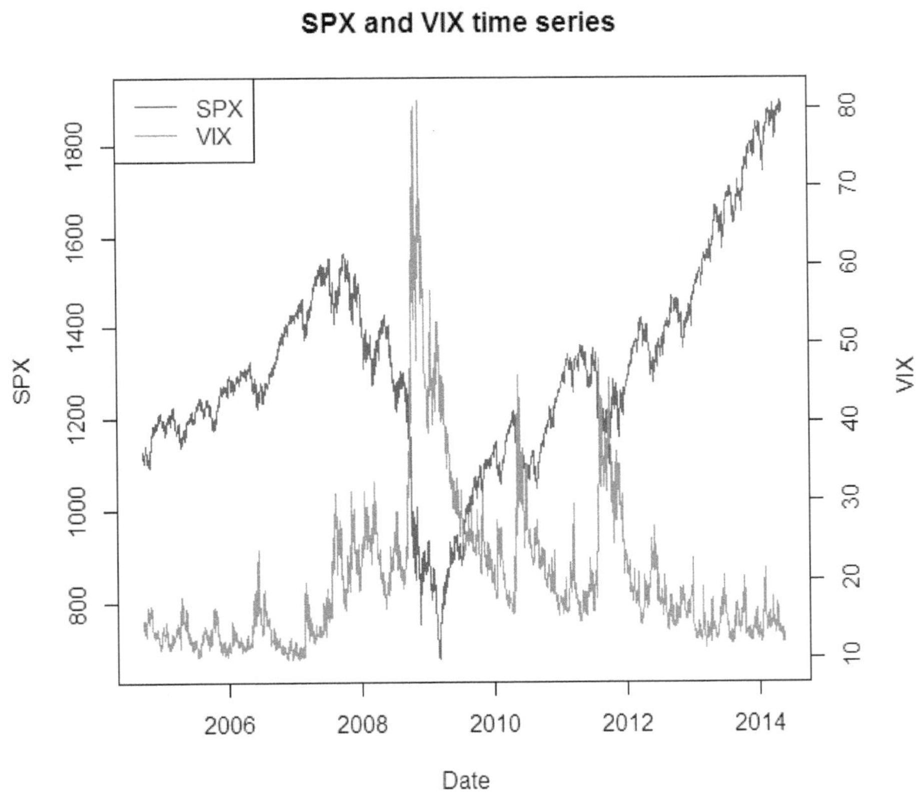


*Figure 3-9. A 2D plot with two Y-axes created using the y2Plot function.*

# Specialized 2D Plots

In the preceding sections, we discusses 2D line plots, which we can use to visualize data in real-world financial applications. In this section, I will show you how to create certain special or application specific graphs in R. I will discuss a variety of special plots that display statistical distributions of data or discrete data, including bar, stair-step, histogram, stem, error bar, and area plots. You will also learn how to create graphs in other coordinate systems, such as pie and polar charts.

## *Bar Plots*

The bar graph is useful for comparing classes or groups of data. In a bar plot, a class or group can contain a single category of data, or it can be broken down further into multiple categories for a greater depth of analysis. A bar plot is often used in exploratory data analysis to illustrate the major features of the distribution of the data in a convenient form. It displays the data using a number of rectangles of the same width, each of which represents a particular category. The length (and hence area) of each rectangle is proportional to the number of cases in the category it represents, for example, age group or religious affiliation. In its simplest form, the format of the *barplot* function is: *barplot*(height), where height is a vector or matrix.

Let us use *barplot* to show the annualized returns in 2013 for some stocks:

```
> library(quantmod)
> tickers <- c("^GSPC","XOM","MSFT","JNJ","GE")
> stks <- new.env()
> getSymbols(tickers, from = "2013-01-01", to = "2014-01-01", env = stks)
> rtns <- eapply(stks, function(x) periodReturn(Ad(x), period = "yearly",
                 type = "arithmetic"))
> rtns <- as.data.frame(rtns)
> colnames(rtns) <- c("XOM", "SPX", "GE", "MSFT", "JNJ")
> barplot(as.matrix(rtns), main = "Simple Bar Plot", xlab = "Stock",
          ylab = "Annual Returns", col = "lightgray")
```

Here, we first download the daily stock price data for several stocks from Yahoo Finance using the *quantmod* package. This produces output shown in Figure 3-10. We then compute the annualized returns using the *periodReturns* function included in the *quantmod* package and convert the result into a data frame object. Finally, we use *barplot* to display the annualized return in a bar graph, as shown in Figure 3-10.

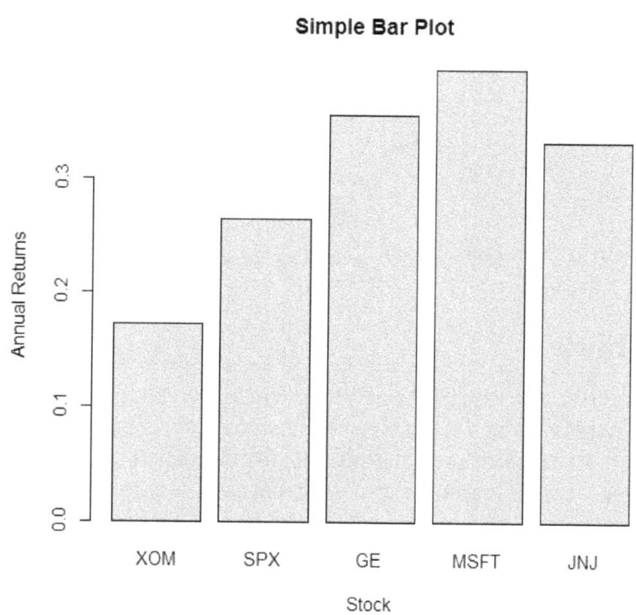


*Figure 3-10. A simple vertical bar plot.*

We can also easily create a horizontal bar chart using the following command:

```
> barplot(as.matrix(rtns), main = "Horizontal Bar Plot", ylab = "Stock",
        xlab = "Annual Returns",col = "gray", horiz = T)
```

This generates the plot shown in Figure 3-11.

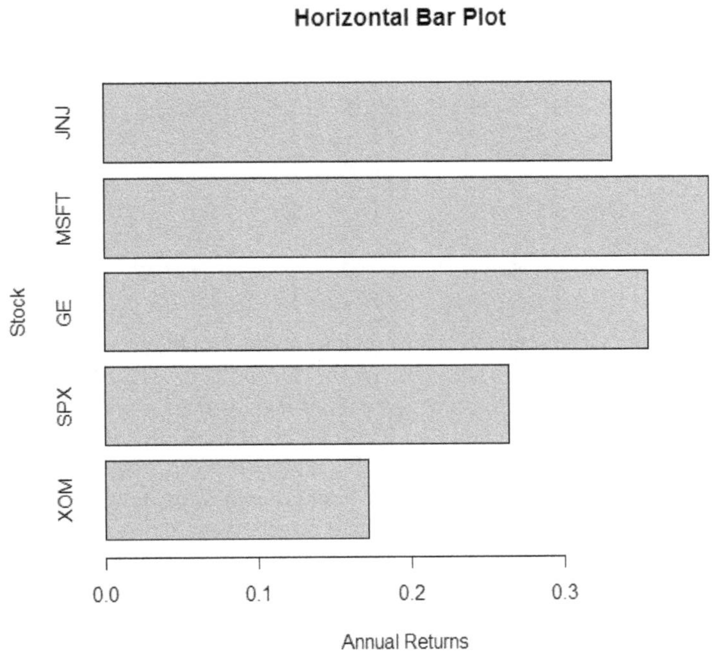


*Figure 3-11. A simple horizontal bar plot.*

If the input argument of the *barplot* function is a matrix rather than a vector, the resulting graph will be a stacked or grouped bar plot. If the argument *beside* = FALSE (the default), then each column of the matrix produces a bar in the plot, with the values in the column giving the heights of stacked sub-bars. If *beside* = TRUE, each column of the matrix represents a group, and the values in each column are juxtaposed rather than stacked.

I will use an example to demonstrate how to create the stacked and grouped bar plots. For this example, we will use the monthly return data for five US stocks from Oct. to Dec. 2013, which is stored in a CSV file:

```
> rtn <- read.table("./inst/extdata/MonthlyRtn.csv", header = T, sep = ","); rtn
  Ticker Month      Return
1   AAPL   Oct 0.096381741
2   AAPL   Nov 0.070052711
3   AAPL   Dec 0.008901793
4   AMZN   Oct 0.164374301
5   AMZN   Nov 0.081284499
6   AMZN   Dec 0.013134531
7     GS   Oct 0.016749845
8     GS   Nov 0.053678750
9     GS   Dec 0.049248204
```

```
10     JPM   Oct 0.004443955
11     JPM   Nov 0.110205664
12     JPM   Dec 0.022020246
13     SPX   Oct 0.044595750
14     SPX   Nov 0.028049470
15     SPX   Dec 0.023562790
```

We need to convert the above data into a matrix that have five columns since the number of levels for *Ticker* is five:

```
> dat <- rtn$Return    # load return data
> dat <- matrix(dat, ncol=5)  # convert data into matrix
> colnames(dat) <- levels(rtn$Ticker)
> rownames(dat) <- c("OCT","NOV", "DEC")
> dat
           AAPL        AMZN          GS          JPM        SPX
OCT 0.096381741 0.16437430 0.01674984 0.004443955 0.04459575
NOV 0.070052711 0.08128450 0.05367875 0.110205664 0.02804947
DEC 0.008901793 0.01313453 0.04924820 0.022020246 0.02356279
```

Double-check the data matrix and original return data to make sure they are consistent. When creating the bar plot, we need to pay special attention to the legend location. By default, *barplot* lacks functionality to generate legend and places it in a proper location. As a result, we need to modify the margin space and handle the clipping carefully. This can be achieved by setting proper arguments for the *par* function. The *par* function is defined to receive parameters through a vector: *c*(*bottom*, *left*, *top*, *right*). The default margin is *c*(5, 4, 4, 2) + 0.1. As a result, we have exploded the right-hand side of the figure to hold a legend. We need to override the default setting using the command:

```
> par(mar=c(5, 5, 4, 7) + 0.1, xpd = T)
```

Here, we set *xpd* = TRUE, which forces all plotting to be clipped to the figure region. Now, we can easily create the stacked bar plot using the following statements:

```
> barplot(dat,col = heat.colors(length(rownames(dat))), width = 2, xlab = "Symbol",
          ylab = "Monthly Return")
> legend("topright", inset = c(-0.15, 0), fill = heat.colors(length(rownames(dat))),
         legend = rownames(dat))
```

which produces the output shown in Figure 3-12. You can see from the results that the individual stocks (AAPL, AMZN, GS, and JPM) outperformed the S&P 500 index (SPX) during the 3-month period span from Oct. to Dec. 2013.

We can also easily create a grouped bar plot by setting the argument *beside* = TURE:

```
> par(mar = c(5, 5, 4, 7) + 0.1, xpd = T)
> barplot(dat, col = heat.colors(length(rownames(dat))), width = 2, xlab = "Symbol",
          ylab = "Monthly Return", beside = T)
> legend("topright", inset = c(-0.15, 0), fill = heat.colors(length(rownames(dat))),
         legend = rownames(dat))
```

which generates the output shown in Figure 3-13.

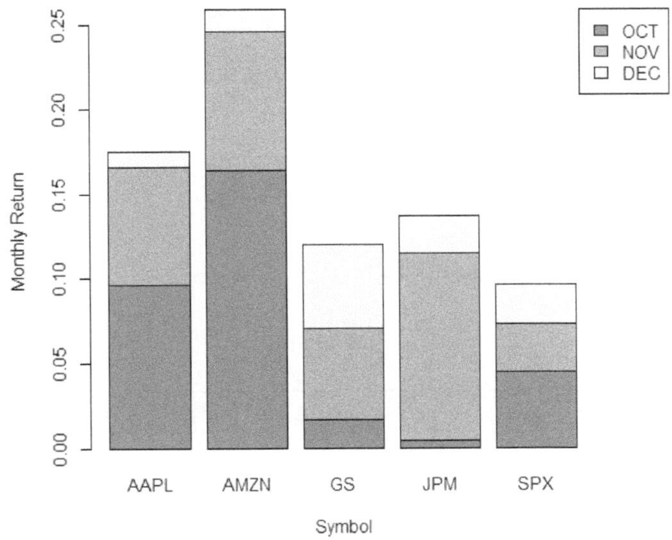


*Figure 3-12. A stacked bar chart.*

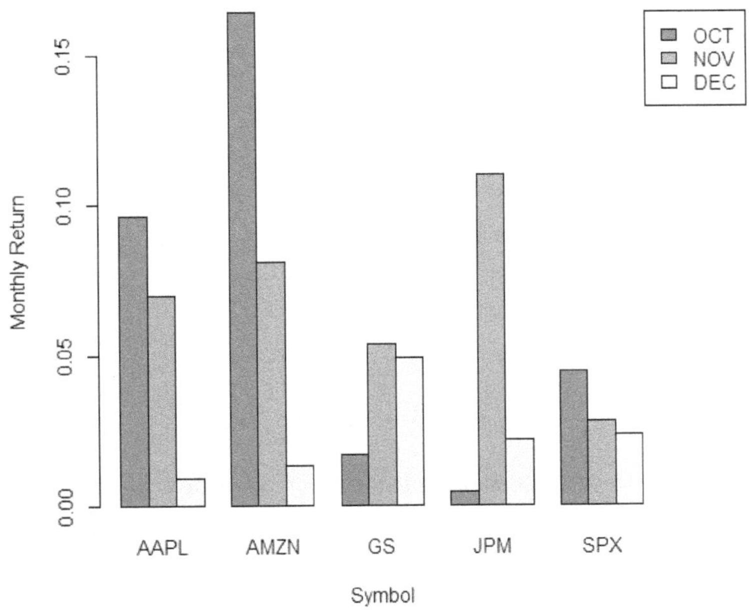


*Figure 3-13. A grouped bar plot.*

## *Stair-Step Plots*

Instead of creating lines that connect the data directly, we can create a plot that emphasizes the discrete nature of the data. We can use the *plot* function to create the stair-step graph by setting type = "*s*", or "*S*". This will draw horizontal lines at the level specified by the Y values. This level will be held constant over the period between the values specified by the elements in X. The stair-step plot is similar to a bar graph with the exception that the vertical lines are not dropped down all the way to the zero value point on the Y-axis.

For example, we can use the following commands to create a stair-step graph:

```
> x <- 1:70/(2 * pi)
> y<- sin(x)  * cos(x)
> plot(x, y, main = "Plot of sin(x)*cos(x)", xlab = "x values",
          ylab = "sin(x)*cos(x)", type = "s")
> lines(x, y, type = "S", col="red")
```

which produces the output shown in Figure 3-14.

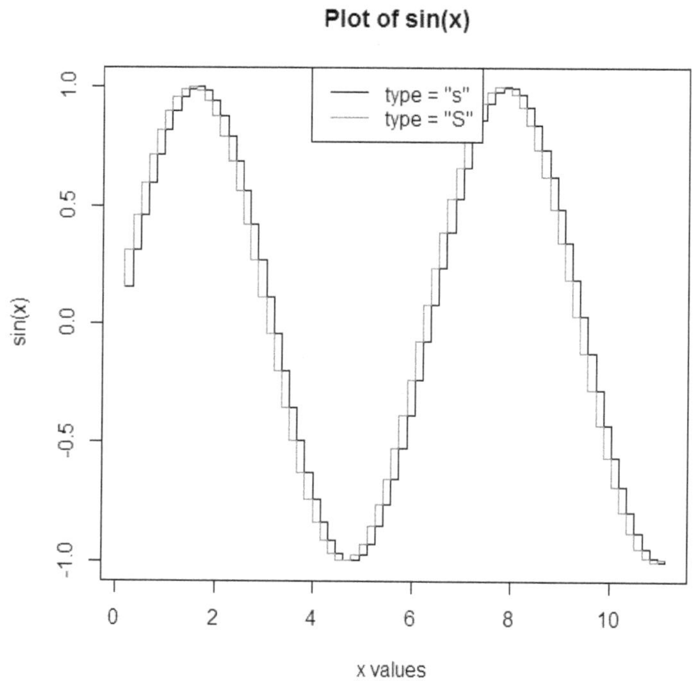


*Figure 3-14. A stair-step plot.*

The above result shows two step types that differ in their X-Y preference: going from $(x1, y1)$ to $(x2, y2)$ with $x1 < x2$. The *type* = "*s*" moves first horizontally, then vertically, whereas *type* = "*S*" moves the other way around.

## *Stem Plots*

Stem plots provide another way of visualizing discrete data sequences, such as sampled time series data. In these types of graphs, vertical lines terminating with a symbol such as a circle specified by the argument *pch* drawn from the zero value point on the Y-axis to the values in the data. We can combine two graphs with type = "*h*" and "*p*" to create a stem plot. For example:

```
> x <- 1:70/(2*pi)
> y <- sin(x)
> plot(x, y, main = "Plot of sin(x)", xlab = "x values",ylab = "sin(x)", type = "h")
```

```
> lines(x, y, type = "p", pch = 7)
```

This will produce the result shown in Figure 3-15.

We can use any of the line styles and terminate our stem plots with any types of symbols. The following code

```
> plot(x, y, main = "Plot of sin(x)", xlab = "x values", ylab = "sin(x)",
       type = "h", lty = 2)
> lines(x, y, type = "p", pch = 18)
```

generates a stem plot in which the lines are dashed and the terminating symbol is a filled triangle as shown in Figure 3-16.

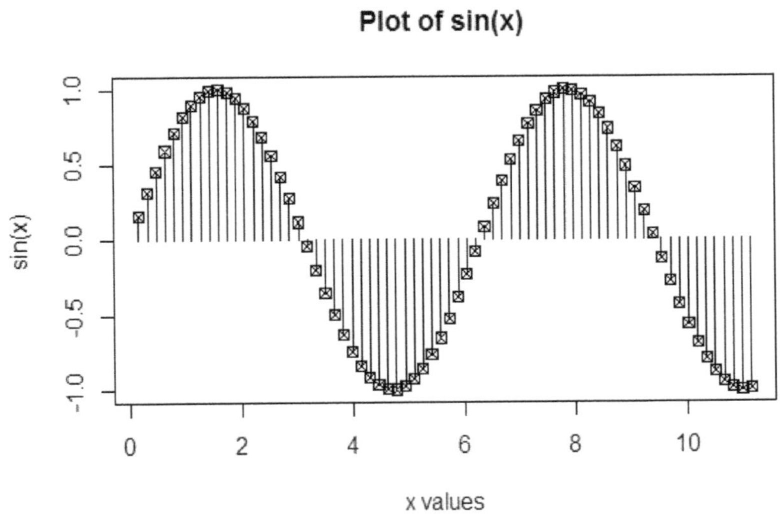


*Figure 3-15. A stem plot.*

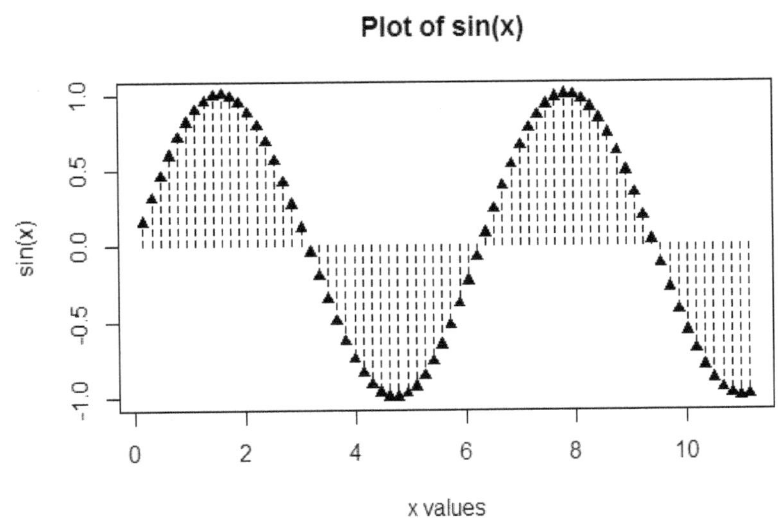


*Figure 3-16. A stem plot with filled terminators and dashed lines.*

## *Error Bar Plots*

We often use error bars to show uncertainty in the accuracy of plotted values. The base R graphics system does not implement plot type with error bars. However, we can easily create a customized R function to achieve this goal.

Add a new function named *errorBar* to the *plotHelper.R* file. Here is the code for this function:

```
errorBar <- function(x, y, error){
  yr <- max(y) - min(y)
  yl <- c(min(y - error) - 0.05 * yr, max(y + error) + 0.05 * yr)
  plot(x, y, ylim = yl, type = "o")
  xb <- (max(x) - min(x)) / length(x) / 20
  if(xb > 0.02) xb = 0.02
  segments(x, y - error, x, y + error)
  segments(x - xb, y - error, x + xb, y - error)
  segments(x - xb, y + error, x + xb, y + error)
}
```

Here, we first set proper limits for Y-axis by taking into account of the Y value range and the error-bar size. We then use the plot function to create the standard line graph. Next, we use the segments function to create the error bars.

To illustrate how to use the above function, we will generate some mean and standard deviation data and plot it with error bars that indicate the range of values that are within three standard deviations of the mean:

```
> source("./R/plotHelper.R")
> x <- 2:20/2
> ymean <- 10 * exp(-x) + 3
> sd <- 1/x
> errorBar(x, ymean, 3 * sd)
```

This produces the result shown in Figure 3-17.

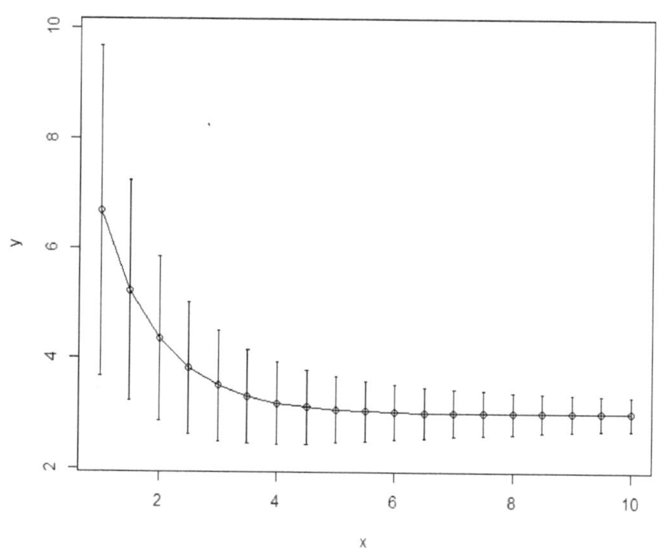


*Figure 3-17. An error-bar graph.*

### *Histograms*

Histograms are a kind of bar graph that is created by first specifying the number of bins that specify a range of values, and then counting the number of occurrences of a data set that fall within each bin. We can use the *hist* function in the base R graphics to create a histogram of the data we pass to it.

Now, we will use histogram to study the SPY (the S&P 500 ETF) return distributions. Assume the SPY return follows a normal (Gaussian) distribution:

$$f(x) = \frac{1}{\sqrt{2\pi\sigma^2}} \exp\left[\frac{(x-\mu)^2}{2\sigma}\right]$$

where $\mu$ denotes for the mean and $\sigma$ for the standard deviation. We can overlap such a distribution onto the SPY daily return data and see what that looks like:

```
> library(quantmod)
> spy <- getSymbols("SPY", from = "2012-01-01", auto.assign = F)
> rtn <- na.omit(ROC(Ad(spy)))
> mu <- mean(rtn)
> sigma <- sd(rtn)
> x <- seq(-5 * sigma, 5 * sigma, length = nrow(rtn))
> hist(rtn, breaks = 50, probability = T)
> lines(x, dnorm(x, mu, sigma), col = "red")
```

Here, the *dnorm* function creates a normal distribution given a range of X values, a mean, and a standard deviation. The above commands produce the output shown in Figure 3-18.

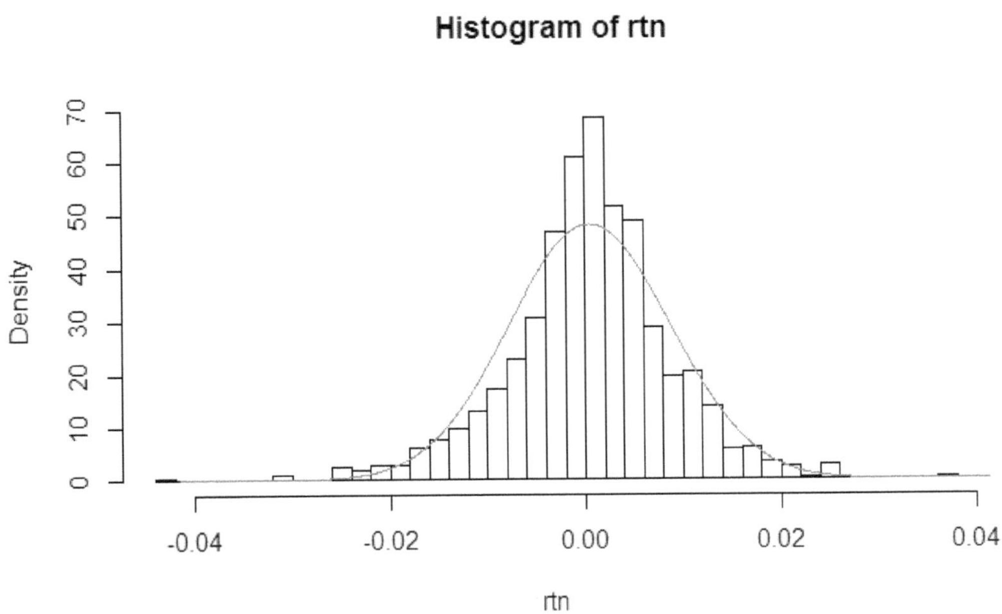


*Figure 3-18. A histogram for SPY returns.*

The results show that the SPY return distribution deviates from the normally distributed. There appears to be more observations that fall around the zero percent range.

## *Area Plots*

The area plot are not implemented in the base R graphics system. However, it is easy to create a customized R function to generate area graphs. This is achieved by combining the *plot* function with the *polygon* function. Add a new function named *areaPlot* to the *plotHelper.R* file. Here is the code for this function:

```
areaPlot <- function(df, xLabel = NULL, yLabel = NULL){
  cols <- c("red", "green", "blue", "yellow", "blueviolet",  "brown", "cyan",
            "cornsilk", "burlywood", "gray")
  x <- c(df[, 1], rev(df[, 1]))
  y <- c(rep(0, nrow(df)), rev(df[, 2]))
  yl = NULL
  if(ncol(df) > 2){
    mi <- min(rowSums(df[, 2:ncol(df)]))
    if(mi > 0) yl <- c(0, max(rowSums(df[, 2:ncol(df)])) + 0.02)
    else  yl <- c(mi - 0.02, max(rowSums(df[, 2:ncol(df)])) + 0.02)
  }
  plot(df[ ,1], df[, 2], col= cols[1], type = "l", ylim = yl, xlab = xLabel,
       ylab = yLabel)
  polygon(x, y, col=cols[1])
  if(ncol(df) > 2){
    df1 <- df[, 2]
    for(i in 3:ncol(df)){
      y <- c(df1, rev(df1 + df[, i]))
      polygon(x, y, col = cols[i - 1])
      df1 <- df1 + df[, i]
    }
  }
}
```

The basic idea here is to draw polygons on the screen. We need to specify the bounds of the polygons. For the first curve, the bottom is the X-axis, and the top is the desired Y values of our curve. For next curve, we need to draw the polygon on top of the previous one, and so on. We also redefined a color sequence, which includes ten colors. You can add or change colors by modifying this color sequence. The function takes the data frame as input with the first column representing the X values and the rest columns representing the Y, Y2,..., Yn values. The other arguments *xLabel* and *yLabel* are optional.

Now, I will show you how to use this function to create area graphs. For example:

```
> source("./R/plotHelper.R")
> x <- seq(0, 7, 0.1)
> y <- sin(x)
> my.df <- data.frame(x = x, y = y)
> areaPlot(my.df,xLabel = "X", yLabel = "Y")
```

Here, we first create a data frame object as the input data. The above commands produce the output shown in Figure 3-19.

When our input data contains more than two columns, a layer in the area plot is draw for each additional column in the input data. The height of *i*th layer in the area plot is determined by summing the values in each row from the 1st to *i*th column in the data.

Now, I will use an example to generate a stacked area plot. Let us consider the OHLC price data for IBM:

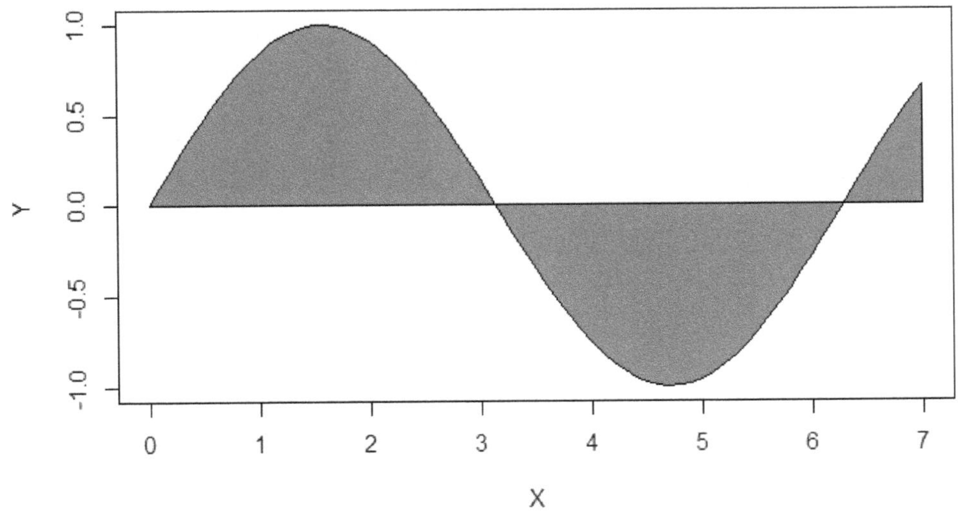


*Figure 3-19. A simple area plot.*

```
> library(Quandl)
> ibm <- Quandl("WIKI/IBM", start_date = "2010-01-01")
> ibm <- ibm[c("Date", "Open", "High", "Low", "Close")]
> areaPlot(ibm, xLabel = "Date", yLabel = "Price")
```

This will generate a four-layered area graph that represents the OHLC stock data for IBM, as shown in Figure 3-20.

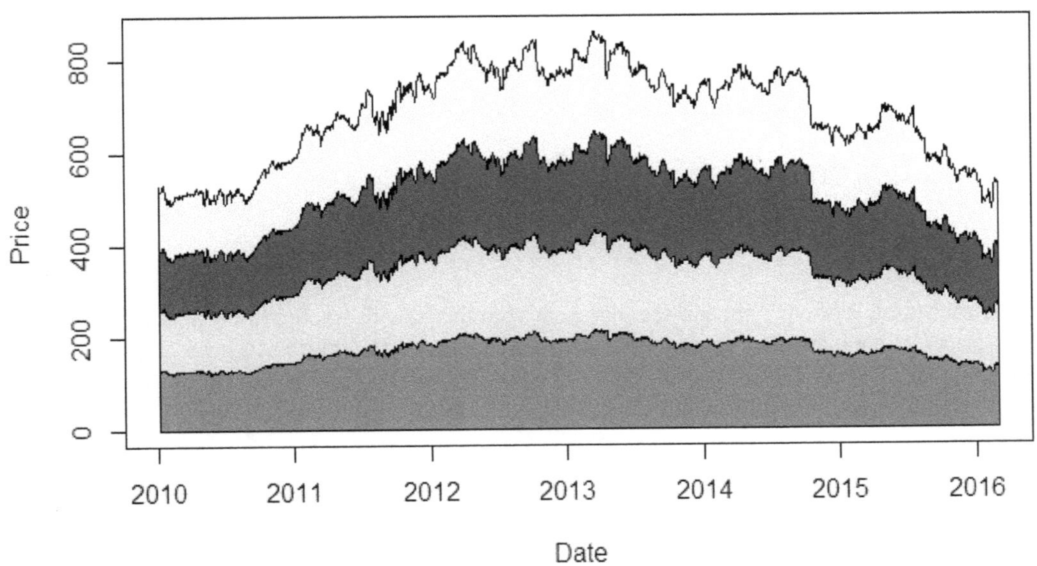


*Figure 3-20. A stacked area plot.*

## *Pie Plots*

The pie charts display the percentage that each element in the data contributes to the sum of all elements. They are useful when we want to show the relative proportion of data elements to one another. For example, let us say we have some data representing the browser market shares from Jan. to May, 2015:

| | | | | | |
|---|---|---|---|---|---|
| **Browser** | MS IE | Chrome | Firefox | Safari | Others |
| **Market Shares** | 0.583 | 0.249 | 0.107 | 0.049 | 0.012 |

We can then create the corresponding pie plot by issuing the following statements:

```
> slices <- c(58.3, 24.9, 10.7, 4.9, 1.2)
> pct <- round(slices/sum(slices) * 100, 1)
> lbls <- c("MS IE",  "Chrome", "Firefox", "Safari", "Others")
> lbls <- paste0(lbls, " ", pct, "%")
> pie(slices, labels = lbls, col = rainbow(length(slices)))
```

This produces the output shown in Figure 3-21.

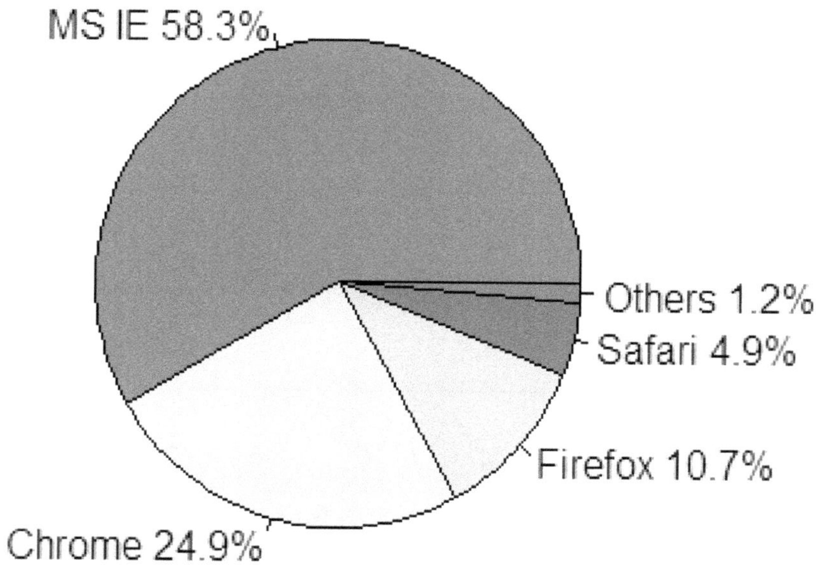


*Figure 3-21. A pie chart.*

From the preceding sections, you can see that even with the base R graphics system, we can still create a wide variety of sophisticated general and specialized graphs. In addition to base graphics, there are several graphics systems available, including the *grid*, *lattice*, and *ggplot2* packages. Each is designed to expand on the capabilities of the base R graphics system.

The *grid* package provides low-level access to graphic primitives, giving you a great deal of flexibility in the creation of graphic output. The *lattice* package provides an intuitive approach for examining multivariate relationships through conditional one-, two-, or three-dimensional graphs called trellis graphs. The *ggplot2* package provides a method of creating innovative graphs based on a comprehensive graphical grammar. In the following section, I will focus on how to use the *ggplot2* package to create various graphs.

# Creating Graphs Using ggplot2

The *ggplot2* package provides a comprehensive, grammar-based system for generating graphs in a unified and coherent manner, allowing us to create new and innovative data visualizations. The power of this approach has led *ggplot2* to become an important tool for visualizing data in R.

In *ggplot2*, we create graphs by chaining together functions using the plus (+) sign. Each function modifies the graph created up to that point. For example:

```
> install_packages("ggplot2")
> library(ggplot2)
> dat <- read.table("./inst/extdata/indices.csv", header = T, sep = ",")
> ggplot(data = dat, aes(x = dat$SPX, y = dat$HYSpread)) +
    geom_point() + labs(title = "HY ~ SPX", x = "SPX", y = "HY") +
    theme_bw()
```

Here, we use the same market data for some indices from a CSV file as we did in preceding sections. The above commands generate the output shown in Figure 3-22.

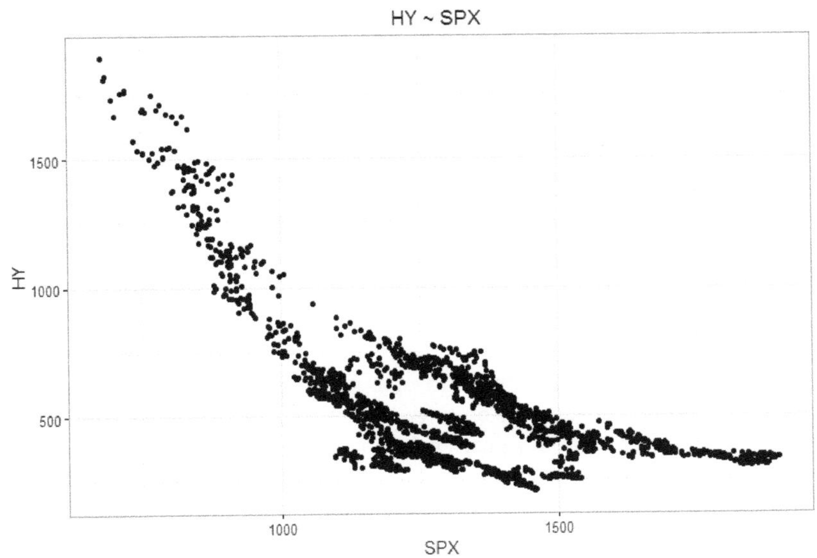


*Figure 3-22. A scatter plot of HY vs SPX.*

You can see that the *ggplot* function initializes the plot and specifies the data source (*dat*) and variables (SPX and HYSpread) to be used. The options in the *aes* function specify what role each variable will play. Here, the SPX values are mapped to prices along the X-axis, and HYSpread values are mapped to the spreads along the Y-axis.

The *ggplot* function sets up the graph but produces no visual output on its own. Geometric objects (or *geoms* for short), which include points, lines, bars, box plots, and shaded regions, are added to the graph using one or more *geom* functions. In this example, the *geom_point* function draws points on the graph and creates a scatter plot. The *labs* function is optional and adds annotations (a title and axis labels).

There are many functions in *ggplot2*, and most can include optional parameters. We can easily expand on the preceding example using the following command:

```
> ggplot(data = dat, aes(x = dat$SPX, y = dat$HYSpread)) +
   geom_point(shape = 5, color = "blue", size = 2) +
   geom_smooth(method = "lm", color = "red", se = FALSE) +
   labs(title = "HY vs SPX", x = "SPY", y = "HY") +
   theme_bw()
```

This generates the output shown in Figure 3-23.

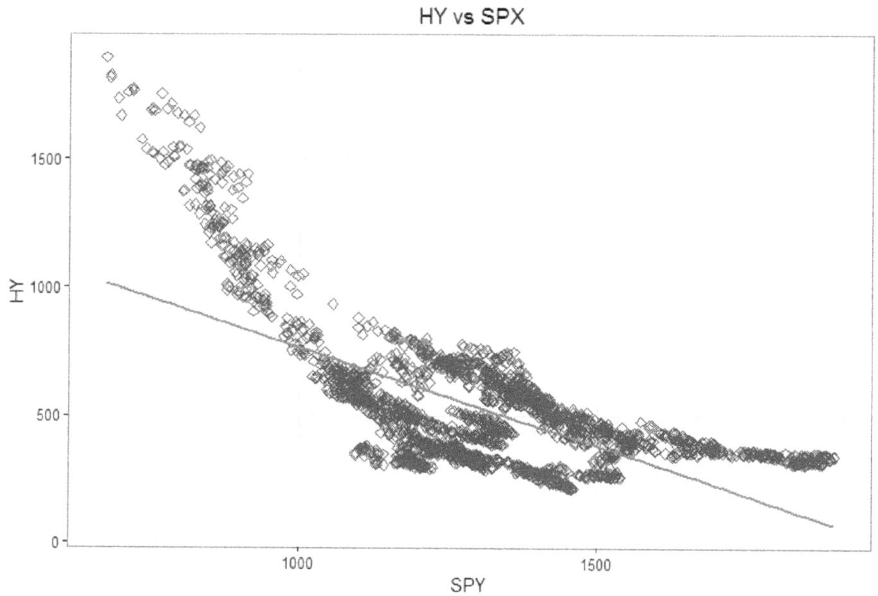


*Figure 3-23. A scatter plot of HY vs SPX with a linear regression line.*

The options to *geom_point* set the point shape to open-diamond (*shape* = 5, or *pch* = 5), double the point's size (*size* = 2), and render them in blue (*color* = "blue"). The *geom_smooth* function adds a smoothed line. Here a red (*color* = "red") linear regression line is added (*method* = "lm"). We also set the *se* argument to FALSE, meaning that we do not want the shaded confidence region on the chart (by default, the regression line includes a 95% confidence region).

The above example shows the basic procedure of creating graphs using *ggplot2*. If you understand and are used to the graphic grammar and structure of *ggplot2*, you will find that *ggplot2* makes constructing graphs simpler, not more complicated comparing to the base R graphics system. If you want to do anything beyond very simple graphs, it is generally better to switch to *ggplot2*. This is because *ggplot2* provides a unified interface and a set of options, instead of constructing graphs piece by piece and special cases required in the base R graphics. Once you learn how *ggplot2* works, you can use that knowledge for everything from scatter plots to histograms to violin plot and maps. In the following sections, I will show you how to create various graphs using the *ggplot2* package.

## Scatter Plots

We often use scatter plots to display the relationship between two continuous variables. In the *ggplot2* package, we can create a scatter graph using the *qplot* function:

```
> dat <- read.table("./inst/extdata/indices.csv", header = T, sep = ",")
```

```
> qplot(dat$SPX, dat$HYSpread)
```

This will generate a similar plot as shown in Figure 3-22. If the two variables are already in the same data frame, we can use the following command:

```
> qplot(data = dat, SPX, HYSpread)
```

This equivalent to the following statement:

```
> ggplot(dat, aes(x = SPX, y = HYSpread)) + geom_point()
```

We can use different shapes in a scatter plot by setting the *shape* (or *pch*) parameter. The Figure 3-4 shows the possible values for *shape*. In Figure 3-23, we set it to open diamonds (*shape* = 5). We can also use the *size* parameter to control the size of the points.

We can also use color or shape to group the data points. For example, in our *dat* data set, we want to group it by year:

```
> dat$Year <- format(as.Date(dat$Date,"%m/%d/%Y"), "%Y")
> dat1<- dat[dat$Year < 2007,]
```

Here, we extract the year part from the Date column and save it into a new column named *Year*, and then subset the data in a 3-year period:

```
> head(dat1, 3)
       Date IGSpread HYSpread     SPX   VIX Year
1 9/21/2004    53.93    363.0 1129.30 13.66 2004
2 9/22/2004    55.18    367.5 1113.56 14.74 2004
3 9/23/2004    54.69    371.2 1108.36 14.80 2004
> tail(dat1, 3)
          Date IGSpread HYSpread     SPX   VIX Year
557 12/27/2006    33.59   264.04 1426.84 10.64 2006
558 12/28/2006    33.58   262.43 1424.73 10.99 2006
559 12/29/2006    33.48   262.86 1418.30 11.56 2006
```

Now, *dat1* has data with three distinct years (from 2004 to 2006). We can then group points on the variable *Year*, by mapping *Year* to color or shape:

```
> ggplot(dat1, aes(x = SPX, y = HYSpread, color = Year)) + geom_point() + theme_bw()
> ggplot(dat1, aes(x = SPX, y = HYSpread, shape = Year)) + geom_point() + theme_bw()
```

The above commands generate the outputs shown in Figure 3-24.

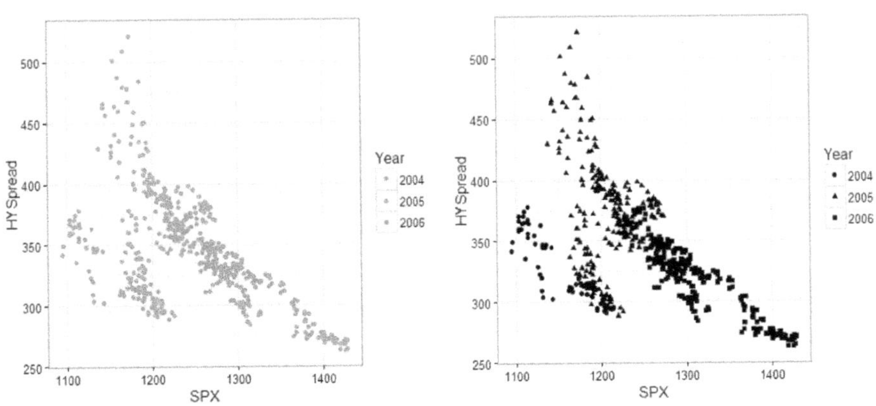


*Figure 3-24. Scatter plots with grouping points by color (left) and shape (right).*

Note that the grouping variable must be categorical, i.e., a factor or character vector. *ggplot2* also allows us to map a variable to both *shape* and *color*. For example:

```
> ggplot(dat1,aes(x = SPX, y = HYSpread, color = Year, shape = Year)) +
        geom_point() + theme_bw()
```

This produces the result shown in Figure 3-25.

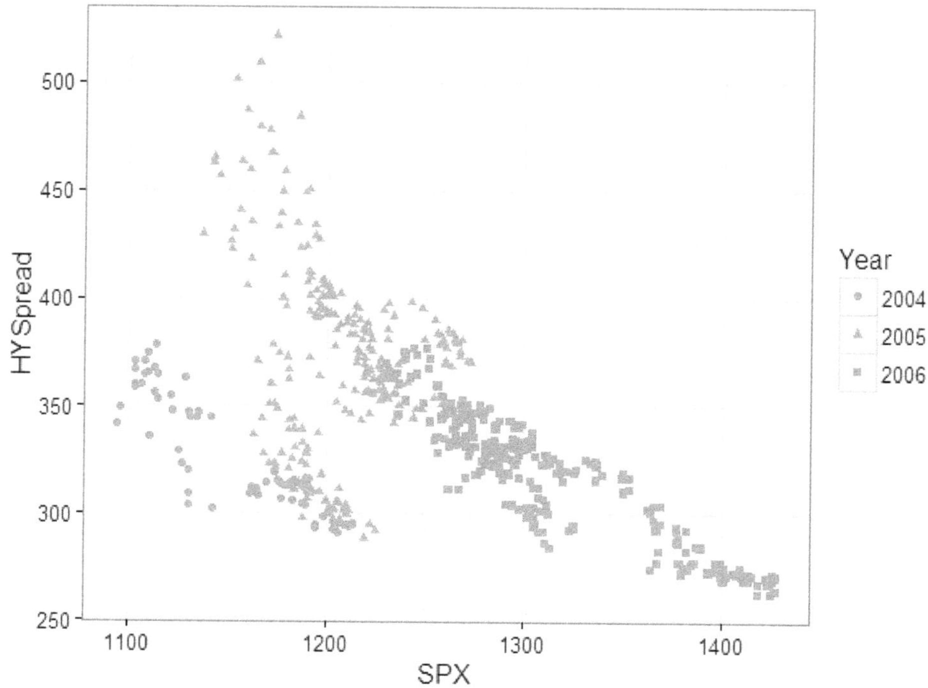


*Figure 3-25. A scatter plot with grouping points by both color and shape.*

In Figure 3-23, we added a linear regression line using the *geom_smooth* function, where the linear regression line does not fit the data well. In fact, *ggplot2* allows us to use different fitting functions when we fit the data. For example, the following code will fit data using different models, including linear (*method* = "*lm*", *formula* = *y* ~ *x*), quadratic (2nd order of polynomials, *method* = "*lm*", formula = y ~ *poly*(*x*, 2)), and locally weighted regression (*method* = "*loess*", *formula* = *y* ~ *x*):

```
> ggplot(data = dat, aes(x = SPX, y = HYSpread)) +
    geom_point(shape = 1, size = 1.5) +
    labs(title = "HY vs SPX", x = "SPX", y = "HY") +
    geom_smooth(method = "lm", formula = y ~ x, color = "red", se = FALSE) +
    geom_smooth(method = "lm", formula = y ~ poly(x,2), color="blue", se = F)+
    geom_smooth(method = "loess", formula = y ~ x, color = "green", se = F) +
    theme_bw()
```

The above code will add three fitting curves to the same scatter plot, as shown in Figure 3-26.

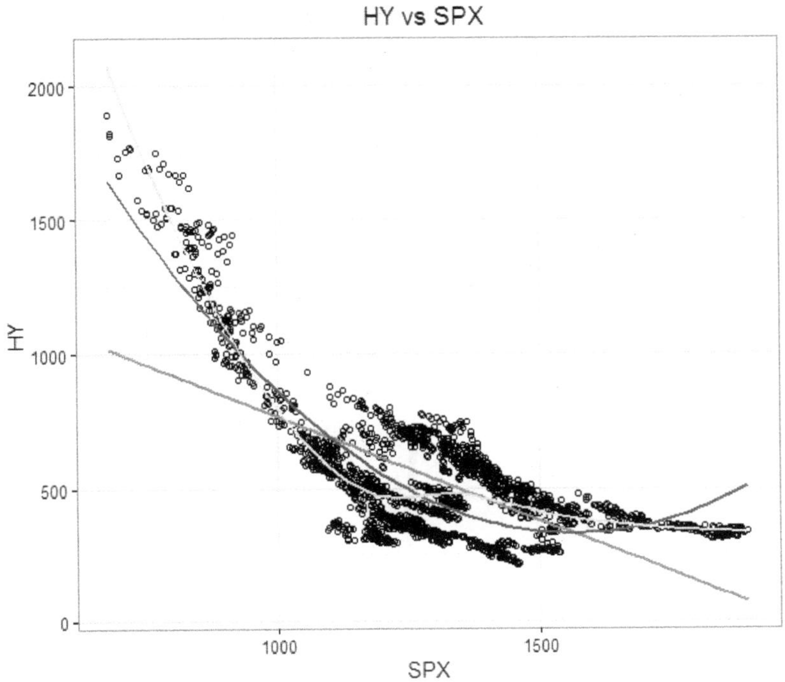


*Figure 3-26. A scatter plot of HY ~ SPX with three fitting curves.*

You can see from the results in the figure that the quadratic fitting (blue) is better than the linear regression (red), and the locally weighted regression (green) gives the best fitting overall. Thus, we will face some issues if our trading strategy is based linear regression. There exists the convexity at very tight credit spread levels (small HY values), because credit spreads have a zero lower bound, once they have tightened to a certain level, no chances of tightening further go down dramatically. Even when further tightening occurs, the absolute value of the move could be very low.

In contrast, in a rally market (i.e., when credit spreads are tightening), equity has unlimited upside. Therefore, at tight spread levels, HY credit performance gets capped while S&P 500 continues to benefit, and we see a curvature in the scatter plot as indicated in Figure 3-26. This why the trading strategies based on linear regression may fail. In this case, we need to make changes to our strategies by taking into account such a convexity effect.

## Line Plots

Creating a simple line graph using *ggplot2* is easy. For example, if we want to create a time-series line plot for SPY, we can issue the following command:

```
> dat$Date <- as.Date(dat$Date, "%m/%d/%Y")
> ggplot(dat, aes(x = Date, y = SPX)) + geom_line() + theme_bw()
```

Since the *Date* column in the data set loaded from a CSV file is a factor object, we need to convert it into a date object. We then use the *geom_line* function to create the line plot, as shown in Figure 3-27.

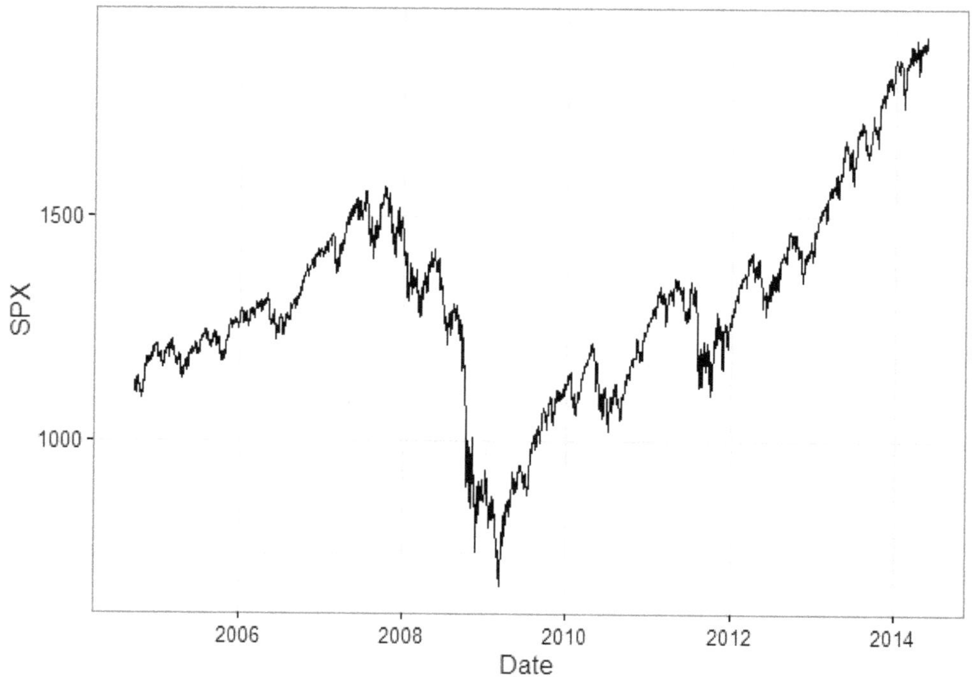


*Figure 3-27. A time-series plot for SPX.*

Sometimes, it is useful to indicate each data point on a line graph. This is helpful when the data records are low. We can easily add symbols (see Figure 3-4) to a line graph by appending a *geom_point* function:

```
> ggplot(dat[dat$Date > "2014-01-01", ], aes(x = Date, y = SPX)) +
    geom_line() + geom_point(shape = 5) + theme_bw()
```

Here we use the subset of *dat* in order to see the symbols on the plot more clearly. This generates the output shown in Figure 3-28.

Be careful when we want to create a line graph with multiple lines. We may want to try a naïve approach to create such a plot. For example, for a small number of variables, we may want to build up the plot manually:

```
> ggplot(dat, aes(Date)) +
    geom_line(aes(y = IGSpread, color = "IGSpread")) +
    geom_line(aes(y = HYSpread, color = "HYSpread")) +
    theme_bw() +
    labs(color = "CDX Indices")
```

The last line of the above code is used to change the legend title; otherwise, we will have an undesired legend title ("IGSpread") on our graph. In general, we can use labs function to set the value of fill, color, shape, or whatever aesthetic is appropriate for the legend.

This produces the results shown in Figure 3-29.

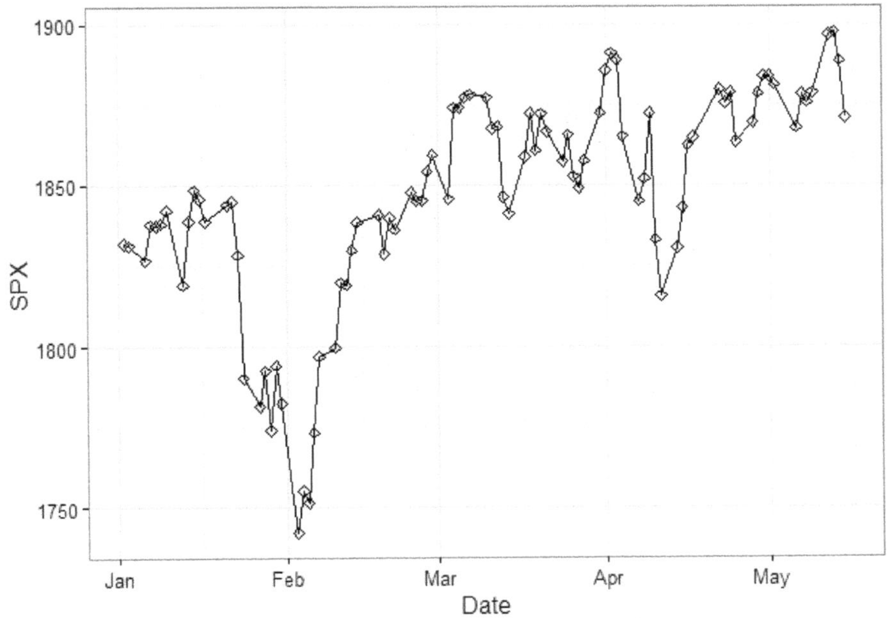


*Figure 3-28. A line plot with symbols.*

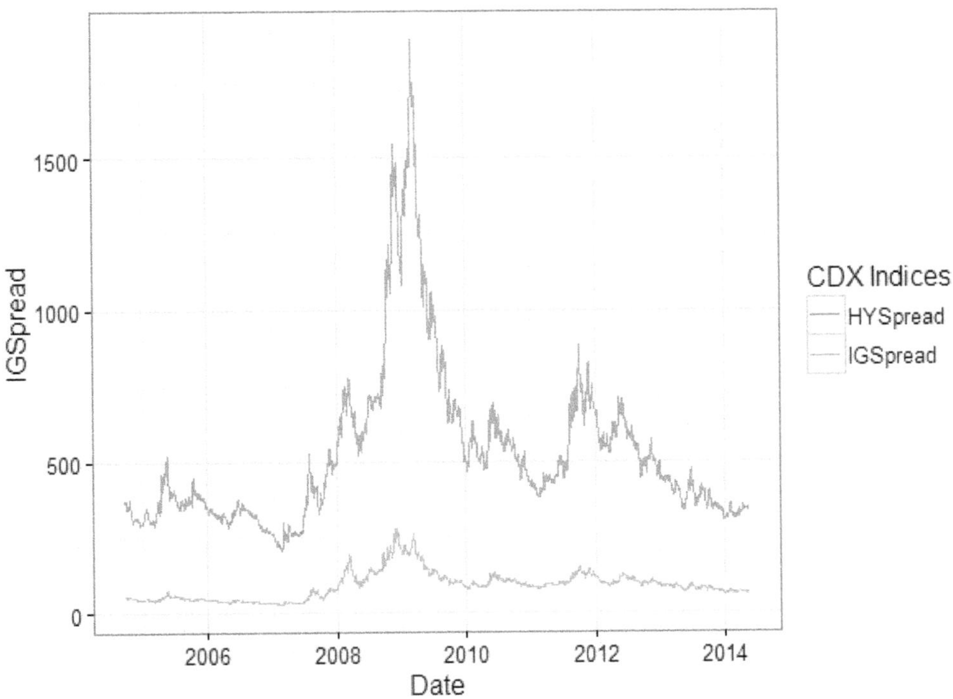


*Figure 3-29. A line plot with multiple lines created manually.*

If we want to show multiple variables on a single line charts, the above manual approach is not recommended. Instead, we should reshape our original data in a format that *ggplot2* will take. For example, if we want to display the open, high, low, and close price time series on a line graph, we can use the following code:

```
> library(ggplot2)
> library(reshape2)
> ibm <- Quandl("WIKI/IBM", start_date = "2015-10-01")
> ibm <- ibm[c("Date", "Open", "High", "Low", "Close")]
> ibm1 <- melt(ibm, "Date")
> colnames(ibm1) <- c("Date", "PriceType", "Price")
> ggplot(ibm1, aes(x = Date, y = Price, colour = PriceType)) +
         geom_line() + theme_bw()
```

Here, we convert the original data into a long format using the melt function from the *reshape2* package. We also rename the default column names (the default names are "Date", "variable", "value") for the converted data (*ibm1*) into more meaningful names. Finally, we use *ggplot* function to create a line graph by setting *color = PriceType*. The above code generate the output shown in Figure 3-30.

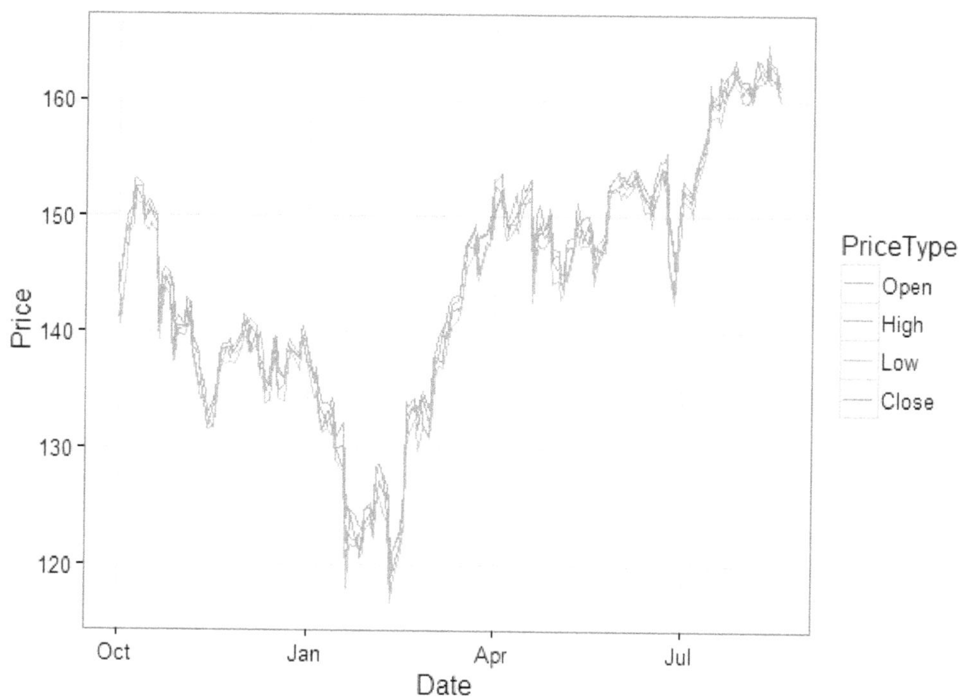


*Figure 3-30. A line graph with multiple lines created using reshaped data.*

Instead of re-typing the above code every time for creating a multiple-line graph, we can implement an R function to do the work automatically. Add a new function named *ggMultipleLines* to the *plotHelper.R* file. Here is the code for this function:

```
ggMultipleLines <- function(df, xcolName, title = NULL, yLabel = NULL,
                            legendTitle = NULL){
  library(reshape2)
  library(ggplot2)
```

```
  if(is.null(yLabel)) yLabel = "value"
  df1 <- melt(df,xcolName)
  g <- ggplot(df1, aes(x= eval(parse(text = xcolName)), y= value, color = variable))
  g <- g + geom_line() + theme_bw()
  g <- g + xlab(xcolName) + ylab(yLabel) + ggtitle(title)
  if(!is.null(legendTitle)) g <- g + labs(color = legendTitle)
  g
}
```

This function takes the standard form of a data frame as input data and converts it into a long format using the melt function. We need also to specify the column name for the *x* variable (it is usually the date column for time series data). The optional arguments, *title*, *yLabel*, and *legendTitle*, allow us to customize our graph.

The following example illustrate how to use the above function to create a multi-line plot:

```
> tks <- c("YAHOO/AMAT","YAHOO/MSFT","YAHOO/INTC")
> stks <- Quandl(tks, start_date = "2015-01-01")
> stk1 <- stks[c("Date", "YAHOO.AMAT - Adjusted Close",
                 "YAHOO.MSFT - Adjusted Close", "YAHOO.INTC - Adjusted Close")]
> colnames(stk1) <- c("Date", "AMAT", "MSFT", "INTC")
> head(stk1)
        Date     AMAT     MSFT     INTC
1 2015-01-02 24.31813 45.19625 34.98996
2 2015-01-05 23.53870 44.78063 34.59541
3 2015-01-06 22.65211 44.12337 33.95066
4 2015-01-07 22.86645 44.68397 34.66277
5 2015-01-08 23.59716 45.99849 35.30753
6 2015-01-09 23.61665 45.61187 35.37489
```

Here, we download the daily stock data for AMAT, MSFT, and INTC from Yahoo Finance using the *Quandl* package. We then extract the *Adjusted Close* price data and save it into a new data frame object named *stk1*, which can be taken as input by our *ggMultipleLines* function:

```
> ggMultipleLines(stk1, xcolName = "Date")
```

This produces the results shown in Figure 3-31 (left). Note that the default Y-axis label is value and the legend title is variable. We can change the default settings using the optional parameters of the *ggMultipleLines* function:

```
> ggMultipleLines(stk1, xcolName = "Date", title = "Stock Price for AMAT, MSFT,
                  INTC", yLabel = "Price", legendTitle = "Stock Ticker")
```

This generates the output shown in Figure 3-31 (right).

The *ggMultipleLines* function provides just the basic structure for creating a graph with multiple lines. You can easily add more customized features to it according to your application requirements.

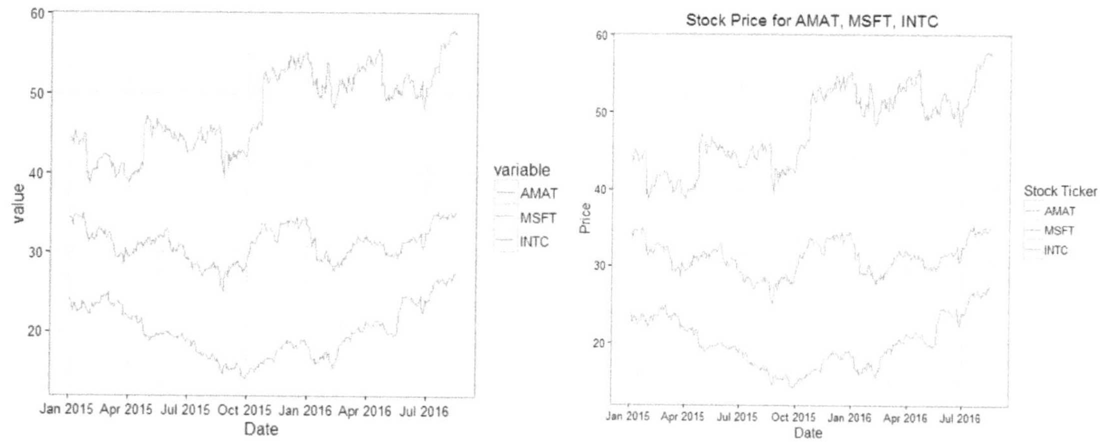


*Figure 3-31. Multi-line graphs created using the ggMultipleLines function.*

# Area Plots

Unlike in the base R graphics system where we have to implement our own *areaPlot* function to create an area graph, *ggplot2* has a built-in function named *geom_area*, which can be used directly to create area plots. For example:

```
> x <- seq(0,7,0.1)
> y <- sin(x)
> df <- data.frame(x = x, y = y)
> ggplot(df, aes(x = x, y = y)) + geom_area(fill = "red")
```

This produces the output shown in Figure 3-32.

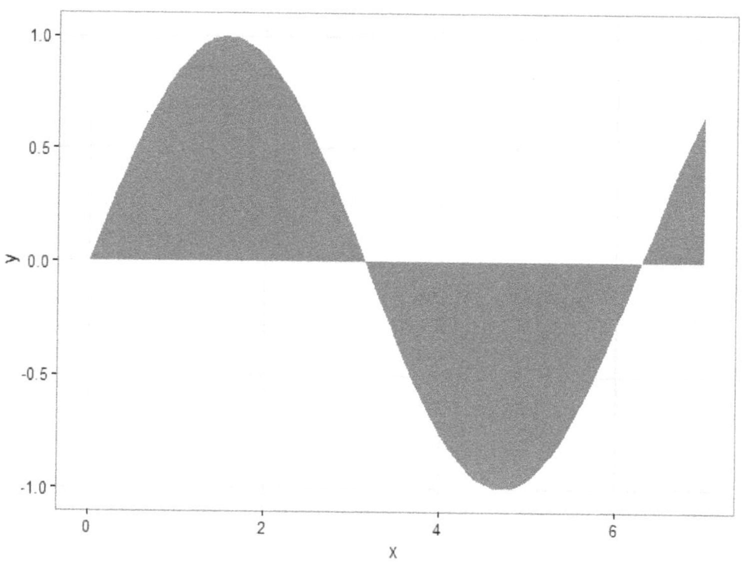


*Figure 3-32. A simple area plot.*

We can also use the *geom_area* function to create a stacked area graph. For example, we can use the data set *stk1* that has been used in creating multiple-line graphs (see Figure 3-31).

```
> stk2 <- melt(stk1, "Date")
> colnames(stk2) <- c("Date", "Ticker", "Price")
> ggplot(stk2, aes(x = Date, y = Price, fill = Ticker)) + geom_area() + theme_bw()
```

The above code generates the result shown in Figure 3-33.

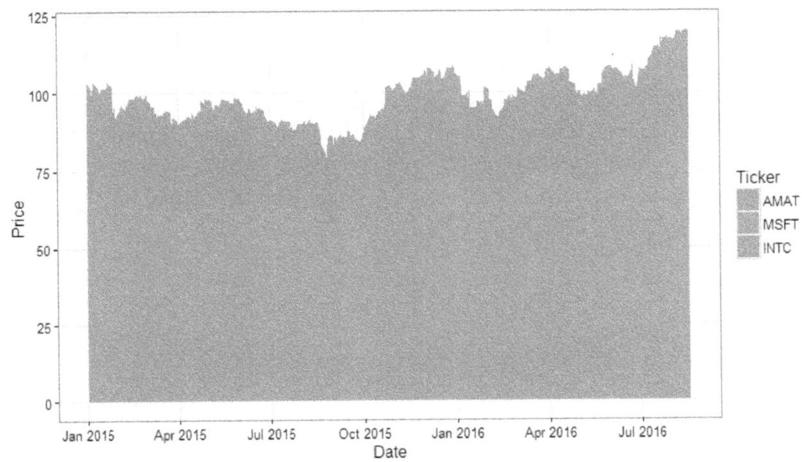


*Figure 3-33. A stacked area graph.*

You may notice there exists one issue in Figure 3-33, that is, the default order of legend items is the opposite of the stacking order. The legend can be reversed by setting the breaks in the scale:

```
> ggplot(stk2, aes(x = Date,y = Price, fill = Ticker)) +
   geom_area(color = "black", alpha = 0.4) + theme_bw() +
   scale_fill_brewer(palette = "Blues", breaks = rev(levels(stk2$Ticker)))
```

This will produce the output shown in Figure 3-34.

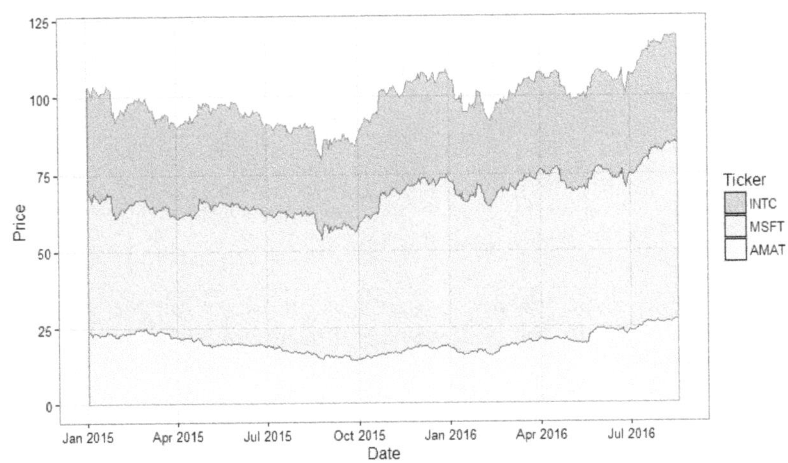


*Figure 3-34. A stacked area plot with reversed legend order.*

## Polar Plots

In most cases, we create various graph applications that make use of the Cartesian coordinate system. *ggplot2* also provides function named *coord_polar* that plot data in the polar coordinates of magnitude and angle. Let us look at an example:

```
> x <- 1:360
> y <- abs(cos(2 * x * pi/180) * sin(2 * x * pi/180))
> df <- data.frame(theta = x, r = y)
> ggplot(df, aes(x = theta, y = r)) + geom_line() + coord_polar() +
   scale_x_continuous(breaks = seq(0, 360, 30))
```

Here, we first create a data frame object using the simple mathematic functions, and then create a line graph in polar coordinates. We also specify the tick spacing along the circle (the X or theta axis) using the *scale_x_continuous* function. The preceding code generates the output shown in Figure 3-35.

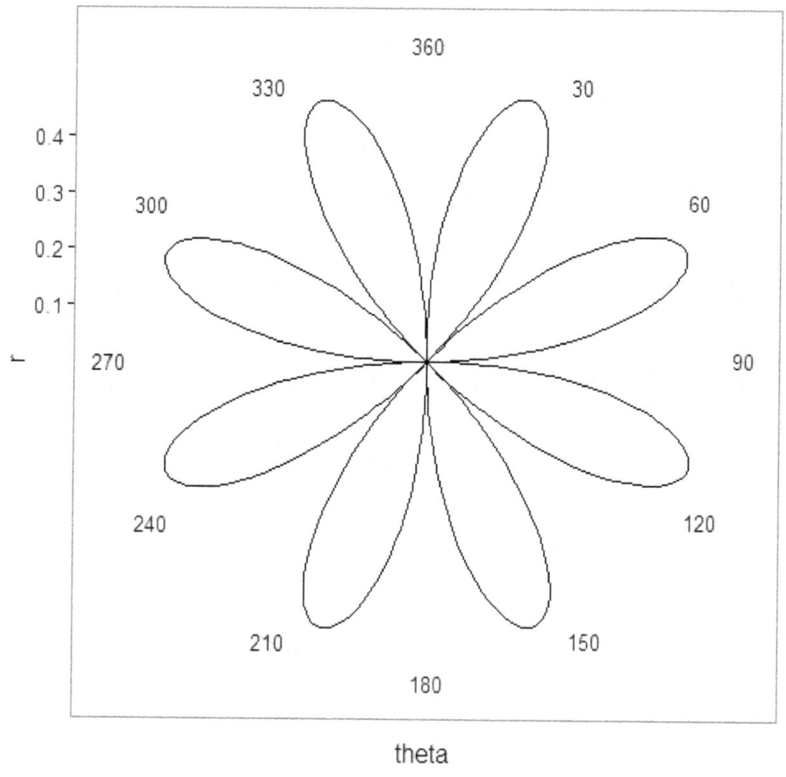


*Figure 3-35. A polar plot.*

If the default polar axis limits, angle direction, or starting angle are not suitable, we may need to modify the arguments so that it provides us with what we want. It is also possible to create a polar graph with multiple lines. For example:

```
> x <-1:360
> y1 <- log(1.001 + sin(2 * x * pi/180))
> y2 <- log(1.001 + cos(2 * x * pi/180))
> df <- data.frame(theta = x, r1 = y1, r2 = y2)
```

```
> df1 <- melt(df, "theta")
> ggplot(df1, aes(x = theta, y = value, color = variable )) +
  coord_polar(start = 3 * pi/2, direction = -1) + geom_line() +
  scale_x_continuous(breaks = seq(0, 360, 30))
```

Here, we first create a data frame with two sets of data and convert it into a long format using the melt function as we did in creating a line graph with multiple lines. Inside the *coord_polar* function, we specifically set the *start* and *direction* arguments. The *start* parameter is used to set the offset of starting point from 12 o'clock in radians and the direction argument is used to set the angular direction: 1 for clockwise and −1 for anticlockwise. Here, we set the starting point (0 or 360) on the east and the direction as anticlockwise.

The preceding statements create the plot shown in Figure 3-36.

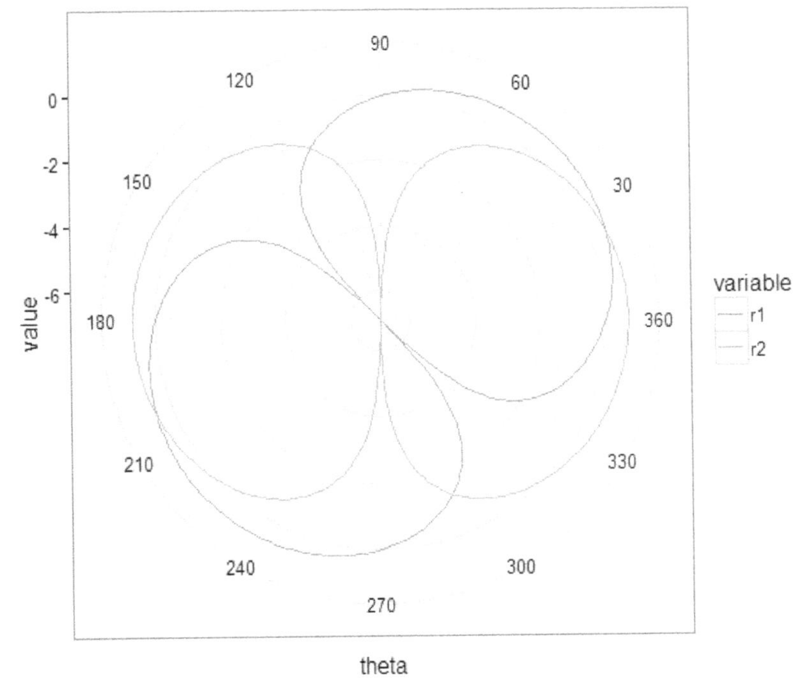


*Figure 3-36. A polar graph with multiple lines.*

You can see that *r* takes negative values, indicating that we can use *coord_polar* to create multiple curves with both positive and negative *r* values on a single polar graph.

# 3D Plots

R has several graphics systems including the base R graphics, the *grid* graphics system, and *ggplot2*. There is considerable overlap of the functionality of these graphics systems, but each has its own strengths and weaknesses. For example, although *ggplot2* is currently probably the most popular R package for creating presentation quality graphs, it does not support 3D plots. However, the generic function *persp* in the base R graphics draws perspective plots of a surface over the X-Y plane. The *plot3D* package based on the *persp* function provide functions for both 2D and 3D plotting. In the following sections, I will illustrate how to use the *plot3D* package to create various static 3D-like graphs. Before using this package, we need to install and load it first:

```
> install_packages("plot3D")
> library(plot3D)
```

## 3D Line Plots

In this section, I will show you how to create a 3D line plot using the *line3D* package. The 3D line graph displays a 3D plot of a set of data points. It is similar to a 2D line plot, except it uses an additional Z component to provide data for the third dimension. Consider the following example:

```
> t <- seq(0, 30, 0.1)
> x <- exp(-t/30) * cos(t)
> y <- exp(-t/30) * sin(t)
> z <- t
> lines3D(x, y, z, ticktype = "detailed", bty = "b2", colvar = NULL,
          Theta = -37, phi = 30)
```

Here, we first create 3D data using a parameter *t*. We also set the other arguments for the *lines3D* function. The *ticktype* parameter has two options: "simple" or "detailed" – "simple" draws just an arrow parallel to the axis to indicate direction of increase; "detailed" draws normal ticks as in 2D plots. *bty* is used to specify the type of the box. The default draws only the back panels. *bty* = "*b2*" draws back panels with gridlines. The *colvar* argument is used for coloring. The default value is mapped to the *z* variable. If set it to NULL, it gives the black color. The *theta* and *phi* define view angles: *theta* gives the azimuthal direction and *phi* the colatitude.

The preceding code produces the output shown in Figure 3-37.

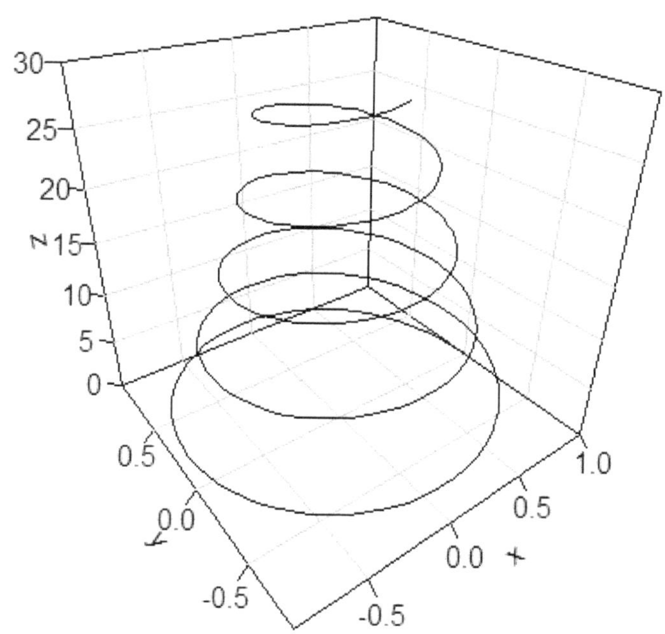


*Figure 3-37. A 3D line plot with a black line.*

We can easily create a 3D line plot with a color-mapped line by setting *colvar* = *z*:

```
> lines3D(x, y, z, ticktype = "detailed", bty = "b2", colvar = z,
          Theta = -37, phi = 30)
```

This gives the result shown in Figure 3-38.

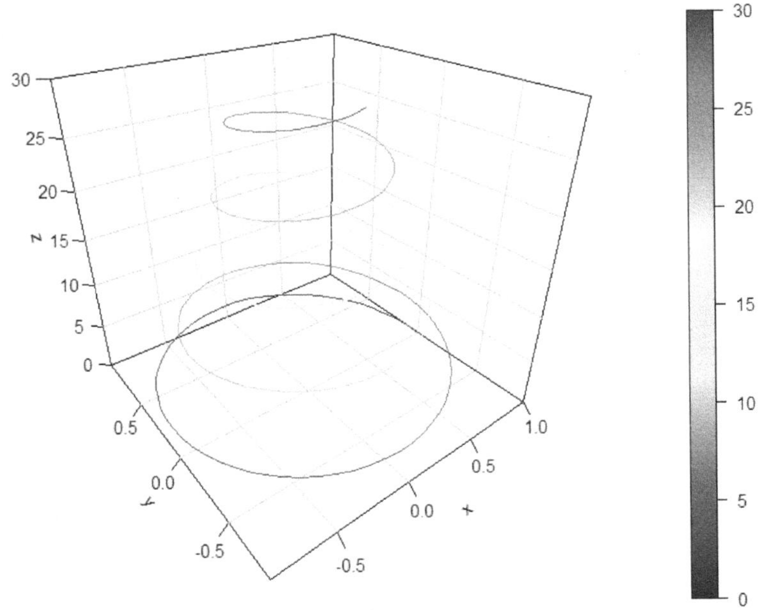


*Figure 3-38. A 3D line graph with a color-mapped line.*

# 3D Scatter Plots

We can create a 3D scatter plot using the *scatter3D* function included in the *plot3D* package. For example, if we want to plot the daily return for IBM as a function of date and price, we can issue the following statements:

```
> ibm <- getSymbols("IBM", from = "2015-01-01", auto.assign = F)
> x <- as.numeric(index(ibm))  # convert Date into numeric
> y <- Ad(ibm)                 # extract Adjusted close price
> z <- ROC(Ad(ibm))            # get return from Adjust close price
> scatter3D(x, y, z, clab = "Return", ticktype = "detailed", bty = "b2", d = 10)
```

Note that the *scatter3D* (or *persp*) does not take the date variable, so we need to convert it into a numeric variable. The *d* parameter (we set *d* = 10 here) inside the *scatter3D* function is used to control the strength of the perspective transformation. *d* > 1 will lessen the perspective effect and d < 1 will enhance the perspective effect.

The above code generates the output shown in Figure 3-39.

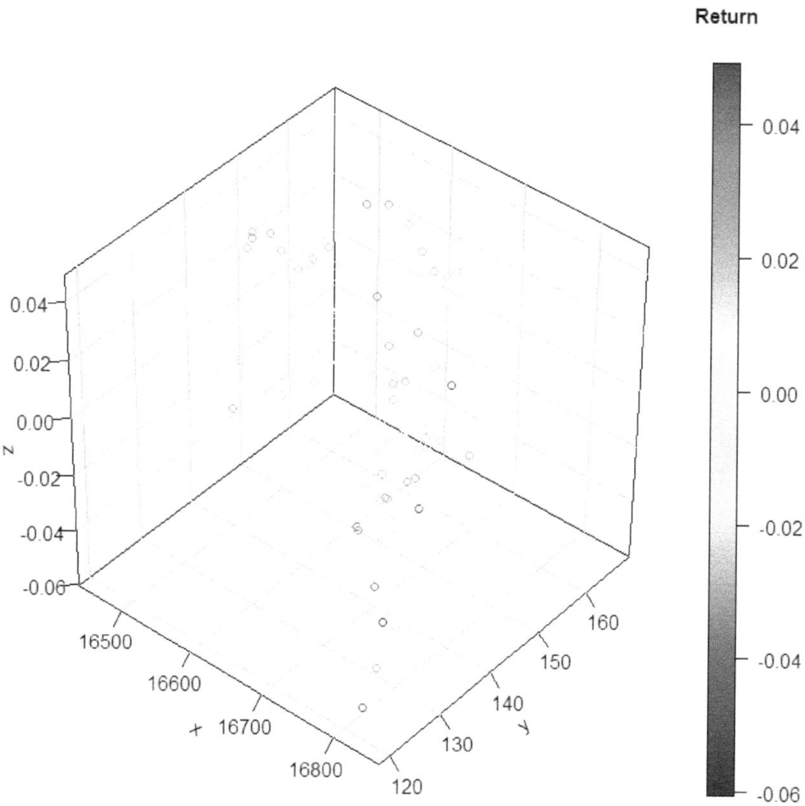


*Figure 3-39. A 3D scatter plot.*

# 3D Surface-Like Charts

Mathematically, a surface graph draws a Z function on a surface for each X and Y coordinate in a region of interest. We can define a surface by the Z-coordinate of points above a rectangular grid in the X-Y plane. The surface plot is formed by joining adjacent points with straight lines. Surface plots are useful for visualizing 2D data arrays or matrices that are too large to display in numerical form, and for graphing functions of two variables.

In this section, I will show you how to use the *plot3D* package to create different types of surface plots. Let us consider an example: creating a single-colored mesh plot for a peaks function. First, we define two math functions, *peaks* and *sinc*, in the *plotHelper.R* file:

```
peaks <- function(x, y){
  z <- 3 * (1 - x)^2 * exp(-x * x - (y + 1)^2) - 10 * (0.2 * x - x^3 - y^5) *
    exp(-x * x - y * y) - (1/3) * exp(-(x + 1)^2 - y * y)
}

sinc <- function(x, y){
  r <- sqrt(x^2 + y^2)
  ifelse(r == 0, 1, sin(r)/r)
}
```

Next, we can use the *peaks* function to create a surface graph:

```
> source("./R/plotHelper.R")
# create grid matrices:
> mx <- seq(-3, 3, 0.2)
> my <- seq(-3, 3, 0.2)
> mxy <- mesh(mx, my)
# create x, y, z grids (z is defined as a peaks function):
> x <- mxy$x
> y <- mxy$y
> z <- peaks(x, y)
> surf3D(x, y, z, ticktype = "detailed", bty = "b2", theta = -37, phi = 30,
         d = 10, facets = F, col = "black")
```

Inside the *surf3D* function, we set the parameter *facets* = FALSE, meaning that the surface facets are colored with a white color and the border will be colored as specified by *col* (= "black" in our example). This effectively create a 3D black-white mesh graph, as shown in Figure 3-40 (left).

You can also create a 3D color-mapped mesh graph using the default colormap (*jet*) with the following command:

```
> surf3D(x, y, z, ticktype = "detailed", bty = "b2", theta = -37, phi = 30,
         d = 10, facets = F)
```

This produces the color-mapped mesh graph shown in Figure 3-40 (right).

The standard 3D surface plot will have color-mapped facets (facets = TRUE) and black mesh lines (using the border parameter):

```
> surf3D(x, y, z, ticktype = "detailed", bty = "b2", theta = -37, phi = 30,
         d = 10, facets = T, border = "black")
```

This will create a standard 3D surface graph shown in Figure 3-41.

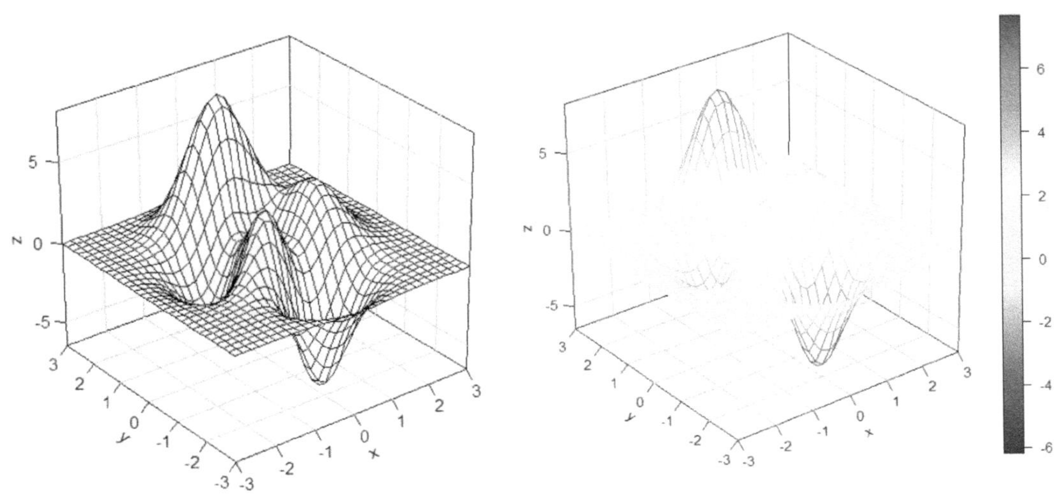


*Figure 3-40. 3D mesh plots: black-white (left) and color-mapped (right).*

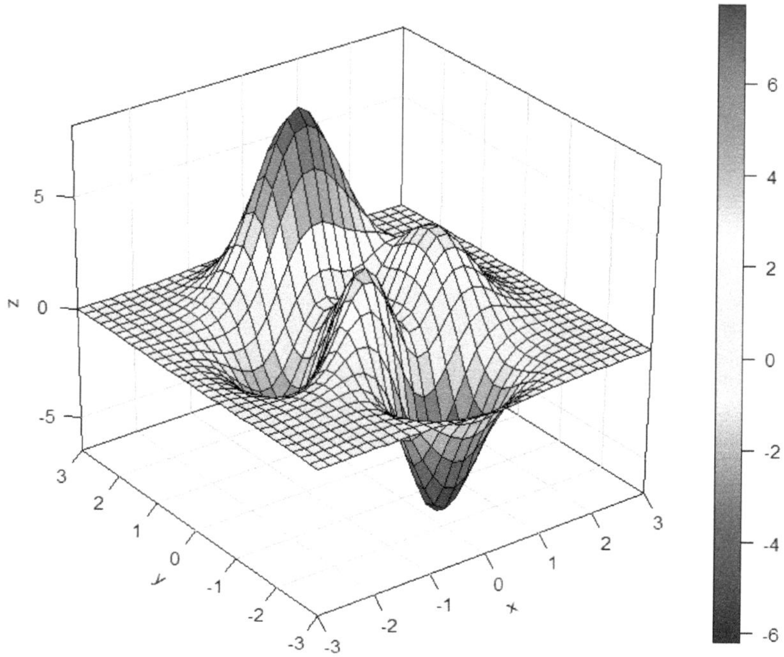


*Figure 3-41. A standard 3D surface plot.*

We can also create a shaded surface graph without mesh lines:

```
> surf3D(x, y, z, ticktype = "detailed", bty = "b2", theta = -37, phi = 30,
        d = 10, facets = T)
```

This generates the output shown in Figure 3-42 (left), in which the mesh lines are no longer visible. As you can see from the figure that the colormap is still coarse, and a single color is clearly visible for each polygon on the surface. We can obtain a surface plot with a much better colormap by regenerating the mesh grids with a finer spacing (from 0.2 to 0.05):

```
> mx <- seq(-3, 3, 0.05)
> my <- seq(-3, 3, 0.05)
> mxy <- mesh(mx, my)
> x <- mxy$x
> y <- mxy$y
> z <- peaks(x, y)
> surf3D(x, y, z, ticktype = "detailed", bty = "b2", theta = -37, phi = 30,
        d = 10, facets = T)
```

This will generate the output shown in Figure 3-42 (right), which has a much smoother color crosses its entire surface.

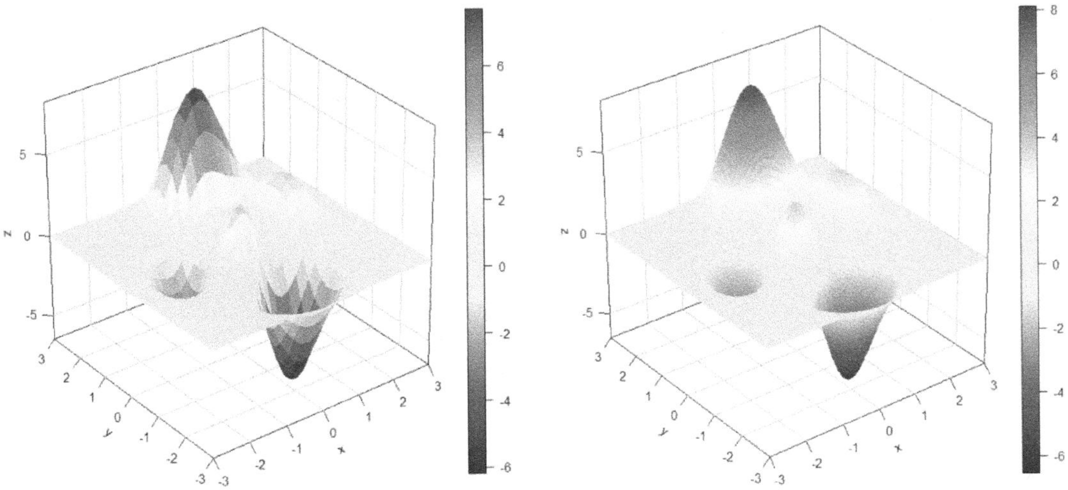

*Figure 3-42. Surface plots without mesh lines: with coarse grids (left) and finer grids (right).*

# Specialized 3D Plots

In the preceding section, we discussed how to create 3D surface-like plots. In this section, I will show you how to use the *plot3D* package to create a variety specialized 3D graphs, including X-Y color, contour, and 3D combination plots.

## *X-Y Color Plots*

Let us first create an X-Y color plot, which is also called the heat plot. We can consider the X-Y color chart a projected surface chart on the X-Y plane. In fact, it is a rectangle mesh grid on the X-Y plane with colors determined by the data values at the grid points. Here, we create the X-Y color chart using each set of four adjacent points to define the polygon. Each polygon is shaded in a single color.

We can create such X-Y plots using the *image2D* function included in the *plot3D* package. By using the same *peaks* function created in the preceding example with finer grids, we can issue the statement:

```
> image2D(z, x, y, border="black")
> image2D(z, x, y)
```

The above commands generate the X-Y color plots with or without grid lines respectively, as shown in Figure 3-43.

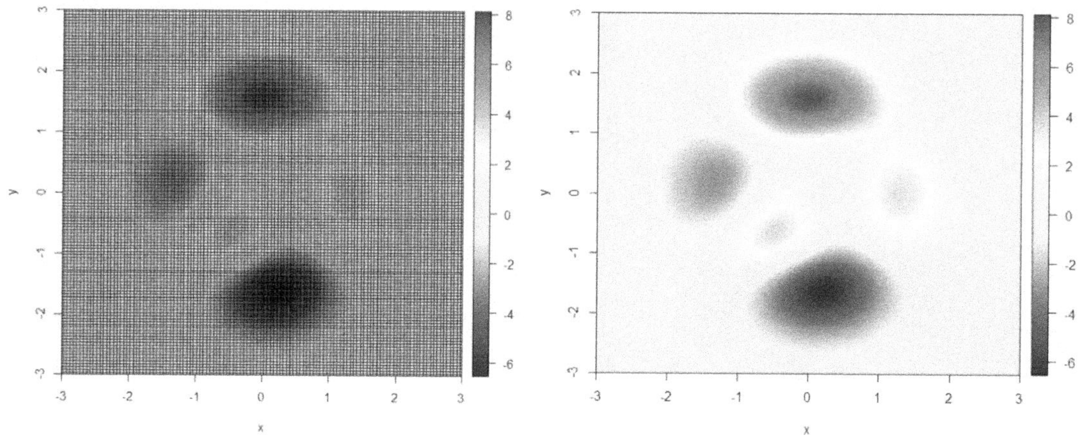


*Figure 3-43. X-Y color graphs with (left) or without grid lines (right).*

## *Contour Plots*

Contour graphs help the visualization of 3D surfaces on a 2D screen. In this case, we plot data values as a function of mesh grid points in the X-Y plane. By using the same *peaks* function, we can use the *contour2D* from the *plot3D* package to create the contour plots:

```
> contour2D(z, mx, my, nlevels = 15, col = "black")
> contour2D(z, mx, my, nlevels = 15)
> image2D(z, mx, my, contour = list(nlevels = 15))
```

Figure 3-44 shows the resulting contour graphs with black lines (left), color-mapped contour lines (center), or color filled contour (right).

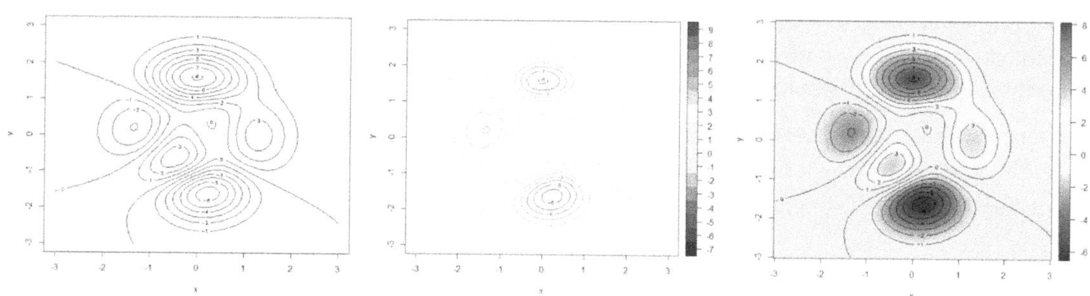

*Figure 3-44. Contour plots with black lines (left), color-mapped contour lines (center), and color-filled contour.*

## *Combination Plots*

Combination graphs are a useful way to exploit the informative properties of various types of graphics plotting methods. In this section, I will show you some examples of typical combinations plots using the *persp3D* function with *contour* and *image* functions. By using the similar approach, we can easily create our own combination plots according to application requirements.

The *persp3D* function from the *plot3D* package allows us to create 3D combination graphs. The following example will use the coarse *peaks* function to speed up the drawing process:

```
> mx <- seq(-3, 3, 0.2)
> my <- seq(-3, 3, 0.2)
> mxy <- mesh(mx, my)
> x <- mxy$x
> y <- mxy$y
> z <- peaks(x, y)
> persp3D(mx, my, z, contour = list(nlevels = 15), zlim = c(-12, 8), d = 10,
    theta = -37, phi = 30, bty = "b2", ticktype = "detailed", border = "black")
```

This creates the 2D surface and contour combination graph shown in Figure 3-45 (left).

We can also create a 3D surface and filled-contour combination plot with the following command:

```
> persp3D(mx, my, z, contour = list(nlevels = 15),image = T, zlim = c(-16, 8),
   d = 10, theta = -37, phi = 30,bty = "b2",ticktype = "detailed", border = "black")
```

Here, we use *persp3D* combining with *contour* and *image* to produce a surface and filled contour combination plot, as shown in Figure 3-45 (center).

Finally, I show you another surface-contour combination plot using the following code:

```
> persp3D(mx, my, z, contour = list(nlevels = 15, side = "z"), d = 10,
          theta =- 37, phi = 30, box = F)
```

This command creates a contour-surface combination graph, in which the contour lines are drawn directly on the 3D surface, as shown in Figure 3-45 (right).

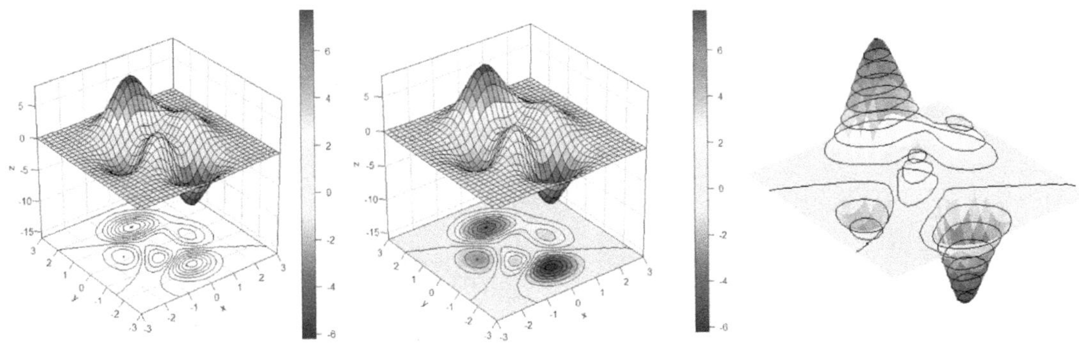

*Figure 3-45. 3D combination plots: surface and contour (left), surface and filled-contour (center), and surface and 3D contour (right)*

## 3D Parametric Surfaces

In the previous sections, you learned how to create simple 3D surfaces. A key feature of this type of surface is that there is at most one Z value for each pair of X and Y values. However, sometimes we may want to create a complex surface of certain shape. We cannot represent this kind of complex surface using a simple function. For certain values of X and Y, this type of surface has more than one Z value. One way to represent such a surface is to use a set of parametric equations. These equations define the X, Y, and Z coordinates of points on the surface in terms of the parametric variables *u* and *v*. We can represent many complex surfaces using parametric equations. For example, the sphere, the torus, and quadric surfaces are all parametric surfaces.

### *Helicoid Surface*

A helicoid is a trace of a line. For any point on the surface, there is a line on the surface passing through it. Helicoids are shaped like screws and can be described in the Cartesian coordinate system by the following parametric equations:

$$x = u \sin v, \qquad y = u \cos v, \qquad z = v$$

We can use the *surf3D* function from the *plot3D* package to easily create a helicoid surface:

```
> library(plot3D)
> mu <- seq(0, 1, 0.1)
> mv <- seq(-3 * pi, 3 * pi, 0.1)
> muv <- mesh(mu, mv)
> x <- muv$x * sin(muv$y)
> y <- muv$x * cos(muv$y)
> z <- muv$y
> surf3D(x, y, z, ticktype = "detailed", bty = "b2", theta = -37, phi = 30,
         d = 10, facets = T, border = "black")
```

Here, we first create a mesh grid in the parametric space and then define the helicoid surface using the parametric equations. Finally, we use the *surf3D* function to generate the parametric surface, as shown in Figure 3-46.

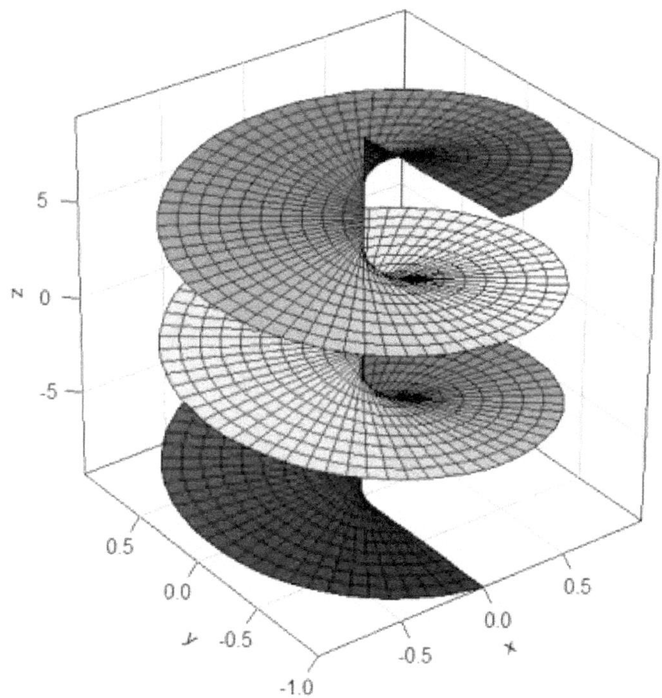


*Figure 3-46. A helicoid surface.*

## *Sphere Surface*

We can represent a sphere surface using a set of parametric equations:

$$x = \cos v * \sin u\,,\quad y = \cos v * \cos u\,,\quad z = \sin v$$

We can then use the *surf3D* function to create a sphere surface:

```
> mu <- seq(0, 2 * pi, length.out = 20)
> mv <- seq(-0.5 * pi, 0.5 * pi, length.out = 20)
> muv <- mesh(mu, mv)
> x <- cos(muv$y) * sin(muv$x)
> y <- cos(muv$y) * cos(muv$x)
> z <- sin(muv$y)
> surf3D(x, y, z, ticktype = "detailed", bty = "b2", theta = -37, phi = 30,
        d = 10, facets = T, border = "black")
```

This produces the output shown in Figure 3-47.

## *Torus Surface*

A torus surface can be described by the following parametric equations:

$$x = (R + r\cos u)\sin v,\quad y = (R + r\cos u)\cos v,\quad z = r\sin u$$

We can use the *surf3D* function to create a torus surface:

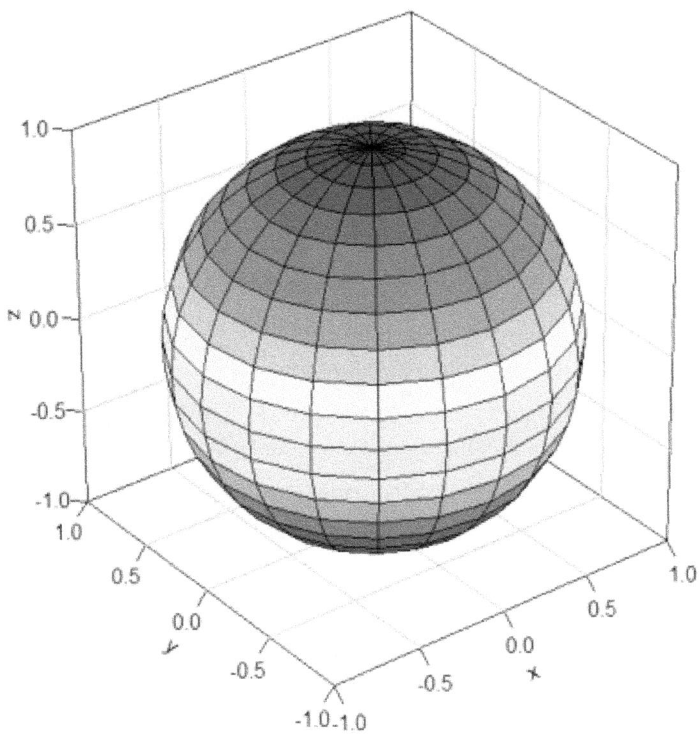


*Figure 4-47. A sphere surface.*

```
>  mu <- seq(0, 2 * pi, length.out = 20)
>  mv <- seq(0, 2 * pi, length.out = 50)
>   muv <- mesh(mu, mv)
>   x <- (1 + 0.3 * cos(muv$x)) * sin(muv$y)
>   y <- (1 + 0.3 * cos(muv$x)) * cos(muv$y)
>   z <- 0.3 * sin(muv$x)
> surf3D(x, y, z, ticktype = "detailed", bty = "b2", theta = -60, phi = 30,
        d = 10, facets = T, border = "black", expand = 0.25)
```

Note that inside the *surf3D* function, we set the *expand* parameter to 0.25, which makes the torus surface looks nice. The *expand* (0 < expand < 1) parameter applies an expansion factor to the Z coordinates to shrink the plotting box in the Z direction. The above code produces the output shown in Figure 3-48.

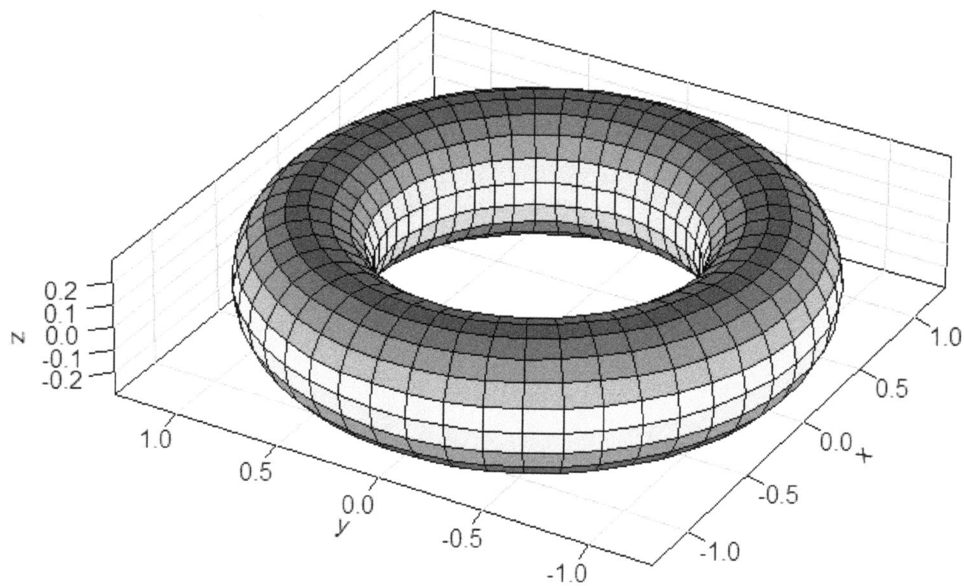


*Figure 3-48. A torus surface.*

## *Quadric Surfaces*

We can also create various quadric surfaces using the *surf3D* function. Here, we will consider four irreducible quadrics: hyperboloid, paraboloid, elliptic cone, and elliptic cylinder.

A hyperboloid surface is described by the following parametric equations:

$$x = a \sin u \cosh v, \quad y = b \cos u \cosh v, \quad z = c \sinh v$$

We can then create the hyperboloid surface using the following code:

```
> mu <- seq(0,2 * pi, length.out = 40)
> mv <- seq(-1, 1, length.out = 20)
> muv <- mesh(mu, mv)
> x <- 0.3 * sin(muv$x) * cosh(muv$y)
> y <- 0.5 * cos(muv$x) * cosh(muv$y)
> z <- 0.5 * sinh(muv$y)
```

```
> surf3D(x, y, z, ticktype = "detailed", bty = "b2", theta = -37, phi = 30,
         d = 10, facets = T, border = "black")
```

The above code produces the output shown in Figure 3-49 (a).

We can represent a paraboloid surface using the following parametric equations:

$$x = a\,v\sinh u\,,\quad y = b\,v\cosh u\,,\quad z = v^2$$

We can then create the paraboloid surface using the following code:

```
> mu <- seq(-2, 2, length.out = 40)
> mv <- seq(-2, 2, length.out = 80)
> muv <- mesh(mu, mv)
> x <- 0.8 * muv$y * sinh(muv$x)
> y <- 0.5 * muv$y * cosh(muv$x)
> z <- muv$y * muv$y
> surf3D(x, y, z, ticktype = "detailed", bty = "b2", theta = -100, phi = 20,
         d = 10, facets = T, border = "black")
```

This will generate the plot shown in Figure 3-49 (b).

An elliptic cone can be described by the following parametric equations:

$$x = a\,v\sin u\,,\quad y = b\,v\cos u\,,\quad z = c\,v$$

We can then create the elliptic cone surface using the following code:

```
> mu <- seq(0, 2 * pi, length.out = 40)
> mv <- seq(-0.5, 0.5, length.out = 20)
> muv <- mesh(mu, mv)
> x <- 1.2 * muv$y * sin(muv$x)
> y <- 0.8 * muv$y * cos(muv$x)
> z <- muv$y
> surf3D(x, y, z, ticktype = "detailed", bty = "b2", theta = -37, phi = 30,
         d = 10, facets = T, border = "black")
```

This will generate the plot shown in Figure 3-49 (c).

We can also represent an elliptic cylinder surface using the following parametric equations:

$$x = a\sin u\,,\quad y = b\sin u\,,\quad z = v$$

We can then create the elliptic cylinder surface using the following code:

```
> mu <- seq(0, 2 * pi, length.out = 40)
> mv <- seq(-0.5, 0.5, length.out = 20)
> muv <- mesh(mu, mv)
> x <- 1.2 * sin(muv$x)
> y <- 0.8 * cos(muv$x)
> z <- muv$y
> surf3D(x, y, z, ticktype = "detailed", bty = "b2", theta = -37, phi = 50,
         d = 10, facets = T, border = "black")
```

The above code generates the output shown in Figure 3-49 (d).

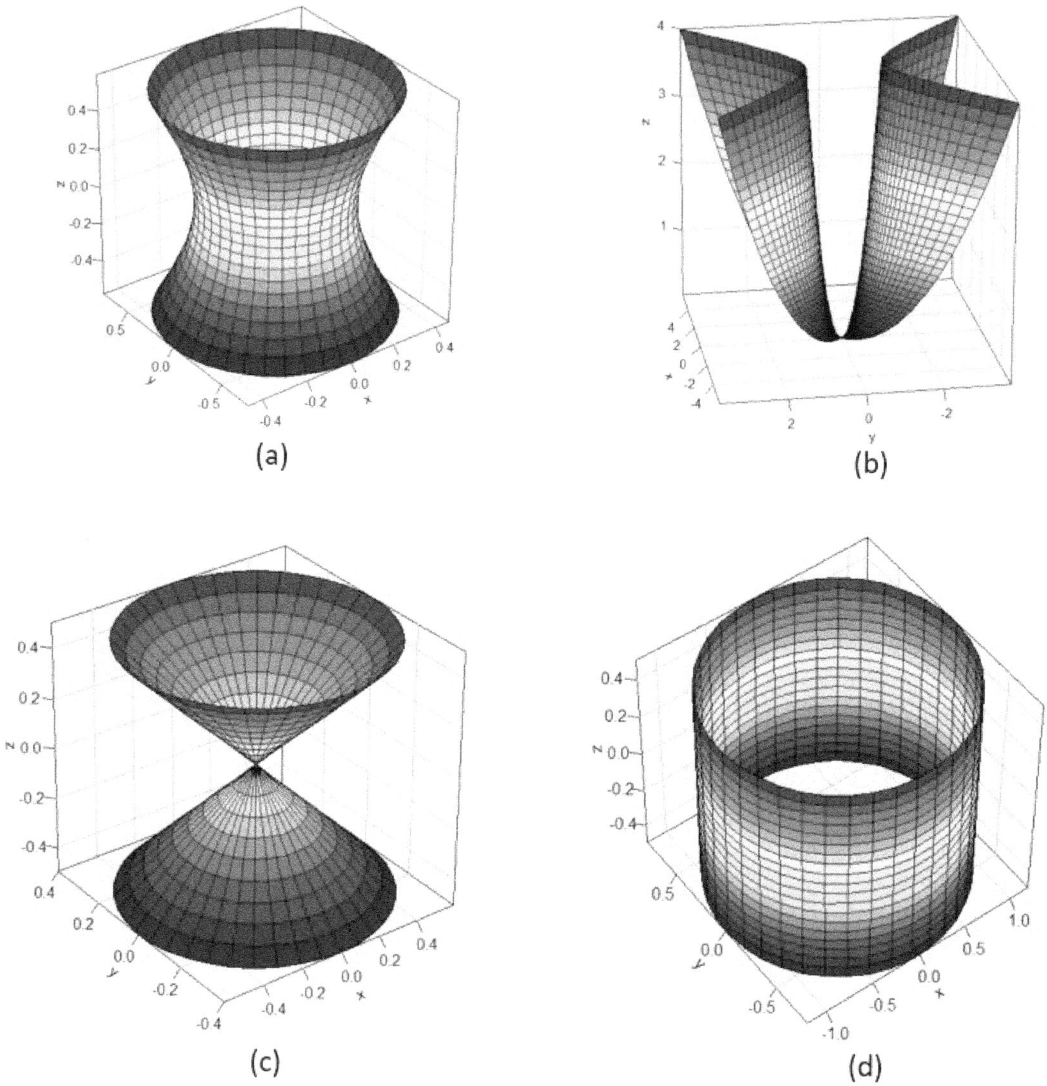


*Figure 3-49. Quadric surfaces: (a) hyperboloid, (b) paraboloid, (c) elliptic cone, and (d) elliptic cylinder.*

# Interactive 3D Plots

In the preceding sections, we have used the *plot3D* package to create various 3D graphs. However, these 3D plots are static and do not allow us to interact with. There are several R packages available, which provide functionality to create interactive 3D graphs. Most of these packages are based on the *rgl* package, which is a 3D real-time rendering system for R using OpenGL (open graphics library). If we create 3D graphs using the *plot3D* package as we did in the preceding sections, we can easily convert them into interactive 3D plots using a new *plot3Drgl* package. I will also show you how to use *rgl* to create 3D interactive plots.

## Using plot3Drgl

There are two ways to create interactive 3D graphs using the *plot3Drgl* package. The first approach is easy: we simply create graphs using the *plot3D* package as usually, and then use the function *plotrgl* function to convert the graphs into interactive plots, in which we can perform rotation and zooming interactively.

For example, we can create a helicoid surface using the following code:

```
> library(plot3D)
> mu <- seq(0, 1, 0.1)
> mv <- seq(-3 * pi, 3 * pi, 0.1)
> muv <- mesh(mu, mv)
> x <- muv$x * sin(muv$y)
> y <- muv$x * cos(muv$y)
> z <- muv$y
> surf3D(x, y, z, ticktype = "detailed", bty = "b2", theta = -37, phi = 30,
         d = 10, facets = T, border = "black")
```

This code will generate the output shown in Figure 3-46. Now, we can convert this 3D graph into an interactive plot using the following statements:

```
> install_package(c("plot3Drgl", "rgl"))
> library(plot3Drgl)
> library(rgl)
> plotrgl()
```

The above commands will create an interactive helicoid surface in a new separate window, as shown in Figure 3-50. In this new window, we can rotate the graph by dragging on it with the left mouse button pressed; zoom the graph by dragging on it with the right mouse button pressed; and move the graph around by dragging on it with the center mouse button pressed. *plotrgl* is the main function in the *plot3Drgl* package that translates the *plot3D* graphs to the *rgl* format.

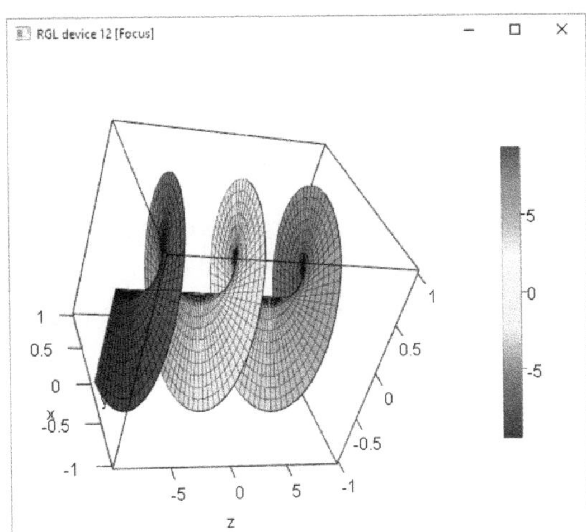


*Figure 3-50. An interactive helicoid surface.*

The second approach is to use the corresponding functions in the *plot3Drgl* package directly to create interactive 3D plots. The available functions in the *plot3Drgl* package can be derived by adding the "rgl" suffix to the corresponding function names in the *plot3D* package. The following list provides the name mapping between these two packages for your reference:

| Function in plot3D | Function in plot3Drgl | Description |
|---|---|---|
| persp3D | persp3Drgl | perspective plot |
| ribbon3D | ribbon3Drgl | a perspective plot as ribbons |
| hist3D | hist3Drgl | 3-D histograms |
| scatter3D | scatter3Drgl | colored points in 3D |
| points3D | points3Drgl | colored points in 3D |
| lines3D | lines3Drgl | colored lines in 3D |
| slice3D | slice3Drgl | slices from 3D data sets |
| slicecont3 | slicecont3Drgl | slices from 3D data sets |
| isosurf3D | isosurf3Drgl | isosurfaces from a full 3-D data set as triangles |
| voxel3D | voxel3Drgl | isosurfaces from a full 3-D data set as points |
| triangle3D | triangle3Drgl | plot 3D function |
| surf3D | surf3Drgl | 3D surface |
| spheresurf3D | spheresurf3Drgl | 3D spherical surface |
| segments3D | segments3Drgl | 3D line segment |
| image3D | image3Drgl | 3D images |
| contour3D | contour3Drgl | 3D contour |
| box3D | box3Drgl | boxes in 3D |
| border3D | border3Drgl | boxes in 3D |
| rect3D | rect3Drgl | rectangles in 3D |
| text3D | text3Drgl | labels in 3D |
| image2D | image2Drgl | images in 2D |
| contour2D | contour2Drgl | 2D contour |
| scatter2D | scatter2Drgl | 2D scatter |
| points2D | points2Drgl | 2D points |
| lines2D | lines2Drgl | 2D lines |
| arrows2D | arrows2Drgl | 2D arrows |
| text2D | text2Drgl | labels in 2D |

You can see from this list that there are a variety of 3D and projected 2D functions in these two packages that we can use to create various static or interactive 3D graphs.

Now, I will demonstrate how to use the *persp3Drgl* function directly to create a 3D curtain plot:

```
> mu <- seq(-8, 8, 0.5)
> mv <- seq(-8, 8, 0.5)
> muv <- mesh(mu, mv)
> x <- muv$x
> y <- muv$y
> z <- sinc(x, y)
> persp3Drgl(mu, mv, z, curtain = T, d = 10, theta = -37, phi = 30, bty = "b2",
            ticktype = "detailed", border = "black")
```

Here, we use the *persp3Drgl* function directly to create the interactive 3D curtain plot by setting curtain = TRUE. The resulting graph is displayed in Figure 3-51, where we show the side, top, and bottom views of the plot by rotating it using the mouse.

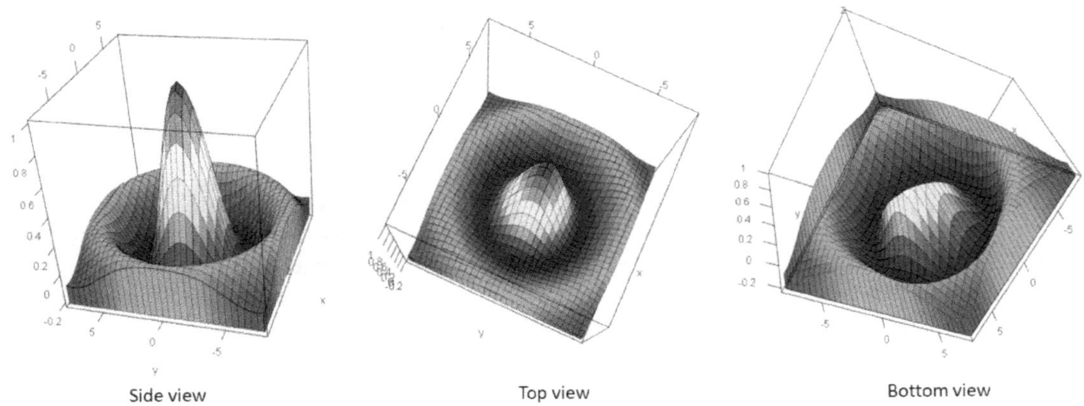


*Figure 3-51. An interactive 3D curtain plot.*

The *plot3D* and *plot3Drgl* packages should provide enough functionality for general 3D plotting applications. However, if we want more flexibility and sophisticated 3D effects in our 3D graphics applications, we may consider using the *rgl* package, which is the topic of next section.

# Using rgl

The core of the *rgl* package is a shared library that acts as an interface between R and OpenGL. *rgl* implements a set of R functions that allow us to create interactive, real-time 3D graphs with lighting and material effects. This package includes solid 3D objects, embedded 3D objects, and surfaces in 3D space, as well as high-level functions corresponding to classic 2D graphics.

The visualization model in *rgl* uses several base object types, including shapes, viewpoint, directional light sources, bounding box, and background. The shapes are basic geometry information and constitute basic building blocks, which support points, lines, triangles, quadrangles, texts, spheres, surfaces, and 3D sprites. The viewpoint surrounding the overall geometry is focused on the center, which provides interactive navigation using the pointing device that controls the view direction, zooming, and field-of-view. With the pointing device, the buttons are by default set as follows: the left mouse button is used to adjust viewpoint position; the middle button is used to adjust field of view angle; and the right or wheel button is used to adjust zoom factor. The light sources define the lighting conditions and the bounding box tracks the range of the geometry and optionally displays axis labeling. The background provides either solid color or an environmental sphere enclosing the scene. This visualization model has been widely used in various 3D graphics systems.

In the following sections, I will show you how to use *rgl* to create various interactive 3D graphs.

## *Scatter Plots*

The *rgl* package provides several functions that allow us to create 3D scatter graphs, including *rgl.points*, *points3d*, and *plot3d*, while the *plot3d* function is more general. Now, let us create our first 3D scatter plot using the *plot3d* function:

```
> ibm <- getSymbols("IBM", from = "2015-01-01", auto.assign = F)
> x <- index(ibm)
> y <- Ad(ibm)
> z <- ROC(Ad(ibm))
> plot3d(x = x, y = y, z = z, size = 2, type = "s", col = "red"))
```

Here, we first download the market data for IBM using the *quantmod* package, and then assign the date variable to *x*, the adjusted close prices to *y*, and daily returns to *z*. Finally, we use the *plot3d* function to create a 3D interactive graph, where we set type = "*s*" for spheres. We can also set it to other types, such as, "*p*" for points, "*l*" for lines, "*h*" for line segments from *z* = 0, and "*n*" for nothing. The output from the above commands is shown in Figure 3-52.

You may notice there are some issues with the results shown in Figure 3-52: the date in the X-axis is represented with numbers, which denotes the number of seconds elapsed since 1/1/1997 (the beginning of the UNIX era), rather than the standard date. We can use the following commands to modify the ticks and tick labels for the X-axis on the current graph:

```
> xl <- x[c(seq(1, length(x), round(length(x)/5)))]
> axes3d(xat = xl, xlab = as.character(xl))
> box3d()
```

This produces the results with the correct date tick labels, as shown in Figure 3-53.

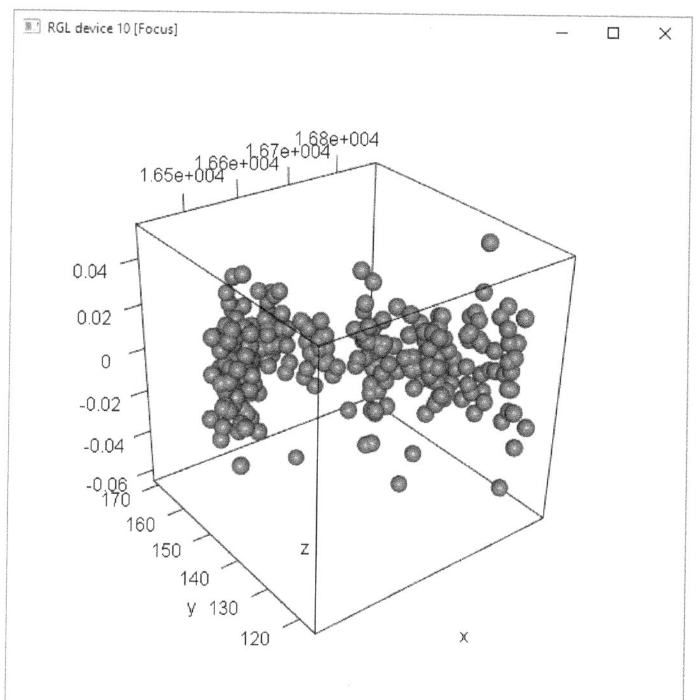


*Figure 3-52. A 3D interactive scatter plot for IBM daily returns.*

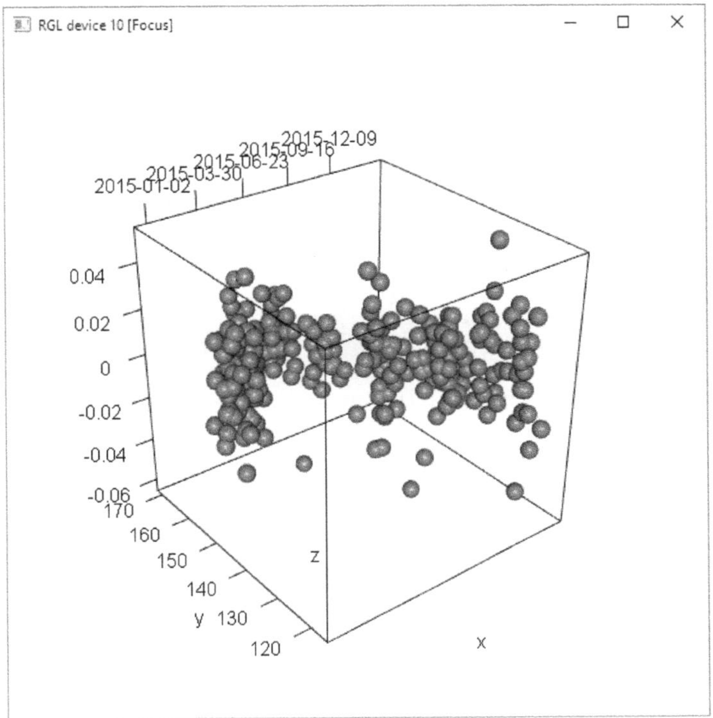


*Figure 3-53. A scatter plot with the right date tick labels.*

Another issue with the above results is the color map. Here, we simply set the color to "*red*", while the default color in *rgl* is "black". This is very different from the *plot3D* and *Plot3Drgl* packages, where we do not need to set the col parameter explicitly: the packages automatically assign the correct color scale to the *z* variable using the "*jet*" colormap, which gives the nice-looking 3D graphs by default. In *rgl*, if we want to obtain the similar colormap effects as in *plot3D*, we need to create our own colormap and assign it to the appreciate variable.

## *Custom Colormap*

In fact, the base R installation already includes several predefined colormaps: *rainbow*, *heat*, *terrain*, *topo*, and *cm*. However, to assign them to the variable with the proper color scale, we still need to do some work. Furthermore, we may sometimes need to create our own custom colormaps to meet the requirements of specific applications. In this section, I will show you how to convert the existing colormaps into a format such that the *rgl* and other graphics systems can take it directly with the right color scaling. I will also illustrate how to create our own customized colormaps. In particular, I will show you how to create the popular Matlab-like colormaps, such as *jet*, *hot*, *spring*, *summer*, *autumn*, *winter*, etc.

Add a new function named *colormapr* to the *plotHelper.R* file. Here is the code for this function:

```
Colormapr <- function(mapName = c("rainbow", "heat", "terrain", "topo", "cm", "jet",
  "spring","summer", "autumn", "winter", "gray", "cool"), zvalue = NULL){
  options(warn = -1)
  cols <- rainbow
```

```
  nm <- tolower(mapName)
  if(nm == "heat") cols <- heat.colors
  else if(nm == "terrain") cols <- terrain.colors
  else if(nm == "topo") cols <- topo.colors
  else if(nm == "cm") cols <- cm.colors
  else if(nm == "jet"){
    cols <- colorRampPalette(c("#00007F", "blue", "#007FFF", "cyan", "#7FFF7F",
                             "yellow", "#FF7F00", "red", "#7F0000"))
  }
  else if(nm == "hot"){
    cols <- colorRampPalette(c(rgb(0, 0, 0), rgb(1, 0, 0),
                             rgb(1, 1, 0), rgb(1, 1, 1)))
  }
  else if(nm == "spring"){
    cols <- colorRampPalette( c(rgb(1,0,1), rgb(1, 1, 0)))
  }
  else if(nm == "summer"){
    cols <- colorRampPalette( c(rgb(0,0.5,0.4), rgb(1, 1, 0.4)))
  }
  else if(nm == "autumn"){
    cols <- colorRampPalette( c(rgb(1,0,0), rgb(1, 1, 0)))
  }
  else if(nm == "winter"){
    cols <- colorRampPalette( c(rgb(0,0,1), rgb(0, 1, 0.5)))
  }
  else if(nm == "gray"){
    cols <- colorRampPalette( c(rgb(0,0,0), rgb(1, 1, 1)))
  }
  else if(nm == "cool"){
    cols <- colorRampPalette( c(rgb(0,1,1), rgb(1, 0, 1)))
  }
  if(!is.null(zvalue)) {
    lh <- length(zvalue)
    cl <- cut(zvalue, breaks = lh)
    cols <- cols(lh)[cl]
  }
  return(cols)
}
```

Note that the *colormapr* function first includes five predefined color palettes in the base R, and then we create additional eight Matlab-like colormaps with various color combinations using the *colorRampPalette* function. The *colorRampPalette* function interpolates a set of given colors to create a new color palette or colormap. If the *zvalue* parameter (usually we map color scale to *z* variable, you can, however, use other variable as well) is provided to the *colormapr* function, the function will map the values with proper color scales. Here, we collect 13 types of colormaps into the single *colormapr* function, which will be convenient for us when we apply them to our graphics applications. The default colormap in this function is rainbow. Following the same procedure, you can add more colormaps to this function as you like.

Here, I will list the colormap names and corresponding color bars for your reference. First, we define a new function named colorbar:

```
colorbar <- function(colormap, xlabel = "") {
  scale = (length(colormap) - 1)/2
  par(mar = c(3, 0.5, 1, 0.5))
```

```
  plot(c(0, 10), c(-1, 1), type = "n", bty = "n", xaxt = "n", xlab = xlabel,
    yaxt = "n", ylab = "", main = "", mgp = c(-0.5, 0, 0))
  for (i in 1:(length(colormap) - 1)) {
    y = (i - 1)/scale -1
    rect(0, y, 10, y + 1/scale, col = colormap[i], border = NA)
  }
}
```

We can then create corresponding color bars using the following statements:

```
par(mfrow=c(1,13))
colorbar(colormapr("rainbow")(100), xlabel = "rainbow")
colorbar(colormapr("heat")(100), xlabel = "heat")
colorbar(colormapr("terrain")(100), xlabel = "terrain")
colorbar(colormapr("topo")(100), xlabel = "topo")
colorbar(colormapr("cm")(100), xlabel = "cm")
colorbar(colormapr("jet")(100), xlabel = "jet")
colorbar(colormapr("hot")(100), xlabel = "hot")
colorbar(colormapr("spring")(100), xlabel = "spring")
colorbar(colormapr("summer")(100), xlabel = "summer")
colorbar(colormapr("autumn")(100), xlabel = "autumn")
colorbar(colormapr("winter")(100), xlabel = "winter")
colorbar(colormapr("cool")(100), xlabel = "cool")
colorbar(colormapr("gray")(100), xlabel = "gray")
```

This produces color bars with corresponding colormap names, as shown in Figure 3-54.

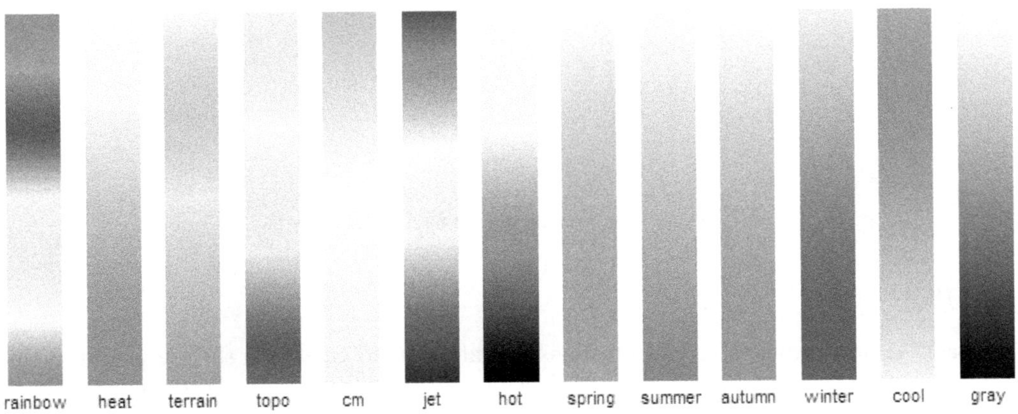


*Figure 3-54. colormaps defined in the colormapr function.*

Now, we can use the colormap function to recreate the scatter graph:

```
> source("./R/plotHelper.R")
> plot3d(x = x, y = y, z = z, size = 2, type = "s", col = colormapr("jet", z))
> xl <- x[c(seq(1, length(x), round(length(x)/5)))]
> axes3d(xat = xl, xlab = as.character(xl))
> box3d()
```

Here, we set *col* = *colormapr*(“*jet*”, *z*), that is, we use the *jet* colormap to set the color scale for the *z* variable.

This will generate the output shown in Figure 3-55. You can see that we now have a scatter plot with nice colormap.

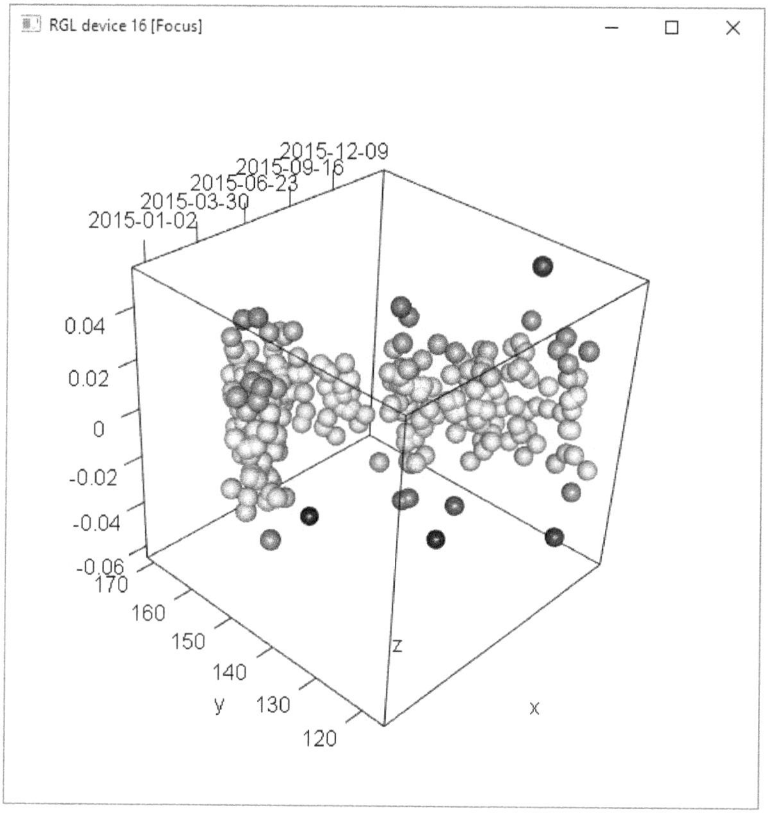


*Figure 3-55. A scatter plot with a jet colormap.*

## *Surface Plots*

The *rgl* package also provides several functions that allow us to create 3D surface graphs, including *rgl.surface*, *surface3d*, and *persp3d*. *persp3D* is a generic function to draw 3D surface plots in a new *rgl* device, while both *rgl.surface* and *surface3d* simply add a 3D surface to the current scene (they will create a new *rgl* device if no current scene exists).

Now, I will use an example to illustrate how to create an interactive 3D surface for a *peaks* function using *rgl*.

```
> source("./R/plotHelper.R")
> library(plot3D)
> # create grid matrices:
> mx <- seq(-3, 3, 0.2)
> my <- seq(-3, 3, 0.2)
> # use the mesh function in the plot3D package to create the mesh matrix:
> mxy <- mesh(mx, my)
> # create x, y, z grids (z is defined as a peaks function):
> x <- mxy$x
```

```
> y <- mxy$y
> z <- peaks(x, y)
> persp3d(x, y, z, col = colormapr("cool", z))
```

Here, even though we are using the *rgl* package to create 3D graphs, I find that it is more convenient to use the mesh function included in the *plot3D* package to construct the mesh matrices than to create these mesh matrices manually. The mesh matrices and the variable assignments are identical to what we have used in creating the 3D surface plot using the *plot3D* package. Finally, we use the *persp3d* function with the *cool* colormap for the *z* variable to create the interactive 3D surface. Now, we can manually rotate, zoom the graph, or change its perspective view with our mouse. A snapshot of this 3D surface created using the preceding commands is shown in Figure 3-56 (left). You can see that the *rgl* create a nice 3D surface with lighting and material effects.

We can add mesh lines to the current 3D surface using the *surface3d* function:

```
> surface3d(x, y, z, col = "black", front = "lines", back = "lines")
```

This will add the mesh lines to both sides of the current surface, as shown in Figure 3-56 (right).

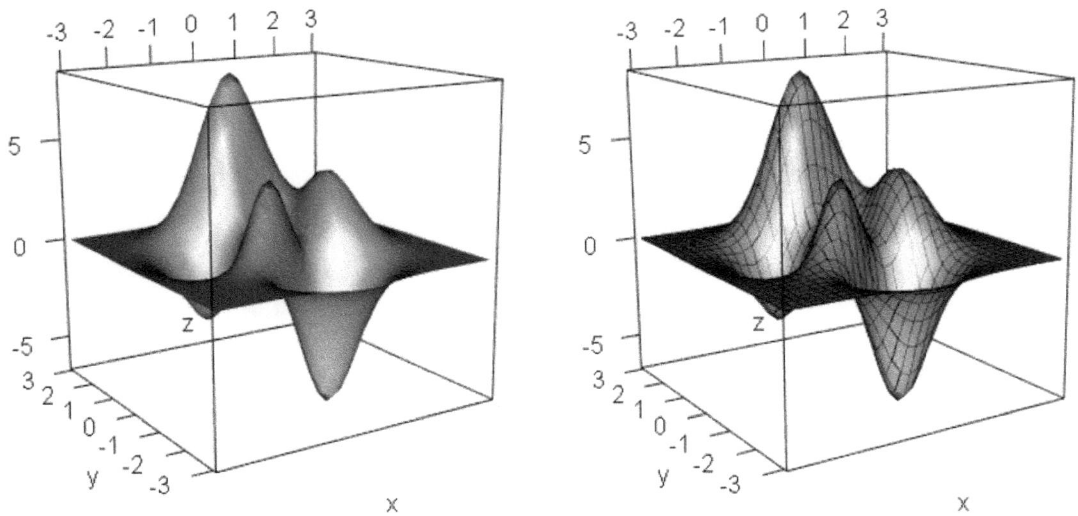


*Figure 3-56. Surface plots created using rgl without (left) and with (right) mesh lines.*

You may notice from the Figure 3-56 that the surface graphs created using *rgl* have no colorbar legend by default, which is different from the graphs with the default colorbar legend if graphs are created using the *plot3D* or *plot3Drgl* packages. For 3D color graphs, the colorbar legend could be very useful because it makes the graphs easier for you to associate color scales with values on the plots. *rgl* has a *legend3d* function, which allows us to add discrete legends to our 3D graphs; however, it does not allow us to add the colorbar legend with continuous color scales.

If we really want to add a colorbar legend to 3D color graphs, we can create it easily with the help of the *fields* package. For your convenience, I implement a simple helper function named *colorbarLegend3d*, which is included in the *plotHelper.R* file. You can use this function to add a colorbar legend to *rgl* 3D graphs. Here is the code for this function:

```
colorbarLegend3d <- function(mapName = c("rainbow", "heat", "terrain",
    "topo", "cm","jet", "hot", "spring", "summer", "autumn", "winter", "gray",
```

```
    "cool"), zvalue){
  library(fields)
  options( warn = -1)
  cl <- colormapr(mapName = mapName)(100)
  par3d(windowRect = c(100, 100, 600, 600))
  bgplot3d(image.plot(legend.only = T, zlim = range(zvalue[!is.na(zvalue)]),
                      col = cl))
}
```

This function takes the colormap name and *zvalue* as the input arguments. Inside this function, we create a colormap with a fixed length of 100. We then resize the *rgl* device window using the *par3d* function to make room for the colorbar legend. Finally, we create the colorbar legend using the *image.plot* function included in the *fields* package, and place the legend as the background of the *rgl* graph using the *bgplot3d* function.

Now, we can use the above function to easily add a colorbar legend to our *rgl* 3D graphs. For example:

```
> source("./R/plotHelper.R")
> mx <- seq(-3, 3, 0.2)
> my <- seq(-3, 3, 0.2)
> mxy <- mesh(mx, my)
> x <- mxy$x
> y <- mxy$y
> z <- peaks(x, y)
> persp3d(x, y, z, col = colormapr("hot", z))
> colorbarLegend3d("hot", z)
```

This produces the output shown in Figure 3-57.

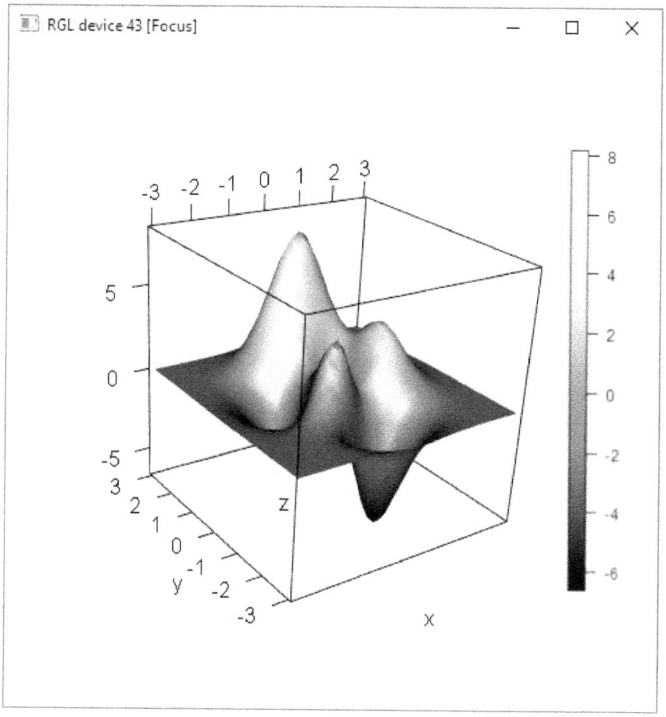


*Figure 3-57. A 3D surface chart with a colorbar legend.*

In the preceding discuss, we created 3D surface graphs by constructing the mesh matrices. In fact, *rgl* allows us to create 3D surface directly using the mathematical functions without constructing the mesh matrices. For example, you can use the *plot3d* function to create a surface plot for a mathematical peaks function:

```
> plot3d(peaks, xlim = c(-3, 3), ylim = c(-3, 3), col = colormapr("rainbow"),
          zlab = "z")
```

This single line code produces a nice-looking 3D interactive surface graph shown in Figure 5-58 (left). However, we now cannot use the *colorbarLegend3d* function directly to add a colorbar legend to this graph because this colorbar function does not know the range of the peaks function. We need to provide the data range for this peaks function manually. From the graph, we know its range is about [-6.5, 8.1], so we can then use the following command to add a colorbar legend:

```
> z <- c(-6.5, 8.1)
> colorbarLegend3d("rainbow", z)
```

This produces the surface plot with a colorbar legend shown in Figure 3-58 (right).

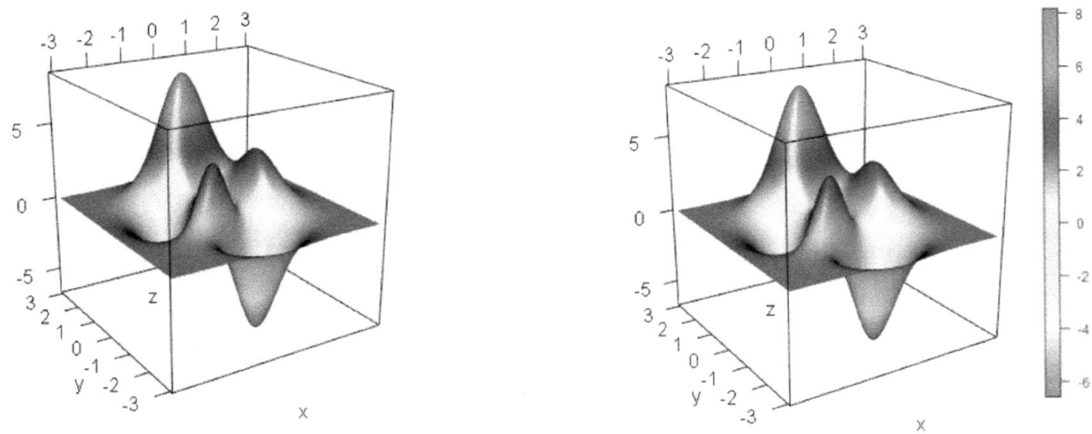


*Figure 3-58. 3D surface plot without (left) and with (right) a colorbar legend.*

# Chapter 4
# Stock Charts and Technical Indicators

Market data for securities, such as price and trading volume, is the primary resource for technical analysis because it reflects every factor affecting the value of a market. Market data visualization and technical analysis play an important role in financial market research and analysis. Technical analysis, unlike fundamental analysis, usually ignores the actual nature of the company, market, currency, or commodity. It is based solely on stock charts, namely, the price and volume information. Stock charts usually show open, high, low, close, and volume data of a security. These charts allow us to plot the change of a stock price over time, analyze the history of stock price changes, and predict the future price movement of a stock based on prior price history.

However, market data does not generate just trend lines and basic chart pattern. Quant traders, analysts, and developers have expanded their studies of market data far beyond those basic elements. They have managed and manipulated market data to develop a number of technical indicators (also called technical analysis indicators), which provide more insight into market action than what we see on the surface.

Stock charts, such as the bar and candlestick charts, can provide a lot of information about a market at a glance, but a technical indicator can put a number on those observations and confirm whether a market is strengthening or weakening or becoming overbought or oversold before it becomes evident on a stock chart. Many analytical software packages or even the market data vendors (including Bloomberg and Reuters) now provide a variety of technical indicators as the computation capabilities of computers have evolved.

We should be very careful when applying these technical indicators in our real-life trading. Most traders and analysts do not rely on only one indicator but often use several indicators together to help making a trading decision because of the misleading information one indicator might provide. An indicator that works in one type of market condition may perform poorly in another market condition. There is no perfect indicator for every market in every period in every market condition.

Nevertheless, we, as a quant analyst, developer, or trader, should be familiar with various technical indicators. In this chapter, I will discuss stock charts using both the standard R graphics and the quantmod package. I also represent some commonly used technical indicators based mainly on the financial analysis capability provided by the *TTR* package. The *TTR* package consists of over 40 technical indicators. In most cases, we do not need to implement these commonly used indicators by ourselves; instead, we simply need to learn how the math and algorithms work behind each indicator and how to use those indicators in our applications.

# Using Standard R Graphics

In the preceding chapter, we discussed various graphics packages and demonstrated how to use them to create various 2D and 3D graphs. We can use the base R graphics or *ggplot2* to represent the financial data in a plot. For example, we can plot the S&P 500 index data easily using the base R graphics:

```
> library(Quandl)
> spx <- Quandl("YAHOO/INDEX_GSPC", start_date = "2010-01-01",
                end_date = "2016-03-01")
> par(mfrow = c(2,1))
> plot(spx$Date, spx$Close, type = "l", xlab = "Date", ylab = "Price",
       main = "SPX Price")
> plot(spx$Date, spx$Volume/1e6, type = "h", xlab = "Date",
       ylab = "Volume (millions)", Main = "SPX Volume")
```

Here, we first load the historical EOD market data for SPX from *Quandl*, and then plot the close price and volume using the plot function of the base R graphics system, as shown in Figure 4-1 (a).

Of course, we can use the *ggplot2* package to create the similar charts with the following commands:

```
> library(ggplot2)
> ggplot(spx, aes(x = Date, y = Close)) + geom_line() + ggtitle("SPX Price") +
        theme_bw()
> ggplot(spx, aes(x = Date, y = Volume)) + geom_bar(stat="identity") +
        ggtitle("SPX Volume") + theme_bw()
```

This produces the output shown in Figure 4-1 (b). Both the *plot* and *ggplot* functions gives similar results. However, if we look at the graphs more closely, we will find some issues. For example, if we just plot the recent one-month price and volume for SPX using *ggplot2*:

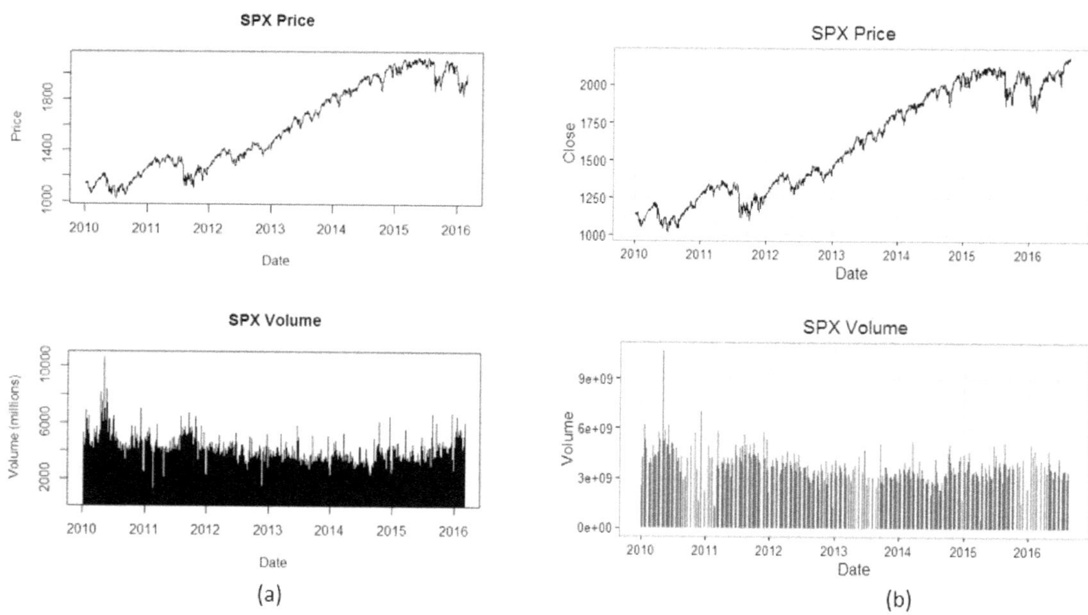


*Figure 4-1. Price and Volume charts for SPX created using the base R graphics (a) and ggplot2 (b).*

```
> ggplot(spx[spx$Date > "2016-02-01",], aes(x = Date, y = Close)) + geom_line() +
```

```
    geom_point(shape = 5) + ggtitle("SPX Price") + theme_bw()
> ggplot(spx[spx$Date > "2016-02-01",], aes(x = Date, y = Volume)) +
    geom_bar(stat = "identity") + ggtitle("SPX Volume")+ theme_bw()
```

This will generate the results shown in Figure 4-2.

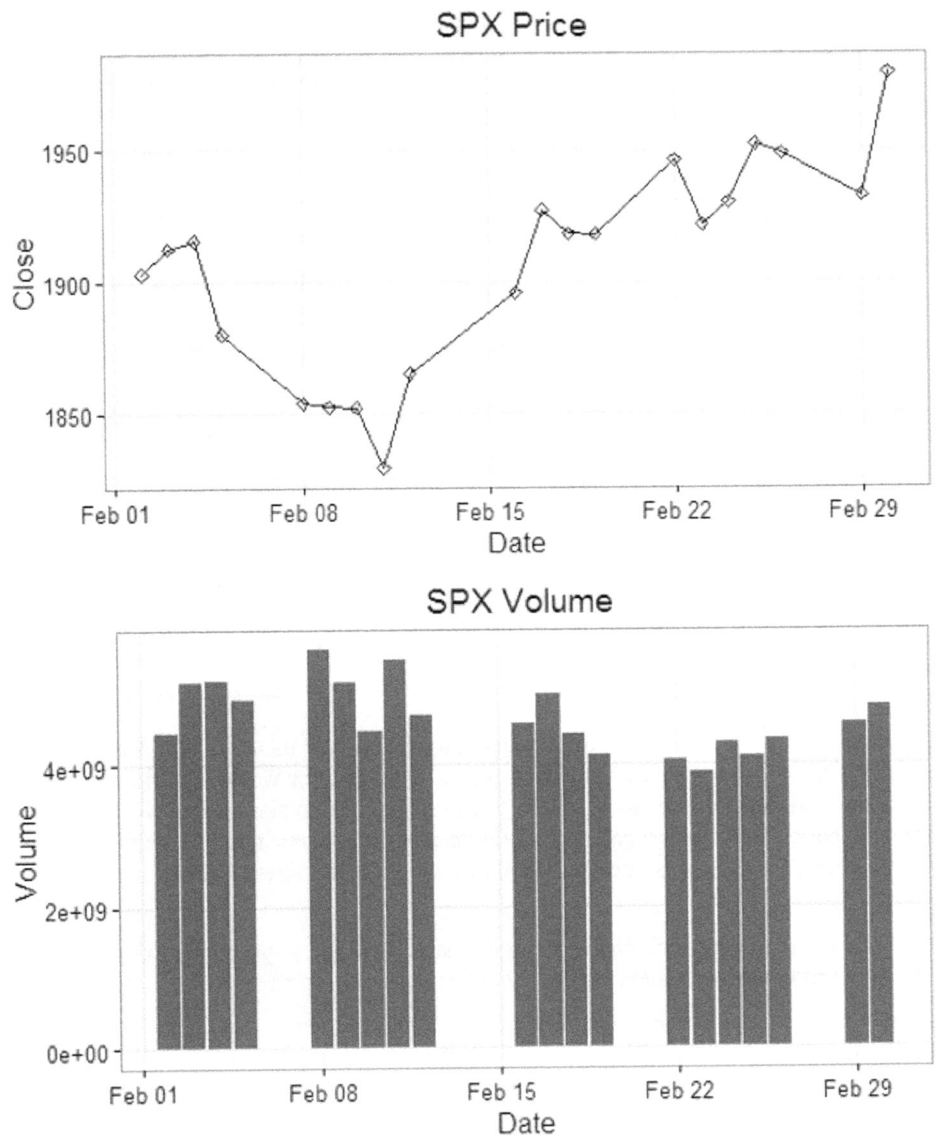


*Figure 4-2. SPX price and volume data for recent month.*

The *plot* function from the base R will produce the similar results as shown in the above figure. Note there are gaps in the charts during weekends and holidays because there is no data for these dates. This will become even worse if we look at the intraday minute-bar data. In Chapter 2, we discussed how to retrieve historical minute-bar data from Google Finance. Let us plot the minute-bar data on a 2D graph:

```
> source("./R/marketdata.R")
> spx <- googleHist1(".INX", "2Y", "1Min")
> spx <- data.frame(Date = index(spx), coredata(spx))
> ggplot(spx[spx$Close > 1500, ], aes(x = Date, y = Close)) + geom_line() +
    ggtitle("SPX Price")
```

Here, we first load the *marketdata.R* file into R because it contains the *googleHist1* function we are going to use, and then load the minute-bar data for SPX ( the symbol .INX in Google Finance is for SPX index). To use *ggplot2*, we also convert the *xts* object into a data frame. Finally, we plot the minute-bar data by filtering out some outliers. The resulted plot is shown in Figure 4-3.

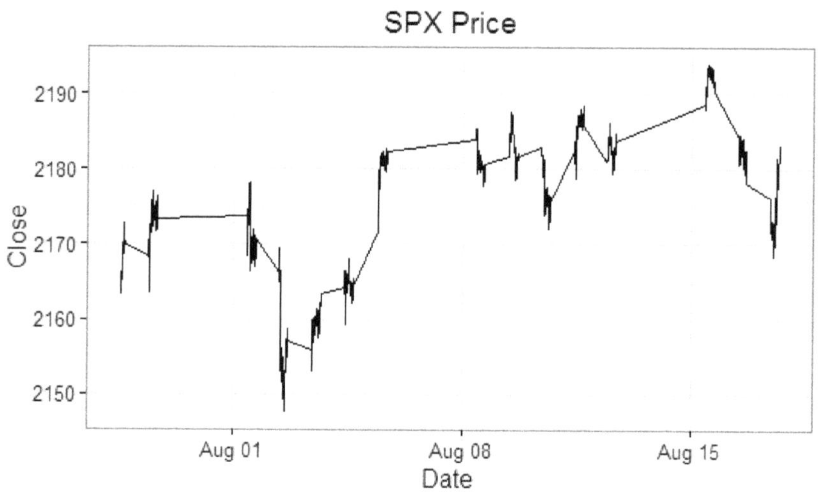


*Figure 4-3. SPX minute-bar data with big data gaps.*

You can see there are many big data gaps because the minute-bar data are only available during the trading hours. In finance, we usually need to remove the data gaps for weekends and holidays, and only show the data on workdays on the stock charts. We may need to do some extra work to remove these data gaps from a stock chart that is created using the base R graphics or *ggplot2*. In fact, we do not need to reinvent the wheel; we can use some specialized financial R packages to generate professional stock charts instead.

It is also possible to create real-time charts using the base R graphics system. For this purpose, add the *getLiveData* function to the *plotHelper.R* file:

```
getLiveData <- function(ticker = "SPY"){
  q <- googleQuote(ticker)
  q <- q[c("Symbol", "LastUpdate", "TradePrice")]
  colnames(q) <- c("Ticker", "Time", "Price")
  q$Time <- strptime(q$Time, format="%H:%M:%S %p")
  return(q)
}
```

This function simply extract the last trade price from Google Finance by calling the *googleQuote* function, which was implemented in Chapter 2 and included the *marketdata.R* file. Next, we implement a new function named *updateLiveData* to update the quote:

```
updateLiveDate <- function(ticker = "SPY", n = 100){
```

```
  q <- GetLiveData(ticker)
  while(1){
    q1 <- getLiveData(ticker)
    if(q1$Time != q$Time){
      q <- rbind(q, q1)
      q <- q[order(q$Time),]
    }
    if(nrow(q) > 5){
      flush.console()
      plot(q$Time, q$Price, type="o", col="blue", lwd = 2,
           main = paste0(ticker,":  trade time = ", q1$Time, ",
                          trade price = ", q1$Price))
      grid()
    }
    if(nrow(q) > n) q <- q[-1, ]
    Sys.sleep(5)
  }
}
```

Here, we call the *getLiveData* function every 5 seconds and display the data in a live stock chart. We can specify how many points we want to plot on the chart by setting the *n* argument. Figure 4-4 shows the live-stock chart for SPY.

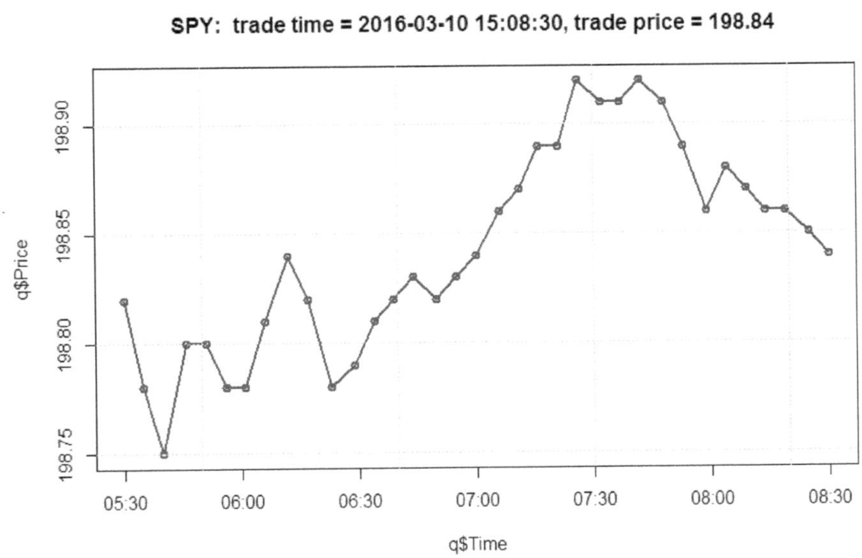


*Figure 4-4. Real-time stock chart for SPY.*

# Using quantmod Package

In Chapter 2, I demonstrated how to use the *quantmod* package to retrieve the market data from different data sources. In fact, *quantmod* provides the ability and functionality to visualize market data with standard financial charting tools. The main function in *quantmod* for financial charting is *chartSeries*. The package also include some charting shortcut functions, such as *lineChart*, *barChart*, and *candleChart*.

## Line Stock Charts

It is easy to create a line stock chart using the *lineChart* function in the quantmod package. For example, we can use the following commands to create a line chart for SPX:

```
> library(quantmod)
> spx <- getSymbols("^GSPC", from = "1900-01-01", auto.assign = F)
> lineChart(spx, TA = NULL, theme = "white")
```

Here, we first load all the available data for SPX (data started from 1/3/1950) from Yahoo using the *quantmod* package, and then generate a line chart for SPX's close price, as shown in Figure 4-5 (left).

We can also use the subset argument to specify a particular period of the data series to view. For example, we can use the following command to display the data in recent month:

```
> lineChart(spx, subset = "2016-02-02::", line.type = "o", theme = "white")
```

Which produces the output shown in Figure 4-5 (right).

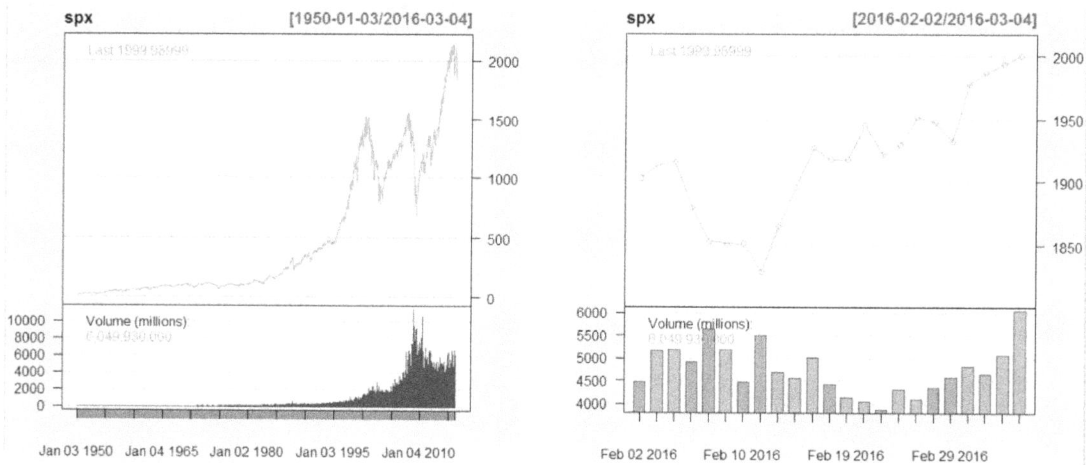


*Figure 4-5. Line charts for SPX.*

It is interesting to compare the above results with those shown in Figure 4-2. In particular, the recent month data in Figure 4-5 (right) has no gaps anymore – the charting tool in *quantmod* automatically removes the weekends and holidays from the date axis.

The *lineChart* function can plot the data not only from *quantmod* but also from the other data sources. For example, we can plot the minute-bar data from Google Finance:

```
> source("./R/marketdata.R")
> spx <- googleHist1(".INX", "2Y", "1Min")
> lineChart(spx, TA = NULL, theme = "white")
```

This produces a minute-bar chart for SPX shown in Figure 4-6.

Comparing to the results shown in Figure 4-3, the data shown in the above plot has no data gaps, and the periods after trading hours are automatically removed from the time axis by the charting tool in *quantmod*.

*Figure 4-6. SPX minute-bar data without data gaps.*

We can specify different the *line.type* parameter to change the line style. For example, we can plot the SPX minute-bar data for the last two hours by setting *line.type* = "*h*" (histogram-like vertical lines) and "*s*" (stair steps) using the following commands:

```
> source("./R/marketdata.R")
> spx <- googleHist1(".INX", "2Y", "1Min")
> lineChart(spx, subset = "last 2 hours", line.type = "h",
            theme = chartTheme("white", up.col = "blue"), TA = NULL)
> lineChart(spx, subset = "last 2 hours", line.type = "s",
            theme = chartTheme("white", up.col = "blue"), TA = NULL)
```

which produces the output shown in Figure 4-7.

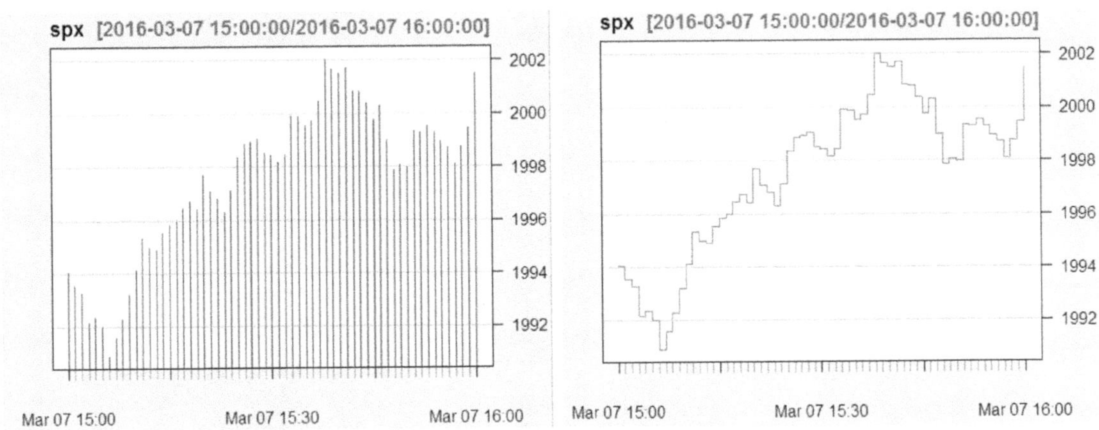


*Figure 4-7. Line charts with vertical lines (left) and stair steps (right).*

## Bar and Candlestick Charts

The *quantmod* package also provides *barChart* and *CandleChart* functions, which allow us to create bar (*hlc* and *hloc*) and candlestick stock charts using the OHLC time series. For example:

```
> source("./R/marketdata.R")
> spy <- googleHist1("SPY", "2Y", "1Min")
> spy <- spy[spy$Close > 170]  # filter out some outliers
> barChart(spy, subset = "last 2 hours", bar.type = "hlc", theme = "white",
           minor.ticks = F)
> barChart(spy, subset = "last 2 hours", bar.type = "ohlc", theme = "white",
           minor.ticks = F)
> candleChart(spy, subset = "last 2 hours", theme = "white", minor.ticks = F)
```

The above commands create the *hlc*, *ohlc* bar charts, and candlestick chart for SPY minute-bar data, as shown in Figure 4-8.

If we do not like appearance of the stock charts created using the current version of the charting tools in *quantmod*, you can try the experimental charting version of the *chart_Series* function (note, *chartSeries* is the current version). The functions in the experimental version is for new version of *chartSeries* in *quantmod*. The interface, behavior, and functionality may change in the final release. Also, these functions, when complete, will revert back to the original *chartSeries* naming convention. So, we must be careful if we use these experimental functions in our applications.

Here, I will illustrate how to use these experimental functions:

```
> spx <- getSymbols("^GSPC",from = "2015-01-01", auto.assign = F)
> cp <- chart_pars()
> cp$mar <- c(4, 2, 0, 2) # set chart margin
> cp$cex <- 0.8           # set font size
> chart_Series(spx, subset = "2016-01-01::", pars = cp, TA = "add_Vo()")
```

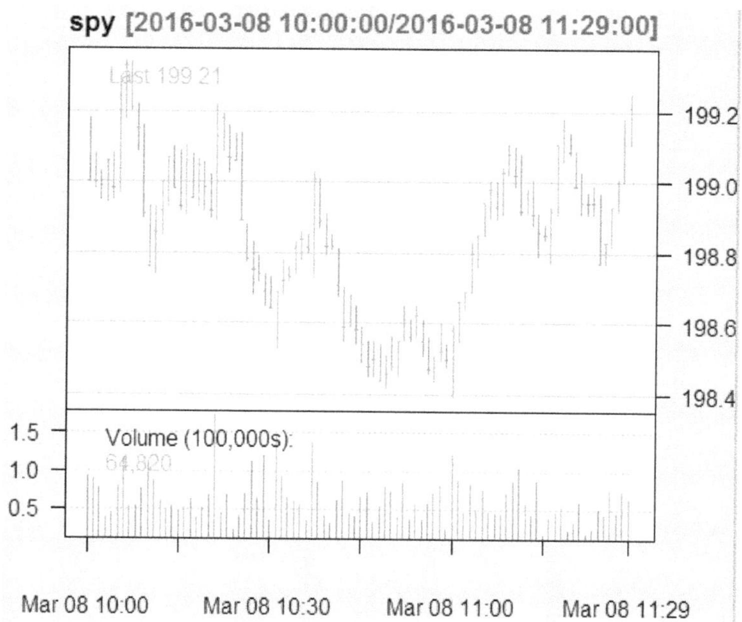

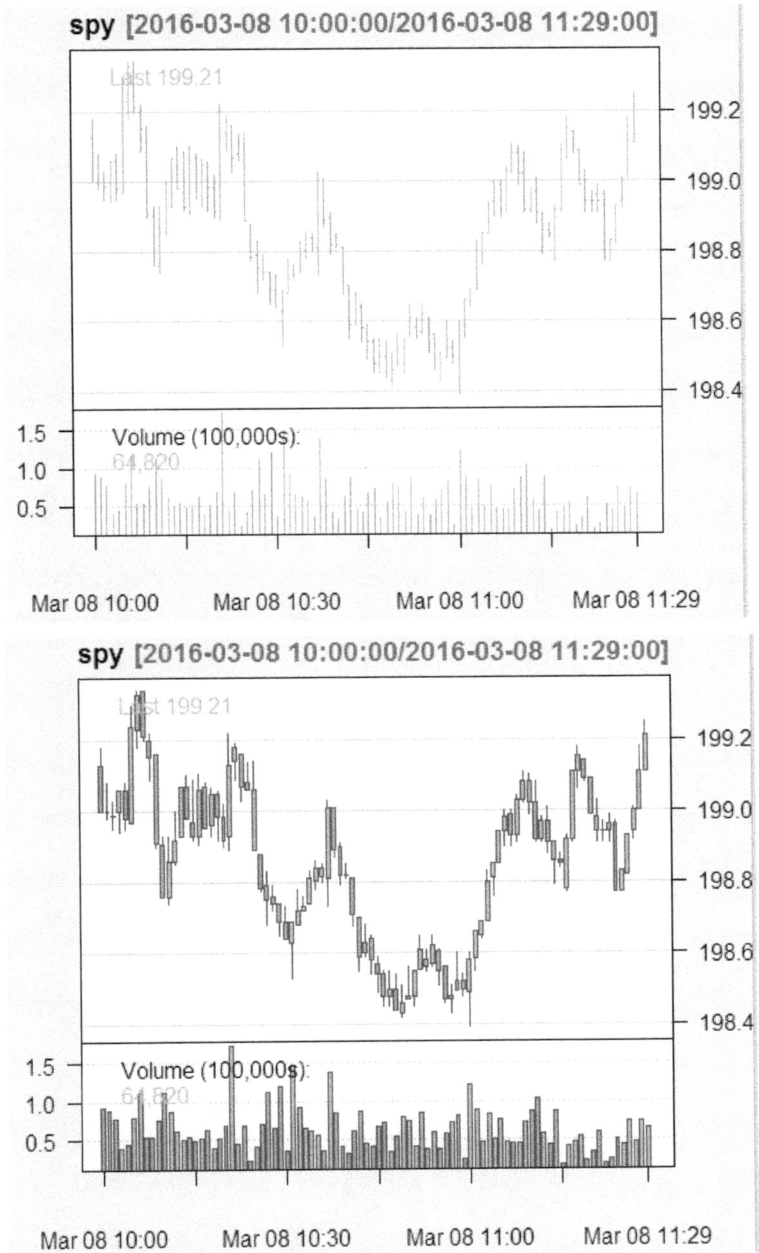


*Figure 4-8. The hlc (top), ohlc (center) bar, and candlestick (bottom) charts for SPY.*

The above command will produce the candlestick chart (the default chart type) shown in Figure 4-9 (top). We can also create a line chart by issuing the following commands:

```
> cp$mar <- c(4, 2, 0, .2)
> ct <- chart_theme()
> ct$rylab <- F     # remove y-axis on right side of the plot to save space
> ct$col$line.col <- c("red", "green", "blue", "black")
```

```
> chart_Series(spx, subset = "2016-01-01::", type = "line", pars = cp,
               TA = "add_Vo()", theme = ct)
```

There generates the line chart shown in Figure 4-9 (center). Similarly, we can create an *ohlc* bar chart by the command:

```
> chart_Series(spx, subset="2016-01-01::", type = "ohlc", pars = cp,
               TA = "add_Vo()", theme = ct)
```

This produces the result shown in Figure 4-9 (bottom).

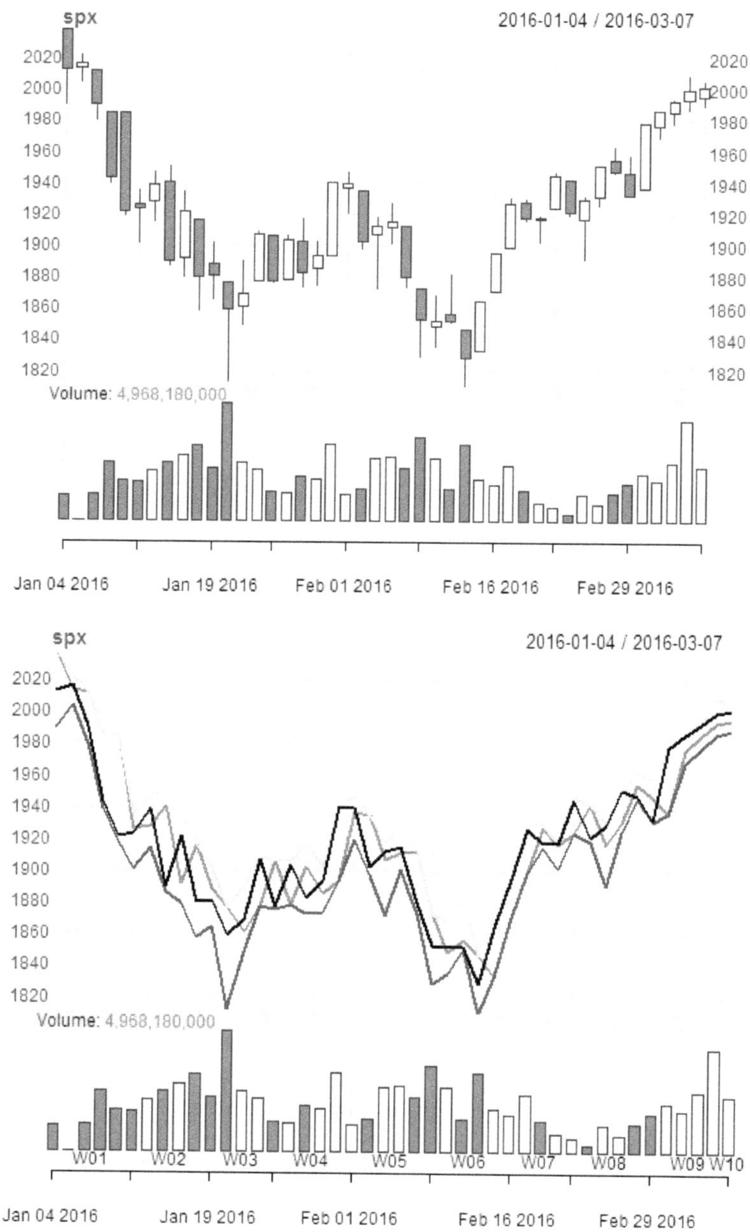

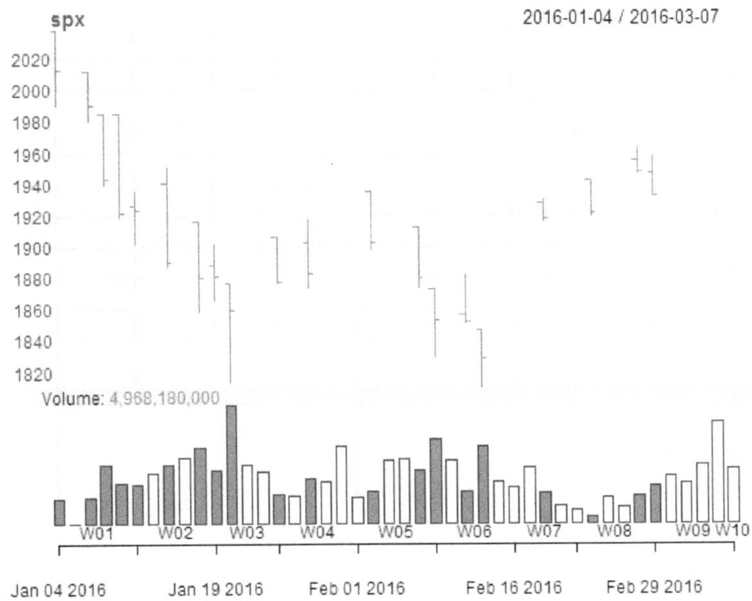


*Figure 4-9. Candlestick (top), line (center), and bar (bottom) charts for SPX.*

# Technical Indicators

Stock charts, such as the bar and candlestick charts presented in the preceding sections, can provide a lot of information about a market at a glance, but a technical indicator can put a number on those observations and confirm whether a market is strengthening or weakening or becoming overbought or oversold before it becomes evident on a stock chart. Many analytical software packages or even the market data vendors (including Bloomberg and Reuters) now provide a variety of technical indicators as the computation capabilities of computers have evolved.

You should be very careful when applying the technical indicators in your real-life trading. Most traders and analysts do not rely on only one indicator but often use several indicators together to help make a trading decision because of the misleading information one indicator might provide. An indicator that works in one type of market condition may perform poorly in another market condition. There is no perfect indicator for every market in every period in every market condition.

Nevertheless, we, as a quant analyst, developer, or trader, should be familiar with various technical indicators. In this section, I will discuss some commonly used technical indicators based mainly on the financial analysis capability provided by the *quantmod* and *TTR* packages. The *TTR* package consists of over 40 technical indicators. In most cases, we do not need to implement these commonly used indicators by ourselves; instead, we simply need to learn how the math and algorithms work behind each indicator and how to use those indicators in our applications.

# Moving Average Based Indicators

Moving averages are often used in analyzing time series data. They are widely applied in finance, especially in technical analysis. They can be also used as a generic smoothing operation, in which case the data need not be a time series.

We can compute moving averages for any time series. In finance, moving averages are often applied to stock prices, returns, or trading volumes. We use them to smooth out short-term fluctuations and highlight longer-term trends or cycles. The threshold between short-term and long-term depends on the application, and the parameters of the moving average will be set accordingly.

A moving average smooths data by replacing each data point with the average of the neighboring data points defined within the time span. This process is equivalent to low pass filters used in digital signal processing.

A simple moving average (SMA) is the mean value of the previous $n$ data points. For example, a 5-day simple moving average of close price is the mean of the previous 5 days' close prices. If those prices are $p_0, p_{-1}, p_{-2}, p_{-3}, p_{-4}$ then the moving average is described by

$$SMA = \frac{p_0 + p_{-1} + p_{-2} + p_{-3} + p_{-4}}{5}$$

In general, for an $n$-day moving average, we have

$$SMA = \frac{p_0 + p_{-1} + \cdots}{n} = \frac{1}{n}\sum_{i=0}^{n-1} p_{-i}$$

When calculating successive values, a new value comes into the sum and an old value drops out, meaning a full summation each time is unnecessary

$$SMA_{today} = MSA_{yesterday} - \frac{p_{-n+1}}{n} + \frac{p_1}{n}$$

In R, you can use the *rollmean* function to calculate the moving average. For example:

```
> source("./R/plotHelper.R")
> ibm <- adjOhlcv("IBM", from = "2016-01-01")
> avg <- rollmean(ibm$IBM.Close, 10, align = "right")
> head(avg, 3)
           IBM.Close
2016-01-15  131.8204
2016-01-19  131.0444
2016-01-20  129.6596
```

Here, we load the adjusted IBM data from *Quandl* and then use the *rollmean* function to calculate the moving average of the close price by setting the moving window to 10. We also set the align argument to "right". The align parameter specifies whether the index of the result should be center- (default), left-, or right-aligned compared to the moving window. We see that the moving average data begins 10 workdays later because there are not enough data points to calculate the average value before that date.

In technical analysis, there are various popular values for $n$, like 10 days, 40 days, or 100 days. The period selected depends on the kind of movement we are concentrating on, such as short, intermediate, or long term. In any case, moving average levels are interpreted as support in a rising market, or resistance in a falling market.

In all cases, a moving average lags behind the latest data point, simply from the nature of its smoothing. An SMA can lag to an undesirable extent and can be disproportionately influenced by old data points' dropping out of the average. We can address this issue by giving extra weight to more recent data points, as done in the weighted and exponential moving averages.

A weighted average is any average that has multiplying factors to give different weights to different data points. In technical analysis, a weighted moving average (WMA) specifically means weights that decrease arithmetically. In an $n$-day WMA the latest day has weight $n$, the second latest $n-1$, etc., down to zero:

$$WMA = \frac{np_0 + (n-1)p_{n-1} + \cdots \quad {}_{\cdots 2} + p_{-n+1}}{n + (n-1) + \cdots} = \frac{2}{n(n+1)} \sum_{i=0}^{n-1} (n-i)p_{-i}$$

We can calculate WMA using the *WMA* function included in the *TTR* package:

```
> wma <- na.omit(WMA(ibm$IBM.Close, n = 10, wts = 1:10))
> head(wma, 3)
               [,1]
2016-01-15 130.9913
2016-01-19 130.0806
2016-01-20 128.1862
```

Here, the same market data for IBM is used as in the preceding SMA example.

One drawback of both the simple and weighted moving averages is that they include data for only the number of periods the moving average covers. For example, a five-day simple or weighted moving average only uses five days' worth of data. Data prior to those five days are not included in the calculation of the moving average.

In some situations, however, the prior data is an important reflection of prices and should be included in a moving average calculation. We can achieve this by using an exponential moving average (EMA).

An EMA uses weight factors that decrease exponentially. The weight for each older data point decreases exponentially, giving much more importance to recent observations while not discarding older observations entirely.

The degree of weight decrease is expressed as a constant smoothing factor $\alpha$, which is a number between 0 and 1. $\alpha$ may be expressed as a percentage, so a smoothing factor of 10% is equivalent to $\alpha = 0.1$. Alternatively, $\alpha$ may be expressed in terms of $n$ time periods, where $\alpha = 2/(n+1)$. For example, $n = 19$ is equivalent to $\alpha = 0.1$.

The observation at a time period $t$ is designated $Y_t$, and the value of the EMA at any time period $t$ is designated $S_t$. $S_1$ is undefined. $S_2$ may be initialized in a number of different ways, most commonly by setting $S_2$ to $Y_1$, though other techniques exist, such as setting $S_2$ to an average of the first 4 or 5 observations. The prominence of the $S_2$ initialization's effect on the resultant moving average depends on $\alpha$; smaller $\alpha$ value makes the choice of $S_2$ relatively more important than larger $\alpha$ value, since a higher $\alpha$ discounts older observations faster.

The formula for calculating the EMA at time periods $t \geq 2$ is

$$S_t = \alpha Y_{t-1} + (1 - \alpha) S_{t-1}$$

This formula can also be expressed in technical analysis terms as follows, showing how the EMA steps towards the latest data point:

$$EMA_{today} = EMA_{yesterday} + \alpha(p_0 - EMA_{yesterday})$$

Where $p_0$ is the current price. Expanding out $EMA_{yesterday}$ each time results in the following power series, showing how the weighting factor on each data point $p_1$, $p_2$, etc., decrease exponentially:

$$EMA = \frac{p_{-1} + (1-\alpha)p_{-2} + (1-\alpha)^2 p_{-3} + \cdots}{1 + (1-\alpha) + (1-\alpha)^2 + \cdots} = \frac{\sum_{i=0}^{\infty}(1-\alpha)^i p_{-i-1}}{\sum_{i=0}^{\infty}(1-\alpha)^i} = \alpha\sum_{i=0}^{\infty}(1-\alpha)^i p_{-i-1}$$

Theoretically, this is an infinite sum, but because $1-\alpha$ is less than one, the terms become smaller and smaller, and can be ignored once they are small enough.

We can also calculate EMA using the *EMA* function included in the *TTR* package:

```
> ema <- na.omit(EMA(ibm$IBM.Close, n = 10))
> head(ema, 3)
                  EMA
2016-01-15 131.8204
2016-01-19 130.9098
2016-01-20 129.0398
```

The *quantmod* package has incorporate some commonly used technical indicators from the *TTR* package. We can easily add the technical indicators to our stock charts through the *TA* argument or using the *addTA* function. Let us take SPX as an example:

```
> spx <- getSymbols("^GSPC", from = "2015-09-01", auto.assign = F)
> chartSeries(spx, theme = "white", minor.ticks = F, yrange = c(1800, 2150),
             TA = NULL)
> addTA(SMA(Cl(spx), n = 10), on = 1, col = "red")
> addTA(WMA(Cl(spx), n = 10,  wts = 1:10), on = 1, col = "green")
> addTA(EMA(Cl(spx), n = 10), on=1, col = "blue")
```

This produces the results shown in Figure 4-10. We can easily compare the different moving average results by plotting them on the same chart.

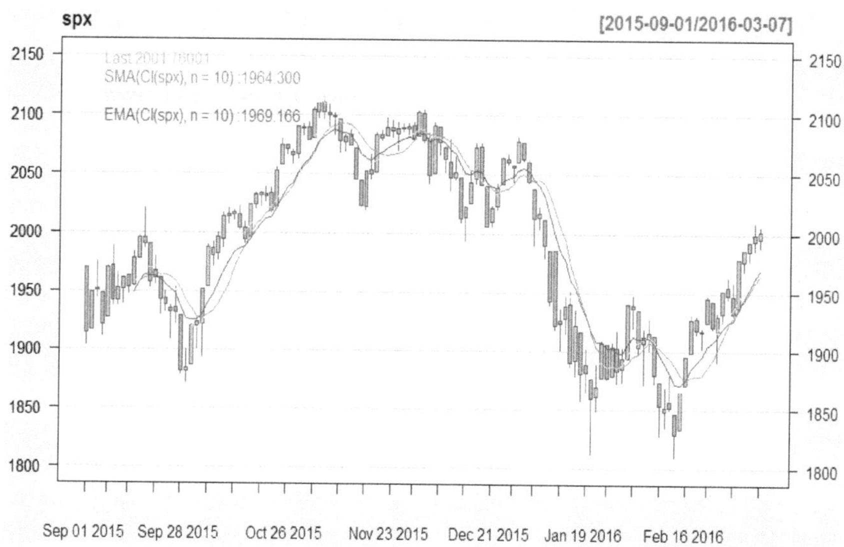


*Figure 4-10. A stock chart for SPX with SMA, WMA, and EMA curves.*

# Envelope and Bollinger Band Indicators

Moving average indicators are a popular trading tool. However, they are prone to providing false signals in choppy markets. The envelope indicator simply calculates "envelope" above and below a moving average using a specified percentage of the stock price as the shift. This creates parallel bands that follow price action. With moving average as the base, the envelope indicator can be used as a trend following indicator. Of course, this indicator is not limited to just trend following, and it can also be used to identify overbought and oversold levels when the trend is relatively flat.

The envelope indicators are designed to encompass most price action. Therefore, we need to pay special attention when the stock prices move above or below the envelopes. Trends often start with strong moves in one direction or another. A surge above the upper envelop shows extraordinary strength, while a plunge below the lower envelop shows extraordinary market weakness. Such strong moves indicate the end of one trend and the beginning of another.

The parameters for the envelope indicator depend on our trading objective and the characteristics of the security we are trading. Traders tend to use shorter moving averages and relatively tight envelopes, while investors tend to prefer longer moving averages with wider envelops.

The stock's volatility will also affect the parameters. Bollinger band indicator has a built-in mechanism that automatically adjusted to the stock's volatility. Bollinger bands use the standard deviation to set bandwidth. Usually, stocks with a high volatility will require wider bands to encompass most price action. Stocks with a low volatility can use narrower bands. A Bollinger band indicator with two standard deviations will encompass 95% of the price action. Then a stock's price going outside the Bollinger bands should not last and should revert back to the moving average. We can then create the trading signals using the Bollinger band indicator. A buy signal will be generated when the stock price falls below the lower Bollinger band, while a sell signal will be created when the price goes outside the upper Bollinger band.

The *quantmod* package allows us to add both the envelope and Bollinger band indicators to our stock charts. First, let us examine the envelope indicator for GS:

```
> gs <- getSymbols("GS", from = "2015-06-01", auto.assign = F)
> chartSeries(gs, theme = "white", minor.ticks = F, yrange = c(140, 230),
              TA = "addEnvelope(20, 5, 'SMA')")
```

Here, we add the envelope indicator to the stock chart by setting the *TA* argument through the *addEnvelope* function, where we set the moving window to 20 workdays, 5% shift, and the SMA (can also be EMA or WMA) as the MA type. The above commands generate the output shown in Figure 4-11.

We can also examine the Bollinger band indicator using the same market data for GS as that we used in the preceding example:

```
> chartSeries(gs, theme = "white", minor.ticks = F, yrange = c(140, 230),
              TA = "addBBands(n = 20, sd = 2, maType = 'EMA')")
```

Here, we use the *addBBands* function to add Bollinger bands to the stock chart by setting parameters: $n = 20$ (corresponding to 20-day moving average), $sd = 2$ (corresponding to 2-standard deviations), and $maType$ = EMA. This produces results shown in Figure 4-12.

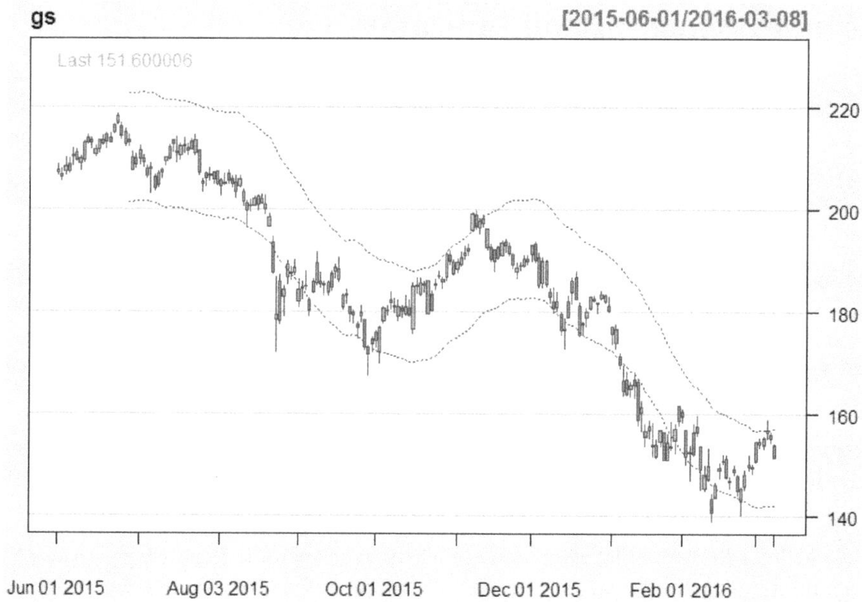


*Figure 4-11. Envelope indicator for GS with a 20-day moving average and a 5% shift.*

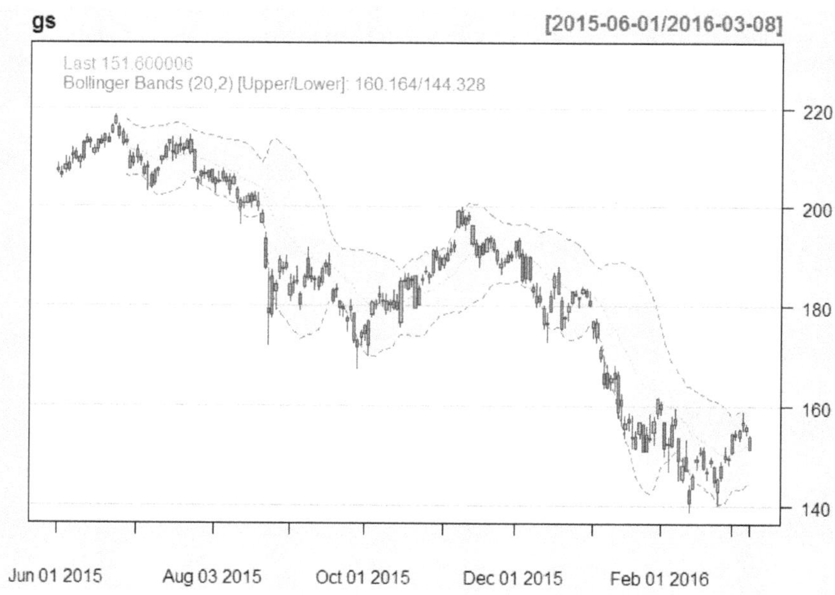


*Figure 4-12. Bollinger bands for GS with a 20-day EMA and 2-standard deviations.*

# MACD and RSI Indicators

The moving average convergence and divergence (MACD) indicator is an oscillating indicator, fluctuating above and below zero. It is both a trend following and momentum indicator. The MACD indicator compares a short period moving average and a long period moving average of prices.

The MACD indicator measures the difference between two EMAs and is depicted as a line. The usual representation of the MACD indicator has another line – a short 9-day EMA of the MACD – plotted together with the MACD on the chart, to act as a trigger indicator.

The trading strategy based on MACD is to look at which side of zero the MACD lines are on. Above zero for a sustained period of time and the trend is likely up; below zero for a sustained period of time and the trend is likely down. Potential buy signals occur when the MACD moves above zero, and potential sell signals when it crosses below zero.

The relative strength index (RSI) is a momentum oscillator that calculates velocity and strength of the stock price movement. This means that the RSI indicator only measures the stock's internal strength (based on its historical data) and should not be confused with its relative strength, which is compared with other stocks, market indices, or sector indices. RSI ranges between 0 and 100, which makes it a convenient indicator to evaluate whether market is currently overbought or oversold. The RSI value about 70 level is generally considered to indicate that security is overbought and value below 30 level is generally considered that security is oversold. However, we should adjust these levels according to the market volatility. For instance, volatile stocks may hit the overbought and oversold levels more frequently than stable stocks if the same levels are used.

The formula for RSI is very simple:

$$RSI = 100 - \frac{100}{1 + RS}, \quad RS = \frac{Average\ Gain}{Average\ Loss}$$

The average gain (loss) is calculated as the sum of all the positive (negative) daily returns over a specified period divided by the total numbers of days. Note that we should use the absolute value of the daily returns when calculating the average loss.

The main problem of the RSI indicator is that the stock may continue to move up despite the indicator hitting the overbought zone, or continue to go down even after the indicator hits the oversold zone. In order to avoid a big loss of using the indicator, Wilder (the inventor of the RSI indicator) developed a new concept called "failure swing" for the RSI. A "bearish failure swing" occurs when the RSI enters the overbought zone (goes above the 70 level) and comes below 70 again. In other words, a short position can be taken only when the RSI cuts the 70 lines from the top. Similarly, a "bullish failure swing" occurs when the RSI enters the oversold zone and comes out. Both the positive and negative failure swings can be clearly seen in the RSI indicator chart.

Now, I will use an example to illustrate how to add the MACD and RSI indicators to the stock chart:

```
> chartSeries(gs, theme = "white", minor.ticks = F, yrange = c(140, 230),
              TA = "addMACD(); addRSI(); addVo()")
```

Here, we add three indicators (MACD, RSI, and Volume) to the stock charts by setting a single *TA* parameter. We also use the default parameters for all three functions: *addMACD*, *addRSI*, and *addVo*. The above code generates the output shown in Figure 4-13.

## On Balance Volume Indicator

Trading volume itself is a valuable indicator, and the on balance volume (OBV) takes a lot volume information and compiles it into a signal indicator. The OBV indicator measures positive and negative volume flows and tends to relate price and volume in the stock market.

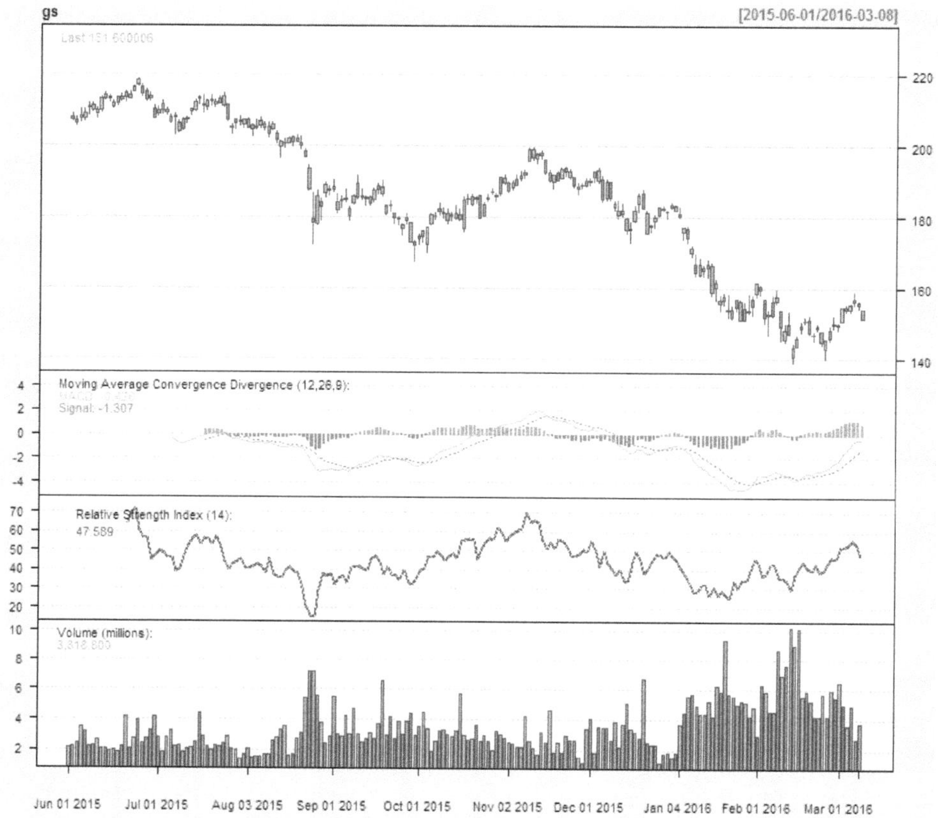


*Figure 4-13. MACD and RSI indicators for GS.*

The OBV can be calculated using the following formula:

$$OBV = OBV_{prev} + \begin{cases} \text{volume} & \text{if close} > \text{close}_{prev} \\ 0 & \text{if close} = \text{close}_{prev} \\ -\text{volume} & \text{if close} < \text{close}_{prev} \end{cases}$$

Since OBV is a cumulative result, the value of OBV depends on the starting point of the calculation. We can use the trading volume to confirm trends. A rising price should be accompanied by a rising OBV; a failing price should be accompanied by a failing OBV.

The OBV indicator is a momentum indicator that uses volume flow to predict changes in stock price. When volume increases sharply without a significant change in the stock price, the price will eventually jump upward, and vice versa. The basic assumption is that OBV changes precede price changes. The theory is that smart money can be seen flowing into the stock by a rising OBV. When the public then moves into the stock, both the stock and the OBV will surge ahead.

If the stock price movement precedes OBV movement, a non-confirmation has occurred. Non-confirmations can occur at bull market tops (when the stock rises without or before the OBV) or at bear market bottoms (when the stock falls without or before the OBV).When the OBV changes to a rising or falling trend, a breakout has occurred. Since OBV breakouts normally precede price breakouts, we should buy long on OBV upside breakouts. On the other hand, we should sell short when the OBV makes a downside breakout. We should hold stock position until the trend changes.

We can now create the OBV indicator using the following command:

```
> chartSeries(gs, theme = "white", minor.ticks = F, yrange = c(140, 230),
              TA = "addOBV(); addVo()")
```

This produces the results shown in Figure 4-14.

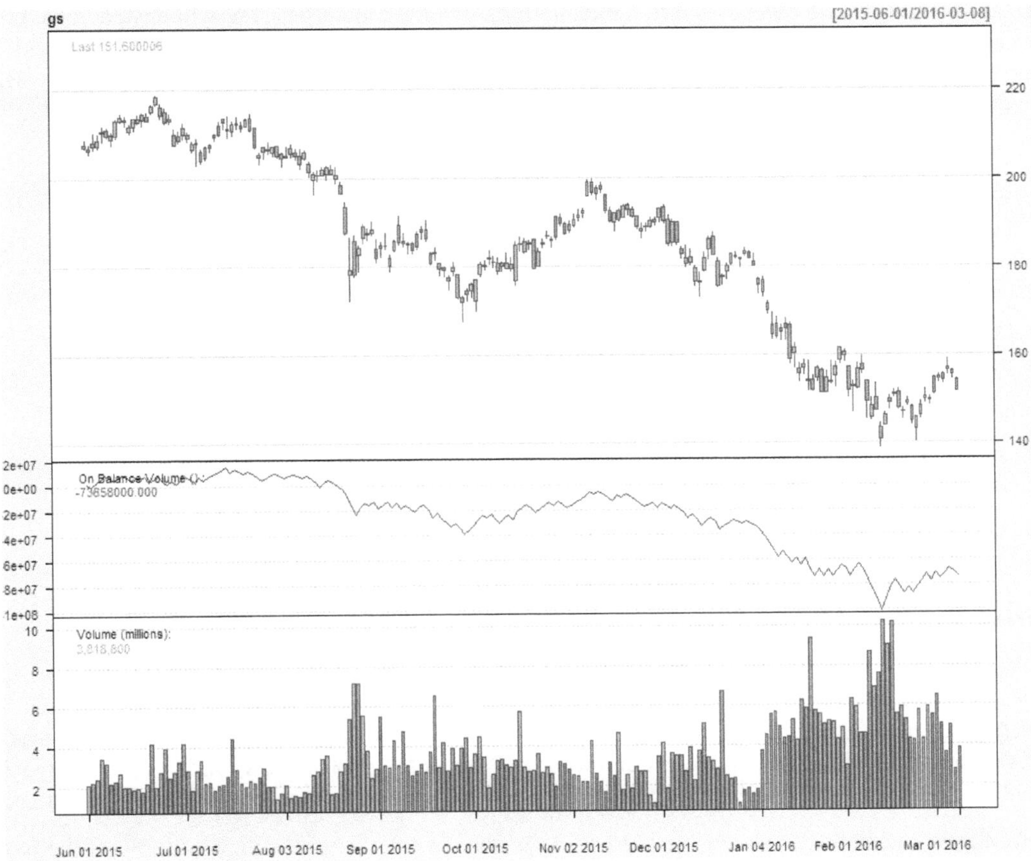


*Figure 4-14. OBV signals for GS.*

## Accumulation/Distribution Indicator

The accumulation/Distribution (A/D) indicator is determined by the changes in price and volume. The volume acts as a weight coefficient at the change of price: the higher the volume is, the greater the contribution of the price change will be in the value of the indicator. This indicator is in fact a variant of the more commonly used OBV indicator. They are both used to confirm price changes by means of measuring the respective volume of sales.

When the value of A/D indicator increases, it means accumulation (buying) of a particular stock, as the overwhelming share of the trading volume is related to an upward trend of prices. When the value of the indicator drops, it means distribution (selling) of the stock, as most of sales take place during the downward price movement.

Divergences between the A/D indicator and the price of the security indicate the upcoming change of prices. As a rule, in case of such divergences, the price tendency moves in the direction in which the indicator moves. Thus, if the indicator is growing, and the price of the security is dropping, a turnaround of price should be expected.

The first step of creating the A/D indicator is to find the close location value (CLV), which looks at the location of the close and compares it to the range for a given period. The CLV will have a value range between +1 and −1. A zero value of CLV means that the price closed halfway between the high and low of the range; a value of +1 means the close is equal to the high of the range; and a value of −1 means the close is equal to the low of the range. The CLV can be calculated using the following formula:

$$CLV = \frac{(Close - Low) - (High - Close)}{High - low}$$

The A/D indicator adds up volume multiplied by the CLV factor:

$$A/D = A/D_{prev} + volume \times CLV$$

The starting point for the A/D is arbitrary, only the shape of the resulting indicator is used, not the actual level of the total.

We can now create the A/D indicator using the following command:

```
> chartSeries(gs, theme = "white", minor.ticks = F, yrange = c(140, 230),
              TA = "addChAD(); addVo()")
```

This generates the output shown in Figure 4-15.

## Williams %R Indicator

The Williams %*R* indicator is a momentum indicator, and is used to measure overbought or oversold levels. This indicator is very similar to the stochastic %*K* indicator, except that the Williams %*R* indicator calculates a negative value between 0, −100 and does not smooth the signals. The trading strategy using this indicator is simple: we sell when %*R* reaches −10% or higher and buy when it reaches −90% or lower. The Williams %*R* indicator works best in trending markets, either bull or bear trends.

The Williams %*R* indicator shows the current close price in relation to the high and low of the past *n* days. We need to determine the highest high and lowest low for the past *n* days. This is the trading range for the past *n* days. Once those values are determined, the Williams %*R* can be calculated using the following formula:

$$\%R = -100 \times \frac{high_{n-days} - close_{today}}{high_{n-days} - low_{n-days}}$$

You can see that the indicator is on a negative scale. A value of −100 means the close today is the lowest low of the past *n* days, and zero means today's close is the highest high of the past *n* days.

We can now create the Williams %*R* indicator using the following command:

```
> chartSeries(gs, theme = "white", minor.ticks = F, yrange = c(140, 230),
              TA = "addWPR(n = 10); addVo()")
```

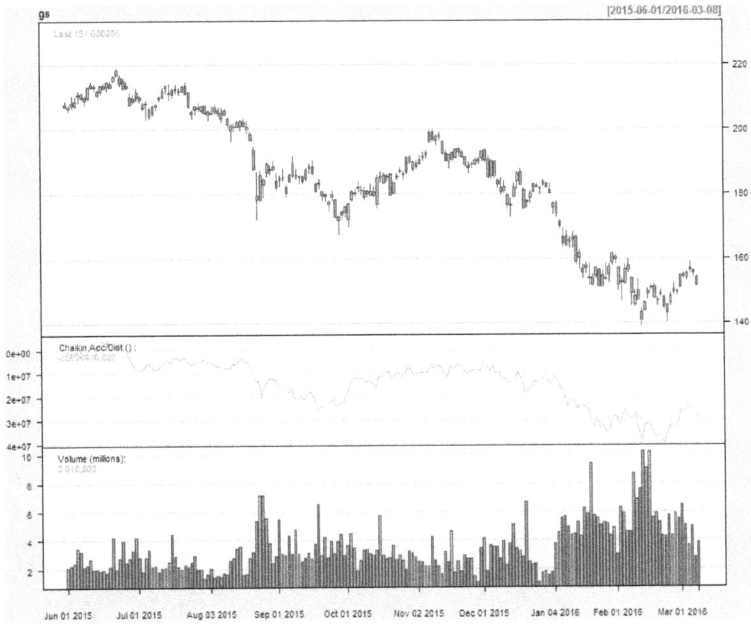


*Figure 4-15. A/D signals for GS.*

Here we set $n = 10$ (the moving window size). The above command produce the output shown in Figure 4-16.

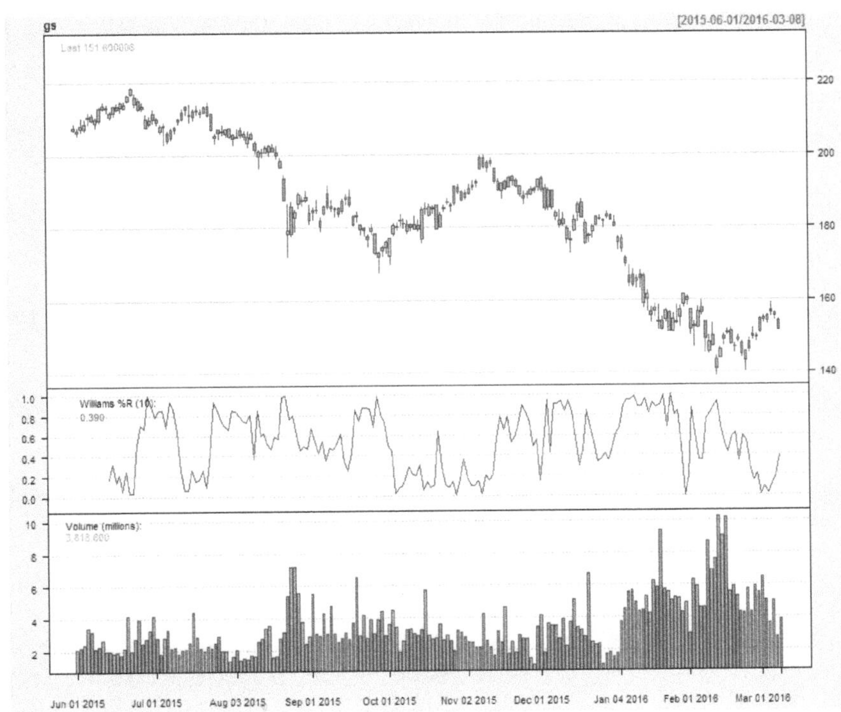


*Figure 4-16. Williams %R signals for GS.*

## Stochastic Indicator

The stochastic indicator formula calculates the simple stochastic indicator (%*K*) and the smoothing stochastic indicator (%*D*). %*D* is a moving average of %*K*. It is a momentum indicator, which uses support and resistance levels. The term stochastic refers to the point of a current price in relation to its price range over a period of time. The indicator attempts to predict price turning points by comparing the stock close price to its price range.

The stochastic indicator is defined by the following formula:

$$\%K = 100 \times \frac{close_{today} - low_{n-days}}{high_{n-days} - low_{n-days}}$$
$$\%D = SMA(\%K, m)$$

You can see that %*D* is the *m*-day simple moving average of %*K* (the last *m* values of %*K*). Usually, this is a SMA, but can be an EMA. The calculation above finds the range between a stock's high and low prices for a given period of time. The current stock close price is then expressed as a percentage of this range with 0% indicating the bottom of the range and 100% indicating the upper limit of the range over the time period covered. The theory behind this indicator is that in an upward-trending market, prices tend to close near their high, and during a downward-trending market, prices tend to close near their low. Transaction signals occur when the %*K* crosses through a moving average %*D* line.

There are several ways to interpret the stochastic indicator results. Three popular trading rules include:

- Buy when the indicator (either %*K* or %*D*) falls below a specific level (e.g., 20) and then rises above that level. Sell when the indicator rises above a specific level (e.g., 80) and then falls below that level.
- Buy when the %*K* line rises above the %*D* line and sell when the %*K* line falls below the %*D* line.
- Look for divergences. For example, the divergence will occur when prices are making a series of new highs and the indicator is failing to surpass its previous highs, and vice versa.

We can now use the following statement to see how the signals from the stochastic indicator look like:

```
> chartSeries(gs, theme = "white", minor.ticks = F, yrange = c(140, 230),
              TA = "addSMI(); addVo()")
```

This produces the output shown in Figure 4-17.

Note that the stochastic indicator has two lines, and the other line is almost invisible. We can change the default setting using the following code:

```
> chartSeries(gs, name = "GS", theme = "white", minor.ticks = F,
              yrange = c(140, 230), TA = "addVo()")
> addTA(SMI(HLC(gs)), col = c("blue", "red"), lwd = c(2,2))
```

Here, we use a separate *addTA* function to create the stochastic indicator interactively. Inside the *addTA* function, we can specify various charting parameters to change the appearance of the chart. This generates the output shown in Figure 4-18.

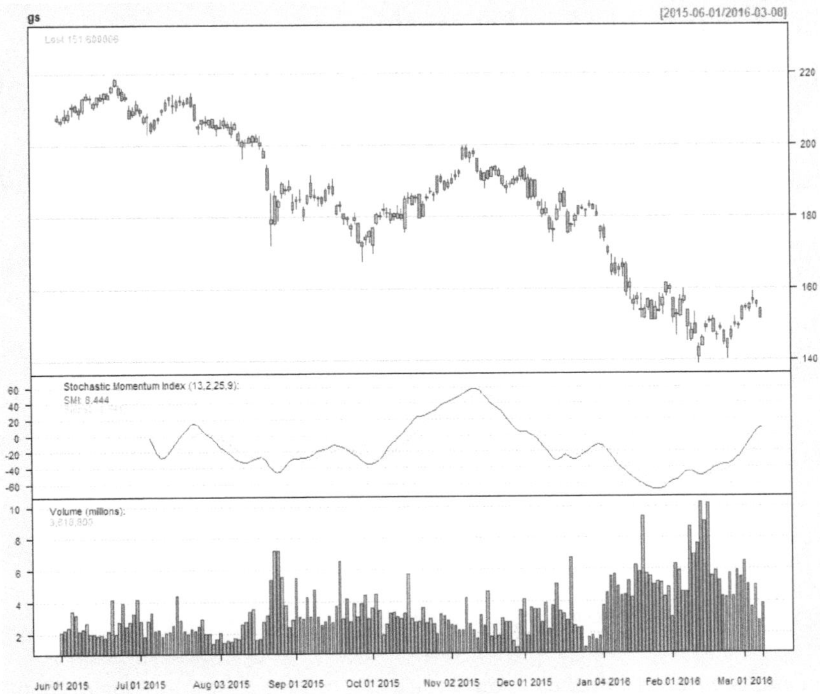


*Figure 4-17. Stochastic signals for GS.*

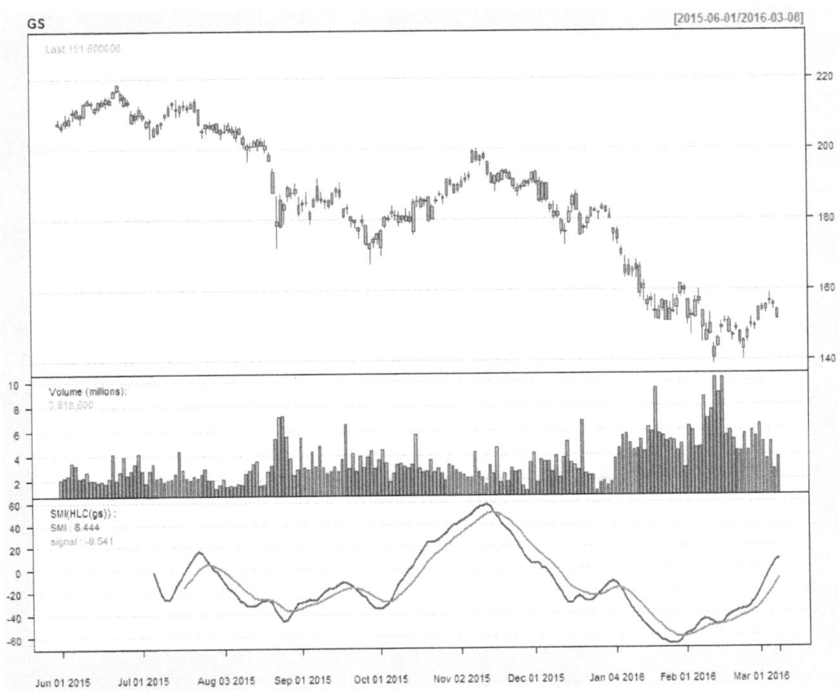


*Figure. 4-18. Stochastic signals for GS created using the addTA function.*

## Commodity Channel Index Indicator

The commodity channel index (CCI) indicator calculates the mean deviation of the daily average price from the moving average. A value above 100 indicates that the commodity is overbought, and a value below -100 indicates that the commodity is oversold.

The CCI indicator is a very commonly used tool for traders in identifying cyclical trends not only in commodities, but also equities and currencies. The CCI can be adjusted to the timeframe of the market traded on by changing the average period.

The assumption behind the CCI indicator is that commodities or stocks move in cycles, with highs and lows coming at periodic intervals.

The CCI indicator can be calculated using the following formula:

$$CCI = \frac{1}{0.015}\frac{price_t - SMA(price_t, n)}{\sigma(price_p, n)}$$

$$price_t = \frac{high + low + close}{3}$$

$$\sigma(price_t, n) = \frac{1}{n}\sum_{i=1}^{n}(|price_{ti} - SMA(price_t, n)\ |)$$

In the above equations, $price_t$ is called the typical price, SMA is the simple moving average of the typical prices for a given period n, and σ is the mean absolute deviation. The factor 0.015 in the CCI formula is for scaling purposes to ensure that approximately 70 ~ 80% of CCI values would fall between −100 to +100. The CCI oscillates around zero. The percentage of CCI values that fall between −100 to +100 will strongly depend on the period *n* used. A shorter CCI will be more volatile with a smaller percentage of value between −100 to +100. Conversely, the longer period used to calculate the CCI, the higher the percentage of values between −100 to +100.

The trading rules using the CCI indicator are based on movements above +100 or below −100 to generate buy and sell signals. When the CCI moves above +100, a stock is considered to be entering a strong uptrend and a buy signal is given. The position should be closed when the CCI moves back below +100. When the CCI moves below −100, the stock is considered to be in a strong downtrend and a sell signal is given. The position should be closed when the CCI moves back above −100.

We can also use the CCI to identify the overbought and oversold levels. A stock can be considered to be oversold when the CCI dips below −100 and overbought when it exceeds +100. From oversold levels, a buy signal might be given when the CCI moves back above −100. From overbought levels, a sell signal might be given when the CCI moves back below +100.

Now, we can create the CCI indicator using the following command:

```
> chartSeries(gs, name = "GS", theme = "white", minor.ticks = F,
              yrange = c(140, 230), TA = "addCCI(15); addVo()")
```

This generates the results shown in Figure 4-19.

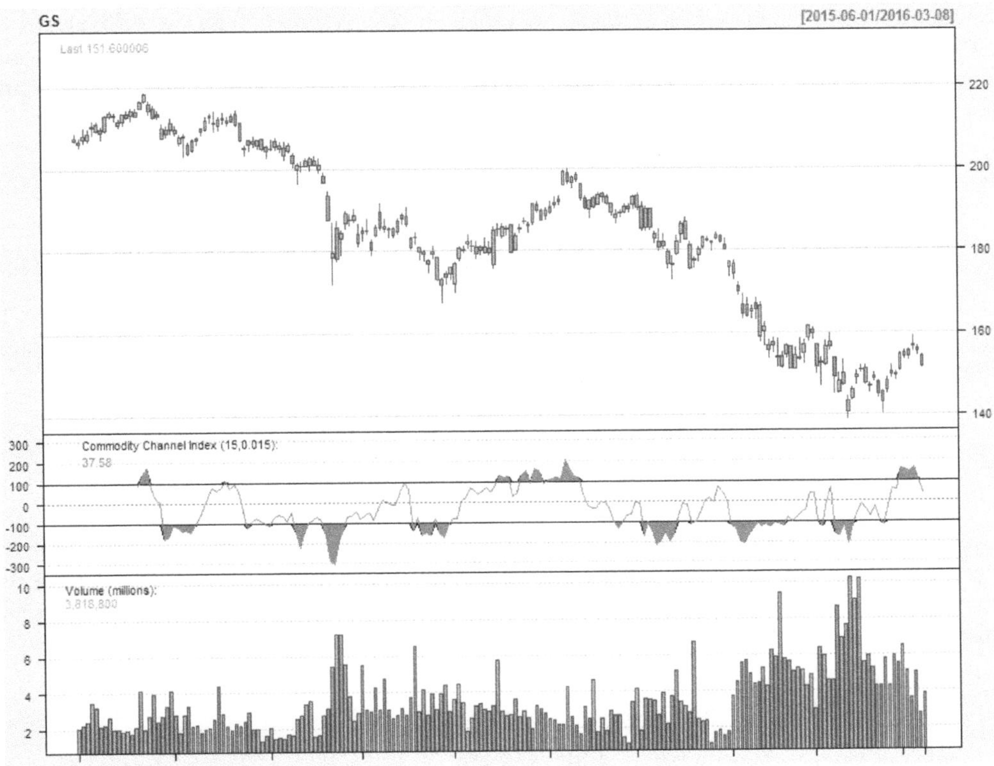


*Figure 4-19. CCI signals for GS.*

The *quantmod* package includes over 30 technical indicators. Here, we discussed just few of them, which are commonly used in technical analysis. You can see that the stock charting functionality with technical analysis indicators in *quantmod* is a powerful quantitative analysis tool, which allows us to examine different stocks for different periods using the specified indicator selected from over 30 built-in technical indicators.

## Add Custom Indicators

The *quantmod* package also allows us to add our own custom indicators to the charts using the *addTA* and *newTA* functions. For example, assume we want to calculate the moving linear regression of the close price versus date for GS over an *n*-day period and would like to add this regression results to our stock chart. First, we need to implement a *selfLinearRegression* function, which is included in the *plotHelper.R* function. Here is the code for this function:

```
selfLinearRegression <- function(xtsData, n = 10){
  rr <- rollapplyr(xtsData, width = n,
                   FUN = function(z){
                     t <- lm(formula = z[, 4] ~ index(z), data = as.data.frame(z),
                             na.rm = T)
                     return(t$coef)
                   },
                   by.column = F)
}
```

Here, the self-regression means that in finance, we usually perform regression for two different securities (i.e., SPX ~ IBM), here we simply perform the close price of a single security vs its own date column. This function takes the *xts* data and moving window size (*n*) as input arguments. The fourth column of the data represents the close price, for example:

```
> head(gs, 3)
           GS.Open GS.High GS.Low GS.Close GS.Volume GS.Adjusted
2015-06-01  207.32  208.82 206.89   207.81   2088200    205.4965
2015-06-02  206.85  207.84 205.65   206.43   2230700    204.1319
2015-06-03  207.52  210.17 206.77   208.29   2417000    205.9711
```

The *selfLinearRegression* function returns the coefficients of the regression: intercept and slope. I will use an example to illustrate how to use this function to create a self-linear regression (SLR) indicator. Here, we will use the same GS data:

```
> source("./R/plotHelper.R")
> rr <- selfLinearRegression(gs, 20)
> slr <- rr[,1] + rr[, 2] * as.numeric(index(gs))
> slrDiff <- gs[, 4] - slr
```

Here, we construct two indicators, *slr* and *slrDiff*, using the regression results. *slr* represents the predicted close price from the linear regression (similar to the moving average), and *slrDiff* represents the difference between the original close price and predicted price. Now, we are ready to add these two indicators to our stock charts.

```
> chartSeries(gs,name = "GS",theme = "white", minor.ticks = F, TA = NULL,
              yrange = c(140, 230))
> addTA(slr, on = 1, col="blue", lwd = 2)
> addTA(slrDiff, col="red", lwd = 2)
```

Here, we overlay the *slr* indicator to the stock chart by setting *on* = 1, and add the *srlDiff* indicator to a new window under the price chart. The above commands produces the output shown in Figure 4-20.

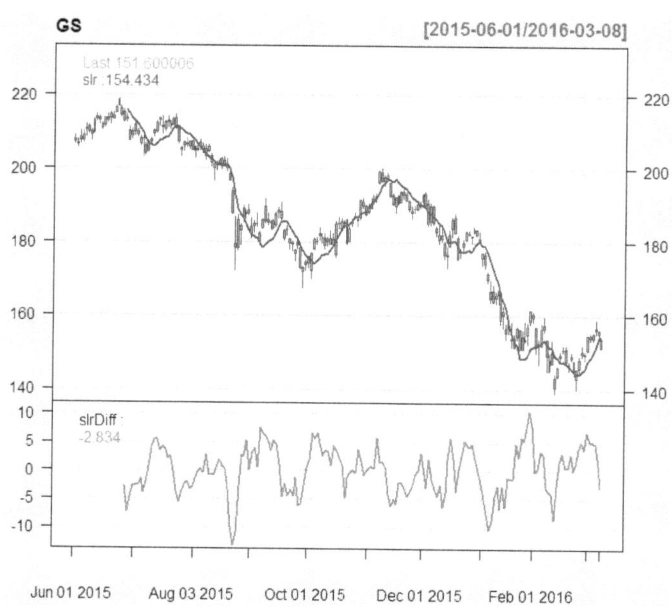


*Figure 4-20. Custom linear regression indicators for GS.*

After testing our custom indicators using *addTA* function, we can now convert them into generic (or built-in like) TA functions using the *newTA* function. First, we need to create the *SLR* and *SLRDiff* functions (included in the *plotHelper.R* file):

```
SLR <- function(xtsData, n = 10){
  xtsData <- as.xts(xtsData)
  rr <- selfLinearRegression(xtsData, n)
  slr <- rr[, 1] + rr[, 2] * as.numeric(index(xtsData))
  return(slr)
}

SLRDiff <- function(xtsData, n = 10){
  xtsData <- as.xts(xtsData)
  slr <- SLR(xtsData, n)
  slrDiff <- xtsData[, 4] - slr
  return(slrDiff)
}
```

Now, we can convert them into generic TA functions:

```
> source("./R/plotHelper.R")
> addSLR <- newTA(FUN = SLR, col = "blue", lwd = 2, on = 1)
> addSLRDiff <- newTA(FUN =SLRDiff, col = "red", lwd = 2)
> chartSeries(gs,name = "GS",theme = "white", minor.ticks = F,
              TA = "addSLR(5); addSLRDiff(5)", yrange = c(140, 230))
```

Notice that we use the *addSLR* and *addSLRDiff* just as they are the built-in TA functions. The above code produces the output with a 5-day moving window shown in Figure 4-21.

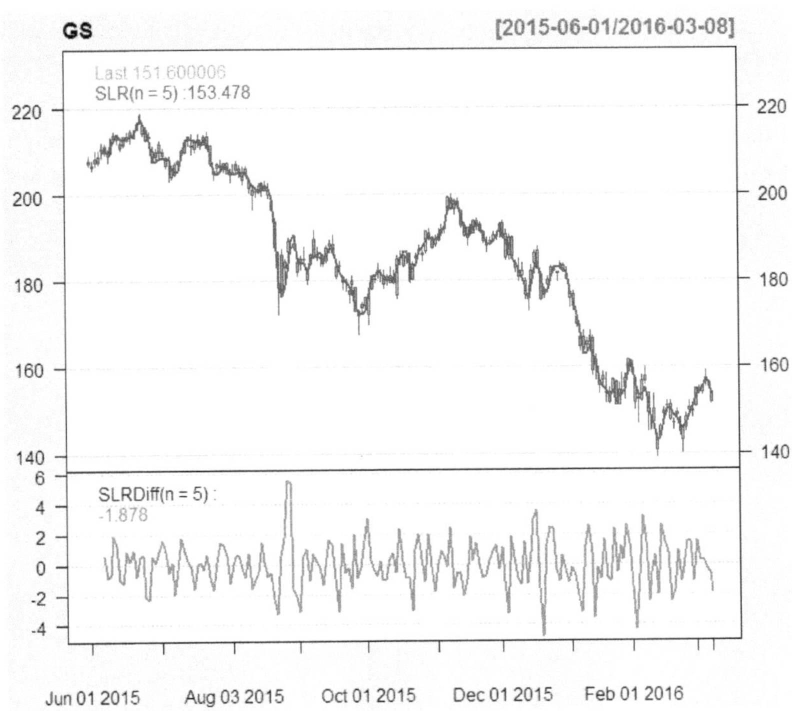


*Figure 4-21. Custom linear regression indicators for GS created using the newTA function.*

Technical indicators can be categorized into two types: leading and lagging indicators. Leading indicators are designed to lead price movements. The majority of leading indicators are oscillators. This means that the values of these indicators are limited within a bounded range. The oscillator will fluctuate into overbought and oversold conditions based on set levels. Some of the more popular leading indicators include CCI, RSI, stochastic, and Williams %*R*. A leading indicator is thought to be powerful during periods of sideways or non-trending trading ranges.

Leading indicators usually generate more signals and create more trading opportunities. Early signaling for entry and exit is the main advantage of the leading indicators, which can act to forewarn against a potential strength or weakness. Because they generate more signals, leading indicators are best used in non-trending markets. In a market that is trending up, the best use of the leading indicators is to help identify oversold conditions for buying opportunities. In a market that is trending down, leading indicators can help identify overbought situations for selling opportunities.

With early signals comes the prospect of higher returns and with higher returns comes the reality of greater risk. More signals and earlier signals mean that the chances of false signals and whipsaws increase. False signals will increase the potential for losses. Whipsaws can generate commissions that can eat away profits and test trading stamina.

Lagging indicators follows price movements and have less predictive qualities. The most well-known lagging indicators include moving average, MACD, envelope, and Bollinger band indicators. The usefulness of these indicators tends to be lower during non-trending periods but highly useful during trending periods. This is because lagging indicators tend to focus more on the trend and generate fewer buy-and-sell signals. This allows us to capture more of the trend instead of being forced out of our positions based on the volatile nature of the leading indicators.

One of the main benefits of lagging indicators is the ability to catch a move and remain in a move. When the market or security in question develops a sustained move, trend-following indicators can be enormously profitable and easy to use. The longer the trend, the fewer the signals and less trading involved.

The benefits of lagging indicators are lost when a security moves in a non-trending range. Another drawback of lagging indicators is that signals tend to be late. By the time a moving average crossover occurs, a significant portion of the move may have already occurred. Late entry and exit points can skew the risk/reward ratio.

# Chapter 5
# Options Pricing

Options are derivative contracts that give the holder the right, but not the obligation, to buy or sell the underlying instrument at a specified price on or before a specified future date. Although the buyer of the option is not obligated to exercise the option, the option seller has an obligation to buy or sell the underlying instrument if the option is exercised. Option trading can provide a variety of benefits including the security of limited risk and the advantage of leverage. Before we start trading options, it is important to understand the factors that determine the value of an option. In this chapter, I will demonstrate how to price various options.

## Introduction to Options

An option, just like a stock or bond, is a security. It is also a binding contract with strictly defined terms and properties. The underlying assets of an option can be stocks, stock indices, currencies, debt instruments, commodities, etc. Options are security derivatives because they derive their value from an underlying asset.

There are two basic types of options: calls and puts. A call option gives the holder the right to buy an underlying asset at a certain price within a specific period of time. The call options are similar to having a long position on a stock. Buyers of the call options hope that the stock will increase before the option expires. A put option gives the holder the right to sell an asset at a certain price within a specific period of time. The put options are very similar to having a short position on a stock. Buyers of the put options hope that the price of the stock will fall before the option expires. There are four types of participants in option markets: buyers of calls, sellers of calls, buyers of puts, and sellers of puts.

The price in the option contract is called the exercise price or strike price; the total cost of an option is called the premium; the date in the contract is called the expiration date, exercise date, or maturity. Options can be categorized into two types: American options and European options according to their exercise characteristics. American options can be exercised at any time between the date of purchase and expiration date. Most exchange-traded options are American options. European options can only be exercised on the expiration date. Both American and European options are standard derivatives or "plain vanilla" options. Other types of options are called exotic or non-standard derivatives, which include Asian, Lookback, and Barrier options among others. Please note that the distinction between American and European options has nothing to do with geographic location.

# Option Payoffs

As mentioned previously, a European call (put) option gives the holder the right but not the obligation to buy (sell) the underlying asset with an initial price *S*, at a given maturity date *T*, and for a fixed price (strike) *K*. Let the price of a European call (put) option be denoted by *c* (*p*). The payoff of a European call at maturity time *T* is:

$$c = \max(S_T - K, 0)$$

where $S_T$ is the price of the underlying asset at maturity. If $S_T < K$, the call will be worthless and the holder will not exercise the right. The payoff of a European put is

$$p = \max(K - S_T, 0)$$

If $S_T > K$, the put will be worthless and the holder will not exercise the right. The call-put parity is the relationship between a European call and put, given by

$$c + Ke^{-rt} = p + S$$

Where *r* is the risk free interest rate and *S* is the underlying asset price.

American call (put) option gives the holder the right but not the obligation to buy (sell) the underlying asset at any time t $(0 < t < T)$ between the date of purchase and expiration date *T*, for a strike price *K*. Let the price of the American call (put) option be denoted by *C* (*P*). The payoff of an American call (put) at maturity *T* is the same as that of corresponding European option. The price boundary and put-call parity for the American option is given by

$$S - K \leq C - P \leq S - Ke^{-rt}$$

# Option Value

In option pricing, the value of an option is a function of both the underlying asset and time: $c_t = f(S_t, t)$. The calculation of the option price (premium) is the option buyers' prime concern. The premium is the fair value of an option contract determined in the competitive market, which the option buyers pay to the option writer (seller).

The intrinsic value of a call option is $\max(S_t - K, 0)$ and that of the put option is $\max(K - S_t, 0)$ for $0 < t < T$. This value represents the profit and loss (*P&L*) we can make by immediately exercising the option. The time value of a call is the difference between the price of the call and its intrinsic value. The time value of an option decreases as the time approaches expiration. The European options do not have time value because they can only be exercised at maturity, at which the time value of the option becomes zero.

The sum of an option intrinsic and time values is the total value of an option. The intrinsic value is the possible profit resulting from selling the option at the current time and does not take a negative value. If the current value of the underlying asset is lower than the strike price the intrinsic value of the call vanishes. For instance, if the premium of a stock call option is $5.5 and the price of the stock is $100 with a strike price of $97, the intrinsic value is $3 and the time value is $2.5. When an option is in-the-money (ITM), the intrinsic value is non-zero. When the strike price is the same as the spot price, the option is at-the-money (ATM) and the intrinsic is zero. Otherwise, the option is out-of-the-money (OTM) when the underlying asset is priced cheaper than the call option's strike price.

Although options have a reputation for being more risky investments that only expert traders or financial institution can understand, they can be useful to the individual investor. Options can provide several key advantages as listed below:

- *Cost Efficiency*: Options have great leveraging power. As such, we can obtain an option position that will mimic a stock position almost identically, but at a huge cost savings. For instance, in order to buy 100 shares of a \$100 stock, we must pay out \$10,000. However, if we were to buy one \$20 call (with each contract representing 100 shares), the total outlay would be only \$2,000. We would then have an additional \$8,000 to use at our discretion. Of course, it is not quite as simple as that. We have to pick the right call option to purchase in order to mimic the stock position properly. However, this strategy, known as stock replacement, is not only viable but also practical and cost efficient.
- *Less Risk*: People usually believe that buying options is more risky than owning equities, but there are also times when options can be used to reduce risk. It really depends on how we use them. Options can be less risky because they require less financial commitment than equities, and they can also be less risky due to their relative imperviousness to the potentially catastrophic effects of gap openings. Options are the most dependable form of hedge, which makes them safer than stocks. When we purchase stocks, a stop-loss-order is frequently placed to protect the position. The stop order is designed to stop losses below a predetermined price. The problem with these orders lies in the nature of the order itself. It is still possible for a considerable loss if the stock has a sudden drop because our order will become a market order when the price drops below the predetermined price level. Had we purchased a put option for protection, we would not have had to suffer the catastrophic loss. Unlike stop-loss orders, options do not shut down when the market closes. They give us insurance 24 hours a day, seven days a week. This is something that stop orders cannot do. This is why options are considered a dependable form of hedging.
- *Possible Higher Returns*: It is easy to figure out that if we spend much less money and make almost the same profit, we will have a higher percentage return. When they pay off, that is what options typically offer to us.

In the following sections, I will show you how to price options.

# Pricing European Options

The price, or cost, of an option is called premium, which is non-refundable whether or not the option is exercised. We pay this premium to the seller in exchange for the right granted by the option. Premiums are priced per share. For example, the premium on a GOOG call option with a strike price of \$800 might be quoted as \$3.4. Since equity option contracts are based on 100 stock shares, this particular contract would cost the buyer $\$3.4\times100$, or \$340 dollars. While supply and demand ultimately determine the option premium, other factors, such as the strike price, interest rate, and time to maturity, do play a role. We can apply these factors to mathematical models to help determine what an option should be worth.

## Black-Scholes Model

The Black-Scholes model is a partial differential equation that governs the price evolution of a European call or put option. For a European option on an underlying stock paying no dividends, the equation is:

$$dS = \mu S dt + \sigma S dz$$

where $\mu$ is the expected instantaneous rate of return on the underlying asset, $\sigma$ is the instantaneous volatility of the rate of return, and $dz$ is a Wiener process. You can find the derivation of the above formula from various textbooks, such as Hull's *Options, Futures, and Other Derivatives*. I will omit the derivation here.

Once the Black-Scholes equation with boundary and terminal conditions is derived for a derivative, we can solve it numerically using standard methods of numerical analysis, such as the finite-difference or Monte Carlo method. In certain cases, it is possible to solve for an exact formula, such as in the case of a European option, which was solved analytically by Black and Scholes. Letting $c$ and $p$ denote the price of European call and put options, respectively, the formula states that

$$c = SN(d_1) - Ke^{-rT}N(d_2)$$

$$p = Ke^{rT}N(-d_2) - SN(-d_1)$$

$$d_1 = \frac{\ln\left(\frac{S}{K}\right) + \left(r + \frac{\sigma^2}{2}\right)T}{\sigma\sqrt{T}}$$

$$d_2 = \frac{\ln\left(\frac{S}{K}\right) + \left(r - \frac{\sigma^2}{2}\right)T}{\sigma\sqrt{T}} = d_1 - \sigma\sqrt{T}$$

where $S$ is the stock price, $K$ the strike price, $r$ the risk-free interest rate, $T$ the time to expiration in years, $\sigma$ the volatility of the relative price change of the underlying stock price, and $N(x)$ the cumulative normal distribution function. The cumulative normal distribution function is given by the integral:

$$N(x) = \frac{1}{\sqrt{2\pi}}\int_{-\infty}^{x} e^{-z^2/2}dz$$

This integral has no analytic solution, so we need to solve it numerically.

## Generalized Black-Scholes Model

We can easily generalize the Black-Scholes model by incorporating a cost-of-carry rate $b$. This model can be used to price European options on stocks, stocks paying a continuous dividend yield, options on futures contracts, and currency options. Here are solutions to this generalized model:

$$c = Se^{(b-r)T}N(d_1) - Ke^{-rT}N(d_2)$$

$$p = Ke^{-rT}N(-d_2) - Se^{(b-r)T}N(-d_1)$$

$$d_1 = \frac{\ln\left(\frac{S}{K}\right) + \left(b + \frac{\sigma^2}{2}\right)T}{\sigma\sqrt{T}}$$

$$d_2 = d_1 - \sigma\sqrt{T}$$

The generalized model will reduce to different models depending how we choose the parameter $b$:

- $b = r$: gives the standard Black-Scholes (1973) stock option model.
- $b = r - q$: gives the Merton (1973) stock option model with continuous dividend yield $q$.
- $b = 0$: gives the Black (1976) futures option model.

- $b = 0$ and $r = 0$: gives the Asay (1982) margined futures option model.
- $b = r - r_f$: gives the Garman and Kohlhagen (1983) currency option model, where $r_f$ is the risk-free rate of the foreign currency.

## Implementation

Even though we can easily find R packages for option pricing, I believe we should at least implement a simple analytic version for vanilla European options. In this section, we will implement the Generalized Black-Scholes model for European vanilla options. Add a new file named *pricingHelper.R* to the subdirectory "[R working directory]/R/". Add the following helper functions to this file:

```
blackScholes <- function(optionType = c("c", "p"), spot = 100, strike = 100,
                         rate = 0.1, carry = 0.04, maturity = 1, vol = 0.3){
  sqrtMaturity <- sqrt(maturity)
  d1 <- log(spot / strike) + (carry + vol * vol * 0.5) * maturity
  d1 <- d1/(vol * sqrtMaturity)
  d2 <- d1 - vol * sqrtMaturity
  optionType <- tolower(optionType)
  option <- NULL
  if(optionType == "p" || optionType == "put"){
    option <- strike * CumNorm(-d2) * exp(-rate * maturity) -
      spot * CumNorm(-d1) * exp((carry - rate) * maturity)
  } else {
    option <- spot * CumNorm(d1) * exp((carry - rate)*maturity) -
      strike * CumNorm(d2) * exp(-rate * maturity);
  }
  return(option)
}

cumNorm <- function(x){
  if(x < 0) return(1-cumNorm(-x))
  pi2 <- 0.39894228
  k <- 1/(1 + 0.2316419 * x)
  cn <- 1 - pi2 * exp(-0.5 * x * x) * ((((1.330274429 * k - 1.821255978) * k
        + 1.781477937) * k - 0.356563782) * k + 0.319381530) * k;
  return(cn)
}

normDensity <- function(x){
  return(exp(-0.5 * x * x)/sqrt(2 * pi))
}
```

The *blackScholes* function returns the call price if the *optionType* parameter is set equal to "*c*" or the put price when set equal to "*p*". The *cumNorm* function implements one of the approximations to the cumulative normal distribution function and the *normDensity* function returns the value of the standard normal density function, which will be used later.

Now, I will use an example to illustrate how to calculate the prices for European options. Let us use the default input parameters: *spot* = 100, *strike* = 100, *rate* = 0.1, *carry* = 0.04, *vol* = 0.3, and *maturity* = 1. We can then calculate the option prices using the following commands:

```
> source("./R/pricingHelper.R")
> call = blackScholes(optionType = "c")
> call
```

```
[1] 12.95233
> put <- blackScholes(optionType = "p")
> put
[1] 9.259623
```

The *blackScholes* function also allows any one of the numerical input parameters to be a vector or sequence. A result vector will be returned and each element corresponds to an evaluation under a given set of parameters. For example, we can calculate the option prices for the following maturities:

```
> maturities <- seq(0.1, 1, 0.1)
```

We can then use these maturities to calculate the price for both call and put options:

```
> source("./R/pricingHelper.R")
> call <- blackScholes(optionType = "c", maturity = maturities)
> put <- blackScholes(optionType = "p", maturity = maturities)
> df <- data.frame(Maturity = maturities, Call = call, Put = put); df
   Maturity      Call      Put
1       0.1  3.954889 3.558076
2       0.2  5.666508 4.879204
3       0.3  6.995539 5.823989
4       0.4  8.121013 6.571386
5       0.5  9.112912 7.191301
6       0.6 10.007453 7.719877
7       0.7 10.826353 8.178756
8       0.8 11.583895 8.582151
9       0.9 12.290099 8.940007
10      1.0 12.952334 9.259623
```

The above results show the time effect (time to expiration or maturity) on both European ATM (at-the-money) call and put options: the options will worth less and less when time approaches expiration date.

Please note that even though the *blackScholes* function can return results for more than one numerical input parameters to be a vector or sequence, but the returned results may contains errors. We need to perform some special vectorization treatment to the function in order to obtain correct results when there are more than one input vector parameters. I will not discuss the code vectorization for the *blackScholes* function further in this book.

## Black-Scholes Greeks

In quantitative finance, the Greeks are the quantities representing the partial derivatives of the generalized Black-Scholes formula introduced in preceding sections. The Greeks are a measure of the sensitivity of the option price to a small change in a parameter of the formula. The name is used because the most of these sensitivities are denoted by Greek letters. Sometimes, we also call these Greeks the risk sensitivities, risk measure, or hedge parameters.

### *Delta*

Delta measures the rate of change of the option price with respect to the underlying asset's price.

$$\Delta_{call} = \frac{\partial c}{\partial S} = e^{(b-r)T} N(d_1) > 0$$

$$\Delta_{put} = \frac{\partial p}{\partial S} = e^{(b-r)T}[N(d_1) - 1] < 0$$

For example, consider a stock option with 6 months to expiration. The stock price is 100, the strike price = 110, the risk-free interest rate is 0.1 per year, the continuous dividend yield is 0.06, and the volatility is 0.3. Then we obtain $c = 5.2515$, and $\Delta_{call} = 0.3898$, $p = 12.8422$, and $\Delta_{put} = -0.5806$.

Delta measures the expected price change of the option given a $1 change in the underlying asset, and can be used in evaluating buying and selling opportunities. Call options have positive deltas with a range of (0, 1) and puts have negative deltas with a range of $(-1, 0)$. For example, a call option has a spot price at $45.2 and has a delta of 0.4. If the underlying stock goes up to 46.2, the option should increase by $0.4. Delta also gives a measure of the probability that an option will expire in the money. In the above example, the call option has a 40% probability of expiring in the money.

Delta can be used to evaluate alternatives when buying options. At-the-money options have deltas of roughly 0.5, meaning that the options have a 50% chance of going up or down. Deep in-the-money options have very high deltas (~ 1), indicating that they will essentially trade dollar for dollar with the stock. Some traders use these as stock substitutes, though there are clearly different risks involved. On the other hand, deep out-of-the-money options have very low deltas (~ 0) and therefore change very little with a $1 move in the underlying stock. Taking into account for commissions and bid/ask spread, low delta options may not make a profit even despite large moves in the underlying. Thus, comparing the delta to the options price across different strikes is one way of measuring the potential returns on a trade.

I have implemented a function named *blackScholesDelta* in the *pricingHelper.R* file to calculate the delta. Here is the code for this function:

```
blackScholesDelta <- function(optionType = c("c", "p"), spot = 100, strike = 100,
                              rate = 0.1, carry = 0.04, maturity = 1, vol = 0.3){
  sqrtMaturity <- sqrt(maturity)
  d1 <- log(spot / strike) + (carry + vol * vol * 0.5) * maturity
  d1 <- d1 /(vol * sqrtMaturity)
  d2 <- d1 - vol * sqrtMaturity
  optionType <- tolower(optionType)
  if (optionType == "p" || optionType == "put")
    option <- (cumNorm(d1) - 1.0) * exp((carry - rate) * maturity)
  else
    option <- cumNorm(d1) * exp((carry - rate) * maturity)
  return(option)
}
```

Now, I will use an example to illustrate how to calculate the delta for European options. Let us use the default input parameters: spot = 100, strike = 100, rate = 0.1, carry = 0.04, and vol = 0.3 to calculate the option delta for different maturities:

```
> source("./R/pricingHelper.R")
> maturities <- seq(0.1, 1, 0.1)
> callDelta <- blackScholesDelta(optionType = "c", maturity = maturities)
> putDelta  <- blackScholesDelta(optionType = "p", maturity = maturities)
> delta <- data.frame(Maturity = maturities, CallDelta = callDelta,
                      PutDelta = putDelta)

> delta
   Maturity CallDelta   PutDelta
1       0.1 0.5324921 -0.4615258
2       0.2 0.5438498 -0.4442219
3       0.3 0.5516440 -0.4305170
```

```
4        0.4 0.5575646 -0.4187211
5        0.5 0.5622716 -0.4081739
6        0.6 0.5661065 -0.3985338
7        0.7 0.5692737 -0.3895961
8        0.8 0.5719074 -0.3812263
9        0.9 0.5741019 -0.3733302
10       1.0 0.5759260 -0.3658385
```

Note that the delta is positive for the call option, white it is negative for the put option.

## *Gamma*

Gamma is the delta's sensitivity to small changes in the underlying asset's price. Gamma is identical for call and put options:

$$\Gamma_{call,put} = \frac{\partial^2 c}{\partial S^2} = \frac{\partial^2 p}{\partial S^2} = \frac{n(d_1)e^{(b-r)T}}{S\sigma\sqrt{T}} > 0$$

where $n(x)$ is the standard normal density:

$$n(x) = \frac{1}{2\pi}e^{-x^2/2}$$

Gamma measures the change in delta for a \$1 change in the price of the underlying asset price. This is really the rate of change of the option price, and is most closely watched by those who sell options, as the gamma gives an indication of potential risk exposure if the stock price moves against the position.

For example, consider a stock option with 6 months to expiration. The stock price is 100, the strike price = 110, the risk-free interest rate is 0.1 per year, the continuous dividend yield is 0.06, and the volatility is 0.3. Then we obtain $c = 5.2515$, and $\Gamma_{call} = 0.01769$, $p = 12.8422$, and $\Gamma_{put} = 0.01769$.

In the *pricingHelper.R* file, I have implemented a function named *blackScholesGamma* to calculate gamma. Here is the code for this function:

```
blackScholesGamma <- function(spot =100, strike = 100, rate = 0.1, carry = 0.04,
                              maturity = 1, vol = 0.3){
  sqrtMaturity <- sqrt(maturity)
  d1 <- log(spot / strike) + (carry + vol * vol * 0.5) * maturity
  d1 <- d1 /(vol * sqrtMaturity)
  option <- normDensity(d1) * exp((carry - rate) * maturity)/
            (spot * vol * sqrtMaturity)
  return(option)
}
```

We can use the above method to calculate gamma for a European option. For example, we can use the default input parameters: spot = 100, strike = 100, rate = 0.1, carry = 0.04, and vol = 0.3 to calculate the option Gamma for different maturities:

```
> source("./R/pricingHelper.R")
> maturities <- seq(0.1, 1, 0.1)
> gamma <- blackScholesGamma(maturity = maturities)
> gamma <- data.frame(Maturity = maturities, Gamma = gamma)
> gamma
   Maturity      Gamma
1       0.1 0.04163320
2       0.2 0.02914579
```

```
3        0.3 0.02356032
4        0.4 0.02020054
5        0.5 0.01788788
6        0.6 0.01616662
7        0.7 0.01481825
8        0.8 0.01372309
9        0.9 0.01280934
10       1.0 0.01203093
```

## *Theta*

Theta is the option's sensitivity to a small change in time to expiration, i.e., the time decay. At time approaches expiration, we can express theta as minus the partial derivative with respect to time:

$$\Theta_{call} = -\frac{\partial c}{\partial T} = -\frac{Se^{(b-r)T}n(d_1)\sigma}{2\sqrt{T}} - (b-r)Se^{(b-r)T}N(d_1) - rKe^{-rT}N(d_2)$$

$$\Theta_{put} = -\frac{\partial p}{\partial T} = -\frac{Se^{(b-r)T}n(d_1)\sigma}{2\sqrt{T}} + (b-r)Se^{(b-r)T}N(-d_1) + rKe^{-rT}N(-d_2)$$

For example, consider a stock option with 6 months to expiration. The stock price is 100, the strike price = 110, the risk-free interest rate is 0.1 per year, the continuous dividend yield is 0.06, and the volatility is 0.3. Then we obtain $c = 5.2515$, and $\Theta_{call} = -8.9963$, $p = 12.8422$, and $\Theta_{put} = -4.3554$. Thus, theta for a one-day time decay is, call: $-8.9963/365 = -0.02465$, put: $-4.3554/365 = -0.01193$.

In the *pricingHelper.R* file, I have implemented a function named *blackScholesTheta* to calculate theta. Here is the code for this function:

```
blackScholesTheta <- function(optionType = c("c","p"), spot =100, strike = 100,
                              rate = 0.1, carry = 0.04, maturity = 1, vol = 0.3){
  sqrtMaturity = sqrt(maturity)
  d1 <- log(spot / strike) + (carry + vol * vol * 0.5) * maturity
  d1 <- d1/(vol * sqrtMaturity)
  d2 <- d1 - vol * sqrtMaturity
  optionType <- tolower(optionType)
  if (optionType == "p" || optionType == "put"){
    p1 <- spot * exp((carry - rate) * maturity) * normDensity(d1) * vol *
          0.5 / sqrtMaturity
    p2 <- (carry - rate) * spot * exp((carry - rate) * maturity) * cumNorm(-d1)
    p3 <- rate * strike * exp(-rate * maturity) * cumNorm(-d2)
    option = p2 + p3 - p1
  } else {
    c1 <- spot * exp((carry - rate) * maturity) * normDensity(d1) *
          vol * 0.5 / sqrtMaturity
    c2 <- (carry - rate) * spot * exp((carry - rate) * maturity) * cumNorm(d1)
    c3 <- rate * strike * exp(-rate * maturity) * cumNorm(d2)
    option = -c1 - c2 - c3
  }
  return(option)
}
```

Now, I will use an example to illustrate how to calculate the theta for European options. Let us use the default input parameters: spot = 100, strike = 100, rate = 0.1, carry = 0.04, and vol = 0.3 to calculate the option theta for different maturities:

```
> source("./R/pricingHelper.R")
> maturities <- seq(0.1, 1, 0.1)
> ctheta <- blackScholesTheta(optionType = "c", maturity = maturities)
> ptheta <- blackScholesTheta(optionType = "p", maturity = maturities)
> theta <- data.frame(Maturity = maturities, CallTheta = ctheta, PutTheta = ptheta)
> theta
   Maturity  CallTheta   PutTheta
1       0.1 -20.469421 -16.533031
2       0.2 -14.724355 -10.850798
3       0.3 -12.109168  -8.297679
4       0.4 -10.508399  -6.758218
5       0.5  -9.387342  -5.697721
6       0.6  -8.538661  -4.908858
7       0.7  -7.862673  -4.291953
8       0.8  -7.304632  -3.792271
9       0.9  -6.831601  -3.376882
10      1.0  -6.422387  -3.024600
```

## *Rho*

Rho is the option's sensitivity to small changes in the risk-free interest rate:

$$\rho_{call} = \frac{\partial c}{\partial r} = TKe^{-rT}N(d_2) > 0$$

$$\rho_{put} = \frac{\partial p}{\partial r} = -TKe^{-rT}N(-d_2) < 0$$

In the case of an option on a futures contract, we have carry ($b$) = 0. The rho will be given by the following formulas:

$$\rho_{call} = -Tc < 0, \;\; \rho_{put} = -Tp < 0$$

When interest rates rise, call prices will rise and put prices will fall. Just the reverse occurs when interest rates fall. Rho is a risk measure that simply tells us by how much call and put prices changes as a result of the rise or fall in interest rates. The rho values for ITM options will be largest due to arbitrary activity with such options. We are willing to pay more for call options and less for put options when interest rates rise because of the interest earnings potential on short sales made to hedge long calls and opportunity costs of not earning that interest.

In the *pricingHelper.R* file, I have implemented a function named *blackScholesRho* to calculate rho. Here is the code for this method:

```
blackScholesRho <- function(optionType = c("c", "p"), spot = 100, strike = 100,
                            rate = 0.1, carry = 0.04, maturity = 1, vol = 0.3){
  sqrtMaturity <- sqrt(maturity)
  d1 <- log(spot / strike) + (carry + vol * vol * 0.5) * maturity
  d1 <- d1 /(vol * sqrtMaturity)
  d2 = d1 - vol * sqrtMaturity
  optionType <- tolower(optionType)
  if (optionType == "p" || optionType == "put"){
    if (carry != 0) option = -maturity * strike * exp(-rate * maturity) *
                             cumNorm(-d2)
    else option <- -maturity * blackScholes("p", spot, strike, rate, 0,
                                              maturity, vol)
```

```
  } else {
    if (carry != 0) option <- maturity * strike * exp(-rate * maturity) *
                              cumNorm(d2)
    else  option <- -maturity * blackScholes("c", spot, strike, rate, 0,
                                             maturity, vol)
  }
  return(option)
}
```

Now, I will use an example to illustrate how to calculate the rho for European options. Let us use the default input parameters: spot = 100, strike = 100, rate = 0.1, carry = 0.04, and vol = 0.3 to calculate the option Rho for different maturities:

```
> source("./R/pricingHelper.R")
> maturities <- seq(0.1, 1, 0.1)
> crho <- blackScholesRho(optionType = "c", maturity = maturities)
> prho <- blackScholesRho(optionType = "p", maturity = maturities)
> rho <- data.frame(Maturity = maturities, CallRho = crho, PutRho = prho); rho
   Maturity   CallRho     PutRho
1       0.1  4.929432  -4.971066
2       0.2  9.743694  -9.860280
3       0.3 14.450658 -14.662708
4       0.4 19.054178 -19.377400
5       0.5 23.557125 -24.004346
6       0.6 27.961919 -28.543953
7       0.7 32.270711 -32.996856
8       0.8 36.485480 -37.363828
9       0.9 40.608079 -41.645728
10      1.0 44.640266 -45.843476
```

## *Vega*

Vega is the option's sensitivity to a small change in the volatility of the underlying asset. Vega is the same for call and put options:

$$Vega_{call,put} = \frac{\partial^2 c}{\partial \sigma^2} = \frac{\partial^2 p}{\partial \sigma^2} = Se^{(b-r)T} n(d_1)\sqrt{T} > 0$$

When any position is taken on options, not only is there risk from changes in the underlying asset but there is risk from changes in implied volatility. Vega is the measure of that risk.

In the *pricingHelper.R* file, I have implemented a function named *blackScholesVega* to calculate Vega. Here is the code for this function:

```
blackScholesVega <- function(spot = 100, strike = 100, rate = 0.1, carry = 0.04,
                             maturity = 1, vol = 0.3){
  sqrtMaturity <- sqrt(maturity)
  d1 <- log(spot / strike) + (carry + vol * vol * 0.5) * maturity
  d1 <- d1/(vol * sqrtMaturity)
  option = spot * normDensity(d1) * exp((carry - rate) * maturity) * sqrtMaturity
  return(option)
}
```

Now, I will use an example to illustrate how to calculate the Vega for European options. Let us use the default input parameters: spot = 100, strike = 100, rate = 0.1, carry = 0.04, and vol = 0.3 to calculate the option Vega for different maturities:

```
> source("./R/pricingHelper.R")
> maturities <- seq(0.1, 1, 0.1)
> vega <- blackScholesVega(maturity = maturities)
> vega <- data.frame(Maturity = maturities, Vega = vega)
> vega
   Maturity     Vega
1       0.1 12.48996
2       0.2 17.48748
3       0.3 21.20429
4       0.4 24.24064
5       0.5 26.83182
6       0.6 29.09992
7       0.7 31.11833
8       0.8 32.93542
9       0.9 34.58522
10      1.0 36.09278
```

# Implied Volatility

For a given option price, we can also calculate the implied volatility based on the Black-Scholes model using various numerical methods, such as the Newton-Raphson and Bisection methods. The Newton-Raphson method requires knowledge of the partial derivative of the option pricing formula with respect to volatility (Vega) when searching for the implied volatility. For some options, such as American and exotic options, Vega is not known analytically. The bisection method can be used to estimate implied volatility when Vera is unknown. In this section, I will implement a bisection method to calculate implied volatility.

In the *pricingHelper.R* file, I have implemented a function named *blackScholesImpliedVol* to calculate the implied volatility for a given option price. Here is the code for this function:

```
blackScholesImpliedVol <- function(optionType = c("c", "p"), spot = 100,
  strike = 100, rate = 0.1, carry = 0.04, maturity = 1, price = 10){
  low <- 0.0
  high <- 4.0
  sqrtMaturity <- sqrt(maturity)
  if (blackScholes(optionType, spot, strike, rate, carry, maturity, high) < price){
    vol <- high
  } else if (blackScholes(optionType, spot, strike, rate, carry, maturity, low) >
             price){
    vol <- low
  } else{
    vol <- (high + low) * 0.5;
    count <- 1;
    while (vol - low > 0.0001 && count < 100000)
    {
      if (blackScholes(optionType, spot, strike, rate, carry, maturity, vol) <
          price){
        low <- vol
      } else if (blackScholes(optionType, spot, strike, rate, carry, maturity, vol)
               > price){
        high <- vol
      }
      vol <- (high + low) * 0.5
      count <- count + 1
```

```
    }
  }
  return(vol)
}
```

Note that unlike other functions, the *blackScholesImpliedVol* function is not vectorized automatically because it involves iterations and comparing a scalar value of price. Therefore, this function cannot take vector or matrix inputs. For illustration purpose, I will not try to vectorize this function. Here, I will use an example to illustrate how to use this function to calculate the implied volatility. Suppose we fix the following parameters: spot = 10, strike = 10.5, rate = 0.1, carry = 0.06. We can then use the following function to calculate the implied volatilities:

```
volTest <- function(){
  mat <-  seq(0.1, 1, 0.1)
  price <- seq(0.15, 0.6, 0.05)
  v <- sapply(1:length(mat), function(i){c(
            blackScholesImpliedVol(optionType = "c", spot = 10, strike = 10.5,
            rate = 0.1, carry = 0.06, maturity = mat[i], price = price[i]),
            blackScholesImpliedVol(optionType = "p", spot = 10, strike = 10.5,
            rate = 0.1,carry = 0.06, maturity = mat[i], price = price[i]))
  })
  vol <- data.frame(Maturity = mat, Price = price, CallVol = v[1, ],
                    PutVol = v[2, ])
  return(vol)
}

> source("./R/pricingHelper.R")
> vol <- volTest()
> vol
   Maturity Price   CallVol     PutVol
1       0.1  0.15 0.2507935 0.00000000
2       0.2  0.20 0.1972046 0.00000000
3       0.3  0.25 0.1755981 0.00000000
4       0.4  0.30 0.1638794 0.05731201
5       0.5  0.35 0.1565552 0.08807373
6       0.6  0.40 0.1516724 0.10980225
7       0.7  0.45 0.1482544 0.12786865
8       0.8  0.50 0.1458130 0.14361572
9       0.9  0.55 0.1442261 0.15802002
10      1.0  0.60 0.1430054 0.17132568
```

We can create 3D graph for implied volatility as a function of strike and maturity. Here, we will use *sapply* (corresponding to for loop) to create such a volatility matrix manually. Add a new function named *volTest3d* to the *pricingHelper.R* file. Here is the code for this function:

```
volTest3d <- function(optionType = c("c", "p"), maturity, strike){
  vol <- sapply(1:length(strike), function(j)
          sapply(1:length(maturity), function(i)
            blackScholesImpliedVol(optionType = optionType, spot = 10, rate = 0.1,
              carry = 0.06, price = 0.5, maturity = maturity[i], strike = strike[j])
            ))
  return(vol)
}
```

Here, inside this function, we use the fixed parameters: spot = 10, rate = 0.1, carry = 0.06, and price = 0.5, and then create a 2D grid with the X-axis for the times to expiration and the Y-axis for the strike price. This function creates a volatility surface as a function of both the time to maturity and the strike for a specified option price.

Now, we can create the 3D plot for the implied volatility using the *plot3Drgl* package:

```
> library(plot3Drgl)
> source("./R/pricingHelper.R")
> x <- seq(0.1, 1, length = 30)
> y <- seq(9.5, 10.5, length = 30)

# create 3D graph for the call option:
> cvol <- volTest3d(optionType = "c", x, y)
> persp3Drgl(x = x, y = y, z = cvol, border = "black", bty = "b2", ticktype =
          "detailed", xlab = "Maturity", ylab = "Strike", zlab = "cVol")

# create 3D graph for the put option:
> pvol <- volTest3d(optionType = "p", x, y)
> persp3Drgl(x = x, y = y, z = pvol, border="black", bty = "b2", ticktype =
            "detailed", xlab = "Maturity", ylab = "Strike", zlab = "pVol")
```

The above code produces the output shown in Figure 5-8.

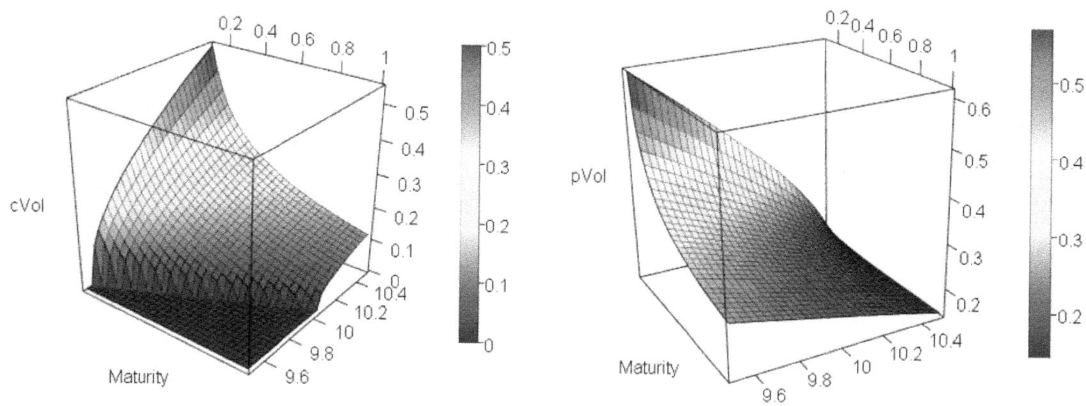


*Figure 5-1. Implied volatility surface for a European call (left) or put (right) option.*

# Pricing American Options

Unlike the European options, American options can be exercised at any time up to its maturity. This flexibility complicates the valuation of American options relative to their European counterparts. In general, American options do not have analytical solutions. However, some excellent closed-form approximations have been proposed. The approximations have become especially popular because they execute quickly compared to numerical methods. In this section, I will present one of such approximations, the Barone-Adesi and Whaley (BAW) method.

# BAW Approximation

The BAW method on an underlying asset with carry rate $b$. When $b \geq r$, the American call price is equal to the European call price and can then be found by using the generalized Black-Scholes formula. The model is fast and accurate for most practical input values. The BAW approximation for American call options can be written in the form:

$$c(S,K,T) = \begin{cases} c_{GBS}(S,K,T) + A_2(S/S^*)^{q_2} & \text{for } S < S^* \\ S - K & \text{for } S \geq S^* \end{cases}$$

Where $c_{GBS}(S,K,T)$ is the generalized Black-Scholes call formula, and

$$A_2 = \frac{S^*}{q_2}\{1 - e^{(b-r)T} N[d_1(S^*)]\}$$

$$d_1(S) = \frac{\ln\left(\frac{S}{K}\right) + \left(b + \frac{\sigma^2}{2}\right)T}{\sigma\sqrt{T}}$$

$$q_2 = \frac{-(N-1) + \sqrt{(N-1)^2 + 4M/L}}{2}$$

$$M = \frac{2r}{\sigma^2}, \quad N = \frac{2b}{\sigma^2}, \quad L = 1 - e^{-rT}$$

For American put, we have:

$$p(S,K,T) = \begin{cases} p_{GBS}(S,K,T) + A_1(S/S^{**})^{q_1} & \text{for } S > S^{**} \\ K - S & \text{for } S \leq S^{**} \end{cases}$$

Where $p_{GBS}(S,K,T)$ is the generalized Black-Scholes call formula, and

$$A_1 = -\frac{S^{**}}{q_1}\{1 - e^{(b-r)T} N[-d_1(S^{**})]\}$$

$$q_1 = \frac{-(N-1) - \sqrt{(N-1)^2 + 4M/L}}{2}$$

where $S^*$ ($S^{**}$) is the critical commodity price for the call (put) option that satisfies

$$S^* - K = c(S^*,K,T) + \{1 - e^{(b-r)T} N[d_1(S^*)]\}\frac{S^*}{q_2}$$

$$K - S^{**} = p(S^{**},K,T) - \{1 - e^{(b-r)T} N[-d_1(S^{**})]\}\frac{S^{**}}{q_1}$$

The above equations for $S^*$ and $S^{**}$ can be solved by using the Newton-Raphson algorithm. Calculating the price for American options is straightforward as long as $S^*$ and $S^{**}$ are known.

# Implementation

The *pricingHelper.R* file contains the implementation of the BAW approximation for American options. Here is the corresponding code listing:

```
americanBAW <- function(optionType = c("c", "p"), spot = 100, strike = 100 ,
```

```
                        rate = 0.1, divYield = 0.1, maturity = 1, vol = 0.3){
  carry <- rate - divYield;
  optionType <- tolower(optionType)
  if (optionType == "p" || optionType == "put")
    return(americanPutBAW(spot, strike, rate, carry, maturity, vol))
  else
    return(americanCallBAW(spot, strike, rate, carry, maturity, vol))
}

americanCallBAW <- function(spot, strike, rate, carry, maturity, vol)
{
  option <- 0
  sqrtMaturity <- sqrt(maturity)
  if (carry >= rate){
    option <- blackScholes("c", spot, strike, rate, carry, maturity, vol)
  } else{
    sk <- americanCallNewtonRaphson(strike, rate, carry, maturity, vol)
    n <- 2.0 * carry / vol / vol
    m <- 2.0 * rate / vol / vol
    k <- 1.0 - exp(-rate * maturity)
    d1 <- log(sk / strike) + (carry + vol * vol * 0.5) * maturity
    d1 <- d1/(vol * sqrtMaturity)
    q2 <- (sqrt((n - 1.0) * (n - 1.0) + 4.0 * m / k) - (n - 1.0)) * 0.5
    a2 <- (sk / q2) * (1.0 - exp((carry - rate) * maturity) * cumNorm(d1))
    if (spot < sk){
      option <- blackScholes("c", spot, strike, rate, carry, maturity, vol) +
                a2 * (spot / sk)^q2
    }  else{
      option <- spot - strike;
    }
  }
  return(option)
}

americanCallNewtonRaphson <- function(strike, rate, carry, maturity, vol )
{
  option <- 0
  sqrtMaturity <- sqrt(maturity)
  n <- 2.0 * carry / vol / vol
  m <- 2.0 * rate / vol / vol
  q2u <- 0.5 * (sqrt((n - 1.0) * (n - 1.0) + 4.0 * m) - (n - 1.0))
  su <- strike / (1.0 - 1.0 / q2u)
  h2 <- (carry * maturity + 2.0 * vol * sqrt(maturity)) * strike / (su - strike)
  si <- strike + (su - strike) * (1.0 - exp(h2))
  k <- 1.0 - exp(-rate * maturity)
  d1 <- log(si / strike) + (carry + vol * vol * 0.5) * maturity
  d1 <- d1/(vol * sqrtMaturity)
  q2 <- 0.5 * (sqrt((n - 1.0) * (n - 1.0) + 4.0 * m / k) - (n - 1.0))
  lhs <- si - strike
  rhs <- blackScholes("c", si, strike, rate, carry, maturity, vol) +
        (1.0 - exp((carry - rate) * maturity) * cumNorm(d1)) * si / q2
  bi <- exp((carry - rate) * maturity) * cumNorm(d1) * (1.0 - 1.0 / q2) +
        (1.0 - exp((carry - rate) * maturity) *
        normDensity(d1) / (vol * sqrtMaturity)) / q2
  while (abs((lhs - rhs) / strike) > 0.000001){
```

```
    si <- (strike + rhs - bi * si) / (1.0 - bi)
    d1 <- log(si / strike) + (carry + vol * vol * 0.5) * maturity
    d1 <- d1/(vol * sqrtMaturity)
    lhs <- si - strike
    rhs <- blackScholes("c", si, strike, rate, carry, maturity, vol) +
      (1.0 - exp((carry - rate) * maturity) * cumNorm(d1)) * si / q2;
    bi <- exp((carry - rate) * maturity) * cumNorm(d1) * (1.0 - 1.0 / q2) +
      (1.0 - exp((carry - rate) * maturity) * normDensity(d1) /
     (vol * sqrtMaturity)) / q2
  }
  option <- si
  return(option)
}

americanPutBAW <- function(spot, strike, rate, carry, maturity, vol)
{
  option <- 0
  sqrtMaturity <- sqrt(maturity)
  if (carry >= rate){
    option <- blackScholes("p", spot, strike, rate, carry, maturity, vol)
  } else{
    sk <- americanPutNewtonRaphson(strike, rate, carry, maturity, vol)
    n <- 2.0 * carry / vol / vol
    m <- 2.0 * rate / vol / vol
    k <- 1.0 - exp(-rate * maturity)
    d1 <- log(sk / strike) + (carry + vol * vol * 0.5) * maturity
    d1 <- d1/(vol * sqrtMaturity)
    q1 <- -(sqrt((n - 1.0) * (n - 1.0) + 4.0 * m / k) + (n - 1.0)) * 0.5
    a1 <- -(sk / q1) * (1.0 - exp((carry - rate) * maturity) * cumNorm(-d1))
    if (spot > sk){
      option <- blackScholes("p", spot, strike, rate, carry, maturity, vol) +
                a1 * (spot / sk)^q1
    } else{
      option <- strike - spot;
    }
  }
  return(option)
}

americanPutNewtonRaphson <- function(strike, rate, carry, maturity, vol){
  option = 0;
  sqrtMaturity <- sqrt(maturity)
  n <- 2.0 * carry / vol / vol
  m <- 2.0 * rate / vol / vol
  q1u <- -0.5 * (sqrt((n - 1.0) * (n - 1.0) + 4.0 * m) + (n - 1.0))
  su <- strike / (1.0 - 1.0 / q1u)
  h1 <- (carry * maturity - 2.0 * vol * sqrtMaturity) * strike/(strike - su)
  si <- su + (strike - su) * exp(h1)
  k <- 1.0 - exp(-rate * maturity)
  d1 <- log(si / strike) + (carry + vol * vol * 0.5) * maturity
  d1 <- d1/(vol * sqrtMaturity)
  q1 <- -0.5 * (sqrt((n - 1.0) * (n - 1.0) + 4.0 * m/k) + (n - 1.0))
  lhs <- strike - si
  rhs <- blackScholes("p", si, strike, rate, carry, maturity, vol) -
        (1.0 - exp((carry - rate) * maturity) * cumNorm(-d1)) * si / q1
```

```
  bi <- -exp((carry - rate) * maturity) * cumNorm(-d1)  * (1.0 - 1.0 / q1) -
        (1.0 + exp((carry - rate) * maturity) * normDensity(-d1) /
        (vol * sqrtMaturity)) / q1
  while (abs((lhs - rhs) / strike) > 0.000001){
    si <- (strike - rhs + bi * si) / (1.0 + bi)
    d1 <- log(si / strike) + (carry + vol * vol * 0.5) * maturity
    d1 <- d1/(vol * sqrtMaturity)
    lhs <- strike - si
    rhs <- blackScholes("p", si, strike, rate, carry, maturity, vol) -
          (1.0 - exp((carry - rate) * maturity) * cumNorm(-d1)) * si / q1
    bi <- -exp((carry - rate) * maturity) * cumNorm(-d1) * (1.0 - 1.0 / q1) -
          (1.0 + exp((carry - rate) * maturity) * normDensity(-d1) /
          (vol * sqrtMaturity)) / q1
  }
  option <- si
  return(option)
}
```

We can use the above *americanBAW* function to calculate the value of an American option using the BAW approximation. Note that this method takes the continuous dividend yield, instead of the carry, as the input parameter for easy comparison with the results in the literature. Both the functions, *americanCallNewtonRaphson* and *americanPutNewtonRaphson*, use a Newton-Raphson algorithm to solve for the critical commodity price for a call and a put, respectively. In our implementation, we do not pay special attention to the code vectorization. Therefore, we need to use the for loop or apply function to carry out the calculations when the input parameters are vectors or matrices.

## Applying BAW Approximation

In this section, I will use an example to illustrate how to price an American option using the BAW approximation presented in the preceding section. Add a new function named *americanOptionTest* to the *pricingHelper.R* file. Here is the code for this function:

```
americanOptionTest <- function(){
  oType <- c(rep("Call",18), rep("Put", 18))
  strike <- rep(100,36)
  spot <- rep(c(90,100,110),12)
  yield <- rep(0.1, 36)
  rate <- rep(0.1, 36)
  mat <- c(rep(0.1,9), rep(0.5,9), rep(0.1,9), rep(0.5,9))
  vol <- rep(c(rep(0.15,3), rep(0.25,3), rep(0.35,3)), 4)
  baw <- c(0.0206, 1.8771, 10.0089, 0.3159, 3.128, 10.3919, 0.9495, 4.3777, 11.1679,
           0.8208, 4.0842, 10.8087, 2.7437, 6.8015, 13.017, 5.0063, 9.5106, 15.5689,
           10,1.877, 0.041,10.2533, 3.1277, 0.4562, 10.8787,4.3777, 1.2402, 10.5595,
           4.0842, 1.0822, 12.4419, 6.8014, 3.3226, 14.6945, 9.5104, 5.8823)
  calc <- sapply(1:36, function(i)
          americanBAW(optionType = oType[i], spot = spot[i], strike = strike[i],
          rate = rate[i], divYield = yield[i], maturity = mat[i], vol = vol[i]))
  df <- data.frame(OptionType = oType, Strike = strike, Spot = spot,
                   DivYield = yield, Rate = rate, Maturity = mat, Vol = vol,
                   BAWValue = baw, Calculated = calc )
  return(df)
}
```

Here, we calculate the price for American call and put options for fixed strike = 100, dividend yield = 0.1, interest rate = 0.1, and varying the parameters of the spot, times to maturity, and volatility. The vector *baw* holds the results of the BAW approximation from the literature. We will make a direct comparison between our calculation and the results from the literature.

Running this example produces the following results:

```
> source("./R/pricingHelper.R")
> df <- americanOptionTest()
> df
   OptionType Strike Spot DivYield Rate Maturity  Vol BAWValue  Calculated
1        Call    100   90      0.1  0.1      0.1 0.15   0.0206  0.02063525
2        Call    100  100      0.1  0.1      0.1 0.15   1.8771  1.87693090
3        Call    100  110      0.1  0.1      0.1 0.15  10.0089 10.00607824
4        Call    100   90      0.1  0.1      0.1 0.25   0.3159  0.31590056
5        Call    100  100      0.1  0.1      0.1 0.25   3.1280  3.12769717
6        Call    100  110      0.1  0.1      0.1 0.25  10.3919 10.39013102
7        Call    100   90      0.1  0.1      0.1 0.35   0.9495  0.94946687
8        Call    100  100      0.1  0.1      0.1 0.35   4.3777  4.37768505
9        Call    100  110      0.1  0.1      0.1 0.35  11.1679 11.16785412
10       Call    100   90      0.1  0.1      0.5 0.15   0.8208  0.82081816
11       Call    100  100      0.1  0.1      0.5 0.15   4.0842  4.08413110
12       Call    100  110      0.1  0.1      0.5 0.15  10.8087 10.80852656
13       Call    100   90      0.1  0.1      0.5 0.25   2.7437  2.74360700
14       Call    100  100      0.1  0.1      0.5 0.25   6.8015  6.80135535
15       Call    100  110      0.1  0.1      0.5 0.25  13.0170 13.01674141
16       Call    100   90      0.1  0.1      0.5 0.35   5.0063  5.00616776
17       Call    100  100      0.1  0.1      0.5 0.35   9.5106  9.51031688
18       Call    100  110      0.1  0.1      0.5 0.35  15.5689 15.56843626
19        Put    100   90      0.1  0.1      0.1 0.15  10.0000 10.00000000
20        Put    100  100      0.1  0.1      0.1 0.15   1.8770  1.87693172
21        Put    100  110      0.1  0.1      0.1 0.15   0.0410  0.04099685
22        Put    100   90      0.1  0.1      0.1 0.25  10.2533 10.25300802
23        Put    100  100      0.1  0.1      0.1 0.25   3.1277  3.12769785
24        Put    100  110      0.1  0.1      0.1 0.25   0.4562  0.45618386
25        Put    100   90      0.1  0.1      0.1 0.35  10.8787 10.87850494
26        Put    100  100      0.1  0.1      0.1 0.35   4.3777  4.37768536
27        Put    100  110      0.1  0.1      0.1 0.35   1.2402  1.24020578
28        Put    100   90      0.1  0.1      0.5 0.15  10.5595 10.55920803
29        Put    100  100      0.1  0.1      0.5 0.15   4.0842  4.08412981
30        Put    100  110      0.1  0.1      0.5 0.15   1.0822  1.08219870
31        Put    100   90      0.1  0.1      0.5 0.25  12.4419 12.44164705
32        Put    100  100      0.1  0.1      0.5 0.25   6.8014  6.80135335
33        Put    100  110      0.1  0.1      0.5 0.25   3.3226  3.32258007
34        Put    100   90      0.1  0.1      0.5 0.35  14.6945 14.69432660
35        Put    100  100      0.1  0.1      0.5 0.35   9.5104  9.51031428
36        Put    100  110      0.1  0.1      0.5 0.35   5.8823  5.88219585
```

You can see from the above results that our calculated results are very close to those from literature. The small discrepancy may come from the accuracy control in solving for the critical commodity price using the Newton-Raphson algorithm.

# Pricing Barrier Options

We usually call the straight call or put options, such as European or American options, non-exotic or vanilla options. Whereas we consider the barrier options a type of exotic option because it is more complex than basic vanilla options. Their payoff depends on whether or not the underlying asset has reached or exceeded a predetermined price. A barrier option can be a knock-out, meaning it can expire worthless if the underlying exceeds a certain price, limiting profits for the holder but limiting losses for the writer. It can also be a knock-in, meaning it has no value until the underlying reaches a certain price. Barrier options are also considered a type of path-dependent option because their value fluctuates as the underlying's price changes during the option's contract term. In other words, a barrier option's payoff is based on the underlying asset's price path.

Barrier options are always cheaper than a similar option without barrier. For example, if we believe that GOOG will go up this year, but are willing to bet that it will not go above $850, then we can buy the barrier and pay less premium than the vanilla option.

## Standard Barrier Option Formulas

Here, we will discuss how to price the standard barrier options using the formulas provided in the literature (D. R. Rich, *Advances in Futures and Options Research*, 7, 267, 1994, and E. G. Haug's book *The complete Guide to Option Pricing Formulas*). The formulas for pricing the standard barrier options use the following common set of factors:

$$A = \phi S e^{(b-r)T} N(\phi x_1) - \phi K e^{-rT} N(\phi x_1 - \phi\sigma\sqrt{T})$$

$$B = \phi S e^{(b-r)T} N(\phi x_2) - \phi K e^{-rT} N(\phi x_2 - \phi\sigma\sqrt{T})$$

$$C = \phi S e^{(b-r)T} \left(\frac{H}{S}\right)^{2(\mu+1)} N(\eta y_1) - \phi K e^{-rT} \left(\frac{H}{S}\right)^{2\mu} N(\eta y_1 - \eta\sigma\sqrt{T})$$

$$D = \phi S e^{(b-r)T} \left(\frac{H}{S}\right)^{2(\mu+1)} N(\eta y_2) - \phi K e^{-rT} \left(\frac{H}{S}\right)^{2\mu} N(\eta y_2 - \eta\sigma\sqrt{T})$$

$$E = K e^{-rT} \left[N(\eta x_2 - \eta\sigma\sqrt{T}) - \left(\frac{H}{S}\right)^{2\mu} N(\eta y_2 - \eta\sigma\sqrt{T})\right]$$

$$F = K \left[\left(\frac{H}{S}\right)^{\mu+\lambda} N(\eta z) + \left(\frac{H}{S}\right)^{\mu-\lambda} N(\eta z - 2\eta\lambda\sigma\sqrt{T})\right]$$

$$x_1 = \frac{\ln\left(\frac{S}{K}\right)}{\sigma\sqrt{T}} + (1+\mu)\sigma\sqrt{T}, \quad x_2 = \frac{\ln\left(\frac{S}{H}\right)}{\sigma\sqrt{T}} + (1+\mu)\sigma\sqrt{T}$$

$$y_1 = \frac{\ln\left(\frac{H^2}{SK}\right)}{\sigma\sqrt{T}} + (1+\mu)\sigma\sqrt{T}, \quad y_2 = \frac{\ln\left(\frac{H}{S}\right)}{\sigma\sqrt{T}} + (1+\mu)\sigma\sqrt{T}$$

$$z = \frac{\ln\left(\frac{H}{S}\right)}{\sigma\sqrt{T}} + \lambda\sigma\sqrt{T}, \quad \mu = \frac{b - \sigma^2/2}{\sigma^2}, \quad \lambda = \sqrt{\mu^2 + \frac{2r}{\sigma^2}}$$

*In Barriers*:

In options are paid for today but first come into existence if the asset price $S$ hits the barrier $H$ before expiration. It is possible to include a pre-specified cash rebate $L$, which is paid out at option expiration if the option has not been knocked in during its lifetime.

Down-and-in call for $S > H$:

Payoff: max($S$–$K$, 0) if $S \leq H$ before $T$ else $L$ at expiration.

$$c_{di(K>H)} = C + E \qquad \eta = 1, \phi = 1$$
$$c_{di(K<H)} = A - B + D + E \qquad \eta = 1, \phi = 1$$

Up-and-in call for $S < H$:

Payoff: max($S$–$K$, 0) if $S \geq H$ before $T$ else $L$ at expiration.

$$c_{ui(K>H)} = A + E \qquad \eta = -1, \phi = 1$$
$$c_{ui(K<H)} = B - C + D + E \qquad \eta = -1, \phi = 1$$

Down-and-in put for $S > H$:

Payoff: max($K$–$S$, 0) if $S \leq H$ before $T$ else $L$ at expiration.

$$p_{di(K>H)} = B - C + D + E \qquad \eta = 1, \phi = -1$$
$$p_{di(K<H)} = A + E \qquad \eta = 1, \phi = -1$$

Up-and-in put for $S < H$:

Payoff: max($K$–$S$, 0) if $S \geq H$ before $T$ else $L$ at expiration.

$$p_{ui(K>H)} = A - B + D + E \qquad \eta = -1, \phi = -1$$
$$p_{ui(K<H)} = C + E \qquad \eta = -1, \phi = -1$$

*Out Barriers*:

Out options are similar to standard options except that the option becomes worthless if the asset price $S$ hits the barrier before expiration. It is possible to include a prespecified cash rebate $L$, which is paid out if the option is knocked out before expiration.

Down-and-out call for $S > H$:

Payoff: max($S$–$K$, 0) if $S > H$ before $T$ else $L$ at hit.

$$c_{do(K>H)} = A - C + F \qquad \eta = 1, \phi = 1$$
$$c_{do(K<H)} = B - D + F \qquad \eta = 1, \phi = 1$$

Up-and-out call for $S < H$:

Payoff: max($S$–$K$, 0) if $S < H$ before $T$ else $L$ at hit.

$$c_{uo(K>H)} = F \qquad \eta = -1, \phi = 1$$
$$c_{uo(K<H)} = A - B + C - D + F \qquad \eta = -1, \phi = 1$$

Down-and-out put for $S > H$:

Payoff: max($K$–$S$, 0) if $S > H$ before $T$ else $L$ at hit.

$$p_{do(K>H)} = A - B + C - D + F \qquad \eta = 1, \phi = -1$$
$$p_{do(K<H)} = F \qquad \eta = 1, \phi = -1$$

Up-and-out put for $S < H$:

Payoff: max($K$−$S$, 0) if $S < H$ before $T$ else $L$ at hit.

$$p_{uo(K>H)} = B - D + F \qquad \eta = -1, \phi = -1$$
$$p_{uo(K<H)} = A - C + F \qquad \eta = -1, \phi = -1$$

# Implementation

The *pricngHelper.R* file contains the implementation of the standard barrier options using the formulas presented in the preceding section. Here is the corresponding code listing:

```
barrierOptions <- function(optionType = c("c", "p"), barrierType = c("downIn",
      "downOut", "upIn", "upOut"), spot = 100, strike = 100, rate = 0.1,
      divYield = 0.06, maturity =1, vol = 0.3, barrierLevel = 90, rebate = 0){
  optionType = tolower(optionType)
  res <- NA
  if(optionType == "c" || optionType == "call"){
    res <- barrierOptionsCall(barrierType, spot, strike, rate, divYield, maturity,
                              vol, barrierLevel, rebate)
  } else if (optionType == "p" || optionType == "put"){
    res <- barrierOptionsPut(barrierType, spot, strike, rate,  divYield, maturity,
                             vol, barrierLevel, rebate)
  }
  return(res)
}

barrierOptionsCall <- function(barrierType, spot, strike, rate, divYield, maturity,
                      vol, barrierLevel, rebate){
  res <- NA
  barrierType <- tolower(barrierType)
  if(barrierType == "downin") {
    if (spot > barrierLevel){
      if (strike >= barrierLevel){
        res <- C(1, 1, barrierLevel, spot, strike, vol, maturity, rate, divYield) +
               E(1, rebate, barrierLevel, spot, strike, vol, maturity,
                 rate, divYield)
      } else{
        res <- A(1, barrierLevel, spot, strike, vol, maturity, rate, divYield) -
               B(1, barrierLevel, spot, strike, vol, maturity, rate, divYield) +
               D(1, 1, barrierLevel, spot, strike, vol, maturity, rate, divYield) +
               E(1, rebate, barrierLevel, spot, strike, vol, maturity, rate,
                 divYield);
      }
    }
  }

  else if(barrierType == "upin"){
    if (spot < barrierLevel){
      if (strike >= barrierLevel){
        res <- A(1, barrierLevel, spot, strike, vol, maturity, rate, divYield) +
               E(-1, rebate, barrierLevel, spot, strike, vol, maturity, rate,
                 divYield)
      } else{
        res <- B(1, barrierLevel, spot, strike, vol, maturity, rate, divYield) -
```

```
            C(-1, 1, barrierLevel, spot, strike, vol, maturity, rate, divYield) +
            D(-1, 1, barrierLevel, spot, strike, vol, maturity, rate, divYield) +
            E(-1, rebate, barrierLevel, spot, strike, vol, maturity, rate,
              divYield)
      }
    }
  }

  else if(barrierType == "downout"){
    if (spot > barrierLevel){
      if (strike > barrierLevel){
        res <- A(1, barrierLevel, spot, strike, vol, maturity, rate, divYield) -
               C(1, 1, barrierLevel, spot, strike, vol, maturity, rate, divYield) +
               F(1, rebate, barrierLevel, spot, strike, vol, maturity, rate,
                 divYield)
      } else{
        res <- B(1, barrierLevel, spot, strike, vol, maturity, rate, divYield) -
               D(1, 1, barrierLevel, spot, strike, vol, maturity, rate, divYield) +
               F(1, rebate, barrierLevel, spot, strike, vol, maturity, rate,
                 divYield)
      }
    }
  }

  else if(barrierType == "upout"){
    if (spot < barrierLevel){
      if (strike > barrierLevel){
        res <- F(-1, rebate, barrierLevel, spot, strike, vol, maturity, rate,
                 divYield)
      } else{
        res <- A(1, barrierLevel, spot, strike, vol, maturity, rate, divYield) -
               B(1, barrierLevel, spot, strike, vol, maturity, rate, divYield) +
               C(-1, 1, barrierLevel, spot, strike, vol, maturity, rate, divYield) -
               D(-1, 1, barrierLevel, spot, strike, vol, maturity, rate, divYield) +
               F(-1, rebate, barrierLevel, spot, strike, vol, maturity, rate,
                 divYield)
      }
    }
  }
  return(res)
}

barrierOptionsPut <- function(barrierType, spot, strike, rate, divYield, maturity,
                              vol, barrierLevel, rebate){
  res <- NA
  barrierType <- tolower(barrierType)
  if(barrierType == "downin"){
    if (spot > barrierLevel){
      if (strike >= barrierLevel){
        res <- B(-1, barrierLevel, spot, strike, vol, maturity, rate, divYield) -
               C(1, -1, barrierLevel, spot, strike, vol, maturity, rate, divYield) +
               D(1, -1, barrierLevel, spot, strike, vol, maturity, rate, divYield) +
               E(1, rebate, barrierLevel, spot, strike, vol, maturity, rate,
                 divYield)
      } else{
```

```
        res <- A(-1, barrierLevel, spot, strike, vol, maturity, rate, divYield) -
               E(1, rebate, barrierLevel, spot, strike, vol, maturity, rate,
                 divYield)
      }
    }
  }

  if(barrierType == "upin"){
    if (spot < barrierLevel){
      if (strike >= barrierLevel){
        res <- A(-1, barrierLevel, spot, strike, vol, maturity, rate, divYield) +
               B(-1, barrierLevel, spot, strike, vol, maturity, rate, divYield) +
               D(-1, -1, barrierLevel, spot, strike, vol, maturity, rate, divYield)+
               E(-1, rebate, barrierLevel, spot, strike, vol, maturity, rate,
                 divYield)
      } else{
        res <- C(-1, -1, barrierLevel, spot, strike, vol, maturity, rate, divYield)+
               E(-1, rebate, barrierLevel, spot, strike, vol, maturity, rate,
                 divYield)
      }
    }
  }

  if(barrierType == "downout"){
    if (spot > barrierLevel){
      if (strike > barrierLevel){
        res <- A(-1, barrierLevel, spot, strike, vol, maturity, rate, divYield) -
               B(-1, barrierLevel, spot, strike, vol, maturity, rate, divYield) +
               C(1, -1, barrierLevel, spot, strike, vol, maturity, rate, divYield) -
               D(1, -1, barrierLevel, spot, strike, vol, maturity, rate, divYield) +
               F(1, rebate, barrierLevel, spot, strike, vol, maturity, rate,
                 divYield)
      } else{
        res <- F(1, rebate, barrierLevel, spot, strike, vol, maturity, rate,
                 divYield)
      }
    }
  }
  if(barrierType == "upout"){
    if (spot < barrierLevel){
      if (strike > barrierLevel){
        res <- B(-1, barrierLevel, spot, strike, vol, maturity, rate, divYield) -
               D(-1, -1, barrierLevel, spot, strike, vol, maturity, rate, divYield)+
               F(-1, rebate, barrierLevel, spot, strike, vol, maturity, rate,
                 divYield)
      } else{
        res <- A(-1, barrierLevel, spot, strike, vol, maturity, rate, divYield) -
               C(-1, -1, barrierLevel, spot, strike, vol, maturity, rate, divYield)+
               F(-1, rebate, barrierLevel, spot, strike, vol, maturity, rate,
                 divYield)
      }
    }
  }
  return(res)
}
```

```
A <- function(phi, barrierLevel, spot, strike, vol, maturity, rate, divYield){
  fac <- vol * sqrt(maturity)
  m <- (rate - divYield - 0.5 * vol * vol) / vol / vol
  x1 <- log(spot / strike) / fac + (1.0 + m) * fac
  return (phi * spot * exp(-divYield * maturity) * cumNorm(phi * x1) -
          phi * strike * exp(-rate * maturity) * cumNorm(phi * x1 - phi * fac))
}

B <- function(phi, barrierLevel, spot, strike, vol, maturity, rate, divYield){
  fac <- vol * sqrt(maturity)
  m <- (rate - divYield - 0.5 * vol * vol) / vol / vol
  x2 <- log(spot / barrierLevel) / fac + (1.0 + m) * fac
  return(phi * spot * exp(-divYield * maturity) * cumNorm(phi * x2) -
         phi * strike * exp(-rate * maturity) * cumNorm(phi * x2 - phi * fac))
}

C <- function(phi, eta, barrierLevel, spot, strike, vol, maturity, rate, divYield){
  hs <- barrierLevel / spot
  fac <- vol * sqrt(maturity)
  m <- (rate - divYield - 0.5 * vol * vol) / vol / vol
  powhs0 <- hs^(2 * m)
  powhs1 <- powhs0 * hs * hs;
  y1 <- log(barrierLevel * barrierLevel / strike / spot) / fac + (1.0 + m) * fac
  return (phi * spot * exp(-divYield * maturity) * powhs1 * cumNorm(eta * y1) -
          phi * strike * exp(-rate * maturity) * powhs0 *
          cumNorm(eta * y1 - eta * fac))
}

D <- function(phi, eta, barrierLevel, spot, strike, vol, maturity, rate, divYield){
  hs <- barrierLevel / spot
  fac <- vol * sqrt(maturity)
  m <- (rate - divYield - 0.5 * vol * vol) / vol / vol
  powhs0 <- hs^(2 * m)
  powhs1 <- powhs0 * hs * hs
  y2 <- log(barrierLevel / spot) / fac + (1.0 + m) * fac
  return (phi * spot * exp(-divYield * maturity) * powhs1 * cumNorm(eta * y2) -
          phi * strike * exp(-rate * maturity) * powhs0 *
          cumNorm(eta * y2 - eta * fac))
}

E <- function(eta, rebate, barrierLevel, spot, strike, vol, maturity, rate,
divYield){
  if (rebate > 0){
    hs <- barrierLevel / spot
    fac <- vol * sqrt(maturity);
    m <- (rate - divYield - 0.5 * vol * vol) / vol / vol
    powhs0 = hs^(2 * m)
    x2 <- log(spot / barrierLevel) / fac + (1.0 + m) * fac
    y2 <- log(barrierLevel / spot) / fac + (1.0 + m) * fac
    return (rebate * exp(-rate * maturity) * (cumNorm(eta * y2 - eta * fac) -
            powhs0 * cumNorm(eta * y2 - eta * fac)))
  }
  else  return(0.0)
}
```

```
F <- function(eta, rebate, barrierLevel, spot, strike, vol, maturity, rate,
divYield){
  if (rebate > 0){
    hs <- barrierLevel / spot
    fac <- vol * sqrt(maturity)
    m <- (rate - divYield - 0.5 * vol * vol) / vol / vol;
    lambda <- sqrt(m * m + 2.0 * (rate - divYield) / vol / vol);
    powHSplus = hs^(m + lambda)
    powHSminus = hs^(m - lambda)
    z = log(barrierLevel / spot) / fac + lambda * fac
    return (rebate * (powHSplus * cumNorm(eta * z) - powHSminus *
                      cumNorm(eta * z - 2.0 * eta * lambda * fac)))
  }
  else return(0.0)
}
```

The implementation for barrier options is straightforward, and you can follow the code easily if you understand the formulas presented in the preceding section. Again, for illustration purpose, we do not perform the code vectorization here. In practical applications, you may need to optimize and vectorize the code.

## Barrier Option Applications

In this section, I will use an example to illustrate how to price the standard barrier options using the code presented in the preceding section.

Add a new helper function named *barrierOptionTest* to the *pricingHelper.R* file. Here is the code for this function:

```
barrierOptionTest <- function(optionType = c("c", "p"), barrierLevel = 90){
  mat <- seq(0.1, 1, 0.1)
  p <- sapply(1:length(mat), function(i) c(
         barrierOptions(optionType = optionType, barrierType = "downin",
           maturity = mat[i], barrierLevel = barrierLevel),
         barrierOptions(optionType = optionType, barrierType = "downout",
           maturity = mat[i], barrierLevel = barrierLevel),
         barrierOptions(optionType = optionType, barrierType = "upin",
           maturity = mat[i], barrierLevel = barrierLevel),
         barrierOptions(optionType = optionType, barrierType = "upout",
           maturity = mat[i], barrierLevel = barrierLevel)))
  df <- data.frame(Maturity = mat, DownIn = p[1, ], DownOut = p[2, ],
                   UpIn = p[3, ], UpOut = p[4, ])
  return(df)
}
```

Here, we use the default values for the following parameters: *spot* = 100, *strike* = 100, *rate* = 0.1, *divYield* = 0.06, *vol* = 0.3, *barrierLevel* = 90, and different maturities. Executing this function for both call and put options, we obtain:

```
> source("./R/pricingHelper.R")
> barrierOptionTest("c")
  Maturity     DownIn DownOut UpIn UpOut
1      0.1 0.04440666 3.910483   NA    NA
2      0.2 0.34306327 5.323445   NA    NA
```

```
3        0.3 0.80206291 6.193476   NA    NA
4        0.4 1.32196272 6.799050   NA    NA
5        0.5 1.86068640 7.252225   NA    NA
6        0.6 2.39982948 7.607623   NA    NA
7        0.7 2.93086961 7.895483   NA    NA
8        0.8 3.44977491 8.134120   NA    NA
9        0.9 3.95470307 8.335396   NA    NA
10       1.0 4.44493474 8.507400   NA    NA

> barrierOptionTest("p")
   Maturity   DownIn    DownOut UpIn UpOut
1       0.1 2.658598 0.89947884   NA    NA
2       0.2 4.435216 0.44398863   NA    NA
3       0.3 5.553516 0.27047255   NA    NA
4       0.4 6.386166 0.18522032   NA    NA
5       0.5 7.054973 0.13632790   NA    NA
6       0.6 7.614533 0.10534363   NA    NA
7       0.7 8.094459 0.08429773   NA    NA
8       0.8 8.512895 0.06925608   NA    NA
9       0.9 8.881928 0.05807957   NA    NA
10      1.0 9.210106 0.04951676   NA    NA
```

Note that there are *NA* values for the *UpIn* and *UpOut* fields because the barrier is lower than the spot. If we enter a barrier that is higher than the spot (say 110), both fields will then have values, but no values for the fields *DownIn* and *DownOut*, as shown in the following:

```
> barrierOptionTest("c", barrierLevel = 110)
   Maturity DownIn DownOut      UpIn      UpOut
1       0.1     NA      NA  3.243091 0.71179838
2       0.2     NA      NA  5.334045 0.33246351
3       0.3     NA      NA  6.797205 0.19833355
4       0.4     NA      NA  7.986674 0.13433890
5       0.5     NA      NA  9.014690 0.09822134
6       0.6     NA      NA  9.931888 0.07556512
7       0.7     NA      NA 10.766068 0.06028414
8       0.8     NA      NA 11.534477 0.04941784
9       0.9     NA      NA 12.248726 0.04137290
10      1.0     NA      NA 12.917110 0.03522427
> barrierOptionTest("p", barrierLevel = 110)
   Maturity DownIn DownOut       UpIn    UpOut
1       0.1     NA      NA 0.07561793 3.482459
2       0.2     NA      NA 0.43960224 4.439602
3       0.3     NA      NA 0.91278267 4.911206
4       0.4     NA      NA 1.39847905 5.172907
5       0.5     NA      NA 1.86676853 5.324532
6       0.6     NA      NA 2.30858479 5.411292
7       0.7     NA      NA 2.72198629 5.456770
8       0.8     NA      NA 3.10762902 5.474522
9       0.9     NA      NA 3.46709922 5.472908
10      1.0     NA      NA 3.80225337 5.457369
```

# Pricing European Options Using RQuantLib

In the preceding sections, we implemented several models to price various options including vanilla European and American options as well as exotic barrier options. You should try to follow our sample code to implement some simple Black-Scholes models by yourself. This way, you will get a better understanding on how the algorithm of pricing options works. Even if you work in a quant group within a financial institution and do not need to create the pricing engine from scratch, implementing some functions for pricing simple vanilla options is always a good practice. This will give you confidence when you use the pricing engines provided by commercial package, internal libraries, or free-source tools.

Options, especially the exotic derivatives, are complex security instruments and usually do not have analytic solutions. We have to use different approximations or various numerical approaches to price them. It is almost impossible to create pricing engines by our own for pricing various complex instruments. In this section, I will show how to use a free open-source tool, *QuantLib*, to price options. *QuantLib* is a financial library written in C++ and has been used as a base reference for modeling of various financial instruments. Of course, we can choose the other packages, such as *fOptions*, to price options. The main reason to use *QuantLib* in this book is that *QuantLib* provides not only the option-pricing tool, but also comprehensive frameworks for pricing fixed-income instruments, quantitative analysis, modeling, trading, and risk management of financial assets.

There is a package called *RQuantLib*, which makes parts of *QuantLib* accessible from R. I should point out that *RQuantLib* version does not have 100 percent support for all of the features in original *QuantLib*, and is quite limited in some areas. For example, the original *QuantLib* implements over 10 types of pricing engines for European option valuations, including analytic, binomial, finite-difference, integral, and Monte Carlo engines. However, in *RQuantLib*, only the analytic approach is provided, which is equivalent to our implementation for the genitalized Black-Scholes-Merton model. Thus, if we need more features than what *RQuantLib* can provide, we may consider creating a SWIG (simplified Wrapper and Interface Generator) R version of *QuantLib*, in which we can access to almost all of the features provided by the original *QuantLib*. In this chapter, for demonstration purpose, I will use *RQuantLib* to price options.

## Scalar Inputs

It is easy to use the *EuropeanOption* function implemented in *RQuantLib* to price European options. This function only allows any numerical input parameter to be a single value scalar. For example:

```
> install.packages("RQuantLib")
> library(RQuantLib)
> eo <- EuropeanOption(type="call", underlying = 100, strike = 100, dividendYield =
                       0.06, riskFreeRate = 0.1, maturity = 0.5, volatility = 0.3)
> eo
Concise summary of valuation for EuropeanOption
   value    delta    gamma     vega    theta      rho   divRho
  9.1129   0.5623   0.0179  26.8318  -9.3873  23.5571 -28.1136
```

Here, the input parameter underlying corresponds to spot. You can see that the *EuropeanOption* function in *RQuantLib* is very similar to the *BlackScholes* function in our own implementation described in previous sections. The only difference is that the *EeropeanOption* function takes the dividend yield as input while our *BlackScholes* function takes the cost of carry as input parameter. However, for options with stock as underlying assets, carry and dividend yield have relationship: $carry = rate - dividendYield$. Therefore, our implementation is practically identical to the *EuropeanOption* function.

The *EuropeanOption* function also gives rise to the Greeks of an option. In addition to first five standard Greeks, the function also returns *divRho*, the sensitivity of the option value for a change in the dividend yield. By comparing the results from the *EuropeanOption* function with those from our *BlackScholes* function, you will find that both functions return identical results, as expected.

## Vector Inputs

*RQuantLib* also provides another function named *EuropeanOptionArrays*, which allows any two of the numerical input parameters to be a vector or sequence. The function returns a list of matrices for the option value (price) as well as each of Greeks. For each of the returned matrices, each element corresponds to an evaluation under the given set of parameters. For example:

```
> spot = seq(10, 200, length=30)
> mat = seq(0.1, 3, length=30)
> call <- EuropeanOptionArrays(type = "call", strike = 100, dividendYield = 0.06,
    riskFreeRate = 0.1, volatility = 0.3, underlying = spot, maturity = mat)
> put <- EuropeanOptionArrays(type = "put",strike = 100, dividendYield = 0.06,
    riskFreeRate = 0.1, volatility = 0.3, underlying = spot, maturity = mat)
```

The results, call and put, contains the following components:

- *value* – (matrix) value (or price) of option.
- *delta* – (matrix) delta greek.
- *gamma* – (matrix) gamma greek.
- vega – (matrix) vega greek.
- *theta* – (matrix) theta greek.
- *rho* – (matrix) rho greek.
- *divRho* – (matrix) dividend rho greeek.
- *parameters* – list with input parameters with which object was created.

We can access input parameters using the following commands:

```
> call$parameters.type
[1] "call"
> call$parameters.strike
[1] 100
> call$parameters.underlying
 [1]  10.00000  16.55172  23.10345  29.65517  36.20690  42.75862  49.31034  55.86207
62.41379  68.96552  75.51724  82.06897  88.62069  95.17241
[15] 101.72414 108.27586 114.82759 121.37931 127.93103 134.48276 141.03448 147.58621
154.13793 160.68966 167.24138 173.79310 180.34483 186.89655
[29] 193.44828 200.00000
```

## Option Prices

We can also access the calculated results by the following statement:

```
> head(call$value, 2)
                          0.1          0.2          0.3          0.4          0.5
10               6.696524e-131 1.710269e-66 6.492657e-45 4.518049e-34 1.553835e-27
16.551724137931  8.214155e-81 2.450920e-41 4.542220e-28 2.206248e-21 2.432712e-17
                          0.6          0.7          0.8          0.9            1
10                3.709001e-23 5.134197e-20 1.193528e-17 8.420206e-16 2.572741e-14
16.551724137931 1.261824e-14 1.132865e-12 3.383195e-11 4.836095e-10 4.118829e-09
                          1.1          1.2          1.3          1.4          1.5
10                4.270787e-13 4.481319e-12 3.301290e-11 1.840616e-10 8.207426e-10
16.551724137931 2.403485e-08 1.055028e-07 3.717048e-07 1.101063e-06 2.837496e-06
                          1.6          1.7          1.8          1.9            2
10                3.050822e-09 9.758449e-09 2.753229e-08 6.987102e-08 1.620134e-07
16.551724137931 6.527087e-06 1.366832e-05 2.646008e-05 4.793195e-05 8.204479e-05
                          2.1          2.2          2.3          2.4          2.5
10                3.476351e-07 6.974916e-07 1.319896e-06 2.372740e-06 4.076607e-06
16.551724137931 1.337535e-04 2.090290e-04 3.148400e-04 4.590983e-04 6.505742e-04
                          2.6          2.7          2.8          2.9            3
10                6.728425e-06 1.071506e-05 1.652627e-05 2.476639e-05 3.616443e-05
16.551724137931 8.987871e-04 1.213881e-03 1.606487e-03 2.087584e-03 2.668363e-03
```

Note that the option value (price) is a 2D matrix with the maturity as columns and underlying (spot) as rows. We can also use the similar command to access the results for Greeks.

In order to see the option price and Greeks change with both the underlying and maturity more clearly, we will plot the option price and Greeks as a function of underlying and maturity on 3D surface graphs. The following statements will create surface graphs for a call and a put option prices:

```
> library(plot3D)
> library(plot3Drgl)
> persp3Drgl(x = spot, y = mat, z = call$value, border = "black", bty = "b2",
    ticktype =  "detailed", xlab = "spot", ylab = "maturity", zlab = "cPrice")
> persp3Drgl(x = spot, y = mat, z = put$value, border = "black", bty = "b2",
    ticktype =  "detailed", xlab = "spot", ylab = "maturity", zlab = "pPrice")
```

which produces the output shown in Figure 5-2.

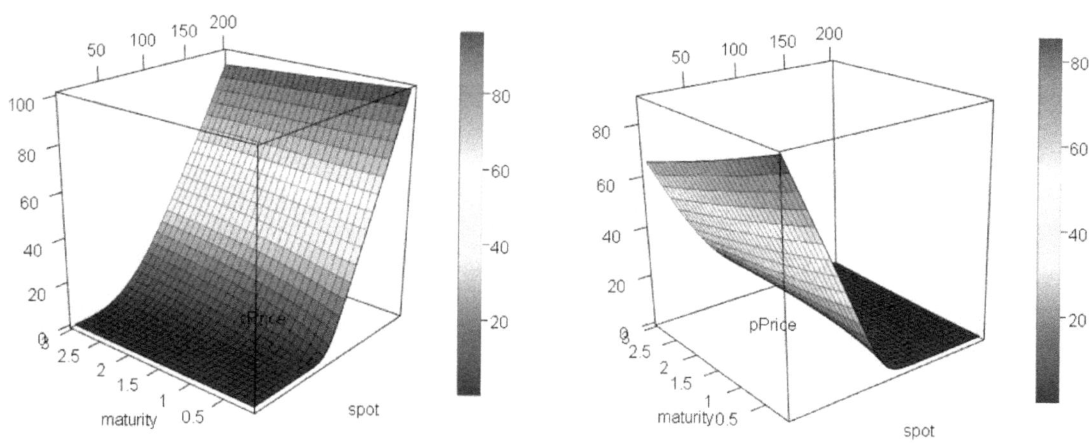


*Figure 5-2. Option prices for a call (left) and a put (right) option as a function of spot and maturity.*

# Delta

Delta represents change in option price for a change in spot. We can extract Delta results use the *call$delta* command and create surface graphs for Delta Greek by issuing the following statements:

```
> persp3Drgl(x = spot, y = mat, z = call$delta, border = "black", bty = "b2",
    ticktype =  "detailed", xlab = "spot", ylab = "maturity", zlab = "cDelta")
> persp3Drgl(x = spot, y = mat, z = put$delta, border = "black", bty = "b2",
    ticktype =  "detailed", xlab = "spot", ylab = "maturity", zlab = "pDelta")
```

This generates the output shown in Figure 5-3.

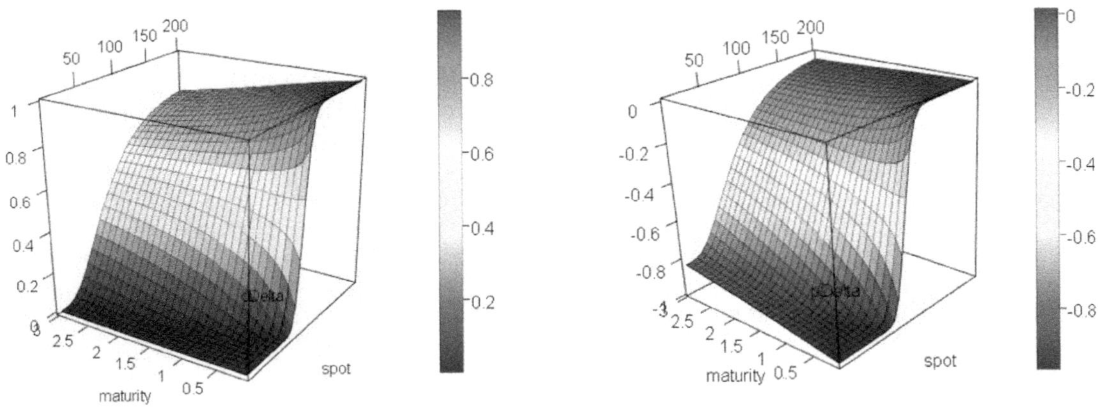


*Figure 5-3. Delta for a call (left) and a put (right) option as a function of spot and maturity.*

We can also create a contour plot for Delta to see how it changes with the maturity and spot:

```
> image2D(z = call$delta, x = spot, y = mat, contour = T, alpha=0.7, resfac = 5,
        xlab = "spot", ylab = "maturity")
```

This produces the result shown in Figure 5-4.

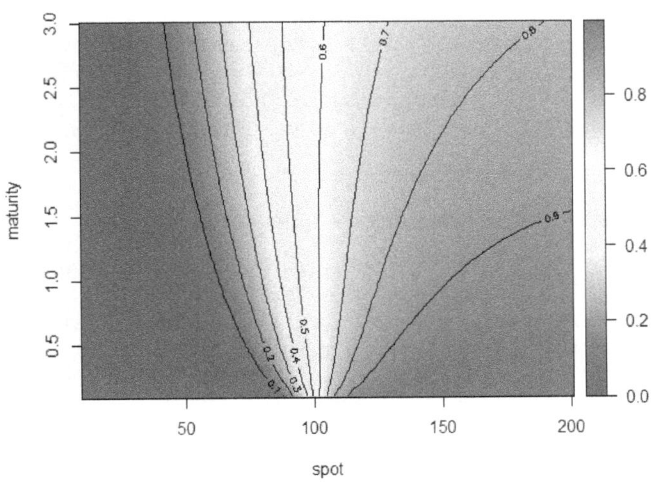


*Figure 5-4. A contour plot for Delta of a call option.*

# Gamma

The Gamma is the same for both the call and put options, and it represents sensitivity of Delta for a change in spot. We can extract the Gamma results with *call$gamma* and create corresponding surface and contour graphs using the commands:

```
> persp3Drgl(x = spot, y = mat, z = call$gamma, border="black", bty = "b2", ticktype
             = "detailed", xlab = "spot", ylab = "maturity", zlab = "Gamma")
> image2D(z = call$gamma, x = spot, y = mat, contour = list(nlevels = 20),
          alpha=0.7, resfac = 5, xlab ="spot", ylab = "maturity")
```

This produces the output shown in Figure 5-5.

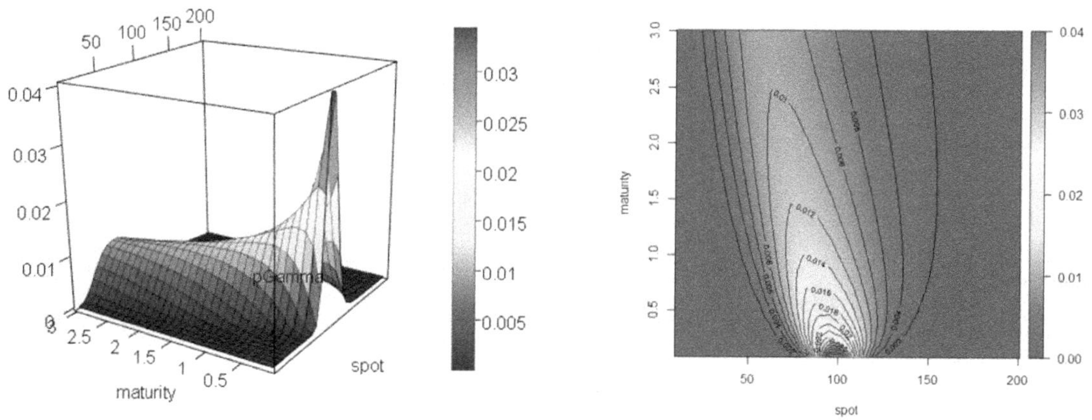


*Figure 5-5. Surface (left) and contour (right) graphs for Gamma.*

# Theta

Theta represents option price change for a change in maturity. We can extract the Theta results with *call$theta* and create corresponding surface graphs using the commands:

```
> persp3Drgl(x = spot, y = mat, z = call$theta, border="black", bty = "b2", ticktype
             = "detailed", xlab = "spot", ylab = "maturity", zlab = "cTheta")
> persp3Drgl(x = spot, y = mat, z = put$theta, border="black", bty = "b2", ticktype
             = "detailed", xlab = "spot", ylab = "maturity", zlab = "pTheta")
```

This creates the surface graphs shown in Figure 5-6.

We can also create contour plots for Theta using the following commands:

```
> image2D(z = call$theta,x = spot,y = mat, contour = list(nlevels = 20), alpha=0.7,
          resfac = 5, xlab = "spot", ylab = "maturity")
> image2D(z = put$theta,x = spot,y = mat, contour = list(nlevels = 20), alpha=0.7,
          resfac = 5, xlab = "spot", ylab = "maturity")
```

The above code generates the results shown in Figure 5-7.

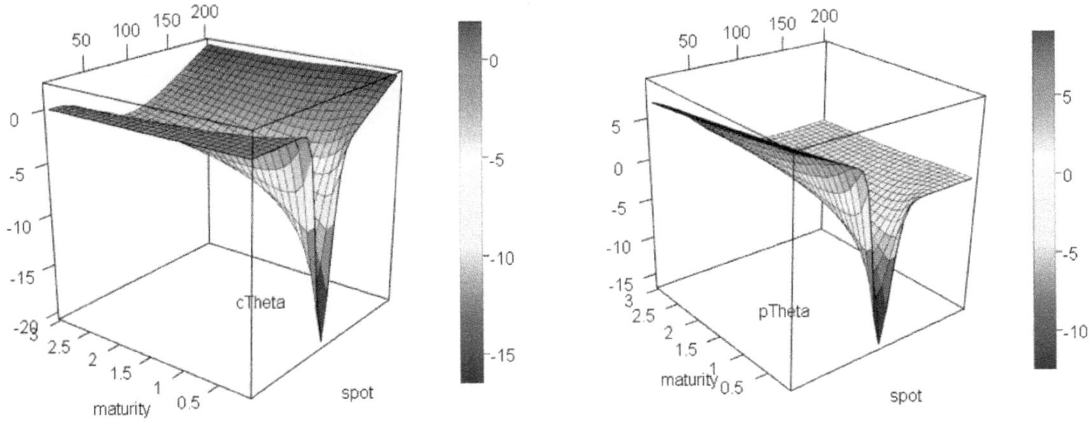


*Figure 5-6. Surface graphs for Theta of a call (left) or a put (right) option.*

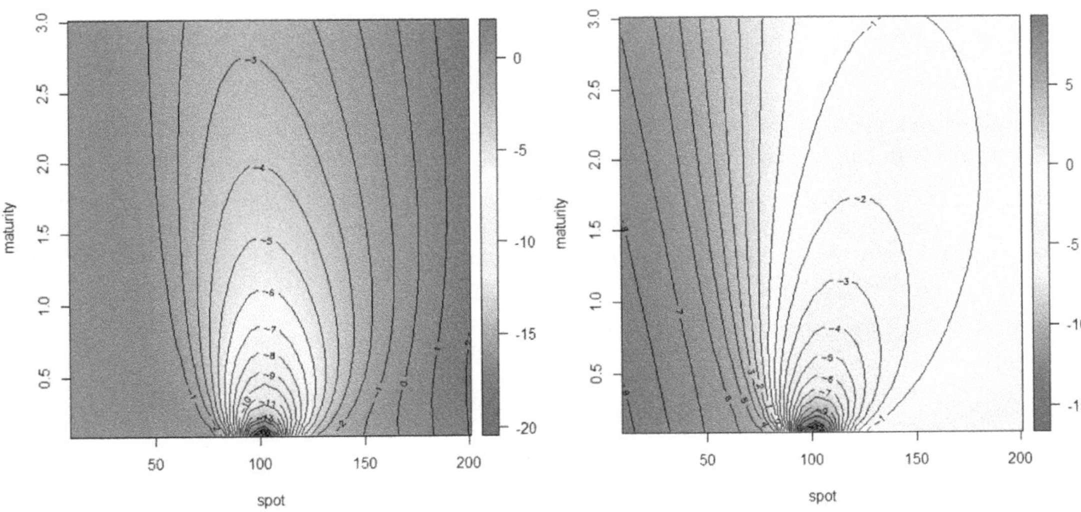


*Figure 5-7. Contour plots for Theta of a call (left) or a put (right) option.*

# Vega

The Vega is the same for both the call and put options, and it represents change in option price for a change in the volatility of the underlying asset. We can extract the Vega results with *call$vega* and create corresponding surface and contour graphs using the commands:

```
> persp3Drgl(x = spot, y = mat, z = put$vega, border = "black", bty = "b2", ticktype
            = "detailed", xlab = "spot", ylab = "maturity", zlab = "Vega")
> image2D(z = put$vega, x = spot, y = mat, contour = list(nlevels = 10), alpha=0.7,
          resfac = 5, xlab = "spot", ylab = "maturity")
```

This produces the output shown in Figure 5-8.

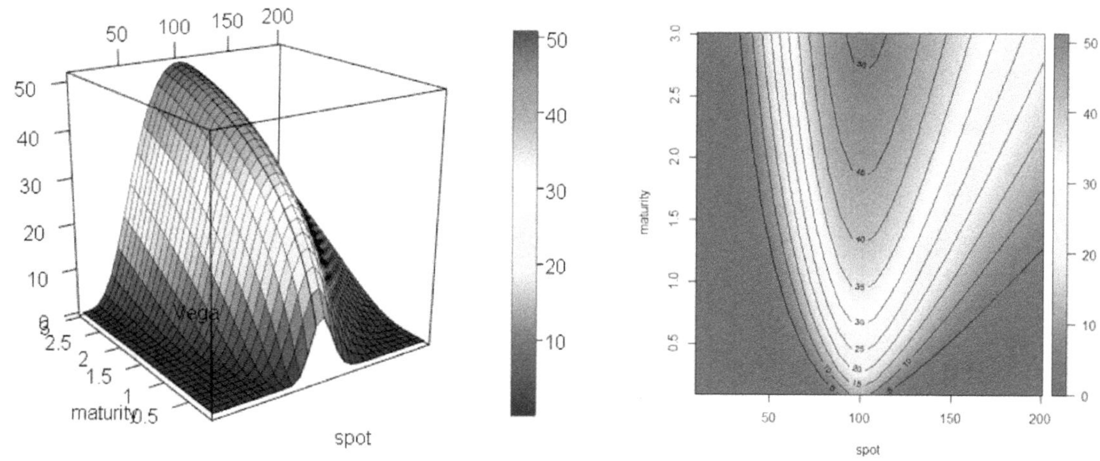


*Figure 5-8. Surface (left) and contour (right) graphs for Vega.*

# Rho

Rho represents the sensitivity of the option price for a change in the risk-free interest rate. We can extract the Rho results with *call$rho* and create corresponding surface graphs using the commands:

```
> persp3Drgl(x = spot, y = mat, z = call$rho, border = "black", bty = "b2", ticktype
            = "detailed", xlab = "spot", ylab = "maturity", zlab = "cRho")
> persp3Drgl(x = spot, y = mat, z = put$rho, border = "black", bty = "b2", ticktype
            = "detailed", xlab = "spot", ylab = "maturity", zlab = "pRho")
```

This generates the output shown in Figure 5-9.

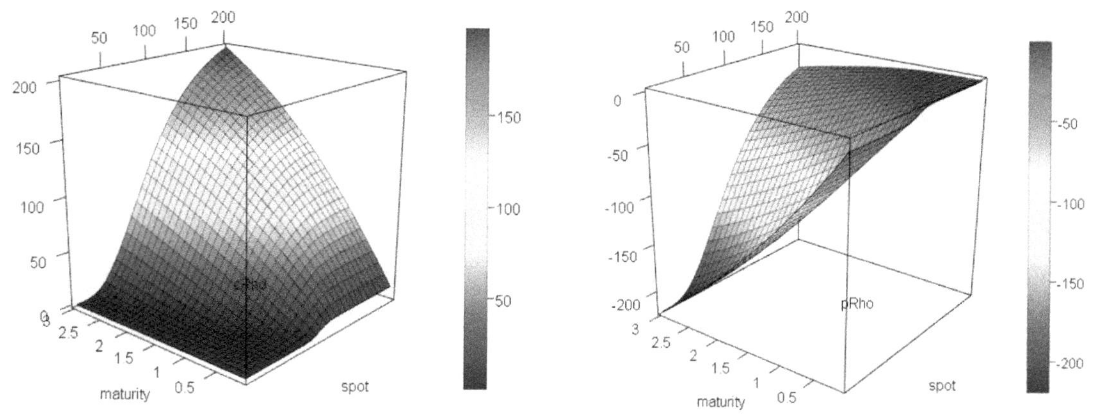


*Figure 5-9. Surface graphs for Rho of a call (left) or a put (right) option.*

We can also create contour plots for Rho using the following commands:

```
> image2D(z = call$rho,x = spot,y = mat, contour = list(nlevels = 10), alpha=0.7,
        resfac = 5, xlab = "spot", ylab = "maturity")
> image2D(z = put$rho,x = spot,y = mat, contour = list(nlevels = 10), alpha=0.7,
```

```
    resfac = 5, xlab = "spot", ylab = "maturity")
```

This produces contour graphs shown in Figure 5-10.

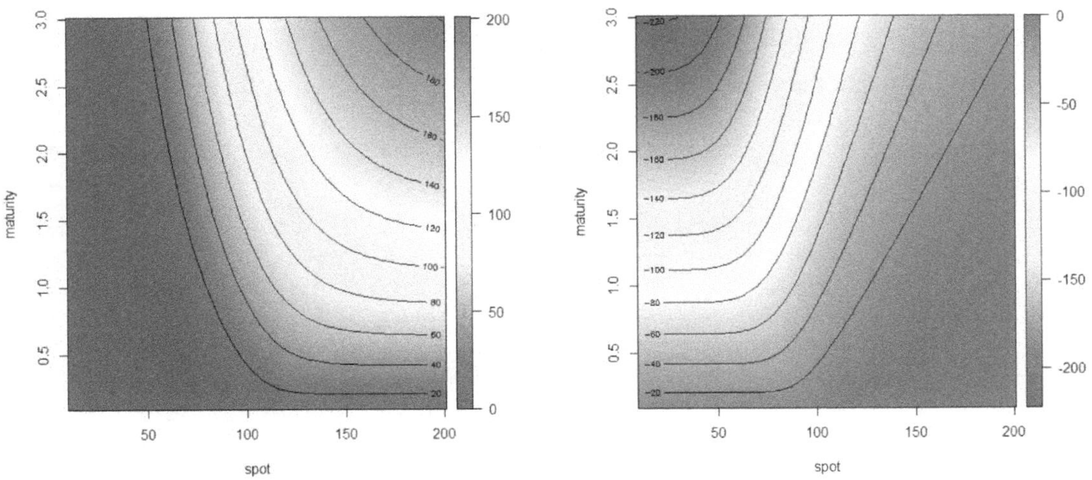


*Figure 5-10. Contour plots for Rho of a call (left) or a put (right) option.*

# Dividend Rho

The dividend Rho represents the sensitivity of the option price for a change in the dividend yield. We can extract the dividend Rho results with *call$divRho* and create corresponding surface graphs using the commands:

```
> persp3Drgl(x = spot, y = mat, z = call$divRho, border="black", bty = "b2",
    ticktype = "detailed", xlab = "spot", ylab = "maturity", zlab = "cDivRho")
> persp3Drgl(x = spot, y = mat, z = put$divRho, border="black", bty = "b2",
    ticktype = "detailed", xlab = "spot", ylab = "maturity", zlab = "pDivRho")
```

This produces the results shown in Figure 5-11.

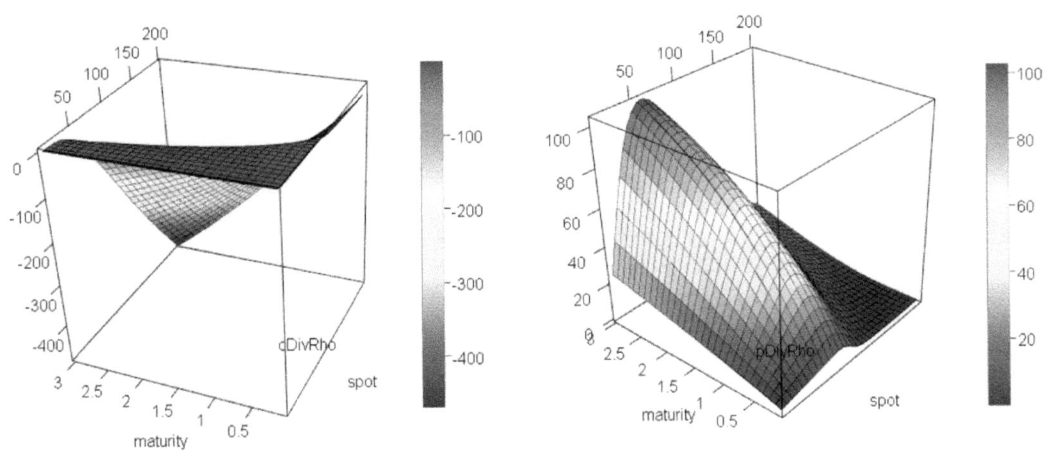


*Figure 5-11. Surface plots for dividend Rho of a call (left) or a put (right) option.*

We can also create contour plots for dividend Rho using the following commands:

```
> image2D(z = call$divRho,x = spot,y = mat, contour = list(nlevels = 10), alpha=0.7,
        resfac = 5, xlab = "spot", ylab = "maturity")
> image2D(z = put$divRho,x = spot,y = mat, contour = list(nlevels = 10), alpha=0.7,
        resfac = 5, xlab = "spot", ylab = "maturity")
```

This generates the output shown in Figure 5-12.

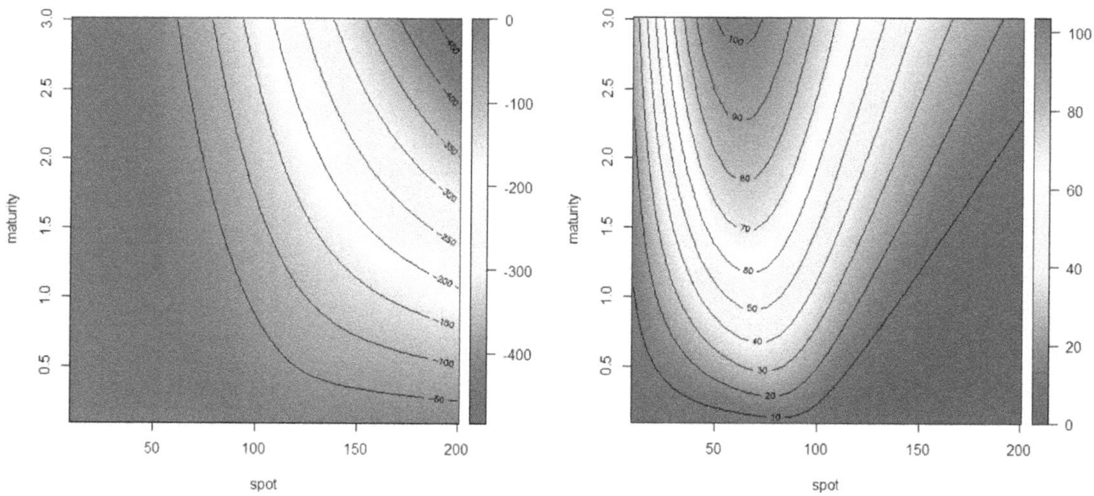


*Figure 5-12. Contour graphs for dividend Rho of a call (left) or a put (right) option.*

# Implied Volatility

The *EuropeanOptionImpliedVolatility* function in *RQuantLib* solves for the implied volatility based on the Newton-Raphson method, given the option price and the other required parameters to value an option. Again, since this function involves iterations and comparing a scalar value of price, it cannot take vector or sequence as input parameters. As we did for our *blackScholesImpliedVol* function, we will use another function named *volTestRQuantLib* to test the *EuropeanOptionImpliedVolatility* function. Here is the code for this function:

```
volTestRQuantLib <- function(){
  mat <-  seq(0.1, 1, 0.1)
  price <- seq(0.15, 0.6, 0.05)
  v <- sapply(1:length(mat), function(i) c(
    tryCatch(EuropeanOptionImpliedVolatility(type="call", value = price[i],
    underlying = 10, strike = 10.5,dividendYield = 0.04, riskFreeRate = 0.1,
    maturity = mat[i], volatility = 0.3), error = function(cond) NA),
    tryCatch(EuropeanOptionImpliedVolatility(type="put", value = price[i],
    underlying = 10, strike = 10.5,dividendYield = 0.04, riskFreeRate = 0.1,
    maturity = mat[i], volatility = 0.3), error = function(cond) NA)
    ))
  vol <- data.frame(Maturity = mat, Price = price, CallVol = v[1, ],
                    PutVol = v[2, ])
  return(vol)
}
```

Executing this function gives the following results:

```
> source("./R/pricingHelper.R")
> volTestRQuantLib()
   Maturity Price   CallVol     PutVol
1       0.1  0.15 0.2508532         NA
2       0.2  0.20 0.1971808         NA
3       0.3  0.25 0.1756172         NA
4       0.4  0.30 0.1638570 0.05729459
5       0.5  0.35 0.1565258 0.08812524
6       0.6  0.40 0.1516229 0.10983901
7       0.7  0.45 0.1482221 0.12780934
8       0.8  0.50 0.1458320 0.14361290
9       0.9  0.55 0.1441666 0.15797678
10      1.0  0.60 0.1430476 0.17130630
```

The above results are consistent with those obtained from our own implementation for implied volatility. This comparison should give you the confidence on how to use the *RQuantLib* to price European options.

# Pricing American Options Using RQuantLib

The real power of using QuantLib pricing engines is to price American and exotic options because these options are complex security instruments and have no analytic solutions. The original *QuantLib* contains over ten types of pricing engines for American option valuation, which including the closed form approximations, finite-difference, binomial, and Monte Carlo approaches. *RQuantLib* implements a function named *AmericanOption* that includes two pricing engines for American option pricing: *BaroneAdesiWhaley* and *CrankNicolson*. The former is a closed-form approximation similar to our implementation for BAW and the latter is a finite difference method.

## Option Prices

In this section, I will use an example to illustrate how to price an American option using the *AmericanOption* function from *RQuantLib*. Add a new function named *americanOptionTestRQuantLib* to the *pricingHelper.R* file. Here is the code for this function:

```
americanOptionTestRQuantLib <- function(){
  oType <- c(rep("call", 18), rep("put", 18))
  strike <- rep(100, 36)
  spot <- rep(c(90, 100, 110), 12)
  yield <- rep(0.1, 36)
  rate <- rep(0.1, 36)
  mat <- c(rep(0.1, 9), rep(0.5, 9), rep(0.1, 9), rep(0.5, 9))
  vol <- rep(c(rep(0.15, 3), rep(0.25, 3), rep(0.35, 3)), 4)
  baw <- c(0.0206, 1.8771, 10.0089, 0.3159, 3.128, 10.3919, 0.9495, 4.3777, 11.1679,
           0.8208, 4.0842, 10.8087, 2.7437, 6.8015, 13.017, 5.0063, 9.5106, 15.5689,
           10,1.877, 0.041,10.2533, 3.1277, 0.4562, 10.8787,4.3777, 1.2402, 10.5595,
           4.0842, 1.0822, 12.4419, 6.8014, 3.3226, 14.6945, 9.5104, 5.8823)
  p <- sapply(1:36, function(i) c(
      (AmericanOption(type = oType[i], underlying = spot[i],strike = strike[i],
        dividendYield = yield[i], riskFreeRate = rate[i], maturity = mat[i],
        volatility = vol[i], engine = "BaroneAdesiWhaley"))$value,
      (AmericanOption(type = oType[i], underlying = spot[i],strike = strike[i],
        dividendYield = yield[i], riskFreeRate = rate[i], maturity = mat[i],
```

```
        volatility = vol[i], engine = "CrankNicolson", timeSteps = 200,
        gridPoints = 199))$value))
  df <- data.frame(Type = oType, Strike = strike, Spot = spot, Yield = yield,
        Rate = rate, Maturity = mat, Vol = vol, BAW = baw, BAWCalc = p[1, ],
        CN = p[2, ])
  return(df)
}
```

Here, we use both the *BaroneAdesiWhaley* and *CrankNicolson* engines to calculate the price for American call and put options for fixed strike = 100, dividend yield = 0.1, interest rate = 0.1, and varying the parameters of the spot, times to maturity, and volatility. The *BAWValue* column in the data frame shows the results from the BAW approximation in the literature. We calculate option prices using these two pricing engines, and compare the calculated results with those in the literature.

Executing the above function produces the following results:

```
> source("./R/pricingHelper.R")
> americanOptionTestRQuantLib()
   Type Strike Spot Yield Rate Maturity  Vol     BAW     BAWCalc          CN
1  call    100   90   0.1  0.1      0.1 0.15  0.0206  0.02063560  0.02049782
2  call    100  100   0.1  0.1      0.1 0.15  1.8771  1.87692069  1.87640480
3  call    100  110   0.1  0.1      0.1 0.15 10.0089 10.00606009 10.01032541
4  call    100   90   0.1  0.1      0.1 0.25  0.3159  0.31590017  0.31525096
5  call    100  100   0.1  0.1      0.1 0.25  3.1280  3.12768316  3.12682858
6  call    100  110   0.1  0.1      0.1 0.25 10.3919 10.39012353 10.39642896
7  call    100   90   0.1  0.1      0.1 0.35  0.9495  0.94947033  0.94821503
8  call    100  100   0.1  0.1      0.1 0.35  4.3777  4.37766904  4.37647441
9  call    100  110   0.1  0.1      0.1 0.35 11.1679 11.16785000 11.17236698
10 call    100   90   0.1  0.1      0.5 0.15  0.8208  0.82082169  0.81132468
11 call    100  100   0.1  0.1      0.5 0.15  4.0842  4.08411689  4.06816109
12 call    100  110   0.1  0.1      0.5 0.15 10.8087 10.80852655 10.80981194
13 call    100   90   0.1  0.1      0.5 0.25  2.7437  2.74360046  2.72219263
14 call    100  100   0.1  0.1      0.5 0.25  6.8015  6.80134160  6.77473397
15 call    100  110   0.1  0.1      0.5 0.25 13.0170 13.01673013 13.00043987
16 call    100   90   0.1  0.1      0.5 0.35  5.0063  5.00615862  4.97336714
17 call    100  100   0.1  0.1      0.5 0.35  9.5106  9.51030764  9.47299305
18 call    100  110   0.1  0.1      0.5 0.35 15.5689 15.56842765 15.53775649
19  put    100   90   0.1  0.1      0.1 0.15 10.0000 10.00000000 10.00034680
20  put    100  100   0.1  0.1      0.1 0.15  1.8770  1.87692247  1.87640479
21  put    100  110   0.1  0.1      0.1 0.15  0.0410  0.04099631  0.04079652
22  put    100   90   0.1  0.1      0.1 0.25 10.2533 10.25300774 10.25973560
23  put    100  100   0.1  0.1      0.1 0.25  3.1277  3.12768538  3.12682854
24  put    100  110   0.1  0.1      0.1 0.25  0.4562  0.45618539  0.45537627
25  put    100   90   0.1  0.1      0.1 0.35 10.8787 10.87850882 10.88355695
26  put    100  100   0.1  0.1      0.1 0.35  4.3777  4.37767141  4.37647425
27  put    100  110   0.1  0.1      0.1 0.35  1.2402  1.24020907  1.23873381
28  put    100   90   0.1  0.1      0.5 0.15 10.5595 10.55921289 10.56340132
29  put    100  100   0.1  0.1      0.5 0.15  4.0842  4.08411682  4.06816091
30  put    100  110   0.1  0.1      0.5 0.15  1.0822  1.08220238  1.07080345
31  put    100   90   0.1  0.1      0.5 0.25 12.4419 12.44164207 12.42898073
32  put    100  100   0.1  0.1      0.5 0.25  6.8014  6.80134134  6.77473281
33  put    100  110   0.1  0.1      0.5 0.25  3.3226  3.32257190  3.29814285
34  put    100   90   0.1  0.1      0.5 0.35 14.6945 14.69431918 14.66811160
35  put    100  100   0.1  0.1      0.5 0.35  9.5104  9.51030684  9.47298884
36  put    100  110   0.1  0.1      0.5 0.35  5.8823  5.88218976  5.84530772
```

In the above table, the *BAWCalc* column represents calculated results from the *BaroneAdesiWhaley* engine and the *CN* column denotes the calculated results from the *CrankNicolson* engine. You can see that the calculated results are consistent with those from literature.

## Greeks

Note that under the pricing framework used in *QuantLib*, the pricing engines based on the closed-form approximation do not provide analytics for all Greeks. This means the *BaroneAdesiWhaley* engine does not return any Greek information. On the other hand, the *CrankNicolson* engine based on finite-difference approach returns the common first derivatives Greeks, such as Delta and Gamma.

We can use the *americanOptionGreeks* function to illustrate how to extract the Greek results. Here is the code for this function:

```
americanOptionGreeks <- function(){
  oType <- c(rep("call",18), rep("put", 18))
  strike <- rep(100,36)
  spot <- rep(c(90,100,110),12)
  yield <- rep(0.1, 36)
  rate <- rep(0.1, 36)
  mat <- c(rep(0.1,9), rep(0.5,9),rep(0.1,9),rep(0.5,9))
  vol <- rep(c(rep(0.15,3),rep(0.25,3),rep(0.35,3)),4)
   g <- sapply(1:36, function(i) c(
     (AmericanOption(type=oType[i], underlying = spot[i],strike = strike[i],
       dividendYield = yield[i], riskFreeRate = rate[i], maturity = mat[i],
       volatility = vol[i], engine = "CrankNicolson",
       timeSteps = 200, gridPoints = 199))$delta,
     (AmericanOption(type=oType[i], underlying = spot[i],strike = strike[i],
       dividendYield = yield[i], riskFreeRate = rate[i], maturity = mat[i],
       volatility = vol[i], engine = "CrankNicolson",
       timeSteps = 200, gridPoints = 199))$gamma))
  df <- data.frame(Type = oType, Strike = strike, Spot = spot, Yield = yield,
        Rate = rate, Maturity = mat, Vol = vol, Delta = g[1, ], Gamma = g[2, ])
  return(df)
}
```

Executing this function produces the following results:

```
> source("./R/pricingHelper.R")
> americanOptionGreeks()
   Type Strike Spot Yield Rate Maturity  Vol      Delta       Gamma
1  call    100   90   0.1  0.1      0.1 0.15 0.01386022 0.008277433
2  call    100  100   0.1  0.1      0.1 0.15 0.50568423 0.083703181
3  call    100  110   0.1  0.1      0.1 0.15 0.98491891 0.012255658
4  call    100   90   0.1  0.1      0.1 0.25 0.09708016 0.024085964
5  call    100  100   0.1  0.1      0.1 0.25 0.51193746 0.050197067
6  call    100  110   0.1  0.1      0.1 0.25 0.89146686 0.021818300
7  call    100   90   0.1  0.1      0.1 0.35 0.18333380 0.026574002
8  call    100  100   0.1  0.1      0.1 0.35 0.51818657 0.035828374
9  call    100  110   0.1  0.1      0.1 0.35 0.81668987 0.021784836
10 call    100   90   0.1  0.1      0.5 0.15 0.16628979 0.025841650
11 call    100  100   0.1  0.1      0.5 0.15 0.50443275 0.037110915
12 call    100  110   0.1  0.1      0.5 0.15 0.82146599 0.024228770
13 call    100   90   0.1  0.1      0.5 0.25 0.29393034 0.021343589
14 call    100  100   0.1  0.1      0.5 0.25 0.51797454 0.022213429
```

```
15 call     100  110   0.1  0.1        0.5 0.25   0.71914059 0.017470663
16 call     100   90   0.1  0.1        0.5 0.35   0.36702857 0.016637036
17 call     100  100   0.1  0.1        0.5 0.35   0.53147893 0.015810027
18 call     100  110   0.1  0.1        0.5 0.35   0.67696592 0.013105550
19  put     100   90   0.1  0.1        0.1 0.15 -0.99652626 0.014160647
20  put     100  100   0.1  0.1        0.1 0.15 -0.48692000 0.083703180
21  put     100  110   0.1  0.1        0.1 0.15 -0.02082640 0.009590872
22  put     100   90   0.1  0.1        0.1 0.25 -0.90138647 0.025404208
23  put     100  100   0.1  0.1        0.1 0.25 -0.48066895 0.050197065
24  put     100  110   0.1  0.1        0.1 0.25 -0.10558343 0.020949701
25  put     100   90   0.1  0.1        0.1 0.35 -0.81219465 0.027217662
26  put     100  100   0.1  0.1        0.1 0.35 -0.47442153 0.035828371
27  put     100  110   0.1  0.1        0.1 0.35 -0.17814186 0.021357903
28  put     100   90   0.1  0.1        0.5 0.15 -0.82417909 0.030816023
29  put     100  100   0.1  0.1        0.5 0.15 -0.46374932 0.037110912
30  put     100  110   0.1  0.1        0.5 0.15 -0.16364221 0.020943326
31  put     100   90   0.1  0.1        0.5 0.25 -0.68209016 0.023050678
32  put     100  100   0.1  0.1        0.5 0.25 -0.45022448 0.022213426
33  put     100  110   0.1  0.1        0.5 0.25 -0.25503649 0.016334141
34  put     100   90   0.1  0.1        0.5 0.35 -0.60516122 0.017497476
35  put     100  100   0.1  0.1        0.5 0.35 -0.43674529 0.015810022
36  put     100  110   0.1  0.1        0.5 0.35 -0.29429093 0.012531198
```

## Implied Volatility

*RQuantLib* uses the finite-difference method to price the American options and then compute the implied volatilities numerically. We can use the *AmericanOptionImpliedVolatility* function from *RQuantLib* to calculate the implied volatility for an American option. Add a new function named *americanOptionVolTest* to the *pricingHelper.R* file. Here is the code for this function:

```
americanOptionvolTest <- function(){
  mat <-  seq(0.1, 1.5, 0.1)
  price <- seq(0.15, 0.85, 0.05)
  v <- sapply(1:length(mat), function(i) c(
    tryCatch(AmericanOptionImpliedVolatility(type = "call", value = price[i],
    underlying = 10, strike = 10.5, dividendYield = 0.04, riskFreeRate = 0.1,
    maturity = mat[i], volatility = 0.3), error = function(cond) NA),
    tryCatch(AmericanOptionImpliedVolatility(type = "put", value = price[i],
    underlying = 10, strike = 10.5, dividendYield = 0.04, riskFreeRate = 0.1,
    maturity = mat[i], volatility = 0.3), error = function(cond) NA)))
  vol <- data.frame(Maturity = mat, Price = price, CallVol = v[1, ],PutVol = v[2, ])
  return(vol)
}
```

Executing this function gives the following results:

```
> source("./R/pricingHelper.R")
> americanOptionvolTest()
   Maturity Price   CallVol     PutVol
1       0.1  0.15 0.2508532         NA
2       0.2  0.20 0.1971808         NA
3       0.3  0.25 0.1756172         NA
4       0.4  0.30 0.1638570         NA
5       0.5  0.35 0.1565258         NA
6       0.6  0.40 0.1516228         NA
```

```
7      0.7  0.45 0.1482221         NA
8      0.8  0.50 0.1458320 0.08736758
9      0.9  0.55 0.1441666 0.11664955
10     1.0  0.60 0.1430476 0.13282119
11     1.1  0.65 0.1423583 0.14606578
12     1.2  0.70 0.1420189 0.15820052
13     1.3  0.75 0.1419731 0.16919763
14     1.4  0.80 0.1421799 0.17950824
15     1.5  0.85 0.1426091 0.18926126
```

# Pricing Barrier Options Using RQuantLib

As discussed previously, the payoff of barrier options depends on whether or not the underlying asset has reached or exceeded a predetermined price. Barrier options are considered a type of path-dependent option because their value fluctuates as the underlying's price changes during the option's contract term. In other words, a barrier option's payoff is based on the underlying asset's price path.

In the original *QuantLib*, there are two types of pricing methods to value the barrier options, including the closed-form and Monte Carlo. *RQuantLib* exposes only one approach based on the closed-form solution, which is similar to our own implementation for barrier options.

Now, I will use an example to illustrate how to use the *BarrierOption* function in *RQuantLib* to value the barrier options. Add a new function named *barrierOptionTestRQauntLib* to the *pricingHelper.R* file. Here is the code for this function:

```
barrierOptionTestRQuantLib <- function(optionType = c("c", "p"), barrierLevel = 90){
  mat <- seq(0.1, 1, 0.1)
  p <- sapply(1:length(mat), function(i) c(
    tryCatch((BarrierOption(type = optionType, barrType = "downin",
      maturity = mat[i], barrier = barrierLevel, underlying = 100,
      strike = 100, dividendYield = 0.06, riskFreeRate = 0.1,
      volatility = 0.3))$value, error = function(cond) NA),
    tryCatch((BarrierOption(type = optionType, barrType = "downout",
      maturity = mat[i], barrier = barrierLevel, underlying = 100,
      strike = 100, dividendYield = 0.06, riskFreeRate = 0.1,
      volatility = 0.3))$value, error = function(cond) NA),
    tryCatch((BarrierOption(type = optionType, barrType = "upin", maturity = mat[i],
      barrier = barrierLevel, underlying = 100, strike = 100, dividendYield = 0.06,
      riskFreeRate = 0.1, volatility = 0.3))$value, error = function(cond) NA),
    tryCatch((BarrierOption(type = optionType, barrType = "upout",
      maturity = mat[i], barrier = barrierLevel, underlying = 100,
      strike = 100, dividendYield = 0.06, riskFreeRate = 0.1,
      volatility = 0.3))$value, error = function(cond) NA)))
  df <- data.frame(Maturity = mat, DownIn = p[1, ], DownOut = p[2, ],
                   UpIn = p[3, ], UpOut = p[4, ])
  return(df)
}
```

Here, we use the following input parameters: *underlying* = 100, *strike* = 100, *riskFreeRate* = 0.1, *dividendYield* = 0.06, *volatility* = 0.3, *barrier* = 90, and different maturities. Executing this function for both call and put options, we obtain:

```
> source("./R/pricingHelper.R")
> barrierOptionTestRQuantLib(optionType = "c", barrierLevel = 90)
```

```
   Maturity     DownIn  DownOut UpIn UpOut
1       0.1 0.0444071 3.910475   NA    NA
2       0.2 0.3430603 5.323442   NA    NA
3       0.3 0.8020655 6.193470   NA    NA
4       0.4 1.3219689 6.799042   NA    NA
5       0.5 1.8606924 7.252219   NA    NA
6       0.6 2.3998328 7.607621   NA    NA
7       0.7 2.9308691 7.895485   NA    NA
8       0.8 3.4497707 8.134126   NA    NA
9       0.9 3.9546957 8.335406   NA    NA
10      1.0 4.4449251 8.507412   NA    NA
> barrierOptionTestRQuantLib(optionType = "p", barrierLevel = 90)
   Maturity   DownIn    DownOut UpIn UpOut
1       0.1 2.658597 0.89947200   NA    NA
2       0.2 4.435218 0.44398095   NA    NA
3       0.3 5.553525 0.27045990   NA    NA
4       0.4 6.386176 0.18520844   NA    NA
5       0.5 7.054978 0.13632256   NA    NA
6       0.6 7.614530 0.10534789   NA    NA
7       0.7 8.094446 0.08431218   NA    NA
8       0.8 8.512873 0.06927962   NA    NA
9       0.9 8.881899 0.05811001   NA    NA
10      1.0 9.210074 0.04955122   NA    NA
```

Note that there are no values for the *UpIn* and *UpOut* fields because the barrier is lower than the spot. If we enter a barrier that is higher than the spot (say 110), both fields will then have values, but no values for the fields *DownIn* and *DownOut*, as shown in the following:

```
> barrierOptionTestRQuantLib(optionType = "c", barrierLevel = 110)
   Maturity DownIn DownOut      UpIn      UpOut
1       0.1     NA      NA  3.243090 0.71179159
2       0.2     NA      NA  5.334038 0.33246421
3       0.3     NA      NA  6.797204 0.19833079
4       0.4     NA      NA  7.986681 0.13432968
5       0.5     NA      NA  9.014705 0.09820570
6       0.6     NA      NA  9.931909 0.07554411
7       0.7     NA      NA 10.766095 0.06025935
8       0.8     NA      NA 11.534506 0.04939127
9       0.9     NA      NA 12.248755 0.04134689
10      1.0     NA      NA 12.917135 0.03520146
> barrierOptionTestRQuantLib(optionType = "p", barrierLevel = 110)
   Maturity DownIn DownOut       UpIn    UpOut
1       0.1     NA      NA 0.07561724 3.482451
2       0.2     NA      NA 0.43959907 4.439600
3       0.3     NA      NA 0.91278507 4.911200
4       0.4     NA      NA 1.39848564 5.172898
5       0.5     NA      NA 1.86677683 5.324523
6       0.6     NA      NA 2.30859306 5.411284
7       0.7     NA      NA 2.72199355 5.456764
8       0.8     NA      NA 3.10763477 5.474518
9       0.9     NA      NA 3.46710326 5.472906
10      1.0     NA      NA 3.80225568 5.457370
```

We can compare these results to those from our direct implementation for the barrier model and find that the results are very consistent.

In this chapter, we discussed how to implement the generalized Black-Scholes-Merton model for pricing European, American, and barrier options. We also presented the detailed procedure on how to use the *RQuantLib* package to value various options and compared the results with those obtained from our own implementation. This should provide you enough background information to understand the mathematics behind the options, implement option models in R, and apply the *RQuantLib* package to evaluate options.

However, all of the above discussions in this chapter is for demonstration purpose only. There is still more work to do to price the real-world options. For example, in our discussion on options pricing, we always use the continuous dividend yield and constant values (or flat term structures) for interest rates and volatility. As we know, in real-world market, the dividends are not paid in a continuous way but in a predetermined format, such as quarterly; both the interest rate and volatility are not constants and we cannot use constant values (or flat term structures) for them.

If you want to value options in real-world market with discrete dividend payments using the interest rate curve and volatility surface, you will need to bootstrap the required dividend, interest rate, and volatility curves from real market data. Since the current version of *RQuantLib* does not exposes the interface to access necessary features, you need to use the original *QuantLib* or its equivalent SWIG R version to evaluate real-world options. If you are interested in this topic, my previous published book "*Practical C# and WPF for Financial Markets*" provided an example on how to price a real-world American option using the C# SWIG version of *QuantLib*. This example will give you an idea for what is required to price options in the real-world market. By following the steps and templates described in that example, you should be able to price various options in real-world markets.

# Chapter 6
# Pricing Fixed-Income Instruments

We usually regard fixed income securities as complex financial instruments. This may be because they have a more complex structure, or include some form of derivative component. Although the fixed income market is more than twice as large as the equity market, it is generally followed less closely by the media and is less well understood by the general investing public.

The major difference between fixed income and equities is in the area of price transparency. Stock prices are publicly known and changes are relayed instantly to all market participants. Thus, in the stock market, we can get a fair market price at the time of our buy or sell stocks. On the other hand, in the fixed income market, such as the bond market, trades are usually executed dealer-to-dealer or dealer-to-investor. This means that there is no central record of all of the transaction prices in the bond market. Therefore, instruments pricing in the fixed income market is more important than that in the equity market.

In this chapter, I will demonstrate how to price some of fixed income instruments, including bond, credit swaps, and interest rates. The purpose of this chapter is more on technical approaches, implementation, and pricing engine applications, rather than an introduction or complete explanation about the fixed income instruments. You can always find good introductions on the topics from other textbooks.

## Simple Bonds Pricing

A bond, or a debt security, is a financial instrument, under which the issuer owes the holders a debt and is obliged to pay them interest (the coupon) and to repay the principal at a maturity date. Interest is usually payable at fixed intervals (annual, semiannual, monthly). Bonds and stocks are both securities, but the major difference between the two is that stockholders have an equity stake in the company (i.e. they are investors), whereas bondholders have a creditor stake in the company (i.e. they are lenders). Being a creditor, bondholders have priority over stockholders. This means they will be repaid in advance of stockholders in the event of bankruptcy. This is the reason why a bond is less risky than an equity. Another difference is that bonds usually have a defined term, or maturity, after which the bond is redeemed, whereas stocks are typically outstanding indefinitely. A standard bond is a fixed coupon bond without any embedded option, delivering its coupons on periodic dates and principal on the maturity date.

In this section, we will discuss simplified or hypothetical bonds, which has flat rate or simple rate curve term structures. We can view bond pricing as a three-step process: obtain the cash flows the bondholder is entitled to; obtain the discount rates for the maturities corresponding to the cash flow dates; and obtain the bond price as the discounted value of the cash flow.

The cash flow of a bond depends on two parameters: maturity and coupon rate. For example, a government bond pays one-half of its coupon rate times its principal value every 6 months up to and including the maturity date. Thus, a bond with a 6% coupon and $1,000 face value maturing on 12/1/2017, will make future coupon payments of 3% of principal value, that is $30 on every June 1 and December 1 between the purchase date and the maturity date.

Then, we need to apply some kind of discounted value type of formula to obtain the current value of the bond. Given that the cash flows are known with certainty ex ante, only the time-value needs to be accounted for, using the present value rule, which can be written in the form:

$$PV(CF_t) = B(0,t)CF_t$$

where $PV(CF_t)$ is the present value of the cash flow $CF_t$ received at date $t$ and $B(0, t)$ is the price at date 0 (today) of $1 to be received on date $t$. $B(t, 0)$ is called discount factor. You might be more familiar with an expression of the kind

$$PV(CF_t) = \frac{CF_t}{[1 + R(0,t)]^t}$$

where $R(0, t)$ is the annual spot rate (or discount rate or interest rate) at date 0 for an investment up to date t. Thus, we can write the price for a bond as

$$PV(\text{bond}) = \sum_{t=1}^{T} \frac{CF_t}{[1 + R(0,t)]^t} = \sum_{t=1}^{T} B(0,t)CF_t \tag{6-1}$$

You may ask how much exactly is worth the $1 received in a year from now? The answer to this question is simply $\$1/[1 + R(0,1)]$. Indeed, note that if we start with $\$1/[1 + R(0,1)]$ and invest it at the rate of $R(0,1)$, we will end up with $1 at the end of the period. Therefore, there is no difference between getting $\$1/[1 + R(0,1)]$ today or $1 in a year from now, so we should be willing to exchange one for the other. In other words, the fair price of a contract that promises to pay $1 in one year from now is $\$1/[1 + R(0,1)]$. It is the present value of $1. Of course, we may extend the principle to obtain the present value of a series of cash flows, which is just the bond pricing formula as shown in the above equation.

# Discounting Factors

There is a very convenient formula that allows us to compute the present value of a series of cash flows when all cash flows and all discount rates across various maturities are identical and equal to $CF$ and $y$. Then the formula become

$$P_0 = \sum_{t=1}^{T} \frac{CF}{(1 + y)^t} = CF \times \frac{1}{y} \times \left[1 - \frac{1}{(1 + y)^T}\right] \tag{6-2}$$

More generally, we have

$$P_0 = C \times \frac{1}{y} \times \left[1 - \frac{1}{(1+y)^T}\right] + \frac{N}{(1+y)^T} \tag{6-3}$$

where $P_0$ is the present value of the bond, $T$ is the maturity of the bond, $N$ is the nominal value of the bond, $C = c \times N$ is the coupon payment, and $c$ is the coupon rate and $y$ is the discount rate.

As an illustration, we consider the problem of valuing a series of cash flows promised by a hypothetical bond with a 5% annual coupon rate, a 10-year maturity and a $1,000 face value. We also assume all discount rates equal to 6%. Before we compute the present value of this bond, denoted by $P_0$, we first identify the cash flows. We have $CF_1 = CF_2 = \ldots = CF_9 = 50$ and $CF_{10} = 1{,}050$. Therefore, the value of this bond is

$$P_0 = \sum_{t=1}^{9} \frac{50}{(1+0.06)^t} + \frac{1050}{(1+0.06)^{10}} = \$926.3991 \tag{6-4}$$

It is useful to note the following result: when the discount rate is equal to the coupon rate, then the bond value is equal to the face value.

The quoted price (or market price) of a bond in the market is usually its clean price, that is, its gross price minus the accrued interest. When we purchase a bond, we are actually entitled to receive all the future cash flows of this bond, until we no longer own it. If we buy the bond between two coupon payment dates, we logically must pay it at a price reflecting the fraction of the next coupon that the seller of the bond is entitled to receive for having held it until the sale. This price is called the gross price or dirty price, which is the sum of the clean price and the portion of the coupon that is due to the seller of the bond. This portion is called the accrued interest. Note that the accrued interest is computed from the settlement data on. In convention, the clean price, dirty price, and accrued interest are calculated for the face value of 100. Therefore, the present value of a bond should be equal to the face value times dirty price divided by 100.

## Pricing Bonds Using RQuantLib

The above example for a bond is very simple. Now we try to reproduce the above results using the bond-pricing engine from *RQuantLib*, which should give us an idea what are the steps we need to take when we price a simple bond using the pricing engine in *QuantLib*.

Add a new fixed-income helper file named *fixedIncomeHelper.R* to the "[R working Directory]/R" directory. Add a new *bondFlatRate* function to this file. Here is the code for this function:

```
bondFlatRate <- function(evalDate, issuedate, maturity, settlementDays, faceValue,
                         rate, coupon, frequency){
  bond <- list(settlementDays = settlementDays,
               issuedate = as.Date(issuedate),
               faceAmount = faceValue,
               accrualDayCounter="ActualActual.Bond",
               paymentConvention="Unadjusted")
  schedule <- list(effectiveDate = as.Date(issuedate),
                   maturityDate = as.Date(maturity),
                   period = frequency,
                   calendar = "UnitedStates/GovernmentBond",
                   businessDayConvention = "Unadjusted",
```

```
                    terminationDateConvention = "Unadjusted",
                    dateGeneration = "Backward",
                    endOfMonth = 0)
  calc <- list(dayCounter = "ActualActual.Bond",
               compounding = "Simple",
               freq = "Annual",
               durationType = "Modified")
  params <- list(tradeDate = as.Date(evalDate),
                 settleDate = as.Date(evalDate) + settlementDays,
                 dt = 0.25,
                 interpWhat = "forward",
                 interpHow = "logLinear")
  setEvaluationDate(as.Date(evalDate))
  flatCurve <- DiscountCurve(params, list(flat = rate))
  b <- FixedRateBond(bond, coupon, schedule, calc, discountCurve = flatCurve)
  return(b)
}
```

Here, we first define a coupon-payment schedule and create a term structure using the flat interest rate, and then construct the fixed rate bond by calling the *FixedRateBond* function. The variables used in the *bondFlatRate* function are rather self-explanatory, and we simply use the template to value the fixed rate bonds.

We can then use the following statements to price the hypothetical bond discussed previously:

```
> source("./R/fixedIncomeHelper.R")
> bondFlatRate("2015-12-16", "2015-12-16", "2025-12-16", 1,1000, 0.06,0.05,"Annual")
Concise summary of valuation for FixedRateBond
 Net present value :  913.7844
       clean price :  91.365
       dirty price :  91.378
    accrued coupon :  0.013889
             yield :  0.061836
          duration :  5.2188
   settlement date :  2015-12-17
        cash flows :
       Date Amount
 2016-12-16     50
 2017-12-16     50
 2018-12-16     50
 2019-12-16     50
 2020-12-16     50
 2021-12-16     50
 2022-12-16     50
 2023-12-16     50
 2024-12-16     50
 2025-12-16     50
 2025-12-16   1000
```

You can see from the above results that the bond engine implemented in *RQuantLib* (version 0.4.2) does provide the correct cash flows, but it gives incorrect values for the net present value (NPV), clean price, dirty price, and accrued amount. For example, our simple analytic calculation for this bond gives NPV = 926.3991 while it is 913.7844 from *RQuantLib*, which generates a 1.38% difference. This is unacceptable. Furthermore, if we set the coupon rate = interest rate (= 0.5 for example), we expect that the NPV should be equal to the face value. However, *RQuantLib* gives NPV = 990.3802, which is not equal to the face value of 1000.

## Creating QuantLib-SWIG R

Note that *RQuantLib* implements an additional wrapper layer on top of the QuantLib-SWIG R code. There may have some issues at this additional wrapper layer. In this case, it is better to use the original QuantLib-SWIG R, instead of the *RQuantLib*.

In practice, generating the QuantLib-SWIG R is not trivial. I found that creating the QuantLib- SWIG R on linux system such as Ubuntu is much easier than creating it on the Windows operating system. Here I will outline the procedure of generating the QuantLib-SWIG R on an Ubuntu system. Do not worry if you are using the Windows PC: you can install an Oracle *VirtualBox* on your Window machine and then install Ubuntu on the *VirtualBox* as a guest system. After that, you can install your application software, such as R, RStudio, etc. on Ubuntu.

First, we need to install *QuantLib* on Ubuntu. We can download the *QuantLib* package in Ubuntu from the https://launchpad.net/ubuntu/+source/quantlib or https://sourceforge.net/projects/quantlit/files websites. Then we can follow the introduction described at http://quantlib.org/install/linux.shtml to install the boost and *QuantLib*.

Next, we need to install the QuantLib-SWIG. If we go to the QuantLib-SWIG's official website at github, we may find that the particular version may miss certain required configure files to setup our linux environment. Therefore, it is better to go to Ubuntu's website to download the latest version (1.7 at that time) of QuanLib-SWIG for Ubuntu at https://launchpad.net/ubuntu/+source/quantlib-swig. Select the latest version and download the original tar.gz file (i.e., quantlib-swig_1.7.Orig.tar.gz). After we download this library and tar ball, we should be able to run individually configure, make, and make install within the QuantLib SWIG directory using the following commands:

```
sudo -s
./configure
make -C R
```

The above build process creates sources for a standard R package that can be installed from this directory by issuing the command:

```
R CMD INSTALL .
```

Now, start *RStudio* and load the QuantLib-SWIG R package using the command:

```
> library(QuantLib)
```

We can then access most features of the original *QuantLib* from R. In the following, I assume that you have successfully loaded the QuantLib-SWIG into R.

## Pricing Bonds Using QuantLib-SWIG R

Now, we can use the bond pricing engines in the QuantLib-SWIG R to reprice the hypothetical bond described in Eq. (6-4). Inside *RStudio* on Ubuntu, we create a new file named *fixedIncomeHelper.R* and add a new function named *bondFlatRate* to this file. We also assume that the file is located at the R working directory. Here is the code for this function:

```
bondFlatRate <- function(evalDate, issueDate, maturity, settlementDays, faceValue,
                        rate, coupon, frequency){
```

```
  evalDate <- toQlDate(evalDate)
  calendar <- UnitedStates("GovernmentBond")
  invisible(Settings_instance()$setEvaluation(d = evalDate))
  issueDate <- toQlDate(issueDate)
  maturity <- toQlDate(maturity)
  settlementDate <- evalDate + settlementDays
  dc <- ActualActual("Bond")
  schedule <- Schedule(issueDate, maturity, Period(frequency), calendar,
                       "Unadjusted", "Unadjusted",
                       copyToR(DateGeneration(),"Backward"), FALSE)
  bond <- FixedRateBond(settlementDays,faceValue,schedule, coupon, dc)
  flateCurve <- FlatForward(settlementDate, QuoteHandle(SimpleQuote(rate)),
                            dc, "Compounded", "Annual")
  ts <- YieldTermStructureHandle(flateCurve)
  engine <- DiscountingBondEngine(ts)
  invisible(Instrument_setPricingEngine(bond, engine))
  df <- data.frame(NPV = Instrument_NPV(bond), CleanPrice = Bond_cleanPrice(bond),
                   DirtyPrice = Bond_dirtyPrice(bond),
                   AccruedAmount = Bond_accruedAmount(bond),
                   Yield = Bond_yield(bond, dc, "Compounded", "Annual"))
  return(df)
}

toQlDate <- function(dateString){
  dt <- as.Date(dateString)
  return(rDate2qlDate(dt))
}

rDate2qlDate<- function(rDate){
  qlDate <- Date(as.numeric(format(rDate, "%d")), format(rDate, "%B"),
                 as.numeric(format(rDate, "%Y")))
  return(qlDate)
}

toDateString <- function(qlDate){
  dt <- toRDate(qlDate)
  return(as.character(dt))
}

toRDate <- function(qlDate){
  d0 <- paste0(Date_dayOfMonth(qlDate), "-", Date_month(qlDate), "-",
               Date_year(qlDate))
  return(as.Date(d0, "%d-%B-%Y"))
}
```

The helper function *toQlDate* is used to convert a date string such as "2015-12-16" to the date format used in *QuantLib*. I also include several other helper functions, *rDate2qlDate*, *toDateString*, and *toRDate*, which allow us to perform various conversions between R date and *QuantLib* date. The code for the *bondFlatRate* function is similar to that used in *RQauntLib* with some differences in syntax. The syntax used in the QuantLib-SWIG R is closer to that used in the original *QuantLib*.

Here, the *bondFlatRate* function takes the face value, discount rate, and coupon rate as inputs and returns the NPV (net present value), clean price, dirty price, accrued amount, and yield to maturity (YTM). Within the function, we first create a *Schedule* object, which generates the coupon payment dates by taking into account a supplied calendar to determine business dates and holidays. We then set a

*FixedRateBond* instance that takes face value of the bond, schedule, and coupon rate as its input parameters. Next, we create a flat term structure for the discount rate because the discount rate is a constant for a simple bond. Finally, the *DiscountingBondEngine* takes the *YieldTermStruture* (or yield curve) as an argument, from which the pricing engine extracts the interest rates required to discount the bond's coupons.

Note that we also define the settlement date using the input parameter, *settlementDays*. The settlement date is the date on which payment is due in exchange for the bond. It is generally equal to the trade date (*evalDate*) plus a number of working days (*settlementDays*). For example, in Japan, *settlementDays* = 3 for Treasury bonds and T-bills. On the other hand, in the United States, *settlementDays* = 1 for Treasury bonds and T-bills. In UK, *settlementDays* = 1 and 2 for Treasury bonds and T-bills respectively. In the Euro zone, *settlementDays* = 3 for Treasury bonds, as it can be 1, 2, or 3 for T-bills, depending on the country under consideration.

We can now execute this function using the following statements:

```
> source("fixedIncomeHelper.R")
> bondFlatRate("2015-12-16", "2015-12-16","2025-12-16", 1, 1000, 0.06,0.05,"Annual")
       NPV CleanPrice DirtyPrice AccruedAmount       Yield
1 926.3991   92.62625   92.63991     0.0136612 0.06001663
```

You can see that our calculation using QuantLib-SWIG R for the net present value is the same as our previous analytic result [see Eq. (6-4)], which is different from what we obtained using *RQuantLib*.

You can also see from the above calculations that the dirty price is consistent with the present value of the bond. In addition, the dirty price is the sum of the clean price and accrued amount. Now, you may ask how does the pricing engine calculate the accrued amount? We know that the evaluation (trade) date is on 12/16/2015, and the settlement days = 1, indicating the settlement date is on 12/17/2015. This means we cannot collect the coupon rate until the settlement date, so we need to pay back one-day coupon to the seller, which is just the one day accrued amount. For the \$100 face value and 5% annual coupon rate, the one-year coupon payment will be \$5. Since we use the *ActualActual* day counter convention in the *bondFlatRate* function. There are 366 days from 12/16/2015 to 12/16/2016. In this case, the accrued interest is equal to $\$5 \times \left(\frac{1}{366}\right) = \$0.0136612$, which is the exact the same result from our calculation.

We can also perform the same calculations when we change the discount rate to 0.05, which is the same as the coupon rate. In this case, we have:

```
> bondFlatRate("2015-12-16", "2015-12-16", "2025-12-16", 1, 1000,0.05,0.05,"Annual")
   NPV CleanPrice DirtyPrice AccruedAmount       Yield
1 1000   99.98634        100     0.0136612 0.05001378
```

You can see the NPV is equal to the face value, as expected.

## Compounding Frequency Conventions

In calculating the present value for a bond, we should pay careful attention to the question of how the interest rate is defined. To apply present value formulas, we must have some information about both the time basis (usually interest rates are expressed on an annual basis) and the compounding frequency.

In general, if we invest \$$x$ amount at the interest rate $R_n$ expressed on an annual basis and compounded $n$ times per year, you would get $x(1+\frac{R_n}{n})^{nT}$ after $T$ years. Then, the effective equivalent annual (i.e., compounded once a year) rate $R_1 = R$ is defined as the solution to

$$x\left(1+\frac{R_n}{n}\right)^{nT} = x(1+R)^T$$

or

$$R = \left(1+\frac{R_n}{n}\right)^{n} - 1 \qquad (6\text{-}5)$$

For example, bond yields are often expressed on a yearly basis with semiannual compounding in the United States and UK, as they are expressed on a yearly basis with annual compounding in France and Germany. One can always convert a bond yield into an effective annual yield (EAY), that is, an interest rate expressed on a yearly basis with annual compounding.

In Eq. (6-5), if we let the compounding frequency increase without bound, we will perform a continuous compounding. In this case, the amount of money obtained per \$$x$ invested after $T$ years is

$$\lim_{n\to\infty} x\left(1+\frac{R_n}{n}\right)^{nT} = xe^{R_cT}$$

where $R_c$ expressed on an annual basis is a continuously compounded rate. This allows us to obtain a very easy derivation of the future or present value of any cash flow, using

$$FV_t(CF_0) = CF_0e^{R_ct}, \qquad PV(CF_t) = CF_te^{-R_ct}$$

Where $FV_t(CF_0)$ is the future value at date $t$ of a cash flow $CF_0$ invested at date 0 at an $R_c$ continuously compounded rate, and $PV(CF_t)$ is the present value at date 0 of a cash flow $CF_t$ received at date $t$.

We can also easily obtain the effective equivalent annual rate R:

$$R = e^{R_c} - 1$$

When R is small, we have $R \approx R_c$ as a first-order approximation. For example, the equivalent annual rate of a 5% continuously compounded interest rate is $R = e^{0.05} - 1 = 5.1271\%$. Note that $R - R^c > 0$, which makes sense; it means that we should invest at a higher rate when compounding is less frequent to generate the same amount of cash at the end of a given period.

## Pricing Bonds with a Rate Curve

In the preceding section, we discussed the frequency compounding. Here, I will show you how to price a bond with an interest curve instead of a constant. In this case, we need to build a curved term structure for the interest rate instead of a flat one. Specifically, we want to consider a simple hypothetical bond with a face value of \$100, which pays 5% coupon semiannually issued on 1/15/2015 and maturity on 1/15/2017. To make things simpler, we assume that we know the interest rates of the treasury as of 1/15/2015. The annualized rates are 0.4% for 6 months, 0.6% for 1 year, 0.65% for 1.5 years, and 0.7% for 2 years. We can calculate the present value for this bond easily using the formula in Eq. (6-1):

$$PV = \frac{2.5}{(1+0.004)^{0.5}} + \frac{2.5}{1+0.006} + \frac{2.5}{(1+0.0065)^{1.5}} + \frac{102.5}{(1+0.007)^2} = 108.53 \qquad (6\text{-}6)$$

Now, we want to reproduce the above result using the pricing engine in *QuantLib*. Add a new function, *bondCurveRate*, to the *fixedIncomeHelper.R* file. Here is the code for this function:

```
bondCurveRate <- function(){
  evalDate <- Date(15, "January", 2015)
  invisible(Settings_instance()$setEvaluation(d = evalDate))
  issueDate <- Date(15, "January", 2015)
  maturity <- Date(15, "January", 2017)
  calendar <- UnitedStates("GovernmentBond")
  settlementDays <- 1
  settlementDate <- evalDate + settlementDays
  settlementDate <- Calendar_adjust(calendar, settlementDate)
  coupon <- 0.05
  dc <- ActualActual("Bond")
  dates <- list(Date(15, "January", 2015), Date(15, "July", 2015),
                Date(15, "January", 2016), Date(15, "July", 2016),
                Date(15, "January", 2017))
  rates <- c(0, 0.004, 0.006, 0.0065, 0.007)
  dateV <- DateVector()
  for(i in 1:5){
    DateVector_push_back(dateV, dates[[i]])
  }
  schedule <- Schedule(issueDate, maturity, Period("Semiannual"), calendar,
    "Unadjusted", "Unadjusted", copyToR(DateGeneration(),"Backward"), FALSE)
  bond <- FixedRateBond(settlementDays, 100, schedule, coupon, dc)
  rateCurve <- ZeroCurve(dateV, rates, dc, calendar, Linear(), "Compounded",
                         "Annual")
  ts <- YieldTermStructureHandle(rateCurve)
  engine <- DiscountingBondEngine(ts)
  invisible(Instrument_setPricingEngine(bond, engine))
  df <- data.frame(NPV = Instrument_NPV(bond), CleanPrice = Bond_cleanPrice(bond),
                   DirtyPrice = Bond_dirtyPrice(bond),
                   AccruedAmount = Bond_accruedAmount(bond),
                   Yield = Bond_yield(bond, dc, "Compounded", "Annual"))
  return(df)
}
```

The key step in this function is to create a curved term structure for the interest rates using the *ZeroCurve* function. This function takes the rate dates and rate data points as its arguments. The zero curve is a special type of yield curve that maps interest rates on zero-coupon bonds to different maturities across time. Zero-coupon bonds have a single payment at maturity, so these curves enable us to price arbitrary cash flows, fixed income instruments, and derivatives. Another type of interest rate curve, the forward curve, is constructed using the forward rates derived from this zero curve.

Zero curves should be separately constructed for government securities and for inter-bank markets. Zero-coupon bonds are available for a limited number of maturities, so we typically construct zero curves with a combination of boostrapping and interpolation techniques in order to build a continuous curve. Inside the *bondCurveRate* function, we use the linear approach to interpolate our zero curve. Once we construct these curves, we can then use them to derive other curves such as the forward curve and to price financial instruments.

We can test the code using the following commands:

```
> source("fixedIncomeHelper.R")
> bondCurveRate()
       NPV CleanPrice DirtyPrice AccruedAmount      Yield
1 108.5359    108.522   108.5359    0.01381215 0.00695278
```

You can see that our calculated result for the present value of the bond is consistent with the analytic result in Eq. (6-6).

## Yield to Maturity

The coupon rate is the stated interest rate on a security, referred to as an annual percentage of the face value. It is commonly paid twice a year in the United States or once a year in France and Germany. Please do not confuse it with the actual current yield. The current yield $y_c$ is obtained using the following formula:

$$y_c = \frac{cN}{P}$$

Where $c$ is the coupon rate, $N$ is the nominal value, and $P$ is the current price.

The yield to maturity (YTM) is the single rate that sets the present value of the cash flows equal to the bond price. More precisely, the bond price $P$ can be obtained by discounting future cash flows back to their present value as indicated in the following formula:

$$P = \sum_{t=1}^{T} \frac{CF_t}{(1+y)^t} \tag{6-7}$$

where $y$ is the yield expressed on a yearly basis and $T$ is the number of periods.

Previously, we calculated the present value for a bond directly using the different interest rates for different periods. Now, we can calculate it again using Eq. (6-7) with a single YTM rate. In our calculated results using *QuantLib*, we have obtained $ytm = 0.00695278$ from the pricing engine in QuantLib, and we can then calculate the present value with Eq. (6-7)

$$P = \frac{2.5}{(1+ytm)^{0.5}} + \frac{2.5}{1+ytm} + \frac{2.5}{(1+ytm)^{1.5}} + \frac{102.5}{(1+ytm)^2} = 108.5376$$

which is consistent with the direct calculation in Eq. (6-6).

In fact, the YTM is the internal rate of return of the series of cash flows. Hence, each cash flow is discounted using the same rate. Generally, there exists a one-to-one correspondence between the price and the YTM of a bond. Therefore, giving the YTM for a bond is equivalent to giving the price for the bond. The YTM is a complex average of pure discount rates that makes the present value of the bond's payment equal to its price. Unless the term structure of interest rates is flat, there is no reason one would consider the YTM on a 10-year bond as the relevant discount rate for a 10-year horizon. We may consider the YTM as just a convenient way of re-expressing the bond price.

# Zero-Coupon Yield Curve

When we attempt to price whatever financial securities, we always need to construct various term structures for the interest rates. The term structure of interest rates is simply the series of interest rates ordered by term-to-maturity at a given time. The nature of interest rate determines the nature of the term structure.

There are several different types of yield curves, including the yield to maturity curve, swap rate curve, the zero-coupon curve, the forward rate curve, etc. The yield to maturity and swap rate curves are market data, whereas zero-coupon and forward rate curves can be constructed using market data.

The zero-coupon yield curve is especially important in practice because it allows us to know the discount factor and price any fixed-income security delivering known cash flows in the future such as a fixed coupon bond. It also allows us to derive other implicit curves such as the forward rate curve and par yield curve.

In Eq. (6-1), we have defined the discount factor $B(0, t)$ as

$$B(0,t) = \frac{1}{[1+R(0,t)]^t} \tag{6-8}$$

where $B(0, t)$ is the market price at date 0 of a bond paying off \$1 at date $t$. $B(0, t)$ is also called the spot zero-coupon rate or discount rate. In practice, when we know the spot zero-coupon yield curve $R(0, t)$, we can obtain spot prices for all fixed income securities with known future cash flows.

If $R(0, t)$ is the rate at which we can invest today in a $t$ period bond, we can define an implied forward rate (also called forward zero-coupon rate) between years $x$ and $y$ as

$$F(0,x,y-x) = \left\{\frac{[1+R(0,y)]^y}{[1+R(0,x)]^x}\right\}^{\frac{1}{y-x}} - 1 \tag{6-9}$$

$F(0,x,y-x)$ is the forward rate as seen from date $t = 0$, starting at date $t = x$, and with residual maturity $y - x$. In practice, it is very common to draw the forward curve $F(0,x,\theta)$ with rates starting at date $x$.

In this section, we want to build the zero-coupon yield curve for three types of market data. First curve is the non-default Treasury zero-coupon curve, which is derived from Treasury bond market prices. The second curve is the interbank zero-coupon yield curve, which is derived from money-market rates, futures contracts rates, and swap rates. The third yield curve is the credit zero-coupon curve for a given rating and economic sector, which is derived from corporate bond market prices. Note that by subtracting the Treasury or the interbank zero-coupon curve from the credit curve, we obtain the credit spread zero-coupon yield curve.

## Treasury Zero-Coupon Yield Curve

We can derive the Treasury zero-coupon curve directly from the current fixed coupon bearing bond prices. This method allows us to recover exactly the prices of the selected bonds. If we need $n$ distinct zero-coupon rates, we need to first collect the prices of $n$ coupon (or even better the zero coupon if existing) bonds. The default-free coupon bonds (like US Treasury bonds) are usually preferred, because they provide information about the risk-free structure of interest rates.

Suppose, we pick up $n$ coupon bonds. We need to figure out the cash flows (coupons and principal) for each bond, and then relate the zero-coupon bond prices to the bond market prices via the cash flows:

$$P_t^j = \sum_{i=1}^{n} CF_{t_i}^j B(t,t_i) \tag{6-10}$$

where $P_t^j$ is the $j$th bond price at date $t$, $CF_{t_i}^j$ is the cash flows of the $j$th bond at date $t_i$, and $B(t,t_i)$ is the zero-coupon bond price at date $t$ of $1 to be received on date $t_i$. Thus, in order to determine the value of the zero-coupon bond price, we need to solve the above linear equation (6-10). The zero-coupon bond prices derived here are not real market values, but, rather, implied zero-coupon bond values consistent with the set of market prices of fixed coupon bonds. From these zero-coupon bond prices, we can easily extract at date $t$ the annual compounded zero-coupon rate $R(t, t_i - t)$ with maturity $t_i - t$ using

$$R(t, t_i - t) = e^{-\frac{1}{t_i - t}\ln[B(t,t_i)]} - 1 \tag{6-11}$$

and its continuously compounded equivalent $R_c(t, t_i - t)$ by using

$$R_c(t, t_i - t) = -\frac{1}{t_i - t}\ln[B(t,t_i)] \tag{6-12}$$

Now, let look at an example. At 1/15/2015, we want to derive the zero-coupon curve until 4-year maturity. For this purpose, we get from the market four bonds with the following features: Bond1: annual coupon: 5%, maturity (years): 1, price: 101; Bond2: 5.5%, 2, 101.5; Bond3: 5%, 3, 99; and Bond4: 6%, 4, 100. Here I will illustrate how to use *QuantLib* to calculate the zero-coupon rate ($R$), continuously compounded equivalent rate ($R_c$), and discount rate ($B$).

Add a new function named *zeroCouponDirect* to the *fixedIncomeHelper.R* file. Here is the code for this function:

```
zeroCouponDirect <- function(){
  evalDate <- Date(15, "January", 2015)
  coupons <- c(0.05, 0.055, 0.05, 0.06)
  bondPrices <- c(101.0, 101.5, 99.0, 100.0)
  maturities <- list( Date(15, "January", 2016),
                      Date(15, "January", 2017),
                      Date(15, "January", 2018),
                      Date(15, "January", 2019))
  invisible(Settings_instance()$setEvaluation(d = evalDate))
  calendar <- UnitedStates()
  dc <- ActualActual("Bond")
  rateHelpers <- RateHelperVector()
  for(i in 1:4){
    quote <- QuoteHandle(SimpleQuote(bondPrices[i]))
    schedule <- Schedule(evalDate, maturities[[i]], Period("Annual"), calendar,
                         "Unadjusted", "Unadjusted", copyToR(DateGeneration(),
                         "Backward"), TRUE)
    helper <- FixedRateBondHelper(quote, 0, 100.0, schedule, coupons[i], dc,
                         "Unadjusted", 100.0, evalDate)
    RateHelperVector_push_back(rateHelpers, helper)
  }
  ts <- PiecewiseLinearZero(evalDate, rateHelpers, dc)
  rmat <- rep(as.Date("1900-01-01"), length = 4)
  discount <- rep(NA, length = 4)
  zeroRate <- rep(NA, length = 4)
  contRate <- rep(NA, length = 4)
  for(i in 1:4){
    years <- DayCounter_yearFraction(dc, evalDate, maturities[[i]])
    rmat[i] <- toRDate(maturities[[i]])
```

```
    discount[i] <- YieldTermStructure_discount(ts, maturities[[i]])
    zz <- YieldTermStructure_zeroRate(ts, years, "Compounded", "Annual")
    zeroRate[i] <- InterestRate_rate(zz)
    contRate[i] <- InterestRate_rate(InterestRate_equivalentRate(zz, dc,
                "Compounded", "Daily", evalDate, maturities[[i]]))
  }
  df <- data.frame(Maturity = rmat, Discount = discount, ZeroRate = zeroRate,
                   ContinuousRate = contRate)
  return(df)
}
```

This function is very simple. First, we define various input parameters according to the QuantLib-SWIG R format, including the maturities, coupons, and prices for the selected four bonds. Then, we create the *FixedRateBondHelper* objects to hold bond properties for each bond and add them to a *RateHelperVector*. Next, we define the discount term structure using the *PiecewiseLinearZero* class, in which the term structure is bootstrapped and interpolated linearly on a number of interest rate instruments. *QuantLib* implemented various bootstrapping and interpolation functions, and we can choose different methods to build the term structures, such as *PiecewiseLogCubicDiscount*, and *PiecewiseCubicZero*.

Finally, we extract the discount factor, annually compounded zero-coupon rate, and continuously compounded rate from the discounting term structure. You may notice that it is more complicated in extracting the useful information from the calculated results in QuantLib-SWIG R. For example, we need to call several *QuantLib* functions to retrieve the continuously compounded rate from the yield term structure. In order to simplify this process, *RQuantLib* adds another wrapper layer to make more R-like *QuantLib* coding. However, *QuantLib* is a very complicated and comprehensive software framework for quantitative finance, it is almost impossible to port all features of the original *QuangLib* in this additional R wrapper layer. This is why *RQauntLib* is only a subset of *QuantLib* and may involve errors in this porting process. Even though QuantLib-SWIG R is hard to use, we can access almost all of the features provided by the original *QuantLib*. When we get used to the coding format, we will realize the power of QuantLib-SWIG R.

We can test the above implementation by issuing the following command:

```
> source("fixedIncomeHelper.R")
> zeroCouponDirect()
    Maturity  Discount   ZeroRate ContinuousRate
1 2016-01-15 0.9619048 0.03960396     0.03884190
2 2017-01-15 0.9119386 0.04717001     0.04609421
3 2018-01-15 0.8536265 0.05417012     0.05275765
4 2019-01-15 0.7890111 0.06103379     0.05924852
```

You can see that the continuously equivalent rate (compounded daily) is always smaller than the corresponding zero-coupon rate (compounded annually). This makes sense; it means that we should invest at a higher rate when compounding is less frequent to generate the same amount of cash at the end of a given period.

This direct method is fairly simple. Unfortunately, finding many distinct linearly independent bonds with the same coupon dates is almost impossible in practice. This is why we need to use a more powerful approach called the bootstrapping technique.

Bootstrapping is the term for building a zero-coupon yield curve from existing market data such as bond prices. Bootstrapping can be regarded as a repetitive double-step procedure.

- Extract directly zero-coupon rates with maturity inferior or equal to one year from corresponding zero-coupon bond prices. We then use interpolation to create a continuous zero-coupon yield curve for maturities inferior or equal to one year.
- Consider the bond with nearest maturity between one and two years. The bond has two cash flows and its price is logically the discounted value of these two cash flows. We know the first discount factor needed to obtain the discounted value of the first cash flow. The unknown variable is the second discount factor. By solving a nonlinear equation, we get this discount factor and corresponding zero-coupon rate. We begin again with the same process considering the next bond with nearest maturity between one and two years. We then use interpolation to create a continuous zero-coupon yield curve for maturities between one and two years, using the zero-coupon rates obtained from market prices.
- Consider the bond with nearest maturity between two and three years and repeat the same process. The unknown factors are always reduced to one and solving one equation enables to determine it as well as the corresponding zero-coupon rate. Repeat the process as necessary…

Here, I will create a helper function called *zeroCouponBootstrap* in the *fixedIncomeHelper.R* file and explain how we can construct a zero-coupon yield curve using the deposit rates and bond prices. The following is the code for this function:

```
zeroCouponBootstrap <- function(curveType = c("DataPoints", "BootStrap")){
  evalDate <- Date(15, "January", 2015)
  invisible(Settings_instance()$setEvaluation(d = evalDate))
  depositeRates <- c(0.044, 0.045, 0.046, 0.047, 0.049, 0.051, 0.053 )
  depositMaturities <- list(Period(1, "Days"),
                            Period(1, "Months"),
                            Period(2, "Months"),
                            Period(3, "Months"),
                            Period(6, "Months"),
                            Period(9, "Months"),
                            Period(12, "Months"))
  bondCoupons <- c(0.05, 0.06, 0.055, 0.05)
  bondPrices <- c(99.55, 100.55, 99.5, 97.6)
  bondMaturities <- list(Period(14, "Months"),
                         Period(21, "Months"),
                         Period(2, "Years"),
                         Period(3, "Years"))
  calendar <- UnitedStates()
  dc <- ActualActual("Bond")
  rateHelpers <- RateHelperVector()
  for(i in 1:length(depositeRates)){
    quote <- QuoteHandle(SimpleQuote(depositeRates[i]))
    helper <- DepositRateHelper(quote, depositMaturities[[i]], 0, calendar,
              "Unadjusted", TRUE, dc)
    RateHelperVector_push_back(rateHelpers, helper)
  }
  for(i in 1:length(bondPrices)){
    quote <- QuoteHandle(SimpleQuote(bondPrices[i]))
    mat <- evalDate + bondMaturities[[i]]
    schedule <- Schedule(evalDate, mat, Period("Annual"), calendar, "Unadjusted",
                         "Unadjusted", copyToR(DateGeneration(), "Backward"), TRUE)
    helper <- FixedRateBondHelper(quote, 0, 100.0, schedule, bondCoupons[i], dc,
                         "Unadjusted", 100.0, evalDate)
    RateHelperVector_push_back(rateHelpers,helper)
```

```
  }
  ts <- PiecewiseLinearZero(evalDate, rateHelpers, dc)
  rmat <- list()
  discount <- list()
  zeroRate <- list()
  contRate <- list()
  curveType <- tolower(curveType)
  mats <- PiecewiseLinearZero_dates(ts)
  if(curveType == "datapoints"){
    for(i in 1:DateVector_size(mats)){
      years <- DayCounter_yearFraction(dc, evalDate, mats[i][[1]])
      disc <- YieldTermStructure_discount(ts, mats[i][[1]])
      zz <- YieldTermStructure_zeroRate(ts, years, "Compounded", "Annual")
      zeror <- InterestRate_rate(zz)
      contr <- InterestRate_rate(InterestRate_equivalentRate(zz, dc, "Compounded",
               "Daily", evalDate, mats[i][[1]]))
      rmat <- c(rmat, as.character(toRDate(mats[i][[1]])))
      discount <- c(discount, disc)
      zeroRate <- c(zeroRate, zeror)
      contRate <- c(contRate, contr)
    }
  } else if(curveType == "bootstrap"){
    d1 <- mats[1][[1]]
    d2 <- mats[12][[1]]
    while(toRDate(d1) <= toRDate(d2)){
      years <- DayCounter_yearFraction(dc, evalDate, d1)
      disc <- YieldTermStructure_discount(ts, d1)
      zz <- YieldTermStructure_zeroRate(ts, years, "Compounded", "Annual")
      zeror <- InterestRate_rate(zz)
      contr <- InterestRate_rate(InterestRate_equivalentRate(zz, dc, "Compounded",
                                 "Daily", evalDate, d1))
      rmat <- c(rmat, as.character(toRDate(d1)))
      discount <- c(discount, disc)
      zeroRate <- c(zeroRate, zeror)
      contRate <- c(contRate, contr)
      d1 <- d1 + Period(1, "Months")
    }
  }
  df <- data.frame(Maturity = unlist(rmat), Discount = unlist(discount),
                   ZeroRate = unlist(zeroRate), ContinuousRate = unlist(contRate))
  df$Maturity <- as.Date(df$Maturity)
  return(df)
}
```

Here, we first create the deposit rates and fixed coupon bonds. We then define the deposit rates using the *DepositRateHelper* and add them to the *RateHelperVector* object named *rateHelpers*. Next, we create a *FixedRateBondHelper* object for each bond and add the bond helper to the *rateHelpers*. The zero-coupon yield curve is then constructed by putting this *rateHelpers* into a bootstrapping and linear interpolation object named *PiecewiseLinearZero*. Finally, we obtain the yield rates from the *ts* (the term structure) object using the *zeroRate* method.

Note that this function allows us to specify the *curveType* parameter, which controls the output results. If we set it to "*DataPoints*", the results are only extracted from the curve at the maturities defined in the deposit rates and bonds. Otherwise, we will get the output monthly. In fact, *QuantLib* generates a continuous yield curve, so we can extract the results at any maturities.

The example shown in the *zeroCouponBootstrap* function using the following deposit rates (zero-coupon) with maturities less or equal to 1 year:

| Maturity | Deposit Rates (%) |
|---|---|
| 1 Day | 4.4 |
| 1 Month | 4.5 |
| 2 Months | 4.6 |
| 3 Months | 4.7 |
| 6 Months | 4.9 |
| 9 Months | 5.1 |
| 12 Months | 5.3 |

and the following bonds priced by the market until 3-year maturity:

| Maturity | Coupon (%) | Price |
|---|---|---|
| 12 Months | 5 | 99.55 |
| 21 Months | 6 | 100.55 |
| 2 Years | 5.5 | 99.5 |
| 3 Years | 5 | 97.6 |

Now, executing the function by setting *curveType* = "*DataPoints*", we obtain the following results:

```
> source("fixedIncomeHelper.R")
> zeroCouponBootstrap("DataPoints")
     Maturity  Discount    ZeroRate ContinuousRate
1  2015-01-15 1.0000000 0.04497958     0.00000000
2  2015-01-16 0.9998795 0.04497958     0.04400000
3  2015-02-15 0.9962640 0.04593983     0.04491860
4  2015-03-15 0.9923917 0.04689073     0.04582744
5  2015-04-15 0.9883865 0.04783488     0.04672901
6  2015-07-15 0.9760859 0.04960025     0.04841259
7  2015-10-15 0.9631592 0.05132240     0.05005224
8  2016-01-15 0.9496676 0.05300000     0.05164689
9  2016-03-15 0.9404565 0.05402896     0.05262371
10 2016-10-15 0.9078081 0.05682578     0.05527405
11 2017-01-15 0.8936192 0.05784917     0.05624209
12 2018-01-15 0.8417482 0.05910559     0.05742929
```

Now, we can get the monthly results by setting *curveType* = "*BootStrap*":

```
> df <- zeroCouponBootstrap("BootStrap"); df
     Maturity  Discount    ZeroRate ContinuousRate
1  2015-01-15 1.0000000 0.04497958     0.00000000
2  2015-02-15 0.9962640 0.04593983     0.04491860
3  2015-03-15 0.9923917 0.04689073     0.04582744
4  2015-04-15 0.9883865 0.04783488     0.04672901
5  2015-05-15 0.9843612 0.04842301     0.04729020
6  2015-06-15 0.9802606 0.04901146     0.04785139
7  2015-07-15 0.9760859 0.04960025     0.04841259
8  2015-08-15 0.9718463 0.05017399     0.04895914
9  2015-09-15 0.9675371 0.05074804     0.04950569
10 2015-10-15 0.9631592 0.05132240     0.05005224
11 2015-11-15 0.9587257 0.05188131     0.05058379
```

```
12 2015-12-15 0.9542282 0.05244050       0.05111534
13 2016-01-15 0.9496676 0.05300000       0.05164689
14 2016-02-15 0.9450893 0.05351435       0.05213530
15 2016-03-15 0.9404565 0.05402896       0.05262371
16 2016-04-15 0.9358986 0.05442805       0.05300233
17 2016-05-15 0.9313041 0.05482729       0.05338095
18 2016-06-15 0.9266737 0.05522669       0.05375957
19 2016-07-15 0.9220081 0.05562623       0.05413819
20 2016-08-15 0.9173081 0.05602593       0.05451681
21 2016-09-15 0.9125745 0.05642578       0.05489543
22 2016-10-15 0.9078081 0.05682578       0.05527405
23 2016-11-15 0.9031022 0.05716680       0.05559673
24 2016-12-15 0.8983723 0.05750793       0.05591941
25 2017-01-15 0.8936192 0.05784917       0.05624209
26 2017-02-15 0.8892578 0.05795381       0.05634102
27 2017-03-15 0.8849031 0.05805847       0.05643996
28 2017-04-15 0.8805552 0.05816313       0.05653889
29 2017-05-15 0.8762142 0.05826781       0.05663782
30 2017-06-15 0.8718803 0.05837250       0.05673676
31 2017-07-15 0.8675534 0.05847719       0.05683569
32 2017-08-15 0.8632339 0.05858190       0.05693462
33 2017-09-15 0.8589216 0.05868662       0.05703355
34 2017-10-15 0.8546168 0.05879134       0.05713249
35 2017-11-15 0.8503196 0.05889608       0.05723142
36 2017-12-15 0.8460301 0.05900083       0.05733035
37 2018-01-15 0.8417482 0.05910559       0.05742929
```

We can also plot the zero-coupon curve and discount yield curve using the above results:

```
> plot(df$Maturity, df$ZeroRate, type="l", col = "blue", main = "Zero-Coupon Yield")
> lines(df$Maturity, df$ContinuousRate, type="l", col = "red")
> grid()
> plot(df$Maturity, df$Discount, type="l", col = "red", main="Discount Yield")
> grid()
```

which generates the results shown in Figure 6-1.

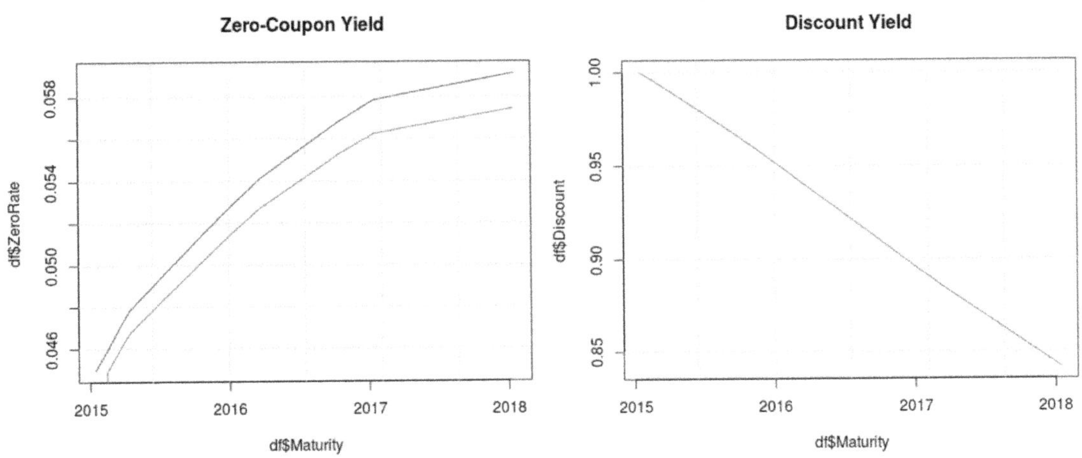


*Figure 6-1. Zero-coupon and discount yield curves.*

From the Figure 6-1 we can see the zero-coupon curve (compounded annually) is always located above its continuously equivalent rate (compounded daily) as expected. The discount rate curve looks like a straight line and decreases with the increase of maturity.

## Interbank Zero-Coupon Yield Curve

Generally, the input basket for deriving the interbank zero-coupon curve contains three types of instruments: money-market rates, futures contracts, and swap rates. Money-market rates have maturities ranging from 1 day to 1 year, such as Euribor and Libor rates. These rates, expressed on an Actual/360 (or 365) basis, are first converted into equivalent zero-coupon rates with Actual/365 (or 30/360) basis. For example, on 1/1/2015, we assume that the 1-month Libor rate was equal to 1.5%. Using the Actual/365 basis, the equivalent zero-coupon rate is given by

$$R\left(0,\frac{1}{12}\right) = \left(1+\frac{31}{360}\times 1.5\%\right)^{\frac{365}{31}} - 1$$

We only need to consider futures contracts depending on money-market rates, for example, 3-month Libor or 3-month Euribor contracts, and find zero-coupon rates from raw data. The price of a 3-month Libor contract is given by 100 minus the underlying 3-month forward rate. For instance, on 3/15/2015, the 3-month Libor rate was 1.5%, and the 3-month Libor contract with maturity date June 2015 had a price equal to 97.5. Hence, on 3/15/2015, the 3-month forward rate, starting on 6/15/2015, is 2.5%. The 6-month spot (or zero-coupon) rate can be obtained as follows:

$$R\left(0,\frac{6}{12}\right) = \left[\left(1+\frac{92}{360}\times 1.5\%\right)\left(1+\frac{92}{360}\times 2.5\%\right)\right]^{\frac{365}{184}} - 1$$

Similarly, from the prices of futures contracts with maturity date September 2015, December 2015 and March 2016, respectively, we can obtain the zero-coupon rates R(0, 9/12), R(0, 1), and R(0, 15/12).

For the swap rates, we consider 3-or-6 month Libor (or Euribor) swap yields with maturities ranging from 1 year to 30 years and find recursively equivalent zero-coupon rates. Swap yields are par yields; so the zero-coupon rate with maturity 2 years R(0, 2) is obtained as the solution to the following equation

$$\frac{Swap(2)}{1+R(0,1)} + \frac{1+Swap(2)}{[(1+R(0,2)]^2} = 1$$

where *Swap*(2) is the 2-year swap yield and R(0, 1) is equal to *Swap*(1). The other zero-coupon rates can be obtained recursively in a similar fashion.

Thus, the input basket for deriving the interbank zero-rate curve contains many different instruments with maturities ranging from 1 day to 30 years. If we need a continuous zero-coupon term structure, we can achieve this using either linear, cubic, log linear, or log cubic interpolations in *QuantLib*.

Add a new helper function named *interbankZeroCoupon* to the *fixedIncomeHelper.R* files. Here is code for this function:

```
interbankZeroCoupon <- function(settlementDate, depositRates, depositMaturities,
                                futPrices, swapRates, swapMaturities){
  calendar <- JointCalendar(UnitedKingdom("Exchange"), UnitedStates("Settlement"))
  settlementDate <- toQlDate(settlementDate)
```

```
fixingDays <- 2
evalDate <- Calendar_advance(calendar, settlementDate, -fixingDays, "Days")
invisible(Settings_instance()$setEvaluation(d = evalDate))
rateHelper <- RateHelperVector()

# Money market - Deposit:
depositDayCounter <- Actual360()
for(i in 1:length(depositRates)){
  quote <- QuoteHandle(SimpleQuote(depositRates[i]))
  helper <- DepositRateHelper(quote, depositMaturities[[i]], 0, calendar,
                              "Unadjusted", TRUE, depositDayCounter)
  RateHelperVector_push_back(rateHelper, helper)
}

# Futures contracts:
futDayCounter <- Actual360()
imm <- IMM_nextDate(settlementDate)
for(i in 1:length(futPrices)){
  helper <- FuturesRateHelper(futPrices[i], imm, 3, calendar, "ModifiedFollowing",
                              TRUE, futDayCounter)
  RateHelperVector_push_back(rateHelper, helper)
  imm <- IMM_nextDate(imm + 1)
}

# Swap rates:
swFrequency <- "Annual"
swDayConvention <- "Unadjusted"
swDayCounter <- Actual360()
swIborIndex <- USDLibor(Period(3, "Months"))
for(i in 1:length(swapRates)){
  helper <- SwapRateHelper(swapRates[i], swapMaturities[[i]], calendar,
        swFrequency, swDayConvention, swDayCounter, swIborIndex)
  RateHelperVector_push_back(rateHelper, helper)
}

# Term structure:
tsDayCounter <- Actual360()
ts <- PiecewiseLinearZero(evalDate, rateHelper, tsDayCounter)

# Retrieve results:
rmat <- list()
discount <- list()
zeroRate <- list()
contRate <- list()
mats <- PiecewiseLinearZero_dates(ts)
for(i in 1:DateVector_size(mats)){
  years <- DayCounter_yearFraction(Actual360(), evalDate, mats[i][[1]])
  disc <- YieldTermStructure_discount(ts, mats[i][[1]])
  zz <- YieldTermStructure_zeroRate(ts, years, "Compounded", "Annual")
  zeror <- InterestRate_rate(zz)
  contr <- InterestRate_rate(InterestRate_equivalentRate(zz, Actual360(),
                             "Compounded", "Daily", evalDate, mats[i][[1]]))
  rmat <- c(rmat, as.character(toRDate(mats[i][[1]])))
  discount <- c(discount, disc)
  zeroRate <- c(zeroRate, zeror)
```

```
    contRate <- c(contRate, contr)
  }
  df <- data.frame(Maturity = unlist(rmat), Discount = unlist(discount),
                   ZeroRate = unlist(zeroRate), ContinuousRate = unlist(contRate))
  df$Maturity <- as.Date(df$Maturity)
  return(df)
}
```

This function takes the money market (deposit), futures contracts, and swap rate market data as input arguments. Note how we create the *FuturesRateHelper* instance with the IMM (international money market) dates. The IMM dates are the four quarterly dates of each year, which most futures and option contracts use as their scheduled maturity date. The dates are the third Wednesday of March, June, September, and December.

The credit default swaps (CDS) also use the IMM dates. From 2002, the CDS market began to standardize CDS contracts so that they would all mature on one of the four IMM dates of March 20, June 20, September 20, and December 20. These IMM dates are used both as maturity dates for the contracts and as the dates for quarterly coupon payments.

We can test this function by creating a test function named *interbandZeroCoupontest*. Here is the code for this function:

```
interbankZeroCouponTest <- function(){
  settlementDate <- "2015-02-18"
  depositRates <- c(0.001375, 0.001717, 0.002112, 0.002581)
  depositMaturities <- list( Period(1, "Weeks"),
                             Period(1, "Months"),
                             Period(2, "Months"),
                             Period(3, "Months"))
  futPrices <- c(99.725, 99.585, 99.385, 99.16, 98.93, 98.715)
  swapRates <- c(0.0089268, 0.0123343, 0.0147985, 0.0165843, 0.0179191)
  swapMaturities <- list(Period(2, "Years"),
                         Period(3, "Years"),
                         Period(4, "Years"),
                         Period(5, "Years"),
                         Period(6, "Years"))
  df <- interbankZeroCoupon(settlementDate, depositRates, depositMaturities,
                            futPrices, swapRates, swapMaturities)
}
```

Here, we simply select few of market data points for demonstration purpose. In practice, we should use all of the relevant market data to build the zero-coupon curve. Running this example generates the following results:

```
> source("fixedIncomeHelper.R")
> df <- interbankZeroCouponTest(); df
    Maturity  Discount    ZeroRate ContinuousRate
1 2015-02-13 1.0000000 0.001375927    0.000000000
2 2015-02-20 0.9999733 0.001375927    0.001374984
3 2015-03-13 0.9998665 0.001718360    0.001716889
4 2015-04-13 0.9996540 0.002113866    0.002111641
5 2015-05-13 0.9993623 0.002583508    0.002580186
6 2015-06-18 0.9991342 0.002497684    0.002494578
7 2015-09-17 0.9980825 0.003203957    0.003198849
8 2015-12-16 0.9965474 0.004077253    0.004068986
9 2016-03-16 0.9944358 0.005072500    0.005059713
```

```
10 2016-06-16 0.9917240 0.006136850    0.006118147
11 2016-09-15 0.9885102 0.007198644    0.007172928
12 2017-02-21 0.9820615 0.008856972    0.008818085
13 2018-02-20 0.9631763 0.012320780    0.012245703
14 2019-02-19 0.9416941 0.014851492    0.014742586
15 2020-02-18 0.9192043 0.016702060    0.016564490
16 2021-02-18 0.8963730 0.018087682    0.017926487
```

We can also plot the results using ggplot2 package:

```
> library(ggplot2)
> ggplot(df, aes(Maturity)) + geom_line(aes(y = ZeroRate, col = "ZeroRate")) +
         geom_line(aes(y = ContinuousRate, col = "ContinuousRate")) +
         labs(col = "Curve Type") + theme_bw() +
         theme(legend.position = c(0.8, 0.2))
> ggplot(df, aes(Maturity)) + geom_line(aes(y = Discount)) + theme_bw()
```

This produces the graph shown in Figure 6-2.

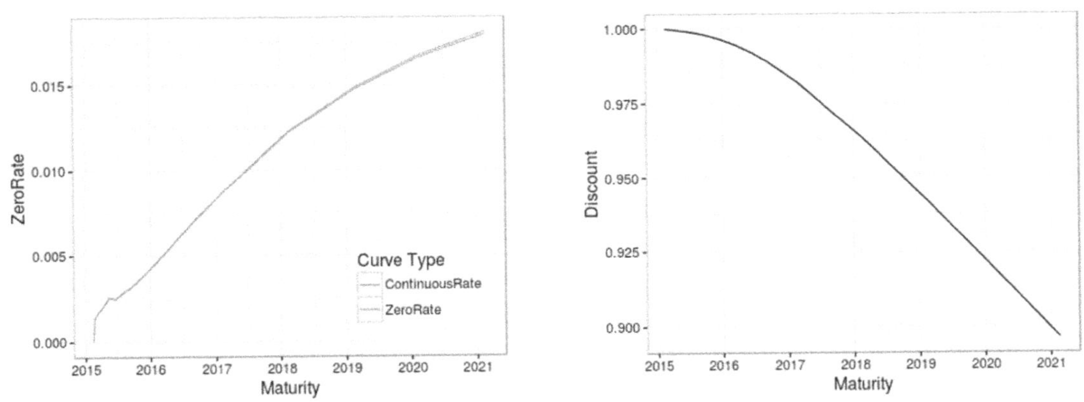


*Figure 6-2. Interbank zero-coupon and discount yield curves.*

# Credit Spread Term Structures

We can derive the term structure of credit spreads for a given rating class and a given sector from market data by the following steps: First, we derive the benchmark zero-coupon yield curve, which can be taken as either the Treasury zero-coupon yield curve or the Interbank zero-coupon yield curve, using the approaches described in the preceding sections. Next, we constitute a homogeneous basket of bonds for the risky class studied, using the same method as we did for deriving the Treasury zero-coupon curve. Finally, we obtain the zero-coupon credit spread curve by subtracting the benchmark zero-coupon yield curve from the risky zero-coupon yield curve.

The nominal spread (*n*-spread) and the zero-volatility spread (*z*-spread) are often used to measure the spread that the investor will receive from a non-Treasury bond over the Treasury yield curve. The nominal spread, or the nominal yield spread, is the simple yield spread for non-Treasury bonds. It measures the difference between the yield of a bond and the yield to maturity of a similar maturity Treasury bond. For example, consider the two 10-year bonds: a Treasury bond with an YTM of 3.5%, and a non-Treasury bond with an YTM of 6%. The *n*-spread = non-Treasury YTM – Treasury YTM = 6%-3.5% = 2.5%. The difference between the YTM for the two bonds is 2.5% (250 bps or basis points). This is the *n*-spread.

A non-Treasury bond usually provides a higher yield compared to a Treasury bond because of the additional risk involved. The *n*-spread is a way to price the bonds. Even though the *n*-spread is easy to calculate, it is not a very strong measure because it does not consider the spot rates for different maturities and it also ignores the effect of embedded options. Due to this reason, the other spread measures such as the *z*-spread are more popular.

The problem with the *n*-spread is that it measures the spread at just one point on the yield curve. The *z*-spread solves this problem by considering the spot yield curve instead of the standard yield curve. Calculating the *z*-spread requires the present value of the cash flows. We start with an assumption for the *z*-spread: taking the Treasury yield rates for each maturity, adding the *z*-spread to it, and using this new rate as a discount rate for each maturity to price the bond. The correct *z*-spread is the one that makes the present value of cash flows equal to the price of the bond:

$$P = \sum_{t=1}^{T} \frac{CF_t}{[1 + R(0,t) + z]^t}$$

where $z$ is called the *z*-spread. The *z*-spread represents the additional risk the investor is taking in the form of credit risk, liquidity risk, and option risk.

In most case, such as the fixed coupon bonds, the *z*-spread will only slightly diverge from the *n*-spread. The difference mainly comes from the shape of the term structure and the bond characteristics. For instance, the difference will be high for amortizing bonds for which the principal is repaid over time, bonds with high coupon, and when the yield curve is steep.

*QuantLib* provides a *z*-spread feature, which allows us to shift the yield curve and to reprice the bonds with specified *z*-spread. First, I will use an example illustrate how to shift a zero-coupon curve by modified the *zeroCouponBootstrap* function in the *fixedIncomeHelper.R* file discussed previously. Here is the code for the modified method named *zeroCouponBootstrapZSpread*:

```
zeroCouponBootstrapZspread <- function(curveType = c("DataPoints", "BootStrap"),
                                        zSpread){
  evalDate <- Date(15, "January", 2015)
  invisible(Settings_instance()$setEvaluation(d = evalDate))
  depositeRates <- c(0.0525, 0.055 )
  depositMaturities <- list(Period(6, "Months"), Period(12, "Months"))
  bondCoupons <- c(0.0575, 0.06, 0.0625, 0.065, 0.0675, 0.068, 0.07, 0.071, 0.0715,
                   0.072,  0.073, 0.0735, 0.074, 0.075, 0.076, 0.076, 0.077, 0.078)
  bondPrices <- rep(100.0, length = length(bondCoupons))
  bondMaturities <- list()
  for(i in 1:length(bondCoupons)){
    bondMaturities <- c(bondMaturities, Period((i+3)*6, "Months"))
  }
  calendar <- UnitedStates()
  dc <- ActualActual("Bond")
  rateHelpers <- RateHelperVector()
  for(i in 1:length(depositeRates)){
    quote <- QuoteHandle(SimpleQuote(depositeRates[i]))
    helper <- DepositRateHelper(quote, depositMaturities[[i]], 0, calendar,
                              "Unadjusted", TRUE, dc)
    RateHelperVector_push_back(rateHelpers, helper)
  }
  for(i in 1:length(bondPrices)){
    quote <- QuoteHandle(SimpleQuote(bondPrices[i]))
    mat <- evalDate + bondMaturities[[i]]
```

```
  schedule <- Schedule(evalDate, mat, Period("Annual"), calendar, "Unadjusted",
                       "Unadjusted", copyToR(DateGeneration(), "Backward"), TRUE)
  helper <- FixedRateBondHelper(quote, 0, 100.0, schedule, bondCoupons[i], dc,
                       "Unadjusted", 100.0, evalDate)
  RateHelperVector_push_back(rateHelpers,helper)
}
ts <- PiecewiseLinearZero(evalDate, rateHelpers, dc)

# ZSpread related code:
tsHandle <- YieldTermStructureHandle(ts)
zsHandle <- QuoteHandle(SimpleQuote(zSpread/10000.0))
zs <- ZeroSpreadedTermStructure(tsHandle, zsHandle)

# Extract results:
rmat <- list()
discount <- list()
zeroRate <- list()
discountZ <- list()
zeroRateZ <- list()

curveType <- tolower(curveType)
mats <- PiecewiseLinearZero_dates(ts)
if(curveType == "datapoints"){
  for(i in 1:DateVector_size(mats)){
    years <- DayCounter_yearFraction(dc, evalDate, mats[i][[1]])
    disc <- YieldTermStructure_discount(ts, mats[i][[1]])
    zz <- YieldTermStructure_zeroRate(ts, years, "Compounded", "Annual")
    zeror <- InterestRate_rate(zz)
    discz <- YieldTermStructure_discount(zs, mats[i][[1]])
    zzSpread <- YieldTermStructure_zeroRate(zs, years, "Compounded", "Annual")
    zeroz <- InterestRate_rate(zzSpread)
    rmat <- c(rmat, as.character(toRDate(mats[i][[1]])))
    discount <- c(discount, disc)
    zeroRate <- c(zeroRate, zeror)
    discountZ <- c(discountZ, discz)
    zeroRateZ <- c(zeroRateZ, zeroz)
  }
} else if(curveType == "bootstrap"){
  d1 <- mats[1][[1]]
  d2 <- mats[12][[1]]
  while(toRDate(d1) <= toRDate(d2)){
    years <- DayCounter_yearFraction(dc, evalDate, d1)
    disc <- YieldTermStructure_discount(ts, d1)
    zz <- YieldTermStructure_zeroRate(ts, years, "Compounded", "Annual")
    zeror <- InterestRate_rate(zz)
    discz <- YieldTermStructure_discount(zs, d1)
    zzSpread <- YieldTermStructure_zeroRate(zs, years, "Compounded", "Annual")
    zeroz <- InterestRate_rate(zzSpread)
    rmat <- c(rmat, as.character(toRDate(d1)))
    discount <- c(discount, disc)
    zeroRate <- c(zeroRate, zeror)
    discountZ <- c(discountZ, discz)
    zeroRateZ <- c(zeroRateZ, zeroz)
    d1 <- d1 + Period(1, "Months")
  }
```

```
  }
  df <- data.frame(Maturity = unlist(rmat), Discount = unlist(discount),
                   ZeroRate = unlist(zeroRate), DiscountZ = unlist(discountZ),
                   ZeroRateZ = unlist(zeroRateZ))
  df$Maturity <- as.Date(df$Maturity)
  return(df)
}
```

The most part of the code in this function is identical to that used in the original *zeroCouponBootstrap* function. Here, we add the *zSpread* parameter as input. The key step is to use the z-spread and the original term structure ts to create a *ZeroSpreadTermStructure* named zs, which will shift the original term structure by an amount of *zSpread*. Note that we divide the input *zSpread* by 10,000, which means that the input *z*-spread should be in units of bps (basis points).

Assuming the *z*-spread is 50 bps, we can obtain the zero-coupon rate and discount curves from original calculations and from the calculation after *z*-spread shift using the following statements:

```
> source("fixedIncomeHelper.R")
> df <- zeroCouponBootstrapZspread("DataPoints", 50.0); df
     Maturity  Discount   ZeroRate DiscountZ  ZeroRateZ
1  2015-01-15 1.0000000 0.05318906 1.0000000 0.05846819
2  2015-07-15 0.9744214 0.05318906 0.9719884 0.05846819
3  2016-01-15 0.9478673 0.05500000 0.9431398 0.06028821
4  2017-01-15 0.8940876 0.05757205 0.8851913 0.06287315
5  2017-07-15 0.8639046 0.06026318 0.8531730 0.06557777
6  2018-01-15 0.8328262 0.06287423 0.8204270 0.06820191
7  2018-07-15 0.8005290 0.06563029 0.7866416 0.07097179
8  2019-01-15 0.7676368 0.06834385 0.7524366 0.07369895
9  2019-07-15 0.7409388 0.06890046 0.7244538 0.07425834
10 2020-01-15 0.7093745 0.07108733 0.6918600 0.07645618
11 2020-07-15 0.6811481 0.07230843 0.6626717 0.07768340
12 2021-01-15 0.6562266 0.07273148 0.6368322 0.07810857
13 2021-07-15 0.6312101 0.07335275 0.6110255 0.07873295
14 2022-01-15 0.6048598 0.07446477 0.5840559 0.07985054
15 2022-07-15 0.5808355 0.07512652 0.5594576 0.08051561
16 2023-01-15 0.5581443 0.07561460 0.5362591 0.08100614
17 2023-07-15 0.5323546 0.07698994 0.5102036 0.08238838
18 2024-01-15 0.5076229 0.07824547 0.4852862 0.08365020
19 2024-07-15 0.4889585 0.07822206 0.4662759 0.08362667
20 2025-01-15 0.4653150 0.07950658 0.4426213 0.08491763
21 2025-07-15 0.4411039 0.08106859 0.4185433 0.08648747
```

We can also plot the zero-coupon rate and discount rate curves with or without z-spread using the following commands:

```
> ggplot(df, aes(Maturity)) + geom_line(aes(y = ZeroRate, col = "ZeroRate"))  +
    geom_line(aes(y = ZeroRateZ, col = "ZeroRateZ")) + labs(col = "Curve Type")+
    theme_bw() + theme(legend.position = c(0.8, 0.2))
> ggplot(df, aes(Maturity)) + geom_line(aes(y = Discount, col = "Discount")) +
    geom_line(aes(y = DiscountZ, col = "DiscountZ")) + labs(col = "Curve Type") +
    theme_bw() + theme(legend.position = c(0.8, 0.8))
```

The above commands produce the results shown in Figure 6-3. You can see that the zero-coupon yield with the *z*-spread is always higher than the original curve, while the discount yield with the *z*-spread is always lower than the original discount curve, as expected.

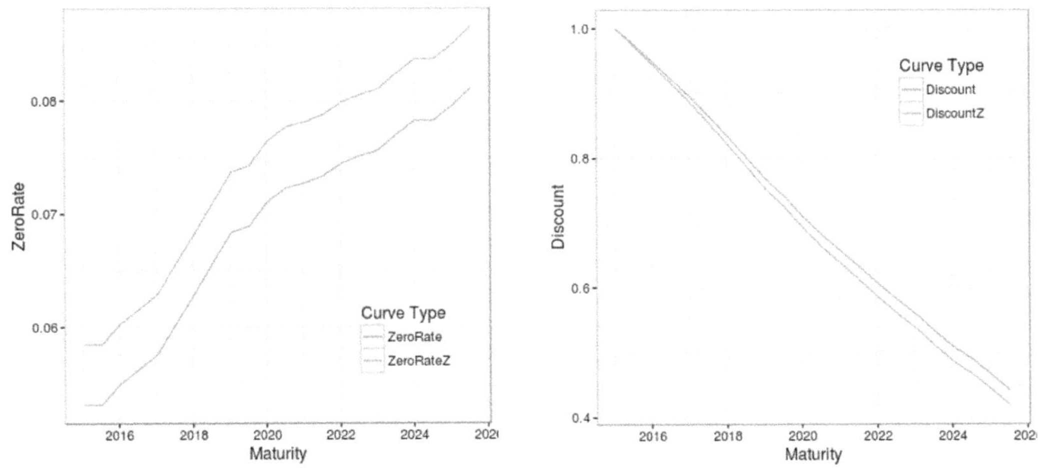


*Figure 6-3. Zero-coupon and discount yield curves with and without the z-spread.*

*QuantLib* also allows us to reprice the bond with the *z*-spread. Here, I will use an example to illustrate how to do it. We need to modify the *bondPriceCurveRate* function implemented previously. Add a new function named *bondPriceCurveRateZSpread* to the *fixedIncomeHelper.R* file. The most part of the code in this method is identical to that used in original *bondPriceCurveRate* method. Here is the code for this function:

```
bondCurveRateZSpread <- function(){
  evalDate <- Date(15, "January", 2015)
  invisible(Settings_instance()$setEvaluation(d = evalDate))
  issueDate <- Date(15, "January", 2015)
  maturity <- Date(15, "January", 2017)
  calendar <- UnitedStates("GovernmentBond")
  settlementDays <- 1
  settlementDate <- evalDate + settlementDays
  settlementDate <- Calendar_adjust(calendar, settlementDate)
  coupon <- 0.05
  dc <- ActualActual("Bond")
  dates <- list(Date(15, "January", 2015), Date(15, "July", 2015),
                Date(15, "January", 2016), Date(15, "July", 2016),
                Date(15, "January", 2017))
  rates <- c(0, 0.004, 0.006, 0.0065, 0.007)
  dateV <- DateVector()
  for(i in 1:5){
    DateVector_push_back(dateV, dates[[i]])
  }
  schedule <- Schedule(issueDate, maturity, Period("Semiannual"), calendar,
    "Unadjusted", "Unadjusted", copyToR(DateGeneration(), "Backward"), FALSE)
  bond <- FixedRateBond(settlementDays,100,schedule, coupon, dc)
  rateCurve <- ZeroCurve(dateV, rates, dc, calendar, Linear(), "Compounded",
                         "Annual")
  ts <- YieldTermStructureHandle(rateCurve)
  engine <- DiscountingBondEngine(ts)
  invisible(Instrument_setPricingEngine(bond, engine))

  zSpreads <- seq(0, 5000, 250)
```

```
  zprices <- rep(NA, length = length(zSpreads))
  leg <- Bond_cashflows(bond)
  for(i in 1:length(zSpreads)){
  zprices[i] <- CashFlows_npv(leg, rateCurve, zSpreads[i]/10000.0, dc,
    "Compounded", "Semiannual", TRUE, settlementDate, evalDate)
  }
  df <- data.frame(ZSpread = zSpreads, BondPrice = zprices)
  return(df)
}
```

Here, we define an array for the *z*-spreads and then extract the leg of cash flows from the original *FixedRateBond* object named bond. *QuantLib* provides a number of functions that calculate the NPV of a series of cash flows. These functions are defined as static functions inside the *CashFlows* class. Here we use the *CashFlows_npv* function to recalculate the bond price for different *z*-spreads. This function takes the cash flow leg and original term structure (*rateCurve*) as inputs.

We can test this function using the following commands:

```
> source("fixedIncomeHelper.R")
> df <- bondCurveRateZSpread(); df
   ZSpread BondPrice
1        0 108.53585
2      250 103.47064
3      500  98.70410
4      750  94.21521
5     1000  89.98470
6     1250  85.99480
7     1500  82.22917
8     1750  78.67277
9     2000  75.31171
10    2250  72.13316
11    2500  69.12528
12    2750  66.27712
13    3000  63.57853
14    3250  61.02011
15    3500  58.59315
16    3750  56.28957
17    4000  54.10185
18    4250  52.02302
19    4500  50.04658
20    4750  48.16649
21    5000  46.37711
```

We can see more clearly the relationship between the bond price and z-spread by plotting it in a graph:

```
> ggplot(df, aes(x = ZSpread, y = BondPrice)) + geom_line() +
  geom_point(shape = 5) + theme_bw()
```

This produces the output shown in Figure 6-4. You can see that the bond price drops with the increase of the *z*-spread, and the bond becomes very cheap when its *z*-spread approaches 5000 bps (near default).

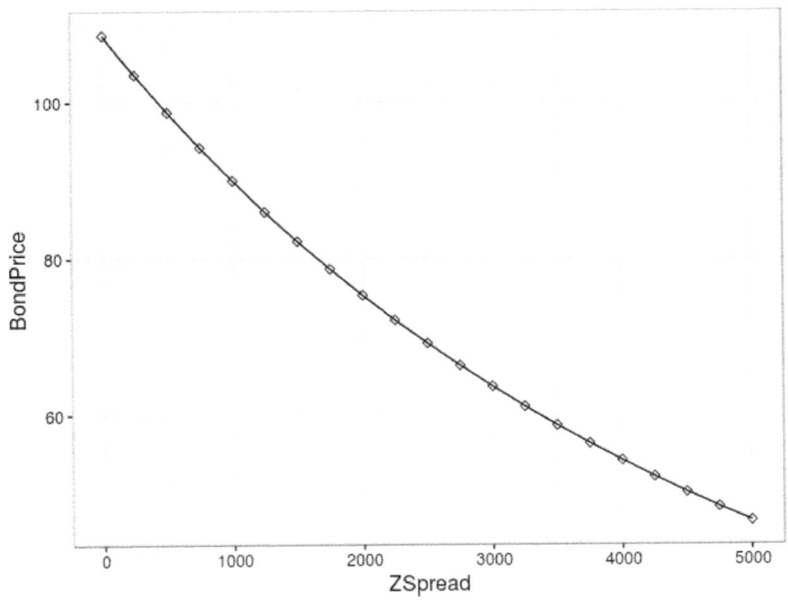


*Figure 6-4. Bond price as a function of the z-spread.*

# CDS Pricing

In the previous sections, we discussed how to build the term structures for interest rate, dividend yield, and volatility, and how to price the fixed coupon bonds. Following the similar procedure, we can also price other types of fixed income instruments. In this section, I will discuss CDS (credit default swap) pricing.

CDS is an agreement between two parties to exchange the credit risk of an issuer (reference entity). The buyer of CDS is said to buy protection, and needs to pay a periodic fee (coupon) and profits if the reference entity has a default event, or if the credit worsens while the swap is outstanding. A credit event includes bankruptcy, failing to pay outstanding debt obligations, or in some CDS contracts, a restructuring of a bond or loan. Buying protection has a similar credit risk position to selling a bond short, or "going short risk".

The seller of CDS is said to sell protection. The seller collects the coupon and profits if the credit of the reference entity remains stable or improves while the swap is outstanding. Selling protection has a similar credit risk position to owning a bond or loan, or "going long risk".

The most commonly traded and therefore the most liquid tenors, or maturity lengths, for CDS contracts are five, seven, and ten years, though liquidity across the maturity curve continues to develop. Standard trading sizes vary depending on the reference entity. For example, in US, $10-20 million notional is typical for investment grade (IG) credits and $2-5 million notional is typical for high yield (HY) credits.

## Hazard Rate and Default Probability

The CDS valuation is similar to other fixed-income instruments, namely, future cash flows are discounted to the present value. What is different in CDS is that the cash flows are further discount by the credit risk. If there is a credit event, the CDS contract is settled and the cash flows then stop. We can consider the valuation of CDS as a scenario analysis where the credit survives or is default. The protection seller (long risk) hopes the credit survives, and discounts the expected annual payments by the probability of this scenario (called the fee leg). The protection buyer (short risk) hopes the credit default, and discounts the expected contingent payment (notional – recovery rate) by the probability of this scenario (called the contingent leg).

CDS usually has a credit curve because the spread demanded for buying or selling protection varies with the length of that protection. Figure 6-5 shows each spread against the time the protection covers (1Y, 2Y,..., 10Y) for IG index on 12/22/2015 to give us a credit curve.

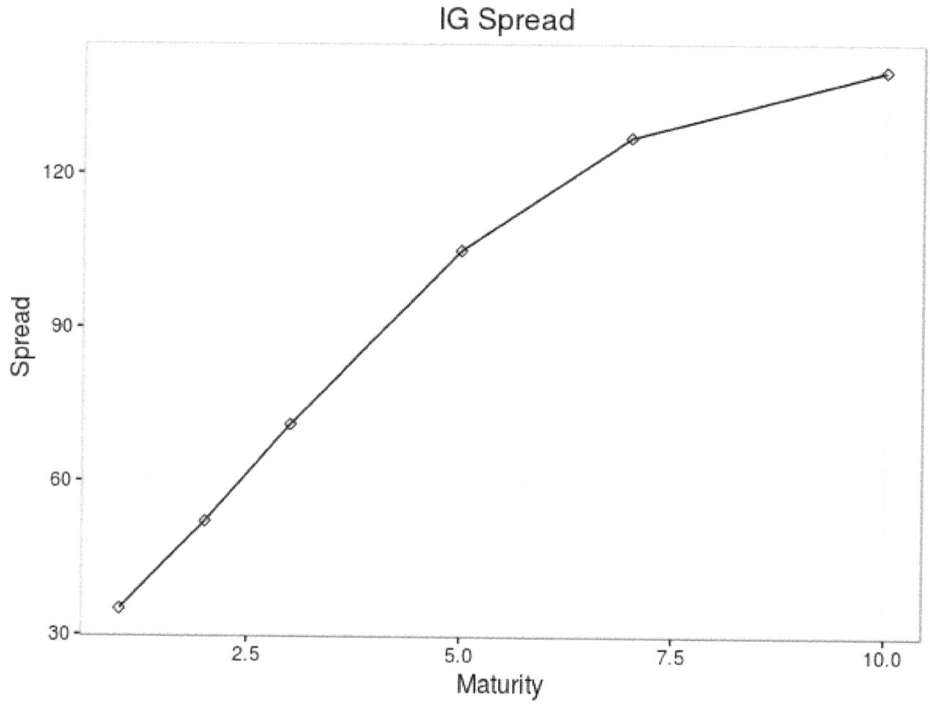


*Figure 6-5. IG spread*

Each point along this credit curve represents a spread that ensures the present value of the expected spread payments (Fee Leg) equals the present value of the payment on default (contingent Leg).

Given that the spread will be paid as long as the credit has not defaulted and the contingent leg payment occurs only if there is a default in a period, we can write for a par CDS contract (with a notional of 1):

$$S_n \sum_{i=1}^{n} \Delta_i \cdot P_{si} \cdot DF_i + accrual\ on\ default = (1 - R) \cdot \sum_{i=1}^{n} \left[P_{s(i-1)} - P_{si}\right] \cdot DF_i \qquad \text{(6-13)}$$

where the left hand side is the present value for fee leg and the right hand side represents the present value for the contingent leg. $S_n$ is the spread for protection to period $n$; $\Delta_i$ is the length of time period $i$ in years; $P_{si}$ is the probability of survival to time $i$; $DF_i$ is the risk-free discount factor to time $i$; $R$ is the recovery rate on default; and the accrual on default is given by

$$\text{Accrual on default} = S_n \sum_{i=1}^{n} \frac{\Delta_i}{2} \cdot \left[P_{s(i-1)} - P_{si}\right] \cdot DF_i$$

We can model survival probabilities by making them a function of a hazard rate. The hazard rate (denoted as $\lambda$) as the conditional probability of default in a period. For the first period $i = 1$, the probability of survival ($P_s$) is the probability of not having defaulted in the period, or $(1 - \lambda)$. So, we can write:

$$P_{s1} = (1 - \lambda_1) \quad \text{for } i = 1$$

For the next period, $i = 2$, the probability of survival is the probability of surviving period 1 and the probability of surviving period 2, i.e.:

$$P_{s2} = (1 - \lambda_1) \cdot (1 - \lambda_2) \quad \text{for } i = 2$$

The probability of default ($P_d$) in a given period is then just the probability of surviving to the start of the period minus the probability of surviving to the end of it, i.e.:

$$P_{d2} = P_{s1} - P_{s2} = (1 - \lambda_1) \cdot \lambda_2$$

This shows how we can build up the probabilities of survival used for CDS pricing in Eq. (6-13). In theory, that means we could calculate a CDS spread from probabilities of survival. In practice, the spread is readily observable in the market and instead we can back out the probability of survival to any time period implied by the market spread, which means we can back out the hazard rates for each period using market spreads.

In terms of pricing a CDS contract, we could in theory solve Eq. (6-13) using a single hazard rate. However, we can also bootstrap a hazard rate implied for each period from the market-observed credit curve. To do this we use the period 1 spread to imply the hazard rate for period 1. For period 2 we use the period 1 hazard rate to calculate the survival probability for period 1 and use the spread observed for period 2 to calculate the hazard rate for period 2. In that way, we are using the market pricing of default risk in period 1 when we price our period 2 CDS contract (i.e. when we back out the survival probability for period 2). Continuing this process, we can bootstrap the hazard rates implied for each period.

Now, let me show you how to calculate the CDS hazard rate and survival probability from the CDS market spread data using *QuantLib*. Add a new helper function called *cdsHazardRate* to the *fixedIncomeHelper.R* file. Here is the code for this method:

```
cdsHazardRate <- function(evalDate, recoveryRate, spreads, tenors,
                          curveType = c("DataPoints", "BootStrap")){
  evalDate <- toQlDate(evalDate)
  periods <- tenorString2Periods(tenors)
  calendar <- TARGET()
  evalDate <- Calendar_adjust(calendar, evalDate)
  invisible(Settings_instance()$setEvaluation(d = evalDate))
  dc <- Actual365Fixed()

  # Dummy curve:
  flatCurve <- FlatForward(evalDate, QuoteHandle(SimpleQuote(0.01)), dc)
  ts <- YieldTermStructureHandle(flatCurve)
  maturities <- DateVector()
  for(i in 1:length(periods)){
    mat <- Calendar_adjust(calendar, evalDate + periods[[i]], "Following")
    DateVector_push_back(maturities, mat)
  }
```

```
instruments <- DefaultProbabilityHelperVector()
for(i in 1:length(periods)){
  qh <- QuoteHandle(SimpleQuote(spreads[i]/10000.0))
  helper <- SpreadCdsHelper(qh, periods[[i]], 0, calendar, "Quarterly",
         "Following", copyToR(DateGeneration(),"TwentiethIMM"),
         dc, recoveryRate, ts)
  DefaultProbabilityHelperVector_push_back(instruments, helper)
}

# Bootstrap hazard rates:
hazardRateStructure <- PiecewiseFlatHazardRate(evalDate, instruments, dc)

rmat <- list()
hazard <- list()
survive <- list()
default <- list()
curveType <- tolower(curveType)
mats <- PiecewiseFlatHazardRate_dates(hazardRateStructure)
if(curveType == "datapoints"){
  for(i in 1:DateVector_size(mats)){
    years <- DayCounter_yearFraction(dc, evalDate, mats[i][[1]])
    haz <- DefaultProbabilityTermStructure_hazardRate(
              hazardRateStructure, mats[i][[1]])
    surv <- DefaultProbabilityTermStructure_survivalProbability(
              hazardRateStructure, mats[i][[1]])
    def <- DefaultProbabilityTermStructure_defaultProbability(
              hazardRateStructure, mats[i][[1]])
    rmat <- c(rmat, as.character(toRDate(mats[i][[1]])))
    hazard <- c(hazard, 100*haz)
    survive <- c(survive, 100*surv)
    default <- c(default, 100*def)
  }
} else if (curveType == "bootstrap"){
  d1 <- mats[1][[1]]
  d2 <- mats[DateVector_size(mats)][[1]]
  while(toRDate(d1) <= toRDate(d2)){
    years <- DayCounter_yearFraction(dc, evalDate, d1)
    haz <- DefaultProbabilityTermStructure_hazardRate(hazardRateStructure, d1)
    surv <- DefaultProbabilityTermStructure_survivalProbability(
              hazardRateStructure, d1)
    def <- DefaultProbabilityTermStructure_defaultProbability(
              hazardRateStructure, d1)
    rmat <- c(rmat, as.character(toRDate(d1)))
    hazard <- c(hazard, 100*haz)
    survive <- c(survive, 100*surv)
    default <- c(default, 100*def)
    d1 <- d1 + Period(1, "Months")
  }
}

df <- data.frame(Maturity = unlist(rmat), Hazard = unlist(hazard),
                 Survive = unlist(survive), Default = unlist(default))
df$Maturity <- as.Date(df$Maturity)
return(df)
```

```
}

tenorString2Periods <- function(tenors){
  periods <- list()
  nn <- as.numeric(substr(tenors, 1, nchar(tenors) - 1))
  ss <- substr(tenors, nchar(tenors), nchar(tenors))
  for(i in 1:length(tenors)){
    if(ss[i] == "M") periods <- c(periods, Period(nn[i], "Months"))
    if(ss[i] == "Y") periods <- c(periods, Period(nn[i], "Years"))
  }
  return(periods)
}
```

Here, the *cdsHazardRate* function uses a dummy flat term structure for the interest rates and takes an array of spread data and recovery rate from market as inputs. We then create a *SpreadCdsHelper* object for the spread at each tenor. Finally, we bootstrap the hazard rates using the *PiecewiseFlatHazardRate* class. The input *curveType* parameter controls the output: if it is set to "*DataPoints*", the results are only shown at the input tenors, otherwise, the monthly continuous curves for hazard rate and survival probability will be interpolated. The helper function, *tenorString2Periods*, converts a string tenor array into a Period list object. This method allows us to input tenors using a simple string array.

We can use an example to illustrate how to calculate the CDS hazard rate and survival probability using the preceding code. Add a new helper function named *testCdsHazard* to the *fixedIncomeHelper.R* file. Here is the code for this function:

```
testCdsHazard <- function(curveType){
  evalDate <- "2015-05-15"
  recoveryRate <- 0.4
  spreads <- c(34.93, 53.60, 72.02, 106.39, 129.39, 139.46)
  tenors <- c("1Y", "2Y", "3Y", "5Y", "7Y", "10Y")
  cdsHazardRate(evalDate, recoveryRate, spreads, tenors, curveType)
}
```

Here, we first specify input parameters. Please note that the elements in spreads must align with the elements in tenors, i.e., the first element in spreads corresponds to the first element in tenors, the second in spreads to the second in tenors, and so on.

Now, we can obtain the results for hazard rate by executing this function using the following commands:

```
> source("fixedIncomeHelper.R")
> df <- testCdsHazard("DataPoints"); df
    Maturity    Hazard   Survive    Default
1 2015-05-15 0.5814708 100.00000  0.0000000
2 2016-06-20 0.5814708  99.36163  0.6383682
3 2017-06-20 1.2413988  98.13578  1.8642176
4 2018-06-20 1.8667885  96.32079  3.6792114
5 2020-06-22 2.7268180  91.18803  8.8119656
6 2022-06-20 3.2643558  85.44009 14.5599091
7 2025-06-20 2.8019856  78.54558 21.4544191
```

We can also use the bootstrap method to calculate the hazard rate, survival, and default probabilities:

```
> df <- testCdsHazard("BootStrap")
my asptr
> head(df)
    Maturity    Hazard   Survive    Default
1 2015-05-15 0.5814708 100.00000 0.00000000
```

```
2 2015-06-15 0.5814708  99.95063 0.04937300
3 2015-07-15 0.5814708  99.90287 0.09713011
4 2015-08-15 0.5814708  99.85354 0.14645516
5 2015-09-15 0.5814708  99.80424 0.19575585
6 2015-10-15 0.5814708  99.75656 0.24344302
> tail(df)
      Maturity   Hazard  Survive  Default
117 2025-01-15 2.801986 79.49187 20.50813
118 2025-02-15 2.801986 79.30292 20.69708
119 2025-03-15 2.801986 79.13264 20.86736
120 2025-04-15 2.801986 78.94455 21.05545
121 2025-05-15 2.801986 78.76295 21.23705
122 2025-06-15 2.801986 78.57574 21.42426
```

To look into these results more closely, we can plot them in graphs:

```
> ggplot(df, aes(x = Maturity, y = Hazard)) + geom_line() +
        labs(title = "Hazard Rate (%)") + theme_bw()
> ggplot(df, aes(x = Maturity, y = Default)) + geom_line() +
        labs(title = "Default Probability (%)") + theme_bw()
```

This produces the output shown in Figure 6-6.

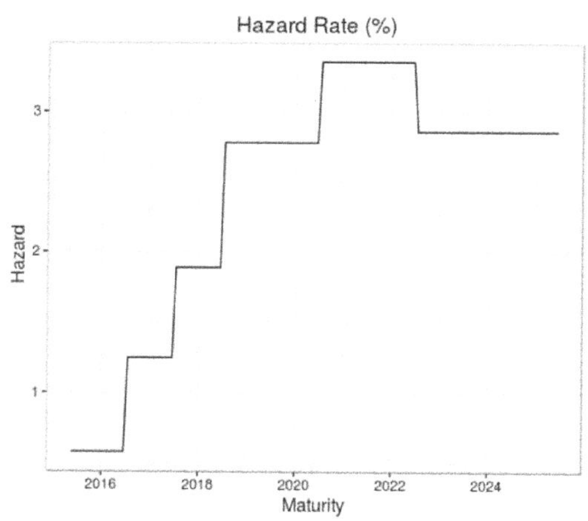


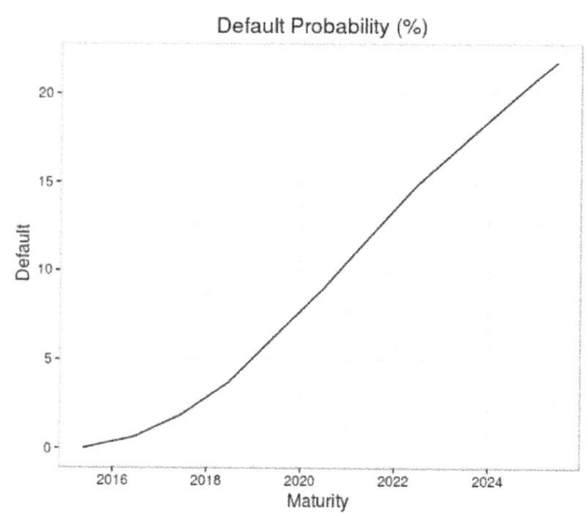


*Figure 6-6. Calculated results for CDS hazard rate (left) and default probability (right).*

You can see that the default probability always increases as time goes on, while the hazard rate is bootstrapped as a piecewise flat curve. *QuantLib* models the hazard rates as a step function, indicating that it holds them constant between changes in spreads. This means that we have constant hazard rates between every period.

## Risky Annuities and Risky Durations

The risky annuity is the present value of a 1 bp risky annuity stream:

$$RiskyAnnuity = A_s \approx 1 \cdot \sum_{i=1}^{n} \Delta_i P_{si} DF_i + 1 \cdot \sum_{i=1}^{n} \frac{\Delta_i}{2} \left[P_{s(i-1)} - P_{si}\right] \cdot DF_i$$

where $A_s$ is the risky annuity for an annuity lasting $n$ periods, given spread level $S$.

The risky duration (DV01) relates to a trade and is the change in mark-to-market (MTM) of a CDS trade for a 1bp parallel shift in spreads. The MTM for a long risk CDS trade with notional = 1 is:

$$MTM_{S\ current} = (S_{Initial} - S_{Current}) \cdot A_{s\ current}$$

$$MTM_{1bp\ shift} = \left(S_{Initial} - S_{Current+1bp}\right) \cdot A_{s\ current+1bp}$$

$$DV01 = MTM_{1bp\ shift} - MTM_{S\ current}$$

Using $S_{Current+1bp} \cdot A_{S\ current+1bp} = S_{Current} \cdot A_{S\ current+1bp} + 1bp \cdot A_{S\ current+1bp}$, we can show that:

$$DV01 = -A_{S\ current+1bp} + (S_{Initial} - S_{Current}) \cdot (A_{S\ current+1bp} - A_{S\ current})$$

For a par trade $S_{Initial} = S_{Current}$, and since the risky annuities do not change by a large amount for a 1bp change in spread, we get:

$$DV01 = -A_{S\ current+1bp} \approx -A_{S}current$$

This means that the risky duration is equal to the risky annuity. This approximation can become inaccurate if we are looking at a trade that is far off-market, where $S_{Initial} - S_{Current}$ becomes significant, causing the risky duration to move away from the risky annuity.

## CDS Pricing Engine

As shown in Eq. (6-13), pricing CDS involves calculating the present value of the two legs of the transaction, i.e., the premium leg or fee leg (the regular fee payments) and the contingent leg (the payment at the time of defaults). If the trade made at the fair spread, the fees associated with these two legs should be equal. However, starting on 4/8/2009, the new ISDA CDS standardization initiatives, i.e. the 100/500 standard fixed coupon CDS contracts, take effect. The 100/500 standard is a change in the practice of trading single name CDS from a traded coupon and *T*+1 accrual period to a bond like fixed coupon (fixed to 100 or 500 bps) with standardized bond like accrual periods, paid upfront, on the settlement of the trade. Here are the key features of the new standard:

- Fixed coupons of 100 bps and 500 bps.
- Buyer pays the full first coupon period (e.g. accrual) for the previous quarterly coupon period *T*+1 fall into.
- Maturity dates always match a quarterly roll date.

We can simply regard the new ISDA standard CDS model as a quoting convention, and it provides a way to map a spread quote into an upfront cash amount, which is the actual "price" or present value of the CDS.

*QuantLib*'s CDS pricing engine enables us to price both the conventional and the new 100/500 fixed coupon CDS contracts. Instead of using the flat rate term structure for the discount curve shown in the previous example for the default probability and hazard rate, here we will use a full ISDA rate curve for building the discount term structure. To achieve this, we add the following helper function named *isdaZeroCurve* to the *fixedIncomeHelper.R* file:

```
isdaZeroCurve <- function(evalDate, ccy = "USD"){
  evalDate <- toQlDate(evalDate)
  calendar <- TARGET()
  rateDate <- Calendar_advance(calendar, evalDate, -1, "Days")
  rateDate1 <- toDateString(rateDate)
  isdaRates <- isdaRate(ccy, rateDate1)
  rateHelper <- RateHelperVector()
  depositMaturities <- list()
  swapMaturities <- list()
  depositRates <- list()
  swapRates <- list()
  depositDayCounter <- Actual360()
  swapDayCounter <- Thirty360()
  for(i in 1:nrow(isdaRates)){
    num <- 0
    if(isdaRates[i, ]$RateType == "Deposit"){
      if(grepl("M", isdaRates[i, ]$Tenor)){
        num <- as.numeric(strsplit(isdaRates[i, ]$Tenor, "M"))
        depositMaturities <- c(depositMaturities, Period(num, "Months"))
        depositRates <- c(depositRates, as.numeric(isdaRates[i, ]$Rate))
      } else if(grepl("Y", isdaRates[i, ]$Tenor)){
        num <- as.numeric(strsplit(isdaRates[i, ]$Tenor, "Y"))
        depositMaturities <- c(depositMaturities, Period(num, "Years"))
        depositRates <- c(depositRates, as.numeric(isdaRates[i, ]$Rate))
      }
    } else if(isdaRates[i, ]$RateType == "Swap"){
      num <- as.numeric(strsplit(isdaRates[i, ]$Tenor, "Y"))
      swapMaturities <- c(swapMaturities, Period(num, "Years"))
      swapRates <- c(swapRates, as.numeric(isdaRates[i, ]$Rate))
    }
  }

  for(i in 1:length(depositRates)){
    helper <- DepositRateHelper(depositRates[[i]], depositMaturities[[i]], 0,
              calendar, "Unadjusted", FALSE, depositDayCounter)
    RateHelperVector_push_back(rateHelper, helper)
  }
  swFixedLegFrequency <- "Semiannual"
  swFixedLegConvention <- "Unadjusted"
  swFloatingLegIndex <- USDLibor(Period(3, "Months"))
  for(i in 1:length(swapRates)){
    qh <- QuoteHandle(SimpleQuote(swapRates[[i]]))
    helper <- SwapRateHelper(qh, swapMaturities[[i]], calendar, swFixedLegFrequency,
              swFixedLegConvention, swapDayCounter, swFloatingLegIndex)
    RateHelperVector_push_back(rateHelper, helper)
  }
  ts <- PiecewiseLogCubicDiscount(rateDate, rateHelper, Actual365Fixed())
  return(ts)
}
```

Here, we first set the *rateDate* to previous workday of the original *evalData*, which is because the ISDA rates on *evalDate* are not available yet, we have to use the rates at the previous workday, i.e., *rateDate*. We then load the ISDA rate curve directly from Markit's website using the *isdaRate* function in the *marketdata.R* file, implemented in Chapter 2. Here, we can specify *ccy* (i.e. "USD", "EUR", "JPY", etc.)

and rate date. Next, we separate the money market (deposit) rates and swap rates. Finally, we use the *PiecewiseLogCubicDiscount* object to build the yield term structure for the discount curve.

Now, we add another helper function named *cdsPV* to the *fixedIncomeHelper.R* file. This function enables us to calculate the present value and fair (or par) spread for a CDS contract. Here is the code for this function:

```
cdsPV <- function(protectionSide =c("Buyer", "seller"), ccy = "USD", evalDate,
                  effectiveDate, maturity, recoveryRate, spreads, tenors, notional,
                  couponFrequency, coupon, flatRate = 0){
  options(digits = 10)
  evalDate <- toQlDate(evalDate)
  effectiveDate <- toQlDate(effectiveDate)
  maturity <- toQlDate(maturity)
  periods <- tenorString2Periods(tenors)
  calendar <- TARGET()
  evalDate <- Calendar_adjust(calendar, evalDate)
  invisible(Settings_instance()$setEvaluation(d = evalDate))
  if(flatRate <= 0){
    rateDate <- toRDate(evalDate)
    curve <- isdaZeroCurve(toDateString(evalDate), ccy)
    ts <- YieldTermStructureHandle(curve)
  }
  else {
    flatCurve <- FlatForward(evalDate, QuoteHandle(SimpleQuote(flatRate)),
                             Actual365Fixed())
    ts <- YieldTermStructureHandle(flatCurve)
  }

  instruments <- DefaultProbabilityHelperVector()
  for(i in 1:length(tenors)){
    qh <- QuoteHandle(SimpleQuote(spreads[i]/10000.0))
    helper <- SpreadCdsHelper(qh, periods[[i]], 1, calendar, couponFrequency,
       "Following", copyToR(DateGeneration(),"TwentiethIMM"), Actual365Fixed(),
       recoveryRate, ts)
    DefaultProbabilityHelperVector_push_back(instruments, helper)
  }

  # Bootstrap hazard rates:
  hazardRateStructure <- PiecewiseFlatHazardRate(evalDate, instruments,
                            Actual365Fixed())
  probability <- DefaultProbabilityTermStructureHandle(hazardRateStructure)

  cdsSchedule <- Schedule(effectiveDate, maturity, Period(couponFrequency),
         calendar, "Following", "Following", copyToR(DateGeneration(),
         "TwentiethIMM"), FALSE)
  cds <- CreditDefaultSwap(protectionSide, notional, coupon/10000.0, cdsSchedule,
         "ModifiedFollowing", ActualActual(), FALSE)
  engine <- MidPointCdsEngine(probability, recoveryRate, ts)
  invisible(Instrument_setPricingEngine(cds, engine))
  surv <- 100.0 * DefaultProbabilityTermStructure_survivalProbability(
          hazardRateStructure, maturity)
  def <- 100.0 * DefaultProbabilityTermStructure_defaultProbability(
         hazardRateStructure, maturity)
  hazard <- 100.0 * DefaultProbabilityTermStructure_hazardRate(hazardRateStructure,
```

```
             maturity)
  npv <- Instrument_NPV(cds)
  fairSpread <- 10000.0 * CreditDefaultSwap_fairSpread(cds)
  df <- data.frame(Maturity = toRDate(maturity), Coupon = coupon,
        SurvivalProb = surv, DefaultProb = def, Hazard = hazard,
        FairSpread = fairSpread, CdsPV = npv)
  return(df)
}
```

The *CdsPV* method takes various input parameters including protection side, evaluation data, effective date, maturity, recovery rate, spreads, notional, and coupon. The optional parameter *flatRate* allows us to specify a flat rate (instead of the default ISDA rate curve) for the discount term structure. The effective date is the date from which the CDS trade provided the buyer of protection with coverage. For the new 100/500 standard trades, this will typically be the most recently passed IMM date. The input spread array (or single spread point) must be paired and aligned with the tenor array. This spread curve at different tenors will be used to calculate the hazard rate and default probability. Note that the spread data are different from the coupon. For conventional CDS contracts, coupon = fair (or par) spread, while for the 100/500 standard CDS contracts, coupon = 100 or 500, depending on the CDS name types. If the CDS name belongs to the IG (investment grade) type, then coupon = 100, otherwise, if the name belongs to the HY (high yield) type, then coupon = 500.

Inside the *cdsPV* function, we use the spread array data to bootstrap the hazard rate and construct the default-probability-term structure, which will be used by the CDS pricing engine. Next, we create the CDS schedule and the *CreditDefaultSwap* instance. Finally, we set the CDS pricing engine using the *MidPointCdsEngine* class. The two important results from the pricing engine are the fair (or par) spread and the present value of the CDS contract. The former is independent of the coupon while the latter does depend on the coupon.

Now, I will use an example to illustrate how to use the *cdsPV* method to calculate the present value and fair spread for a CDS contract. First, we check a CDS contract with a single 5Y spread. Add a new helper function named *testCsvPV0*. Here is the code for this function:

```
testCdsPV0 <- function(coupon = 100){
  evalDate <- "2009-06-15"
  effectiveDate <- "2009-03-20"
  maturity <- "2014-06-20"
  protectionSide = "Buyer"
  spreads <- 210
  tenors <- "5Y"
  recoveryRate <- 0.4
  flatRate <- 0.032329
  notional <- 10000
  df <- cdsPV(protectionSide, "USD", evalDate, effectiveDate, maturity,
        recoveryRate, spreads, tenors, notional, "Quarterly", coupon, flatRate)
  return(df)
}
```

This function sets the default CDS contract with a single 5Y spread data point (= 210 bps), a 100 bps coupon, a buyer protection, and a flat rate of 0.032329. Running this function, we obtain:

```
> source("fixedIncomeHelper.R")
> testCdsPV0(coupon = 100)
    Maturity Coupon SurvivalProb DefaultProb      Hazard FairSpread       CdsPV
1 2014-06-20    100  83.95709325 16.04290675 3.485825996 199.756237 444.8020329
```

You can see from the calculation that the buyer needs to pay the present value of $444.8 (the upfront cash value) for the CDS contract with a notional of $10000 and a fixed coupon of 100 bps. This contract is under the new ISDA100/500 standard. However, the conventional CDS contract with coupon = the fair spread should have no upfront fee, i.e. the present value should be zero. We can double check the results by entering the fair spread value of 199.756237 in the coupon field and recalculate the CDS present value:

```
> testCdsPV0(coupon = 199.756237)
    Maturity     Coupon SurvivalProb DefaultProb      Hazard FairSpread         CdsPV
1 2014-06-20 199.756237  83.95709325 16.04290675 3.485825996 199.756237 -4.04098e-08
```

You can see the present value is basically zero, i.e. the buyer does not need to pay any upfront for a conventional CDS contract. Please note that all of the CDS contracts for North American Corporates must use the new 100/500 standard agreement after 4/8/2009.

For CDS buyers or sellers, the present value of a CDS contract is all what they are care about. However, as a quant analyst or quant developer, we want to know more about the CDS contracts, such as how to calculate the accrual amount and risky annuity (or DV01). We also want to know the dirty price and clean price for a notional of $100, just like a bond with a face value of $100. This can be achieved easily using the following helper function named *cdsPrice*:

```
cdsPrice <- function(protectionSide = c("Buy", "Seller"), ccy = "USD", evalDate,
     effectiveDate, maturity, recoveryRate, spreads, tenors, couponFrequency,
     coupon, flatRate = 0){
  notional <- 100
  numDays <- as.numeric(as.Date(evalDate) - as.Date(effectiveDate)) + 1
  accrual <- coupon * numDays /360.0/100.0
  cdsDf <- cdsPV(protectionSide, ccy, evalDate, effectiveDate, maturity,
    recoveryRate, spreads, tenors, notional, couponFrequency, coupon, flatRate)
  upfront <- as.numeric(cdsDf$CdsPV)
  cleanPrice <- 100
  dirtyPrice <- 100
  if(protectionSide == "Buyer"){
    accrual <- -accrual
    dirtyPrice <- 100 - upfront
    cleanPrice <- dirtyPrice + accrual
  } else{
    dirtyPrice <- 100 + upfront
    cleanPrice <- dirtyPrice - accrual
  }
  cdsDf1 <- cdsPV(protectionSide, ccy, evalDate, effectiveDate, maturity,
            recoveryRate, spreads + 1.0, tenors, notional, couponFrequency, coupon,
            flatRate)
  dv01 <- as.numeric(cdsDf1$CdsPV) - as.numeric(cdsDf$CdsPV)
  df <- data.frame(Accrual = accrual, Upfront = upfront, CleanPrice = cleanPrice,
       DirtyPrice = dirtyPrice, RiskAnnuity = dv01)
}
```

Here, we first calculate accrual between the effective date and the evaluation date plus one business day ($T$+1 rule). For buyer, the dirty price for CDS with a notional of $100 should be 100 – upfront, while the clean price should be equal to the dirty price with the accrual removal. Similar derivation applies to the seller side. Next, in order to obtain the risky annuity (or DV01): we calculate the PV for a 1 bp parallel shift in spreads, and the difference of the PVs with and without 1 bp shift in spreads will be the risky (see the definition of the risky annuity in the preceding section). Thus, this helper function enables us to extract several important quantities, which are widely used in CDS trading.

Add a new helper function named *testCdsPrice0* to the *fixedIncomeHelper.R* file. Here is the code for this function:

```
testCdsPrice0 <- function(spreads = 210){
  evalDate <- "2009-06-15"
  effectiveDate <- "2009-03-20"
  maturity <- "2014-06-20"
  protectionSide = "Buyer"
  tenors <- "5Y"
  coupon = 100
  recoveryRate <- 0.4
  flatRate <- 0.032329
  df <- cdsPrice(protectionSide, "USD", evalDate, effectiveDate, maturity,
        recoveryRate, spreads, tenors, "Quarterly", coupon, flatRate)
  return(df)
}
```

Executing this function produces the following results:

```
> source("fixedIncomeHelper.R")
> testCdsPrice0(210)
       Accrual     Upfront  CleanPrice  DirtyPrice   RiskAnnuity
1 -0.2444444444 4.448020329 95.30753523 95.55197967 0.04064365949 199.756237
```

You can see that for this CDS contract, the clean price is 95.31, which is less than 100. This is because its fair spread (199.76) is well above the coupon (100) level. If the fair spread is less than the coupon, we expect the clean price will be above 100. For example, if we change the spread from 210 to 90, we will obtain the following results:

```
> testCdsPrice0(90)
       Accrual       Upfront  CleanPrice  DirtyPrice  RiskAnnuity
1 -0.2444444444 -0.6723511894 100.4279067 100.6723512 0.0447284814
```

Which confirm our expectation: clean price > 100.

In the preceding discussion, we always use a single spread data point as input. In practice, the market quoted CDS data are often a spread curve. Our helper functions implemented above also allow us to take the spread curve with corresponding tenor array as input parameters. In this case, the *QuantLib* will bootstrap the hazard rates using the spread curve to calculate the default probability. The CDS pricing engine will then use this default probability to calculate the present value and various other quantities for a CDS contract.

For example, we can set a new CDS contract with a spread curve specified using the following function:

```
testCdsPV1 <- function(){
  evalDate <- "2015-05-15"
  effectiveDate <- "2015-03-20"
  maturity <- "2018-06-20"
  protectionSide = "Buyer"
  spreads <- c(34.93, 53.60, 72.02, 106.39, 129.39, 139.46)
  tenors <- c("1Y", "2Y", "3Y", "5Y", "7Y", "10Y")
  recoveryRate <- 0.4
  coupon <- 100
  notional <- 10000
  flatRate <- 0
  df <- cdsPV(protectionSide, "USD", evalDate, effectiveDate, maturity,
        recoveryRate, spreads, tenors, notional, "Quarterly", coupon, flatRate)
```

```
  return(df)
}
```

Here, we simply set the maturity about 3 years from the evaluation date, i.e. we want to enter a 3Y CDS contract. The spread data should be the market data on the previous workday of the evaluation date. We also set the *flateRate* = 0, indicating that we will use the *isdaZeroCurve* function to construct the yield term structure. Executing this function generates the following results:

```
> source("fixedIncomeHelper.R")
> testCdsPV1()
    Maturity Coupon SurvivalProb DefaultProb      Hazard  FairSpread         CdsPV
1 2018-06-20    100  96.32850372 3.671496282 1.864790327 68.53020416 -99.40594806
```

We can also calculate the other quantities for a CDS contract with a spread curve using the following helper function:

```
testCdsPrice1 <- function(){
  evalDate <- "2015-05-15"
  effectiveDate <- "2015-03-20"
  maturity <- "2018-06-20"
  protectionSide = "Buyer"
  spreads <- c(34.93, 53.60, 72.02, 106.39, 129.39, 139.46)
  tenors <- c("1Y", "2Y", "3Y", "5Y", "7Y", "10Y")
  recoveryRate <- 0.4
  coupon <- 100
  flatRate <- 0
  df <- cdsPrice(protectionSide, "USD", evalDate, effectiveDate, maturity,
        recoveryRate, spreads, tenors, "Quarterly", coupon, flatRate)
  return(df)
}
```

This produces the following results:

```
> source("fixedIncomeHelper.R")
> testCdsPrice1()
        Accrual       Upfront  CleanPrice  DirtyPrice   RiskAnnuity
1 -0.1583333333 -0.9940594806 100.8357261 100.9940595 0.03034013884
```

Here, we have discussed the basic procedure for pricing CDS contracts using the *QuantLib* CDS pricing engine. In order to apply this pricing engine in our real-word CDS trading, there is still a lot of calibration work need to be done. In practice, the CDS pricing requires very high accuracy (up to 7 to 9 decimal) because CDS contracts usually involve a very large notional, meaning that a small discrepancy in CDS price may leads to a big difference in P&L (profit and loss). In this sense, it is better to use the ISDA standard CDS model directly. However, regardless of whatever pricing engine you are going to use, I believe that the concept and procedure for CDS pricing presented here will be useful for your real-world applications.

In this chapter, we discussed how to price some of fixed-income instruments. The basic steps are clear: specifying cash flows; build various term structures for discount curves, yield curves, credit risk, and volatility; and select proper pricing engines. Using this procedure, you should be able to price other types of fixed-income instruments, such as callable and convertible bonds, swaps, and swaptions etc., without much trouble.

# Chapter 7
# Linear Analysis

Linear analysis is a widely used statistical tool in finance and trading. In this chapter, I will discuss two linear analysis techniques: linear regression and principal component analysis (PCA). In statistics, simple linear regression is a least squares estimator of a linear regression model with a single explanatory variable. In other words, simple linear regression fits a straight line through the set of n data points in such a way that minimizes the sum of squared residuals of the model. On the other hand, the PCA is a statistical procedure that uses an orthogonal transformation to convert a set of observations of possible correlated variables into a set of values of linearly uncorrelated variables called principal components. This transformation is defined in such a way that the first principal component has the largest possible eigenvalue.

In this chapter, I will present the relevant mathematical background for the simple 2D linear regression and 2D PCA. I will then illustrate how to perform simple and multivariable linear analysis using R.

## Simple Linear Regression

Simple linear regression refers to the fact that the resultant (or dependent) variable is related to a single predictor (or independent variable). The slope of the fitted line is equal to the correlation between these two variables corrected by the ratio of standard deviations of these variables.

We can construct a simple linear regression by fitting a straight line through a scatter plot of the prices for a pair of stocks. Suppose we have two stocks, $x$ and $y$, which have $n$-day prices $(x_0, y_0)$, $(x_1, y_1)$,..., $(x_n, y_n)$. The linear function that describes $x$ and $y$ is:

$$y_i = a + bx_i + \varepsilon_i$$

The goal here is to find the equation of the straight line

$$y = a + bx$$

which should provide a best fit for the data points. We can use the least-squares approach to achieve this goal. The least-squares technique minimizes the sum of squared residual of the linear regression model. We can get the parameters $a$ (the intercept) and $b$ (the slope) in the preceding equation from solving the following minimization problem:

$$\min_{a,b} \sum_{i=1}^{n} \epsilon_i^2 = \min_{a,b} \sum_{i=1}^{n} (y_i - a - bx_i)^2$$

Taking derivative to the above equation relative to $a$ and $b$ and setting them to zero generates the following equations:

$$\sum_{i=1}^{n} (y_i - a - bx_i) = 0$$

$$\sum_{i=1}^{n} x_i(y_i - a - bx_i) = 0$$

Solving these equation gives

$$b = \frac{\overline{xy} - \bar{x}\bar{y}}{\overline{x^2} - \bar{x}^2}, \qquad a = \bar{y} - b\bar{x}$$

where $\bar{u}$ is the average value of the time series $u_1, u_2, \ldots, u_n$.

## R-Squared

R-squared, also called the coefficient of determination, is a statistical measure that indicates how well the data fit a statistical model such as a linear regression. An R-Squared ~ 1 means that the regression line fits the data very well. In finance, R-Squared represents the percentage of a fund or stock's movements that can be explained by movements in a benchmark index. For equities, the benchmark is the S&P 500 while the T-bill is usually used as the benchmark for fixed-income securities.

In a simple linear regression, R-squared equals to the square of the Pearson correlation coefficient between the observed and modeled data values of the dependent variable. The Pearson correlation $r$ can be calculated using the following equation:

$$r = \frac{\sum_{i=1}^{n}(x_i - \bar{x})(y_i - \bar{y})}{\sqrt{\sum_{i=1}^{n}(x_i - \bar{x})^2 \sum_{i=1}^{n}(y_i - \bar{y})^2}}$$

where $\bar{u}$ is the average value of the time series $u_1, u_2, \ldots, u_n$.

In general, a data set has $n$ values marked $y_1, \ldots, y_n$, each associated with a predicted (modeled) value $f_1, \ldots, f_n$, then the variability of a data set can be measured using three sums of squares formula:

- The total sum of squares: $SS_{tot} = \sum_{i=1}^{n}(y_i - \bar{y})^2$
- The regression sum of squares: $SS_{reg} = \sum_{i=1}^{n}(f_i - \bar{y})^2$
- The sum of squares of residuals: $SS_{res} = \sum_{i=1}^{n}(y_i - f_i)^2$

The most general definition of R-squared (the coefficient of determination) is

$$R^2 = 1 - \frac{SS_{res}}{SS_{tot}}$$

There are some common problems associated with the R-squared: every time we add a predictor to a model, the R-squared increases even if due to chance, and never decreases, leading to a fault fact that a model with more terms may appear to have a better fit simply because it has more terms. Another problem is that if a model has too many predictors, it begins to simulate the random noise in the data, which is called overfitting and may produce misleadingly high R-squared values.

In order to resolve these problems, we can introduce a modified R-squared named the adjusted R-squared. Adjusted R-squared aims to adjust for the number of predictors in a model relative to the number of data points. It can be negative and its value is always less than or equal to that of R-squared. Unlike R-squared, the adjusted R-squared increases only when the increase in R-squared is more than one would expect to see by chance. The adjusted R-squared is defined as:

$$R_{adj}^2 = R^2 - (1 - R^2)\frac{p}{n - p - 1}$$

where $p$ is the total number of predictors in the model (not including the constant term), and $n$ is the sample size.

## What are Alpha and Beta?

In finance, Alpha and Beta are important tools when we try to figure out if our investments are performing well. Alpha is a measure of an investment's performance compared to a benchmark, such as the S&P 500 index. It is an estimate of the return based usually on the growth of earnings per share. On the other hand, Beta is based on the volatility, namely the movement of the fund or stock relative to its benchmark. If it goes up more when its benchmark goes up, then it has a higher beta. A beta of one means it moves just like its benchmark.

As discussed previously, the simple linear regression for the returns of a stock and a benchmark index is a mathematical process to produce a single straight line that best represents all the data points in a scatter chart. We can use two parameters, intercept and slope, to describe this regression line. Mathematically, we believe that the intercept is the Alpha and the slope is the Beta. Please note that both Alpha and Beta depend strongly on the date period we are choosing; they can have dramatically different values for different periods.

In the following section, we will look at how to calculate Alpha and Beta and how the linear regression looks like on the charts.

## Linear Regression in R

To perform a linear regression using R, we need to understand the syntax for defining regression models. Suppose that $y$ is the dependent variable and $x_1, x_2, \ldots, x_n$ are independent variables. Then we can define the general format for a linear model using the following formula:

$$y = a_0 + a_1 x_1 + a_2 x_2 + \cdots + a_n x_n$$

The basic syntax for a regression analysis in R is

$$lm(y \sim x_1 + x_2 + \cdots + x_n)$$

Now, I will use an example to illustrate how to perform a simple linear regression in R. First, we need to load some data into R:

```
> idxdata <- read.csv("./inst/extdata/indices.csv", head = T, sep = ",")
> idxdata$Date <- as.Date(idxdata$Date, "%m/%d/%Y")
> head(idxdata)
        Date IGSpread HYSpread     SPX   VIX
```

```
1 2004-09-21    53.93    363.0 1129.30 13.66
2 2004-09-22    55.18    367.5 1113.56 14.74
3 2004-09-23    54.69    371.2 1108.36 14.80
4 2004-09-24    55.11    374.5 1110.11 14.28
5 2004-09-27    54.59    370.5 1103.52 14.62
6 2004-09-28    54.15    365.5 1110.06 13.83
```

This file contains EOD data for CDX indices (IG and HY), SPX, and VIX. Now we can use this data to perform a linear regression analysis:

```
> reg <- lm(idxdata$HYSpread ~ idxdata$SPX); reg

Call:
lm(formula = idxdata$HYSpread ~ idxdata$SPX)

Coefficients:
(Intercept)  idxdata$SPX
  1542.2195      -0.7756
```

The coefficients gives the regression lines:

$$HY = 1542.2195 - 0.7756 \times SPY$$

Now we can add a regression line to a scatter plot of HY and SPX:

```
> plot(idxdata$SPX, idxdata$HYSpread, col ="blue", main = "HY ~ SPX", xlab = "SPY",
      ylab = "HY")
> grid()
> abline(reg, col = "red", lw = 3)
```

This produces output shown in Figure 7-1.

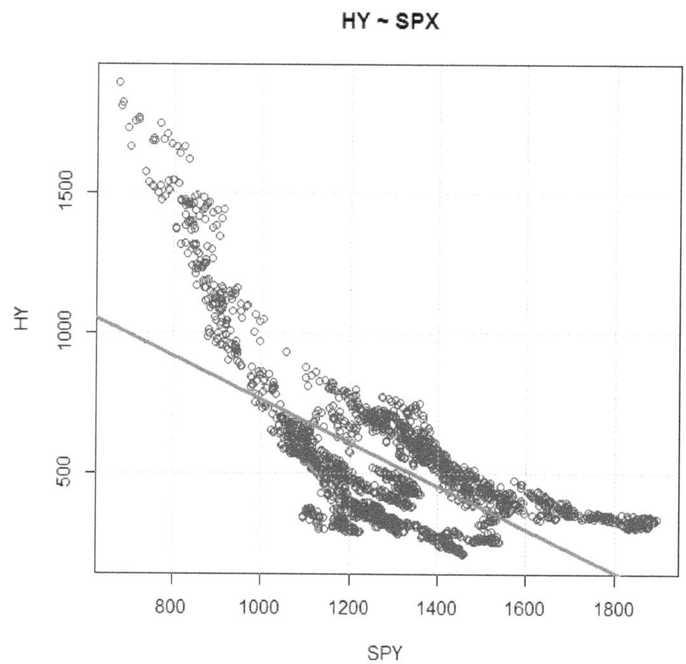


*Figure 7-1. Simple linear regression for HY and SPX.*

We can get more information from the regression results. For example, we can use the summary command to obtain a complete statistical summary of the model:

```
> summary(reg)

Call:
lm(formula = idxdata$HYSpread ~ idxdata$SPX)

Residuals:
    Min      1Q  Median      3Q     Max 
-361.63 -176.98    1.92  128.23  876.08 

Coefficients:
              Estimate Std. Error t value Pr(>|t|)    
(Intercept) 1542.21954   23.54808   65.49   <2e-16 ***
idxdata$SPX   -0.77563    0.01776  -43.67   <2e-16 ***
---
Signif. codes:  0 '***' 0.001 '**' 0.01 '*' 0.05 '.' 0.1 ' ' 1 

Residual standard error: 199.4 on 2364 degrees of freedom
Multiple R-squared:  0.4465,	Adjusted R-squared:  0.4462 
F-statistic:  1907 on 1 and 2364 DF,  p-value: < 2.2e-16
```

The *Residuals* section gives the difference between the original HY data and the predicted HY values from linear regression. The above results also provide estimates for the model's coefficients along with the standard deviation, and a *t*-value and probability for a null hypotheses that the coefficients have values of zero. At the bottom of the results, we find the standard deviation about the regression, the R-squared, the adjusted R-squared, and an *F*-test result on the null hypothesis.

We can evaluate the regression results using the graphical methods provided by R linear regression:

```
> layout(matrix(1:4, 2, 2))
> plot(reg)
```

This produces the output shown in Fig 7-2.

The graphs at the top of Figure 7-1 shows the relationship between the residual errors (left) or the square root of the standardized residuals (right) and fitted values. We expect both of these two quantities are randomly distributed around the horizontal axis without a distinct trend. However, our results clearly show a downtrend then an up-trend, which means a simple linear-regression model may not be a good fit for representing the relationship between HY and SPY. The graph in the lower left is a standard Q-Q plot, which should suggest that the residual errors are normally distributed. You can see there are too many data points in our results located above the theoretical line. Finally, the graph in the lower right shows the points leverage, which is a measure of its importance in determining the regression results. A smaller distances means that removing the points has little effect on the regression results. Distances larger than one are suspicious and suggest the presence of a possible outlier or a poor model. In our case, we see so many data points located outside of the $[-1, +1]$ range, indicating the model is very poor.

One particular issue that tends to deviate from the linear regression model in credit (HY) versus equity (SPX) is the convexity exhibited by credit spreads at very tight levels. The problem is as follows: since the credit spreads have a zero lower bound, once they have tightened to a certain level, even when further tightening occurs, the absolute value of the move could be very low. In contrast, in a rallying market (i.e., when spreads are tightening), equity has unlimited upside. Therefore, at tight spread levels, HY credit performance gets capped while SPX continues to benefit, and we see a curvature in the scatter plot as shown in Figure 7-1.

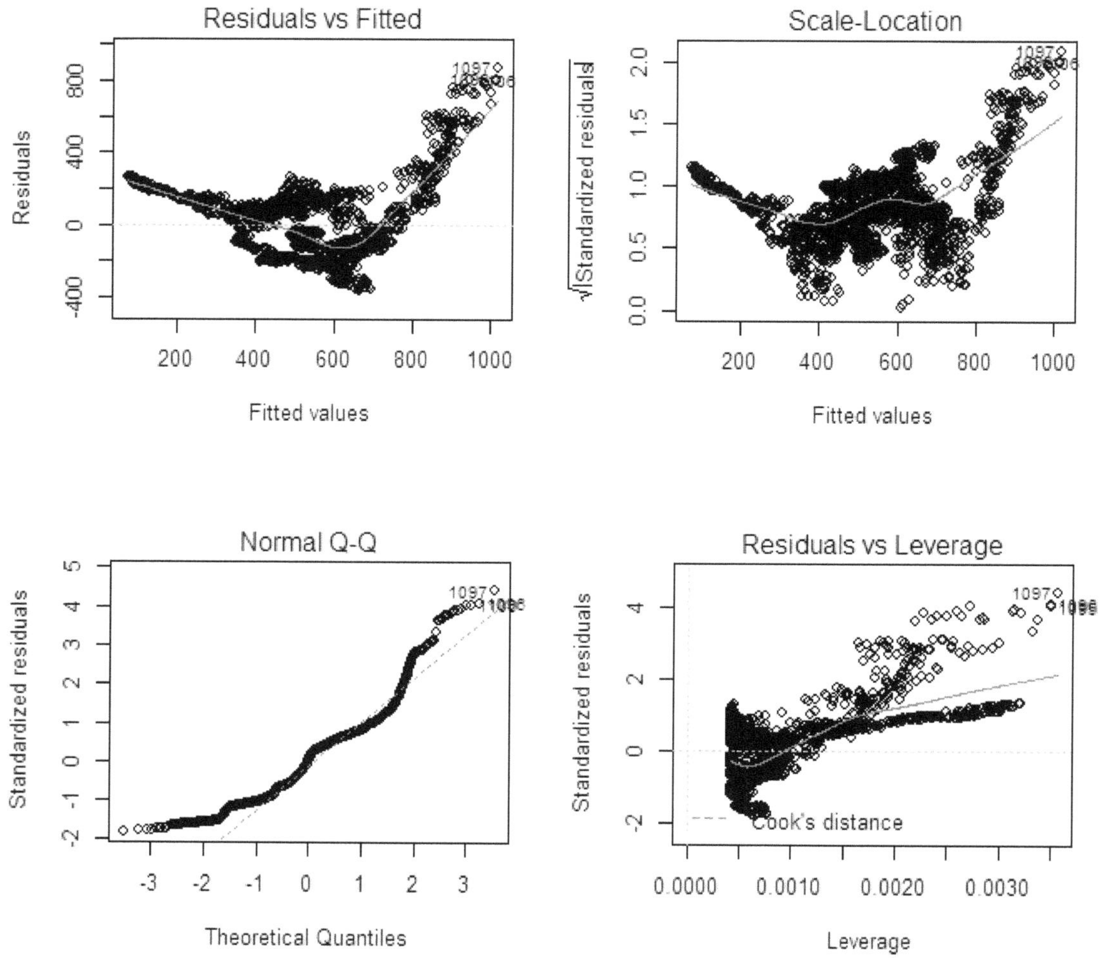


*Figure 7-2. Residual analysis for a linear regression.*

In order to address this issue, we can use a quadratic regression to calculate the residuals – such a regression includes a second-degree term that should control for the convexity. The *lm* function in R also allows us to add a quadratic term. For example, assume we have the following model:

$$y = a_0 + a_1 x + a_2 x^2$$

The syntax for such a quadratic regression analysis in R is

$$lm(y \sim x + I(x^2))$$

Note that the identity function *I( )* allows terms in the model to include normal mathematical symbols. We can then perform a quadratic regression for HY and SPX in R:

```
> reg1 <- lm(idxdata$HYSpread ~ idxdata$SPX + I(idxdata$SPX^2))
> summary(reg1)
```

```
Call:
lm(formula = idxdata$HYSpread ~ idxdata$SPX + I(idxdata$SPX^2))

Residuals:
   Min     1Q Median     3Q    Max
-355.6 -120.3  -34.6  130.3  422.7

Coefficients:
                   Estimate Std. Error t value Pr(>|t|)
(Intercept)       4.399e+03  6.852e+01   64.20   <2e-16 ***
idxdata$SPX      -5.197e+00  1.033e-01  -50.29   <2e-16 ***
I(idxdata$SPX^2)  1.658e-03  3.844e-05   43.14   <2e-16 ***
---
Signif. codes:  0 '***' 0.001 '**' 0.01 '*' 0.05 '.' 0.1 ' ' 1

Residual standard error: 149.1 on 2363 degrees of freedom
Multiple R-squared:  0.6904, Adjusted R-squared:  0.6901
F-statistic:  2634 on 2 and 2363 DF,  p-value: < 2.2e-16
```

You can see that the quadratic regression indeed outperform the linear regression in our case because the R-squared increases from 0.4465 (linear) to 0.6904 (quadratic). We can plot the quadratic regression curve on the HY ~ SPX scatter graph:

```
> plot(idxdata$SPX, idxdata$HYSpread, col = "blue", main = "HY ~ SPX",
       xlab = "SPX", ylab = "HY")
> grid()
> lines(idxdata$SPX, reg1$fitted.values, col = "red", lw = 3)
```

This generates the graph shown in Figure 7-3.

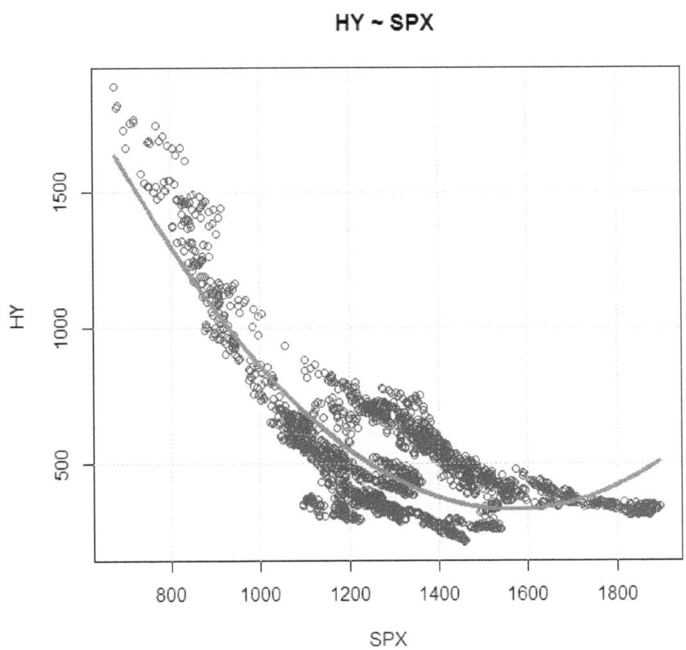


*Figure 7-3. A quadratic regression for HY and SPX.*

Note that the quadratic regression fits data better than the linear regression does. In fact, when we discuss the linear models in R, the "linear" term does not mean a straight line. Instead, a linear model can contain additive terms, each containing a single multiplicative parameter. Thus, the following equations represents different linear models:

$$y = a_0 + a_1 x^3, \quad y = a_0 + a_1 x_1 + a_2 \log(x_2)$$

However, the equation

$$y = a_0 + a_1 x_1 + a_{21} x^{a_{22}}$$

is not a linear model.

# Simple 2D PCA

PCA is a mathematical procedure that intends to replace a number of correlated variables with a new set of variables that are linearly uncorrelated. It is a way of identifying patterns in data, and expressing the data in such a way as to highlight their similarities and differences. Since patterns in data is hard to find in data of high dimension, PCA is a powerful tool for analyzing data. The other main advantage of PCA is that once we have found these patterns in the data, we can compress the data by reducing the number of dimensions, without much loss of information.

In 2D case, PCA is very simple to analyze. Suppose we have a collection of data points ($x_0$, $y_0$), ($x_1$, $y_1$),…, ($x_n$, $y_n$). In order for the PCA to work properly, we first need to subtract the mean from each data series. Therefore, all the $x$ values have $\bar{x}$ (the mean of the $x$ values of all the data points) subtracted, and all the $y$ values have $\bar{y}$ subtracted. The new data points correspond to a translation: $(x, y) \to (x - \bar{x}, y - \bar{y})$. In the new data space with the mean subtracted, the covariance matrix can be simply expressed in the form:

$$\sigma = \begin{pmatrix} \overline{x^2} & \overline{xy} \\ \overline{xy} & \overline{y^2} \end{pmatrix}, \quad \text{where: } \overline{x^2} = \frac{1}{n-1} \sum_{i=1}^{n} x_i x_i, \ \overline{xy} = \frac{1}{n-1} \sum_{i=1}^{n} x_i y_i$$

The PCA components are just the eigenvectors of the covariance matrix. For a 2D covariance matrix, we can easily find the analytic solution for the eigenvalues and eigenvectors. The eigenvalues can be found by finding the roots of

$$\det \begin{pmatrix} a - \lambda & b \\ b & c - \lambda \end{pmatrix} = 0, \qquad \text{with } a = \overline{x^2}, b = \overline{xy}, c = \overline{y^2}$$

This equation has two roots, and they are:

$$\lambda_{\pm} = \frac{(a + c) \pm d}{2}, \quad d = \sqrt{(a - c)^2 + 4b^2}$$

Corresponding to each eigenvalue, $\lambda_i$, there will be an eigenvector $e_i$ that can be obtained by solving a set of linear equations. For 2D case, we need to solve

$$\begin{pmatrix} a - \lambda & b \\ b & c - \lambda \end{pmatrix} \begin{pmatrix} x \\ y \end{pmatrix} = \begin{pmatrix} 0 \\ 0 \end{pmatrix}$$

We can write the normalized eigenvectors in the form:

$$\frac{1}{\sqrt{2d[d \pm (c - a)]}} \begin{pmatrix} \pm 2b \\ d \pm (c - a) \end{pmatrix}$$

Any non-zero multiple of these vectors is, of course, also an eigenvector. It is important to note that these eigenvectors are unit eigenvectors, i.e. their lengths are 1. This is very important for PCA. Usually, the eigenvector with the highest eigenvalue is the principal component of the data set. In 2D PCA case, we always pick the eigenvector with the higher eigenvalue and neglect the eigenvector with the lower eigenvalue.

# PCA in R

There are many packages and functions, which can be used to perform the PCA analysis in R. Here, we will use the *prcomp* function from the *stats* package. For easy comparison between regression and PCA, we will use the same data set as we used in the simple regression analysis.

Now, we will apply PCA to analyze the relationship between HY and SPX. We can use a subset of *idxdata*:

```
> sh <- data.frame(SPX = idxdata$SPX, HY = idxdata$HYSpread)
> head(sh)
      SPX    HY
1 1129.30 363.0
2 1113.56 367.5
3 1108.36 371.2
4 1110.11 374.5
5 1103.52 370.5
6 1110.06 365.5
```

We can then perform the PCA analysis for HY and SPX using the following command:

```
> pca <- prcomp(sh, center = T)
> pca
Standard deviations:
[1] 323.8234 142.0644

Rotation:
           PC1       PC2
SPX  0.6250655 0.7805723
HY  -0.7805723 0.6250655
```

Note that we set the center input argument to *true* in the *prcomp* function, indicating that the data should be shifted to be zero centered. The output from this function gives the standard deviations of the principal components and a rotation matrix. The columns of the rotation matrix contain the eigenvectors and the first column is the first principal component.

We can also use the *summary* function to examine the importance of the principal components:

```
> summary(pca)
Importance of components:
                            PC1      PC2
Standard deviation     323.8234 142.0644
Proportion of Variance   0.8386   0.1614
Cumulative Proportion    0.8386   1.0000
```

The first row describes again the standard deviation associated with each principal component. The second row shows the proportion of the variance in the data explained by each component while the third row describes the cumulative proportion of explained variance. We can see that the first principal component accounts for about 84% of the variance of the data.

Just as we did in the linear regression, we can overlap a PCA line on the HY-SPX scatter plot. Add a new helper file named *analysisHelper.R* to the [*Working directory*]/*R*/ directory. Add a new helper function named *pca2dProcess* to this file. Here is the code for this function:

```
pca2dProcess <- function(origData, isYtoPredict = T){
  pca <- prcomp(origData, center = T)
  f1 <- pca$rotation[1, 1]
  f2 <- pca$rotation[2, 1]
  xa <- pca$center[1]
  ya <- pca$center[2]
  b <- f2/f1
  a <- ya - b * xa
  if(isYtoPredict == T) origData$PcaPrediction <- a + b * origData[, 1]
  else origData$PcaPrediction <- (origData[, 2] - a)/b
  return(origData)
}
```

This function generates the predicted values from PCA, which are decoded from the first principal component and the *center* values used in PCA. The *isYtoPredict* argument is used to specify whether we want the predict *y* (if it is set to *TRUE*) or *x* (if it is set to *FASLE*) values. The default value for this argument is *TRUE*, i.e, we want to predict *y* values.

We can then add a PCA line to the scatter plot using the commands:

```
> sh1 <- pca2dProcess(sh)
> head(sh1)
      SPX    HY PcaPrediction
1 1129.30 363.0      749.6469
2 1113.56 367.5      769.3028
3 1108.36 371.2      775.7964
4 1110.11 374.5      773.6111
5 1103.52 370.5      781.8406
6 1110.06 365.5      773.6735

> plot(sh1$SPX, sh1$HY, col = "blue", main = "HY ~ SPY", xlab = "SPX", ylab = "HY")
> grid()
> lines(sh1$SPX, sh1$PcaPrediction, type = "l", col = "red")
```

The above commands generate the graph shown in Figure 7-4.

# Comparing Linear Regression with PCA

In the preceding sections, we discussed the simple linear regression and 2D PCA. Comparing the linear regression results in Figure 7-1 with the PCA results in Figure 7-4, we will find that they are very similar. Here, we will plot both results on the same chart for a direct comparison, which can be easily achieved by issuing the following commands:

```
> plot(sh1$SPX, sh1$HY, col = "blue", main = "HY ~ SPY", xlab = "SPX", ylab = "HY")
> grid()
> lines(sh1$SPX, sh1$PcaPrediction, type = "l", col = "red")
> abline(reg, col = "darkgreen")
```

Here, the *reg* object contains the linear regression results. The above commands produces the output shown in Figure 7-5.

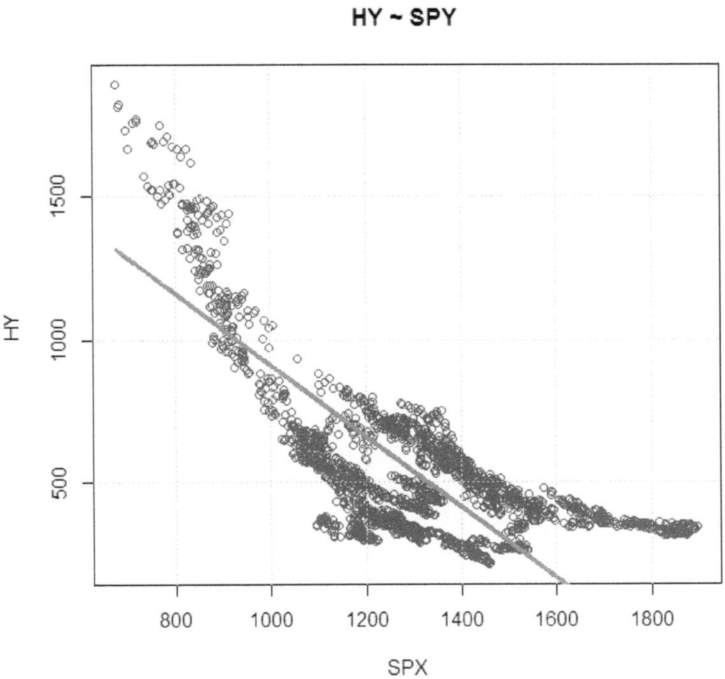


*Figure 7-4. PCA analysis for HY and SPX.*

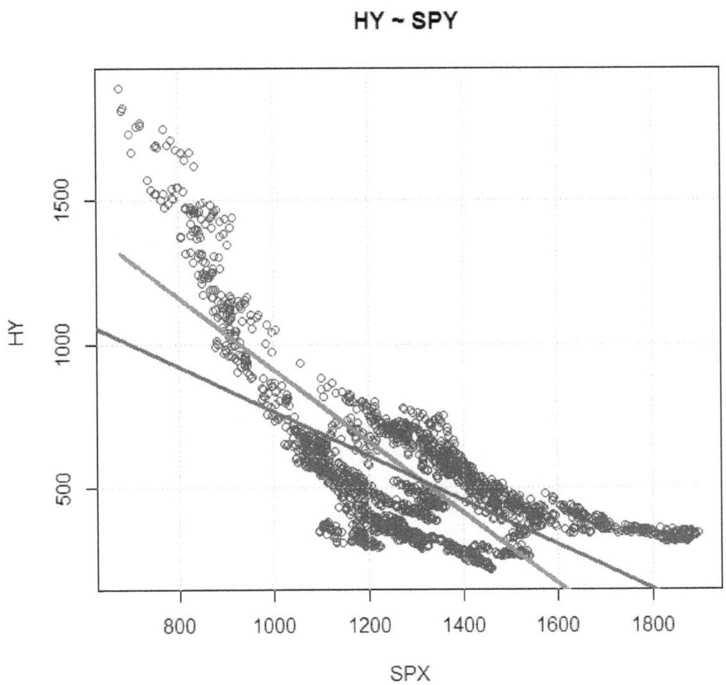


*Figure 7-5. Linear regression (green line) and PCA (red line) results for HY and SPX.*

You can see that the difference between the linear regression and PCA is significant.

By comparing the results from regression and PCA, we may still wonder what is fundamental difference between the linear regression and the PCA? First, I should point out that the linear regression is not symmetric between $y \sim x$ and $x \sim y$. We can use the following data set to examine it:

```
> head(sh)
      SPX    HY
1 1129.30 363.0
2 1113.56 367.5
3 1108.36 371.2
4 1110.11 374.5
5 1103.52 370.5
6 1110.06 365.5
```

*sh* is a subset of the original dataset: *idxdata*, which contains only the SPX and HY data.

```
> reg <- lm(sh$HY ~ sh$SPX); reg

Call:
lm(formula = sh$HY ~ sh$SPX)

Coefficients:
(Intercept)       sh$SPX
  1542.2195      -0.7756

> reg1 <- lm(sh$SPX ~ sh$HY); reg1

Call:
lm(formula = sh$SPX ~ sh$HY)

Coefficients:
(Intercept)        sh$HY
  1610.3409      -0.5756
```

We see the regression of HY ~ SPX gives different regression coefficients than those from regression of SPX ~ HY. We can also make a direct comparison visually by adding these two regression lines to the HY-SPX scatter plot. For this end, we need to convert the SPX ~ HY regression results

$$SPX = a + b \times HY$$

into

$$HY = \frac{1}{b}(SPY - a)$$

We know from the SPX ~ HY regression result *reg1*: $a = 1610.3409$ and $b = -0.5756$, which gives:

$$HY = 2797.6736 - 1.7373 \times SPX$$

While the results of the HY ~ SPX regression gives:

$$HY = 1542.2195 - 0.7756 \times SPX$$

These two regressions give two very different regression lines. We can add these two regression lines to the HY ~ SPX scatter graph using the following commands:

```
> plot(sh$SPX, sh$HY, col = "blue", main = "HY ~ SPY", xlab = "SPX", ylab = "HY")
> grid()
```

```
> abline(reg, col = "red")
> lines(sh$SPX, 2797.6736 - 1.7373*sh$SPX, type = "l", col = "darkgreen")
```

This produces the output shown in Figure 7-6. We clearly see from this figure that the linear regression of HY ~ SPX (or $y \sim x$) is not the same as that of SPX ~ HY (or $x \sim y$). The reason for this asymmetry is that the linear regression of $y \sim x$ minimizes error perpendicular to the independent axis (vertical red lines in Figure 7-6). If we want to regress $x \sim y$, it would minimize error perpendicular to $Y$-axis (horizontal green lines in Figure 7-6). In general, these two regressions give different results.

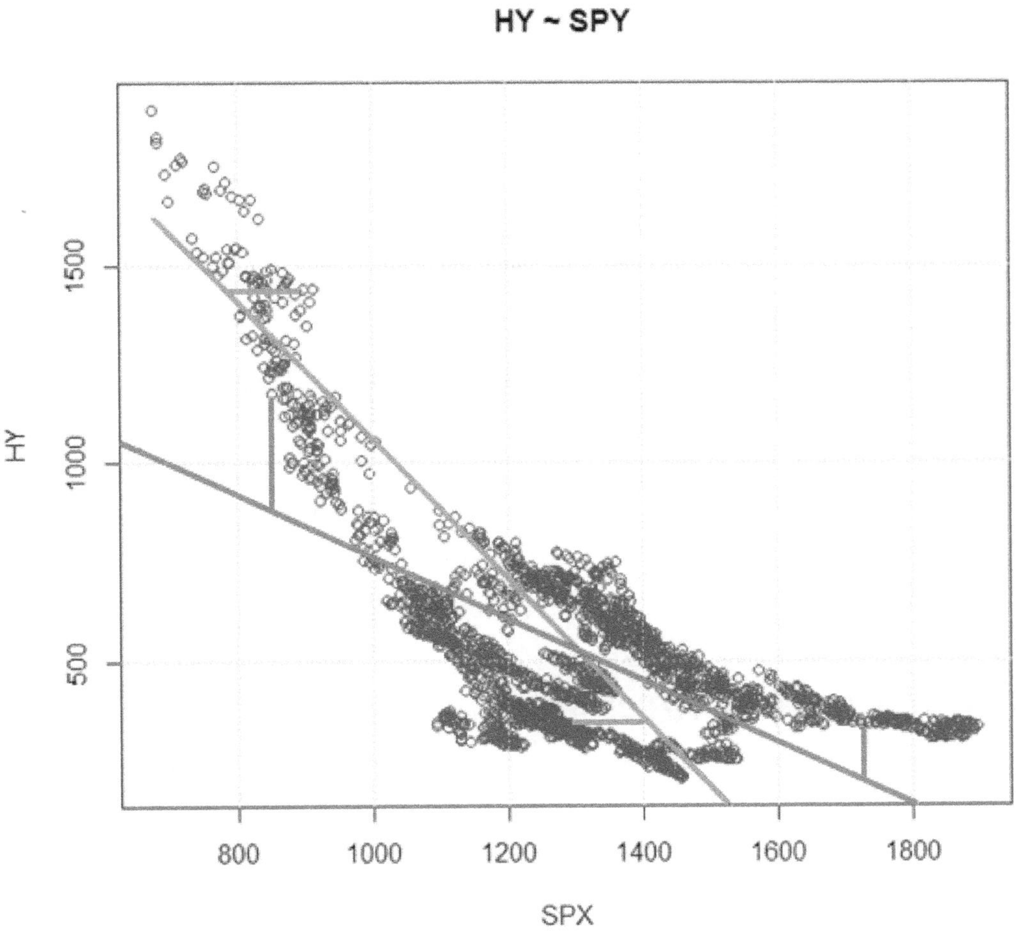


*Figure 7-6. Linear regressions of HY ~ SPX (red) and SPX ~ HY (green).*

On the other hand, the PCA effectively minimizes error orthogonal to the principal component axis, as shown in Figure 7-7 (red lines). Therefore, the PCA results are always symmetric between ($y \sim x$) and ($x \sim y$).

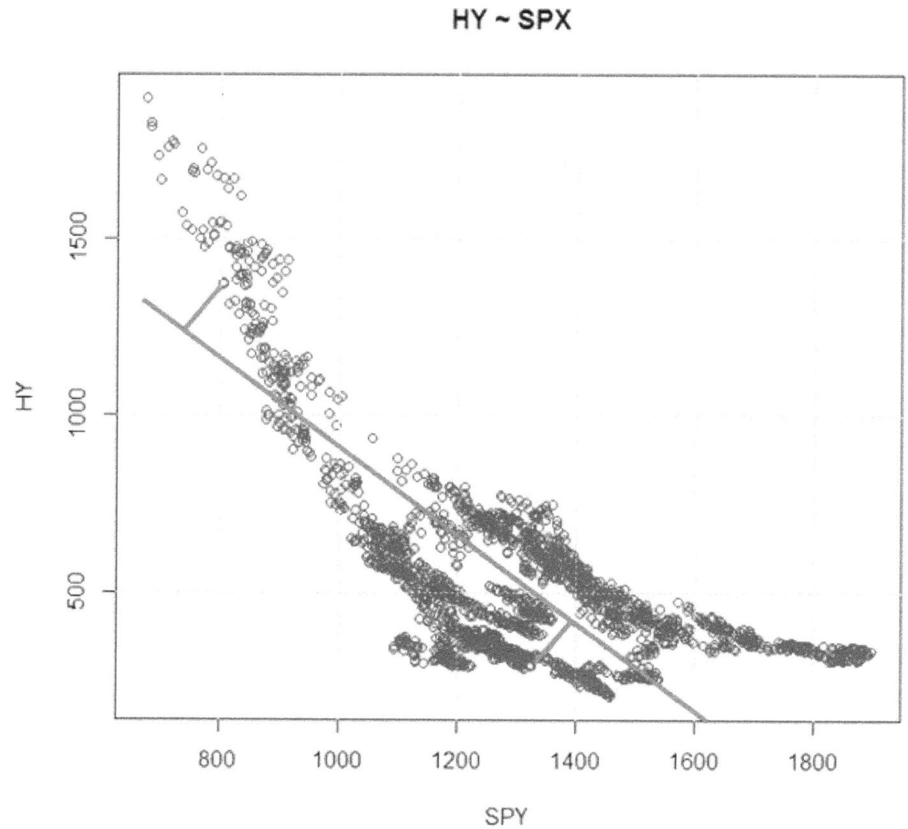


*Figure 7-7. PCA for HY ~ SPX and SPY ~ HY.*

# Multiple Linear Regressions

In the preceding sections, we discussed the simple linear regression: the dependent variable $y$ depends only on a single independent variable $x$. In practice, the dependent variable can depend on several independent variables. The purpose of the multivariable linear regression is to find the relationship between the dependent and multiple independent variables. For example, the CDS high yield (HY) spread can depend not only on the equity index (SPX) but also on volatility (VIX), interest rate, and other factors. A real estate agent such as Zillow attempts to collect information for each listing the size of the house, the number of bedrooms, and the average income in the respective neighborhood according to census data. Once this information has been compiled for various houses we would like to see whether and how these variables relate to the price for which a house is sold.

Mathematically, a multiple linear regression (MLR) model consists of $p$ independent variables:

$$y_i = b_1 x_{i1} + b_2 x_{i2} + \cdots + b_p x_{ip} + \varepsilon_i$$

where $x_{ij}$ is the $i$th observation on the $j$th independent variable. We can obtain the least squares parameter estimates from $p$ normal equations. The residual can be written as

$$\varepsilon_i = y_i - b_1 x_{i1} - \cdots - b_p x_{ip}$$

The normal equations become

$$\sum_{i=1}^{n}\sum_{k=1}^{p} X_{ij}X_{ik}\hat{b}_k = \sum_{i=1}^{n} X_{ij}y_i, \quad j = 1,2,\dots,p$$

In matrix notation, the above equation can be written as

$$(X^T X)\hat{b} = X^T Y$$

where the *ij* element of $X$ is $x_{ij}$, the *j* element of the column vector Y is $y_j$, and the *j* element of $\hat{b}$ is $b_j$. Thus, $X$ is the $n\times p$, $Y$ is the $n\times 1$, and $\hat{b}$ is the $p\times 1$ matrix. The solution is

$$\hat{b} = (X^T X)^{-1} X^T Y$$

# MLR for Indices

Here, we will perform a MLR analysis for HY, SPX, and VIX with HY as the dependent variable and SPX and VIX as the independent variables. First, we need to extract the market data from the original dataset of *idxdata*:

```
> svh <- data.frame(Date = idxdata$Date, SPX = idxdata$SPX, VIX = idxdata$VIX,
                    HY = idxdata$HYSpread)
> head(svh)
        Date     SPX   VIX    HY
1 2004-09-21 1129.30 13.66 363.0
2 2004-09-22 1113.56 14.74 367.5
3 2004-09-23 1108.36 14.80 371.2
4 2004-09-24 1110.11 14.28 374.5
5 2004-09-27 1103.52 14.62 370.5
6 2004-09-28 1110.06 13.83 365.5
```

Now, we can perform the MLR analysis for this dataset:

```
> reg <- lm(svh$HY ~ svh$SPX + svh$VIX)
> reg

Call:
lm(formula = svh$HY ~ svh$SPX + svh$VIX)

Coefficients:
(Intercept)      svh$SPX      svh$VIX
   494.5112      -0.2735      19.3608
```

This gives the regression coefficients, i.e., the predicted HY values can be expressed in the form:

$$HY = 494.5122 - 0.2735 \times SPX + 19.3608 \times VIX$$

We can obtain more information by using the *summary* command:

```
> summary(reg)

Call:
lm(formula = svh$HY ~ svh$SPX + svh$VIX)

Residuals:
    Min      1Q  Median      3Q     Max
```

```
-600.65  -74.31  -16.58   75.75  622.25

Coefficients:
             Estimate Std. Error t value Pr(>|t|)
(Intercept) 494.51124   22.22553   22.25   <2e-16 ***
svh$SPX      -0.27352    0.01359  -20.12   <2e-16 ***
svh$VIX      19.36080    0.31123   62.21   <2e-16 ***
---
Signif. codes:  0 '***' 0.001 '**' 0.01 '*' 0.05 '.' 0.1 ' ' 1

Residual standard error: 122.8 on 2363 degrees of freedom
Multiple R-squared:  0.7901, Adjusted R-squared:   0.79
F-statistic:  4449 on 2 and 2363 DF,  p-value: < 2.2e-16
```

From these results we can see that the MLR analysis improves the regression results dramatically, the R-squared increases from 0.4465 for a simple linear regression of HY ~ SPY to the current value of 0.7901. We can represent this more clearly by direct comparing the original HY spreads and the predicted HY spreads from MLR:

```
> plot(svh$Date, svh$HY, type = "l", col = "blue", main = "HY ~ SPX + VIX",
       xlab = "Date", ylab = "HY")
> lines(svh$Date, reg$fitted.values, type = "l", col = "red")
> legend("topleft", c("HY", "Regression"), lty = c(1, 1), col = c("blue", "red"))
> grid()
```

The above commands generate the output shown in Figure 7-8.

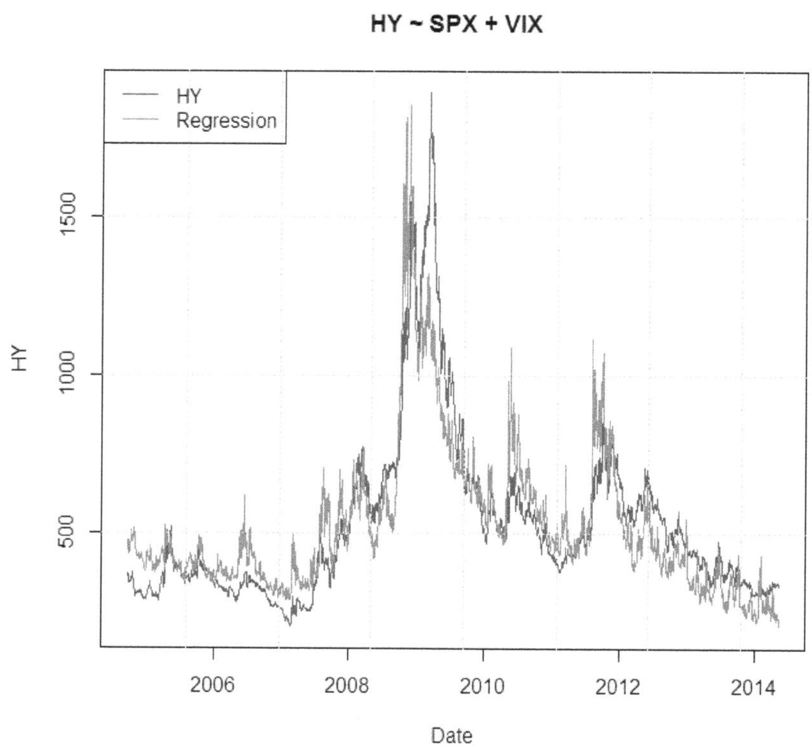


*Figure 7-8. Multiple regression results for HY vs SPX and VIX*

The results shown in Figure 7-8 indicate that the MLR analysis provides a reasonable fit to HY. We can also create a scatter graph for HR ~ MLR (the predicted HY values from MLR analysis) and add a regression line to the scatter plot. First, create another sub-dataset:

```
> hp <- data.frame(HY = svh$HY, MLR = reg$fitted.values)
> head(hp)
     HY      MLR
1 363.0 450.0959
2 367.5 475.3107
3 371.2 477.8947
4 374.5 467.3484
5 370.5 475.7335
6 365.5 458.6497
```

We then perform another simple linear regression for HY ~ MLR using the above dataset:

```
> slr <- lm(hp$HY ~ hp$MLR)
```

We expect *slr* should gives the same R-squared:

```
> summary(slr)
Call:
lm(formula = hp$HY ~ hp$MLR)
Residuals:
    Min      1Q  Median      3Q     Max
-600.65  -74.31  -16.58   75.75  622.25

Coefficients:
             Estimate Std. Error t value Pr(>|t|)
(Intercept) 8.227e-13  6.155e+00    0.00        1
hp$MLR      1.000e+00  1.060e-02   94.34   <2e-16 ***
---
Signif. codes:  0 '***' 0.001 '**' 0.01 '*' 0.05 '.' 0.1 ' ' 1

Residual standard error: 122.8 on 2364 degrees of freedom
Multiple R-squared:  0.7901, Adjusted R-squared:  0.7901
F-statistic:  8901 on 1 and 2364 DF,  p-value: < 2.2e-16
```

Indeed, we have the same R-squared, as expected. Now, we can create the scatter plot for HY and MLR with a regression line:

```
> plot(hp$MLR, hp$HY, col = "blue", main = "HY ~ MLR", xlab = "MLR", ylab = "HY")
> abline(slr, col = "red")
```

This produces the output shown in Figure 7-9.

## MLR for Stocks

We can also perform the MLR analysis for stocks. For example, taking MS as dependent variable, GS, C, and XLE as independent variables. First, we need to load the market data into R:

```
> library(quantmod)
> tks <- c("MS", "GS", "C", "XLE")
> stocks <- lapply(tks, function(tk) Ad(na.omit(getSymbols(tk, from = "2004-09-21",
                    To = "2016-01-01", auto.assign = FALSE))))
> stks <- do.call(merge.xts, stocks)
> colnames(stks) <- tks
```

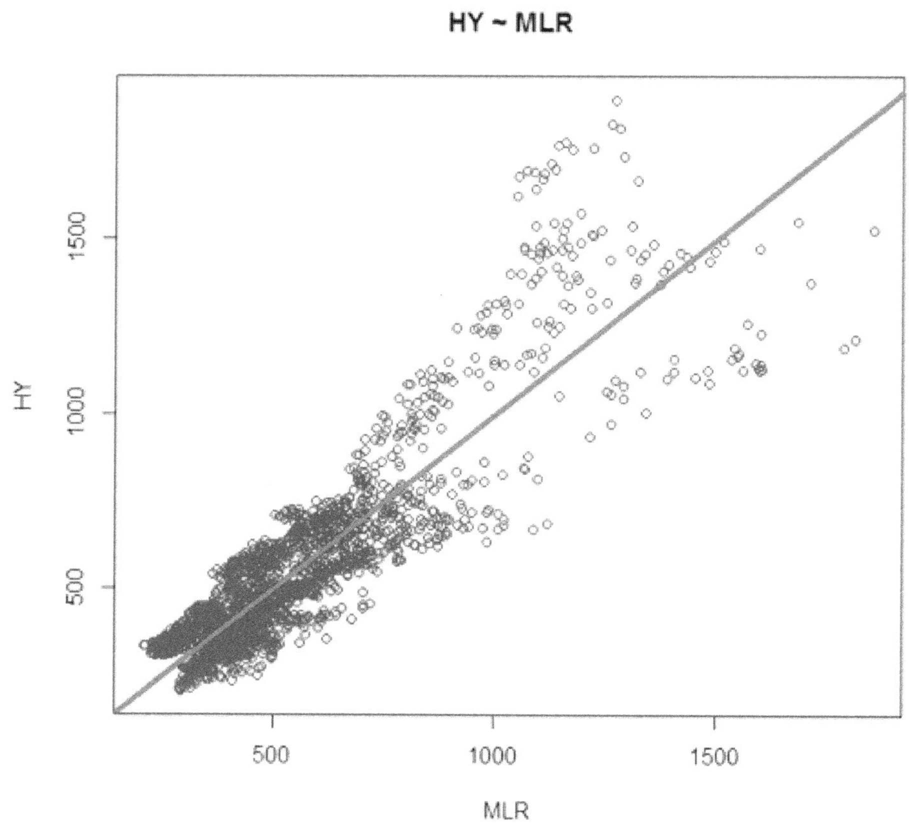


*Figure 7-9. Regression results for HY ~ MLR.*

```
> head(stks)
                 MS       GS        C      XLE
2004-09-21 36.24343 83.09762 374.6251 28.26122
2004-09-22 33.71096 81.77541 364.2029 28.08240
2004-09-23 34.26451 81.49521 360.0996 27.82230
2004-09-24 34.61739 81.85422 362.3154 28.13929
2004-09-27 33.74556 81.21501 357.8839 28.12304
2004-09-28 33.80091 81.48645 363.6284 28.60259
```

Here, we first get the adjusted close prices for all stocks under considered using the *lappy* function from Yahoo Finance, then use the *do.call* function to merge the date into an *xts* object with aligned dates. Note that you may have slightly different data values from the data shown here because the adjusted stock price may change when new stock split or dividend information becomes available. Now, we can apply MLR to this dataset:

```
> mlr <- lm(stks$MS ~ stks$GS + stks$C + stks$XLE)
> mlr

Call:
lm(formula = stks$MS ~ stks$GS + stks$C + stks$XLE)

Coefficients:
```

```
(Intercept)      stks$GS       stks$C     stks$XLE
   -2.25364      0.19241      0.05699     -0.04048

> summary(mlr)

Call:
lm(formula = stks$MS ~ stks$GS + stks$C + stks$XLE)

Residuals:
     Min       1Q   Median       3Q      Max
-10.8554  -1.5304   0.0035   1.4337   8.8032

Coefficients:
              Estimate Std. Error t value Pr(>|t|)
(Intercept) -2.2536418  0.2180738  -10.33   <2e-16 ***
stks$GS      0.1924149  0.0015004  128.24   <2e-16 ***
stks$C       0.0569943  0.0003083  184.89   <2e-16 ***
stks$XLE    -0.0404758  0.0040033  -10.11   <2e-16 ***
---
Signif. codes:  0 '***' 0.001 '**' 0.01 '*' 0.05 '.' 0.1 ' ' 1

Residual standard error: 2.227 on 2965 degrees of freedom
Multiple R-squared:  0.9663, Adjusted R-squared:  0.9663
F-statistic: 2.833e+04 on 3 and 2965 DF,  p-value: < 2.2e-16
```

From the regression coefficients, we have the following relations:

$$MS = -2.25364 + 0.19241 \times GS + 0.05699 \times C - 0.04048 \times XLE$$

This regression creates a high R-squared of 0.9663, indicating the regression predicted values are highly correlated with original MS prices. This can be seen more clearly when we plot them on the same graph:

```
> plot(as.Date(index(stks)), as.numeric(stks$MS), type="l",  col = "blue",
       main = "MS ~ GS + C + XLE", xlab = "Date", ylab = "MS Price")
> grid()
> lines(as.Date(index(stks)), mlr$fitted.values, type = "l", col = "red")
> legend("topright", c("MS", "MLR"), lty = c(1, 1), col = c("blue", "red"))
```

This produces the output shown in Figure 7-10.

We can also add the regression line to the scatter plot of MS ~ MLR:

```
> reg <- lm(df$MS ~ mlr$fitted.values)
> plot(mlr$fitted.values, df$MS, col = "blue", main = "MS ~ MLR", xlab = "MLR",
       ylab = "MS")
> abline(reg, col = "red")
> grid()
```

This produces the results shown in Figure 7 – 11.

We see from Figures 7-10 and 7-11 that the predicted values from MLR have a very high correlation relative to the original MS data with an R-squared = 0.9663.

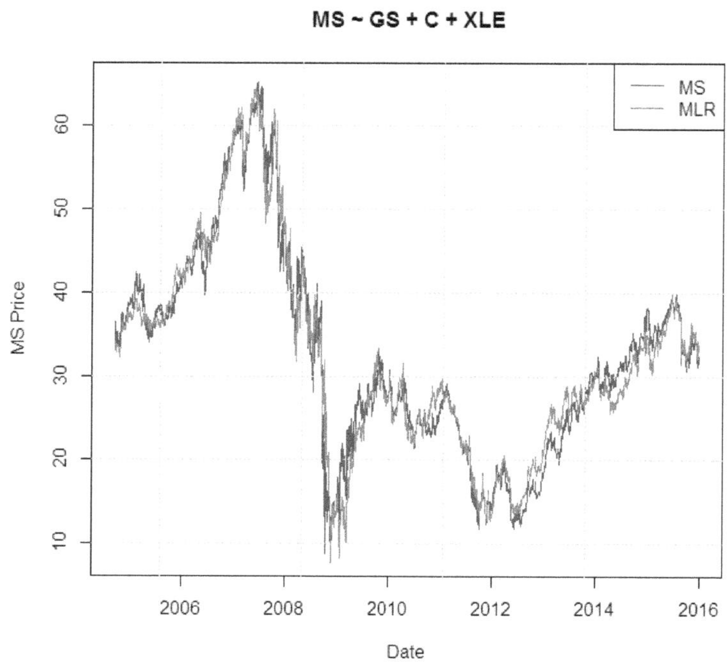


*Figure 7-10. MS stock price and MLR values.*

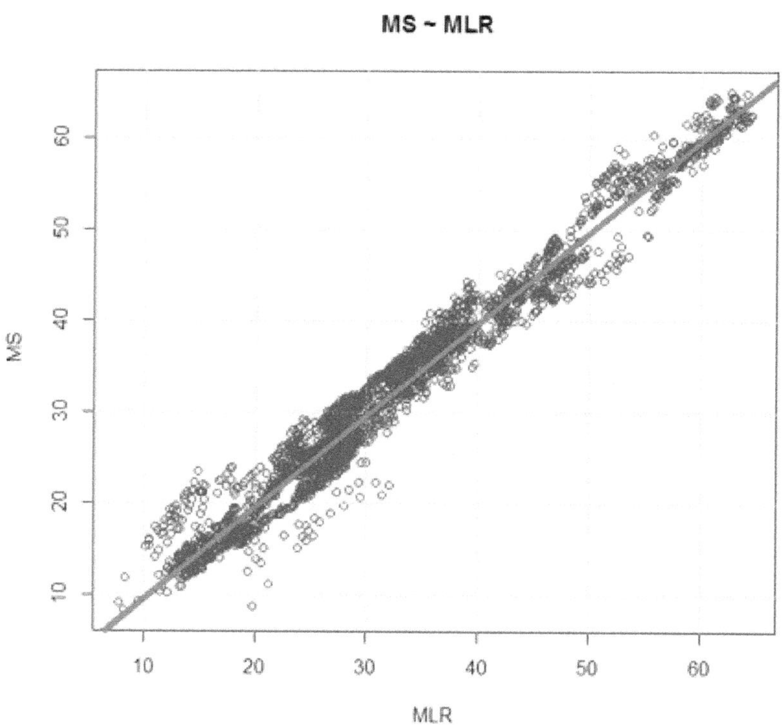


*Figure 7-11. Regression results for MS ~ MLR.*

# Multiple PCA

Previously, we have discussed the simplest PCA case: a simple 2D PCA. Just like the multiple linear regression, we can also perform a PCA computation with multiple variables (i.e., the number of variables > 2) using the *prcomp* function from the *stats* package.

## PCA for Indices

Here, we will perform a multiple PCA analysis for HY, IG, SPX and VIX with HY as the dependent variable and IG, SPX, and VIX as the independent variables. We extract data for PCA from the original *idxdata*:

```
> isv <- data.frame(IG = idxdata$IGSpread, SPX = idxdata$SPX, VIX = idxdata$VIX)
> head(isv)
     IG     SPX   VIX
1 53.93 1129.30 13.66
2 55.18 1113.56 14.74
3 54.69 1108.36 14.80
4 55.11 1110.11 14.28
5 54.59 1103.52 14.62
6 54.15 1110.06 13.83
```

Now, we can perform PCA for this dataset:

```
> pca <- prcomp(isv, center = T, scale. = T)
> pca
Standard deviations:
[1] 1.5296439 0.7327263 0.3511435

Rotation:
           PC1        PC2         PC3
IG   0.6008241 -0.4302517 -0.67371644
SPX -0.5087688 -0.8558801  0.09286298
VIX  0.6165750 -0.2869716  0.73313207
> summary(pca)
Importance of components:
                          PC1    PC2    PC3
Standard deviation     1.5296 0.7327 0.3511
Proportion of Variance 0.7799 0.1790 0.0411
Cumulative Proportion  0.7799 0.9589 1.0000
```

Note that we set both arguments *center* and *scale.* to TRUE when we perform PCA using the *prcomp* function. In our case, this is necessary to scale the variables to have unit variance before PCA because our input variables have very different data ranges. We can extract these center and scaling parameters using the following commands:

```
> pca$center
       IG        SPX        VIX
  89.45037 1305.46152   20.25820
> pca$scale
      IG       SPX      VIX
 44.48189 230.79662  10.08152
```

From the summary section, we see that the first PCA component accounts for about 78% variance, so for a simplicity's sake, we will consider the first PCA component only:

```
> pca1 <- data.frame(Pca = 0.6008241 * (isv$IG  - pca$center[1])/pca$scale[1] -
                          0.5087688 * (isv$SPX - pca$center[2])/pca$scale[2] +
                          0.6165750 * (isv$VIX - pca$center[3])/pca$scale[3])
```

Note how we construct the first PCA component: since the PCA solution is for preprocessed data, we have to use the centered and scaled data to construct the component. Now, we can examine the correlation between HY and the first PCA component:

```
> reg <- lm(idxdata$HYSpread ~ pca1$Pca)
> summary(reg)

Call:
lm(formula = idxdata$HYSpread ~ pca1$Pca)

Residuals:
    Min      1Q  Median      3Q     Max
-387.01  -55.99   -6.30   52.22  526.28

Coefficients:
            Estimate Std. Error t value Pr(>|t|)
(Intercept)  529.659      1.891   280.1   <2e-16 ***
pca1$Pca     164.503      1.237   133.0   <2e-16 ***
---
Signif. codes:  0 '***' 0.001 '**' 0.01 '*' 0.05 '.' 0.1 ' ' 1

Residual standard error: 91.99 on 2364 degrees of freedom
Multiple R-squared:  0.8822, Adjusted R-squared:  0.8821
F-statistic: 1.77e+04 on 1 and 2364 DF,  p-value: < 2.2e-16
```

The above results show that the correlation between HY and the first PCA component is very high because of a high R-squared value of 0.8822.

We can plot HY and its predicted values on the same graph for a direct comparison:

```
> plot(idxdata$Date, idxdata$HYSpread, type="l", col = "blue",
       main = "HY ~ IG + SPY + VIX", xlab = "Date", ylab = "HY")
> grid()
> lines(idxdata$Date, reg$fitted.values, col = "red")
```

This produces the outputs shown in Figure 7-12.

We can also add a PCA line on a scatter plot of HY ~ first PCA component of IG, SPY, and VIX:

```
> reg1 <- lm(df$HY ~ mlr$fitted.values)
> plot(reg$fitted.values, idxdata$HYSpread, col = "blue",
       main = "HY ~ IG + SPY + VIX", xlab = "PCA", ylab = "HY")
> abline(reg1, col = "red")
> grid()
```

This produces the outputs shown in Figure 7-13.

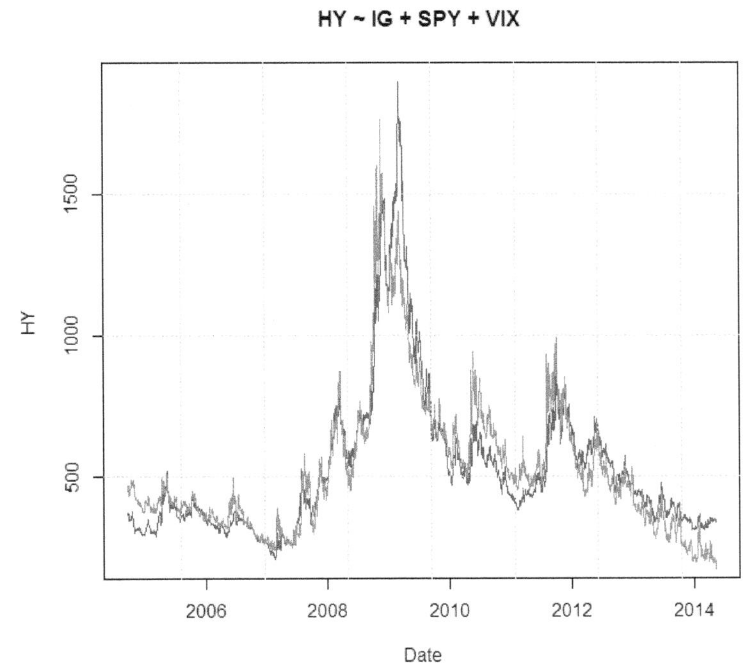


*Figure 7-12. HY and its values predicted from the first PCA component of IG, SPX, and VIX.*

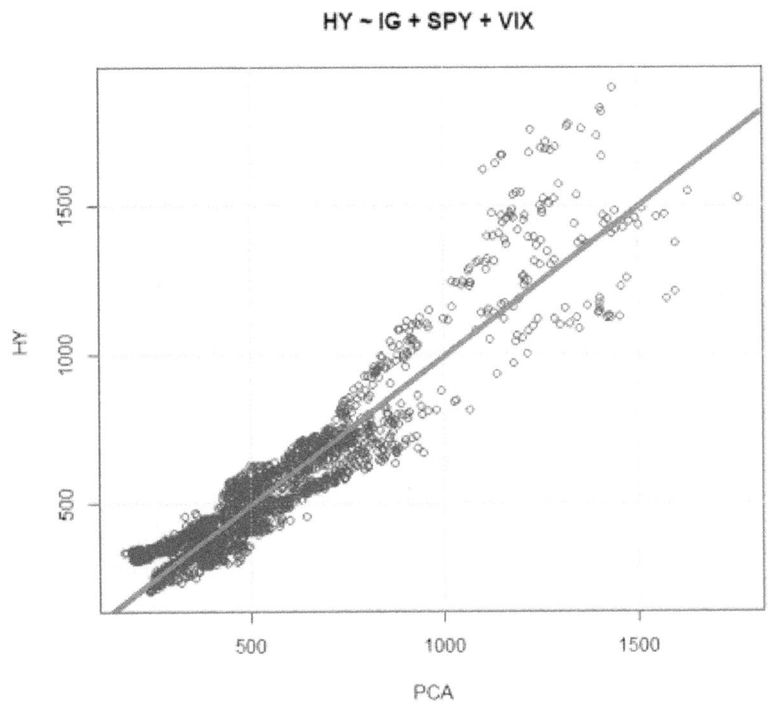


*Figure 7-13. Regression results for HY ~ PCA.*

# PCA for Stocks

We can also perform the PCA analysis for stocks. For example, taking MS as dependent variable, GS, C, and XLE as independent variables. We can use the same stock dataset, *stks*, as what was used previously when we discussed the multiple regression for stocks. We extract data for independent variable from the original *stks* data:

```
> pcaData <- stks[,-1]
> head(pcaData)
                 GS        C      XLE
2004-09-21 83.09762 374.6251 28.26122
2004-09-22 81.77541 364.2029 28.08240
2004-09-23 81.49521 360.0996 27.82230
2004-09-24 81.85422 362.3154 28.13929
2004-09-27 81.21501 357.8839 28.12304
2004-09-28 81.48645 363.6284 28.60259
```

Now, we can perform PCA for this dataset:

```
> pca <- prcomp(pcaData, center = T, scale. = T)
> pca
Standard deviations:
[1] 1.3104948 1.0132951 0.5058029

Rotation:
           PC1          PC2        PC3
GS   0.5078173 -0.690205554  0.5154977
C   -0.4826657 -0.723611285 -0.4933766
XLE  0.7135512  0.001732141 -0.7006009
> summary(pca)
Importance of components:
                          PC1    PC2     PC3
Standard deviation     1.3105 1.0133 0.50580
Proportion of Variance 0.5725 0.3423 0.08528
Cumulative Proportion  0.5725 0.9147 1.00000
```

Note that we set both arguments *center* and *scale.* to TRUE when we perform PCA using the *prcomp* function. In our case, this is necessary to scale the variables to have unit variance before PCA because our input variables have very different data ranges. We can extract these center and scaling parameters using the following commands:

```
> pca$center
       GS         C       XLE
142.45960 158.43790  58.72229
> pca$scale
       GS         C       XLE
 35.01892 167.55585  15.19448
```

From the summary section, we see that the first PCA component accounts for only 57.3% of variance, while the second PCA component accounts for about 34.2% of variance. This means that we need to consider both the first and second components, which account for about 91.47% of variance:

```
> pca1 <- data.frame(PCA1 = as.numeric(
                        0.5078173 * (stks$GS  - pca$center[1])/pca$scale[1] -
                        0.4826657 * (stks$C   - pca$center[2])/pca$scale[2] +
                        0.7135512 * (stks$XLE - pca$center[3])/pca$scale[3]),
```

```
              PCA2 = as.numeric(
                     -0.690205554 * (stks$GS  - pca$center[1])/pca$scale[1] -
                      0.723611285 * (stks$C   - pca$center[2])/pca$scale[2] +
                      0.001732141 * (stks$XLE - pca$center[3])/pca$scale[3])
              )
```

Note how we construct the first two PCA components: since the PCA solution is for preprocessed data, we have to use the centered and scaled data to construct the PCA components. Now, we can examine the correlation between HY and the first two PCA components:

```
> reg <- lm(stks$MS ~ pca1$PCA1 + pca1$PCA2)
> summary(reg)

Call:
lm(formula = stks$MS ~ pca1$PCA1 + pca1$PCA2)

Residuals:
     Min       1Q   Median       3Q      Max
-10.9732  -1.4955  -0.0424   1.5022   8.2298

Coefficients:
             Estimate Std. Error t value Pr(>|t|)
(Intercept)  31.81093    0.04154   765.8   <2e-16 ***
pca1$PCA1    -1.62641    0.03170   -51.3   <2e-16 ***
pca1$PCA2   -11.56207    0.04100  -282.0   <2e-16 ***
---
Signif. codes:  0 '***' 0.001 '**' 0.01 '*' 0.05 '.' 0.1 ' ' 1

Residual standard error: 2.263 on 2966 degrees of freedom
Multiple R-squared:  0.9652, Adjusted R-squared:  0.9651
F-statistic: 4.108e+04 on 2 and 2966 DF,  p-value: < 2.2e-16
```

The above results show that the correlation between MS and the first two PCA components is very high because of a high R-squared value of 0.9652.

We can plot MS and its predicted values on the same graph for a direct comparison:

```
> plot(as.Date(index(stks)), as.numeric(stks$MS), type="l", col = "blue",
       main = "MS ~ GS + C + XLE", xlab = "Date", ylab = "MS")
> grid()
> lines(as.Date(index(stks)), reg$fitted.values, col = "red")
> legend("topright", c("MS", "MLR"), lty = c(1, 1), col = c("blue", "red"))
```

This produces the output shown in Figure 7-14.

We can also add a PCA line on a scatter plot of MS ~ first two PCA components of GS, C, and XLE:

```
> reg1 <- lm(stks$MS ~ reg$fitted.values)
> plot(as.numeric(reg$fitted.values[,1]), as.numeric(stks$MS), col = "blue",
       main = "MS ~ GS + C + XLE", xlab = "PCA", ylab = "MS")
> abline(reg1, col = "red")
> grid()
```

This produces the outputs shown in Figure 7-15.

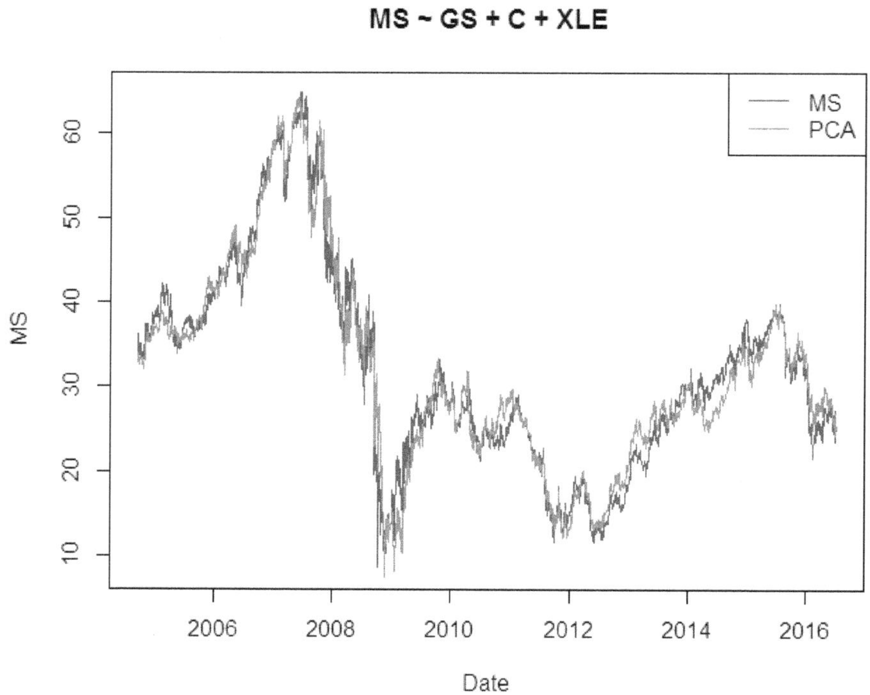


*Figure 7-14. MS and its values predicted from the first two PCA components of GS, C, and XLE.*

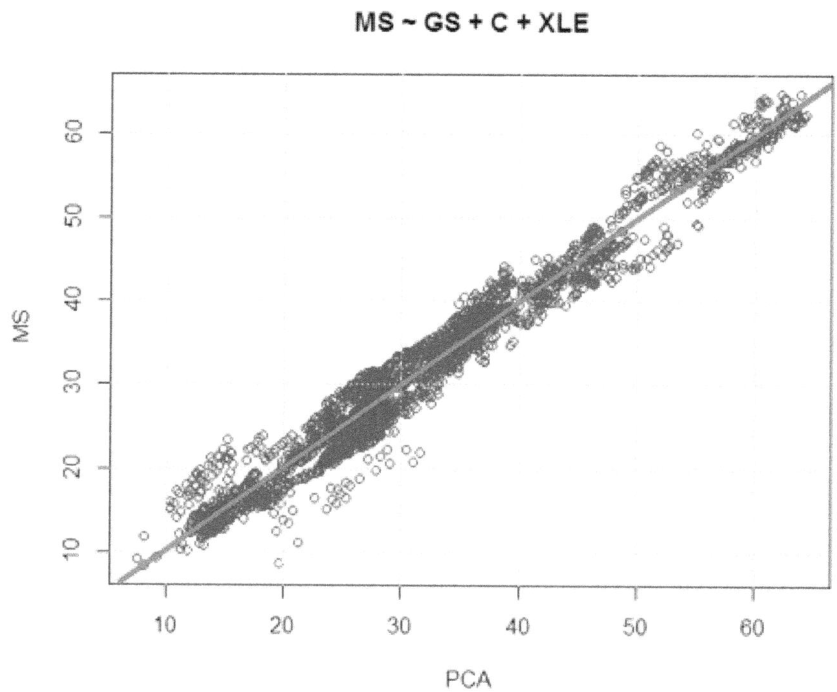


*Figure 7-15. Regression results for MS ~ PCA.*

In this chapter, we presented two linear analysis techniques, linear regression and PCA, which are the most commonly used methods in quantitative analysis in finance. There are many other linear and nonlinear analysis approaches, such as moving average, cointegration, technical indicators, and machine learning, which will be discussed in following chapters.

# Chapter 8
# Time Series Analysis

A time series is a sequence of numerical data points in successive order, usually occurring in uniform intervals. Most financial data, such as stock prices, trading volume, interest rates, and currency exchange rates, all belong to the time series data. We can use the time series analysis to examine how a given security variable changes over time or how it changes compared to other variables over the same time period. In addition, since the adjacent data points in a time series are typically dependent, we can also use the time series analysis to study this dependence.

In this chapter, we will introduce some common modeling techniques in time series analysis, including the autoregressive moving average (ARMA), the autoregressive integrated moving average (ARIMA), and the volatility modeling generalized autoregressive conditional heteroscedasticity (GARCH). We will also investigate the stationarity of a time series using different approaches, including the augmented Dickey-Fuller (ADF) unit root test and the Johansen test.

## Autocorrelation

As mentioned above, the consecutive points in a time series are typically dependent, that is, the time series possesses some kind of self-correlation. We will call this correlation the autocorrelation (or serial correlation). The autocorrelation function (ACF) will tell us how sequential points in a time series affect each other. We can define ACF in the following formula:

$$\rho_k = \frac{E[(y_t - \bar{y})(y_{t+k} - \bar{y})]}{E[(y_t - \bar{y})^2]} = \frac{\text{Cov}(y_t, y_{t+k})}{\text{Var}(y_t)}$$

where $\bar{y} = E(y_t)$ is the expected (or average) value in a time series. *Cov*(…) and *Var*(…) denote the covariance and variance respectively. Note that $\rho_0 = 1$, i.e., the first lag of $k = 0$ always gives a value of unity.

In time series analysis, we often use the autocorrelation plot (or correlogram) to show the relationship of the $\rho_k$ and the lag $k$. The correlogram allows us to see the correlation structure in each lag and to detect any autocorrelation subsequent to the removal of any deterministic or seasonality effects.

For an ACF to make sense, the time series must be a weakly stationary series. This means that the autocorrelation for any particular lag is the same regardless of where we are in time. For a weakly stationary time series, it should satisfy the following conditions: the mean $E(y_t)$ is the same for all $t$, the variance of $y_t$ is the same for all $t$, and the covariance (and also correlation) between $y_t$ and $y_{t+k}$ is the same for all $t$. Many stationary time series have recognizable AFC patterns. Most series that we encounter in practice, however, are not stationary. A continual upward (or downward) trend, for example, is a violation of the requirement that the mean is the same for all $t$. Distinct seasonal patterns also violate that requirement.

Now, we will consider the autocorrelation for some common time series.

## White Noise

The white noise time series is a simple collection of uncorrelated random variables $\{w_t\}$, with a mean of zero and finite variance $\sigma_w^2$. In particular, if the values $w_i$ are drawn from a standard normal distribution, i.e. $w_t \sim N(0, \sigma^2)$, then the series is called Gaussian white noise. The designation "white" originates from the analogy with white light and indicates that all possible periodic oscillations are present with equal strength.

We also require the noise to be independent and identically distributed random variables with mean 0 and variance $\sigma_w^2$. Figure 8-1 shows a collection of 1000 such random variables, with $\sigma_w^2 = 1$, plotted in the order in which they are drawn. We can generate this figure using the following R commands:

```
> set.seed(1)
> w <- rnorm(1000, 0, 1)
> plot.ts(w, main = "Gaussian white noise")
```

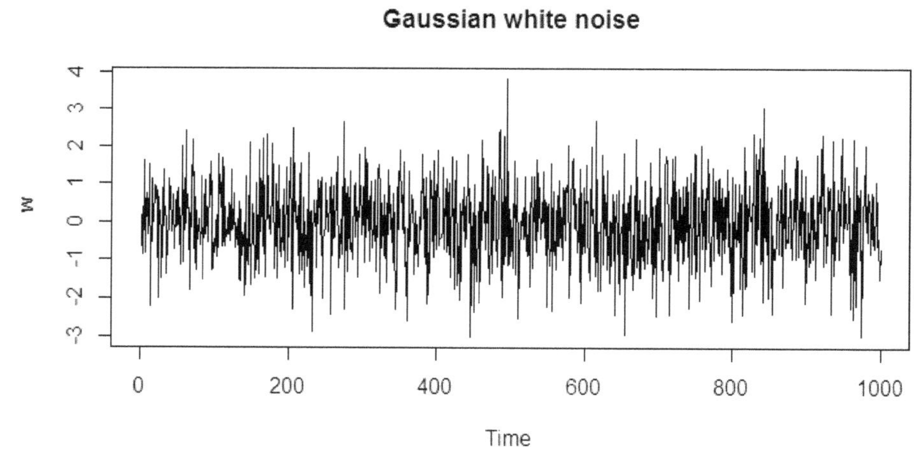


*Figure 8-1. Gaussian white noise with 1000 random variables.*

By definition, we know that the mean of the white noise is zero and there is no autocorrelation:

$$\overline{w} = E(w_t) = 0, \quad \rho_k = Cor(w_t, w_{t+k}) = \begin{cases} 1 & \text{if } k = 0 \\ 0 & \text{if } k \neq 0 \end{cases}$$

From the above properties, we know that the white noise series is a stationary time series. We can now generate a correlogram for the white noise, plotted in R using the *acf* function:

```
> acf(w)
```

This generates output shown in Figure 8-2.

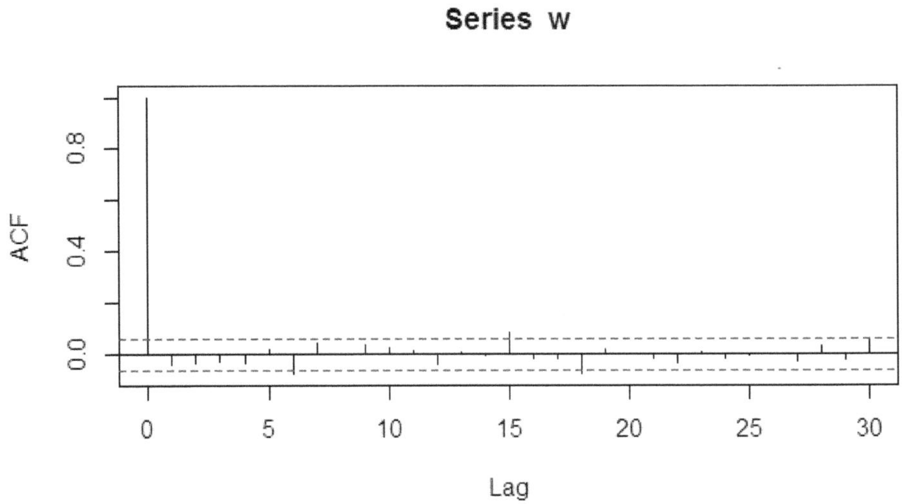


*Figure 8-2. Correlogram of Gaussian white noise.*

We see from Figure 8-2 that at lag $k = 6$, 15, and 18, we have three peaks that different from zero at the 5% level (within the blue dotted lines). However, this may be due to the variation in discrete sampling from the normal distribution.

# Random Walk with Drift

A random walk is another time series where the current point value is equal to the previous point with a random step up or down. We often use this model to analyze the price-movement trend as seen in the stock market. We can describe a random walk model with drift using the following formula:

$$y_t = \delta + y_{t-1} + w_t$$

where $w_t$ is the white noise, the constant $\delta$ is called the drift, and when $\delta = 0$ the above equation describes simply a random walk. The term random walk comes from the fact that, when $\delta = 0$, the value of the time series at time $t$ is the value of the series at time $t - 1$ plus a completely random movement determined by $w_t$. Note that we may rewrite the above equation as a cumulative sum of white noise variables (with initial condition $y_0 = 0$):

$$y_t = t\delta + \sum_{i=1}^{t} w_i$$

Because $\mathrm{E}(w_i) = 0$ for all $t$, and $\delta$ is a constant, we have:

$$\bar{y} = E(y_t) = t\delta + \sum_{i=1}^{t} E(w_i) = t\delta$$

which is a straight line with slope $\delta$. The autocorrelation function of a random walk can be derived as follows:

$$\rho_k = \frac{t\sigma^2}{\sqrt{t\sigma^2(t+k)\sigma^2}} = \frac{1}{\sqrt{1+k/t}}$$

The above result implies that the autocorrelation is almost unity for a short term lags (small $k$) if the random walk model is a long time series (large $t$). That is, a random walk has a very high autocorrelation that does not decrease rapidly as the lag increases.

We now use an example to illustrate a random walk model in R.

```
> set.seed(3)
> w <- rnorm(300, 0, 1)
> y <- cumsum(w)
> wd <- w + 0.2
> yd <- cumsum(wd)
> plot.ts(yd, ylim=c(-10, 80), main = "Random walk")
> lines(0.2*(1:300), lty="dashed")
> lines(y, col="red")
```

The above commands generate output shown in Figure 8-3, which shows 300 observations created from the model with $\delta = 0$ and $\delta = 0.2$. For comparison, we also superimposed a straight line $0.2t$ on the graph.

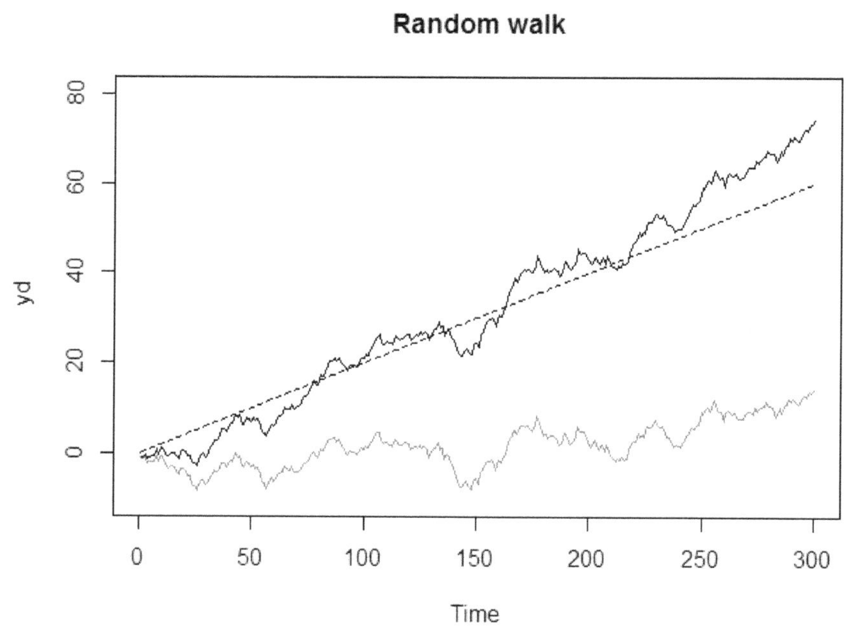


*Figure 8-3. Random walk with drift $\delta = 0.2$ (black line), without drift (red line), and a straight line with slope = 0.2 (black dashed line).*

It is also easy to draw the correlogram for the random walk series:

```
> par(mfrow=c(2,1))
> acf(y)
> acf(yd)
```

This produces output shown in Figure 8-4.

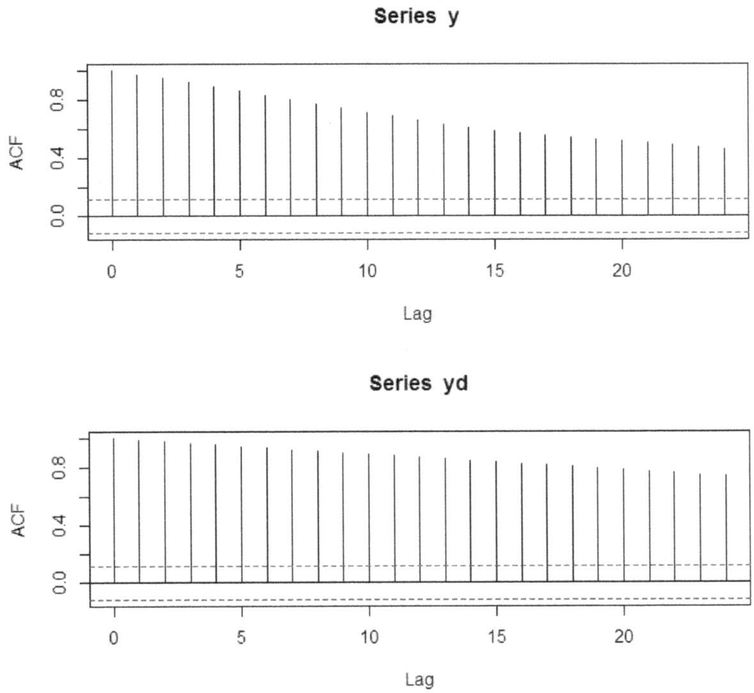


*Figure 8-4. Correlograms for random walk models without drift (top) and with drift* $\delta = 0.2$ *(top).*

Note that the ACF plot for random walk models decreases slowly as the lags increase. In addition, the correlogram plot has several notable features: first, since the correlation is unity for lag $k = 0$, we will always have a line of height equal to unity at lag $k = 0$, which provides us with a reference point upon which to judge the remaining autocorrelations at subsequent lags. Then, the dotted blue lines in the figure represent boundaries upon which if values fall outside of these, we have evidence against the null hypothesis that our correlation at lag $k$ is equal to zero at the 5% level.

If we create a series of the difference of elements from the random walk series, we should have a white noise time series:

```
> diff <- diff(y)
> plot.ts(diff, type="l")
```

This produces the result shown in Figure 8-5. You can see that the values oscillate around zero, leading to a zero mean. Similarly, the difference of *yd* will also generate a similar white noise, but its values will oscillate around the drift $\delta$, resulting in a mean equal to $\delta$.

Once we have create the difference time series, we can create a correlogram to see how close this is to a white noise model:

```
> acf(diff)
```

This generates the output shown in Figure 8-6.

We see from this figure that there is no statistically significant peaks at 5% level, indicating that the difference of the random walk model indeed represents a white noise series.

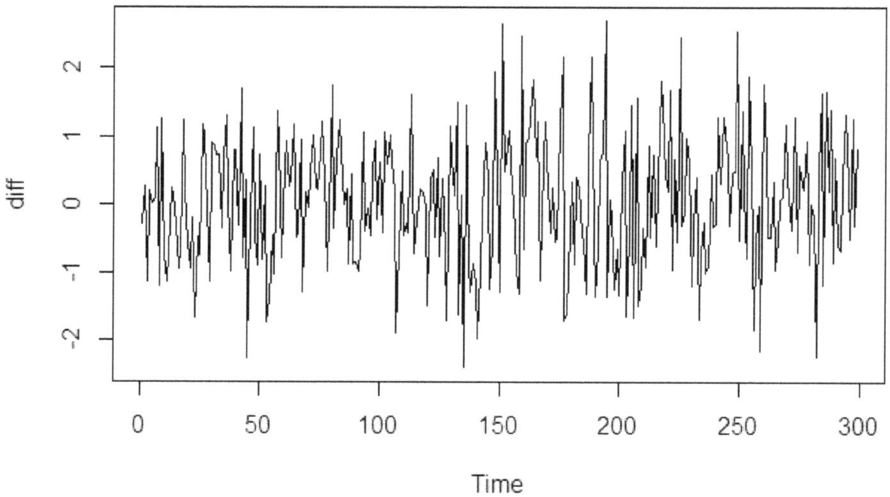


*Figure 8-5. Difference of a random walk.*

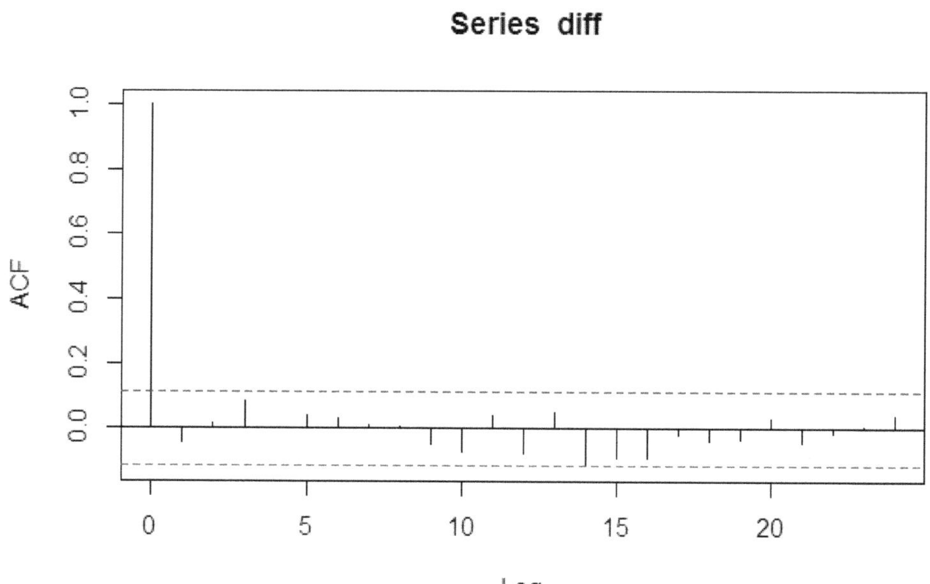


*Figure 8-6. Correlogram of the difference series from a random walk model.*

## Model for Financial Data

Now, I will use the S&P 500 index price as an example to illustrate how to fit the financial data using the autocorrelation function. First, we need to load the stock data:

```
> library(quantmod)
> getSymbols("^GSPC", from = "2012-06-01", to = "2014-06-01")
> plot(Cl(GSPC))
```

Figure 8-7 depicts the close price of S&P 500 index, showing that the time series has an up-trend with some random fluctuations. This behavior is very similar to the random walk model with a drift (see Figure 8-3).

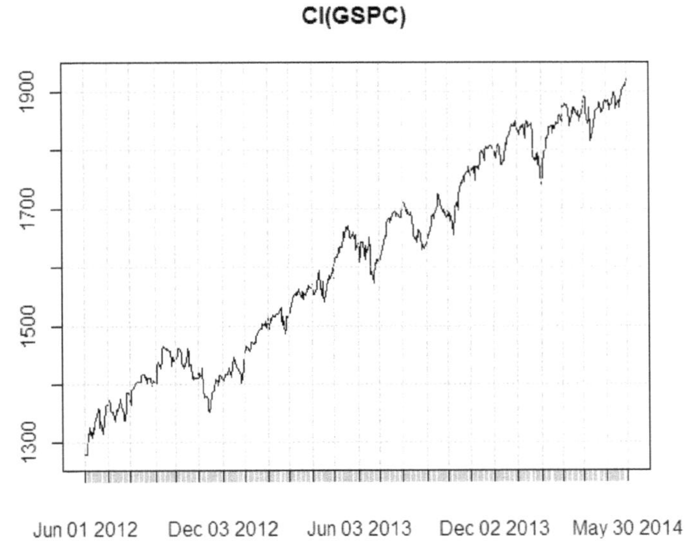


*Figure 8-7. Close price of the S&P 500 index.*

We can now generate a correlogram for the S&P 500 index, plotted in R using the *acf* function:

```
> acf(Cl(GSPC))
```

This produces the output shown in Figure 8-8.

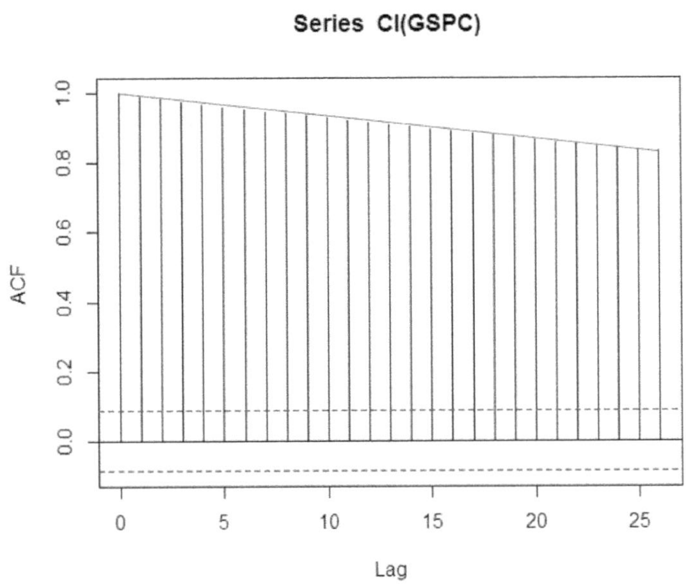


*Figure 8-8. A correlogram for the price of the S&P 500 index.*

Note that the ACF plot for S&P 500 decreases slowly in an almost linear fashion (see the red line in the figure) as the lags increase, which is clear indication of a trend. This correlogram is also similar to the random walk model as shown in Figure 8-4

In order to see whether a random walk model is a good fit to the S&P 500 index, we need to examine its return. Here, we will use the log return instead of the simple return:

```
> rtn <- diff(log(Cl(GSPC)))
> plot(rtn)
> acf(rtn, na.action = na.pass)
```

The above commands generate the outputs shown in Figure 8-9 (return) and Figure 8-10 (ACF of the return).

You can see that the return of the S&P 500 index behaves like a white noise model because the return oscillates around zero (Figure 8-9) and the majority of the lag peaks do not differ from zero at the 5% level except of the peak at $k = 4$ where the peak is slightly below the 5% level. Although it is difficult to justify the existence of this peak beyond that of random variation, it may indicate the existence of a longer-lag process. Thus, it is hard to conclude that a random walk is a good model for the S&P 500 index. We will discuss it using more sophisticated models in the following sections.

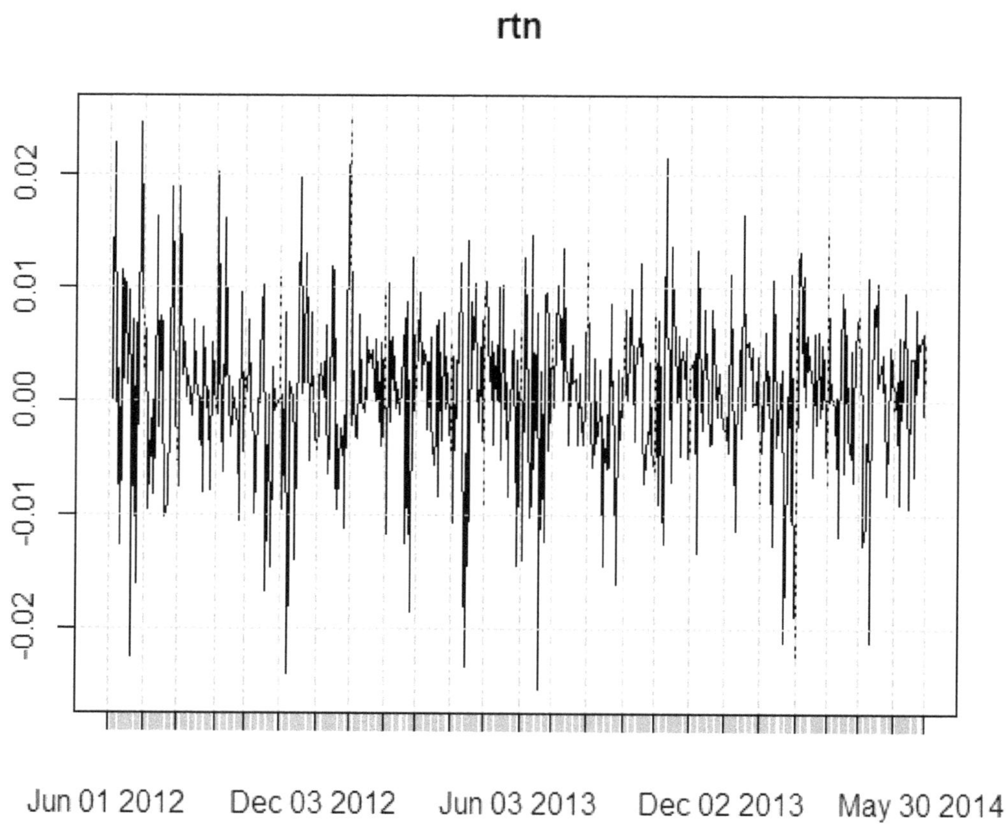


*Figure 8-9. The daily log return of the S&P 500 index.*

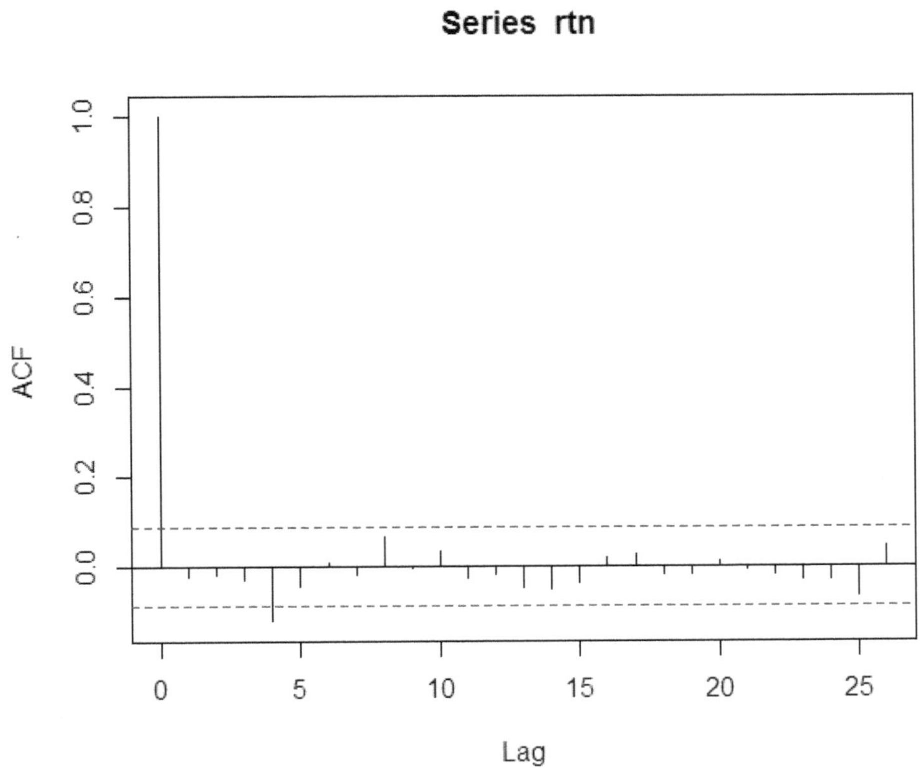


*Figure 8-10. A correlogram for the return of the S&P 500 index.*

# Model Selection

In order to determine the best model from a group of statistical models, we need to set some criterion. Here, I will briefly discuss two commonly used techniques in time series analysis: Akaike information criterion (AIC) and Bayesian information criterion (BIC).

## AIC

AIC is a measure of the relative quality of statistical models for a given time series. Given a set of models for the time series, AIC provides a means of selecting a model from a set of models.

Suppose that we have a statistical model of some time series. Let $L$ be the maximum value of the likelihood function for the model; let $k$ be the number of estimated parameters in the model. Then, the AIC value of the model is given by the following formula:

$$AIC = 2k - 2\ln(L)$$

Given a set of candidate models for the series, the preferred model is the one with the minimum AIC value. Thus, AIC rewards goodness of fit, but it also includes a penalty that is an increasing function of the number of estimated parameters.

To apply AIC in practice, we begin with a set of candidate models, and then find the models' corresponding AIC values. There will always be information lost due to using a candidate model to represent the real model. We wish to select the model that minimizes the information loss. We cannot choose with certainty, but we can minimize the estimated information loss.

The second order information criterion, often called AICc, takes into account the sample size by increasing the relative penalty for model complexity with small data sets. It is defined as

$$AICc = AIC + \frac{2k(k+1)}{n-k-1} = \frac{2kn}{n-k-1} - 2\ln(L)$$

where $n$ denotes the sample size. As $n$ gets larger, AICc converges to AIC. Thus, it is always better to use AICc regardless of the sample size.

## BIC

BIC is another popular criterion for model selection among a finite set of models. The model is based on the likelihood function and it is closely related to AIC. BIC is defined as

$$BIC = -2\ln(L) + k\ln(n)$$

where $L$ is the maximum value of the likelihood function of the model, $n$ is the number of data points in the series, and $k$ is the number of free parameters to be estimated.

BIC is an asymptotic result derived under the assumptions that the data distribution is in an exponential family. It generally penalizes free parameters more strongly than AIC, though it depends on the sample size and relative magnitude of $n$ and $k$.

Note that AIC and BIC were originally derived under different assumptions and are useful in different settings. AIC was derived under the assumption that the true model requires an infinite number of parameters and attempts to minimize the information lost by using a given finite dimensional model to approximate it. BIC was derived as a large-sample approximation to Bayesian selection among a fixed set of finite dimensional models. This difference leads to different asymptotic properties. As the sample size grows, selection based on AIC becomes equivalent to that based on the maximum likelihood. However, BIC does not become equivalent to maximum likelihood selection. As a result, BIC is consistent for selection among a fixed family of models, whereas AIC will favor more complex models when given more data. This makes sense, as AIC was designed to approximate infinite dimensional models, but it is not ideal for selection among a fixed set of model.

# ARIMA Model

ARIMA is an important class of linear time series models, which was proposed by Box and Jenkins in 1976. It is a generalization of an autoregressive moving average (ARMA) model. This model is from statistical models perspectives and is often fitted to time series data either to better understand the data or to predict future points in the series (forecasting). The ARIMA model assumes that the current value can depend only on the past value of the time series itself or on past values of some error terms. It is more robust and efficient in financial time series forecasting especially short-term prediction than even the most popular neural network techniques.

We can use ARIMA model to reduce a non-stationary series to a stationary series using a sequence of differencing steps. An ARIMA($p$, $d$, $q$) model can be obtained from a corresponding ARMA(p, q) model.

If a time series $\{y_t\}$ follows an ARMA($p$, $q$) process after it is differenced $d$ times (denoting by $\nabla^d y_t$), the series is then an ARIMA($p$, $d$, $q$) time series. We can write an ARIMA($p$, $d$, $q$) process in the form:

$$(1 - \alpha_1 \boldsymbol{B} - \alpha_2 \boldsymbol{B}^2 - \cdots - \alpha_p \boldsymbol{B}^p)(1 - \boldsymbol{B})^d y_t = (1 + \beta_1 \boldsymbol{B} + \beta_2 \boldsymbol{B}^2 + \cdots + \beta_q \boldsymbol{B}^q)$$

Where $\boldsymbol{B}$ is the backward shift operator, that is, $\boldsymbol{B} y_t = y_{t-1}$. Note that $\nabla = 1 - \boldsymbol{B}$. In fact:

$$\nabla y_t = y_t - y_{t-1} = (1 - \boldsymbol{B}) y_t$$
$$\nabla^2 y_t = y_t - 2y_{t-1} + y_{t-2} = (1 - \boldsymbol{B})^2 y_t$$
$$\nabla^d y_t = \cdots = (1 - \boldsymbol{B})^d y_t$$

If there is a non-linear trend in a time series, we can always reduce it to a stationary white noise by using repeated differencing.

The ARIMA model consists of set of activities for identifying, estimating, and diagnosing the model with time series data. The ARIMA model can deduce to different models depending on parameter settings. For example, It will become an autoregressive (AR) model of order $p$ if we set $d = q = 0$; it will reduce to a moving average (MA) model of order $q$ if we set $p = d = 0$; while it will be the ARMA($p$, $q$) model if we set $d = 0$.

## AR Model

In this model, the current value depends linearly on the past terms, with coefficients for each term. It is essentially a regression model where the past terms are the predictors. An AR model of order $p$ (or ARIMA(p, 0, 0)) can be expressed in the following form:

$$y_t = \alpha_1 y_{t-1} + \alpha_2 y_{t-2} + \cdots + \alpha_p y_{t-p} + w_t$$

where $w_t$ is the random error, $\alpha_i$ is the constant coefficient with $\alpha_p \neq 0$ for a $p$-order autoregressive process. Note that the random walk is simply an AR(1) model with $\alpha_1 = 1$, that is, the autoregressive model is an extension of the random walk model.

An AR model of order $p$ can be rewritten in the form using the backward shift operators:

$$(1 - \alpha_1 \boldsymbol{B} - \alpha_2 \boldsymbol{B}^2 - \cdots - \alpha_p \boldsymbol{B}^p) y_t = w_t$$

It is straightforward to make predictions with the AR($p$) model if the coefficients $\alpha_i$ are determined:

$$\hat{y}_t = \alpha_1 y_{t-1} + \alpha_2 y_{t-2} + \cdots + \alpha_p y_{t-p}$$

This way, we can make $n$-step ahead forecasts by producing $\hat{y}_t, \hat{y}_{t+1}, \hat{y}_{t+2}, \cdots, \hat{y}_{t+n}$.

In order to determine whether an AR($p$) process is stationary or not, we need to solve the characteristic equation. The characteristic equation is simply the autoregressive model:

$$1 - \alpha_1 \boldsymbol{B} - \alpha_2 \boldsymbol{B}^2 - \cdots - \alpha_p \boldsymbol{B}^p = 0$$

In order for a particular autoregressive process to be stationary we need all of the absolute values of the roots of this equation to be greater than unity. This is a useful property, which allows us to quickly examine whether an AR($p$) process is stationary or not.

Let us consider some AR(p) processes. For a random walk, it is a AR(1) process with $\alpha_1 = 1$ and $\alpha_i = 0$ for $i > 1$. In this case, the characteristic equation becomes $1 - \boldsymbol{B} = 0$, which has a solution of $\boldsymbol{B} = 1$. Thus, the random walk is not a stationary process. However, an AR(1) process can become stationary if we chose a different parameter $\alpha_1 = 1/2$, which gives solution $\boldsymbol{B} = 2 > 1$.

Let us consider a simple AR(1) process. This is similar to a random walk, except that $\alpha_1$ does not have to equal to unity. Assuming $\alpha_1 = 0.5$, we can use the following R commands to create such a process:

```
> set.seed(1)
> y <- arima.sim(n = 100, list(ar = 0.5))
> layout(1: 2)
> plot(y)
> acf(y)
```

The above commands generate the outputs shown in Figure 8-11.

Now we want to fit the above AR(1) process using the *forecast* package to see if we can recover the underlying parameters. This method gives the best order $p$ of the autoregressive model, the coefficient estimates for $\alpha_i$, as well as the AIC, AICc, and BIC values:

```
> install.packages("forecast")
> library(forecast)
> auto.arima(y)
Series: y
ARIMA(1,0,0) with non-zero mean

Coefficients:
         ar1  intercept
      0.5126     0.2753
s.e.  0.0881     0.1845

sigma^2 estimated as 0.8392:  log likelihood=-132.27
AIC=270.54   AICc=270.79   BIC=278.35
```

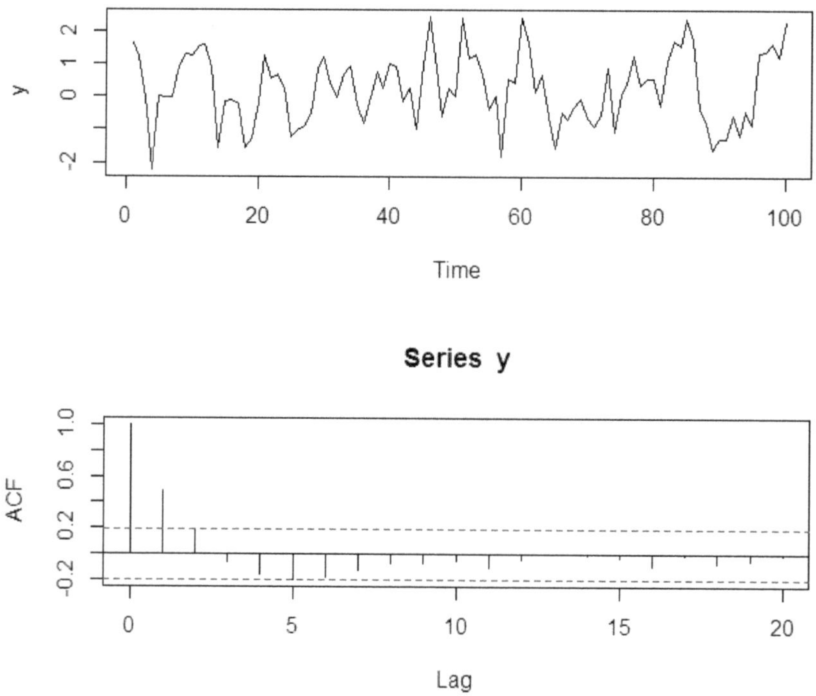


*Figure 8-11. AR(1) model with* $\alpha_1 = 0.5$ *(top) and associated correlogram (bottom).*

Note that the *auto.arima* function has successfully determined that our underlying time series model is an AR(1) (or ARIMA(1, 0, 0)) process and the corresponding coefficient is 0.5126, which is slightly higher than the real value of $\alpha_1 = 0.5$.

## Moving Average Model

A moving average (MA) model is similar to an autoregressive model, except that instead of being a linear combination of past time series values, it is a linear combination of the past white noise terms:

$$y_t = w_t + \beta_1 w_{t-1} + \beta_2 w_{t-2} + \cdots + \beta_q w_{t-q}$$

where $\{w_t\}$ is the white noise with $E(w_t) = 0$ and variance of $\sigma^2$. The above model can be rewritten in the following form using the backward shift operators:

$$y_t = (1 + \beta_1 \boldsymbol{B} + \beta_2 \boldsymbol{B}^2 + \cdots + \beta_q \boldsymbol{B}^q) w_t$$

Note that the mean of an MA($q$) (or ARIMA(0, 0, $q$)) process is zero because the mean is simply a sum of means of white noise terms, which are all themselves zero. In fact, we have:

$$\bar{y} = E(y_t) = \sum_{i=0}^{q} \beta_i E(w_i) = 0$$

The variance and the ACF function for a MA($q$) process can be expressed in the form:

$$Var(y_t) = \sigma_w^2(1 + \beta_1^2 + \beta_2^2 + \cdots + \beta_q^2)$$

$$ACF:\ \rho_k = \begin{cases} 1 & \text{if } k = 0 \\ \sum_{i=0}^{q-k} \beta_i \beta_{i+k} / \sum_{i=0}^{q} \beta_i^2 & \text{if } k = 1, 2, \cdots, q \\ 0 & \text{if } k > q \end{cases}$$

with $\beta_0 = 1$.

For a simple MA(1) process, we have:

$$Var(y_t) = \sigma_w^2(1 + \beta_1^2), \quad \rho_1 = \frac{\beta_1}{1 + \beta_1^2}$$

Suppose that an MA(1) model is described by $y_t = w_t + 0.5w_{t-1}$. Thus, the coefficient $\beta_1 = 0.5$ and the theoretical ACF is given by $\rho_1 = 0.4$, and $\rho_k = 0$ for all lags $k > 1$. In practice, a sample series would not usually provide such a clear pattern. For example, we can simulate a time series with 100 sample points using the same MA(1) model:

```
> set.seed(2)
> y <- arima.sim(n = 100, list(ma = 0.5))
> layout(1:2)
> plot(y)
> acf(y)
```

The above commands produce the outputs shown in Figure 8-12.

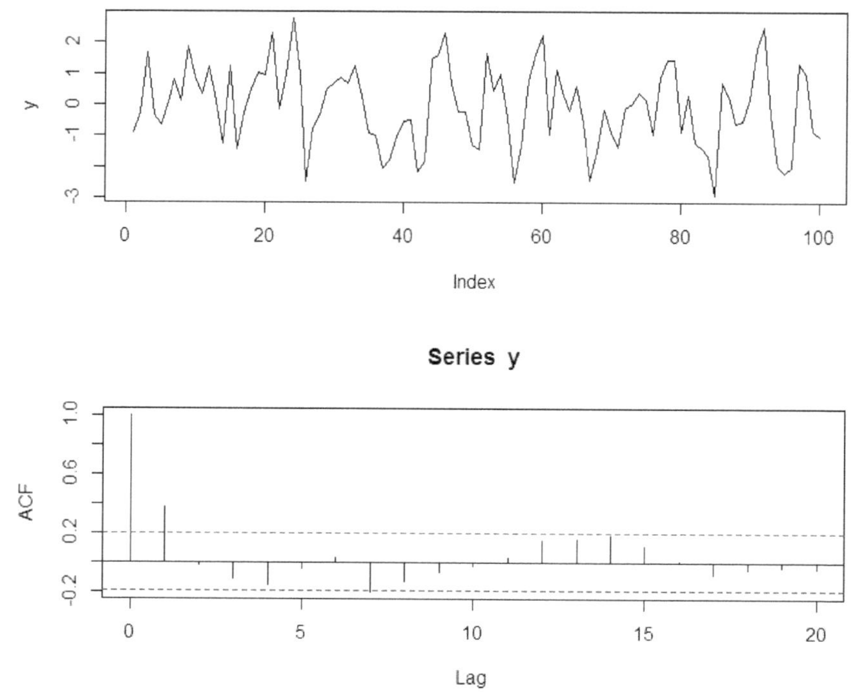


*Figure 8-12. MA(1) model with* $\beta_1 = 0.5$ *(top) and associated correlogram (bottom).*

We see a peak at lag $k = 1$ followed by generally non-significant values for lags $k > 1$. Note that the sample ACF does not match the theoretical pattern of the underlying MA(1) model, which is that all autocorrelations for lags $k > 1$ will be zero. A different sample would have a slightly different ACF (as shown in Figure 8-12), but would likely have the same broad features.

We can fit the above MA(1) process using the *auto.arima* function in the *forecast* package to see if we can recover the underlying parameters:

```
> auto.arima(y)
Series: y
ARIMA(0,0,1) with zero mean

Coefficients:
         ma1
      0.4219
s.e.  0.0867

sigma^2 estimated as 1.346:  log likelihood=-156.35
AIC=316.7   AICc=316.83   BIC=321.92
```

Note that the *auto.arima* function has successfully determined that our underlying time series model is an MA(1) (or ARIMA(0, 0, 1)) process and the corresponding coefficient is 0.4219, which is slightly lower than the real value of $\beta_1 = 0.5$.

Now consider an MA(2) model: $y_t = w_t + 0.7w_{t-1} + 0.5w_{t-1}$. Because this is an MA(2) (or ARIMA(0, 0, 2)) process, the theoretical ACF will have nonzero values only at lags $k = 1$ and 2, which can be easily calculated: $\rho_1 = 0.6034, \rho_2 = 0.2874$. Again, a sample time series would not behaves quite so perfectly as theory. We can simulate a sample time series with 200 data points for the same MA(2) model in R:

```
> set.seed(1)
> y <- arima.sim(n = 200, list(ma = c(0.7, 0.5)))
> layout(1:2)
> plot(y)
> ic <- acf(y)
```

This produces the outputs shown in Figure 8-13.

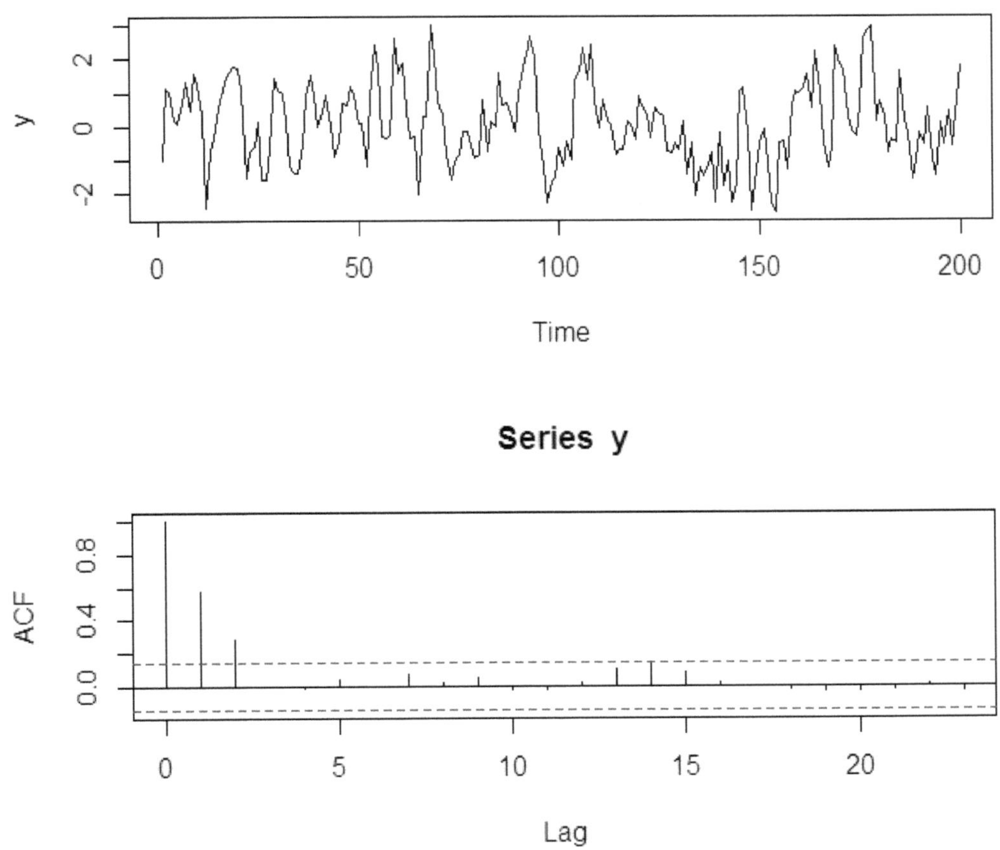


*Figure 8-13. MA(2) model with $\beta_1 = 0.7$ and $\beta_2 = 0.5$ (top) and associated correlogram (bottom).*

We can see from Figure 8-13 that there are two statistically significant peaks at lags $k = 1$ and 2 followed by non-significant values for other lags. Note again that due to sampling error, the sample ACF does not match the theoretical pattern exactly.

We can also fit the above MA(2) process using the *auto.arima* function in the *forecast* package to see if we can recover the underlying parameters:

```
> auto.arima(y, max.p=0)
Series: y
ARIMA(0,0,2) with zero mean
```

```
Coefficients:
         ma1     ma2
      0.6735  0.5145
s.e.  0.0625  0.0596

sigma^2 estimated as 0.8782:  log likelihood=-270.21
AIC=546.43   AICc=546.55   BIC=556.32
```

You can see that the *auto.arima* function has successfully determined that our underlying time series model is an MA(2) (or ARIMA(0, 0, 2)) process and the corresponding coefficients are (0.6735, 0.5145), which is are consistent with the real values of $\beta_1 = 0.7$ and $\beta_2 = 0.5$.

## Autoregressive Moving Average Model

ARMA models form a class of linear time series models, which can be derived from the ARIMA models by setting $d = 0$. By allowing the order of an ARMA model to increase, we can approximate any linear time series model with desirable accuracy. In fact, ARMA($p$, $q$) model is a linear combination of two linear models, AR($p$) and MA($q$):

$$y_t = \alpha_1 y_{t-1} + \alpha_2 y_{t-2} + \cdots + \alpha_p y_{t-p} + w_t + \beta_1 w_{t-1} + \beta_2 w_{t-2} + \cdots + \beta_q w_{t-q}$$

where $\{w_t\}$ is the white noise with $E(w_t) = 0$ and variance $= \sigma^2$. The above model reduces to AR($p$) model if $p \neq 0$ and $q = 0$. Similarly, if we set $p = 0$ and $q \neq 0$, we recover the MA($q$) model. In practice, an ARMA model often requires fewer parameters than an AR($p$) or MA($q$) model along.

ARMA models are a special class of more general ARIMA models without differencing operations. Consider a simple ARMA(1, 1) model with coefficients $\alpha_1 = 0.6$ and $\beta_1 = 0.3$. This model contains an AR(1) model a MA(1) model:

$$y_t = 0.6y_{t-1} + w_t + 0.3w_{t-1}$$

We can then perform the simulation for this model in R:

```
> set.seed(1)
> y <- arima.sim(n = 200, list(ar = 0.6, ma = 0.3))
> layout(1:2)
> plot(y)
> acf(y)
```

This produces the outputs shown in Figure 8-14.

We can also determine the coefficients and their standard errors using the *arima* function in R:

```
> arima(y, order=c(1,0,1))

Call:
arima(x = y, order = c(1, 0, 1))

Coefficients:
         ar1     ma1  intercept
      0.6094  0.2587     0.1367
s.e.  0.0745  0.0913     0.2130

sigma^2 estimated as 0.8882:  log likelihood = -272.34,  aic = 552.68
```

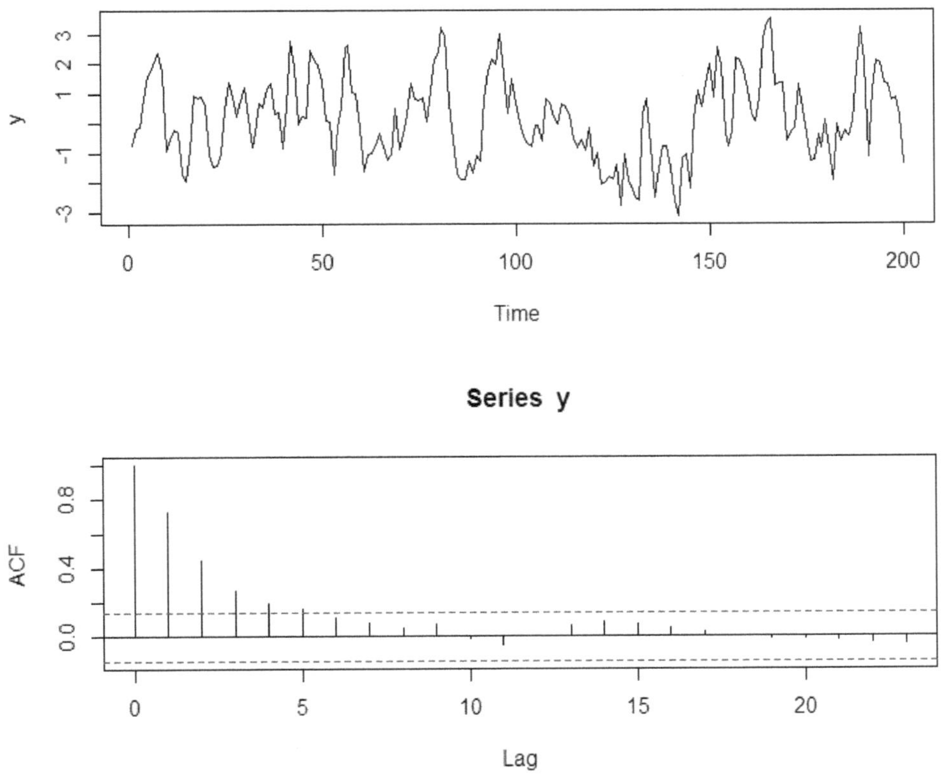


*Figure 8-14. ARMA(1,1) model with $\alpha_1 = 0.6$ and $\beta_1 = 0.3$ (top) and associated correlogram (bottom).*

This gives $\alpha_1 = 0.6094$ and $\beta_1 = 0.2587$, which should compare to the real value of the ARMA(1, 1) model with $\alpha_1 = 0.6$ and $\beta_1 = 0.3$.

For an ARMA(2, 2) model, which is an AR(2) model combined with a MA(2) model, we need to specify four parameters: $\alpha_1$, $\alpha_2$, $\beta_1$, and $\beta_2$. Here, we set $\alpha_1 = 0.8$, $\alpha_2 = -0.5$, $\beta_1 = 0.6$, and $\beta_2 = -0.4$:

```
> set.seed(1)
> y <- arima.sim(n = 500, list(ar = c(0.8, -0.5), ma = c(0.6, -0.4)))
> plot(y, type = "l")
> acf(y)
```

This generates the outputs shown in Figure 8-15. We can fit an ARMA(2, 2) model to the data:

```
> arima(y, order = c(2, 0, 2))

Call:
arima(x = y, order = c(2, 0, 2))

Coefficients:
         ar1      ar2     ma1      ma2  intercept
      0.8283  -0.5139  0.5488  -0.4512     0.0060
s.e.  0.0761   0.0392  0.0871   0.0869     0.0726
sigma^2 estimated as 1.027:  log likelihood = -719.95,  aic = 1451.91.
```

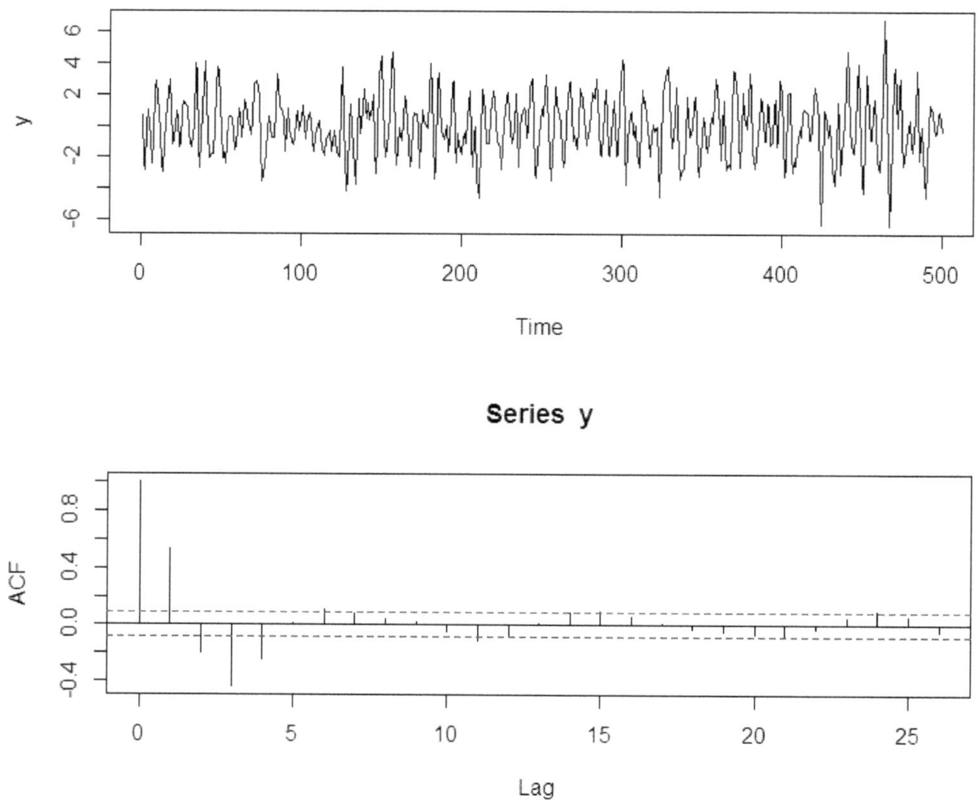


*Figure 8-15. ARMA(2, 2) model with* $\alpha_1 = 0.8$, $\alpha_2 = -0.5$, $\beta_1 = 0.6$, *and* $\beta_2 = -0.4$ *(top) and associated correlogram (bottom).*

You can see that the signs and values of the coefficients are consistent with the true coefficients.

Now, we want to simulate an ARMA(4, 3) process:

$$y_t = 0.3y_{t-1} + 0.9y_{t-2} + 0.1y_{t-3} - 0.8y_{t-4} + w_t + 0.9w_{t-1} + 0.8w_{t-2} + 0.72w_{t-3}$$

We can easily create this model in R:

```
> set.seed(2)
> y <- arima.sim(n=1000, list(ar = c(0.3, 0.9, 0.1, -0.8), ma = c(0.9, 0.8, 0.72)))
> layout(1:2)
> plot(y, type = "l")
> acf(y)
```

This produces the outputs shown in Figure 8-16.

We can now fit the above ARMA(4, 3) (or ARIMA(4, 0, 3)) process using the *auto.arima* function in the *forecast* package to see if we can recover the underlying parameters:

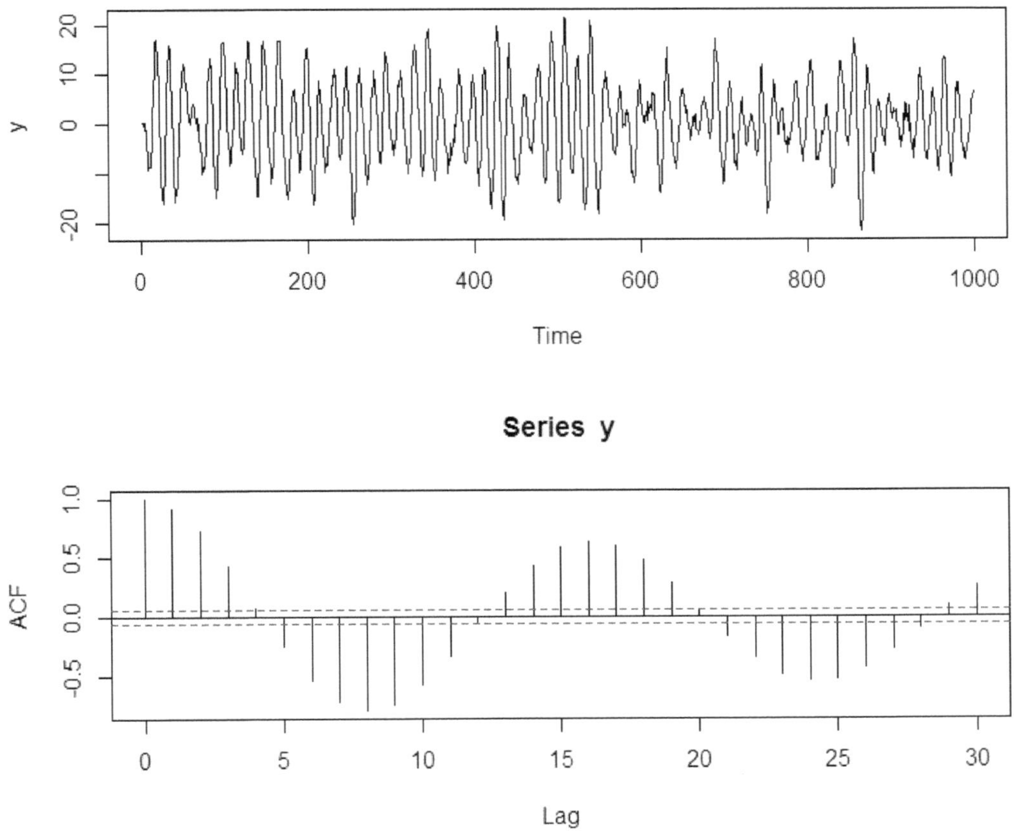


*Figure 8-16. ARMA(4, 3) model (top) and associated correlogram (bottom).*

```
> fit <- auto.arima(y)
> fit
Series: y
ARIMA(4,0,3) with non-zero mean

Coefficients:
         ar1     ar2     ar3      ar4     ma1     ma2     ma3  intercept
      0.3314  0.8765  0.0906  -0.7818  0.8996  0.8270  0.7257     0.4081
s.e.  0.0208  0.0244  0.0241   0.0206  0.0243  0.0236  0.0248     0.2211

sigma^2 estimated as 0.9656:  log likelihood=-1403.22
AIC=2824.44   AICc=2824.62   BIC=2868.61
```

We can see that the order of the original ARMA(4, 3) model is recovered ($p$ = 4, and $q$ =3) and the corresponding coefficients are also consistent with those of the original model.

We can also plot the correlogram of the residuals of the model to see if it looks like a white noise model:

```
> acf(resid(fit))
```

This produces the result shown in Figure 8-17. You can see that the correlogram indeed looks like a white noise model because there are no significant peaks outside the 5% level.

Now, we can perform the Ljung-Box test for 30 lags to confirm the white noise model:

```
> Box.test(resid(fit), lag=30, type = "Ljung-Box")

        Box-Ljung test

data:  resid(fit)
X-squared = 28.697, df = 30, p-value = 0.5335
```

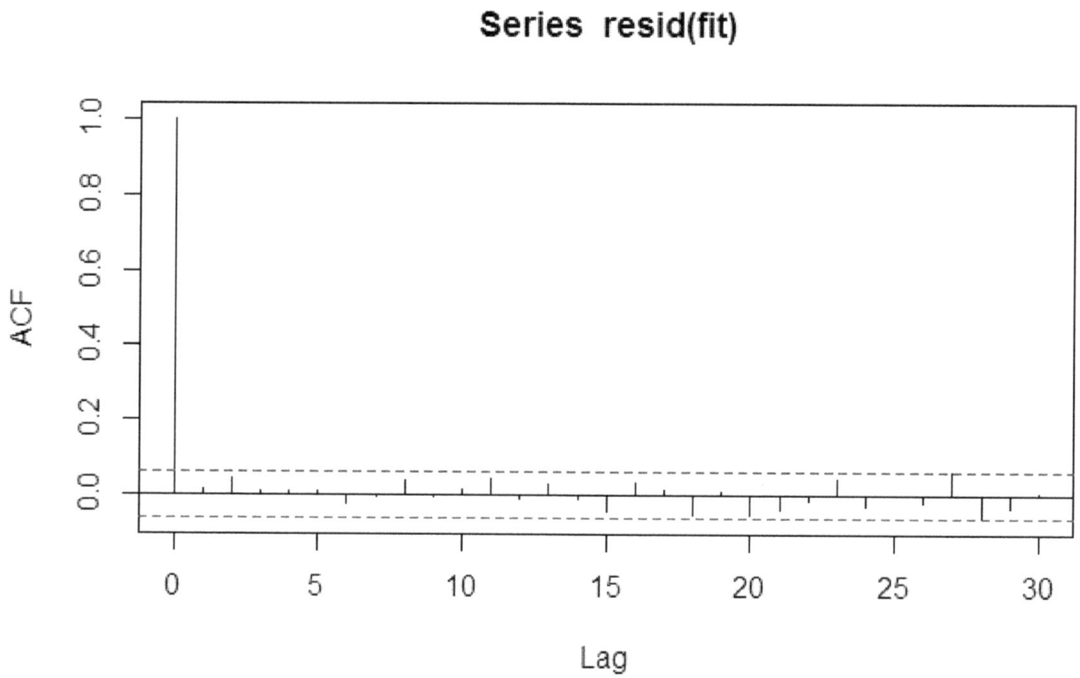


*Figure 8-17. Correlogram of the residuals of the best fitting ARMA(4, 3) model based on BIC.*

Note that the $p$-value is greater than 0.05, meaning that the residuals are independent at the 95% level and thus the ARMA(4, 3) model provides a good fit to our original series.

Now, we want to apply the above procedure to the return of the S&P 500 index with a longer period of data starting from 1980-01-01 to 2016-01-01:

```
> library(quantmod)
> getSymbols("^GSPC", from = "1980-01-01", to = "2016-01-01")
> spx <- na.omit(diff(log(Ad(GSPC))))
> layout(1:2)
> plot(spx, type="l")
> acf(spx)
```

This generates outputs shown in Figure 8-18.

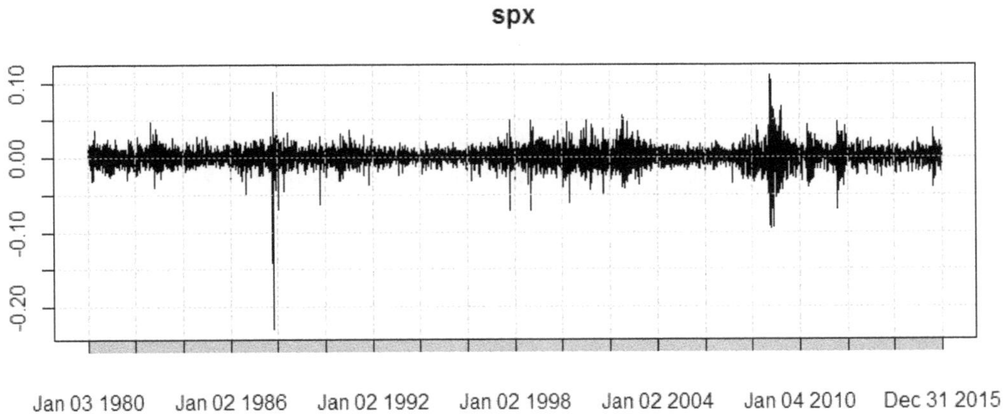


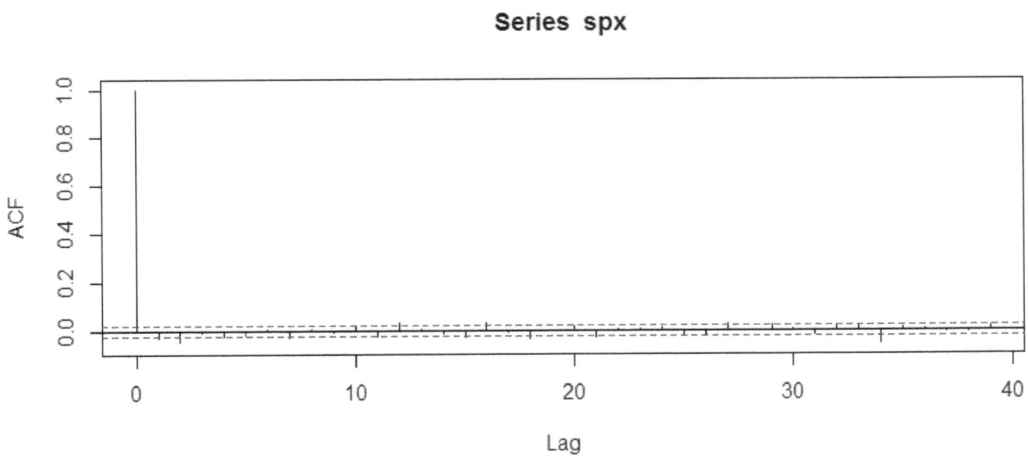


*Figure 8-18. SPX log return (top) and corresponding correlogram (bottom).*

We want to obtain the preferred model for the SPX return using the *auto.arima* function:

```
> fit <- auto.arima(spx)
> fit
Series: spx
ARIMA(2,0,1) with non-zero mean

Coefficients:
         ar1      ar2      ma1  intercept
      0.6523  -0.0188  -0.6807      3e-04
s.e.  0.1118   0.0133   0.1114      1e-04

sigma^2 estimated as 0.0001263:  log likelihood=27871.21
AIC=-55732.43   AICc=-55732.42   BIC=-55696.86
```

which gives an ARMA(2, 1) (or (ARIMA(2, 0, 1)) model for the SPX daily return.

Now we perform a Ljung-Box test for the residuals of the fitted model to the SPX return:

```
> Box.test(resid(fit), lag=30, type = "Ljung-Box")

        Box-Ljung test

data:  resid(fit)
X-squared = 77.632, df = 30, p-value = 4.302e-06
```

You can see that the $p$-value is less than 0.05, indicating that the residuals are not a white noise model. Thus, there is additional autocorrelation in the residuals that is not explained by the fitted ARMA(2, 1) model. This means that an ARMA(2, 1) model cannot explain the autocorrelations in the SPX return.

In practice, ARMA models usually cannot provide good fits for the stock returns. We have to take into account the conditional heteroscedasticity and use a combination of ARIMA and GARCH models.

## ARIMA Model Applications

In the preceding sections, we discussed several simple variations of ARIMA models, including AR($p$), MA($q$), and ARMA($p$, $q$) models. We used these simple models to create simulated data sets, fitted models to recover parameters, and applied these models to the SPX daily return. In this section, we will discuss the general ARIMA($p$, $d$, $q$) model.

The ARIMA model consists of a set of activities for identifying, estimating, and diagnosing the model with time series data. It can reduce a non-stationary series to a stationary series using a sequence of differencing steps. For example, if we apply the difference operator $\nabla$ to a random walk series $\{y_t\}$, which is a non-stationary series, we will obtain a white noise with a constant drift:

$$\nabla y_t = y_t - y_{t-1} = \delta + w_t$$

ARIMA basically performs this operation, but does so repeatedly, $d$ times, in order to reduce a non-stationary series to a stationary one. Here, we will consider non-stationary series with stochastic trends and fit ARIMA models to these time series. We will ignore seasonality effects, which need to be simulated using more complex seasonal ARIMA (SARIMA) model.

Let us consider a simple ARIMA(1, 1, 1) model with one AR term and one MA term, which is applied to the variable $\nabla y_t = y_t - y_{t-1}$. This model has the autoregressive coefficient $\alpha = 0.8$ and the moving average coefficient $\beta = -0.6$. Here is the R code to create such a time series:

```
> set.seed(1)
> y <- arima.sim(n = 1000, list(order = c(1,1,1), ar = 0.8, ma = -0.6))
> layout(1:2)
> plot(y)
> acf(y)
```

This produces the outputs shown in Figure 8-19.

Now, we can use the *auto.arima* function to see if we can recover the above ARIMA(1, 1, 1) model:

```
> aic.fit <- auto.arima(y, approximation = FALSE, ic = "aic")
> aic.fit
Series: y
ARIMA(2,1,2)

Coefficients:
          ar1     ar2     ma1      ma2
      -0.1073  0.7623  0.2801  -0.6682
```

```
s.e.   0.0724  0.0604  0.0857   0.0793

sigma^2 estimated as 1.064:  log likelihood=-1448.28
AIC=2906.55   AICc=2906.61   BIC=2931.09
```

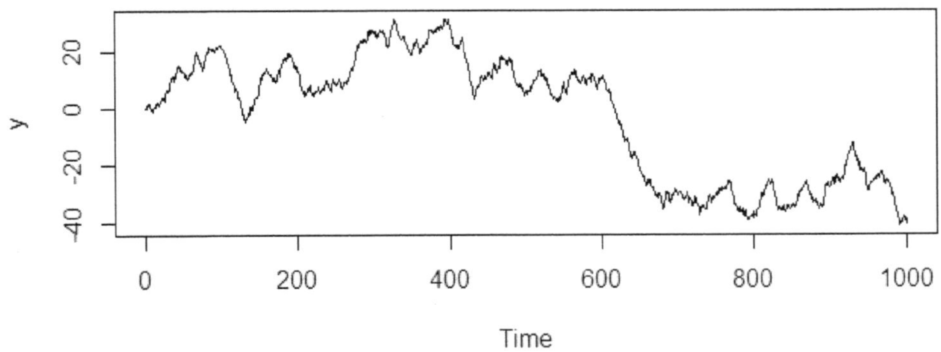


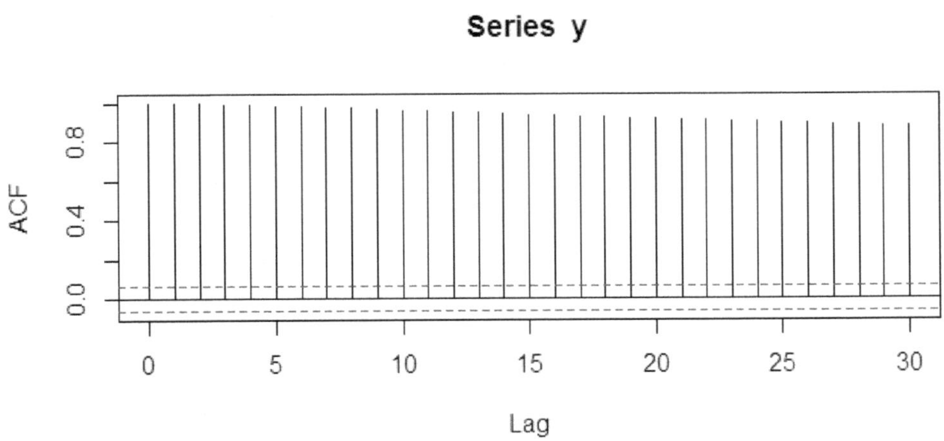


*Figure 8-19. ARIMA(1, 1, 1) model (top) and corresponding correlogram (bottom).*

You can see that the function based on AIC gives an ARIMA(2, 1, 2) model, which is different from the original ARIMA(1, 1, 1) model. Generally, we cannot presume that the simulated ARIMA model is truly of the order we specify. This is because the fact that we take a sample from the specified model (in our case, the ARIMA(1, 1, 1) model) and due to randomness, the best fitting model for the particular sample drawn may not the one from which the simulation is drawn.

However, we do get the right model if we switch to BIC:

```
> bic.fit <- auto.arima(y, approximation = FALSE, ic = "bic")
> bic.fit
Series: y
ARIMA(1,1,1)

Coefficients:
         ar1      ma1
```

```
      0.7972  -0.6502
s.e.  0.0714   0.0912

sigma^2 estimated as 1.075:  log likelihood=-1454.07
AIC=2914.13   AICc=2914.16   BIC=2928.86
```

Note that both the ARIMA(2, 1, 2) and the ARIMA(1, 1, 1) models have a very small difference in the AIC or BIC values, we thus expect both models will give a good fit to the original series.

We can easily validate the models using the *tsdiag* function:

```
> tsdiag(aic.fit)
> tsdiag(bic.fit)
```

which generates the outputs shown in Figures 8-20 (based on AIC) and 8-21 (based on BIC).

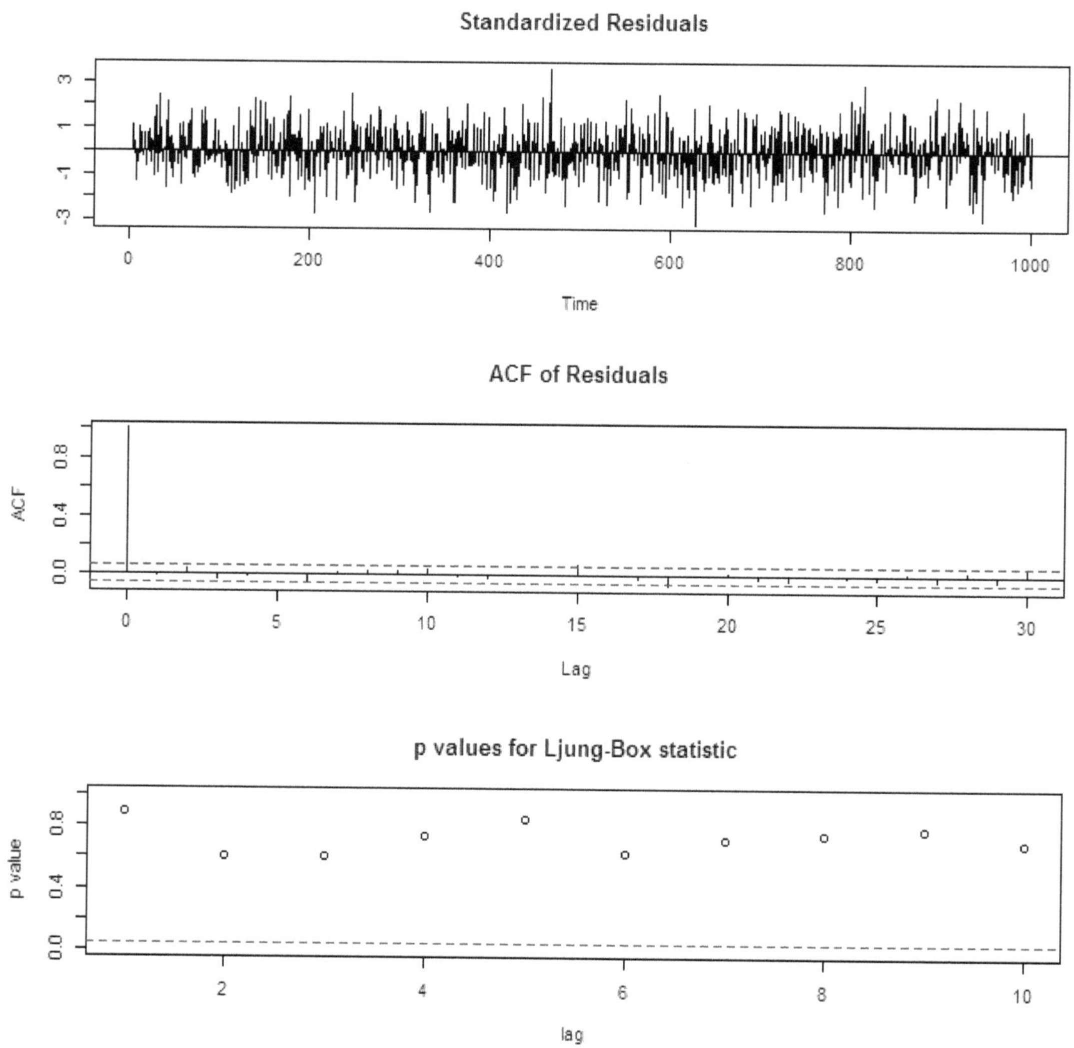


*Figure 8-20. Diagnostics of ARIMA(2, 1, 2) based on AIC.*

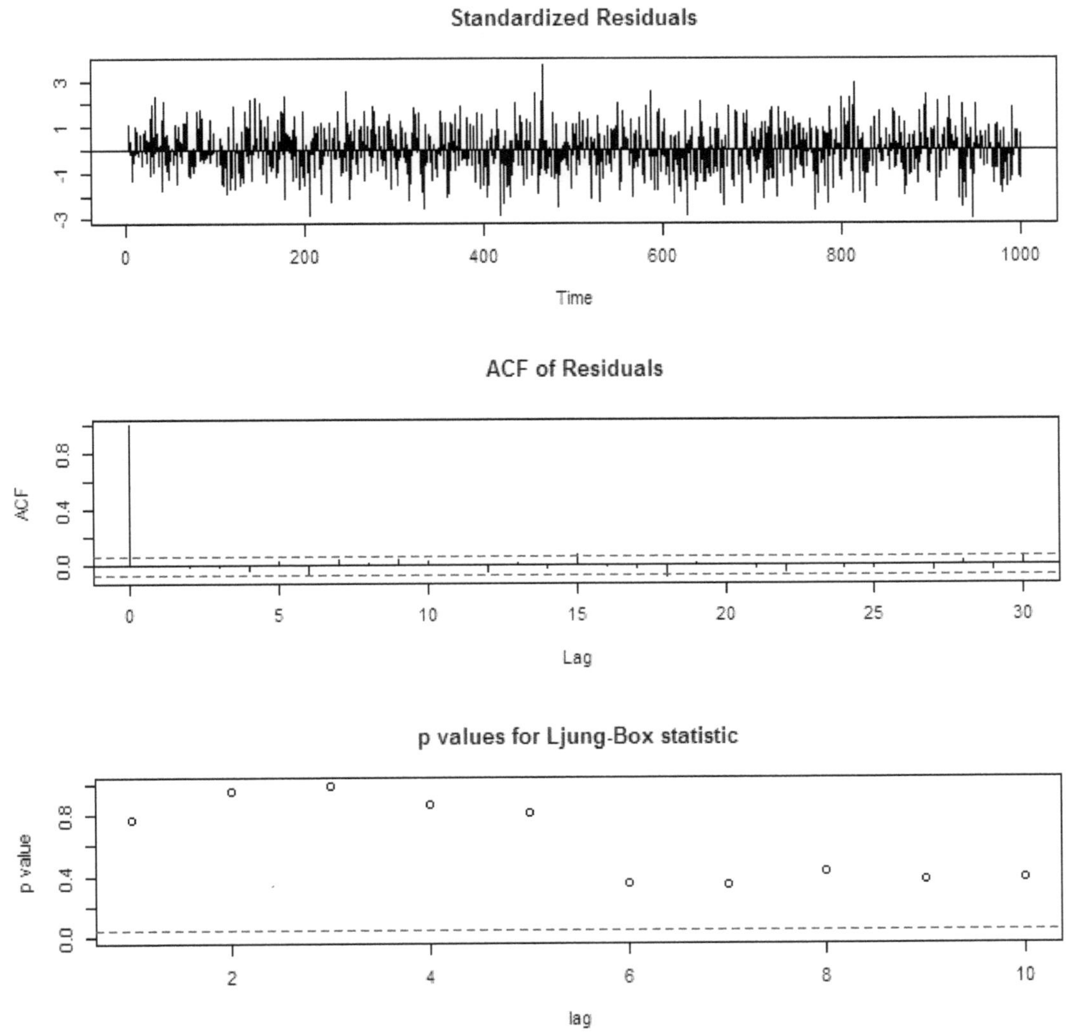


*Figure 8-21. Diagnostics of ARIMA(1, 1, 1) based on BIC.*

You can see that both models look good since the standardized residuals do not show volatility clusters, no significant autocorrelations between the residuals according to the ACF plots, and the Ljung-Box test for autocorrelation shows high p- values (> 0.05), so the residuals are simply white noises.

In order to see how well these two models represent the original series in sample, we can plot the raw data of *y* versus the fitted values:

```
> plot(y)
> lines(fitted(aic.fit), col = "red")
> lines(fitted(bic.fit), col = "green")
```

The output from the above commands is shown in Figure 8-22. You can see that both models fit the original data very well.

In addition, we can calculate common measures of accuracy using the *accuracy* function:

```
> accuracy(aic.fit)
                      ME     RMSE       MAE       MPE     MAPE
Training set -0.02365897 1.029111 0.8203498 -4.048141 14.42001
                  MASE         ACF1
Training set 0.9639163 -0.004438652
> accuracy(bic.fit)
                      ME     RMSE       MAE       MPE     MAPE
Training set -0.02420573 1.035184 0.8265849 -3.815855 14.30091
                  MASE        ACF1
Training set 0.9712426 0.009530211
```

This returns the mean error, root mean squared error, mean absolute error, mean percentage error, mean absolute percentage error, and mean absolute scaled error.

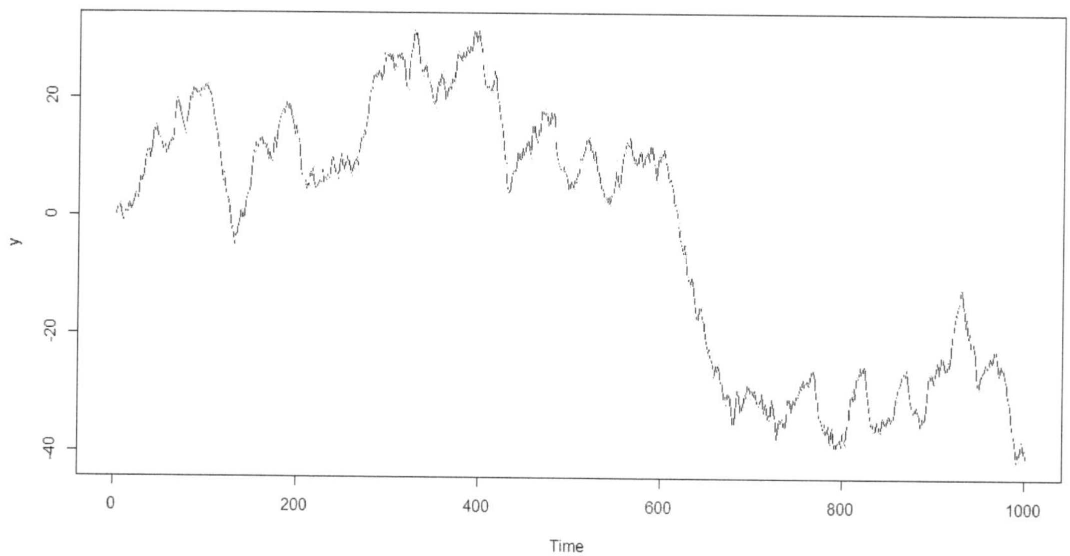


*Figure 8-22. Original data (black) vs ARIMA(2, 1, 2) (red) and ARIMA(1, 1, 1) (green) models.*

Now, we want to apply the ARIMA($p$, $d$, $q$) model to the SPX index. First, we need to reload the SPX price data:

```
> library(quantmod)
> getSymbols("^GSPC", from = "2007-01-01", to = "2016-01-01")
> sp <- Ad(GSPC)
> plot(sp)
```

The price data of SPX is plotted in Figure 8-23, from which we can clearly see several up- and down-trends during the period of 1/1/2007 to 1/1/2016.

Here, we want to fit the data using the *auto.arima* function:

```
> sp.arima <- auto.arima(sp, approximation = FALSE)
> sp.arima
Series: ft
ARIMA(1,1,1)
```

*Figure 8-23. SPX price.*

```
Coefficients:
         ar1      ma1
      0.5726  -0.6529
s.e.  0.1460   0.1354

sigma^2 estimated as 272.1:  log likelihood=-9561.89
AIC=19129.78   AICc=19129.79   BIC=19146.96
```

We see the preferred model is ARIMA(1, 1, 1). The full model is then given by

$$y_t - y_{t-1} = 0.5726(y_{t-1} - y_{t-2}) - 0.6529w_{t-1} + w_t$$

We can create a residual plot for this model:

```
> plot(sp.arima$residuals)
```

The output of the preceding command is shown in Figure 8-24.

We can also validate the model to plot time series diagnostics using the *tsdiag* function:

```
> tsdiag(ft.arima)
```

The output of the above command is shown in Figure 8-25. This model looks good since there are no significant peaks in the ACF plot and the Ljung-Box test for autocorrelation shows high p-value (> 0.05) at all lags.

We can also use the *forecast* function from the *forecast* package to predict 30 days ahead for the price series of FTSE:

```
> plot(forecast(ft.arima, h = 30))
```

The output of the preceding command is shown in Figure 8-26.

We can see the point forecasts for the next 30 days with 95% (dark blue) and 99% (light blue) error bands.

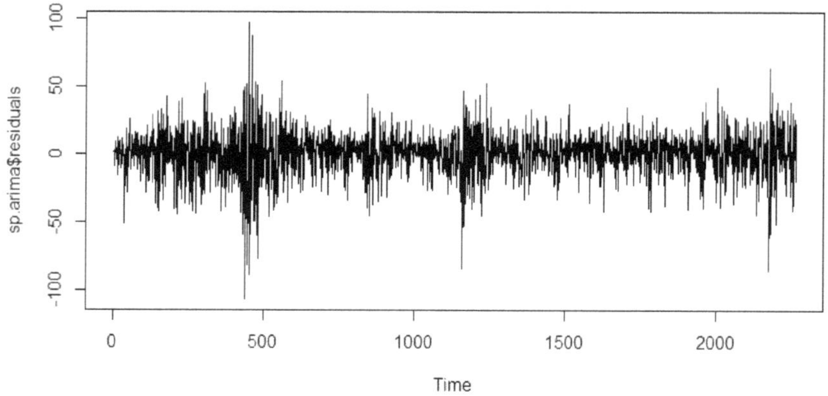


*Figure 8-24. Residual plot of the ARIMA(1, 1, 1) model for FTSE.*

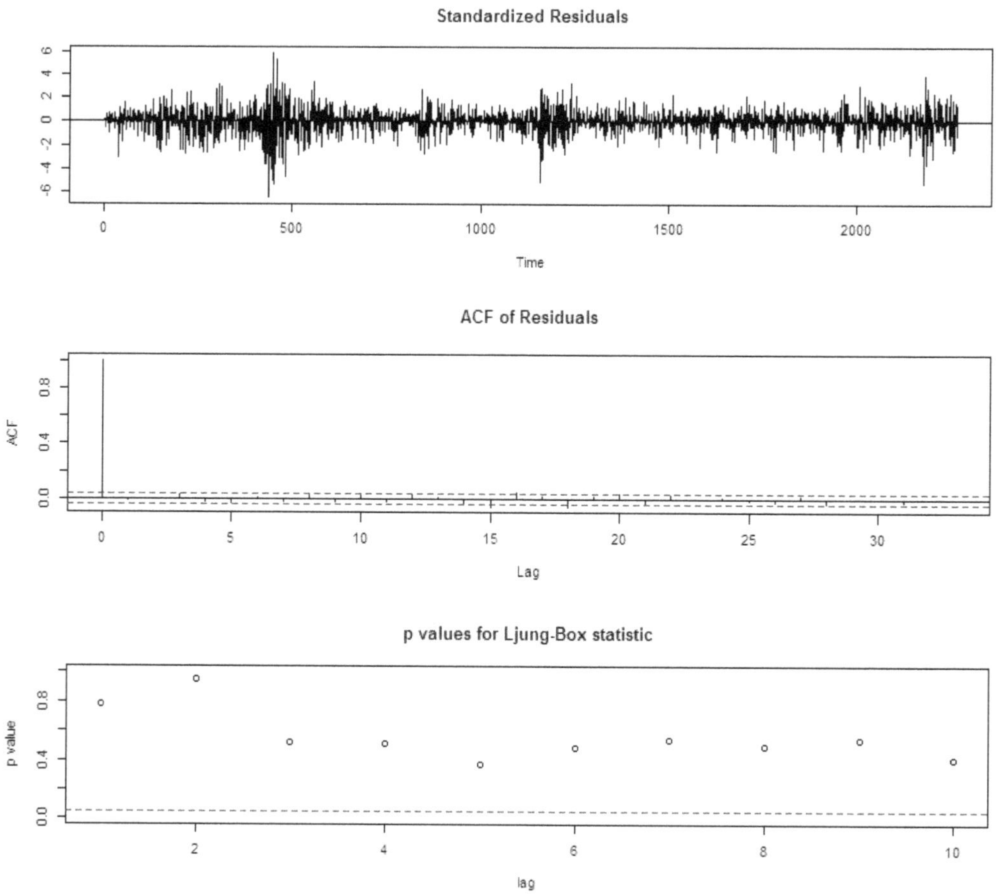


*Figure 8-25. Diagnostics of the ARIMA(1, 1, 1) model for SPX.*

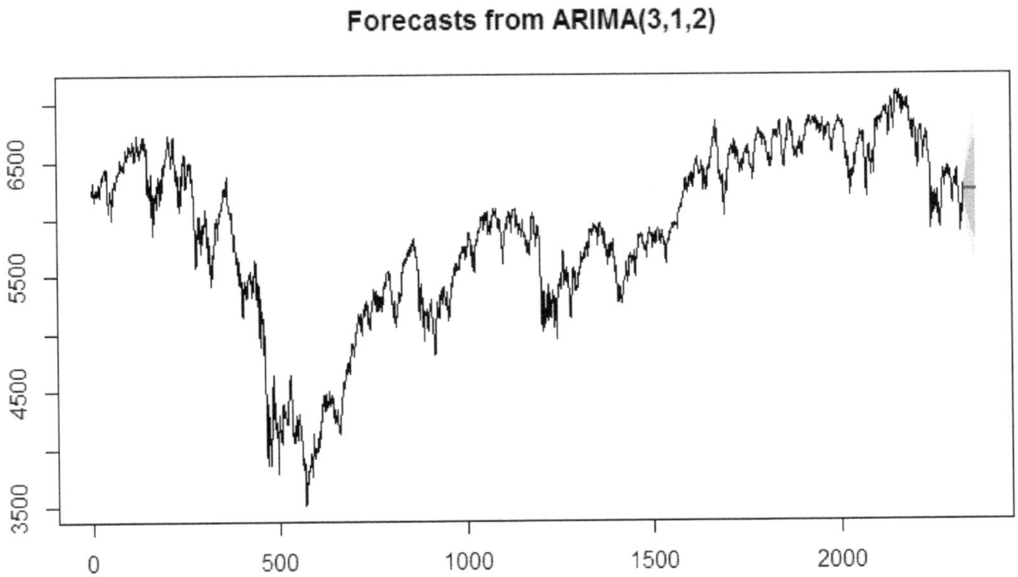


*Figure 8-26. 30-day forecast of SPX daily prices using the ARIMA(1, 1, 1) model.*

# GARCH Model

As mentioned previously, we use ARIMA models to simulate the conditional expectation of a process, given its past. For such a process, the conditional variance is constant. We see from the residual plot of the SPX price in Figures 8-24 and 8-25 that the residuals show some cluster of volatility. It is important to remember that ARIMA models are a method to simulate the data linearly, and the forecast width remains constant because the models do not reflect changes or incorporate new information. That is, ARIMA models provide best linear forecast for the series, and thus play little role in forecasting model nonlinearly. In order to model volatility, we need to use autoregressive conditional heteroscedasticity (ARCH) or generalized ARCH (GARCH) methods.

You may wonder how we know if ARCH/GARCH is necessary for the time series in concern. First, check if residual plot displays any cluster of volatility. Next, check the squared residual plot. If there are clusters of volatility, we need to use ARCH/GARCH to model the volatility of the series to reflect more recent changes and fluctuations in the series. Finally, ACF of squared residuals will help confirm if the residuals are dependent and can be predicted. If the residuals are white noise, they are independent with zero mean, normally distributed, and the ACF of squared residuals shows no significant lags.

Let us check the squared residuals for the SPX price:

```
> res2 <- sp.arima$residuals^2
> layout(1:2)
> plot(res2)
> acf(res2)
```

The output of the preceding commands is shown in Figure 8-27.

You can see that the squared residuals show cluster of volatility at some points in time and corresponding ACF has significant peaks at most lags. In this case, we need to use ARCH/GARCH to model the volatility of the series. As indicated by its name, this approach concerns with the conditional variance of the series.

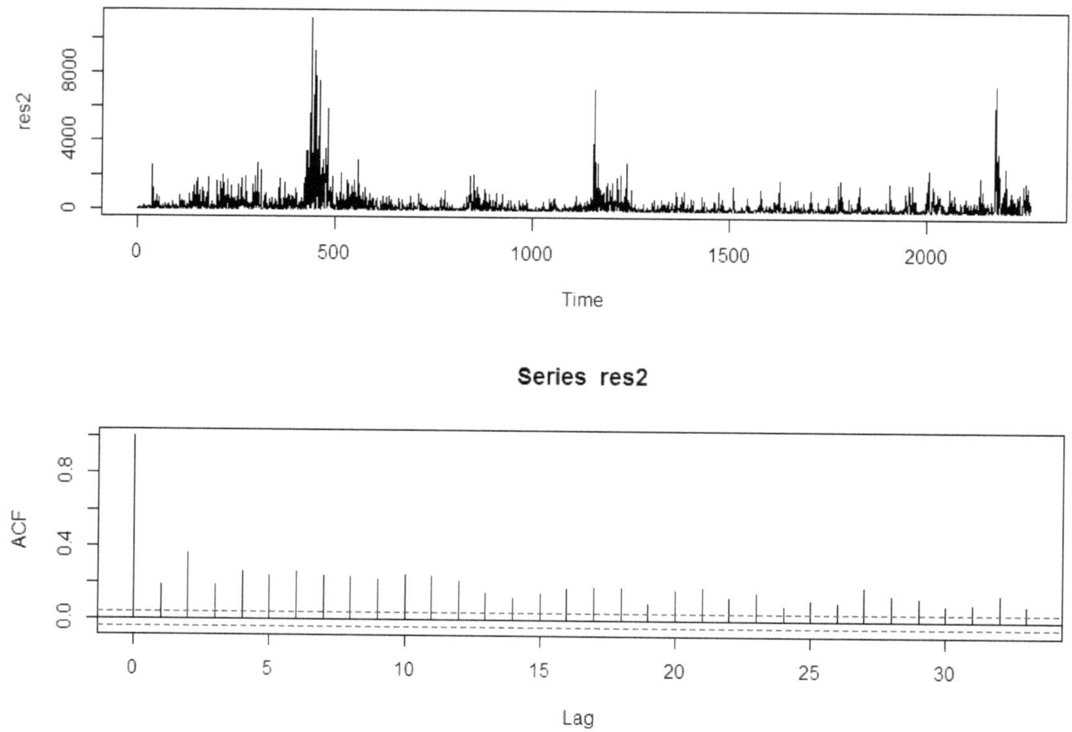


*Figure 8-27. Squared residuals of SPX (top) and associated correlogram.*

ARCH models assume the variance of the current error term (or innovation) to be a function of the actual sizes of the previous time periods' error terms, that is, the variance is related to the squares of the previous innovations. Suppose we wish to model a time series using an ARCH process. Let $\varepsilon_t$ denote the error terms (such as the residuals of SPX). There $\varepsilon_t$ can then be split into a white noise piece $w_t$ and a time-dependent standard deviation $\sigma_t$:

$$\varepsilon_t = \sigma_t w_t$$

The series $\sigma_t$ is modelled by

$$\sigma_t = \alpha_0 + \alpha_1 \varepsilon_{t-1}^2 + \alpha_2 \varepsilon_{t-2}^2 + \cdots + \alpha_q \varepsilon_{t-q}^2 = \alpha_0 + \sum_{i=1}^{q} \alpha_i \varepsilon_{t-i}^2$$

where $\alpha_i$ are parameters of the model. We call $\{\varepsilon_t\}$ an autoregressive conditional heteroskedastic model of order $q$, denoted by ARCH($q$). Substituting for $\sigma_t$, we have:

$$\varepsilon_t = w_t \sqrt{\alpha_0 + \sum_{i=1}^{q} \alpha_i \varepsilon_{t-i}^2}$$

We can think of ARCH($q$) as applying an AR($q$) model to the variance of the series.

The $\sigma_t^2$ in a GARCH model is defined as follows

$$\sigma_t^2 = \alpha_0 + \sum_{i=1}^{q} \alpha_i \varepsilon_{t-i}^2 + \sum_{i=1}^{p} \beta_i \sigma_{t-i}^2$$

where $\alpha_i$ and $\beta_i$ are parameters of the model. In this case, we call $\{\varepsilon_t\}$ a generalized autoregressive conditional heteroskedastic model of order $p$, $q$, denoted by GARCH($p$, $q$).

For a simple GARCH(1, 1) model, it just contains a single autoregressive lag and a single moving average lag:

$$\varepsilon_t = \sigma_t w_t, \quad \alpha_t^2 = \alpha_0 + \alpha_1 \varepsilon_{t-1}^2 + \beta_1 \sigma_{t-1}^2$$

In practice, we usually model the financial time series by following a two-phase procedure. First, we select the "best" ARIMA model to simulate the linear data of the time series. The residuals of this linear ARIMA model will contain only the nonlinear or volatility clustering data. Next, we use GARCH to model the nonlinear patterns of the residuals. We then apply this hybrid model, which combines an ARIMA with GARCH error components, to analyze the time series and to forecast the values of approximation series. In this procedure, we consider the error (or residual) term $\varepsilon_t$ of the ARIMA model as to follow a GARCH process of order $p$, $q$.

In the preceding section, we have identified that ARIMA(1, 1, 1) is a preferred linear model for the SPX price series. Now, we will use a simple GARCH(1, 1) model and the *garch* function in the *tseries* package to simulate the residuals of ARIMA(1, 1, 1) for SPX. Here is the R code for this process:

```
> sp.garch <- garch(sp.arima$residuals, order = c(1, 1), trace = FALSE)
> summary(sp.garch)

Call:
garch(x = sp.arima$residuals, order = c(1, 1), trace = FALSE)

Model:
GARCH(1,1)

Residuals:
    Min      1Q  Median      3Q     Max
-5.6793 -0.4959  0.1168  0.6432  3.0569

Coefficient(s):
    Estimate  Std. Error  t value Pr(>|t|)
a0   7.32201     1.24338    5.889 3.89e-09 ***
a1   0.09988     0.01025    9.748  < 2e-16 ***
b1   0.87142     0.01363   63.938  < 2e-16 ***
---
Signif. codes:  0 '***' 0.001 '**' 0.01 '*' 0.05 '.' 0.1 ' ' 1

Diagnostic Tests:
        Jarque Bera Test

data:  Residuals
X-squared = 262.88, df = 2, p-value < 2.2e-16
```

```
        Box-Ljung test

data:  Squared.Residuals
X-squared = 3.9171, df = 1, p-value = 0.0478
```

Thus, the full hybrid model of ARIMA(1, 1, 1)-GARCH(1, 1) for the SPX price series is given by

$$ARIMA: \quad y_t - y_{t-1} = 0.5726(y_{t-1} - y_{t-2}) - 0.6529\varepsilon_{t-1}$$

$$GARCH: \quad \sigma_t^2 = 7.32201 + 0.09988\varepsilon_{t-1}^2 + 0.87142\sigma_{t-1}^2, \quad \text{with } \varepsilon_t = \sigma_t w_t$$

where $\varepsilon_t$ is the residual term of the ARIMA(1, 1, 1) model and $w_t$ is the white noise process.

In order to test for a good fit, we can plot the correlogram of the GARCH(1, 1) residuals and the squared residuals:

```
> layout(1:2)
> acf(sp.garch$residuals, na.action = na.pass)
> acf(sp.garch$residuals^2, na.action = na.pass)
```

The output of the preceding commands is shown in Figure 8-28.

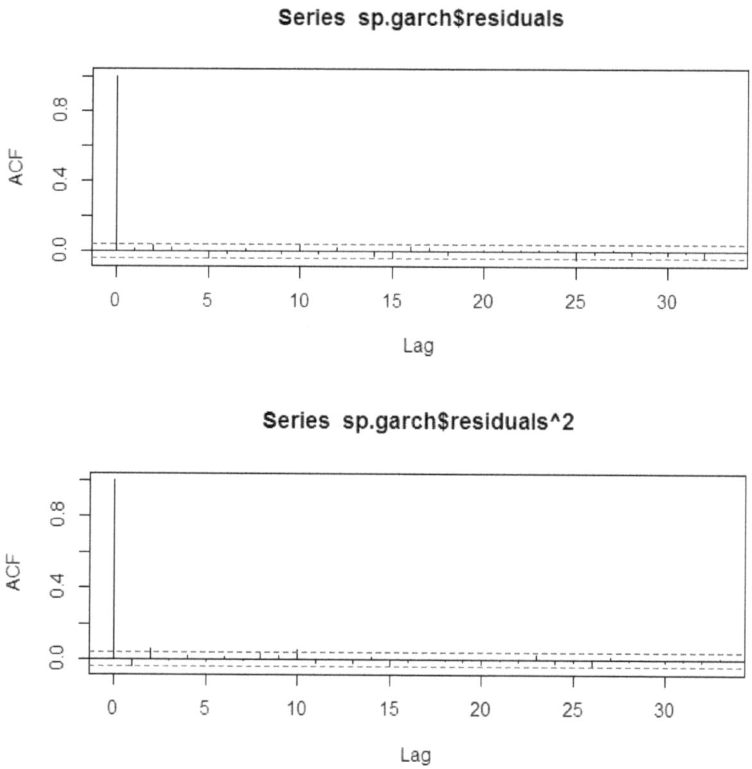


*Figure 8-28. Correlograms of GARCH residuals (top) and squared residuals (bottom).*

You can see the correlogram for both GARCH residuals and squared GARCH residuals looks like a realization of a white noise process, indicating that the GARCH(1, 1) model is a good fit to the ARIMA residuals. We have thus explained the autocorrelation present in the squared residuals using the hybrid ARIMA(1, 1, 1)-GARCH(1, 1) model.

# Cointegration

In the preceding sections, we discussed the univariate time-series models and their characteristics, as well as how to apply these models to analyze financial data. In this section, I will introduce you the concept of cointegration. The idea behind cointegration is to find a linear combination between two or more time series that yields a stationary time series. In finance, we can implement a mean-reverting trading strategy for a stationary data series, in which all we need to do is to buy low, wait for reversion to the mean price, and then sell at this higher price. However, most price series in finance are not mean reverting. We need to identify the stationary series in order for the mean-reversion strategy to be profitable. Fortunately, we can construct a stationary price series by combining two or more individual price series that are not stationary into a portfolio whose net value is mean reverting. We call this combined process the cointegration.

## Testing for Stationarity

We can test for the stationarity of a time series using the Augmented Dickey Fuller (ADF) Test. If a price series were indeed stationary, we would expect a dependency between the current prices and the future prices: if the price is above the mean, the next price move will tend to go down towards the mean. Similarly, if the price is below the mean, the upcoming price will go up towards the mean. The ADF test is simply based on this observation.

We can describe the price changes using a linear model:

$$\Delta y_t = \lambda y_{t-1} + \mu + \beta t + \alpha_1 \Delta y_{t-1} + \alpha_2 \Delta y_{t-2} + \cdots + \alpha_k \Delta y_{t-k} + \varepsilon_t$$

where $\Delta y_t = y_t - y_{t-1}$. The ADF test will find out if $\lambda = 0$. If the hypothesis $\lambda = 0$ can be rejected, that means the next move $\Delta y_t$ depends on the current level $y_{t-1}$, and therefore the series is not a random walk. On the other hand, if the null-hypothesis cannot be rejected, which indicates the price changes are completely independent, and therefore the series follows a random walk. The test statistic is the regression coefficient $\lambda$ (with $y_{t-1}$ as the independent variable and $\Delta y_t$ as dependent variable) divided by the standard error of the regression fit: $\lambda/SE$. ADF test will tell us about the distribution of this test statistic and the critical values, so we can look up for the value of $\lambda/SE$ whether the hypothesis can be rejected at, say, the 95% probability level.

Note that since we expect the ratio of $\lambda/SE$ to be more negative than the critical value for the hypothesis to be rejected. The critical values depend on the sample size, and whether we assume that the price series has a non-zero mean (drift term) $-\lambda/SE$ or a steady trend term $-\beta t/\lambda$.

The ADF test has been implemented in several R packages, including *tseries*, *fUnitRoots*, *uroot*, and *urca*. Here we will use the *ur.df* function included in the *urca* package to determine the stationarity for time series. In the following example, we will apply the ADF test to the ETF of S&P 500 index: SPY:

```
> install.packages("urca")
> library(urca)
> library(quantmod)
> getSymbols("SPY", to = "2016-01-01")
> spy <- Ad(SPY)
> plot(spy)
```

The output of the preceding command is shown in Figure 8-29.

*Figure 8-29. SPY daily prices.*

You can see that the SPY price shows some trends. In the *ur.df* function, we can specify three different types: *none* (no drift and no trend, i.e., the coefficients $\mu = \beta = 0$ in the linear model equation), *drift* ($\mu \neq 0, \beta = 0$), and *trend* ($\mu \neq 0, \beta \neq 0$). Here, we will use a regression with a constant and a trend in our unit root test.

```
> spy.adf <- ur.df(spy, type = "trend", selectlags = "AIC")
> summary(spy.adf)

###############################################
# Augmented Dickey-Fuller Test Unit Root Test #
###############################################

Test regression trend


Call:
lm(formula = z.diff ~ z.lag.1 + 1 + tt + z.diff.lag)

Residuals:
    Min      1Q  Median      3Q     Max
-8.5870 -0.6931  0.0857  0.7630 10.8171

Coefficients:
              Estimate Std. Error t value Pr(>|t|)
(Intercept)  1.702e-01  1.238e-01   1.375   0.1693
z.lag.1     -2.643e-03  1.377e-03  -1.919   0.0551 .
tt           1.951e-04  8.221e-05   2.374   0.0177 *
z.diff.lag  -5.151e-02  2.101e-02  -2.452   0.0143 *
```

```
---
Signif. codes:  0 '***' 0.001 '**' 0.01 '*' 0.05 '.' 0.1 ' ' 1

Residual standard error: 1.476 on 2260 degrees of freedom
Multiple R-squared:  0.005147,      Adjusted R-squared:  0.003826
F-statistic: 3.897 on 3 and 2260 DF,  p-value: 0.008624


Value of test-statistic is: -1.9187 2.4312 2.8176

Critical values for test statistics:
      1pct  5pct 10pct
tau3 -3.96 -3.41 -3.12
phi2  6.09  4.68  4.03
phi3  8.27  6.25  5.34
```

where we simply use the AIC value to determine lags inside the *ur.df* function. The above output shows the summary results returned from the ADF test. It also includes a usual $F$ type test for the hypothesis $\phi_3 = (\mu, \beta, \lambda) = (\mu, 0, 0)$, that is, we set zero restrictions on the time trend and the lagged value terms. The test statistic gives the following values: $tau3 = -1.9187$, $phi2 = 2.4312$, $phi3 = 2.8176$. While the critical *phi3* values at significant levels 1%, 5%, and 10% are 8.27, 6.25, and 5.34, respectively. Hence, the null hypothesis cannot be rejected, indicating that the SPY daily price data does contain a unit root. This finding is reiterated by a tau3 ratio of -1.9187, which is not more negative even than 10% significant level ($-3.12$).

From the above analysis, we cannot reject a unit root. Next, we examine whether the SPY series is a random walk with or without drift. The relevant test statistic is *phi2* ($\phi_2$) = 2.4312, which has to be compared with the critical values. These values are 6.09, 4.68, and 4.03 for significant levels of 1%, 5%, and 10%, respectively. We can therefore conclude that the SPY series behaves more like a random walk, which is not a stationary series.

The *urca* package provides more functions for testing stationarity of time series, including the *ur.pp* function for Phillips-Perron test, the *ur.ers* function for Elliott-Rothenberg-Stock test, the *ur.sp* function for Schmidt-Phillips test, and the *ur.kpss* function for Kwiatkowski-Phillips-Schmidt-Shin test. I will not discuss these functions here, and you can check them by yourself to see how they work.

## Cointergrating Time Series

In the preceding section, we introduced a test statistic to evaluate whether a time series is a random walk or stationary (mean-reverting) series. Unfortunately, not many price series are intrinsically stationary or mean reverting by definition. Usually, most price series follow a random walk or consist of alternating trends and sideways periods. However, we can construct a stationary series based on a linear combination of two or more non-stationary price series. Here, I will describe two approaches of doing this.

The first approach is the covariate (or cointegrated) Augmented Dickey-Fuller test, which combine two or more stationary price series to form a cointegrated and stationary price series linearly. First, we perform an ordinary linear regression to fit the two or more price series. We then apply the normal ADF test as described in the preceding section to test for stationarity for the combined series. This approach was first proposed by Eagle and Granger in 1987 and is widely used in financial applications.

Consider two price series of SPY and IWM: SPY is the S&P 500 ETF Trust and IWM is the iShares Russell 2000 index ETF. We expected that these two series are cointegrated and can be combined to form a stationary price series. We have loaded the SPY data in the preceding section and need to load the price data for IWM:

```
> getSymbols("IWM", to = "2016-01-01")
> iwm <- Ad(IWM)
> plot(spy, ylim = c(30,210), main = ("SPY and IWM"))
> lines(iwm, col = "red")
> legend("topleft", c("SPY", "IWM"), col = c("black", "red"), lty = c(1,1))
```

This produces the output shown in Figure 8-30.

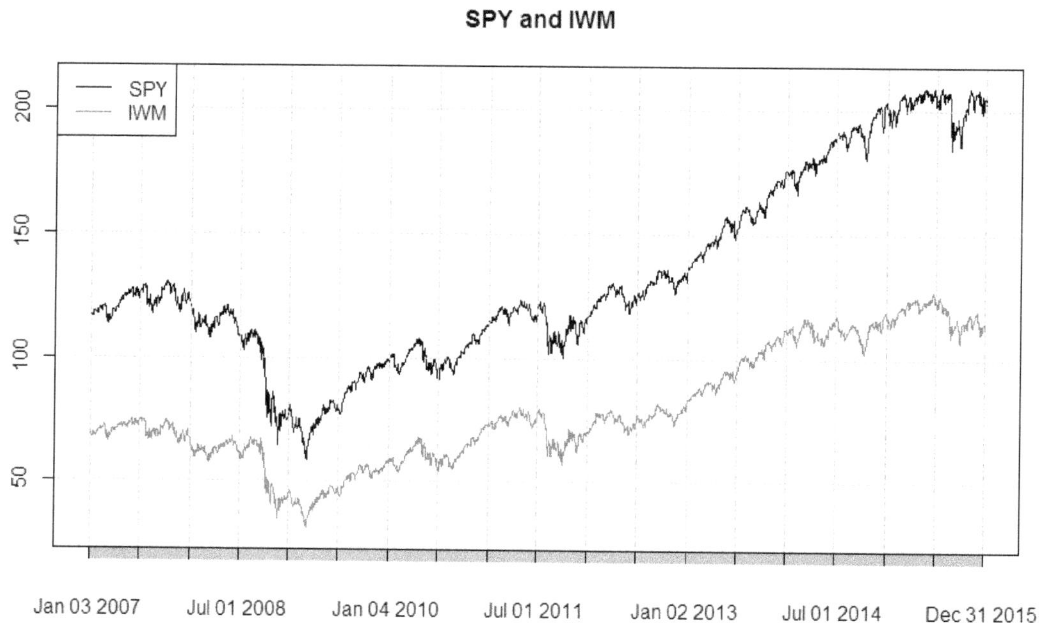


*Figure 8-30. Price data for SPY (black) and IWM (red).*

ETFs provide a fertile ground for finding cointegrating price series and they are thus good candidates for pairing trading. SPY and IWM are equity index based, so they seem likely to cointegrate, as shown in Figure 8-30.

We can use the *lm* function to perform a linear regression:

```
> lm(spy ~ iwm + 1)

Call:
lm(formula = spy ~ iwm + 1)

Coefficients:
(Intercept)          iwm
      4.468        1.626
```

This regression gives: $spy = 4.468 + 1.626\ iwm$. We call the coefficient of *iwm* (1.626) the hedge ratio. As expected, the plot of the residual = $spy - 4.468 - 1.626\ iwm$ shown in Figure 8-31 look like a stationary series. In this case, there seem no mean (mean = 0) and trend in the residual series. We can thus use the following R code to test the stationarity for the residual series:

```
> res <- ur.df(spy-4.468-1.626*iwm, type = "none", selectlags = "AIC")
> summary(res)

###############################################
# Augmented Dickey-Fuller Test Unit Root Test #
###############################################

Test regression none


Call:
lm(formula = z.diff ~ z.lag.1 - 1 + z.diff.lag)

Residuals:
    Min      1Q  Median      3Q     Max
-5.4376 -0.4457 -0.0127  0.4558  4.2294

Coefficients:
            Estimate Std. Error t value Pr(>|t|)
z.lag.1    -0.006749   0.002760  -2.445   0.0145 *
z.diff.lag -0.022305   0.021055  -1.059   0.2895
---
Signif. codes:  0 '***' 0.001 '**' 0.01 '*' 0.05 '.' 0.1 ' ' 1

Residual standard error: 0.7637 on 2262 degrees of freedom
Multiple R-squared:  0.003326,      Adjusted R-squared:  0.002445
F-statistic: 3.775 on 2 and 2262 DF,  p-value: 0.02309


Value of test-statistic is: -2.4454

Critical values for test statistics:
      1pct  5pct 10pct
tau1 -2.58 -1.95 -1.62
```

Note that the ADF test statistic is $-2.4454$, certainly more negative than the critical value at the 95% level of $-1.95$. We can thus reject the null hypothesis that $\lambda$ is zero. In order words, SPY and IWM are cointegrating with 95% certainty.

The other test approach is the Johansen test. Here, we want to form a stationary price series out of an arbitrary number of price series. We can rewrite the linear model using vectors and matrices for the data and their coefficients:

$$\Delta Y_t = \Lambda Y_{t-1} + M + A_1 \Delta Y_{t-1} + A_2 \Delta Y_{t-2} + \cdots + A_k \Delta Y_{t-k} + \varepsilon_t$$

where $\Lambda$ and $A$ are matrices and $Y_t$ is in vector representation. Similar to the ADF test, we need to examine whether our null hypothesis that $\Lambda = 0$ can be rejected and at what certainty. Let $r$ be the rank of $\Lambda$ and $n$ the number of price series. The number of independently combined series, which can be formed by various linear combinations of the cointegrating price series, is equal to $r$. The Johansen test will compute $r$ based on eigenvector deposition of $\Lambda$ to test whether we can reject the $n$ null hypothesis for $r = 0, r \leq 1, r \leq 2, \cdots, r \leq n-1$. If all these hypothesis are rejected, then we have $r = n$. We can use the eigenvectors as the hedge ratios for the individual price series to form a combined stationary series.

*Figure 8-31. Stationarity of residuals of linear regression between SPY and IWM.*

In order to demonstrate the application of the Johansen test, we choose three stocks in financial sector: Morgan Stanley (MS), Goldman Sachs (GS), and Citigroup (C). First, we need to load the stock data:

```
> getSymbols(c("MS", "GS", "C"), from = "2010-01-01", to ="2016-01-01")
> ms <- Ad(MS)
> gs <- Ad(GS)
> c <- Ad(C)
> plot(ms/mean(ms), main = "Mean normalized prices for MS, GS, and C")
> lines(gs/mean(gs), col = "red")
> lines(c/mean(c), col = "blue")
> legend("topleft", c("MS", "GS", "C"), col = c("black", "red", "blue"),
        lty = c(1,1,1))
```

Here, to see the correlation among these stocks more directly, we plot stock prices normalized by their mean values, as shown in Figure 8-32. From this figure, we can see that these three stocks do look quite cointegrating.

We can now perform a Johansen test for these three stocks:

```
> prices <- na.omit(merge(ms, gs, c))
> result <- ca.jo(prices, type = "eigen", ecdet = "const")
> summary(result)
######################
# Johansen-Procedure #
######################
```

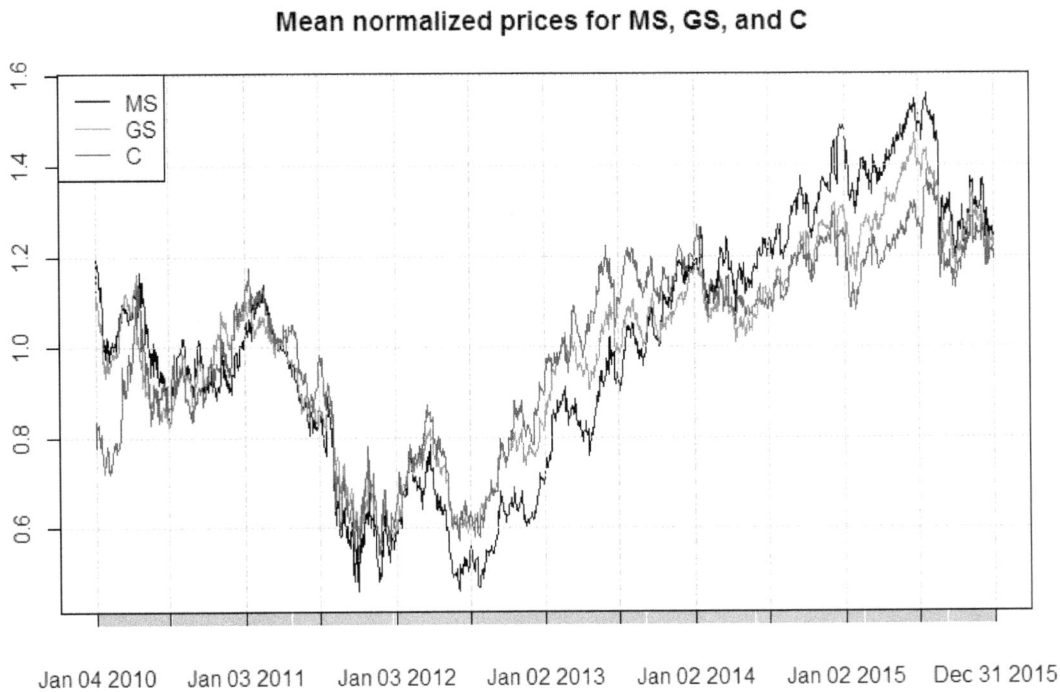


*Figure 8-32. Stock prices for MS, GS, and C.*

```
Test type: maximal eigenvalue statistic (lambda max) , without linear trend and
constant in cointegration

Eigenvalues (lambda):
[1] 2.642957e-02 8.168871e-03 9.715186e-04 1.545611e-20

Values of teststatistic and critical values of test:

          test 10pct  5pct  1pct
r <= 2 |  1.47  7.52  9.24 12.97
r <= 1 | 12.37 13.75 15.67 20.20
r = 0  | 40.39 19.77 22.00 26.81

Eigenvectors, normalised to first column:
(These are the cointegration relations)

               MS.Adjusted.l2 GS.Adjusted.l2 C.Adjusted.l2     constant
MS.Adjusted.l2      1.0000000      1.0000000     1.0000000    1.0000000
GS.Adjusted.l2     -0.4516686     -0.1637052     0.3606371    0.7796766
C.Adjusted.l2       0.8659341     -0.2430729    -0.2563534 -12.4328208
constant            2.8858745      9.1624896   -70.7779856  84.9808773

Weights W:
(This is the loading matrix)

              MS.Adjusted.l2 GS.Adjusted.l2 C.Adjusted.l2      constant
MS.Adjusted.d   -0.001349717   -0.012263341 -0.0007970018 2.953496e-19
```

```
GS.Adjusted.d      0.020126378    0.007337092 -0.0042570875  9.486685e-19
C.Adjusted.d      -0.026902132   -0.002691330 -0.0012572397 -3.646637e-19
```

The above results returned from the Johansen test provide various useful information, including eigenvalues, eigenvectors, test statistic, and critical values. From the $r <= 2$ result, we see that we cannot reject the null hypothesis because the test statistic value 1.47 is much lower than even 90% confidence critical value (7.52), indicating that we cannot form a stationary time series without combination. For $r <= 1$ we have $12.37 < 13.75$, which tells us that there is also no good linear combination of only two stocks to form a stationary time series. However, we have $40.39 > 26.81$ for $r = 0$, meaning that we have over 99% confidence to form a stationary series with a linear combination by all of the three stocks.

Next question is how to construct the stationary series when we reject one of the above null hypothesis. In our case ($r = 0$), the first column in the eigenvector matrix $(1, -0.4517, 0.8659, 2.8859)$ corresponds to the largest eigenvalue 0.02643, i.e. MS $-0.4517$*GS + 0.8659*C + 2.8859 will be the stationary time series we are looking for. Note that we have included a constant term in the combined series to make sure the series will be mean reverting about zero.

We usually call this stationary series the spread. We can plot it to visually double-check if this series is stationary or mean reverting:

```
> spread = ms - 0.4517*gs + 0.8659*c + 2.8859
> plot(spread)
```

This produces the output shown in Figure 8-33. You can see that the combined series does show the mean-reverting behavior.

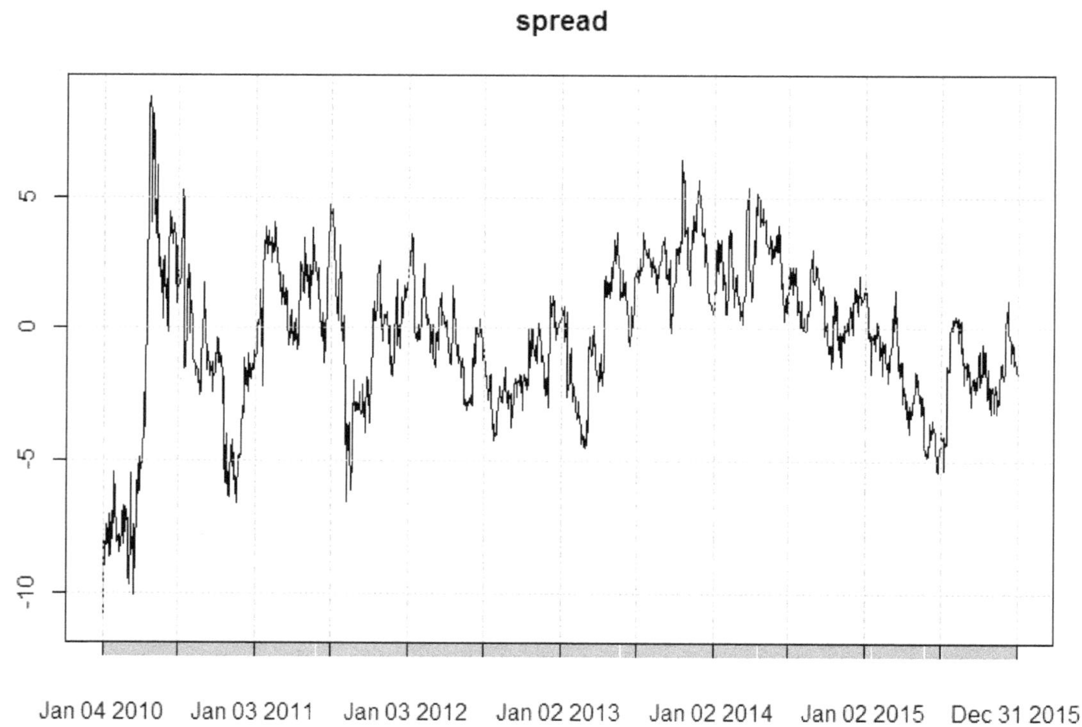


*Figure 8-33. A stationary time series formed by a linear combination of MS, GS, and C*

# Chapter 9
# Machine Learning

In recent years, the machine-learning (ML) technique has become one of the most promising fields in quantitative finance. We can categorize ML into unsupervised and supervised learning. Unsupervised learning is a type of ML algorithm used to draw inferences from data sets consisting of input data without labeled responses. The most common unsupervised learning method is cluster analysis, which is used for exploratory data analysis to find hidden patterns or grouping in data.

Supervised learning is a type of ML algorithm that uses a known dataset (called a training dataset) to make predictions. The training dataset includes input data and response values, from which the supervised learning algorithm seeks to build a model that can make predictions of the response values for a new dataset. Supervised learning consists of two types of algorithms: classification and regression. We use the classification for categorical response values, for example, the direction of the next day's stock price movement; while we use the regression for continuous response values, that is, we attempt to predict both the direction and magnitude of a value (i.e., the future stock price).

Supervised learning is widely used in quantitative finance for predicting the future stock prices. In this chapter, I will concentrate on the supervised learning and present several commonly used ML algorithms in finance, including the K-nearest neighbors (KNN), random forests, support vector machines (SVM), and neural networks.

## KNN Classifier

The KNN classifier is one of the simplest machine learning algorithms. It is a non-parametric algorithm, which can be used for either classification or regression. Non-parametric means that it makes no assumption about the underlying data or its distribution. It has applications in a variety of fields, ranging from the healthcare industry, IT industry with pattern recognition, to the finance field.

### KNN Model

The KNN algorithm is simply based on the idea that objects that are near each other will also have similar characteristics. Thus, if we know the characteristic features of one of the objects, we can also predict it for its nearest neighbor. This indicates that any new instance can be classified by the majority vote of its *k*-neighbors, where *k* is a positive integer, usually a small number.

The KNN algorithm looks for $k$ nearest records with in the training dataset and uses the majority of the classes of the identified neighbors for classifying a new record. It is commonly based on the Euclidean distance between a test sample and the specified training samples. Let $x_i$ be an input sample with $p$ features $(x_{i1}, x_{i2}, \ldots, x_{ip})$, $n$ be the total number of input samples $(i = 1,2,\cdots,n)$, and $p$ the total number of features $(j = 1,2,\cdots,p)$. The Euclidean distance between sample $x_i$ and $x_l$ $(l = 1,2,\cdots,n)$ is given by the following formula

$$d(\mathbf{x}_i, \mathbf{x}_l) = \sqrt{(x_{i1} - x_{l1})^2 + (x_{i2} - x_{l2})^2 + \cdots + \left(x_{ip} - x_{lp}\right)^2}$$

If we use the KNN algorithm for classification, for each data point, the algorithm finds the $k$ closest observations, and then classifies the data point to the majority. For example, if $k = 4$, and the four nearest observations to a specific data point belong to the classes A, B, C, and B respectively, the KNN will classify this data point into class B. If $k$ is an even number, there might be ties. To avoid this, we can add weights to the observations, so that observations with a shorter distance are more influential in determining which class the data point belongs to.

# KNN Model for Classification

We can use the KNN model for both the classification and regression problems. In this section, I will illustrate how to use the KNN classification method to predict the stock market moving direction. In order to apply the KNN algorithm to the stock price prediction, we consider the use of global stock data as input features to predict the today's stock moving direction for the FTSE 100 index. The FTSE 100 index is a share index of the 100 companies listed on the London Stock Exchange with the highest market capitalization. Specifically, we are interested in the correlation between the Nikkei 225 (N225) index and the FTSE index. The market for the N225 index, listed on Tokyo Stock Exchange, is closed right before the opening of the UK markets. As the connection between world-wide economics are tightened by globalization, we believe that the N225 index, which has a strong temporal correlation with the upcoming UK trading day, should be useful in predicting the market direction of the FTSE index.

We use the stock data with the open, high, low, and close prices and the daily returns for both FTSE and N225 as the independent variables, and the today's market move direction for FTSE as the dependent variable. We define the market direction as the sign of the FTSE return, and assign two values ("UP", "DOWN") to represent the market direction: "UP": market up for the positive return, "DOWN": market down for the negative return.

Note that in predicting today's FTSE market direction, we can use today's N225 market data as predictors because the Tokyo stock market has already been closed before the opening of the London Market. However, we cannot use today's FTSE data to predict today's FTSE market direction because today's FTSE data are not available yet before market closing. Keeping this in mind, we can now prepare our market data using the *processFtseN225Data* function, which is implemented in the, *machineLearning.R*, located at "[WORK DIRECTORY]/R/" directory. Here is the code for this function:

```
processFtseN225Data <- function(){
  library(dplyr)
  #getSymbols(c("^FTSE", "^N225"), from = "2010-01-01", to = "2016-01-01")
  FTSE.data <- read.csv("./inst/extdata/ftse100.csv")
  FTSE <- xts(FTSE.data[,-1], order.by = as.Date(FTSE.data[,1], format="%m/%d/%Y"))
  ftse <- na.omit(merge(FTSE$FTSE.Open, FTSE$FTSE.High, FTSE$FTSE.Low,
                        FTSE$FTSE.Close ))
```

```
  ftse$FTSE.Rtn <- dailyReturn(Cl(FTSE)) * 100
  getSymbols("^N225", from="2010-01-01",to="2016-01-01")
  n225 <- na.omit(merge(N225$N225.Open, N225$N225.High, N225$N225.Low,
                        N225$N225.Close))
  n225$N225.Rtn <- dailyReturn(Cl(N225)) * 100
  d1 <- na.omit(merge(ftse,n225))
  d1 <-  data.frame(Date = index(d1), coredata(d1))
  d1$Direction <- "NA"
  for (i in 1:nrow(d1)){
    val <- d1$FTSE.Rtn[i]
    if(val > 0) d1$Direction[i] = "UP"
    else d1$Direction[i] = "DOWN"
  }
  d1$N225.Open <- lead(d1$N225.Open)
  d1$N225.High <- lead(d1$N225.High)
  d1$N225.Low <- lead(d1$N225.Low)
  d1$N225.Close <- lead(d1$N225.Close)
  d1$N225.Rtn <- lead(d1$N225.Rtn)
  d1$Direction = lead(d1$Direction)
  dat <- d1[-nrow(d1),]
  return(dat)
}
```

Since Yahoo does not provide historical data for FTSE recently, we load the data from a csv file. Note that in order to use today's N225 market data, we use the *lead* command to offset one-day relative to the FTSE data, which is equivalent to use today's N225 data as yesterday's data in the UK market because today's N225 data is already available before today's FTSE market opens. We also offset the *Direction* field by one-day using the same lead function, that is, we want to use yesterday's market data to predict today's market direction for FTSE. Now, we can load the market data into the R working space:

```
> source("./R/machineLearning.R")
> fn <- processFtseN225Data()
Head(fn, 10)
         Date FTSE.Open FTSE.High FTSE.Low FTSE.Close    FTSE.Rtn N225.Open N225.High N225.Low N225.Close   N225.Rtn Direction
1  2010-01-04    5412.9    5500.3   5410.8     5500.3  1.61465951  10719.44  10791.04 10655.57   10681.83  0.2537829        UP
2  2010-01-05    5500.3    5536.4   5480.7     5522.5  0.40361791  10709.55  10768.61 10661.17   10731.45  0.4645282        UP
3  2010-01-06    5522.5    5536.5   5497.7     5530.0  0.13580806  10742.75  10774.00 10636.67   10681.66 -0.4639638      DOWN
4  2010-01-07    5530.0    5551.7   5499.8     5526.7 -0.05967098  10743.30  10816.45 10677.56   10798.32  1.0921538        UP
5  2010-01-08    5526.7    5549.3   5494.8     5534.2  0.13570485  10770.35  10905.39 10763.68   10879.14  0.7484436      DOWN
6  2010-01-12    5538.1    5549.6   5459.9     5498.7 -0.71143357  10795.48  10866.62 10729.86   10735.03 -1.3246394      DOWN
7  2010-01-13    5498.7    5509.7   5450.9     5473.5 -0.45829367  10778.07  10909.94 10774.25   10907.68  1.6082807        UP
8  2010-01-14    5473.5    5521.9   5473.5     5498.2  0.45126875  10917.41  10982.10 10878.83   10982.10  0.6822709      DOWN
9  2010-01-15    5498.2    5527.0   5450.4     5455.4 -0.77844188  10887.61  10895.10 10781.03   10855.08 -1.1566052        UP
10 2010-01-18    5455.4    5504.0   5454.3     5494.4  0.71488801  10866.83  10866.83 10749.47   10764.90 -0.8307602        UP
```

Note that today's "*UP*" or "*DOWN*" in the *Direction* column is determined by the sign of the next day's FTSE return (the *FTSE.Rtn* column), that is, we want to use today's data to predict the next day's market direction. The KNN algorithm will identify k-nearest neighbors in the training data set in terms of the Euclidean distance with respect to the day for which prediction is to be done. Once we identify the k-nearest neighbors, the classification for that day's market direction is simply the majority of the next day's classes of those identified neighbors. This predictive model will be applied on the test data sample for identifying the next day's market direction.

Here, we will use the *caret* package to perform the KNN classification. The *caret* package is a great R package that provides general interface to nearly 150 machine-learning algorithms. The package provides various functions to sample the data for training and testing, preprocessing, and evaluating the model etc.

We first need to split data into the training and test data sets:

```
> fn.train <- with(fn, fn[Date >= "2010-01-01" & Date <= "2014-12-31",])
> fn.test <- with(fn, fn[Date >= "2015-01-01",])
```

Next, we can train our KNN model using the *train* function:

```
> set.seed(1)
> fn.knn <- train(Direction ~ ., data = fn.train[,-1], method = "knn",
                  trControl = trainControl(method = "repeatedcv", repeats = 3),
                  preProcess = c("center","scale"), tuneLength = 50)
```

Here, we use a shortcut formula *Direction* ~ . to indicate that all of the columns in the data set (except for *Direction* itself) should be used as predictors. We can also explicitly list the predictors using the formula like this: *outcome* ~ *var1* + *var2* + .... Note also that we do not want to include the *Date* column as a predictor, so we exclude it in the data assignment.

Inside the *trainControl*, we specify the resampling method as "*repeatedcv*", and set repeats = 3, indicating that we want to perform three repetitions of 10 fold cross validation. The KNN model also requires data to be normalized or scaled. Here, we choose both *center* and *scale* for data preprocessing, where the method = "*center*" subtracts the mean of the predictor's data from the predictor values while the method = "*scale*" divides by the standard deviation.

The following is the output of the KNN fit:

```
> fn.knn
k-Nearest Neighbors

1205 samples
  10 predictor
   2 classes: 'DOWN', 'UP'

Pre-processing: centered (10), scaled (10)
Resampling: Cross-Validated (10 fold, repeated 3 times)
Summary of sample sizes: 1085, 1084, 1084, 1084, 1084, 1086, ...
Resampling results across tuning parameters:

  k   Accuracy   Kappa
   5  0.5435449  0.08333035
   7  0.5372134  0.07059155
   9  0.5427647  0.08077888
  11  0.5515387  0.09767723
  13  0.5615112  0.11727098
  15  0.5585063  0.11111462
  17  0.5626406  0.11956816
  19  0.5604368  0.11514041
  21  0.5615272  0.11687402
  23  0.5610133  0.11611863
  25  0.5698424  0.13384297
  27  0.5775698  0.14946869
  29  0.5858987  0.16602897
  31  0.5875630  0.16944180
  33  0.5875701  0.16950867
  35  0.5939315  0.18262317
  37  0.5955545  0.18550668
  39  0.5936076  0.18140388
  41  0.5927581  0.17948866
  43  0.5886351  0.17120988
```

```
 45  0.5869706  0.16774032
 47  0.5928018  0.17940073
 49  0.5941724  0.18170738
 51  0.5988624  0.19120506
 53  0.5963693  0.18591905
 55  0.6035849  0.20030258
 57  0.6002814  0.19317500
 59  0.6033163  0.19917574
 61  0.6077563  0.20832944
 63  0.6008370  0.19419350
 65  0.6019527  0.19627477
 67  0.5977813  0.18745452
 69  0.5994410  0.19044237
 71  0.5997143  0.19071725
 73  0.5991633  0.18948622
 75  0.5969434  0.18500131
 77  0.5963971  0.18392700
 79  0.5988973  0.18896021
 81  0.5933531  0.17747159
 83  0.5927998  0.17668206
 85  0.5936332  0.17825559
 87  0.5933485  0.17754364
 89  0.5927883  0.17630908
 91  0.5905729  0.17137130
 93  0.5861514  0.16274152
 95  0.5866909  0.16366597
 97  0.5897465  0.16994734
 99  0.5878089  0.16627042
101  0.5858482  0.16204231
103  0.5833665  0.15715902

Accuracy was used to select the optimal model using  the largest value.
The final value used for the model was k = 61.
```

The above results are based on repeated cross validation. Note that the optimal model for the training data set is the one with 61 nearest neighbors. We can also plot the accuracy as a function of the *k* number:

```
> plot(fn.knn)
```

This produces the output shown in Figure 9-1.

Now, we can use the trained model to make prediction for the test data set:

```
> fn.knn.predict <- predict(fn.knn, newdata = fn.test[,-1])
> confusionMatrix(fn.knn.predict, fn.test$Direction)
Confusion Matrix and Statistics

          Reference
Prediction DOWN UP
      DOWN   94 72
      UP     25 50

               Accuracy : 0.5975
                 95% CI : (0.5326, 0.66)
    No Information Rate : 0.5062
    P-Value [Acc > NIR] : 0.002732
```

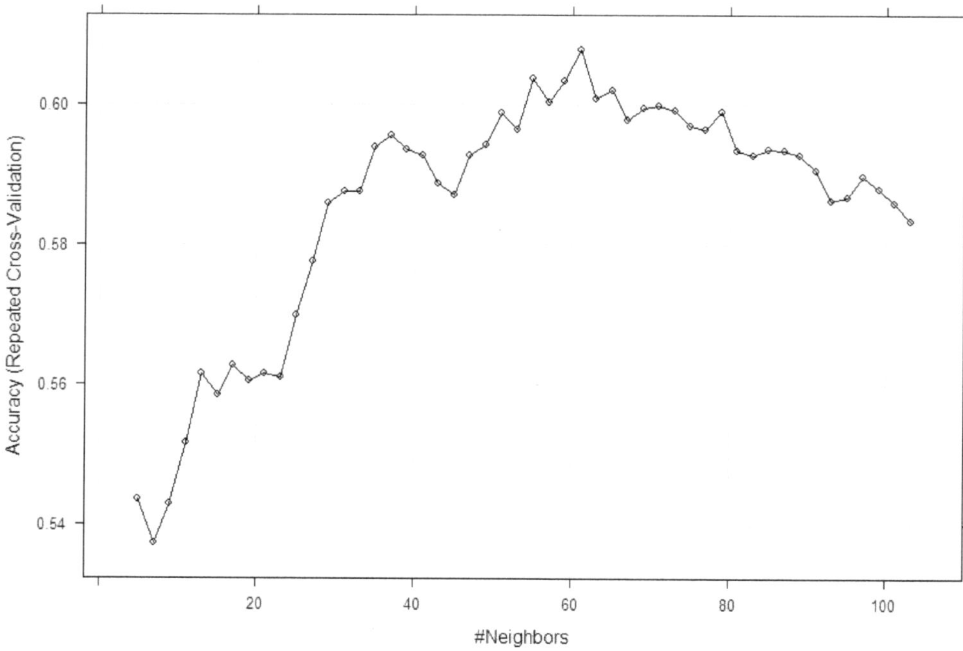


*Figure 9-1. Accuracy vs number of nearest neighbors for training data.*

```
Kappa : 0.1988
 Mcnemar's Test P-Value : 3.003e-06

            Sensitivity : 0.7899
            Specificity : 0.4098
         Pos Pred Value : 0.5663
         Neg Pred Value : 0.6667
             Prevalence : 0.4938
         Detection Rate : 0.3900
   Detection Prevalence : 0.6888
      Balanced Accuracy : 0.5999

       'Positive' Class : DOWN
```

We see from the above results that the prediction accuracy is about 61%, indicating that the trained model has good prediction power. If we do not use the N225 index in the above calculation, we would not get any better result than the random guessing (50%). Our results show strong interconnection between the FTSE index and the N225 index that close right before the beginning of UK trading hours.

We can also extract the detailed prediction results and compare with the real market move direction:

```
> fn.test$Predict <- fn.knn.predict
> head(fn.test, 20)
```

```
           Date FTSE.Open FTSE.High FTSE.Low FTSE.Close   FTSE.Rtn N225.Open N225.High N225.Low N225.Close     N225.Rtn Direction Prediction
1233 2015-01-02    6566.1    6607.9   6510.6     6547.8 -0.2787087  17325.68  17540.92 17219.22   17408.71 -0.24101283      DOWN       DOWN
1234 2015-01-05    6547.8    6576.7   6404.5     6417.2 -1.9945572  17101.58  17111.36 16881.73   16883.19 -3.01872716      DOWN       DOWN
1235 2015-01-06    6417.2    6452.7   6328.6     6366.5 -0.7900672  16808.26  16974.61 16808.26   16885.33  0.01267903        UP       DOWN
1236 2015-01-07    6366.5    6459.7   6366.5     6419.8  0.8371916  17067.40  17243.71 17016.09   17167.10  1.66872385        UP         UP
1237 2015-01-08    6419.8    6580.8   6419.8     6570.0  2.3396399  17318.74  17342.65 17129.53   17197.73  0.17842769      DOWN         UP
1238 2015-01-09    6570.0    6570.2   6471.4     6501.1 -1.0487047  16970.88  17087.71 16828.27   17087.71 -0.63973285        UP       DOWN
1239 2015-01-13    6501.4    6558.8   6465.2     6542.2  0.6275617  16961.82  17036.72 16770.56   16795.96 -1.70736737      DOWN       DOWN
1240 2015-01-14    6542.2    6542.2   6353.7     6388.5 -2.3493655  16872.95  17141.98 16856.22   17108.70  1.86198505        UP         UP
1241 2015-01-15    6388.5    6498.8   6298.2     6498.8  1.7265368  16812.96  16864.34 16592.57   16864.16 -1.42932586        UP       DOWN
1242 2015-01-16    6498.8    6553.2   6443.3     6550.3  0.7924540  17000.78  17039.80 16911.58   17014.29  0.89022462        UP         UP
1243 2015-01-19    6550.3    6598.9   6548.0     6585.5  0.5373830  17071.65  17366.30 17066.77   17366.30  2.06891818        UP         UP
1244 2015-01-20    6585.5    6640.4   6585.5     6620.1  0.5253982  17308.72  17329.03 17181.55   17280.48 -0.49417728        UP       DOWN
1245 2015-01-21    6620.1    6728.0   6620.1     6728.0  1.6298832  17306.64  17355.74 17229.21   17329.02  0.28088954        UP         UP
1246 2015-01-22    6728.0    6808.2   6726.2     6796.6  1.0196210  17520.63  17532.06 17460.76   17511.75  1.05447668        UP         UP
1247 2015-01-23    6796.6    6841.7   6796.6     6832.8  0.5326149  17285.71  17471.94 17285.71   17468.52 -0.24686550        UP       DOWN
1248 2015-01-26    6832.8    6855.9   6790.1     6852.4  0.2868531  17649.40  17768.41 17633.47   17768.30  1.71612282      DOWN         UP
1249 2015-01-27    6852.4    6865.0   6773.5     6811.6 -0.5954090  17615.93  17850.59 17615.93   17795.73  0.15437429        UP       DOWN
1250 2015-01-28    6811.6    6863.0   6777.1     6825.9  0.2099331  17666.91  17778.83 17575.10   17606.22 -1.06491704      DOWN       DOWN
1251 2015-01-29    6825.9    6825.9   6750.2     6810.6 -0.2241434  17788.74  17808.47 17661.10   17674.39  0.38719225      DOWN       DOWN
1252 2015-01-30    6810.6    6844.0   6749.4     6749.4 -0.8986021  17536.61  17628.40 17459.45   17558.04 -0.65830594        UP       DOWN
```

We see from the above results that we can predict the next day's market move direction after today's market close. This information is important and of great interest because successful prediction of the stock moving direction may affects our decision to buy or sell a stock. It will also be very useful in our trading strategy development.

## Confusion Matrix

In the field of machine learning, the confusion matrix, also known as the contingency table or the error matrix, is a specific table layout that allows us to examine the performance of the machine-learning algorithm. Each column of the matrix represents the instances in a predicted class while each row represents the instances in an actual class (or vice-versa). The simplest description of the machine-learning algorithm is the overall prediction accuracy, which is computed by dividing the total correctness (i.e., the sum of the major diagonal) by the total number of data records in the confusion matrix. In addition, accuracies of individual classes can be computed in a similar manner. However, this case is a little more complex in that we have a choice of dividing the number of correctness in that class by either the total number of records in the corresponding row or the corresponding column.

Let us consider the confusion matrices for the training and prediction data sets:

```
# Confusion Matrix for the training set:
          Reference
Prediction DOWN  UP  Total
      DOWN  327 196    523
      UP    277 432    709
      Total 604 628   1232
```

```
# Confusion Matrix for the test set:
          Reference
Prediction DOWN  UP  Total
      DOWN  108  83    191
      UP     11  39     50
      Total 119 122    241
```

In the confusion matrix for the training data set, the total in each column represents the number of records for the expected (or actual) class. In this example, there are total of 604 and 628 records for the expected class *DOWN* and *UP* respectively. While the total in each row represents the number of records for the predicted class. You can see from the above results that there are total of 523 and 709 records for the predicted class *DOWN* and *UP* respectively.

In this confusion matrix, of the 604 actual class *DOWN*, the KNN algorithm predicts that 327 are class *DOWN* and 277 are class *UP*, which is slightly better than 50%. While of the 628 actual class *UP*, it predicts that 196 are class *DOWN*, and 432 are class, which is a reasonably good prediction.

In the confusion matrix for the test data set, of the 119 actual class DOWN, the KNN algorithm predicts that 108 for class *DOWN* and 11 *UP*. Of the 122 actual class UP, it predicts that 83 is *DOWN* and 39 *UP*.

In the confusion matrices, all correct predictions are located in the diagonal of the table, so it is easy to visually inspect the table for errors, as they will be represented by values outside the diagonal of the table.

We can extract the accuracy directly from the confusion matrices manually. We know that the accuracies from the KNN algorithm are 0.6161 and 0.61 for the training and prediction data sets respectively. We can extract the accuracy from the confusion matrix by dividing the total correctness (i.e., the sum of the major diagonal) by the total number of data records in the confusion matrix:

$$Accuracy_{training} = \frac{327 + 432}{1232} = 0.6160714$$

$$Accuracy_{prediction} = \frac{108 + 39}{241} = 0.6099585$$

which are consistent with those obtained from the results directly from the KNN algorithm. You can see that the confusion matrix is a good description for the performance of the classification model on a set of test data for which the true classification values are known.

## KNN Model for Regression

As mentioned previously, we can also apply the KNN model to regression problems. In this section, we will use the same data set used in the preceding section to predict the next day's FTSE close price value. To this end, we need to make some changes to the original data set *fn*. First, we change the name of the *Direction* column to *Expected*, i.e. the expected close price value:

```
> fnReg <- fn
> colnames(fnReg)[colnames(fnReg)=="Direction"] <- "Expected"
```

Next, we need offset the FTSE close prices by one day and place them into the *Expected* column:

```
> fnReg$Expected <- lead(fnReg$FTSE.Close)
> fnReg <- fnReg[-nrow(fnReg),]   #Remove the last row with NA
> head(fnReg)
```

```
        Date FTSE.Open FTSE.High FTSE.Low FTSE.Close    FTSE.Rtn N225.Open N225.High N225.Low N225.Close   N225.Rtn Expected
1 2010-01-04    5412.9    5500.3   5410.8     5500.3  1.61465951  10719.44  10791.04 10655.57   10681.83  0.2537829   5522.5
2 2010-01-05    5500.3    5536.4   5480.7     5522.5  0.40361791  10709.55  10768.61 10661.17   10731.45  0.4645282   5530.0
3 2010-01-06    5522.5    5536.5   5497.7     5530.0  0.13580806  10742.75  10774.00 10636.67   10681.66 -0.4639638   5526.7
4 2010-01-07    5530.0    5551.7   5499.8     5526.7 -0.05967098  10743.30  10816.45 10677.56   10798.32  1.0921538   5534.2
5 2010-01-08    5526.7    5549.3   5494.8     5534.2  0.13570485  10770.35  10905.39 10763.68   10879.14  0.7484436   5498.7
6 2010-01-12    5538.1    5549.6   5459.9     5498.7 -0.71143357  10795.48  10866.62 10729.86   10735.03 -1.3246394   5473.5
```

Comparing the *Expected* column with the *FTSE.Close* column, we see that they are indeed offset by one day, which ensure that we use today's market data of FTSE and N225 to predict the next day's FTSE close price.

Following the same procedure as used in preceding section, we need to split the market data into training and test portions. Here, we want to use the last 60 days' data as the test set:

```
> fnReg.train <- head(fnReg, -60)
```

```
> fnReg.test <- tail(fnReg, 60)
```

Next, we can train our KNN model using the *train* function from the caret package:

```
> set.seed(1)
> fnReg.knn <- train(Expected ~ ., data = fnReg.train[, -1], method = "knn",
                     trControl = trainControl(method = "repeatedcv", repeats = 3),
                     tuneLength = 20)
```

The following is the output of the KNN fit:

```
> fnReg.knn
k-Nearest Neighbors

1384 samples
  10 predictor

No pre-processing
Resampling: Cross-Validated (10 fold, repeated 3 times)
Summary of sample sizes: 1245, 1246, 1247, 1244, 1246, 1246, ...
Resampling results across tuning parameters:

  k   RMSE       Rsquared
   5   72.38262  0.9832634
   7   73.22541  0.9828401
   9   74.53708  0.9821892
  11   75.83467  0.9815238
  13   77.29232  0.9808194
  15   78.86102  0.9800470
  17   80.70710  0.9790931
  19   82.56277  0.9781681
  21   84.61414  0.9771009
  23   86.75711  0.9759724
  25   89.01906  0.9747057
  27   91.07481  0.9735752
  29   93.29457  0.9723065
  31   95.83354  0.9708248
  33   97.91363  0.9695673
  35  100.11237  0.9682106
  37  101.95932  0.9670638
  39  104.17858  0.9656309
  41  106.19996  0.9643133
  43  108.27178  0.9629405

RMSE was used to select the optimal model using  the smallest value.
The final value used for the model was k = 5.
```

The above results show that the optimal model is the one with five nearest neighbors. From the high R-squared value (0.983), we know that the KNN model fits to the training data set well, which can be see more clearly by plotting the fitting results on a graph:

```
> plot(fnReg.train$Expected, type="l", ylab = "FTSE Price")
> lines(predict(fnReg.knn, newdata = fnReg.train[, -1]), col="red")
> legend("topleft", c("Training Data", "Prediction"), col = c("black", "red"),
         lty = c(1, 1))
```

This produces the output shown in Figure 9-2.

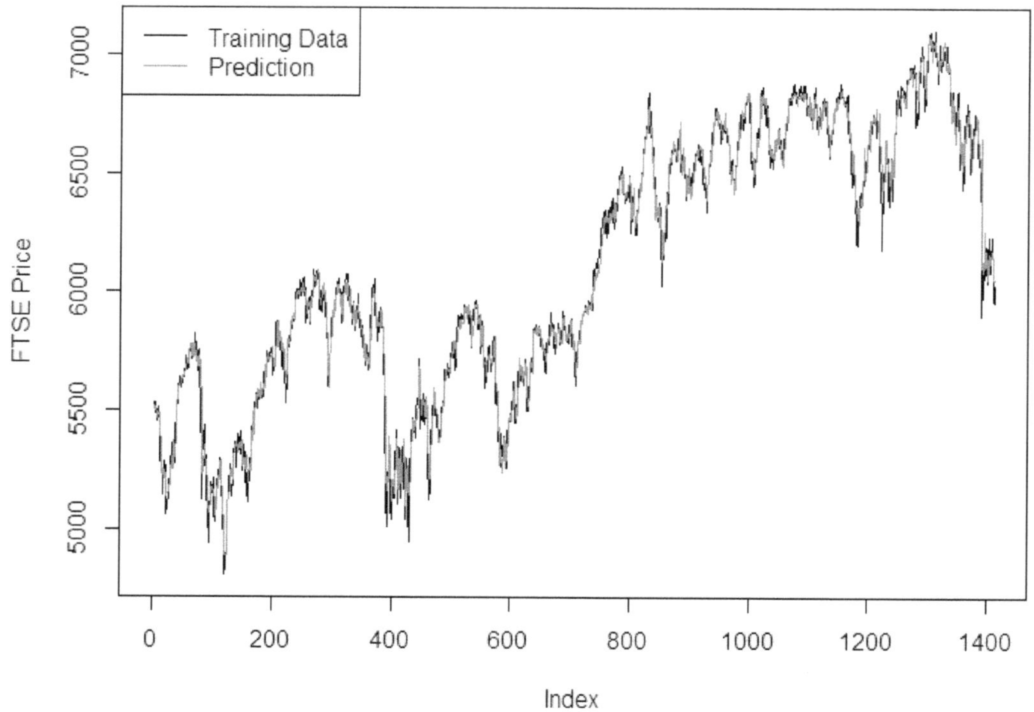


*Figure 9-2. Prediction from the KNN model for the training data set.*

Now, we can use the trained model to predict for the test data set:

```
> fnReg.predict <- predict(fnReg.knn, newdata = fnReg.test[, -1])
```

We can examine the performance of the KNN model for the test set using the *defaultSummary* function from the caret package:

```
> modelValues <- data.frame(obs = fnReg.test$Expected, pred = fnReg.predict)
> defaultSummary(modelValues)
      RMSE    Rsquared
208.8675446   0.1137484
```

We see that the prediction for the test data set is not very good because it shows a large RMSE (root-mean-square error) and a small R-squared. For comparison, we can plot the prediction results for the test data set:

```
> plot(fnReg.test$Expected, type = "l", ylim = c(4500, 7500), ylab = "FTSE Price")
> lines(fnReg.predict, col = "red")
> legend("topright", c("Test Data", "Prediction"), col = c("black", "red"),
         lty = c(1, 1))
```

This generates results shown in Figure 9-3.

Here, I simply present the procedure on how to apply the KNN method to regression problems. For this particular data set, the prediction is not satisfactory. This may suggest that we need to include more features in our data set or to use more advanced machine-learning approaches.

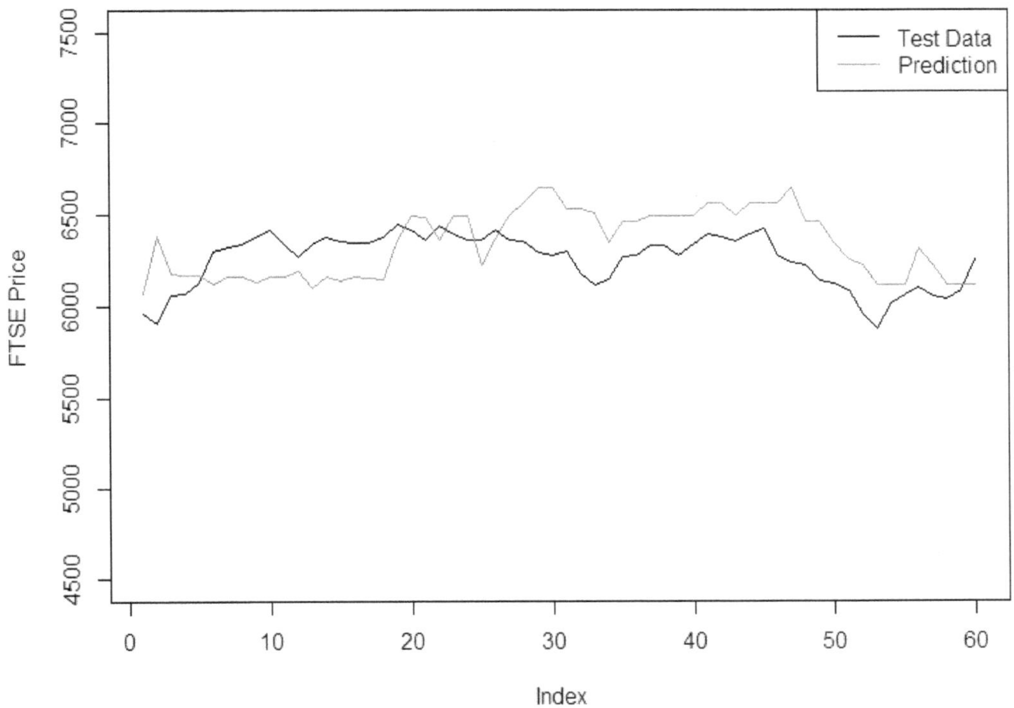


*Figure 9-3. Prediction from the KNN model for the test data set.*

# Random Forest

Random forest is an ensemble-based learning technique for both the classification and regression. It consists of a collection or ensemble of simple decision trees, and gives a prediction based on the majority voting (for classification problems) or averaging (for regression problems) predictions made by each tree in the ensemble using some input data.

## Random Forest Algorithm

The random forest method is based on the principle that a group of "weak learners" can be combined to form a "strong learner". We use independent subsets of variables in the process of growing large number of simple regression trees. Random forests randomly choose variables to split, and a bootstrapped sample of the dataset builds the decision trees. The training algorithm for random forests applies the general techniques of bootstrap aggregating, or bagging, to tree learners.

The algorithm of random forests is very much like the bagging algorithm. Let $N$ be the number of observations and assume that the response variable is binary:

1. Take a random sample of size $N$ with replacement from the data (bootstrap sample).
2. Take a random sample without replacement of the predictors.
3. Construct a split by using predictors selected in Step 2.
4. Repeat Steps 2 and 3 for each subsequent split until the tree is as large as desired.

5. Drop the out-of-bag data down the tree. Store the class assigned to each observation along with each observation's predictor value.
6. Repeat Steps 1-5 a large number of times (e.g. 1000).
7. For each observation in the dataset, count the number of trees that it is classified in one category over the number of trees.
8. Assign each observation to a final category by a majority vote over the set of trees.

This bootstrapping procedure leads to better model performance because it decreases the variance of the model, without increasing the bias. This means that while the predictions of a single tree are highly sensitive to noise in its training set, the average of many trees is not as long as the trees are not correlated. Simply training many trees on a single training set would give strong correlated trees, while bootstrap sampling avoids correlations among the trees by showing them different training sets.

The number of samples or trees is a free parameter. Typically, we use a few hundred to several thousand trees depending on the size and nature of the training set. An optimal number of trees can be found using cross-validation, or by observing the out-of-bag error.

## Random Forest for Classification

In this section, I will illustrate how to apply the random forest method to classification problems using the same data set, *fn*, which has been used in the KNN model previously.

We first need to split data into the training and test data sets:

```
> fn.train <- with(fn, fn[Date <= "2014-12-31",])
> fn.test <- with(fn, fn[Date >= "2015-01-01",])
```

Next, we can train our random forest model using the *train* function by setting its *method* to *rf*:

```
> set.seed(1)
> fn.rf <- train(Direction ~ ., data = fn.train[,-1], method = "rf",
                trControl = trainControl(method = "repeatedcv", repeats = 3),
                preProcess = c("center","scale"), tuneLength = 50)
```

The following is the output of the random forest fit:

```
> fn.rf
Random Forest

1205 samples
  10 predictor
   2 classes: 'DOWN', 'UP'

Pre-processing: centered (10), scaled (10)
Resampling: Cross-Validated (10 fold, repeated 3 times)
Summary of sample sizes: 1085, 1084, 1084, 1084, 1084, 1086, ...
Resampling results across tuning parameters:

  mtry  Accuracy   Kappa
   2    0.5613188  0.1180254
   3    0.5674117  0.1300751
   4    0.5707058  0.1367682
   5    0.5643490  0.1237011
   6    0.5635063  0.1223799
```

```
 7    0.5696132  0.1343256
 8    0.5643443  0.1235905
 9    0.5673978  0.1298264
10    0.5651754  0.1255139

Accuracy was used to select the optimal model using  the largest value.
The final value used for the model was mtry = 4.
```

The above results show that the optimal model is the one with *mtry* = 4, where *mtry* is the number of variables randomly sampled as candidates at each split.

We can also plot the accuracy as a function of the *mtry* number:

```
> plot(fn.rf)
```

This produces the output shown in Figure 9-4.

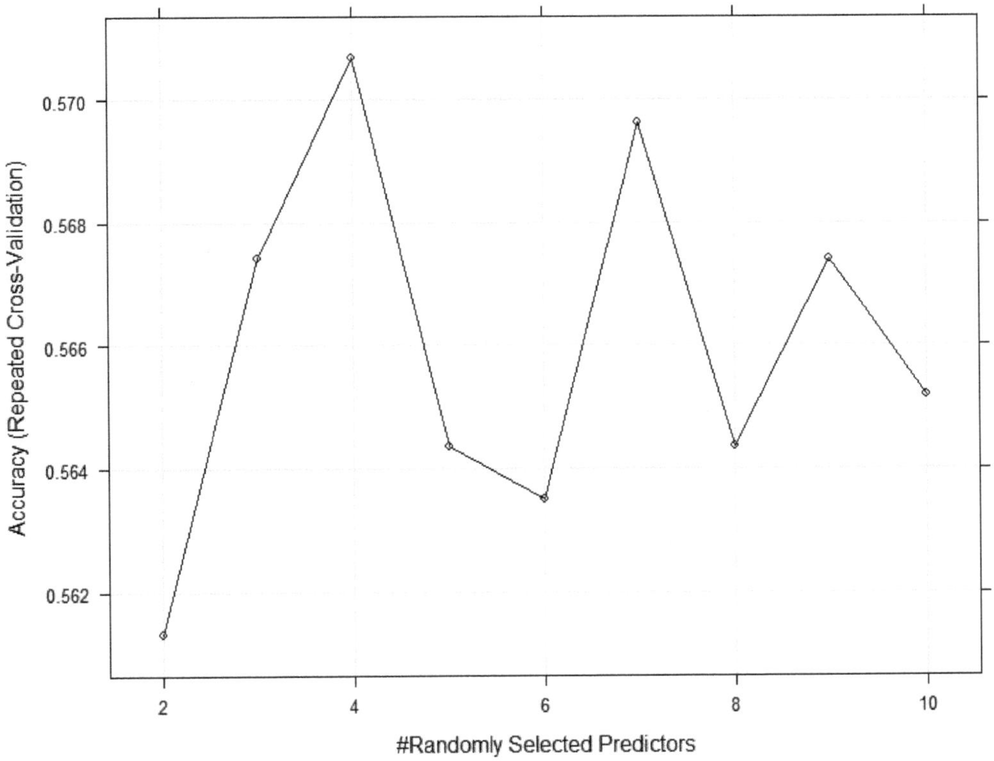


*Figure 9-4. Accuracy vs mtry for training data.*

Now, we can use the trained model to predict for the test data set:

```
> fn.rf.predict <- predict(fn.rf, newdata = fn.test[,-1])
> confusionMatrix(fn.rf.predict,fn.test$Direction)
Confusion Matrix and Statistics

          Reference
Prediction DOWN UP
      DOWN   71 63
```

```
      UP     48 59

               Accuracy : 0.5394
                 95% CI : (0.4743, 0.6036)
    No Information Rate : 0.5062
    P-Value [Acc > NIR] : 0.1670

                  Kappa : 0.0801
 Mcnemar's Test P-Value : 0.1839

            Sensitivity : 0.5966
            Specificity : 0.4836
         Pos Pred Value : 0.5299
         Neg Pred Value : 0.5514
             Prevalence : 0.4938
         Detection Rate : 0.2946
   Detection Prevalence : 0.5560
      Balanced Accuracy : 0.5401

       'Positive' Class : DOWN
```

We see from the above results that the prediction accuracy is about 54%, indicating that the trained model has some prediction power. This accuracy is not as good as that from the KNN method, where the accuracy is about 60%.

## Random Forest for Regression

We can also apply the random forest method to regression problems. In this section, we will use the same data set used in the KNN regression previously to predict the next day's FTSE close price value. Specifically, we want to predict the FTSE close prices for the last 60 days in the data set.

Here, we can train our random forest model using the *train* function from the caret package:

```
> set.seed(1)
> fnReg.rf <- train(Expected ~ ., data = fnReg.train[, -1], method = "rf",
                    trControl = trainControl(method = "repeatedcv", repeats = 3),
                    tuneLength = 20)
```

The following is the output of the random forest fit:

```
> fnReg.rf
Random Forest

1384 samples
  10 predictor

No pre-processing
Resampling: Cross-Validated (10 fold, repeated 3 times)
Summary of sample sizes: 1245, 1246, 1247, 1244, 1246, 1246, ...
Resampling results across tuning parameters:

  mtry  RMSE      Rsquared
   2    58.04400  0.9891612
   3    57.98132  0.9891871
   4    58.08253  0.9891546
```

```
   5     58.34743  0.9890492
   6     58.58388  0.9889612
   7     58.63312  0.9889431
   8     58.85706  0.9888605
   9     58.93493  0.9888290
  10     59.06008  0.9887810

RMSE was used to select the optimal model using  the smallest value.
The final value used for the model was mtry = 3.
```

The above results indicate that the optimal model is the one with *mtry* = 3. This model has a smaller RMSE (57.98132) and larger R-squared (0.9891871) compared to the KNN model where RMSE = 72.38262 and R-squared = 0.9832634. This means that the random forest model is better than the KNN model for the training data set.

Now, we can examine if the random forest model gives a better prediction for the test data set:

```
> fnReg.predict <- predict(fnReg.rf, newdata = fnReg.test[, -1])
> modelValues <- data.frame(obs = fnReg.test$Expected, pred = fnReg.predict)
> defaultSummary(modelValues)
      RMSE   Rsquared
92.1977694  0.6594446
```

We see that the predicted results for the test set is improved significantly comparing to the KNN model where RMSE = 208.87 and R-squared = 0.11, which can be seen more clearly in a plot:

```
> plot(fnReg.test$Expected, type = "l", ylim = c(4500, 7500), ylab = "FTSE Price")
> lines(fnReg.predict, col = "red")
> legend("topright", c("Test Data", "Prediction"), col = c("black", "red"),
         lty = c(1, 1))
```

This produces the output shown in Figure 9-5.

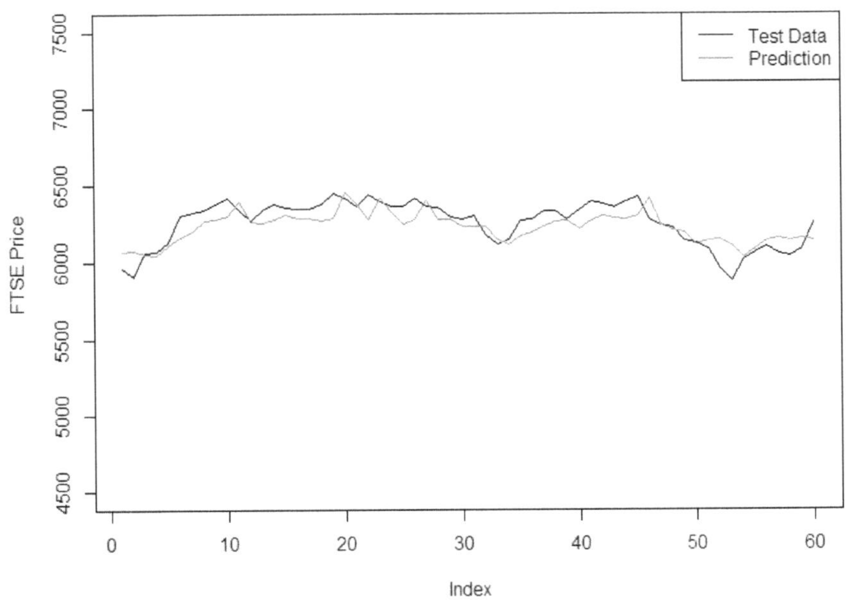


*Figure 9-5. Prediction from the random forest model for the test data set.*

# Support Vector Machine

In machine learning, the support vector machine (SVM) is a supervised learning model with associated algorithms that analyze data and recognize patterns, used for both classification and regression analysis. SVM was originally used as a discriminative classifier defined by separating hyperplane. The SVM algorithm is based on finding the hyperplane that gives the largest minimum distance to the data points in the training data set. This distance is called margin in the SVM theory. Therefore, the optimal separating hyperplane maximizes the margin of the training data. In addition to performing linear classification, SVM can efficiently perform a nonlinear classification using the kernel trick, implicitly mapping their inputs into high-dimensional feature space.

The large-margin separation and the kernel function are two key features of SVM. The large-margin separation means that only the relative position or similarity of the data points to each other is important. Such a similarity can be computed using a so-called kernel function. The simplest kernel function is the dot-product between two feature vectors (known as the linear kernel), which leads to a linear decision boundary between the two classes. Nonlinear kernels, such as the polynomial and Gaussian kernels, provide additional flexibility for large-margin separation between different classes.

SVM can be applied not only to the classification problems but also to the case of regression by introducing an alternative loss function. Still it contains all the main features that characterize maximum margin algorithm: a nonlinear function is learned by linear learning machine mapping into high dimensional kernel induced feature space. The loss function in SVM should be modified to include a distance measure. This type of function is often called epsilon intensive loss function. Using the epsilon intensive loss function ensures existence of the global minimum.

There are two steps for the SVM training. The first step is to transform input data to a high-dimensional feature space by specifying a kernel function. The next step is to solve a quadratic optimization problem to fit an optimal hyperplane to classify the transformed features into different classes. The number of transformed features is determined by the number of support vectors.

## SVM for Classification

In this section, I will use an example to illustrate how to use the SVM model in the *caret* package to predict the next day's stock price direction. Here, we will use the same data set *fn* that was used previously for classification problems when we discussed the KNN and random forest models.

Now, we can train our SVM model using the *train* function by setting its *method* to *svmLinear*, i.e. SVM with a linear kernel:

```
> ctrl <- trainControl(method = "repeatedcv", repeats = 10)
> fn.svm <- train(Direction ~ ., data = fn.train[,-1], method = "svmLinear",
            trControl = ctrl, preProcess = c("center","scale"))
```

The following is the output of the SVM fit:

```
> fn.svm
Support Vector Machines with Linear Kernel

1205 samples
  10 predictor
   2 classes: 'DOWN', 'UP'

Pre-processing: centered (10), scaled (10)
```

```
Resampling: Cross-Validated (10 fold, repeated 10 times)
Summary of sample sizes: 1085, 1085, 1086, 1084, 1084, 1084, ...
Resampling results:

  Accuracy   Kappa
  0.5951005  0.1842688

Tuning parameter 'C' was held constant at a value of 1
```

Note that for SVM with a linear kernel, the *train* function uses a default value of $C = 1$, where $C$ is a parameter for tuning the cost function. We see accuracy = 0.595 from SVM, which is slightly better than that from the random forest method (where accuracy = 0.567).

Now, we can use the trained model to predict for the test data set:

```
> fn.svm.predict <- predict(fn.svm, newdata = fn.test[,-1])
> confusionMatrix(fn.svm.predict,fn.test$Direction)
Confusion Matrix and Statistics

          Reference
Prediction DOWN  UP
      DOWN   34  14
      UP     85 108

               Accuracy : 0.5892
                 95% CI : (0.5242, 0.652)
    No Information Rate : 0.5062
    P-Value [Acc > NIR] : 0.005893

                  Kappa : 0.1722
 Mcnemar's Test P-Value : 1.989e-12

            Sensitivity : 0.2857
            Specificity : 0.8852
         Pos Pred Value : 0.7083
         Neg Pred Value : 0.5596
             Prevalence : 0.4938
         Detection Rate : 0.1411
   Detection Prevalence : 0.1992
      Balanced Accuracy : 0.5855

       'Positive' Class : DOWN
```

We see from the above results that the prediction accuracy is about 59%, indicating that the trained model has some prediction power. Again, this accuracy is not as good as that from the KNN method, where the accuracy is about 60%.

In order to improve the prediction accuracy, we can use a SVM model with a nonlinear kernel. The following example uses a SVM with a radial base function kernel:

```
> ctrl <-  trainControl(method = "repeatedcv", repeats = 3)
> fn.svm <- train(Direction ~ ., data = fn.train[,-1], method = "svmRadial",
          trControl = ctrl, preProcess = c("center","scale"), tuneLength = 10)
> fn.svm
Support Vector Machines with Radial Basis Function Kernel

1205 samples
```

```
  10 predictor
   2 classes: 'DOWN', 'UP'

Pre-processing: centered (10), scaled (10)
Resampling: Cross-Validated (10 fold, repeated 3 times)
Summary of sample sizes: 1084, 1085, 1084, 1085, 1084, 1085, ...
Resampling results across tuning parameters:

  C       Accuracy   Kappa
    0.25  0.6113456  0.2134304
    0.50  0.6093897  0.2099084
    1.00  0.6088433  0.2086362
    2.00  0.6024887  0.1960291
    4.00  0.6002872  0.1924064
    8.00  0.5925253  0.1779038
   16.00  0.5826034  0.1592527
   32.00  0.5698577  0.1344269
   64.00  0.5645936  0.1245210
  128.00  0.5604499  0.1169141

Tuning parameter 'sigma' was held constant at a value of 0.2472114
Accuracy was used to select the optimal model using  the largest value.
The final values used for the model were sigma = 0.2472114 and C = 0.25.
```

Here, the *tuneLength* parameter in the *train* function is set to 10 to assign 10 arbitrary values for the *C* (cost) parameter of the radial kernel. This parameter controls the complexity of the boundary between support vectors. The radial kernel also requires setting a smoothing parameter, *sigma*, in which we let *train* function use its default method of calculating an analytically derived estimate for *sigma*. We see that the optimal model is the one with *C* = 0.25 and *sigma* = 0.247, which gives an accuracy = 0.61135. This result is slightly better than that from the linear SVM method.

Now, we can use the trained model to predict for the test data set:

```
> fn.svm.predict <- predict(fn.svm, newdata = fn.test[,-1])
> confusionMatrix(fn.svm.predict,fn.test$Direction)
Confusion Matrix and Statistics

          Reference
Prediction DOWN UP
      DOWN   72 52
      UP     47 70

               Accuracy : 0.5892
                 95% CI : (0.5242, 0.652)
    No Information Rate : 0.5062
    P-Value [Acc > NIR] : 0.005893

                  Kappa : 0.1787
 Mcnemar's Test P-Value : 0.687673

            Sensitivity : 0.6050
            Specificity : 0.5738
         Pos Pred Value : 0.5806
         Neg Pred Value : 0.5983
             Prevalence : 0.4938
         Detection Rate : 0.2988
```

```
   Detection Prevalence : 0.5145
      Balanced Accuracy : 0.5894

       'Positive' Class : DOWN
```

This gives an accuracy of 0.5892, which is the same as that obtained from the linear SVM.

## SVM for Regression

As mentioned previously, we can also apply SVM to regression problems. In this section, we will use the same data set *fnReg* to predict the next day's FTSE close price value. Specifically, we want to predict the FTSE close prices for the last 60 days in the data set.

Here, we can train our SVM model using the *train* function from the caret package:

```
> set.seed(1234)
> fnReg.svm <- train(Expected ~ ., data = fnReg.train[, -1], method = "svmLinear",
               trControl = trainControl(method = "repeatedcv", repeats = 3))
> fnReg.svm
Support Vector Machines with Linear Kernel

1384 samples
  10 predictor

No pre-processing
Resampling: Cross-Validated (10 fold, repeated 3 times)
Summary of sample sizes: 1247, 1245, 1246, 1244, 1245, 1245, ...
Resampling results:

  RMSE      Rsquared
  56.67272  0.9898198

Tuning parameter 'C' was held constant at a value of 1
```

Here, we use the linear SVM method to train the training data set. The above results are slightly better than those obtained from the random-forest regression.

Now, we examine if the SVM model gives a better prediction for the test data set:

```
> fnReg.predict <- predict(fnReg.svm, newdata = fnReg.test[, -1])
> modelValues <- data.frame(obs = fnReg.test$Expected, pred = fnReg.predict)
> defaultSummary(modelValues)
RMSE   Rsquared
65.7114293  0.8115933
```

This result is much better than that obtained from the KNN (RMSE = 208.87, R-squared = 0.11) or random forest (RMSE = 92.71, R-squared = 0.66) model, which can be seen more clearly in a plot:

```
> plot(fnReg.test$Expected, type = "l", ylim = c(4500, 7500), ylab = "FTSE Price")
> lines(fnReg.predict, col = "red")
> legend("topright", c("Test Data", "Prediction"), col = c("black", "red"),
         lty = c(1, 1))
```

This produces the output shown in Figure 9-5.

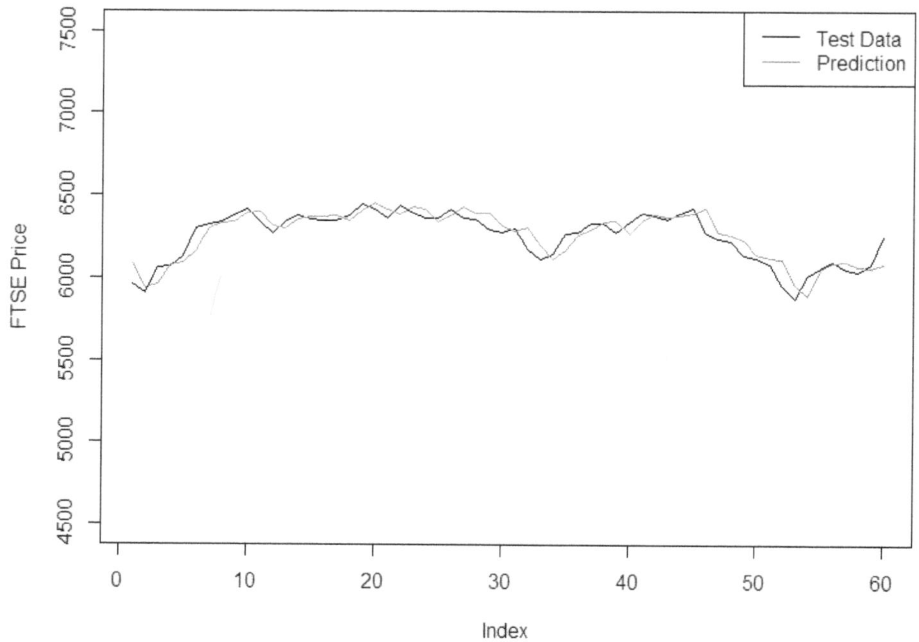


*Figure 9-6. Prediction from the linear SVM model for the test data set.*

# Artificial Neural Networks

In machine learning, artificial neural networks (ANNs) are a family of models inspired by biological neural networks. ANNs are generally presented as systems of interconnected neurons that exchange messages between each other. The connections have numeric weights that can be tuned based on experience, making neural nets adaptive to inputs and capable of learning.

In numeric computation and related symbol manipulation, modern computers usually outperform humans. However, humans can intuitively solve complex perceptual problems much more quickly than the world's fastest computer does. For instance, human can easily recognize a man in a crowd from a mere glimpse of his face. Why is there such a remarkable difference in their performance? The biological neural system is completely different from the von Neumann architecture of computers.

Inspired by biological neural networks, ANNs are massively parallel computing systems consisting of an extremely large number of simple processors with many interconnections. ANN models attempt to use some organizational principles believed to be used in the human brain. However, the human brain as a whole is far too complex to model. Rather, ANNs study individual cells that make up the human brain.

## Introduction to Neural Networks

ANN is basically a mathematical model of what goes in our brain. Let us consider a supervised learning problem where we have access to labeled training examples $(x_i, y_i)$. ANNs provide a way of defining a complex, nonlinear form of hypotheses $h_{W,b}(x)$, with parameters, the weight $W$ and bias $b$, that we can fit to our data.

The simplest possible ANN consists of a single neuron, as shown in Figure 9-7.

This neuron is a computational unit that takes $(x_1, x_2, \dots, x_n)$ as inputs. The output $h_{W,b}(x)$ can be written in the form:

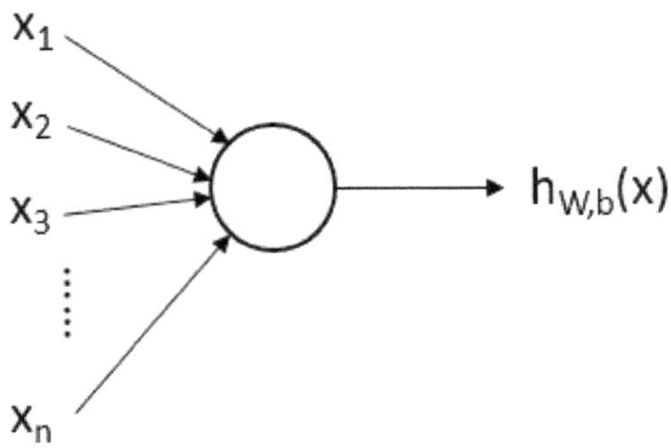


*Figure 9-7. The simplest ANN with a single neuron.*

$$h_{W,b}(x) = f\left(\sum_{i=1}^{n} W_i x_i + b\right)$$

where *f* is called the activation function, which limits the output of a neuron. The activation function plays an important role in the schema of a neuron. It can be chosen as a unit step, piecewise linear, sigmoid, or Gaussian function. The sigmoid function is by far the most frequently used in ANNs. It is a strictly increasing function that exhibits smoothness and has the desired asymptotic properties. The standard sigmoid function is the logistic function, defined by

$$f(z) = \frac{1}{1 + e^{-z}}$$

Figure 9-8 shows the sigmoid function. Note that the output signals can fall anywhere in the range from 0 to 1.

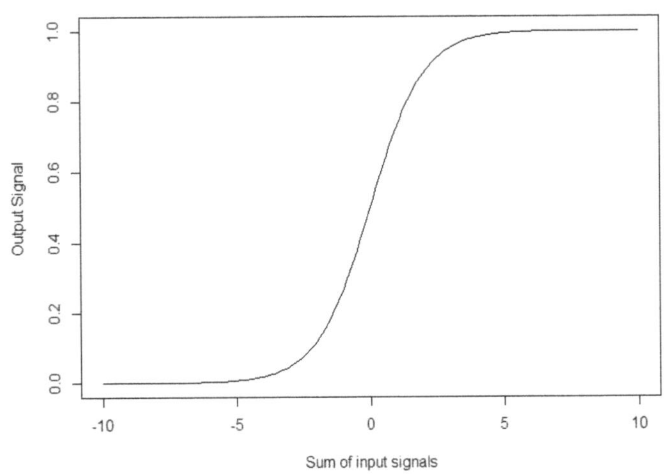


*Figure 9-8. Sigmoid activation function.*

Thus, the single neuron corresponds exactly to the input-output mapping defined by logistic regression. Although the sigmoid is perhaps the most commonly used activation function, other activation functions can also be used in some neural network algorithms, including linear, saturated linear, hyperbolic tangent, and Gaussian functions.

It is important to recognize that for many of the activation functions, the range of input values that affect the output signal is relatively narrow. For example, in the case of the sigmoid, the output signal is always 0 or always 1 for an input signal below -5 or above +5, respectively. The compression of the signal in this way results in a saturated signal at the high and low ends of very dynamic inputs. Because this essentially squeezes the input values into a smaller range of outputs, such activation functions are sometimes called squashing functions.

The solution to the squashing problem is to transform all neural network inputs such that the feature values fall within a small range around 0. Typically, this is done by standardizing or normalizing the inputs. By limiting the input values, the activation function will have action across the entire range, preventing large-valued features such as Dow Jones index price (~17,800) from dominating small-valued features such as the stock price of IBM (~ 150).

We can construct a neural network by hooking many of the simple neurons so that the output of a neuron can be the input of another, as shown in Figure 9-9.

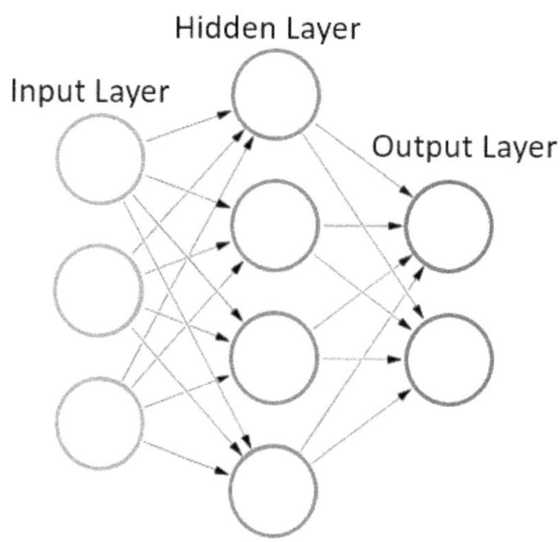


*Figure 9-9. A multilayer neural network.*

In Figure 9-9, each circle represents a neuron and an arrow represents a connection from the output of one neuron to the input of another. We call the leftmost layer of the network the input layer, the rightmost layer the output layer, and the middle layer of nodes the hidden layer.

In the following sections, we will demonstrate how to use the so-called multilayer feed-forward network that is the best choice for predicting the stock price movement. In a feed forward ANN, neurons are only connected forward. Each layer of the neural network contains connections to the next layer, but there are no connections back, as shown in Figure 9-9. Multilayer feed forward ANNs use a variety of learning techniques, the most popular being back-propagation, where the weights and biases are updated in the direction of the negative gradient of predefined error-function. The error is then fed back through the network. Using this information, the algorithm adjusts the weights of each connection in order to reduce the value of the error function by a small amount. After repeating this process for a sufficiently large number of training cycles, the network will usually converge to some state where the error of the calculations is small. In this case, one would say that the network has learned a certain target function.

## Neural Networks for Classification

In this section, I will use an example to illustrate how to use the neural network model (*nnet*) in the *caret* package to predict the next day's stock price direction. This model lets us construct standard ANNs with one hidden layer of sigmoid function neurons. It can be used for both the classification and regression problems. There are two tuning parameters in this model, number of hidden units (*size*) and weight decay (*decay*). We can optimize these two parameters automatically using the *train* function from the *caret* package. Here, we will use the same data set *fn* that was used previously for classification problems.

As mentioned previously, neural networks work best when the input data are scaled to a narrow range around zero. We can examine our original *fn* data using the *str* command:

```
> str(fn)
'data.frame':  1446 obs. of  12 variables:
 $ Date      : Date, format: "2010-01-04" "2010-01-05" "2010-01-06" "2010-01-07" ...
 $ FTSE.Open : num  5413 5500 5522 5530 5527 ...
 $ FTSE.High : num  5500 5536 5536 5552 5549 ...
 $ FTSE.Low  : num  5411 5481 5498 5500 5495 ...
 $ FTSE.Close: num  5500 5522 5530 5527 5534 ...
 $ FTSE.Rtn  : num  0 0.403 0.137 -0.06 0.136 ...
 $ N225.Open : num  10719 10710 10743 10743 10770 ...
 $ N225.High : num  10791 10769 10774 10816 10905 ...
 $ N225.Low  : num  10656 10661 10637 10678 10764 ...
 $ N225.Close: num  10682 10731 10682 10798 10879 ...
 $ N225.Rtn  : num  0.254 0.465 -0.464 1.092 0.748 ...
 $ Direction : chr  "UP" "UP" "DOWN" "UP" ...
```

Here we see the data values anywhere from around zero up to over 10 thousands. Typically, the solution to this problem is to rescale the data with a normalization or standardization function. Here, we will manually normalize our data to a [0, 1] range using the following function:

```
> normalizeData <- function(x) {
    return((x - min(x)) / (max(x) - min(x)))
  }
```

After executing this code, we can apply the above function to every column in the original data using the *lapply* function:

```
> fnx <- fn
> fnx$Date <- fnx$Direction <- NULL
> fnx <- as.data.frame(lapply(fnx, normalizeData))
> head(fnx)
  FTSE.Open FTSE.High  FTSE.Low FTSE.Close  FTSE.Rtn N225.Open N225.High  N225.Low N225.Close  N225.Rtn
1 0.2641729 0.2819301 0.2736763  0.3022282 0.4748689 0.2019377 0.2031963 0.1983699  0.1984432 0.5917886
2 0.3022282 0.2978813 0.3044879  0.3118704 0.5158622 0.2011639 0.2014375 0.1988108  0.2023478 0.6033282
3 0.3118704 0.2979255 0.3119561  0.3151512 0.4887610 0.2037613 0.2018601 0.1968820  0.1984298 0.5524876
4 0.3151512 0.3046442 0.3129039  0.3137066 0.4687603 0.2038043 0.2051887 0.2001010  0.2076099 0.6376946
5 0.3137066 0.3035775 0.3106952  0.3169787 0.4887136 0.2059205 0.2121627 0.2068808  0.2139696 0.6188743
6 0.3186452 0.3037368 0.2953313  0.3015190 0.4025538 0.2078865 0.2091227 0.2042184  0.2026296 0.5053603
```

In order to normalize the data, we first exclude the *Date* and *Direction* columns. Note that the data in the *fnx* data frame are all normalized to the [0, 1] range.

We now need to split data into the training and test data sets:

```
> x.train <- head(fnx, -241)
> x.test <- tail(fnx, 241)
> y.train <- as.data.frame(head(fn,-241))$Direction
> y.test <- as.data.frame(tail(fn,241))$Direction
```

Now, we can train our neural network model using the *train* function by setting its *method* to *nnet*:

```
> set.seed(1234)
> ctrl <- trainControl(method = "repeatedcv", repeats = 5, number = 5)
> fn.nn <- train(x = x.train, y = y.train, method = "nnet",
         trControl = ctrl, tuneLength = 10, trace = F)
```

The following is the output of the *nnet* fit:

```
> fn.nn
Neural Network

1205 samples
  10 predictor
   2 classes: 'DOWN', 'UP'

No pre-processing
Resampling: Cross-Validated (5 fold, repeated 5 times)
Summary of sample sizes: 964, 964, 964, 964, 964, 964, ...
Resampling results across tuning parameters:

  size  decay         Accuracy   Kappa
   1    0.0000000000  0.5936727  0.1763348
   1    0.0001000000  0.5747818  0.1319909
   1    0.0002371374  0.5985012  0.1882540
   1    0.0005623413  0.5908614  0.1700646
   1    0.0013335214  0.5747638  0.1332888
  ......
   9    0.0001000000  0.5903663  0.1745178
   9    0.0002371374  0.5839076  0.1624882
   9    0.0005623413  0.5925253  0.1792181
   9    0.0013335214  0.5945157  0.1833190
   9    0.0031622777  0.5976816  0.1896583
   9    0.0074989421  0.5965047  0.1875507
   9    0.0177827941  0.6029805  0.1992008
   9    0.0421696503  0.6132703  0.2212579
   9    0.1000000000  0.6063172  0.2064515
  11    0.0000000000  0.5867045  0.1688778
  11    0.0001000000  0.5847169  0.1637310
  11    0.0002371374  0.5840688  0.1635985
  11    0.0005623413  0.5857224  0.1664805
  11    0.0013335214  0.5901948  0.1758761
  11    0.0031622777  0.5887127  0.1716291
  11    0.0074989421  0.5955198  0.1854714
  11    0.0177827941  0.6061402  0.2061683
  11    0.0421696503  0.6094528  0.2139131
  ......

Accuracy was used to select the optimal model using  the largest value.
The final values used for the model were size = 9 and decay = 0.04216965.
```

We see that the optimal model is the one with *size* = 9 and *decay* = 0.042, which gives an accuracy of 0.6133 for the training set.

We can also visualize the network topology using the following R code:

```
> library(devtools)
>source_url('https://gist.githubusercontent.com/fawda123/7471137/raw/466c1474d0a505f
f044412703516c34f1a4684a5/nnet_plot_update.r')
> plot.nnet(fn.nn)
```

This produces the output shown in Figure 9-10, which shows that our ANN model contains 10 inputs, 19 neurons at the hidden layer, 2 bias, and 1 output. Note also that the thicknesses of the connection lines represent the weight magnitude, the black color lines represent positive weights, and the gray color line represent negative weights. We see from the weights in the figure that the N225 return is the most important feature in determining the market moving direction of FTSE. This information will be very useful for evaluating the ANN model performance.

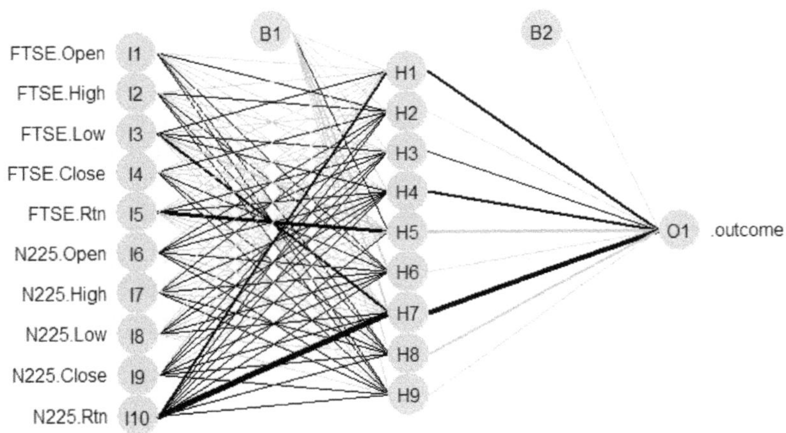


*Figure 9-10. Neural network topology for predicting FTSE market direction.*

Now, we can use the trained model to predict for the test data set:

```
> fn.nn.predict <- predict(fn.nn, newdata = x.test)
> confusionMatrix(fn.nn.predict,y.test)
Confusion Matrix and Statistics

          Reference
Prediction DOWN UP
      DOWN   84 59
      UP     35 63

               Accuracy : 0.61
                 95% CI : (0.5453, 0.6719)
    No Information Rate : 0.5062
    P-Value [Acc > NIR] : 0.0007648

                  Kappa : 0.2217
 Mcnemar's Test P-Value : 0.0176792

            Sensitivity : 0.7059
```

```
         Specificity : 0.5164
      Pos Pred Value : 0.5874
      Neg Pred Value : 0.6429
          Prevalence : 0.4938
      Detection Rate : 0.3485
Detection Prevalence : 0.5934
   Balanced Accuracy : 0.6111

    'Positive' Class : DOWN
```

For this particular problem, we see that the accuracy from *nnet* for the test data set is better than that from other machine learning methods, such as KNN (0.5975), random forest (0.5394), and SVM (0.5892).

In order to improve the prediction accuracy from ANN models, we may adjust control parameters to retrain the model, or we may consider using neural network models with multiple hidden layers. Here, our purpose is just to show you how to apply the ANN model to the classification problems.

## Neural Network for Regression

ANNs are commonly used for classification because of the relationship to logistic regressions: they typically use a logistic activation function and output values from 0 to 1 (sigmoid) or from $-1$ to $+1$ (bipolar sigmoid) like logistic regression. However, the worth of ANNs to model complex, nonlinear hypotheses is desirable for many real world problems, including regression.

Here, I will use the same normalized data set *fnx*, which is used for classification problems in the preceding section, to predict the next day's FTSE close price value. Specifically, we want to predict the FTSE close prices for the last 60 days in the data set. Let us first preprocess the training and test data:

```
> xy <- fnx
> xy$Expected <- lead(xy$FTSE.Close)
> xy<- xy[-nrow(xy),]
```

Here, we offset the FTSE close prices by one day and place them into the *Expected* column. Next, we need to split the market data into training and test portions:

```
> xy.train <- head(xy, -60)
> xy.test <- tail(xy, 60)
```

We can then train our ANN model using the *train* function from the caret package:

```
> set.seed(12345)
> ctrl <- trainControl(method = "repeatedcv", repeats = 3, number = 5)
> fnReg.nn <- train(Expected ~ ., data = xy.train, method = "nnet",
             trControl = ctrl, tuneLength = 5, trace = F)
> fnReg.nn
Neural Network

1385 samples
  10 predictor

No pre-processing
Resampling: Cross-Validated (5 fold, repeated 3 times)
Summary of sample sizes: 1109, 1108, 1108, 1107, 1108, 1107, ...
Resampling results across tuning parameters:
```

```
size  decay   RMSE        Rsquared
1     0e+00   0.02999684  0.9848316
1     1e-04   0.03007921  0.9847517
1     1e-03   0.03084047  0.9840240
1     1e-02   0.03351267  0.9814054
1     1e-01   0.04166035  0.9742469
3     0e+00   0.02535672  0.9890596
3     1e-04   0.02523162  0.9891870
3     1e-03   0.02558962  0.9888679
3     1e-02   0.02932364  0.9856210
3     1e-01   0.03711060  0.9786812
5     0e+00   0.02555556  0.9888889
5     1e-04   0.02496387  0.9894143
5     1e-03   0.02559807  0.9888947
5     1e-02   0.02921566  0.9857238
5     1e-01   0.03623766  0.9794047
7     0e+00   0.02524936  0.9891498
7     1e-04   0.02499465  0.9893847
7     1e-03   0.02540837  0.9890499
7     1e-02   0.02906629  0.9858450
7     1e-01   0.03568607  0.9799671
9     0e+00   0.02516978  0.9892325
9     1e-04   0.02504601  0.9893452
9     1e-03   0.02538774  0.9890690
9     1e-02   0.02909306  0.9858126
9     1e-01   0.03535365  0.9802845

RMSE was used to select the optimal model using  the smallest value.
The final values used for the model were size = 5 and decay = 1e-04.
```

We see that the optimal model is the one with five neurons at the hidden layer and the decay parameter = 1e-4, which gives a very high R-squared (0.9894).

We can also visualize the network topology using the following R code:

```
> plot.nnet(fnReg.nn)
```

This command produces the output shown in Figure 9-11.

Now, we examine if our trained ANN model gives a better prediction for the test data set:

```
> fnReg.predict <- predict(fnReg.nn, newdata = xy.test)
> modelValues <- data.frame(obs = xy.test$Expected, pred = fnReg.predict)
> defaultSummary(modelValues)
      RMSE   Rsquared
0.03576801 0.81599207
```

The high R-squared value indicates that our ANN model has a very good prediction power, which can be seen more clearly in a plot:

```
> plot(xy.test$Expected, type = "l", ylim = c(0, 1), ylab = "Normalized FTSE Price")
> lines(fnReg.predict, col = "red")
> legend("topright", c("Test Data", "Prediction"), col = c("black", "red"),
         lty = c(1, 1))
```

Figure 9-12 shows the output from the above commands.

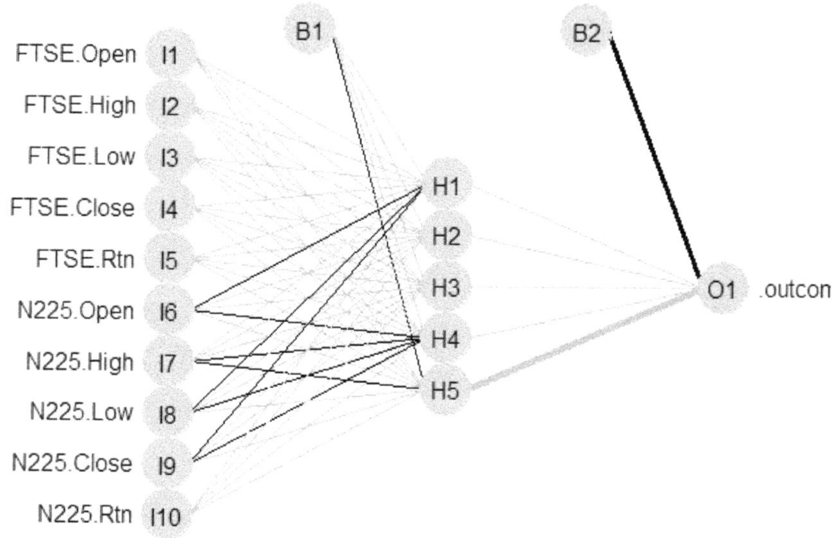


*Figure 9-11. Neural network topology for predicting next day's FTSE close price.*

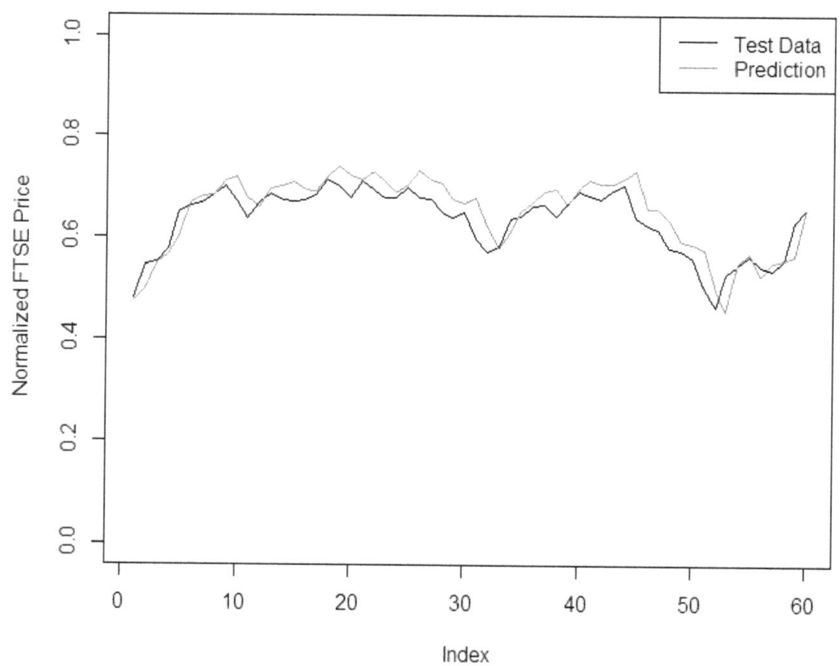


*Figure 9-12. Prediction from the ANN model for normalized FTSE close prices.*

You may notice that the data shown in Figure 9-12 are normalized FTSE close prices. If we want to show the prediction for the original prices, we need to encode the data by reversing the normalization formula using the following commands:

```
> FTSE.min <- min(fn$FTSE.Close)
> FTSE.max <- max(fn$FTSE.Close)
> expected <- FTSE.min + xy.test$Expected*(FTSE.max - FTSE.min)
> predicted <- FTSE.min + fnReg.predict*(FTSE.max - FTSE.min)
> plot(expected, type = "l", ylim = c(4500, 7500), ylab = "FTSE Price")
> lines(predicted, col = "red")
> legend("topright", c("Expected", "Predicted"), col = c("black", "red"),
        lty = c(1, 1))
```

This produces the output shown in Figure 9-13.

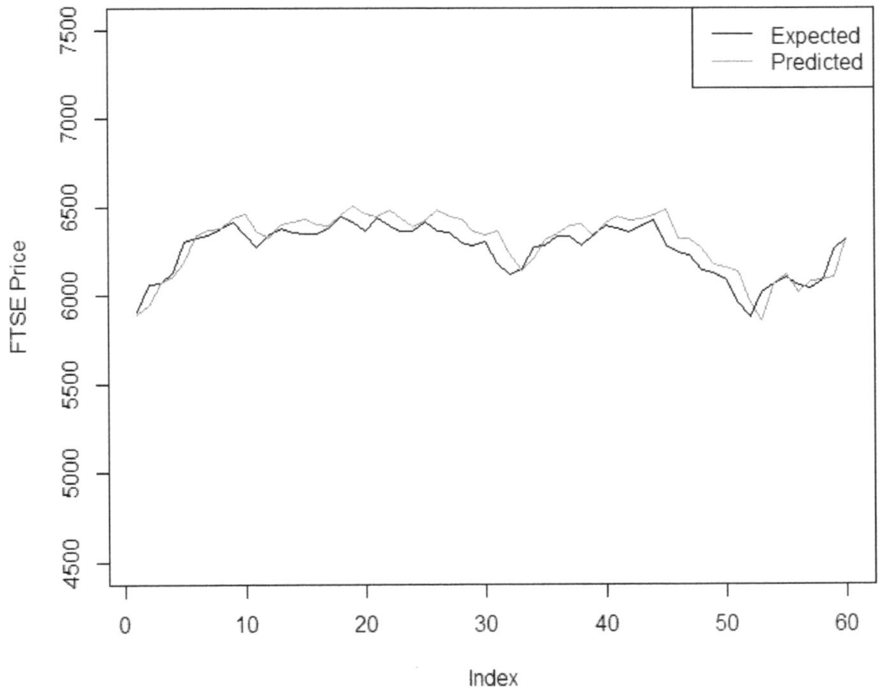


*Figure 9-13. Prediction from the ANN model for original FTSE close prices.*

The results in Figure 9-13 shows that the prediction for the next day's FTSE close price fits well to the expected close price. In order to compare with other models, we can calculate the RMSE and R-squared for predicted price for the original data:

```
> modelValues <- data.frame(obs = expected, pred = predicted)
> defaultSummary(modelValues)
      RMSE   Rsquared
82.2031150  0.8159921
```

We see that the results from the ANN model are better than those from the other machine learning models, such as KNN and random forest; and are very close to the SVM results where we have R-squared = 0.8116.

You may notice that for simplicity's sake, we normalized the training and test data sets using the minimum and maximum values from the entire *fnx* data set. In practice, we cannot do that because the test set should be assumed to be the future data, which is yet not available when we are training the ANN models. We should always use the parameters from the training set to normalize our data.

The examples presented in this chapter are used for demonstration purposes only. In order to apply machine-learning techniques to real-world stock market, we may need to include much more features than the stock prices, such as volume, PE ratio, volatility, moving average, risk premium, interest rate, S&P 500 index, and other sector related data. In our ANN examples, we only use a single hidden layer to construct our network, whereas for more complicated real-world problems, we may need multiple hidden layers. However, by following the procedure presented in our examples, you should be able to apply the neural network and other machine learning techniques to your financial applications without any difficulty.

# Chapter 10
# Trading Strategies and Backtesting

Quantitative trading is usually considered as the rocket science in finance because it is an extremely sophisticated area of quantitative finance. It can take a significant amount of time to gain the necessary knowledge to develop your own trading strategies. It also requires strong background in math, physical modeling, and statistics, as well as extensive programming expertise. A successful quantitative trading system consists several major components, including trading strategy development, backtesting, automatic algorithm execution, and risk management.

The key step for quantitative trading is to develop and identify the trading strategies. Some strategies do require advanced background knowledge on math and finance, while most trading ideas can easily be found through various public resources, such as blogs, books, magazines, and online communities. After identifying our trading strategies, we need to backtest them to see how they would have performed in the past. Even if we find a strategy with all the historical performance data available, we still need to backtest it ourselves, which ensures that we understand the strategy completely and can reproduce its results.

In this chapter, I will show you how to develop several trading strategies using the simple quantitative analysis techniques, including the moving average, linear regression, and region switching, as well as the commonly used technical indicators. I will also present a long-short based backtesting framework, which allows us to examine the historical performance of our trading strategies.

## Trading Strategy Identification

All quantitative trading processes begin with an initial period of research. Reference books, financial courses, blogs, and online trader forums can save your valuable time, but quantitative trading can also be a "do it yourself" career. Contrary to common belief, building strategies can be easy and quick. In fact, you can find good strategies through various public sources. You may question why traders are keen to publicize their trading strategies if the strategies are profitable. The reason lies in the fact that the fundamentals of the published strategies are quite well known to professional traders, so they can discuss the principles of the strategies publicly. However, they will not often discuss the exact parameters and optimization methods that they have carried out. These optimizations are the key to turning a relatively mediocre strategy into a highly profitable one. In fact, one of the best ways to build our own unique strategies is to find similar strategies from public sources and then perform our own optimization procedure.

Many of the trading strategies can be broadly divided into the mean-reversion and momentum categories. A mean-reverting strategy attempts to exploit the fact that a stock price eventually returns to its long-term average price after a temporary deviation. The strategy takes advantage of such price movement, that is, buying low and selling high. On the other hand, momentum strategies are devised on the promise that strong moves in the market in either direction will be most likely followed by higher highs and lower lows. Trend-following strategies attempt to capitalize on big market movements by buying stocks that are showing an upward trend and selling stocks that are on a downward trend.

To illustrate the difference between these two strategies, take for example the chart created using the following R commands:

```
> library(quantmod)
> getSymbols("IBM", from = "2012-01-01", to = "2013-08-01")
> chartSeries(IBM, theme = "white", minor.ticks = F)
> addTA(SMA(Cl(IBM), n = 40), on = 1, col = "blue")
```

This produces the output shown in Figure 10-1.

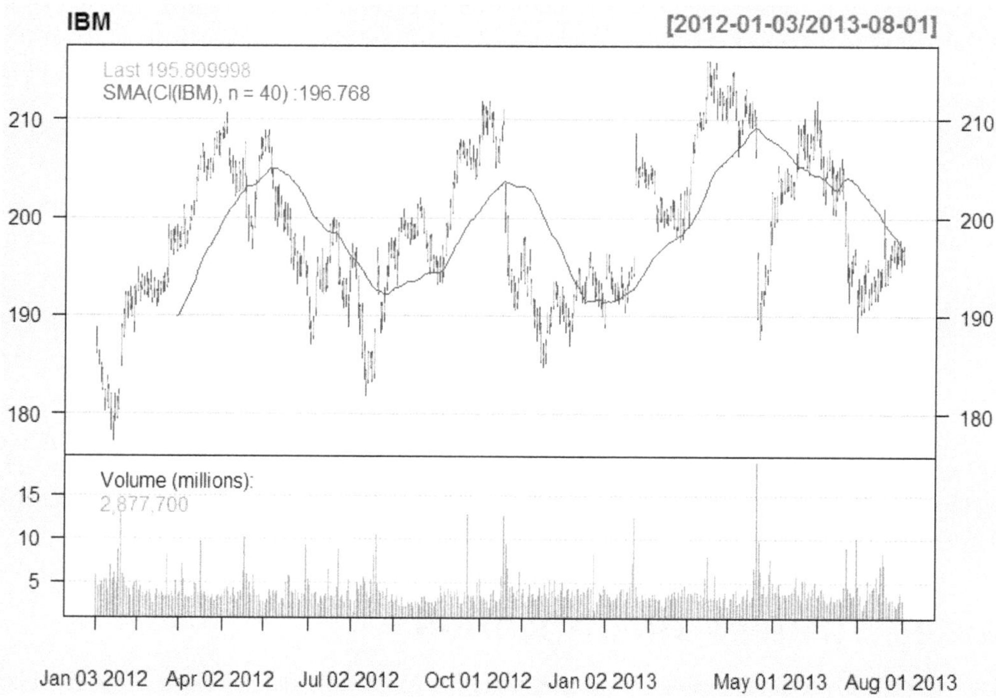


*Figure 10-1. IBM stock price from 1/3/2012 to 7/31/2013.*

You can see from Figure 10-1 that IBM is very mean-reversion during the period of 1/3/2012 to 8/1/2013. It was moving in a range of 180 to 215. Additionally, its 40-day moving average serves as a guide on its mean or average. In this case, we can enter a short position when the price of the stock moves above MA; and take on a long position when the price moves below MA. A mean reversion strategy like this will prove to be very profitable if the stock has been oscillating in this price range.

Figure 11-2 shows GS stock price and 200 MA in a period of 3 years from 7/31/2012 to 7/31/2015. This chart is created using the following R code:

```
> getSymbols("GS", from = "2011-01-01", to = "2015-07-31")
> gs <- GS["2012-07-31::2015-07-31"]
> chartSeries(gs, theme = "white", minor.ticks = F)
> addTA(SMA(Cl(GS), n = 200), on = 1, col = "blue")
```

*Figure 11-2. GS stock price from 7/31/2012 to 7/31/2015.*

You can see that GS is a good candidate for momentum strategies for the period of 7/31/2012 to 7/31/2015. A good momentum strategy would exploit this opportunity the moment the stock made higher highs. For example, you can go long once the price goes above the 200 MA and exit the position once the price is below the MA.

You may notice that we do not distinguish between the momentum and the trend-following strategies. Strictly speaking, even though both momentum and trend-following have many similarities, they are in fact are two different non-competing techniques aimed at identifying chances to buy on the upswing and sell on the downswing, serving to support or reject each other.

Momentum investing relies on predictive (forward-looking) fundamental analysis, such as sales and earnings. Momentum is the acceleration in stock prices that can be due to earnings, sentiment, news, greed, or fear. Momentum traders will take a long or short position in the stock in the hope that its momentum will continue in either an upward or downward direction in the time frame they are trading.

Some traders have a different definition for momentum strategies. They believe that momentum is the observation that stock prices have performed well relative to other stock prices (peers) on average continue to outperform, and that prices that have performed relatively poorly tend to continue to underperform. Here, the word relative is crucial as momentum is calculated by ranking a stock's price movement against other stocks.

Trend-following strategies take a backward-looking approach and focus on the price. Trend-following traders ignore predictions, whatever they are based on. They believe that any change in fundamentals, such as sales and earnings, will eventually reflect on the price. Compared to the momentum strategies with relative stock prices, trend-following concentrates on the absolute price change (i.e., stock price changes against market). Momentum always takes long position relative past outperformance and short relative past underperformance, while trend following involves increasing your investment exposure during market upswings and decreasing exposure during downswings.

In this book, we will ignore the subtle difference between the momentum and trend-following strategies and will use momentum to represent the strategies of buying high and selling low.

Another important aspect of quantitative trading is the frequency of the trading strategies. Low frequency trading (LFT) generally refers to any strategy that holds positions longer than a trading day. Correspondingly, high frequency trading (HFT) generally refers to a strategy that holds positions intraday. Ultra-high frequency trading (UHFT) refers to strategies that hold positions on the order of seconds or milliseconds. In this chapter, we will only discuss the low frequency trading.

# Trading Signals

In Chapters 7-9, we discussed various quantitative analysis approaches used in finance, including moving average, linear analysis, PCA, a variety of technical indicators, and advanced machine learning techniques. These analysis techniques are very powerful when we use them to study the market trends, price pattern, and correlation between different stocks. However, the ultimate goal of the quantitative analysis is to generate the trading signals. In this section, I will show you how to create the trading signals using different quantitative analysis methods.

## Signals from Moving Average

For practical trading, traders often use the Bollinger band-like model based on the moving average, where we enter a position only when the price deviates by more than *SignalIn* standard deviations from the mean. *SignalIn* is a free parameter to be optimized in a training data set, and the mean and standard deviation can be computed within a moving window, whose length again can be optimized. We can exit positions when the price returns to *SignalOut* standard deviations from the mean. We often set *SignalOut* = 0, which means we will exit when the price returns back to its current mean. If we set the moving window size to a short period, and small *SignalIn* and *SignalOut*, we will get a shorter holding period and more trades.

Figure 11-3 shows the Bollinger bands based on the 40-day MA for IBM, which is created using the following R code:

```
> chartSeries(IBM, theme = "white", minor.ticks = F, yrange = c(170, 230),
              TA = "addBBands(n = 40, maType = 'SMA')")
```

In this case, we can extract the trading signal by defining the so-called *Z*-score:

$$Signal = \frac{price - mean}{standard\ deviation}$$

Note that this signal is a rolling signal, that is, we should compute it for each moving window. We can use the *rollapply* function in R to calculate this MA based rolling Z-score easily.

Add a new file named *strategyHelper.R* to the "[WORKING Directory]/R/" directory, and add a new function, *maZscore*, to this file:

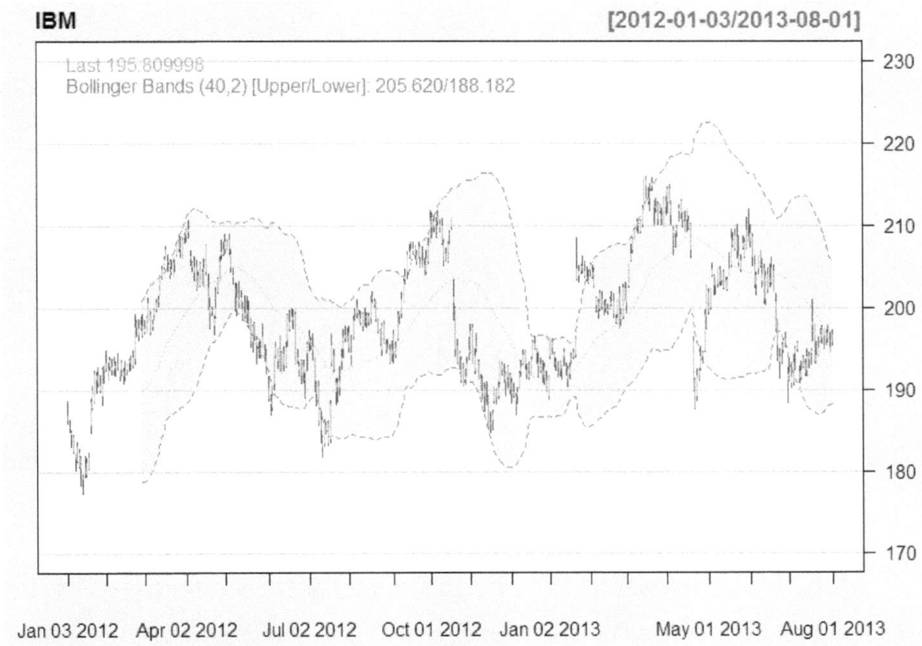


*Figure 11-3. Bollinger bands based on the 40 MA for IBM.*

```
maZscore <- function(x, n){
  ma <- rollapply(x, n, mean)
  std <- rollapply(x, n, sd)
  zs <- (x - ma)/std
  return(zs)
}
```

Inside this function, we calculate the moving average, standard deviation, and Z-score (or the signal). We can then use this function to calculate the *Z*-score for IBM:

```
> source("./R/strategyHelper.R")
> zscore <- maZscore(Cl(IBM), 40)
> plot(zscore)
```

Figure 10-4 shows the signal, which corresponds to the Bollinger bands shown in Figure 10-3.

We see that using the Z-score signal in Figure 10-4 is much easier than using the original Bollinger bands.

# Signals from Linear Regression

We can also create the trading signals from the linear regression. In this case, the signal is defined by

$$Signal = \frac{price - priceLR}{standard\ deviation}$$

where *priceLR* is the predicted price by the linear regression. Note that this signal is a rolling signal, that is, we should compute it for each moving window.

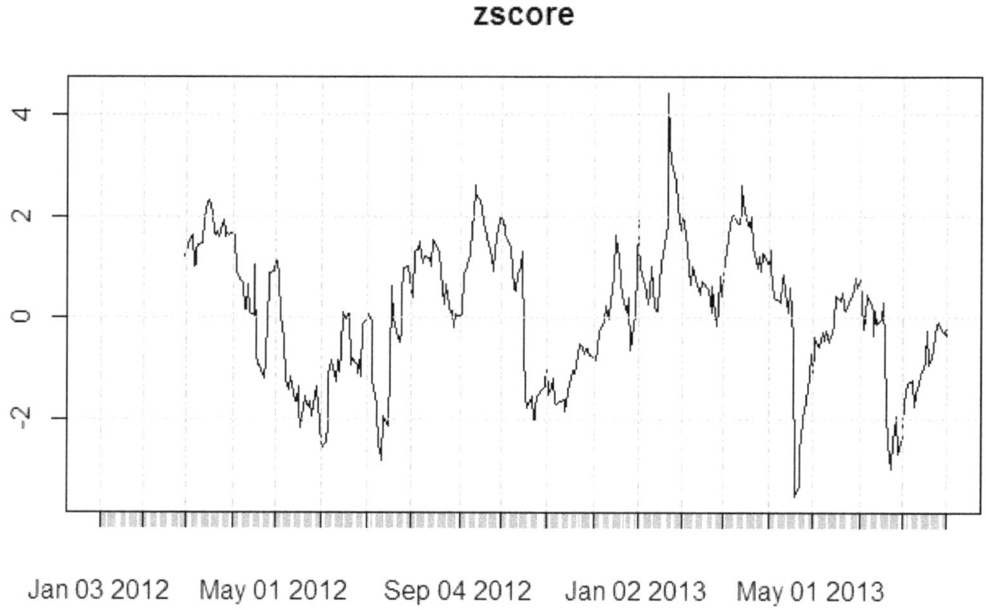


*Figure 10-4. Z-score signal based on the 40 MA for IBM.*

Add a new function, *lrZscore*, to the *strategyHelper.R* file. Here is the code for this function:

```
lrZscore <- function(x, n){
  lr <- rollapply(x, n, FUN = function(y){
    t <- lm(formula = y ~ row(y)); return(t$coef)
    },
    by.column = F)
  fit <- lr[, 1] + lr[, 2]*n
  std <- rollapply(x, n, sd)
  zs <- (x - fit)/std
  colnames(zs) <- "Zscore"
  zs$FittedValues <- fit
  return(zs)
}
```

Here, we simply perform a linear regression for stock price relative to its row number, i.e. a self-regression. We can then extract the trading signal for IBM based on a linear regression using the above function:

```
> source("./R/strategyHelper.R")
> zscore <- lrZscore(Cl(IBM), 40)
> plot(zscore$Zscore, main = "Linear regression Zscore for IBM")
> plot(Cl(IBM))
> lines(zscore$FittedValues, col="red")
```

Figure 11-5 shows the regression results for IBM and the trading signal based on the linear regression with a moving window = 40.

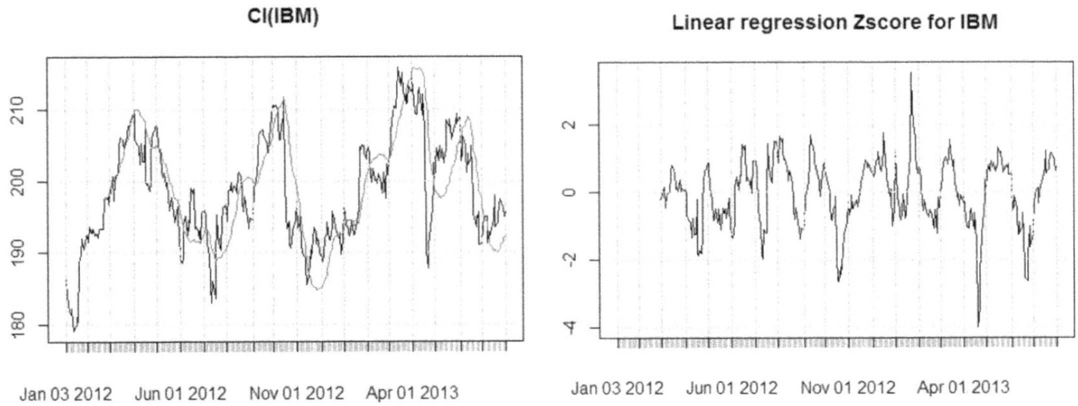


*Figure 11-5. Linear regression (left) and trading signal for IBM.*

## Signals from RSI

RSI (relative strength Index) indicator is a momentum oscillator that measures the speed and change of price movement. RSI oscillates between 0 and 100. Traditionally, RSI is considered overbought when above 70 and oversold when below 30. We can calculate RSI using the following formula

$$RSI = 100 - \frac{100}{1 + RS}, \quad RS = \frac{Average\ Gain}{Average\ Loss}$$

Note that RSI has been broken down into its basic components: RS, average gain, and average loss. The losses are expressed as positive values, not negative values.

In order to extract the trading signal from the RSI indicator, we need to renormalize it into a proper value range of $[-2, +2]$:

$$Signal = \frac{RSI - 50}{25}$$

We can see that the signal will be $-2$ when RSI reaches its minimum value 0, and it is equal to +2 when RSI is at its maximum value of 100.

Add a new helper function, *rsiSignal*, to the *strategyHelper* file:

```
rsiSignal <- function(x, n){
  rsi <- RSI(x, n)
  signal <- (rsi - 50)/25
  return(signal)
}
```

Here, we can then apply the above function to IBM close prices:

```
> source("./R/strategyHelper.R")
> sig <- rsiSignal(Cl(IBM), 14)
> plot(sig)
```

Figure 10-6 shows the RSI signal for IBM with a moving window = 14. You can see that the signal indeed oscillates from $-2$ to +2.

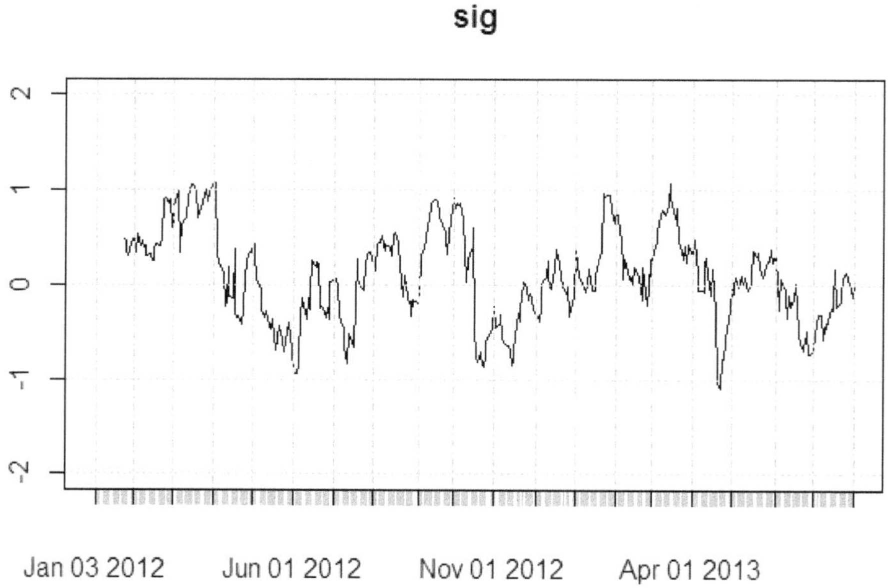


*Figure 10-6. Trading signal based on RSI for IBM.*

# Signals from Williams %R

The Williams %R is a momentum indicator that shows the level of the close price relative to the highest high for a given moving window (or look-back period). Williams %R oscillates from $-100$ to $0$. Readings from 0 to $-20$ are considered overbought, and readings from $-80$ to $-100$ are considered oversold. You can compute Williams %R using the following formula

$$WilliamsR = -100 \times \frac{highest\ high - Close}{highest\ high - lowest\ low}$$

where both the highest high and the lowest low are calculated for a given moving window. In order to extract the trading signal from the Williams %R indicator, we need to renormalize it by

$$Signal = \frac{WilliamsR}{25} + 2 = -4 \times \frac{highest\ high - Close}{highest\ high - lowest\ low} + 2$$

Thus, the normalized signal will be in the range of $[-2, +2]$.

Add a new function, *wprSignal*, to the *strategyHelper.R* file. Here is the code for this function:

```
wprSignal <- function(x.hlc, n){
  wpr <- WPR(x.hlc, n)
  sig <- wpr*4 - 2
  return(sig)
}
```

We can then apply the above function to IBM:

```
> source("./R/strategyHelper.R")
> wpr <- wprSignal(IBM[, c("IBM.High", "IBM.Low", "IBM.Close")], 14)
> plot(wpr)
```

This produces the output shown in Figure 10-7.

Figure 10-7 shows the Williams %R signal for IBM with a moving window = 14. You can see that the signal from Williams %R indeed oscillates from −2 to +2.

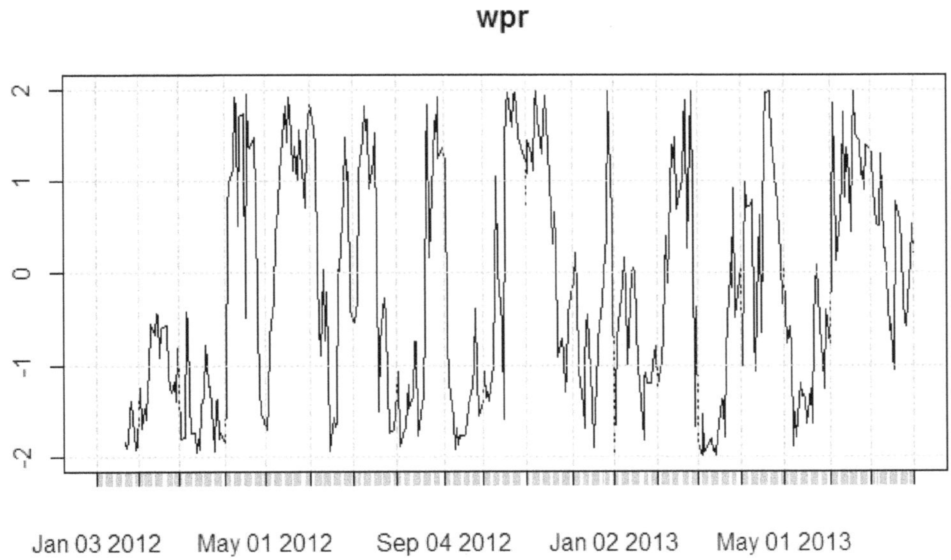


*Figure 10-7. Trading signal based on Williams % R for IBM.*

Here, we simply create several trading signals using different techniques, including moving average, linear regression, and technical indicators. Following the same procedure presented here, you can create your own trading signals using other technical indicators and advanced quantitative analysis approaches, such as machine learning and neural networks. Here, we scale all signals into a similar value range and make them symmetric above the zero line, so that we can easily implement a unified backtesting system that can handle different trading signals.

# Backtest System Implementation

In this section, we will build a backtest system that allows us to backtest the historical performance using the trading signals. Typically, we can use this system to calculate the daily and accumulated P&L (profit and loss) and other risk measures of the performance for a given trading strategy. For simplicity's sake, we will neglect the stop-loss mechanism and the transaction costs, which includes brokers' commission and the bid/ask spreads. In addition, we assume that the orders can be filled fully at a specified price (i.e., the close price). We all know that in practice, this is impossible. We have to use the proper algorithms to execute our orders, such as the popular TWAP (time-weighted average price) or VWAP (volume-weighted average price) algorithms. A practical real-world trading system including the real-time order execution algorithms will be discussed in another one of my books, *Practical C# for Real-Time Trading System*.

## P&L Computation

Here, we will implement a simple long/short method to compute the P&L (profit and loss). We can use the Bollinger band-like technique, where we enter into a position only when the price deviates by more than the entry *Z*-score point (called *zin*) from the mean. We treat *zin* as a free parameter, and it can be optimized in a training set. We compute the *Z*-score within a look-back moving window, whose period again can be a free parameter to be optimized. We can exit our position when the price mean-reverts to the exit Z-score point (called *zout*), where $zout < zin$. Note that if $zout = 0$, this means we will exit when the price mean-reverts to the current mean value. At any one time, we can have either zero or one unit (long or short) invested, so it is very easy to allocate capital to this strategy or to manage its risk. If we set the moving window to a short period, and a small *zin* and *zout* magnitude, we will get a shorter holding period and more trades.

Now, we will implement this long-short strategy. Add a new function named *longShortStrategy* to the *strategyHelper.R* file. Here is the code for this function:

```
longShortStrategy <- function(price, zin, zout){
  colnames(price) <- c("Price", "Zscore")

  #Long positions:
  price$PosLong <- NA
  price$PosLong[price$Zscore < -zin] <- 1
  price$PosLong[price$Zscore > -zout] <- 0
  price$PosLong[1] <- 0            #Flat on the first day
  price$PosLong[nrow(price)] <- 0  #Flat on the last day
  price$PosLong <- na.locf(price$PosLong)

  #Short positions:
  price$PosShort <- NA
  price$PosShort[price$Zscore > zin] <- -1
  price$PosShort[price$Zscore < zout] <- 0
  price$PosShort[1] <- 0
  price$PosShort[nrow(price)] <- 0
  price$PosShort <- na.locf(price$PosShort)

  price$Position <- as.numeric(Lag(price$PosLong + price$PosShort))
  price$Position[1] <- 0

  price$Equity <- c(0, cumsum(diff(price$Price, na.pad = F)*price$Position[-1]))
  price$Return <- c(0, cumsum(ROC(price$Price, na.pad = F)*price$Position[-1]))
  price$ReturnDaily <- c(0, ROC(price$Price, na.pad = F)*price$Position[-1])
  price$RetHold <- c(0, cumsum(ROC(price$Price, na.pad = F)))
  price$RetDailyHold <- c(0, ROC(price$Price, na.pad = F))

  return(as.xts(price))
}
```

The function takes the *price* (a data frame or *xts* object), which contains both the price and *Z*-score data, *zin*, and *zout* as inputs. First, we enter a long position when *Z*-score < - *zin* and flat the position when *Z*-score > −*zout*. The following code

```
price$PosLong <- na.locf(price$PosLong)
```

is a key statement. The *na.locf* function starts with the second row of the *price$PosLong* field, and replaces any *NA* value by the most recent non-*NA* value prior to it. We do the similar thing for the short position. Once *PosLong* and *PosShort* are computed, we combine them to obtain the net trading position. In order to avoid look-forward bias, we also lag our final net position signal by one day to reflect that we cannot trade on the same day as our position signal fires. Finally, we use the net position signal to calculate the equity curve for one share of stock, cumulative return, and daily returns of a fully invested account. For comparison, we also calculate the returns for a passive "buy-and-hold" strategy, in which we buys stock at the beginning and hold it for the entire period of the investment.

Based on this basic *longShortStrategy* function, we can easily add more features to it, such as stop loss control and transaction costs.

We can use the above function to backtest the long-short trading strategy for IBM. In the preceding section, we discussed various trading signals for IBM. As an example, we will test the trading signal based on moving average:

```
> source("./R/strategyHelper.R")
> zscore <- maZscore(Cl(IBM), 40)
> price <- na.omit(data.frame(Price = Cl(IBM), Zscore <- zscore[,1]))
> strategy <- longShortStrategy(price, 2, 0)
> tail(strategy)
```

| | Price | Zscore | PosLong | PosShort | Position | Equity | Return | ReturnDaily | RetHold | RetDailyHold |
|---|---|---|---|---|---|---|---|---|---|---|
| 2013-07-25 | 197.22 | -0.16334173 | 1 | 0 | 1 | 50.67001 | 0.2550261 | 0.0030977858 | 0.002487652 | 0.0030977858 |
| 2013-07-26 | 197.35 | -0.09181161 | 1 | 0 | 1 | 50.80002 | 0.2556851 | 0.0006589705 | 0.003146623 | 0.0006589705 |
| 2013-07-29 | 196.21 | -0.26315330 | 1 | 0 | 1 | 49.66002 | 0.2498918 | -0.0057932826 | -0.002646660 | -0.0057932826 |
| 2013-07-30 | 196.01 | -0.25625811 | 1 | 0 | 1 | 49.46000 | 0.2488719 | -0.0010198971 | -0.003666557 | -0.0010198971 |
| 2013-07-31 | 195.04 | -0.42220256 | 1 | 0 | 1 | 48.49000 | 0.2439109 | -0.0049610230 | -0.008627580 | -0.0049610230 |
| 2013-08-01 | 195.81 | -0.21742572 | 0 | 0 | 1 | 49.26001 | 0.2478511 | 0.0039401613 | -0.004687419 | 0.0039401613 |

Here, we first calculate the *Z*-score using the *maZscore* function implemented in the preceding section based on moving average. We then construct the input data and set *zin* = 2 and *zout* = 0. Finally, we compute the equity curve and the returns. We can plot the results to see the performance of our simple strategy:

```
> plot(strategy$Return, main = "Cumulative returns for IBM", ylim = c(-0.1, 0.27))
> lines(strategy$RetHold, col = "red")
```

This generates the output shown in Figure 10-8. We see that our strategy does outperform the simple "buy-and-hold" strategy.

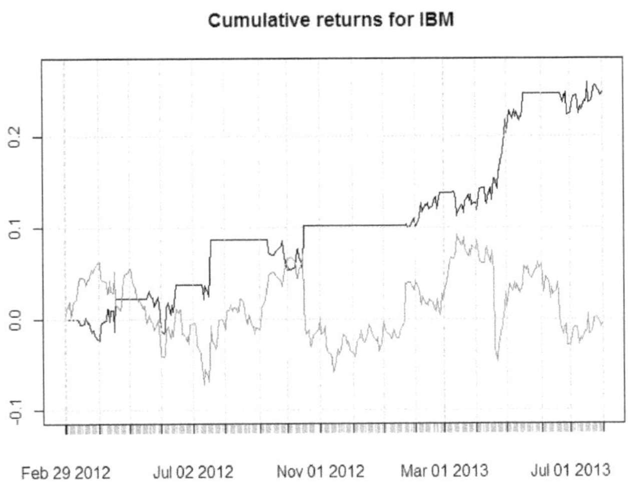


*Figure 10-8. Cumulative returns for IBM based on a moving average strategy.*

We can also calculate the other quantities easily:

```
> numTrades <- sum(abs(diff(strategy$Position, na.pad = F)))
> numTrades      #Number of trades
[1] 15
> Pnl.oneShare <- sum(diff(strategy$Price) * strategy$Position, na.rm = T)
> Pnl.oneShare  #P&L for one share of investment
[1] 49.26001
> rtn <- 100 * sum(ROC(strategy$Price) * strategy$Position, na.rm=T)
> rtn            #Percentage return of fully invested account
[1] 24.78511
```

# Risk Measures

In order to backtest the historical performance of a strategy, in addition to the P&L (or returns), we need to calculate a few important risk measures. The standard risk metrics for quantitative strategies are the Sharpe ratio and the maximum drawdown. The Sharpe ratio is defined as the average of the excess daily returns divided by the standard deviation of those excess daily returns. Here, the excess returns refer to the return of the strategy above the risk-free rate.

Fortunately, we do not need to implement performance-related functions by ourselves in R. The *PerformanceAnalytics* package makes our lives easier. It is a powerful library of functions specifically designed for evaluating the performance and risk characteristics of financial assets. Yet in order to use this package, we need to install it first:

```
> install.packages("PerformanceAnalytics")
> library(PerformanceAnalytics)
```

We can then use the package and the daily return data to perform various risk analysis. First, we can obtain the performance summary using the following code:

```
> ret <- strategy$ReturnDaily  #get daily return data
> ret$RetDailyHold <- strategy$RetDailyHold
> head(ret)
           ReturnDaily RetDailyHold
2012-02-29           0  0.000000000
2012-03-01           0  0.004058257
2012-03-02           0  0.006459118
2012-03-05           0  0.009262369
2012-03-06           0 -0.017089323
2012-03-07           0  0.002582129
> charts.PerformanceSummary(ret, main = "Performance Summary")
```

This produces the output shown in Figure 10-9.

We see that the maximum drawdown from our moving-average based strategy is much smaller than that of the buy-and-hold strategy. The maximum drawdown characterizes the largest peak-to-trough drop in the cumulative return curve over a particular period. The historical backtest results will show the past maximum drawdown, which is a good guide for the future drawdown performance of the strategy.

The risk measures that depend on the maximum drawdown can be directly observable at the end of the given period because they are functions of the price data, and thus can be traded. For example, the price of a futures contract on maximum drawdown can serve as an important risk measure indicator that could be quoted by the market. When the market is in a bubble, the prices of drawdown contracts would be significantly higher. On the other hand, when the market is stable, or when it exhibits mean reversion behavior, the prices of drawdown contracts would become cheaper.

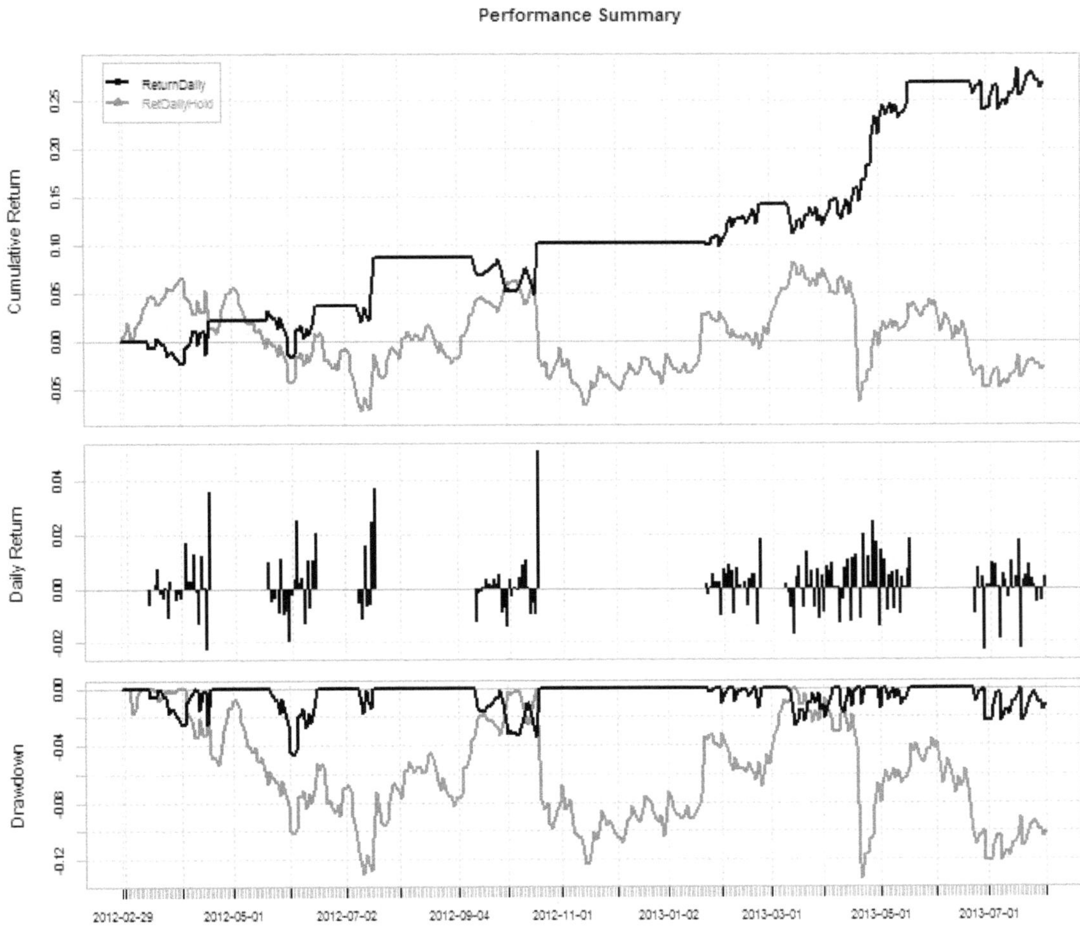


*Figure 10-9. Cumulative return, daily return, and drawdown for IBM.*

The *PerformanceAnalytics* package also allows us to extract drawdown parameters in a table:

```
> table.Drawdowns(ret$ReturnDaily)
        From     Trough         To   Depth Length To Trough Recovery
1 2012-05-22 2012-06-04 2012-06-15 -0.0470     18         9        9
2 2012-09-13 2012-10-16 2012-10-17 -0.0348     25        24        1
3 2013-03-12 2013-03-14 2013-04-05 -0.0267     18         3       15
4 2012-03-21 2012-04-03 2012-04-10 -0.0252     14        10        4
5 2012-04-11 2012-04-17 2012-04-18 -0.0251      6         5        1

> table.Drawdowns(ret$RetDailyHold)
        From     Trough         To   Depth Length To Trough Recovery
1 2013-03-15 2013-04-22       <NA> -0.1338     98        26       NA
2 2012-04-04 2012-07-12 2013-03-14 -0.1298    236        69      167
3 2012-03-06 2012-03-06 2012-03-12 -0.0171      5         1        4
```

```
4 2012-03-19 2012-03-20 2012-03-26 -0.0086      6          2        4
5 2012-03-27 2012-03-27 2012-03-29 -0.0028      3          1        2
```

Another important risk measure is the annualized Sharpe ratios, which can be computed using the daily returns. It shows the annualized performance of our trading strategy. From these yearly results, we can see more clearly how our strategy performs:

```
> table.AnnualizedReturns(ret)
                          ReturnDaily RetDailyHold
Annualized Return              0.1825      -0.0189
Annualized Std Dev             0.1173       0.1770
Annualized Sharpe (Rf=0%)      1.5549      -0.1068
```

The preceding results show that our trading strategy gives an 18.25% return each year and an annualized Sharpe ratio of 1.5549 (for simplicity's sake, here we neglect the risk-free rate).

Value at risk (VaR) is another measure of the risk investments. It determines the possibility of losing a certain amount of money over a certain period. VaR is an industry standard for measuring downside risk. VaR statistic has three components: a time period, a confidence level, and a loss amount (or loss percentage). Here is the code to calculate VaR for a given return series:

```
> VaR(ret, p = 0.95)
     ReturnDaily RetDailyHold
VaR -0.006649175   -0.0197185
```

This result shows that with 95% confidence, we expect that the worst daily loss will not exceed 0.665% for our moving-average based strategy; while for the buy-and-hold strategy, we expect the worst daily loss will not exceed 1.97%, indicating that our strategy is much better than the buy-and-hold strategy.

# Pairs Trading

Pairs trading is a market-neutral trading strategy, that is, the P&L or returns from this strategy is uncorrelated with the market direction. Regardless of whether the market goes up or down, in good times or bad the market neutral strategy performs in a steady manner, and results are typically achieved with a lower volatility. Thus, the pairs trading can help to hedge sector- and market-risk. For example, if the whole market crashes, and the two stocks plummet along with the market, the trade should result in a gain on the short position and a loss on the long position, leaving the profit close to zero in spite of large move. We can create this strategy by matching a long position with a short position in a pair of highly correlated stocks. We categorize the market neutral strategy as a statistical arbitrage and convergence trading strategy.

At any given time, a portfolio with a pair of stocks is associated with a quantity called spread (or price ratio). We can compute the spread using the prices of the two stocks, and the spread forms a new time series. Pairs trading involves going long on the under-performer while simultaneously going short on the over-performer when the spread is substantially away from its mean value. When the spread reverts to its mean value, we will close the positions. The strategy's P&L is derived from the difference in price change between the two stocks, rather than from the direction in which each moves.

Pairs trading is based on the idea of relative pricing. The underlying premise in relative pricing is that stocks with similar characteristics should be priced more or less the same. The pairs trading is a mean-reverting strategy, betting that the prices will eventually revert to their historical trends. It is also a substantially self-funding strategy, since the short sale proceeds may be used to create the long position.

# Pairs Identification

The key to success in pairs trading lies in the identification of stock pairs. First, we can apply an empirical approach based on the stock fundamentals or alternatively on a pure statistical approach based on historical market data. We can find suitable pairs by checking stocks that have something in common. Because of similar market risks, competing companies within the same sector are usually good pair candidates. Examples of potentially correlated pairs including QQQ and SPY, DIA and SPY, Coca-Cola (KO) and Pepsi (PEP), Exxon Mobile (XOM) and Chevron (CVX), etc.

Next, we need to verify whether the pairs are mean-reverting based on statistical evidence from historical data. We can use various statistical techniques for detecting the mean reversion or stationarity for the spread time series of the pairs, including augmented Dickey-Fuller (ADF) test. We can also examine cointegration of a stock pairs using cointegrated augmented Dickey-Fuller (CADF) test and Johansen test. We have presented the detailed explanation about these stationary test approaches in Chapter 8.

Here, I will use a simple correlation method to identify possible pair stocks. The correlation (or R-squared) is a term from linear regression analysis that describes the strength of the relationship between a dependent variable and an independent variable. If we can find two stocks that are correlated enough, any changes in correlation may be followed by a reversion to their mean trend, which may create a trading opportunity.

Let us consider the QQQ and SPY ETFs:

```
> library(quantmod)
> getSymbols(Symbols = c("QQQ", "SPY"), from ="2010-01-01", to = "2016-01-01")
> etfs <- na.omit(merge(Ad(QQQ), Ad(SPY)))
> colnames(etfs) <- c("QQQ","SPY")
> plot(etfs$QQQ/mean(etfs$QQQ), main = "Normalized stock prices for QQQ and SPY")
> lines(etfs$SPY/mean(etfs$SPY), col = "red")
> legend("topleft", c("QQQ", "SPY"), col = c("black", "red"), lty = c(1,1))
> correl <- rollapply(etfs, 100, FUN = function(y){
    t <- cor(as.numeric(y[,1]), as.numeric(y[,2])); return(t)}, by.column = F)
> plot(correl, main = "Correlation between QQQ and SPY", ylim = c(0, 1))
```

Figure 10-10 (left) shows the QQQ and SPY ETFs' stock prices (normalized for comparison) that tend to move together for the most part, as indicated by the rolling correlation between the two price series over a moving window = 100 as shown in Figure 10-10 (right).

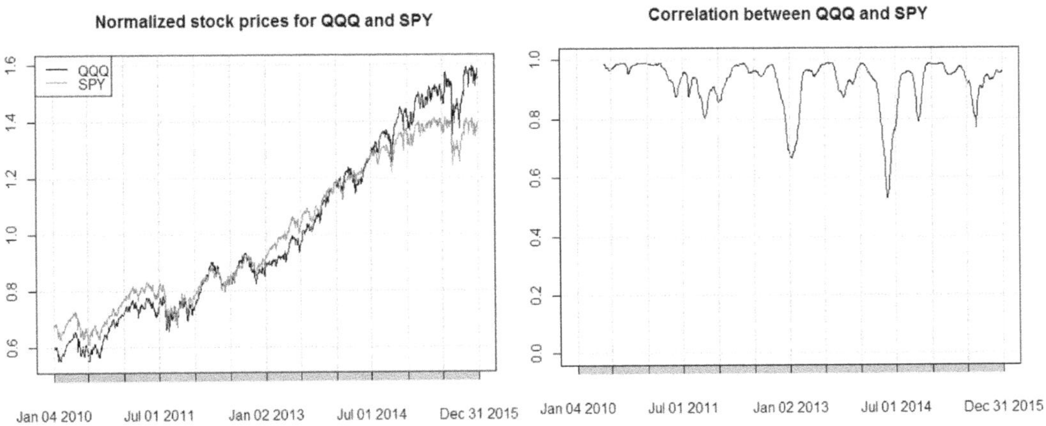


*Figure 10-10. Stock Prices and correlation for QQQ and SPY.*

The correlation between two stock price series is a relative statistical measure of the degree to which these two stocks tend to move together. Values of the correlation coefficient range from −1 to +1. When it is equal to −1, the two series have perfect negative correlation and move in opposite directions; while perfect positive correlation (+1) exists if the two series move in the same direction. Pairs trading attempts to look for stocks with a high degree of correlation. We usually use correlations of 0.8 or above as a benchmark for pairs trading, and consider a correlation less than 0.5 as weak correlated. Ideally, good correlation should present over multiple periods.

You can see from Figure 10-10 that the average rolling correlation between QQQ and SPY is 0.927 and the overall (i.e., when the moving window = the number of data points) correlation is 0.991, indicating that QQQ and SPY are highly correlated.

Now let us check another pair: IBM and INTC:

```
> getSymbols(Symbols = c("IBM", "INTC"), from = "2010-01-01", to = "2016-01-01")
> stocks <- na.omit(merge(Ad(IBM), Ad(INTC)))
> colnames(stocks) <- c("IBM", "INTC")
> plot(stocks$IBM/mean(stocks$IBM), ylim = c(0.6, 1.6),
       main="Normalized stock prices for IBM and INTC")
> lines(stocks$INTC/mean(stocks$INTC), col = "red")
> legend("topleft", c("IBM", "INTC"), col = c("black", "red"), lty = c(1,1))
> correl <- rollapply(stocks, 100, FUN = function(y){
    t <- cor(as.numeric(y[,1]), as.numeric(y[,2])); return(t)}, by.column = F)
>  plot(correl, main = "Correlation between IBM and INTC", ylim = c(-1, 1))
```

This produces the output shown in Figure 10-11. You can see that the prices of IBM and INTC do not move together and sometimes they move in opposite direction. Their correlation oscillates between −1 and +1. The average rolling correlation = 0.375 and the overall correlation = 0.269, meaning that IBM and INTC have very weak correlation.

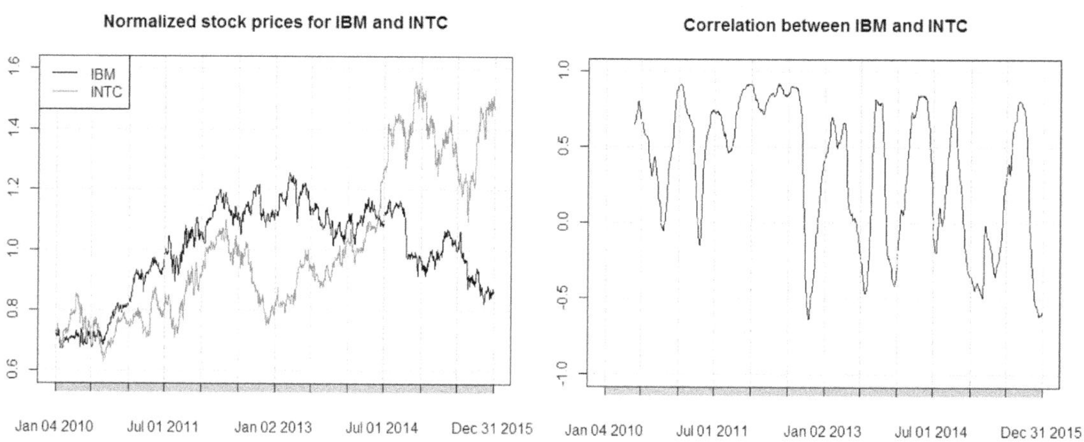


*Figure 10-11. Stock Prices and correlation for IBM and INTC.*

After determining the correlation coefficients, we can use the results as a filter to find the pairs that show the most potential for pairs trading.

## Signals for Pairs Trading

Once we find correlated pairs, we can determine if the relationship is mean reverting; that is, when price goes diverge, will it revert to its statistical mean? In Chapter 8 when we discussed the time series, we construct a portfolio as the weighted sums of the constituent price series, where the weights are the hedge ratios we found from linear regression or from the eigenvalues of the Johansen test:

$$y = h_1 y_1 + h_2 y_2 + \cdots + h_n y_n$$

where $y$ is a stationary time series and $h_i$ is the hedge ratio that tells us the number of shares of each stock. In the case of just two stocks, this reduces to a spread:

$$y = y_1 - h y_2$$

Note that in the above price spread equation, if we set $h = 1$, then the price ratio $y_1/y_2$ is stationary. In this case, the price spread is a direct price difference between two stocks, which is equivalent to using the price ratio. But this is just a special case, we usually do not expect such a price ratio forms the stationary time series. However, many traders still prefer to use the price ratio as the signal for pairs trading because of its simplicity. Here, we define the price ratio as

$$price\ ratio = \frac{price\ of\ stock\ 1}{price\ of\ stock\ 2}$$

Here, we will try to generate trading signals using both the price ratio and price spread for a pair of two stocks.

Add a new function named *priceRatioSignal* to the *strategyHelper.R* file. Here is the code for this function:

```
priceRatioSignal <- function(x, n){
  ratio <- x[,1]/x[,2]
  ma <- rollapply(ratio, n, mean)
  std <- rollapply(ratio, n, sd)
  zs <- (ratio - ma)/std
  x$Signal <- zs
  x <- na.omit(x)
  return(x)
}
```

This function takes a data frame (or *xts*) object and the size of moving window as the inputs, it also assume that the prices for stock 1 and stock 2 are contained in the first and second columns of the input data, respectively.

Consider an example for a pair of ETFs, QQQ and SPY, whose data has been stored in the *etfs* data set. We can easily generate the trading signal using the preceding function:

```
> source("./R/strategyHelper.R")
> ratio.signal <- priceRatioSignal(etfs, 14)
> head(ratio.signal)
                QQQ      SPY     Signal
2010-01-22 41.13985 96.18021 -0.4018966
2010-01-25 41.27960 96.67339 -0.6672382
2010-01-26 41.31686 96.26828  0.9071377
2010-01-27 41.64292 96.72624  1.6634650
2010-01-28 40.57157 95.61657 -1.9431163
2010-01-29 39.86355 94.57735 -2.4162288
```

```
> plot(ratio.signal$Signal, minor.ticks = F, col = "blue")
```

Figure 10-12 shows the trading signal for QQQ and SPY based on the price ratio.

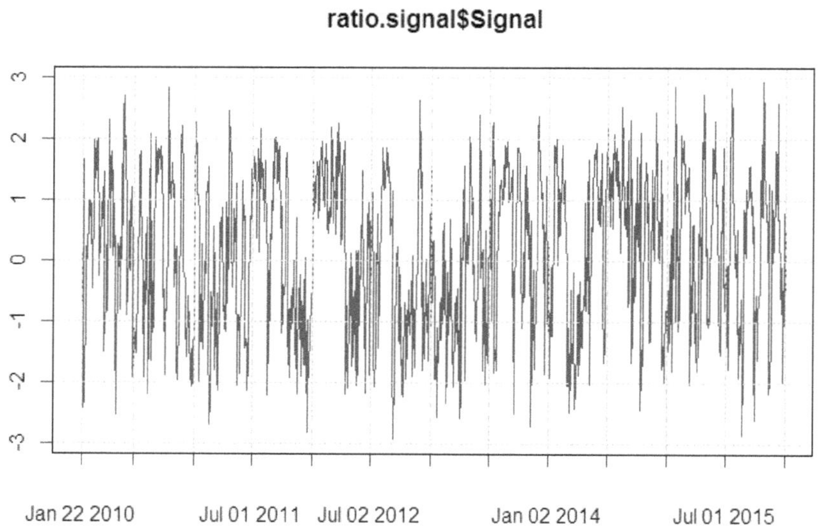


*Figure 10-12. Trading Signal for QQQ and SPY based on the price ratio.*

Now, we can also use the price spread as a trading signal. However, we need to dynamically recalculate the hedge ratio (beta) every day using a short moving window in order to adapt to the changing level of the stock pairs over time. Add a new function named *priceSpreadSignal* to the *strategyHelper.R* file. Here is the code for this function:

```
priceSpreadSignal <- function(x, n){
  lr <- rollapply(x, n, FUN = function(y){
    t <- lm(formula = y[,1] ~ y[,2]); return(t$coef)
  }, by.column = F)
  x$Spread <- x[,1] - lr[,2]*x[,2]
  x <- na.omit(x)
  ma <- rollapply(x$Spread, n, mean)
  std <- rollapply(x$Spread, n, sd)
  zs <- (x$Spread - ma)/std
  x$Signal <- zs
  x <- na.omit(x)
  return(x)
}
```

Here, we use the first stock as the dependent variable and the second stock as the independent variable when we carry out the linear regression. We define the spread as

$$spread = price1 - \beta \times price2$$

for each moving window. We then calculate the Z-score for the spread within the moving window as the trading signal.

Let us use the above function to generate the trading for QQQ and SPY based on the price spread:

```
> source("./R/strategyHelper.R")
```

```
> spread.signal <- priceSpreadSignal(etfs, 14)
> head(spread.signal)
                QQQ      SPY   Spread    Signal
2010-02-10 40.07782 94.24269 1.253981 1.0549484
2010-02-11 40.68336 95.22906 2.615565 1.4235782
2010-02-12 40.76721 95.14980 4.549604 1.6802001
2010-02-16 41.28891 96.64697 4.803251 1.5509789
2010-02-17 41.52181 97.10494 5.925110 1.6286599
2010-02-18 41.78266 97.67739 2.361115 0.7950526
> plot(spread.signal$Signal, minor.ticks = F, col = "blue")
```

This produces the output shown in Figure 10-13.

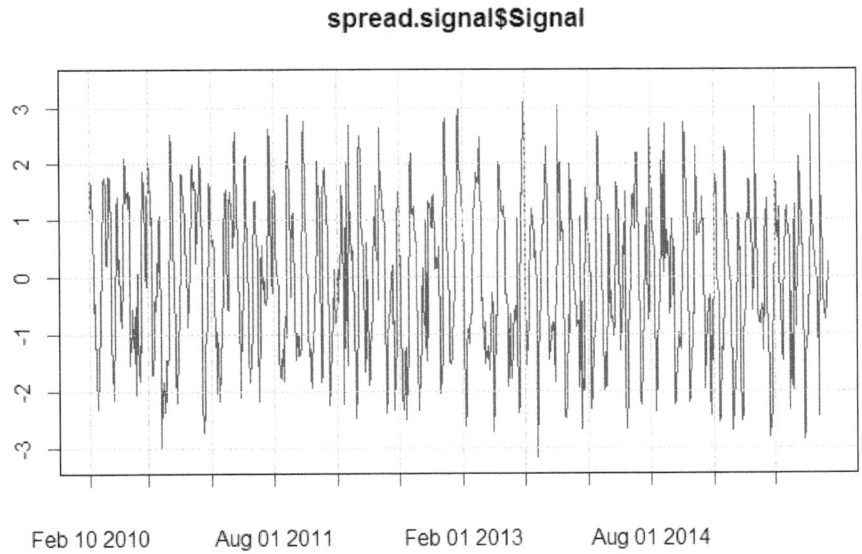


*Figure 10-13. Trading signal for QQQ and SPY based on the price spread.*

# Market Neutral

Here I will show you how to construct a market neutral position using the trading signal. We have two choices: beta neutral or dollar neutral. The beta neutral targets a zero total beta of a pair portfolio (i.e., the beta of the long side equals the beta of the short side). While the dollar neutrality has the virtue of simplicity, but may not be market neutral. We can use the linear regression to calculate the beta or hedge ratio to make the beta neutral strategy.

Add a new function named *rollingBeta* to the *strategyHelper.R* file. Here is the code for this function:

```
rollingBeta <- function(x, n){
  lr <- rollapply(x, n, FUN = function(y){
    t <- lm(formula = y[,1] ~ y[,2]); return(t$coef)
  }, by.column = F)
  return(na.omit(lr[,2]))
}
```

Now, we can calculate the overall beta and the rolling beta:

```
> lm(etfs[,1] ~ etfs[,2])
```

```
Call:
lm(formula = etfs[, 1] ~ etfs[, 2])

Coefficients:
(Intercept)    etfs[, 2]
   -14.9988       0.5869

> source("./R/strategyHelper.R")
> beta <- rollingBeta(etfs, 100)
> mean(beta)
[1] 0.5414415
```

We see that for the specified period (100 trading days here), the average rolling beta = 0.541 and the overall beta = 0.587, indicating that QQQ will change 0.541% relative to a 1% movement of SPY, that is, SPY has a higher volatility.

In order to create a market neutral position, we need to construct a hedge position using the beta as the hedge ratio. For example, if the total notional we want to invest in the long-short strategy is $N$ and the hedge ratio is β, then the investments in the first stock and second stock, $N_1$ and $N_2$, can be calculate using the following formula:

$$N_1 = \frac{N}{1+\beta}, \quad N_2 = \frac{\beta N}{1+\beta}$$

In the above formula, we will obtain the dollar neutrality if we set $\beta = 1$.

Here, for the simplicity's sake, we will use the constant beta (average rolling beta or the overall beta) as the hedge ratio to determine the relative notional size of the two stocks. However, the rolling beta between stock pairs does vary over time, which is because the two stocks do not always move together. Sometimes, one stock may move faster than the other and vice versa. Therefore, we can use the rolling beta as the dynamical hedge ratio to over- or under-weight the notional. I will leave this dynamic beta hedge problem for your exercise.

## P&L for Pairs Trading

We can now compute the P&L for pairs trading using a constant hedge ratio. Add a new function named *pairPnL* to the *strategyHelper.R* file. Here is the code for this function:

```
pairPnL <- function(x, zin, zout, h){
  h1 <- 1/(1+h)
  h2 <- h/(1+h)
  x1 <- merge(x[,1], x$Signal)
  x2 <- merge(x[,2], x$Signal)
  pnl1 <- longShortStrategy(x1, zin, zout)
  pnl2 <- longShortStrategy(x2, zin, zout)
  pnl <- data.frame(Date = index(pnl1), Price1 = as.numeric(pnl1$Price))
  pnl$Price2 <- as.numeric(pnl2$Price)
  pnl$Signal <- pnl1$Zscore
  pnl$ReturnDaily <- h1*as.numeric(pnl1$ReturnDaily) -
                     h2*as.numeric(pnl2$ReturnDaily)
  pnl$Return <- cumsum(pnl$ReturnDaily)
  return(xts(pnl[,-1], order.by = pnl[,1]))
}
```

Here, we calculate the P&L of these two stocks separately using the hedge ratio and the *longShortStrategy* function. Note that we reverse the sign of the returns for the second stock, that is, we want to short the second stock if the first stock is long at a given date, and vice versa.

Let us consider an example for a pair of QQQ and SPY. We will use the preceding function and the pair-trading signal to computer returns for this pair. For the signal based on the price ratio, we have:

```
> source("./R/strategyHelper.R")
> library(PerformanceAnalytics)
> pnl.ratio <- pairPnL(ratio.signal, 2, 0, 0.54)
> charts.PerformanceSummary(pnl.ratio$ReturnDaily, main = "Performance Summary")
```

This produces the cumulative returns for the pair trading of QQQ and SPY, which is shown in Figure 10-14.

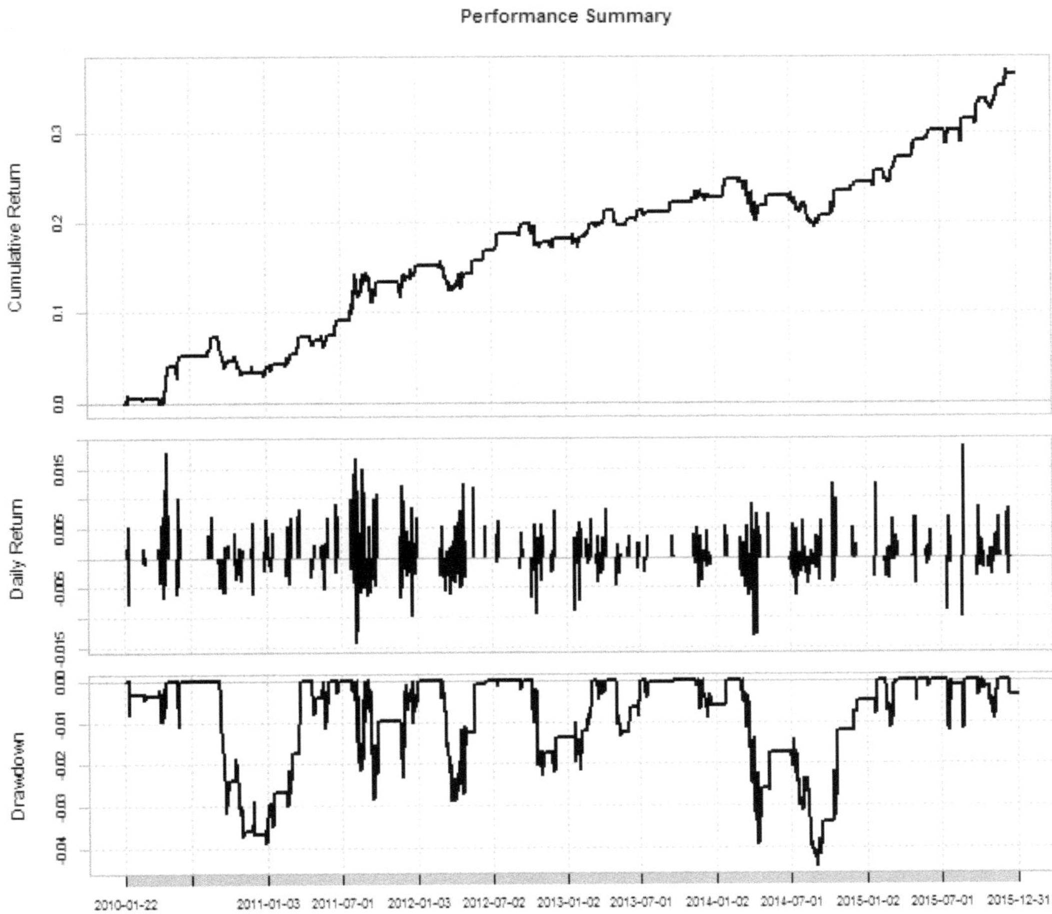


*Figure 10-14. Cumulative returns for pair trading of QQQ and SPY using price-ratio signal.*

We can also calculate the risk measure parameters, for example, the Sharpe ratio:

```
> table.AnnualizedReturns(pnl.ratio$ReturnDaily)
                          ReturnDaily
```

```
Annualized Return              0.0539
Annualized Std Dev             0.0411
Annualized Sharpe (Rf=0%)      1.3115
```

We can also compute the P&L for the pair using the price-spread signal with different input parameters:

```
> pnl.spread <- pairPnL(spread.signal, 0.5, 0.2, 0.48)
> charts.PerformanceSummary(pnl.spread$ReturnDaily, main = "Performance Summary")
```

This generates the output shown in Figure 10-15.

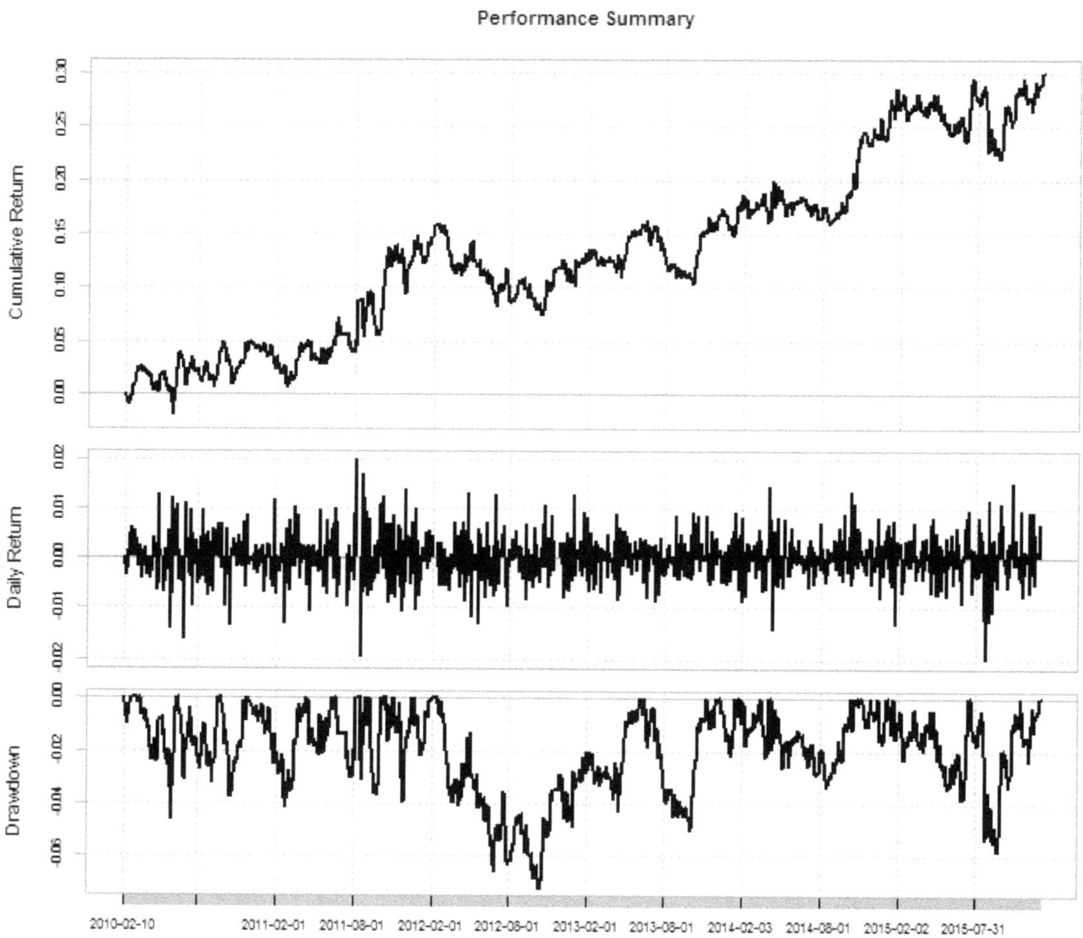


*Figure 10-15. Cumulative returns for pair trading of QQQ and SPY using price-spread signal.*

The corresponding Sharpe ratio is given by:

```
> table.AnnualizedReturns(pnl.spread$ReturnDaily)
                          ReturnDaily
Annualized Return              0.0455
Annualized Std Dev             0.0650
Annualized Sharpe (Rf=0%)      0.7001
```

In this section, we just present the detailed procedures for pairs trading and do not pay attention to maximize the returns and Sharpe ratio by optimizing the pairs-trading models. In practice, we can tune various parameters, such as the size of the moving window used in creating the trading signal, the entry/exit *Z*-scores, and the hedge ratio.

Note that pairs trading also involves investment risks, such as model risk and execution risk. The model risk occurs when the model used to create the pairs trading strategy does not perform as expected. This can be due to a number of factors such as inaccurate research, unsound logic, changing circumstances, and misinterpreted results. The execution risk can negatively affect the return for a pair trade. Here, our backtest completely ignores this type of risk. The execution risk refers to the possibility that the strategy will not be executed as planned. For example, we may experience slippage in price or may receive a partial fill on an order, resulting in reduced profit potential.

# Regime-Switching Model

Figure 10-16 shows the weekly returns of S&P 500 index and its volatility index (VIX). We see that the return and volatility vary greatly over time, suggesting that there may exist different regimes, and the mean return and volatility are higher in one regime than in the other.

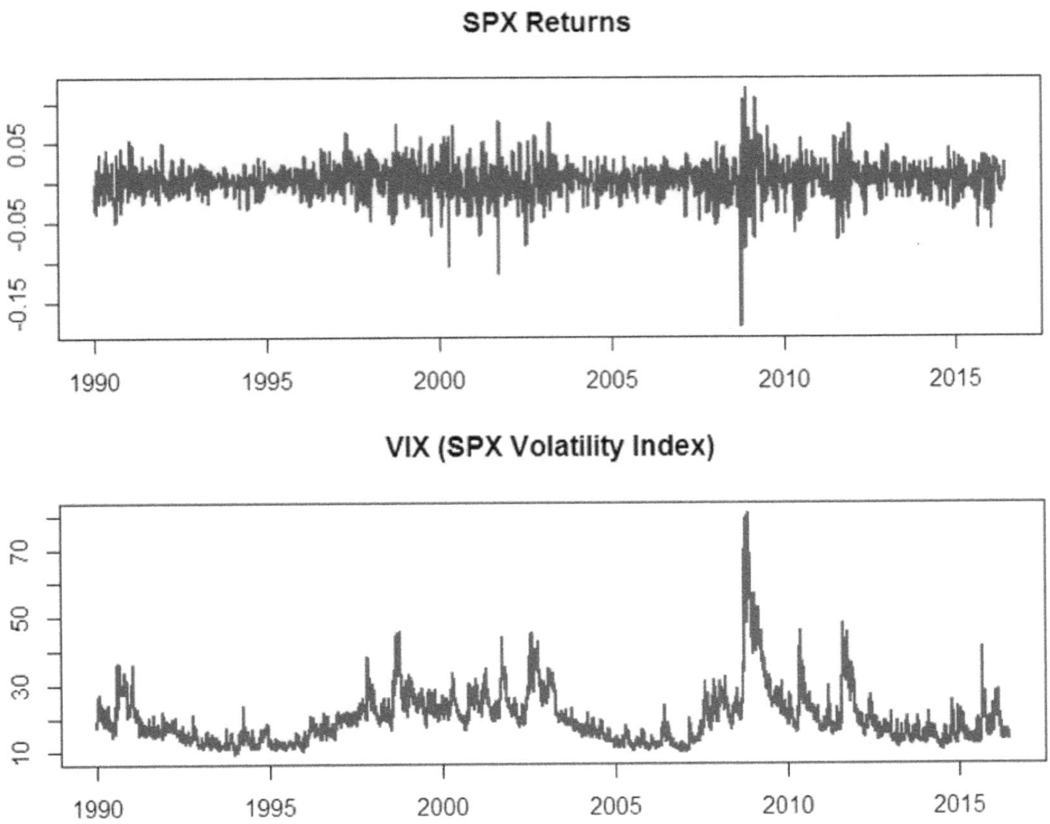


*Figure 10-16. Weekly returns of SPX (top) and VIX (bottom) from 1/1/1990 to 6/1/2016.*

We can define regimes using the mean return and volatility, with each regime representing different economic situation. Identification of different regimes is important for understanding the time series properties of stock returns and may be valuable for developing profitable trading strategy.

# Hidden Markov Model

The regime-switching model, also known as the Hidden Markov switching model, is a nonlinear time series model, which involves multiple structures that can be characterize the time series behaviors in different regimes. The main feature of this model is the possibility for some or all parameters of the model to switch across different regimes (states) according to Markov process, which governed by a state variable $s_t$. We assume that the state variable evolves according to a first-order Markov chain, with transition probability

$$\Pr(s_t = j | s_{t-1} = i) = p_{ij}$$

which indicates the probability of switching from state $i$ at time $t-1$ into state $j$ at $t$. Usually these probabilities are grouped together into a transition matrix

$$P = \begin{bmatrix} p_{11} & p_{21} \\ p_{12} & p_{22} \end{bmatrix} = \begin{bmatrix} p & 1-q \\ 1-p & q \end{bmatrix}$$

where for simplicity's sake, we only consider two regimes in the model. The ergodic probability (i.e. the unconditional probability) of being in state $s_t = 1$ is given by $\pi_1 = (1-p)/(2-p-q)$.

We can use the hidden Markov model (HMM) to determine the state transition probabilities and the distribution parameters for each state, that is, it can work out all the details that are "hidden" from an observer of a process. All we really need to do is to specify how many states in the model.

We can model the stock return series as a mixture of Gaussian distribution and discrete Markov chain. In a certain regime, stock series follow geometric Brownian motion with drift, which means stock returns have Gaussian distribution and regimes are changing by the discrete Markov process.

In a bull market, the stock return has a low volatility while it has high volatility in a bear market. In this case, we have two economic states, i.e. bull and bear, and each state has different mean return and volatility. The regime switching occurs randomly in this model. However, the switching probability is fixed and consistent through out the stock return series. We can then use the above transition matrix to describe this situation.

We can use the *depmixS4* package to specify and fit the HMM model. The package uses the expectation-maximization (EM) algorithm to perform optimization. We can do the model fitting using this package in two steps: first, we specify models through the *depmix* function, and then use the *fit* function to fit the models with specified constraints.

Here, we will take SPX as an example. The inputs for the HMM model will be SPX return and volatility index VIX. Add a new function named *hmmSPX* to the *strategyHelper.R* file. Here is the code for this function:

```
hmmSPX <- function(){
   getSymbols(symbols = c("^GSPC", "^VIX"), from = "2000-01-01", to ="2016-06-01")
   rtn <- ROC(Cl(GSPC))
   dat <- na.omit(merge(rtn, Cl(VIX)))
   colnames(dat) <- c("SpxReturn","VIX")
   set.seed(123)
   hmm <- depmix(list(SpxReturn ~ 1, VIX ~ 1), data = dat, nstates = 2,
```

```
                family = list(gaussian(), gaussian()))
  hmmFit <- fit(hmm, verbose = FALSE)
  res <- list(hmmFit, rtn, Cl(VIX))
  return(res)
}
```

Sourcing in this function and running it, we have:

```
> source("./R/strategyHelper.R")
> hmm <- hmmSPX()
> hmmFit <- hmm[[1]]
> rtn <- hmm[[2]]
> vix <- hmm[[3]]
```

We can examine the transition matrix:

```
> summary(hmmFit)
Initial state probabilties model
pr1 pr2
  0   1

Transition matrix
        toS1  toS2
fromS1 0.991 0.009
fromS2 0.011 0.989

Response parameters
Resp 1 : gaussian
Resp 2 : gaussian
    Re1.(Intercept) Re1.sd Re2.(Intercept) Re2.sd
St1           0.001  0.006          14.628  2.359
St2           0.000  0.015          25.966  7.726
```

The above transition matrix gives us the probability of switching from one state to the next. We can obtain the probabilities for each state over our data set by post-processing the model:

```
> result <- posterior(hmmFit)
> head(result)
  state           S1        S2
1     2 0.0000000000 1.0000000
2     2 0.0078588037 0.9921412
3     2 0.0025525879 0.9974474
4     2 0.0057936018 0.9942064
5     2 0.0001158573 0.9998841
6     2 0.0002329353 0.9997671
```

In order to see how the states switch over the entire data set, we can plot various quantities together:

```
> dt <- index(rtn); dt <- dt[-1]
> layout(matrix(c(1, 2, 3, 4, 5), ncol = 1),heights = c(1.2, 1, 1, 1, 1.2), TRUE)
> par(mar = c(1, 4, 2, 1.5))
> plot(index(rtn), as.numeric(rtn),ty = "l",main = "Return", xlab = "",
       ylab = "Return", panel.first = grid(), mgp = c(2, 0.4,0))
> par(mar = c(1, 4, 0.6, 1.5))
> plot(index(vix), as.numeric(vix), ty = "l", xlab = "", ylab = "VIX",
       panel.first = grid(), mgp = c(2, 0.4, 0))
> par(mar = c(1, 4, 0.6, 1.5))
> plot(dt, result$S1, ty = "l", xlab = "", ylab = "State 1", panel.first = grid(),
```

```
      mgp = c(2, 0.4, 0))
> par(mar = c(1, 4, 0.6, 1.5))
> plot(dt, result$S2, ty = "l", xlab = "", ylab = "State 2", panel.first = grid(),
      mgp = c(2, 0.4, 0))
> par(mar = c(4, 4, 0.6, 1.5))
> plot(dt, result$state,ty = "l",xlab = "Date", ylab = "HMM State",
      mgp = c(2, 0.4, 0))
```

This generates the output shown in Figure 10-17. We see from the results that the state 1 corresponds to the low volatility while the state 2 to the high volatility. The final state gives us the noise-free signal of the HMM model.

## Average True Range Indicator

In the preceding section, we use the return and volatility to identify different regimes for SPX using the HMM model. For common stocks, we can calculate their volatilities using their historical price data. Instead, we can also use the volatility technical indicator called average true range (ATR), which provides a degree of price volatility. The average true range is an $n$-day smoothed moving average of the true range (TR) values. In practice, we usually use a 14-period smoothing.

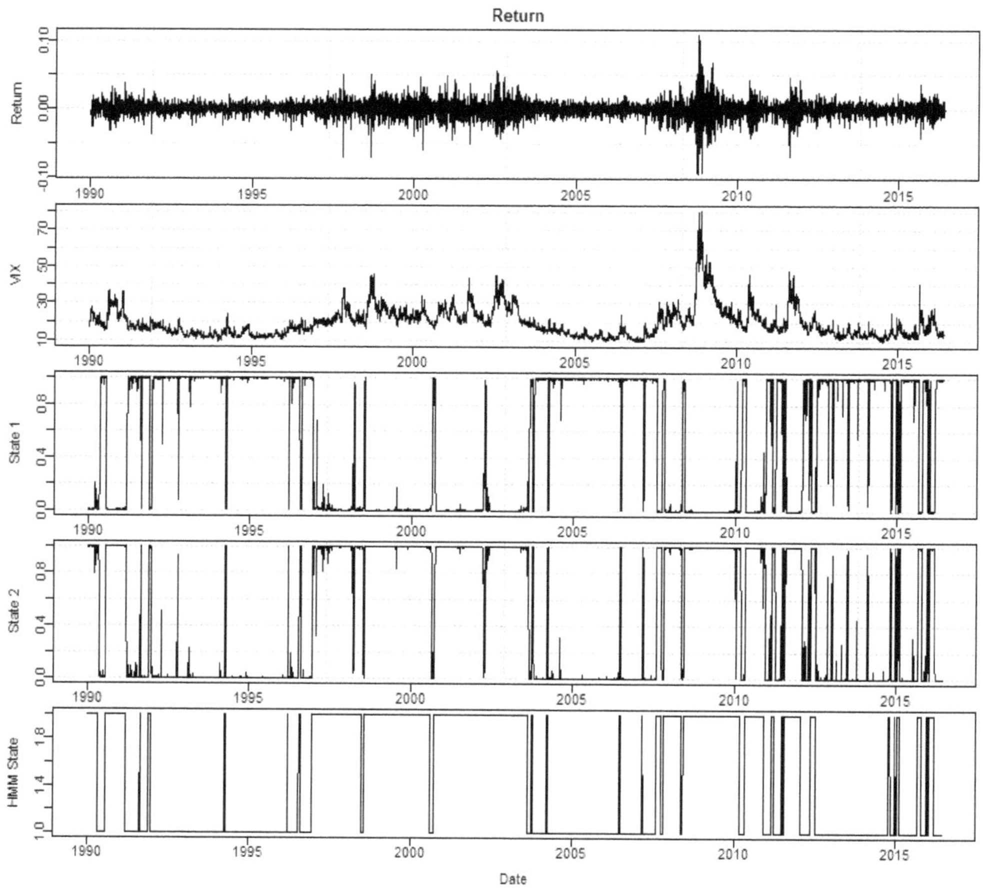


*Figure 10-17. Results from hidden Markov model for SPX.*

The range of a day's trading is simply *high – low*. The true range extends it to yesterday's closing price if it was outside of today's range:

$$TR = \max\left[(high - low), \text{abs}\left(high - close_{prev}\right), \text{abs}(low - close_{prev})\right]$$

We can calculate the ATR at time *t* using the following formula based on the exponential moving average:

$$ATR_t = \frac{1}{n}\left[ATR_{t-1}(n-1) + TR_t\right]$$

We can calculate the first ATR value using the arithmetic mean formula:

$$ATR = \frac{1}{n}\sum_{i=1}^{n} TR_i$$

The *TTR* package includes the ATR indicator, which allows us to calculate the ATR values based on stock's high, low, and close price data. For example, we can use the following code to calculate ATR for SPX:

```
> atr <- ATR(HLC(GSPC), 14)
> plot(index(atr$atr), as.numeric(atr$atr), type = "l", col = "blue",
       main = "ATR for SPX")
```

This produces the output shown in Figure 10-18.

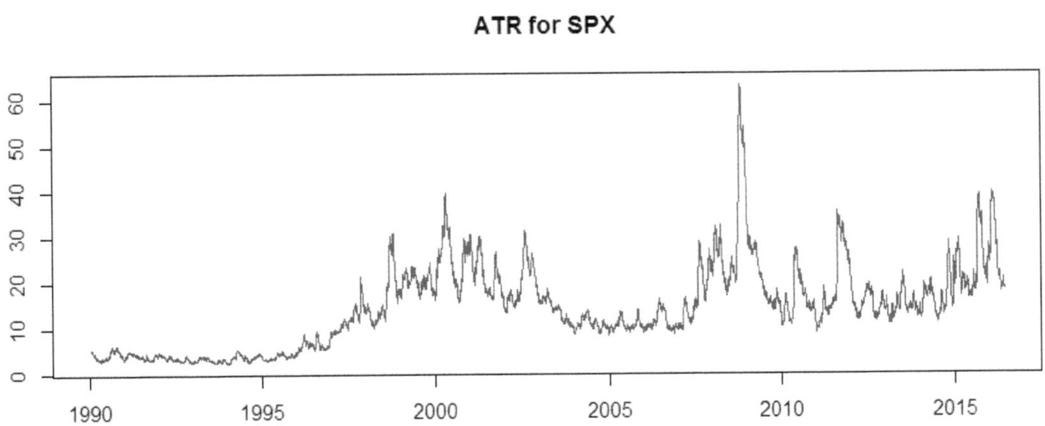


*Figure 10-18. ATR for SPX.*

We see that this ATR curve is very similar to the SPX volatility (VIX) curve in Figure 10-17. Therefore, we can use the stock return and its ATR value as inputs of the HMM model.

## Regime-Switching Strategy

As mentioned previously, in a bull market, the stocks tend to have a low volatility while they tend to have a high volatility in a bear market. These two different economic states can be identified using the HMM model. The HMM state values clearly tell us that we would have a high volatility state when the HMM state value = 2 and a low volatility state when the HMM state value = 1.

Now, we can use the HMM state information to implement a simple trading strategy: we will long the stock when the HMM state value = 1 (bull market); and short the stock when the HMM state value = 2 (bear market). Add a new function named *hmmPnL* to the *strategyHelper.R* file. Here is the code for this function:

```
hmmPnL <- function(ticker, startDate, endDate){
  options(warn = -1)
  stock <- getSymbols(ticker, from = startDate, to = endDate, auto.assign = F)
  rtn <- ROC(Cl(stock), n = 1, type = "discrete")
  atr <- (ATR(HLC(stock), n = 14))$atr
  modelData <- na.omit(merge(rtn, atr))
  colnames(modelData) <- c("Return","ATR")
  set.seed(1)
  hmm <- depmix(list(Return ~ 1, ATR ~ 1), data = modelData, nstates=2,
                family=list(gaussian(), gaussian()))
  hmmFit <- fit(hmm, verbose = FALSE)
  hmmPost <- posterior(hmmFit)
  pnl <- merge(modelData$Return, hmmPost$state)
  colnames(pnl) <- c("Return","HmmState")
  pnl$Signal <- 0
  pnl$Signal[pnl$HmmState == 1] <- 1
  pnl$Signal[pnl$HmmState == 2] <- -1
  pnl$Signal <- Lag(pnl$Signal)
  pnl$Signal[1] <- 0
  pnl$ReturnHmm <- cumsum(pnl$Return*pnl$Signal)
  pnl$ReturnDailyHmm <- pnl$Return*pnl$Signal
  pnl$ReturnHold <- cumsum(pnl$Return)
  pnl$ReturnDailyHold <- pnl$Return
  return(pnl)
}
```

Here, we first calculate the ATR values for the specified stock and then extract the HMM state information from the HMM model. Finally, we compute the P&L for both the regime-switching and buy-and-hold strategies.

Let us consider SPY using the HMM model:

```
> source("./R/strategyHelper.R")
> pnl <- hmmPnL("SPY", "2000-01-01", "2016-06-01")
> getSymbols("SPY", from = "2000-01-01", to = "2016-06-01")
> layout(1:2)
> plot(index(SPY), as.numeric(Cl(SPY)), ty = "l", col = "blue",
       main = "Stock Price for SPY", xlab = "Date", ylab = "Price")
> plot(index(pnl), as.numeric(pnl$ReturnHmm), ty = "l", col = "blue",
       main = "Cumulative Return for SPY", xlab = "Date",
       ylab = "Cumulative Return", ylim = c(-1,2))
> lines(index(pnl), as.numeric(pnl$ReturnHold), col = "red")
> legend("topleft", c("Regime Switching", "Buy-and-hold"), col = c("blue", "red"),
         lty = c(1, 1))
```

This produces the output shown in Figure 10-19.

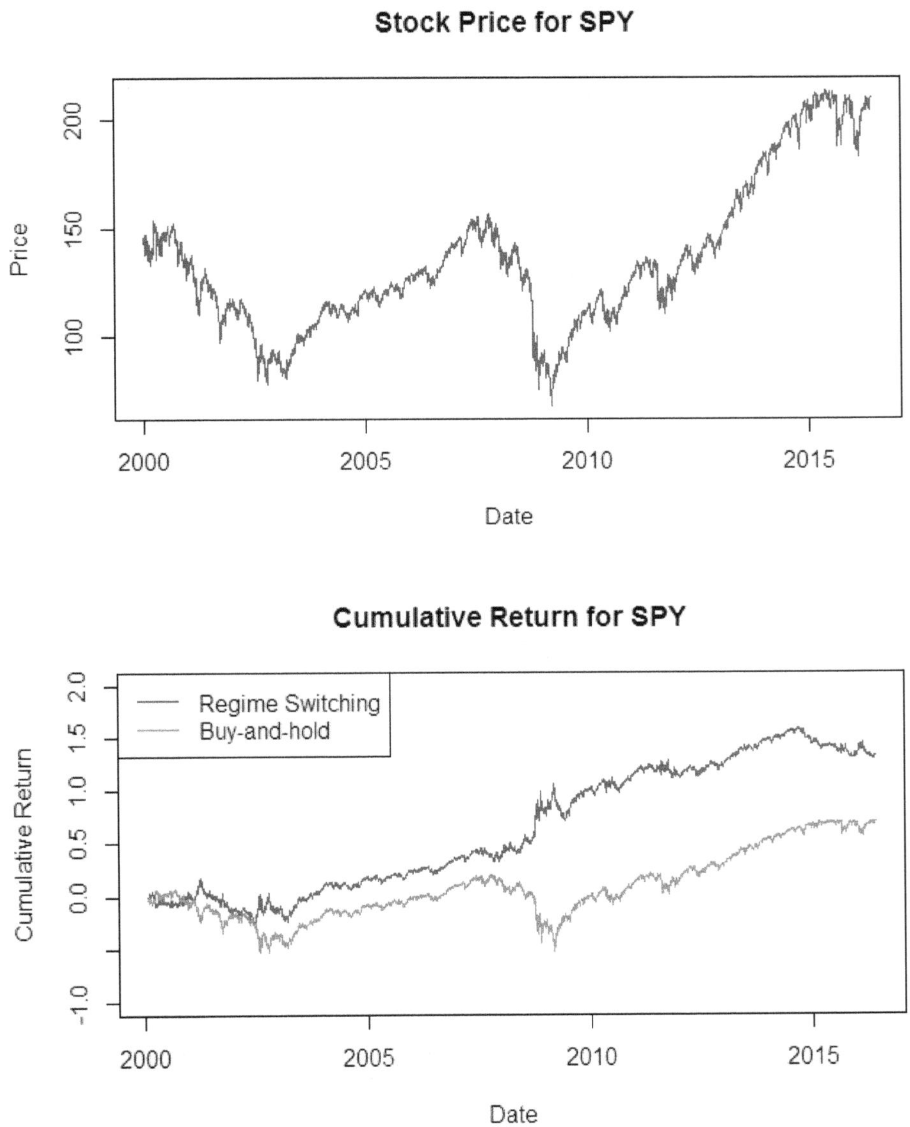


*Figure 10-19. Stock price and cumulative returns for SPY.*

We see from the results in Figure 10-19 that the regime-switching model outperforms the buy-and-hold strategy significantly, especially during the periods of financial crisis (around 2002 and 2008). The region-switching model works well for most index ETFs, including QQQ, DIA, and most Select Sector SPDR ETFS.

However, the gold related indices or ETFs are usually exhibit an opposite trend: in a bear stock market, the gold price usually goes up while it goes down in a bull market. We can use the HMM model to examine this for SPDR Gold Trust ETF (GLD):

```
> source("./R/strategyHelper.R")
> gld <- hmmPnL("GLD", "2000-01-01", "2016-06-01")
```

```
> plot(index(gld), -as.numeric(gld$ReturnHmm), type = "l", col = "blue",
       main = "Cumulative Return for GLD")
> lines(index(gld), as.numeric(gld$ReturnHold), col = "red")
> legend("topleft", c("Regime Switching", "Buy-and-Hold"), col = c("blue", "red"),
         lty = c(1, 1))
```

Note that we plot the negative return from the HMM model, which is equivalent to reverse the sign of HMM state values. The above code generates the output shown in Figure 10-20.

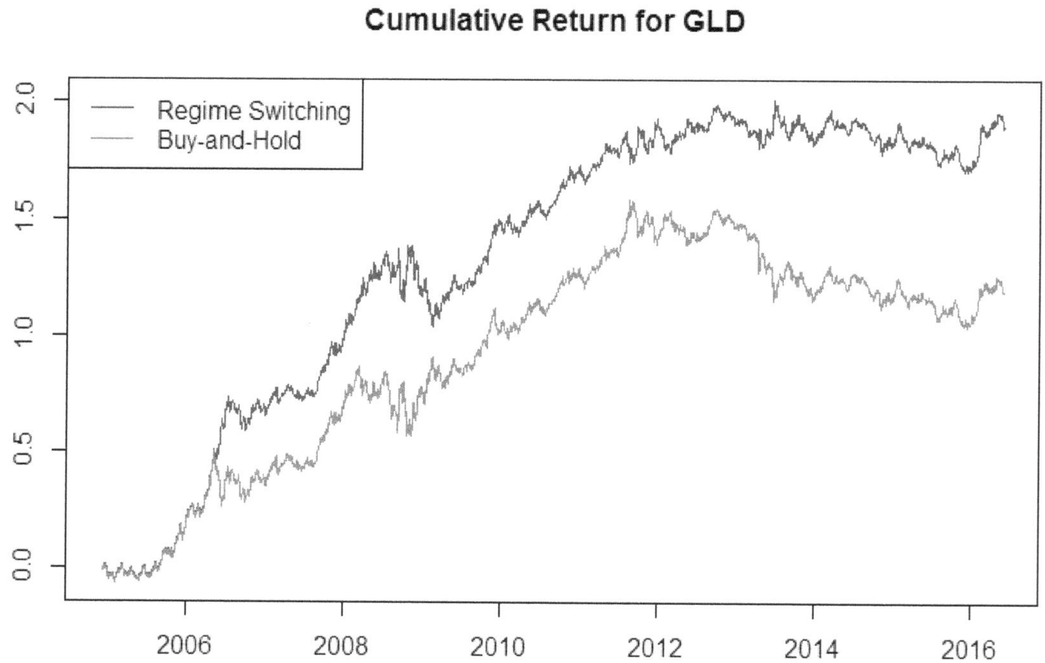


*Figure 10-20. P&L for GLD.*

# R Packages for Trading System

If you read through this chapter, you should have a better understanding about trading strategy backtesting. It involves several components: creation of the trading signals based on historical data; implementation of the trade entry and exit rules; and P&L computation. Of course, there is another important component, which is not discussed in this book, that is, the order execution.

If you are an individual trader and simply trading stocks and ETFs, you can implement and backtest your trading strategies easily by following the procedure presented in this book, because R provides various functions and chart capabilities for serving your basic needs. However, if you have complex multi-asset classes and multi-currency portfolios, you may consider using advanced packages, such as *quantstrat*. This package provides a generic infrastructure to model and backtest signal-based quantitative strategies. It is a high-level abstraction layer (built on *xts*, *FinancialInstrument*, *blotter*, etc.), which allows you to build and test strategies in very few lines of code. The package uses *FinancialInstrument* to specify instruments and currencies, and use *blotter* to keep track of transactions, valuations, and P&L across portfolios and accounts. However, the *quantstrat* package is not an execution platform in and of itself.

For financial institutions, there are custom tools for doing that while for independent quantitative traders, Interactive Brokers is probably the best bet.

The signal-based strategy model in *quantstrat* first creates the security instruments that contains market data. The model then generates indicators that are quantitative values derived from market data (e.g. moving average, RSI, MACD, Bollinger bands, customized functions, etc.). We should apply indicators to market data in a vectorized (for fast backtesting) or streaming (for live execution) fashion.

Next, we can generates trading signals based on the interaction between indicators and market data (e.g. crossovers, thresholds, multiples, etc.). These signals are points in time at which we may want to take some action, even though we may not able to. Like indicators, signals may be applied in a vectorized or streaming fashion.

Trading rules use market data, indicators, signals, and current account/portfolio characteristics to generate orders. Notice that trading rules about position sizing, fill simulation, order generation/ management, etc. are separate from the indicator and signal generation process. Unlike indicators and signals, trading rules are generally evaluated in a path-dependent fashion and are aware of all prior market data and current positions at the time of evaluation.

In the following sections, we will backtest several simple strategies using *quantstrat*.

# Using Standard Indicators

In this section, I will show you how to backtest a trading strategy using *quantstrat* with standard technical indicators from the *TTR* package, specifically the Bollinger band indicator (*BBands*).

To use *quantstrat*, we first need to install the package:

```
> install.packages(pkgs = c("FinancialInstrument", "blotter", "quantstrat"),
                   repos="http://R-Forge.R-project.org")
> library(quantstrat)
```

Next, we need to initialize a currency and a stock instrument, and load historic market data:

```
> ticker = "IBM"
> currency("USD")
> stock(ticker, currency = "USD", multiplier = 1)
> initDate <- "2011-01-01"
> endDate <- "2012-12-31"
> initEq <- 1.0e6
> Sys.setenv(TZ = "UTC")
> getSymbols(ticker, from = initDate, to = endDate, adjust = TRUE,
             index.class = "POSIXct")
```

Note that *quantstrat* uses *blotter* functions for instrument initialization and the currency and stock instrument objects are stored in the *.instrument* environment in *blotter*. To load market data into R, we must set the timezone and use a *POSIX* time-date index class. Here, we will use the dividend and split adjusted OHLC market data by setting *adjust* = *TRUE*.

Next, we need to initialize the portfolio, account, orders, and strategy:

```
> qs.strategy <- "qsBBands"
> rm.strat(qs.strategy)
> initPortf(qs.strategy, symbols = ticker, initDate=initDate)
> initAcct(qs.strategy, portfolios = qs.strategy, initDate = initDate,
          initEq = initEq)
```

```
> initOrders(portfolio = qs.strategy, initDate = initDate)
> strategy(qs.strategy, store = T)
> addPosLimit(portfolio = qs.strategy, ticker, initDate, 100, 1)
```

Note that the function *rm.strat* removes any strategy, portfolio, account, or order book object with the specified strategy name, which facilitates re-running the code for debugging. Here, the *blotter* functions are used for portfolio and account initialization. The function *initOrders* sets up an order container for the portfolio while the *strategy* function creates a strategy object.

The *addPosLimit* function works with *osMaxPos* to set and enforce position-sizing limits. If *levels* = 1, then all order sizing will be in complete control of the strategy rules, up to the maximum position specified using *addPosLimit*'s *maxpos* and *minpos* arguments. Note that simply setting a position limit will not do anything, the strategy entry rules also need to specify the use of order sizing function *osMaxPos*, most typically as an argument to *ruleSignal*.

From here, we add indicators:

```
> add.indicator(strategy = qs.strategy, name = "BBands", arguments =
                list(HLC = quote(HLC(mktdata)), maType = "SMA", n = 20, sd = 2),
                label = "BBands")
```

Here, the name of the indicator must be an R function or the name of the standard indicator from the *TTR* package, and the *arguments* field is used to pass parameters to the indicator function.

Now, we can add the trading signals to our strategy:

```
> add.signal(strategy = qs.strategy, name="sigCrossover",
             arguments = list(columns = c("Close", "up"), relationship = "gt"),
             label = "Cl.gt.UpperBand")
> add.signal(strategy = qs.strategy, name="sigCrossover",
             arguments = list(columns = c("Close", "dn"), relationship = "lt"),
             label = "Cl.lt.LowerBand")
> add.signal(strategy = qs.strategy, name="sigCrossover",
             arguments = list(columns = c("High", "Low", "mavg"),
             relationship = "op"), label = "Cross.Mid")
```

*quantstrat* supports several different signal types, including *sigCrossover*, *sigComparison*, *sigThreshold*, *sigFormula*, etc. Here, we add three *sigCrossover* signals to our strategy. Specifically, *sigCrossover* returns *TRUE* on the period in which there is a crossover in the direction specified by *relationship*, and *NA* otherwise.

Next, we add trading rules to our strategy:

```
> add.rule(strategy = qs.strategy, name = 'ruleSignal',
           arguments = list(sigcol="Cl.gt.UpperBand", sigval = TRUE,
           orderqty = -100, ordertype='market', orderside = "short",
           osFUN = osMaxPos, TxnFees = -2), type = 'enter')
> add.rule(strategy = qs.strategy, name = 'ruleSignal',
           arguments = list(sigcol = "Cl.lt.LowerBand", sigval = TRUE,
           orderqty= 100, ordertype = 'market', orderside = "long",
           osFUN = osMaxPos, TxnFees = -2), type = 'enter')
> add.rule(strategy = qs.strategy, name = 'ruleSignal',
           arguments = list(sigcol = "Cross.Mid", sigval = TRUE, orderqty= 'all',
           ordertype = 'market', orderside = NULL, osFUN = osMaxPos), type = 'exit')
```

Here, we enter a short position when the close price crosses above the upper band of the Bollinger bands, and a long position when the close price crosses below the lower band. We flat all of our positions when the close price crosses the center of the Bollinger bands. Note that we add a transaction cost of 2 dollars for a 100-share round-trip trade, which is the cost from Interactive Brokers.

The *strategy* object now contains a complete set of quantitative trading signals and rules, which are ready to be applied to a portfolio of assets. Next, we can call the *applyStrategy* function to generate transactions in the specified portfolio.

```
applyStrategy(strategy = qs.strategy , portfolios = qs.strategy)
```

The above function uses the R core function *get* to load market data for each symbol during strategy evaluation unless the user passes *mktdata* in the call to *applyStrategy*.

Now, we can examine the transaction details using the following command:

```
> getTxns(Portfolio = qs.strategy, Symbol = ticker)
           Txn.Qty Txn.Price Txn.Fees Txn.Value Txn.Avg.Cost Net.Txn.Realized.PL
2011-01-01       0    0.0000        0      0.00       0.0000             0.00000
2011-03-02     100  152.5421       -2  15254.21     152.5421            -2.00000
2011-03-04    -100  154.1327        0 -15413.27     154.1327           159.05659
2011-03-10    -100  154.3137       -2 -15431.37     154.3137            -2.00000
2011-03-11     100  154.7041        0  15470.41     154.7041           -39.04882
2011-03-17     100  146.8465       -2  14684.65     146.8465            -2.00000
2011-03-25    -100  154.4660        0 -15446.60     154.4660           761.94864
2011-04-25    -100  159.6949       -2 -15969.49     159.6949            -2.00000
2011-05-17     100  163.1165        0  16311.65     163.1165          -342.16055
2011-06-02     100  158.8975       -2  15889.75     158.8975            -2.00000
......          .....             .....          .....                .....
```

This provides the useful information about our trades, including the position size, transaction fees, price per share, and net realized P&L.

The *mktdata* object is a special variable created during the execution of *applyStrategy*. It is a time series object, which contains the historic price data and the calculated indicators, signals, and rules:

```
> tail(mktdata, 10)
           IBM.Open IBM.High IBM.Low IBM.Close IBM.Volume IBM.Adjusted dn.BBands mavg.BBands up.BBands pctB.BBands Cl.gt.UpperBand Cl.lt.LowerBand Cross.Mid
2013-12-17   177.36   177.49  175.12    175.76    5471900     162.9151  171.6609    178.3688  185.0767   0.3326226              NA              NA        NA
2013-12-18   176.45   178.74  174.85    178.70    5697700     165.6402  172.0444    177.9803  183.9163   0.4536443              NA              NA         1
2013-12-19   177.88   180.54  177.88    180.22    5927000     167.0492  172.7403    177.6897  182.6390   0.6875993              NA              NA        NA
2013-12-20   180.12   182.00  180.02    180.02    7653500     166.8638  173.3721    177.5022  181.6323   0.8847168              NA              NA        NA
2013-12-23   181.05   182.93  180.61    182.23    4079900     168.9123  173.3968    177.4948  181.5929   1.0403210               1              NA        NA
2013-12-24   181.96   183.50  181.91    183.22    1613600     169.8299  173.0017    177.6802  182.3586   1.0553644              NA              NA        NA
2013-12-26   183.56   185.56  183.51    185.35    3325700     171.8043  172.4104    178.0278  183.6453   1.1033712              NA              NA        NA
2013-12-27   185.84   186.50  184.56    185.08    3381600     171.5540  171.8841    178.3473  184.8106   1.0440522              NA              NA        NA
2013-12-30   185.32   186.70  184.67    186.41    3018600     172.7868  171.4101    178.6530  185.8959   1.0021267              NA              NA        NA
2013-12-31   186.49   187.79  186.30    187.57    3619700     173.8620  170.9727    179.1108  187.2490   0.9982184              NA              NA        NA
```

It is very helpful to understand strategy processing and debug by inspecting *mktdata*.

Next, we need to update our portfolio, account, and equity using the following code:

```
> updatePortf(qs.strategy)
> updateAcct(qs.strategy)
> updateEndEq(qs.strategy)
```

Now, we can create a performance plot using the *chart.Posn* function from the *blotter* package:

```
> myTheme <- chart_theme()
> myTheme$col$dn.col <- "blue"
> myTheme$col$dn.border <- "gray"
> myTheme$col$up.border <- "gray"
> chart.Posn(Portfolio=qs.strategy, Symbol = ticker, theme = myTheme)
> plot(add_BBands(on = 1, sd = 2, n = 20))
```

This generates the output shown in Figure 10-21.

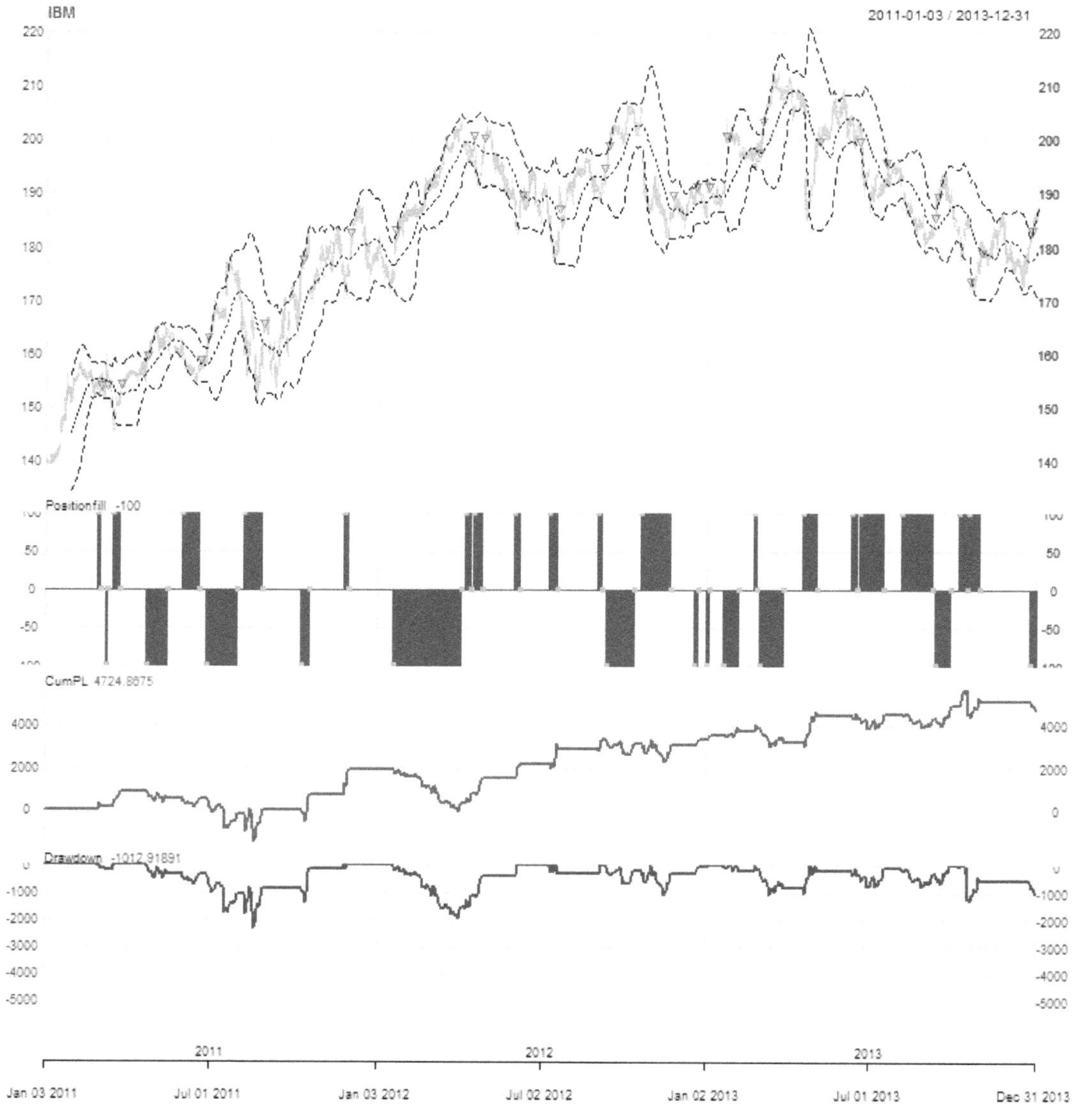


*Figure 10-21. Performance summary of the Bollinger band strategy for IBM.*

Figure 10-21 shows the stock price with Bollinger bands and trading marks, position, P&L, and drawdown.

We can use the *getOrderBook* function to retrieve the order book object:

```
> obook <- getOrderBook(qs.strategy)
> head(obook$qsBBands$IBM)
```

```
                    Order.Qty Order.Price         Order.Type Order.Side Order.Threshold Order.Status Order.StatusTime
2011-03-01 00:00:00 "100"     "152.361155265144" "market"   "long"     NA              "closed"     "2011-03-02 00:00:00"
2011-03-03 00:00:00 "all"     "155.704200147509" "market"   "long"     NA              "closed"     "2011-03-04 00:00:00"
2011-03-09 00:00:00 "-100"    "157.971002104563" "market"   "short"    NA              "closed"     "2011-03-10 00:00:00" ......
2011-03-10 00:00:00 "all"     "154.313651504592" "market"   "short"    NA              "closed"     "2011-03-11 00:00:00"
2011-03-16 00:00:00 "100"     "145.72267681343"  "market"   "long"     NA              "closed"     "2011-03-17 00:00:00"
2011-03-24 00:00:00 "all"     "152.427818151389" "market"   "long"     NA              "closed"     "2011-03-25 00:00:00"
```

We can also check the trading statistics:

```
> t(tradeStats(qs.strategy))
                   IBM
Portfolio          "qsBBands"
Symbol             "IBM"
Num.Txns           "59"
Num.Trades         "29"
Net.Trading.PL     "4724.867"
Avg.Trade.PL       "179.9955"
Med.Trade.PL       "208.9459"
Largest.Winner     "1258.95"
Largest.Loser      "-1571.547"
Gross.Profits      "9576.231"
Gross.Losses       "-4356.363"
Std.Dev.Trade.PL   "593.1125"
Percent.Positive   "65.51724"
Percent.Negative   "34.48276"
Profit.Factor      "2.198217"
Avg.Win.Trade      "504.0122"
Med.Win.Trade      "471.6495"
Avg.Losing.Trade   "-435.6363"
Med.Losing.Trade   "-268.5564"
Avg.Daily.PL       "179.9955"
Med.Daily.PL       "208.9459"
Std.Dev.Daily.PL   "593.1125"
Ann.Sharpe         "4.817534"
Max.Drawdown       "-2312.048"
Profit.To.Max.Draw "2.043585"
Avg.WinLoss.Ratio  "1.156956"
Med.WinLoss.Ratio  "1.75624"
Max.Equity         "5737.786"
Min.Equity         "-1436.092"
End.Equity         "4724.867"
```

This provides detailed information about our trades. We can also retrieve the account information using the *getAccount* function:

```
> acct <- getAccount(qs.strategy)
> last(acct$summary, 5)
       Additions Withdrawals Realized.PL Unrealized.PL Interest Gross.Trading.PL
2013-12-24     0           0           0             0        0           0.0000
2013-12-26     0           0           0          -213        0        -213.0005
2013-12-27     0           0           0            27        0          27.0004
2013-12-30     0           0           0          -133        0        -133.0002
2013-12-31     0           0           0          -116        0        -116.0003
           Txn.Fees Net.Trading.PL Advisory.Fees Net.Performance  End.Eq
2013-12-24       -2        -2.0000             0         -2.0000 1005160
2013-12-26        0      -213.0005             0       -213.0005 1004947
2013-12-27        0        27.0004             0         27.0004 1004974
2013-12-30        0      -133.0002             0       -133.0002 1004841
```

```
2013-12-31          0       -116.0003                 0       -116.0003 1004725
```

We can use the *xyplot* function from the *lattice* package to display the entire account summary multivariate time series:

```
> library(lattice)
> xyplot(acct$summary, type = "h", col = 4)
```

This produces the output shown in Figure 10-22.

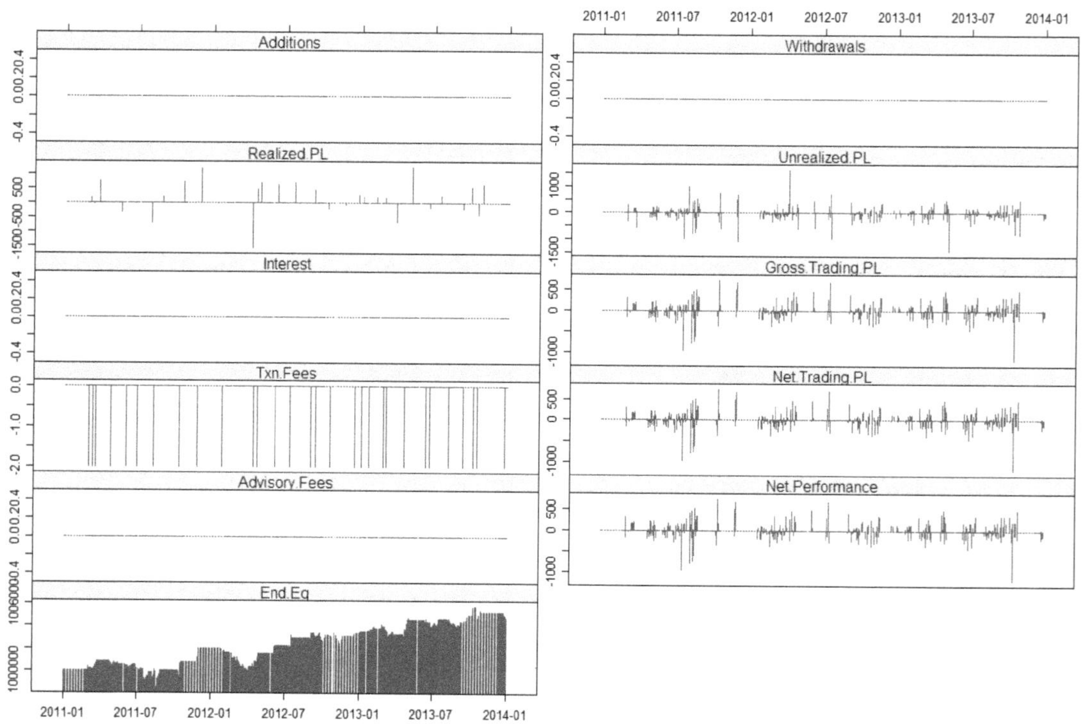


*Figure 10-22. Account summary of the Bollinger band strategy for IBM.*

With the full portfolio-level equity time series, we can perform any type of performance and risk analysis. We can easily create the equity curve using the following code:

```
> eq <- acct$summary$End.Eq
> plot(eq, minor.ticks = F, col = "blue", main = "BBands strategy equity curve")
```

This produces the equity curve shown in Figure 10-23.

We can also extract the returns from the equity data and examine the strategy performance:

```
> rtn <- Return.calculate(eq, method = "log")
> charts.PerformanceSummary(rtn, main = "BBands strategy performance")
```

This produces the output shown in Figure 10-24.

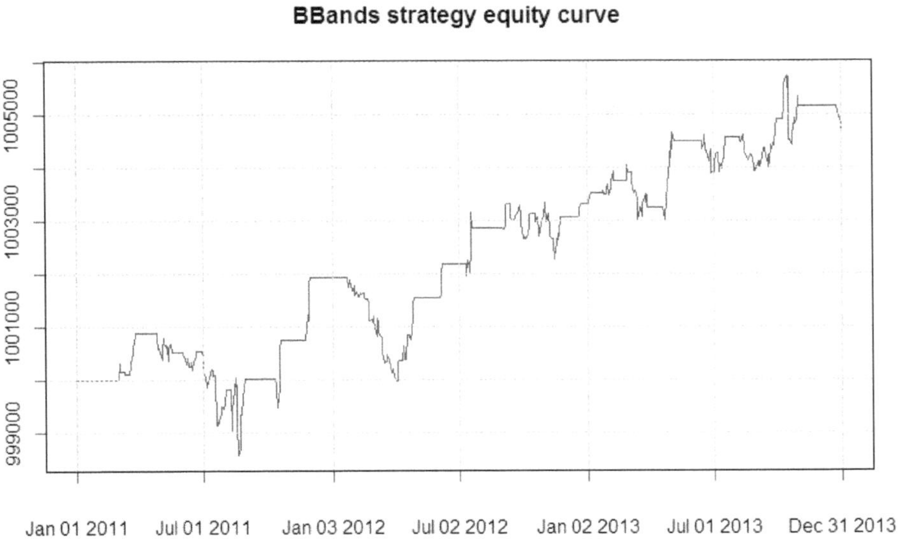


*Figure 10-23. Equity curve of the Bollinger band strategy for IBM.*

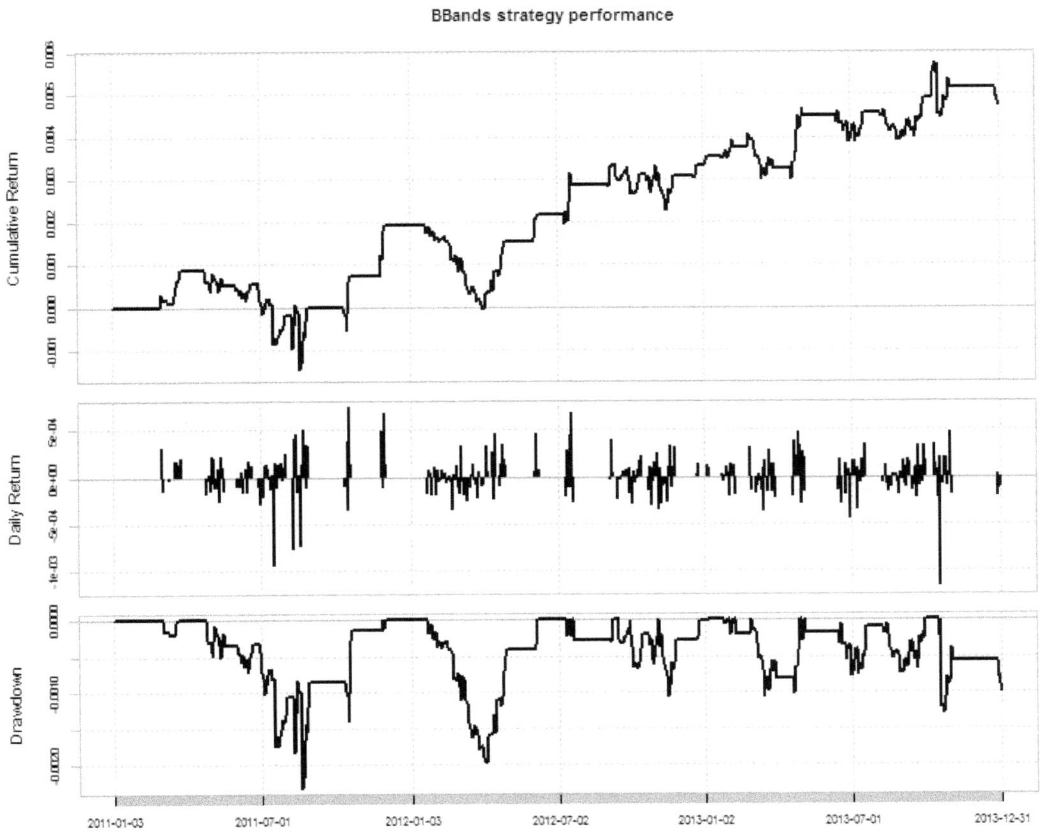


*Figure 10-24. Bollinger band strategy performance for IBM.*

## Using Custom Indicators

In the preceding section, we presented the detailed procedure on how to use *quantstrat* and the built-in indicators from the *TTR* package to evaluate strategies. Here, we will discuss using the custom indicators. For simplicity's sake, we are going to use the *Z-score* based on moving average to generate trading signals. As discussed previously, we implemented the *maZscore* function to calculate this *Z-score*. We can then use this function as our indicator.

First, we need to add the following code to perform necessary initialization:

```
> source("./R/strategyHelper.R")
> zin = 2
> zout = 0
> ticker = "IBM"
> currency("USD")
> stock(ticker, currency = "USD", multiplier = 1)
> initDate <- "2012-01-01"
> endDate <- "2013-08-01"
> initEq <- 22000
> Sys.setenv(TZ = "UTC")
> getSymbols(ticker, from = initDate, to = endDate, index.class = "POSIXct")
> qs.strategy <- "qsZscore"
> rm.strat(qs.strategy)
> initPortf(qs.strategy, symbols = ticker, initDate=initDate)
> initAcct(qs.strategy, portfolios = qs.strategy, initDate = initDate,
          initEq = initEq)
> initOrders(portfolio = qs.strategy, initDate = initDate)
> strategy(qs.strategy, store = T)
> addPosLimit(portfolio = qs.strategy, tikcer, initDate, 100, 1 )
```

The above code snippet is similar to that used in the preceding example. Next, we will need to add our custom indicator, signals, and rules to our strategy:

```
> #Add indicator:
> add.indicator(strategy = qs.strategy, name = "maZscore",
               arguments = list(x = quote(Cl(mktdata)), n = 40), label="Zscore")

> #Add signals:
> add.signal(strategy = qs.strategy, name = "sigThreshold", label = "longEntryCond",
            arguments = list(column = "Zscore", threshold = -zin,
            relationship = "lt", cross = T))
> add.signal(strategy = qs.strategy, name = "sigThreshold", label = "longExitCond",
            arguments = list(column = "Zscore", threshold = -zout,
            relationship = "gt", cross = T))
> add.signal(strategy = qs.strategy, name = "sigThreshold",label = "shortEntryCond",
            arguments = list(column = "Zscore", threshold = zin,
            relationship = "gt", cross = T))
> add.signal(strategy = qs.strategy, name = "sigThreshold", label = "shortExitCond",
            arguments = list(column = "Zscore", threshold = zout,
            relationship = "lt", cross = T))

> #Add trading rules:
> add.rule(strategy = qs.strategy, name = "ruleSignal",
          arguments = list(sigcol = "longEntryCond", sigval = T, orderqty = 100,
          ordertype = "market", orderside = "long", osFUN = osMaxPos),
          type = "enter", path.dep = T)
```

```
> add.rule(strategy = qs.strategy, name = "ruleSignal",
          arguments = list(sigcol = "longExitCond", sigval = T, orderqty = "all",
          ordertype = "market", orderside = "long", osFUN = osMaxPos),
          type = "exit", path.dep = T)
> add.rule(strategy = qs.strategy, name = "ruleSignal",
          arguments = list(sigcol = "shortEntryCond", sigval = T, orderqty = -100,
          ordertype = "market", orderside = "short", osFUN = osMaxPos),
          type = "enter", path.dep = T)
> add.rule(strategy = qs.strategy, name = "ruleSignal",
          arguments = list(sigcol = "shortExitCond", sigval = T, orderqty = "all",
          ordertype = "market", orderside = "short", osFUN = osMaxPos),
          type = "exit", path.dep = T)
```

Note that we create our custom indicator by setting *name* = "*maZscore*", which is the name of our function used to calculate *Z-score*. We then use the *sigThreshold* with its argument *cross* being set to *TRUE* to create trading signals. We enter a long position when *Z-score* is below $-zin$ and flat the long position when Z-score is moving above the $-zout$ level. Alternatively, we enter a short position when *Z-score* is above *zin* and flat the short position when *Z-score* is below the *zout* level. We then add the trading rules corresponding to the signals.

Finally, we can call the *applyStrategy* function to generate transactions in our specified portfolio:

```
> applyStrategy(strategy = qs.strategy , portfolios = qs.strategy)
> updatePortf(qs.strategy)
> updateAcct(qs.strategy)
> updateEndEq(qs.strategy)
```

Now, we can examine the performance of our strategy:

```
> myTheme <- chart_theme()
> myTheme$col$dn.col <- "blue"
> myTheme$col$dn.border <- "gray"
> myTheme$col$up.border <- "gray"
> chart.Posn(qs.strategy, Symbol = "IBM", theme = myTheme)
```

This generates the output shown in Figure 10-25.

We can also retrieve the equity and returns generated from our strategy using the following code:

```
> acct <- getAccount(qs.strategy)
> eq <- acct$summary$End.Eq
> rtn <- Return.calculate(eq, method = "log")
> charts.PerformanceSummary(rtn, main = "Z-score strategy performance")
```

This produces the output shown in Figure 10-26. We see that the results in Figure 10-26 are almost identical to those obtained from our manual calculation as shown in Figure 10-9. However, *quantstrat* provides a complete infrastructure that allows us to model and backtest trading strategies as well as automatically update the portfolio, account, and order book in a systematic fashion.

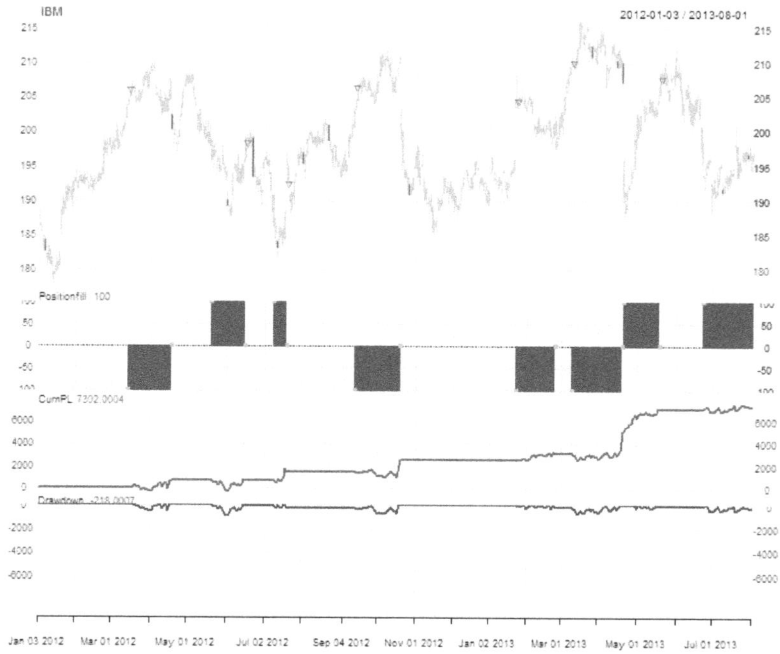


*Figure 10-25. Performance summary of our Z-score strategy for IBM.*

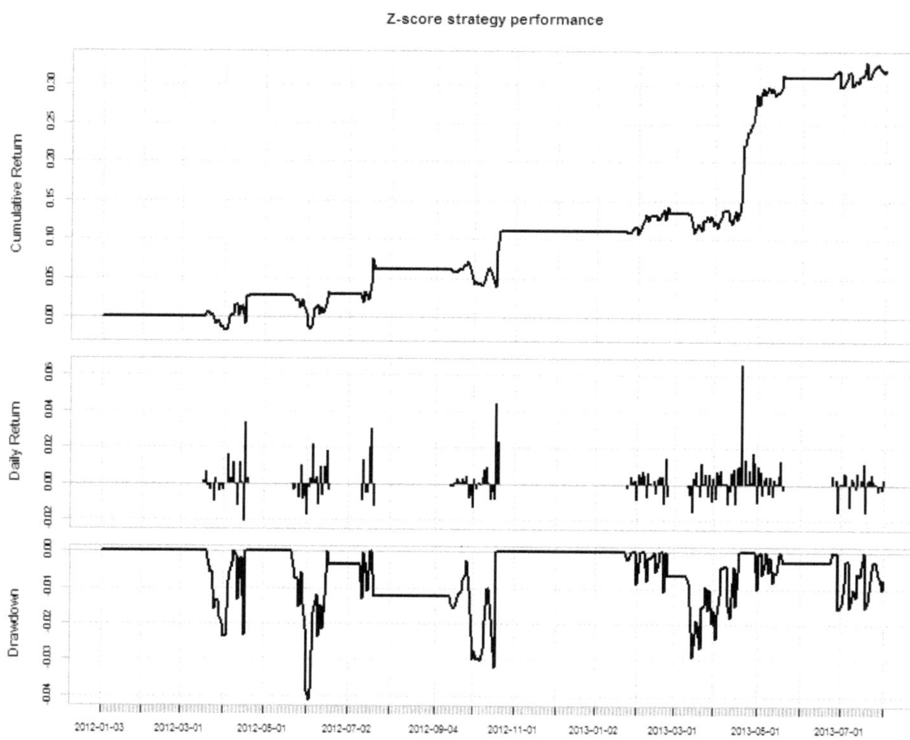


*Figure 10-26. Z-score strategy performance for IBM.*

# Multi-Asset Portfolios

The real power of the *quantstrat* framework comes from its ability to apply a quantitative trading strategy to a multi-asset portfolio, and analyze performance and risk at both the component and portfolio level. Here, we consider a multi-asset portfolio that contains four index EFTs and nine common stocks. We use the 10-month simple moving average (SMA) as the trading signal, and the following buy-sell rules: enter a long position when the monthly close price is above the 10-month SMA and flat the long position when the monthly close price is below the 10-month SMA.

First, we need to download market data from yahoo:

```
> currency("USD")
> Sys.setenv(TZ = "UTC")
> initDate <- "2000-01-01"
> endDate <- "2015-01-01"
> initEq <- 100000
> symbols <- c("SPY", "QQQ", "DIA", "IWM", "AAPL", "AMZN", "IBM", "MSFT", "INTC",
             "JPM", "GS", "MS", "C")
> getSymbols(symbols, from = initDate, to = endDate,
           index.class = c("POSIXt", "POSIXct"), adjust = T)
> for(symbol in symbols) {
    stock(symbol, currency = "USD", multiplier = 1)
    x <- get(symbol)
    x <- to.monthly(x, indexAt = "endof", drop.time = FALSE)
    colnames(x) <- gsub("x", symbol, colnames(x))
    assign(symbol, x)
  }
```

Here, we download the daily market data for 13 assets from Yahoo and convert them into the monthly data. Note that when converting to monthly data, we need to use "*endof*" and set *drop.time = FALSE*. Next, we need to initialize our multi-asset strategy, portfolio, and account:

```
> rm.strat("multiAsset")
> qs.multiAsset <- strategy("multiAsset")
> initPortf("multiAsset", symbols = symbols, initDate = initDate)
> initAcct("multiAsset", portfolios = "multiAsset", initDate = initDate,
         initEq = initEq)
> initOrders(portfolio = "multiAsset", initDate = initDate)
```

We then set the position limits so we do not add to the position every month when close is above 10-month SMA:

```
> for(symbol in symbols) {
    addPosLimit("multiAsset", symbol, timestamp = initDate, maxpos = 100)
  }
```

Next, we add the indicator, signals, and trading rules:

```
> #Add the 10-month SMA indicator
> qs.multiAsset <- add.indicator(qs.multiAsset, name = "SMA",
                   arguments=list(x=quote(Cl(mktdata)), n=10), label="SMA10")

> #Add signals:
> qs.multiAsset <- add.signal(qs.multiAsset, name = "sigCrossover",
    arguments=list(columns = c("Close", "SMA10"), relationship = "gte"),
    label = "Cl.gt.SMA")
> qs.multiAsset <- add.signal(qs.multiAsset, name = "sigCrossover",
```

```
    arguments = list(columns = c("Close", "SMA10"), relationship = "lt"),
    label = "Cl.lt.SMA")

> #Add trading rules:
> qs.multiAsset <- add.rule(qs.multiAsset, name="ruleSignal",
    arguments = list(sigcol = "Cl.gt.SMA", sigval = TRUE, orderqty = 100,
    ordertype="market", orderside = "long", pricemethod = "market",
    TxnFees = -2, osFUN = osMaxPos), type = "enter", path.dep = TRUE)
> qs.multiAsset <- add.rule(qs.multiAsset, name = "ruleSignal",
    Arguments = list(sigcol = "Cl.lt.SMA", sigval = TRUE, orderqty = "all",
    Ordertype = "market", orderside = "long", pricemethod = "market"),
    type = "exit", path.dep = TRUE)
```

The signals and trading rules are very simple: we long the stocks only. We also include the transaction cost ($2 for a 100-share round-trip trade) to our strategy. Note that the strategy created in *quantstrat* does not depend on assets, so it can be apply to any asset or any multi-asset portfolio.

We can now apply our strategy to a multi-asset portfolio:

```
> applyStrategy(strategy = qs.multiAsset, portfolios = "multiAsset")
> updatePortf("multiAsset")
> updateAcct("multiAsset")
> updateEndEq("multiAsset")
```

Now, we can examine the results:

```
> tradeStats("multiAsset")[,c("Num.Trades","Net.Trading.PL","Max.Drawdown")]
     Num.Trades Net.Trading.PL Max.Drawdown
AAPL          7      11102.461    -1819.242
AMZN         10      20967.998    -9075.002
C            14       3616.060    -9508.710
DIA          12      10593.226    -1432.697
GS           13       8893.533    -8531.493
IBM          18       1499.416    -5822.553
INTC         12       1474.098    -1092.630
IWM          14       5272.808    -1978.780
JPM          14       1478.678    -2255.252
MS           12        148.362    -2468.070
MSFT         17       1319.894    -1190.978
QQQ          13       5794.550    -1378.626
SPY           6      14535.604    -1829.927
```

We can plot the total performance of our portfolio:

```
> pr <- PortfReturns("multiAsset")
> pr$Total <- rowSums(pr, na.rm=TRUE)
> charts.PerformanceSummary(pr$Total)
```

This produces the output shown in Figure 10-27.

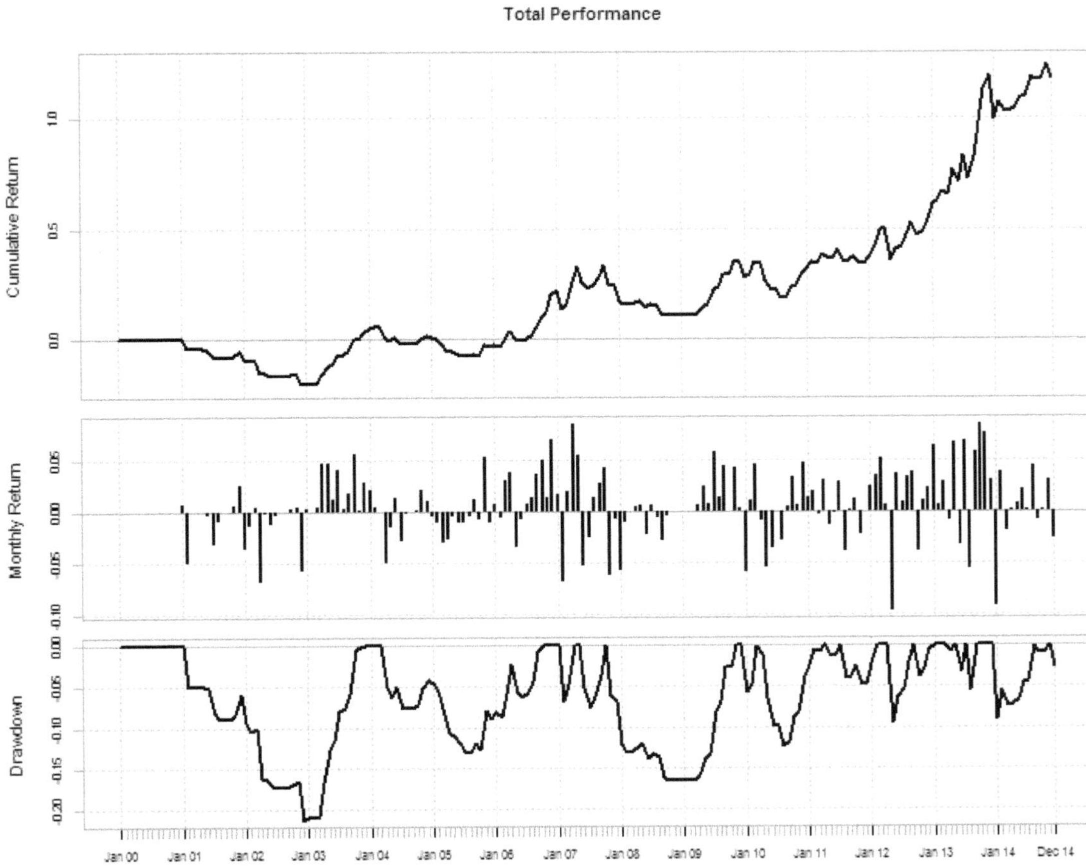


*Figure 10-27. Total performance for a multi-asset portfolio.*

We can also easily evaluate the performance for any individual asset in our portfolio:

```
> myTheme <- chart_theme()
> myTheme$col$dn.col <- "blue"
> myTheme$col$dn.border <- "gray"
> myTheme$col$up.border <- "gray"
> chart.Posn(Portfolio = "multiAsset", Symbol = "AMZN", theme = myTheme)
> plot(add_SMA(on = 1, n = 10))
```

This generates the output shown in Figure 10-28.

We can also compare the cumulative returns by asset:

```
> prl <- PortfReturns("multiAsset")
> chart.CumReturns(prl, legend.loc = "topleft", main = "Cumulative Returns",
                   colorset = rich12equal)
```

This produces the output shown in Figure 10-29.

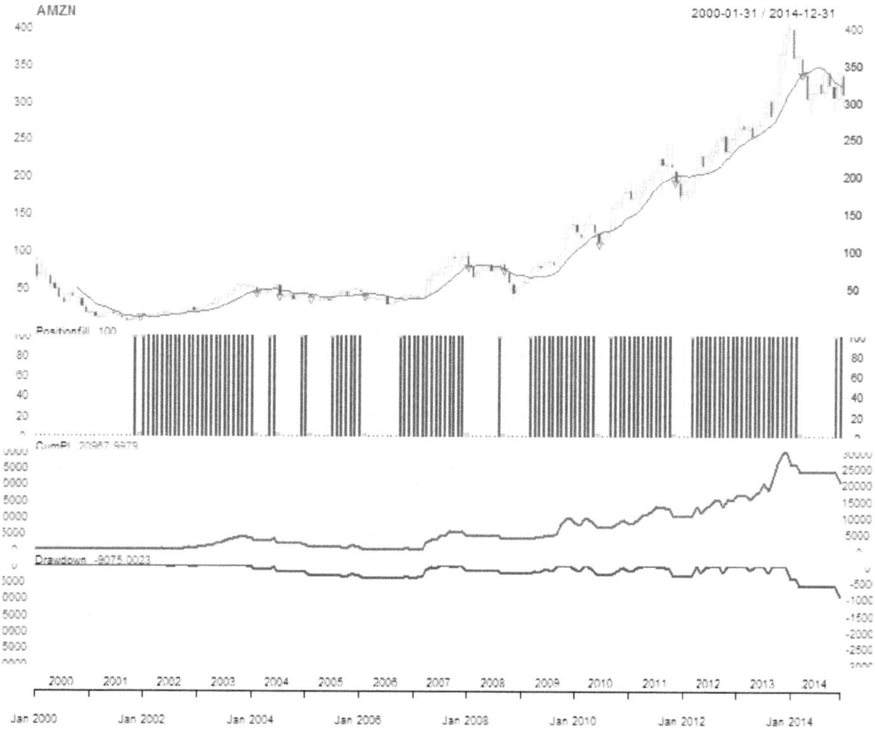


*Figure 10-28. Strategy performance for AMZN.*

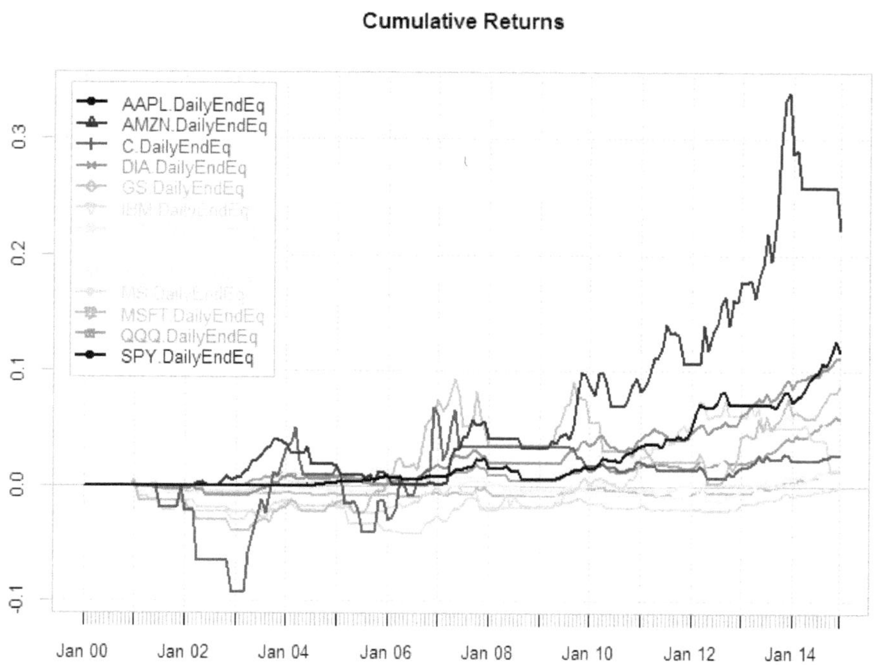


*Figure 10-29. Cumulative returns by asset.*

We can perform a return distribution analysis using the *chart.Boxplot* function from the *PerformanceAnalytics* package:

```
> chart.Boxplot(pr, colorset = rich12equal)
```

This generates the output shown in Figure 10-30.

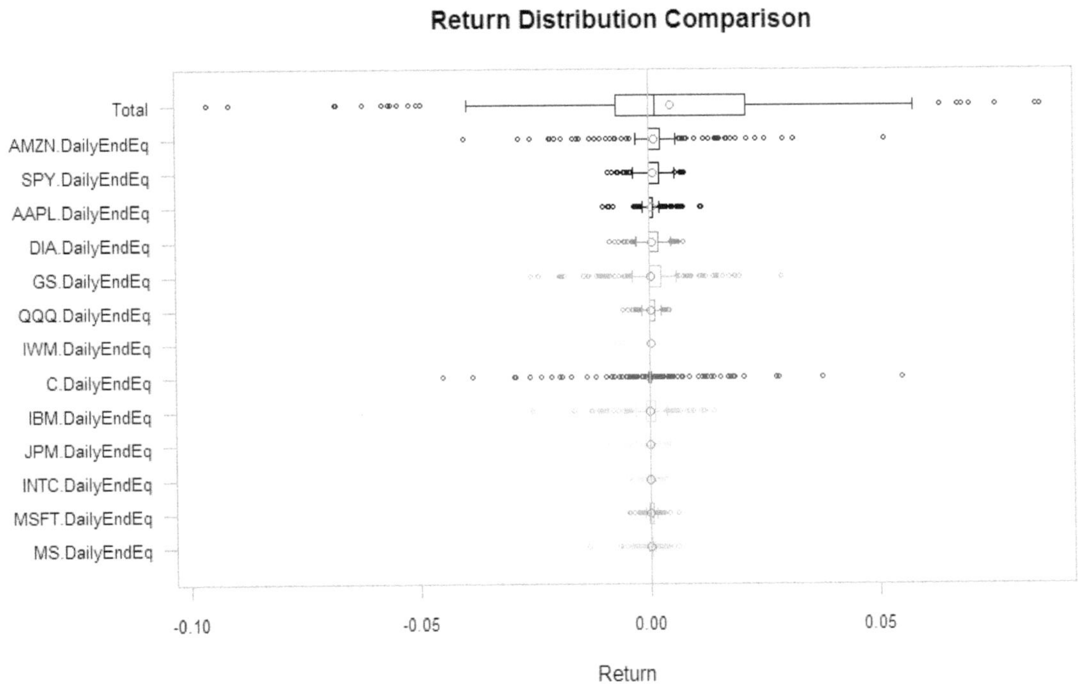


*Figure 10-30. Return distribution analysis for a multi-asset portfolio.*

We can extract the annualized returns and Sharpe ratios:

```
> t(table.AnnualizedReturns(pr))
                 Annualized Return Annualized Std Dev Annualized Sharpe (Rf=0%)
AAPL.DailyEndEq             0.0074             0.0095                    0.7773
AMZN.DailyEndEq             0.0135             0.0339                    0.3985
C.DailyEndEq                0.0018             0.0349                    0.0518
DIA.DailyEndEq              0.0070             0.0091                    0.7771
GS.DailyEndEq               0.0056             0.0254                    0.2211
IBM.DailyEndEq              0.0009             0.0173                    0.0493
INTC.DailyEndEq             0.0010             0.0040                    0.2467
IWM.DailyEndEq              0.0035             0.0087                    0.4008
JPM.DailyEndEq              0.0010             0.0065                    0.1492
MS.DailyEndEq               0.0001             0.0075                    0.0096
MSFT.DailyEndEq             0.0009             0.0044                    0.1981
QQQ.DailyEndEq              0.0039             0.0058                    0.6594
SPY.DailyEndEq              0.0097             0.0100                    0.9718
Total                       0.0534             0.1070                    0.4985
```

# Chapter 11
# **Portfolio Optimization**

A portfolio in finance refers to any collection of assets such as stocks, bonds, cash, etc. Portfolios may be held by individuals, hedge funds, banks, and other financial institutions. Expected return and risk are the most important parameters with regard to optimal portfolios. The goal of portfolio optimization is to find the best asset allocation strategy that maximizes portfolio's return and minimizes its risk. Modern portfolio theory assumes that if we want to achieve a higher expected return, we have to take on more risk, that is, there is always a trade-off between expected return and risk.

Portfolio optimization involves identifying portfolios that satisfy three criteria: minimizing risk, matching or exceeding expected return, and satisfying basic feasibility requirements. In this chapter, we will discuss portfolio optimization using several different techniques, including Markowitz's classical mean-variance method, mean-CVaR (conditional value at risk), and the *portfolioAnalytics* package.

## Theoretical Background

Modern portfolio theory (MPT) is a theory on how risk-averse investors can construct portfolios to optimize or maximize expected return based on a given level of market risk, emphasizing that risk is an inherent part of higher reward. According to the theory, it is possible to construct an efficient frontier of optimal portfolios that offers the maximum possible expected return for a given level of risk.

We can define the return $R_t$ of a portfolio at time $t$ as the total value $T_t$ of the portfolio divided by the total value at an earlier time $t-1$, i.e.

$$R_t = \frac{T_t - T_{t-1}}{T_{t-1}} = \frac{T_t}{T_{t-1}} - 1 \qquad 11\text{-}1$$

MPT provides a method to analyze how good a given portfolio is based on only the mean and variance of the returns. Consider a portfolio with $n$ different assets. Let $\mu_i$ and $\sigma_i^2$ be the corresponding mean and variance and $\sigma_{ij}$ the covariance between $R_i$ and $R_j$. Suppose the relative amount of the value of the portfolio invested in asset $i$ is $x_i$. If $R$ is the return of the entire portfolio, we then have:

$$\mu = E[R] = \sum_{i=1}^{n} \mu_i x_i \qquad \text{11-2}$$

$$\sigma^2 = Var[R] = \sum_{i=1}^{n}\sum_{j=1}^{n} \sigma_{ij} x_i x_j \qquad \text{11-3}$$

$$\sum_{i=1}^{n} x_i = 1 \qquad \text{11-4}$$

$$x_i \geq 0, \quad i = 1, 2, \cdots, n \qquad \text{11-5}$$

Condition 11-5 is the same as saying that only long positions are allowed, hence if short sale should be included in the model, we need to ignore this condition. For different choices of $x_1, x_2, \cdots, x_n$, we will get different combinations of $\mu$ and $\sigma^2$. We call the set of all possible $(\mu, \sigma^2)$ combinations the attainable set. Those $(\mu, \sigma^2)$ with minimum $\sigma^2$ for a given $\mu$ or more and maximum $\mu$ for a given $\sigma^2$ or less are called the efficient set or efficient frontier. Since we want a high profit and a small risk, we need to choose a portfolio that gives a $(\mu, \sigma^2)$ combination in the efficient set.

# Efficient Frontier

The efficient set or efficient frontier shows us the minimum risk that can be achieved at each level of expected return for a given set of risky securities. In order to calculate the efficient frontier, we need to have an estimate of the expected returns and the covariance matrix for the set of risky assets that will be used to build the optimal portfolio. These parameters are usually difficult to forecast and the optimal portfolio calculation is extremely sensitive to these parameters. For this reason, an efficient frontier based portfolio is hard to successfully implement in practice. However, a familiarity with the concept is still very useful, and will help us to develop intuition about diversification and relationship between risk and return.

We need two inputs to calculate the efficient frontier for a portfolio with *n* assets. First, we need the expected returns of each asset. The vector of expected returns will be denoted by $\bar{R}$. The other input is the variance-covariance matrix for the *n* assets, which will be designated as *S*. We also need a unity matrix *I* with the same length as the vector $\bar{R}$.

Once we have this information, we can perform the following calculations:

$$A = I'S^{-1}I > 0, \qquad B = I'S^{-1}\bar{R}, \qquad C = \bar{R}'S^{-1}\bar{R}, \qquad \Delta = AC - B^2 > 0$$

Using these values, we can calculate the variance at each level of expected return using the following equation:

$$\sigma^2 = \frac{A\mu^2 - 2B\mu + C}{\Delta} \qquad \text{11-6}$$

We see from this equation that the efficient frontier is a parabolic function in the mean-variance space. Using the standard deviation $\sigma$ rather than the variance, we have:

$$\sigma = \sqrt{\frac{A\mu^2 - 2B\mu + C}{\Delta}} \qquad 11\text{-}7$$

We can calculate the covariance matrix and the mean return using the historical return time series. The diagonal of the covariance matrix is the variance of our securities. Therefore, if we take the square root of the diagonal, we can obtain the standard deviation of each asset.

As an example, we consider nine SPRD ETFs: XLE (energy), XLF (Financials), XLI (industrials), XLK (technology), and XLU (utilities), XLY (consumer discretionary), XLP (consumer staples), XLV (health care), and XLB (materials). Add a new file named *portfolioHelper.R* to the "[*Working Directory*]/*R*/" folder. Add a new helper function named *getFrontier* to this file. Here is the code for this function:

```
getFrontier <- function(tickers){
  getSymbols(tickers, from = "2000-01-01", to= "2016-01-01", adjust = T)
  rtn <- na.omit(do.call(merge, lapply(tickers, FUN = function(x)
                                     monthlyReturn(Cl(get(x))))))

  colnames(rtn) <- tickers
  R1 <- colMeans(rtn)                  #Get mean returns
  S <- cov(rtn)                        #Get covariance matrix
  S1 <- solve(S)                       #Get inverse of S
  std <- sqrt(diag(S))                 #Get vector of security standard deviation
  I <- cbind(rep(1, length(R1)))       #Define unity vector

  A <- t(I)%*%S1%*%I
  B <- t(I)%*%S1%*%R1
  C <- t(R1)%*%S1%*%R1
  D <- A*C - B^2

  #Define efficient frontier:
  mu <- c(1:400)/20000
  minVar <- (A*mu^2 -2*B*mu + C)/D
  minStd <- sqrt(minVar)

  plot(minStd, mu, type = "l", ylab = "mean", xlab = "Standard Deviation",
       main = "Efficient Frontier", col = "blue")
  points(std, R1, pch = 18, col = "red")
  textxy(std, R1, labs = tickers)
}
```

Here, we first load market data from Yahoo and extract corresponding monthly returns. We then calculate the mean returns, covariance matrix, and standard deviations. Next, we create the efficient frontier using Eqs 11-6 and 11-7. Finally, we display the efficient frontier on a plot:

```
> install.packages("calibrate")
> library(calibrate)
> source("./R/portfolioHelper.R")
> tickers <- c("XLE","XLF","XLI","XLK","XLU","XLY","XLP","XLV","XLB")
> getFrontier(tickers)
```

Here, we use the *textxy* function from the *calibrate* package to label data points on a plot. The above code generates the output shown in Figure 11-1.

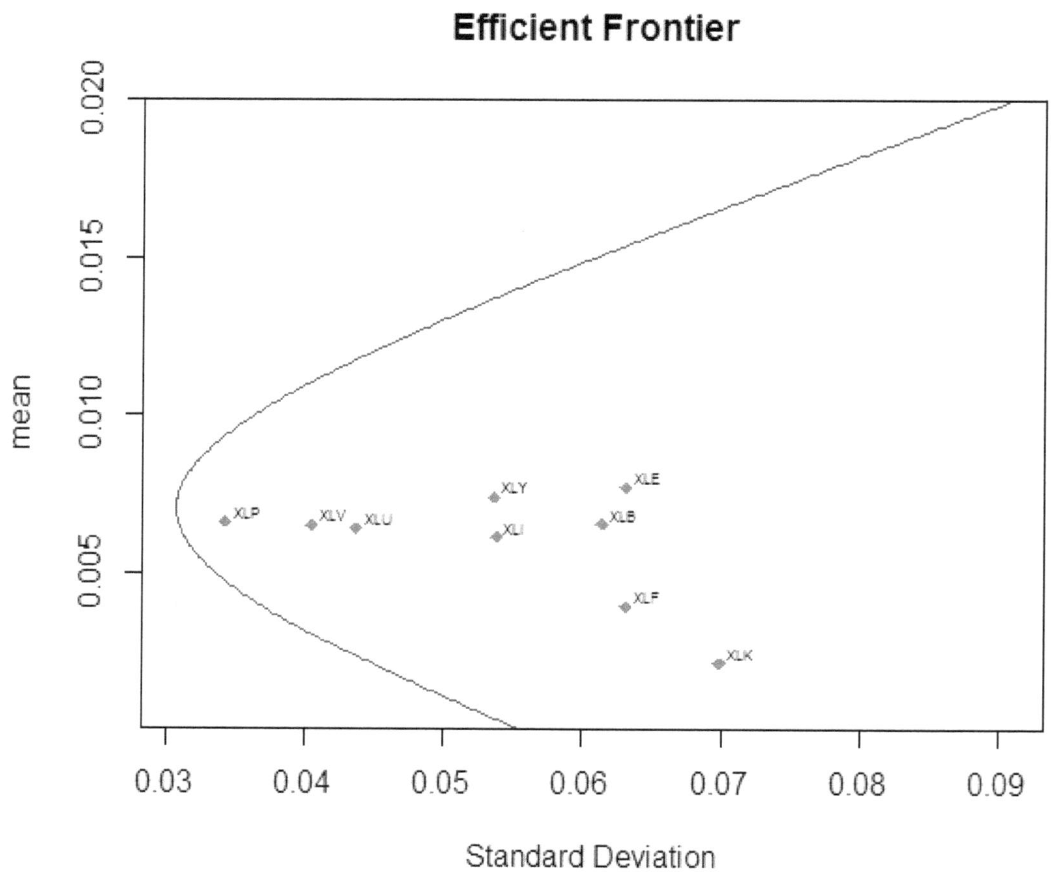


*Figure 11-1. Efficient frontier for SPRD ETFs.*

## Portfolio Weights

In the preceding section, we showed how to calculate and plot the efficient frontier for a set of risky assets. In this section, we discuss the calculation for the portfolio weights for each of the assets at any point on the efficient frontier.

A point of particular interest on the efficient frontier is so-called the global minimum variance portfolio. This portfolio is the point on the efficient frontier that has the minimum variance or standard deviation. We can solve for the mean and variance of the global minimum variance portfolio by setting the derivative of Eq. 11-6 for the variance to zero and solving for $\mu$:

$$\frac{2A\mu - 2B}{\Delta} = 0, \quad \rightarrow \mu_g = \frac{B}{A}, \quad \sigma_g^2 = \frac{1}{A} \qquad \text{11-8}$$

Finally, the portfolio weights for the global minimum variance portfolio are given by:

$$W_g = \frac{S^{-1}I}{A} \tag{11-9}$$

We need two points on the efficient frontier to calculate any other point. We already have the global minimum variance portfolio as a first point. The second easy point to calculate is the tangency portfolio for the case where the risk-free rate is set to zero.

The equations for the expected return, standard deviations, and weights for this portfolio are given below:

$$W_d = \frac{S^{-1}\bar{R}}{B}, \quad \mu_d = W_d'\bar{R}, \quad \sigma_d^2 = W_d'SW_d \tag{11-10}$$

The two-fund separation theorem states that all minimum variance portfolios on the efficient frontier are combinations of only two distinct portfolios. Therefore, any two points on the mean variance frontier will span the entire set.

To calculate any point on the frontier, we can use the minimum variance portfolio and the tangency portfolio when risk-free rate = 0. With the portfolio weights for the two portfolios calculated above, we can find the weights for any point on the efficient frontier:

$$W^* = (\lambda A)W_g + (\gamma B)W_d, \quad \lambda = \frac{C - \mu B}{\Delta}, \quad \gamma = \frac{\mu A - B}{\Delta} \tag{11-11}$$

We can also calculate the mean return, variance, and standard deviation for this point:

$$\mu^* = W^{*\prime}\bar{R}, \quad \sigma^{*2} = W^{*\prime}SW^*, \quad \sigma^* = \sqrt{W^{*\prime}SW^*} \tag{11-12}$$

As an example, we can calculate the portfolio weights for the portfolio discussed in the previous example. Add a new function named *getFrontierWeights* to the *portfolioHelper.R* file. Here is the code for this function:

```
getFrontierWeights <- function(tickers){
  getSymbols(tickers, from = "2000-01-01", to= "2016-01-01", adjust = T)
  rtn <- na.omit(do.call(merge, lapply(tickers, FUN = function(x)
                                 monthlyReturn(Cl(get(x))))))

  colnames(rtn) <- tickers
  R1 <- colMeans(rtn)                 #Get mean returns
  S <- cov(rtn)                       #Get covariance matrix
  S1 <- solve(S)                      #Get inverse of S
  std <- sqrt(diag(S))                #Get vector of security standard deviation
  I <- cbind(rep(1, length(R1)))      #Define unity vector

  A <- t(I)%*%S1%*%I
  B <- t(I)%*%S1%*%R1
  C <- t(R1)%*%S1%*%R1
  D <- A*C - B^2

  #Define efficient frontier:
  mu <- c(100:250)/20000
  minVar <- (A*mu^2 -2*B*mu + C)/D
  minStd <- sqrt(minVar)
```

```
    #Calculate global minimum variance portforlio:
    mug <- B/A
    stdg <- 1/sqrt(A)
    wg <- (S1 %*% I)/as.numeric(A)

    #Calculate tengency portfolio:
    wd <- (S1 %*% R1)/as.numeric(B)
    mud <- t(wd) %*% R1
    stdd <- sqrt(t(wd) %*% S %*% wd)

    #An arbitray expected return with mean return = 0.011
    lambda <- (C - 0.011*B)/D
    gamma <- (0.011*A - B)/D
    wstar <- as.numeric(lambda*A)*wg + as.numeric(gamma*B)*wd
    mustar <- t(wstar) %*% R1
    stdstar <- sqrt(t(wstar) %*% S %*% wstar)

    #Plot results:
    plot(minStd, mu, type = "l", ylab = "mean", xlab = "Standard Deviation",
         main = "Efficient Frontier", col = "blue")
    points(stdg, mug, pch = 4, col = "blue")
    textxy(stdg, mug, labs = "Global")
    points(stdd, mud, pch = 8, col = "red")
    textxy(stdd, mud, labs = "Tangency")
    points(stdstar, mustar, pch = 5, col = "darkgreen")
    textxy(stdstar, mustar, labs = "Arbitray")

    #Output weights as a list:
    out <- list(wg, wd, wstar)
}
```

Here, we simply implement code for computing the global minimum variance, tangency, and arbitrary (with mean return = 0.01) portfolios using Eqs. (11-8) – (11-12). We can obtain the efficient frontier and its weights by issuing the following statements:

```
> source("./R/portfolioHelper.R")
> tickers <- c("XLE","XLF","XLI","XLK","XLU","XLY","XLP","XLV","XLB")
> wt <- getFrontierWeights(tickers)
```

This produces the output shown in Figure 11-2.

We can also obtain the weights for the global minimum variance portfolio:

```
> wt[[1]]
           [,1]
XLE  0.10075565
XLF -0.11069515
XLI -0.19349599
XLK  0.03058747
XLU  0.14371718
XLY  0.15659430
XLP  0.62964649
XLV  0.32565610
XLB -0.08276605
```

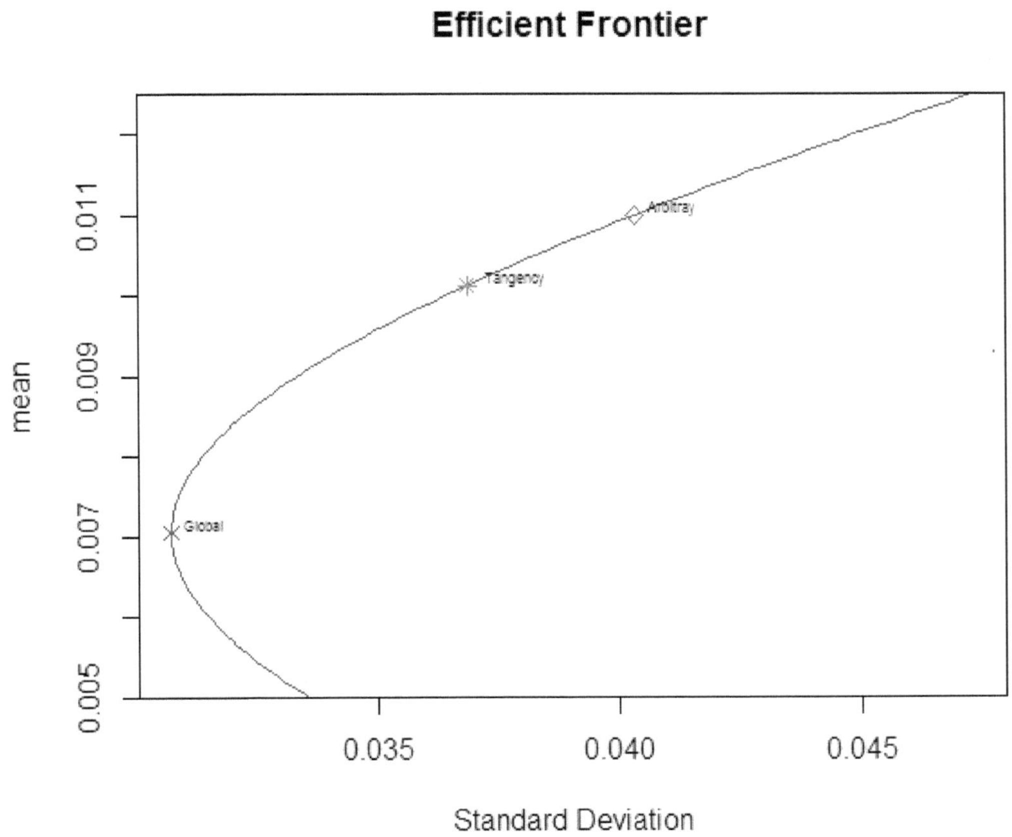


*Figure 11-2. Efficient frontier with global minimum variance, tangency, and arbitrary portfolios.*

Here are the weights for the tangency portfolio:

```
> wt[[2]]
           [,1]
XLE  0.23364168
XLF -0.47599830
XLI -0.05074008
XLK -0.32498165
XLU  0.06106536
XLY  0.67662253
XLP  0.54968322
XLV  0.49336991
XLB -0.16266268
```

The following are the weights for the arbitrary portfolio with the mean return = 0.01:

```
> wt[[3]]
           [,1]
XLE  0.27124931
XLF -0.57938153
XLI -0.01033920
XLK -0.42561008
```

```
XLU  0.03767434
XLY  0.82379399
XLP  0.52705309
XLV  0.54083403
XLB -0.18527395
```

You may notice that the above weights have some negative values, meaning that we allow the short-sell positions in our portfolio. The weights may also have some components whose absolute values are greater than one, indicating that the portfolio allows leveraging.

If the portfolio does not allow short sell, we need to impose the conditions in Eqs. 11-4 and 11.5. This will be the topic of next section: quadratic programming.

# Quadratic Programming

In the preceding section, we simply presented an overview of Markowitz's theory based on mean-variance portfolio optimization. In our manual implementation for the MPT model, we did not include the constraint in Eq. 11.5 that ensures only long positions in our portfolio. In order to apply various constraints to our portfolio, we need to use the quadratic programming (QP) approach.

## QP Model

Quadratic programming is an optimization problem wherein one either minimizes or maximizes a quadratic objective function of a finite number of decision variables subject to a finite number of linear inequality and/or equality constraints. A quadratic function of a finite number of variables $x = (x_1, x_2, \cdots, x_n)^T$ is any function of the form

$$f(x) = \alpha + \sum_{i=1}^{n} c_i x_i + \frac{1}{2}\sum_{i=1}^{n}\sum_{j=1}^{n} q_{ij} x_i x_j \qquad 11\text{-}13$$

Using matrix notation, the above expression becomes

$$f(x) = \alpha + c^T x + \frac{1}{2} x^T Q x \qquad 11\text{-}14$$

where

$$c = \begin{pmatrix} c_1 \\ c_2 \\ \vdots \\ c_n \end{pmatrix}, \quad Q = \begin{pmatrix} q_{11} & q_{12} & \cdots & q_{1n} \\ q_{21} & q_{22} & \cdots & q_{2n} \\ \vdots & \vdots & \ddots & \vdots \\ q_{n1} & q_{n2} & \cdots & q_{nn} \end{pmatrix}$$

The factor of one half preceding the quadratic term in the function $f$ is included for the sake of convenience since it simplifies the expressions for the first and second derivatives of $f$. We also assume that the matrix $Q$ is symmetric. Thus, the standard form of the QP model will be:

$$\text{minimize } c^T x + \frac{1}{2} x^T Q x, \quad \text{subject to } Ax \le b, \; x \ge 0 \qquad 11\text{-}15$$

Here, the decision variable $x$ is an $n$-dimensional column vector, Q is an $n \times n$ symmetric matrix, and the constraints are defined by an $m \times n$ $A$ matrix and an $m$-dimensional column vector $b$ of right-hand-side coefficients. We also assume that a feasible solution exists and that the constraint region is bounded.

When the objective function $f(x)$ is strictly convex for all feasible points, the problem has a unique local minimum that is also the global minimum. A sufficient condition to guarantee strictly convexity is for $Q$ to be positive definite.

## QP Solvers

We will not try to find solution for the QP problems manually; instead, we will use powerful R packages to do it. There are several R packages available to solve quadratic programming problems. Here, we will use the *quadprog* package.

The *quadprog* package contains a QP solver that implements the dual method of Goldfard and Idnani for solving QP problems of the standard form:

$$\text{min:} \ -c^T x + \frac{1}{2} x^T Q x, \qquad s.t. \ \ Ax \geq x_0 \qquad \text{11-16}$$

In order to use the *quadprog* package to solve the QP problems, we need to convert the QP problem specified in Eq.11-15 into the standard form (Eq. 11-19) for the solver.

The function *solve.QP* in the package is used to solve the QP problems. This function takes 6 arguments as its inputs: *Dmat, dvec, Amat, bvec, meq,* and *factorized. Dmat* is equivalent to the $Q$ matrix in 11-16; *dvec* corresponds to the $c^T$ vector; *Amat* to the $A$ matrix that defines the constraints; and *bvec* to the vector that holds the values of $x_0$. The *meq* argument indicates that the first *meq* constraints are treated as equality constraints and all further as inequality constraints (its default value is zero). Finally, the *factorized* argument is simply a logical flag, that is, if TRUE, it is passing $R^{-1}$(where $Q = R^T R$) instead of the matrix $Q$ in the argument *Dmat.*

Let us consider a simple example: that is, we want to minimize the following function:

$$f(x_1, x_2) = \frac{1}{2} x_1^2 + x_2^2 - x_1 x_2 - 2x_1 - 6x_2$$

subject to the following conditions:

$$x_1 + x_2 \leq 2, \quad -x_1 + 2x_2 \leq 2, \quad 2x_1 + x_2 \leq 3, \quad x_1 \geq 0, \quad x_2 \geq 0$$

We can easily extract corresponding coefficients in the matrix form as in Eq.11-16:

$$c = (2, 6), \quad Q = \begin{pmatrix} 1 & -1 \\ -1 & 2 \end{pmatrix}, \quad A = \begin{pmatrix} -1 & -1 \\ 1 & -2 \\ -2 & -1 \\ 1 & 0 \\ 0 & 1 \end{pmatrix}, \quad x0 = \begin{pmatrix} -2 \\ -2 \\ -3 \\ 0 \\ 0 \end{pmatrix}$$

Now, I will show you how to use the *solve.QP* function from the *quadprog* package to solve the QP problem specified in the above example.

First, enter the coefficient matrices:

```
> install_packages("quadprog")
```

```
> library(quadprog)
> c = c(2, 6)
> Q = matrix(c(1, -1, -1, 2), nrow = 2, ncol = 2, byrow = T)
> A = matrix(0, nrow = 5, ncol = 2)
> A[1,] = c(-1, -1)
> A[2,] = c( 1, -2)
> A[3,] = c(-2, -1)
> A[4,] = c( 1,  0)
> A[5,] = c( 0,  1)
> x0 = c(-2, -2, -3, 0, 0)
```

We can then use the *solve.QP* function to solve our QP problem:

```
> x <- solve.QP(Q, c, t(A), x0)
> x$solution
[1] 0.6666667 1.3333333
> x$value
[1] -8.222222
```

The solution to our QP problem is $x_1 = 0.6666667, x_2 = 1.3333333$, and the corresponding value of the quadratic function at the solution is $f(x_1, x_2) = -8.222222$.

## Portfolio Optimization Using QP Solver

Now, we can apply the QP solver to portfolio optimization problems. Suppose we create a portfolio that contains several stocks. We want to determine how much of each stock to include in our portfolio, that is, we want to calculate the portfolio weights.

Here, we will reformulate our portfolio optimization problem described in Eqs.11-2 – 11-5 using the standard form of the QP solver. To take into account the risk of deviations in our portfolio return, we define the quadratic term in the matrix form: $x^T Qx$, where $Q$ is the covariance matrix of the returns. To solve the portfolio allocation problem, we will try to determine the weight $x = (x_1, x_2, \cdots, x_n)$ so that the risk function is minimized. Additionally, we need to add more constraints to the model:

$$\text{min:}\ \ f(x) = x^T Qx \qquad \text{11-17a}$$

$$\sum_{i=1}^{n} x_i \mu_i \geq r_{min}, \quad \text{(total return limit)} \qquad \text{11-17b}$$

$$\sum_{i=1}^{n} x_i = 1, \quad \text{(Total weights normalized)} \qquad \text{11-17c}$$

$$x_i \leq x_0, \ \ i = 1,2, \cdots, n, \quad \text{(max allocation limit)} \qquad \text{11-17d}$$

$$x_i \geq 0, \ \ i = 1,2, \cdots, n, \quad \text{(no short sell)} \qquad \text{11-17e}$$

Here, we want to minimize the risk function *f*(*x*) subject to the conditions 11-17b – 11.17e. Condition 11-17b indicates that we require a minimum expected return from our portfolio. For example, we may demand a minimum expected monthly return of 1%. The condition in 11-17c is simply a weight normalization, i.e. we require the total weight be unity. In condition 11-17d, we set a maximum allocation limit (i.e. 30%), which is the maximum weight allowed for any one security (for reducing concentration). We can use this condition to avoid the positions with leverage. The last condition in 11-17e means that our portfolio does not allow the short-sell positions, and requires the weight for each security in our portfolio to be non-negative.

Now, we will implement the portfolio optimization problem described in Eqs.11-17a – 11-17e and use the QP solver to find corresponding solutions. Add a new function named *getPortfolioQP* to the *portfolioHelper.R* file. Here is the code for this function:

```
getPortfolioQP <- function(tickers, minRtn, maxAllocation){
  getSymbols(tickers, from = "2000-01-01", to= "2016-01-01", adjust = T)
  rtn <- na.omit(do.call(merge, lapply(tickers, FUN=function(x)
                                    monthlyReturn(Cl(get(x))))))
  colnames(rtn) <- tickers
  R1 <- colMeans(rtn)                #Get mean returns
  R1 <- matrix(R1, nrow = 1)         #Convert to mean matrix
  S <- cov(rtn)                      #Get covariance matrix
  n <- ncol(S)

  #Add equality condition first: Sum_i(x_i) = 1
  Amat <- matrix(1,nrow = n)
  bvec <- 1
  meq <- 1

  #Add non-equality condition: minimum return: Sum_i(x_i*mu_i) >= minRtn
  Amat <- cbind(Amat,t(R1))
  bvec <- c(bvec, minRtn)

  #Add max allocation to the constraints: x_i <= maxAllocation, i = 1,2,...,n
  Amat <- cbind(Amat, -diag(n))
  bvec <- c(bvec, rep(-maxAllocation, n))

  #Add no short-sell constraints: x_i >= 0, i = 1,2,...,n
  Amat <- cbind(Amat, diag(n))
  bvec <- c(bvec, rep(0, n))

  res <- solve.QP(Dmat = S, dvec = rep(0, n), Amat = Amat, bvec = bvec, meq = meq)
  return(res)
}
```

The preceding code is straightforward and easy to follow. Here, we will use an example to demonstrate how to apply this function to portfolio optimization problems. The portfolio used here is the same as that used in the preceding example. First, we consider a portfolio with a positive total return (*minRtn* = 0) and without limitation on maximum allocation (*maxAllocation* = 1):

```
> source("./R/portfolioHelper.R")
> require(quadprog)
> tickers <- c("XLE","XLF","XLI","XLK","XLU","XLY","XLP","XLV","XLB")
> gp <- getPortfolioQP(tickers, minRtn = 0, maxAllocation = 1)
> gp$solution
[1]  1.427103e-02  1.793169e-17 -5.497970e-17
[4]  0.000000e+00  1.687945e-01  3.858422e-19
[7]  5.576936e-01  2.592409e-01  1.274330e-17
```

Note that we set the constraints that all the weights sum up to unity (Eq.11-17c) and that the weights are positive (Eq.11-17e). We also implicitly set the constraint on the solution that has no leverage (i.e. no weight component has an absolute value greater than unity).

Note from the solution that the weight for XLP is about 0.5577, that is, we put 55.77% of our portfolio into XLP. While assets XLF, XLI, XLK, XLY, and XLB have zero weight. From the risk management's point of view, we may not be comfortable with such a heavy allocation on a single asset. We can impose a constraint on the maximum allocation to 20%, i.e. no single asset in our portfolio takes up more than 20%:

```
> gp <- getPortfolioQP(tickers, minRtn = 0, maxAllocation = 0.2)
> gp$solution
[1] 1.602739e-01 2.816926e-19 0.000000e+00
[4] 3.972606e-02 2.000000e-01 2.000000e-01
[7] 2.000000e-01 2.000000e-01 1.117950e-17
```

# PortfolioAnalytics Package

The *PortfolioAnalytics* package provides numerical solutions for portfolio problems with complex constraints and object sets. It implements a common interface to specify constraints and objectives that can be solved by any supported solver. Currently supported optimization methods include random portfolios, differential evolution, particle swarm optimization, generalized simulated annealing, as well as linear and quadratic programming solvers.

## Standard Deviation as Risk

The *PortfolioAnalytics* package requires the following steps to solve a portfolio optimization problem: initializing the portfolio, adding the constraints, and adding the objectives, which can be achieved using the functions from the package: *portforlio.spec*, *add.constraint*, and *add.objective*, respectively.

Let us consider an example. First, we need install various packages and load them into R:

```
library(PortfolioAnalytics)

#The following packages contain the optimzation algorithms used by
#PortfolioAnalytics:
library(ROI)
library(ROI.plugin.quadprog)
library(ROI.plugin.glpk)
```

Next, we need to load the monthly return data for our portfolio, which is the same as in preceding example:

```
> tickers <- c("XLE","XLF","XLI","XLK","XLU","XLY","XLP","XLV","XLB")
> getSymbols(tickers, from = "2000-01-01", to= "2016-01-01", adjust = T)
> rtn <- na.omit(do.call(merge, lapply(tickers, FUN=function(x)
                                       monthlyReturn(Cl(get(x))))))
> colnames(rtn) <- tickers
```

Next, we need to set up an initial portfolio with some basic constraints:

```
> init = portfolio.spec(assets = tickers)
> init <- add.constraint(portfolio = init, type = "full_investment")
> init <- add.constraint(portfolio = init, type = "long_only")
```

Here, we add the full-investment constraint, which is a special case of the leverage constraint that the weights must sum to unity. The *long_only* constraint is a special case of a box constraint where the lower bound of the weights for each asset is equal to zero and the upper bound is equal to unity.

Next, we need to create a new portfolio object:

```
> minSD <- add.objective(portfolio = init, type = "risk", name = "StdDev")
```

Note that we assign a new name, *minSD*, for our portfolio. This way, we can reuse our *init* portfolio for other new portfolio optimization problems, which is useful for testing multiple portfolios with different objectives using the same constraints as the constraints only need to be specified once and several new portfolios can be created using an initial portfolio object.

The *name* argument in the *add.objective* function can be any valid R function. The *PortfolioAnalytics* provides several functions that can be specified as the name argument, including *StdDev* (standard deviation), *ES* (expected shortfall), *ETL* (expected tail loss), *CVaR* (conditional value at risk), etc. We see that the *add.constraint* and *add.objective* functions are very flexible and modular so that we can add constraints and objectives to portfolio objects easily.

Now that we have our portfolio set up with desired constraints and objectives, we can then use the *optimize.portfolio* function to run the optimization:

```
> minSD.optim <- optimize.portfolio(R = rtn, portfolio = minSD,
                                    optimize_method = "ROI", trace = T)
```

Here, we use the *ROI* (R optimization infrastructure) as our optimization method, which includes linear and quadratic programming solvers. We can also use other valid solvers such as *DEoptim* (different evolution), *GenSA* (generalized simulated annealing), *pso* (particle swarm optimization), and *random portfolios*. Now, we can examine the solution from the ROI solver:

```
> minSD.optim
***********************************
PortfolioAnalytics Optimization
***********************************

Call:
optimize.portfolio(R = rtn, portfolio = minSD, optimize_method = "ROI",
    trace = T)

Optimal Weights:
   XLE    XLF    XLI    XLK    XLU    XLY    XLP    XLV    XLB
0.0143 0.0000 0.0000 0.0000 0.1688 0.0000 0.5577 0.2592 0.0000

Objective Measure:
 StdDev
0.03204
```

Note that the above results are identical to those obtained using the QP solver for the portfolio without maximum allocation limit in the preceding section.

We can also set the maximum allocation limit to 20% by changing our initial portfolio:

```
> init1 = portfolio.spec(assets = tickers)
> init1 <- add.constraint(portfolio = init1, type = "full_investment")
> init1 <- add.constraint(portfolio = init1, type = "box", min = 0, max = 0.2)
```

```
>
> minSD1 <- add.objective(portfolio = init1, type = "risk", name = "StdDev")
> minSD1.optim <- optimize.portfolio(R = rtn, portfolio = minSD1,
                                     optimize_method = "ROI", trace = T)
> minSD1.optim
***********************************
PortfolioAnalytics Optimization
***********************************

Call:
optimize.portfolio(R = rtn, portfolio = minSD1, optimize_method = "ROI",
    trace = T)

Optimal Weights:
   XLE    XLF    XLI    XLK    XLU    XLY    XLP    XLV    XLB
0.1603 0.0000 0.0000 0.0397 0.2000 0.2000 0.2000 0.2000 0.0000

Objective Measure:
 StdDev
0.03601
```

The above results are also identical with those obtained using the QP solver directly in the preceding section.

# Expected Shortfall as Risk

In classical Markowitz mean-variance portfolio optimization, we optimize the portfolios by minimizing variance (or standard deviation). In the distribution of portfolio returns, variance is a double edged blade: there is a downside (portfolio loss) and an upside (portfolio gain) to the variance distribution. Minimizing the variance penalizes for both the downside and the upside of the distribution. Whereas the ES, ETL or CVaR method optimizes portfolio and only penalizes for the loss, not the gain in the portfolio return distribution. Thus, this method is usually a better risk measure because it describes a downside risk measure.

In this section, we will use *ES* as our risk measure. We can reuse the initial portfolio object created in the preceding section:

First, we want to minimize the risk:

```
> meanES <- add.objective(portfolio = init, type = "risk", name = "ES")
```

Next, we want to achieve the maximum possible return:

```
> meanES <- add.objective(portfolio = meanES, type = "return", name = "mean")
```

We can then find solution using the ROI solver:

```
> meanES.optim <- optimize.portfolio(R = rtn, portfolio = meanES,
                                     optimize_method = "ROI", trace = TRUE)
> meanES.optim
***********************************
PortfolioAnalytics Optimization
***********************************

Call:
optimize.portfolio(R = rtn, portfolio = meanES, optimize_method = "ROI",
```

```
    trace = TRUE)

Optimal Weights:
   XLE    XLF    XLI    XLK    XLU    XLY    XLP    XLV    XLB
0.1347 0.0000 0.0000 0.0000 0.0000 0.1139 0.5531 0.1983 0.0000

Objective Measure:
    mean
0.006837

     ES
0.07851
```

Similarly, we can perform optimization for our portfolio with the maximum allocation limit (20%):

```
> meanES1 <- add.objective(portfolio = init1, type = "risk", name = "ES")
> meanES1 <- add.objective(portfolio = meanES1, type = "return", name = "mean")
> meanES1.optim <- optimize.portfolio(R = rtn, portfolio = meanES1,
                                      optimize_method = "ROI", trace = TRUE)
> meanES1.optim
***********************************
PortfolioAnalytics Optimization
***********************************

Call:
optimize.portfolio(R = rtn, portfolio = meanES1, optimize_method = "ROI",
    trace = TRUE)

Optimal Weights:
XLE XLF XLI XLK XLU XLY XLP XLV XLB
0.2 0.0 0.0 0.0 0.2 0.2 0.2 0.2 0.0

Objective Measure:
    mean
0.006937

     ES
0.08838
```

# Efficient Frontier

We can also create efficient frontiers using the *PortfolioAnalytics* package easily. The package also provides various visualization tools for optimal portfolios. For instance, we can use the *chart.Weights* function to plot the weights of the optimal portfolio. We can extract efficient frontiers from *optimize.portfolio* objects or create them from a portfolio object, and then chart efficient frontiers in risk-reward space with *chart.EfficientFrontier*. We can also plot the weight along the efficient frontier using the *chart.EF.Weights* function.

In the preceding section, we create the *init* portfolio object. Here, we can reuse it to create the efficient frontier:

```
> ef.create = create.EfficientFrontier(rtn, portfolio = init,  type = "mean-ES",
                                       match.col = "ES")
```

Of course, we can also extract the efficient frontier directly from the *meanES.optim* object:

```
> ef.extract <- extractEfficientFrontier(meanES.optim, match.col ="ES")
```

As expected, *ef.create* and *ef.extract* are identical. We can print out the weights of the 25 portfolios (default) on the efficient frontier:

```
> summary(ef.create, digits = 6)
**************************************************
PortfolioAnalytics Efficient Frontier
**************************************************

Call:
create.EfficientFrontier(R = rtn, portfolio = init, type = "mean-ES",
    n.portfolios = 25, match.col = "ES")

Efficient Frontier Points: 25

Weights along the efficient frontier:
        XLE XLF XLI XLK      XLU      XLY      XLP      XLV XLB
1  0.000000   0   0   0 0.084917 0.051743 0.563732 0.299608   0
2  0.025629   0   0   0 0.056593 0.064502 0.574764 0.278512   0
3  0.055555   0   0   0 0.033236 0.073092 0.576362 0.261754   0
4  0.085482   0   0   0 0.009879 0.081682 0.577959 0.244997   0
5  0.112723   0   0   0 0.000000 0.096738 0.568428 0.222110   0
6  0.137995   0   0   0 0.000000 0.116534 0.550740 0.194731   0
7  0.161846   0   0   0 0.000000 0.138339 0.532321 0.167495   0
8  0.172646   0   0   0 0.000000 0.178595 0.507178 0.141581   0
9  0.204115   0   0   0 0.000000 0.189629 0.492683 0.113573   0
10 0.212333   0   0   0 0.000000 0.233536 0.466209 0.087921   0
11 0.220551   0   0   0 0.000000 0.277444 0.439736 0.062270   0
12 0.228769   0   0   0 0.000000 0.321351 0.413262 0.036618   0
13 0.245644   0   0   0 0.000000 0.351710 0.402646 0.000000   0
14 0.312503   0   0   0 0.000000 0.316804 0.370693 0.000000   0
15 0.357133   0   0   0 0.000000 0.313033 0.329833 0.000000   0
16 0.378005   0   0   0 0.000000 0.342542 0.279453 0.000000   0
17 0.397200   0   0   0 0.000000 0.374400 0.228400 0.000000   0
18 0.413777   0   0   0 0.000000 0.409924 0.176299 0.000000   0
19 0.430354   0   0   0 0.000000 0.445448 0.124198 0.000000   0
20 0.446931   0   0   0 0.000000 0.480972 0.072096 0.000000   0
21 0.463509   0   0   0 0.000000 0.516496 0.019995 0.000000   0
22 0.560208   0   0   0 0.000000 0.439792 0.000000 0.000000   0
23 0.706805   0   0   0 0.000000 0.293195 0.000000 0.000000   0
24 0.853403   0   0   0 0.000000 0.146597 0.000000 0.000000   0
25 1.000000   0   0   0 0.000000 0.000000 0.000000 0.000000   0

Risk and return metrics along the efficient frontier:
       mean       ES      out
1  0.006609 0.077517 0.077517
2  0.006656 0.077573 0.077573
3  0.006703 0.077720 0.077720
4  0.006749 0.077868 0.077868
5  0.006796 0.078161 0.078161
6  0.006843 0.078600 0.078600
7  0.006890 0.079322 0.079322
8  0.006937 0.080239 0.080239
9  0.006983 0.081301 0.081301
10 0.007030 0.082526 0.082526
```

```
11 0.007077 0.083752 0.083752
12 0.007124 0.084977 0.084977
13 0.007171 0.086350 0.086350
14 0.007218 0.088429 0.088429
15 0.007264 0.090625 0.090625
16 0.007311 0.092850 0.092850
17 0.007358 0.095365 0.095365
18 0.007405 0.098450 0.098450
19 0.007452 0.101535 0.101535
20 0.007498 0.104620 0.104620
21 0.007545 0.107706 0.107706
22 0.007592 0.112296 0.112296
23 0.007639 0.119381 0.119381
24 0.007686 0.127338 0.127338
25 0.007732 0.136450 0.136450
```

Now, we can plot the efficient frontier using the *chart.EfficientFrontier* function:

```
> chart.EfficientFrontier(ef.create, match.col = "ES", xlim = c(0.07,0.15),
                          ylim=c(0.006,0.008), type="l")
```

This produces the output shown in Figure 11-3.

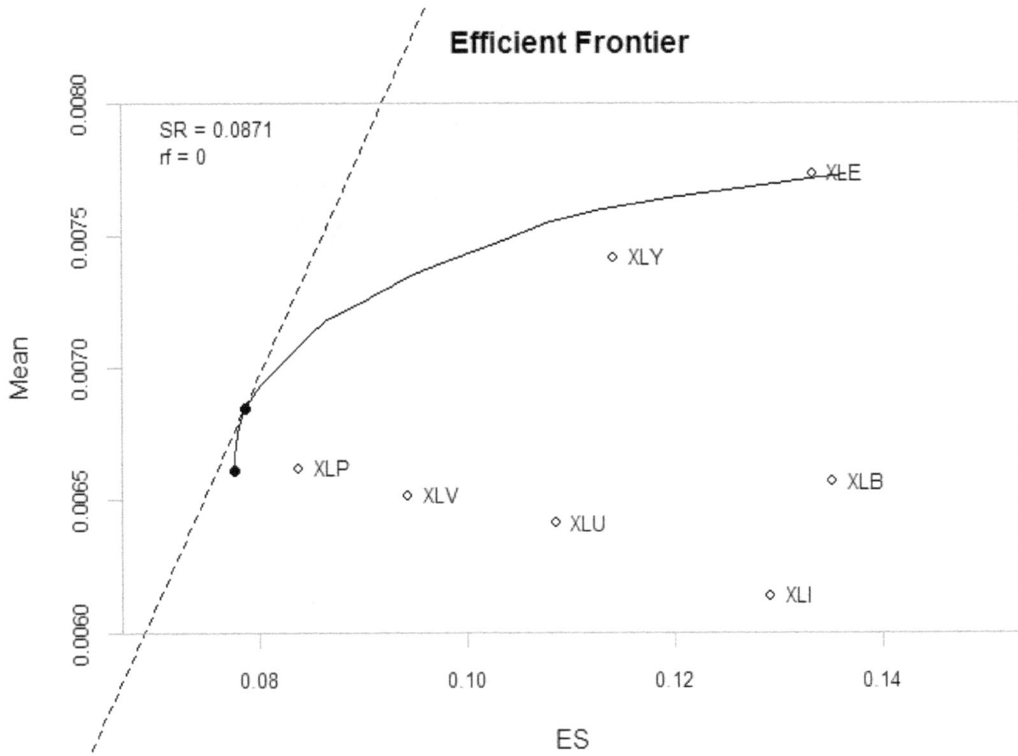


*Figure 11-3. Efficient frontier of an optimal mean-ES portfolio for SPRD ETFs.*

In this chart, the efficient frontier is the convex curve drawn with a solid line. The dashed line is created by taking the tangent to the efficient frontier starting from the risk-free rate. This is the capital allocation line and the locus of the portfolios that can be built linearly combining the risk-free asset with the tangent portfolio on the efficient frontier. If there is no leverage, the optimal portfolios that include the risk-free assets are those that lie on the straight segment between the origin (0, 0) and the tangency point on the efficient frontier. If the investment in risk-free asset is not allowed, all optimal portfolios lie on the efficient frontier.

We can also plot the weights by asset along the efficient frontier:

```
> chart.EF.Weights(ef, main= "Weights on the Efficient Frontier", match.col="ES")
```

This produces the output shown in Figure 11-4.

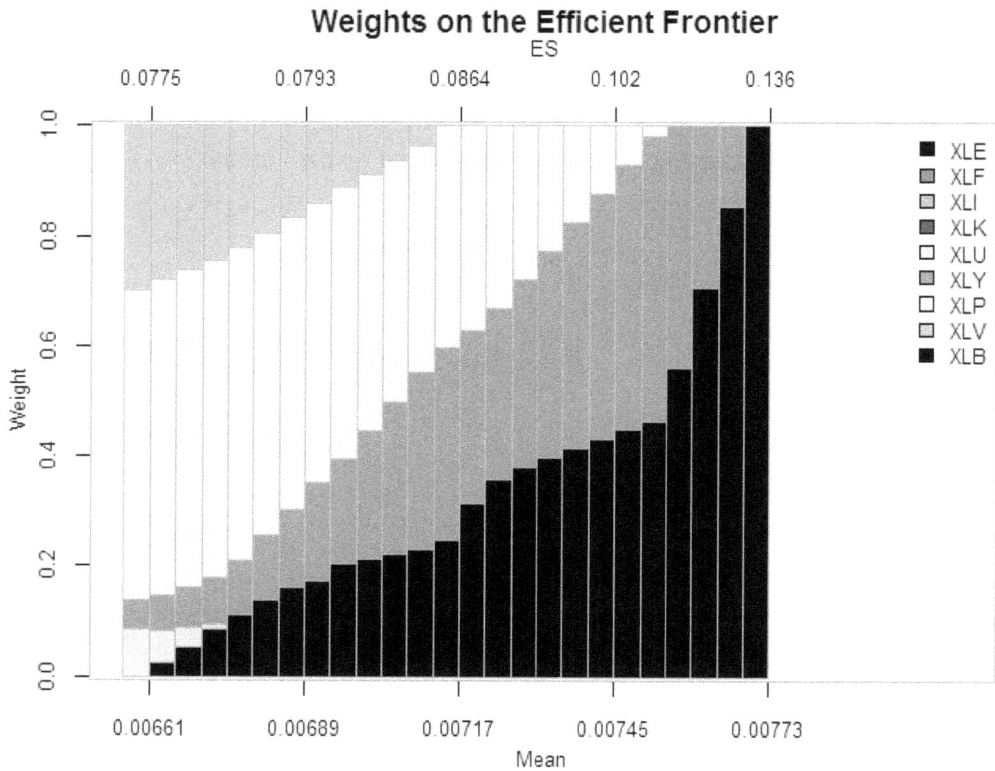


*Figure 11-4. Weights on the efficient frontier.*

This chart shows the weight on the vertical axis, the mean return on the lower horizontal axis, and the expected shortfall on the upper horizontal axis. Each column represents one of the 25 portfolios on the efficient frontier and the colored segments in each column represent individual asset as defined in the legend.

We can also use the *plot* function to generate a chart of the optimal weights and the optimal portfolio on risk-return space:

```
> plot(meanES.optim, risk.col = "ES", return.col = "mean", chart.assets = T)
```

This generates the output shown in Figure 11-5.

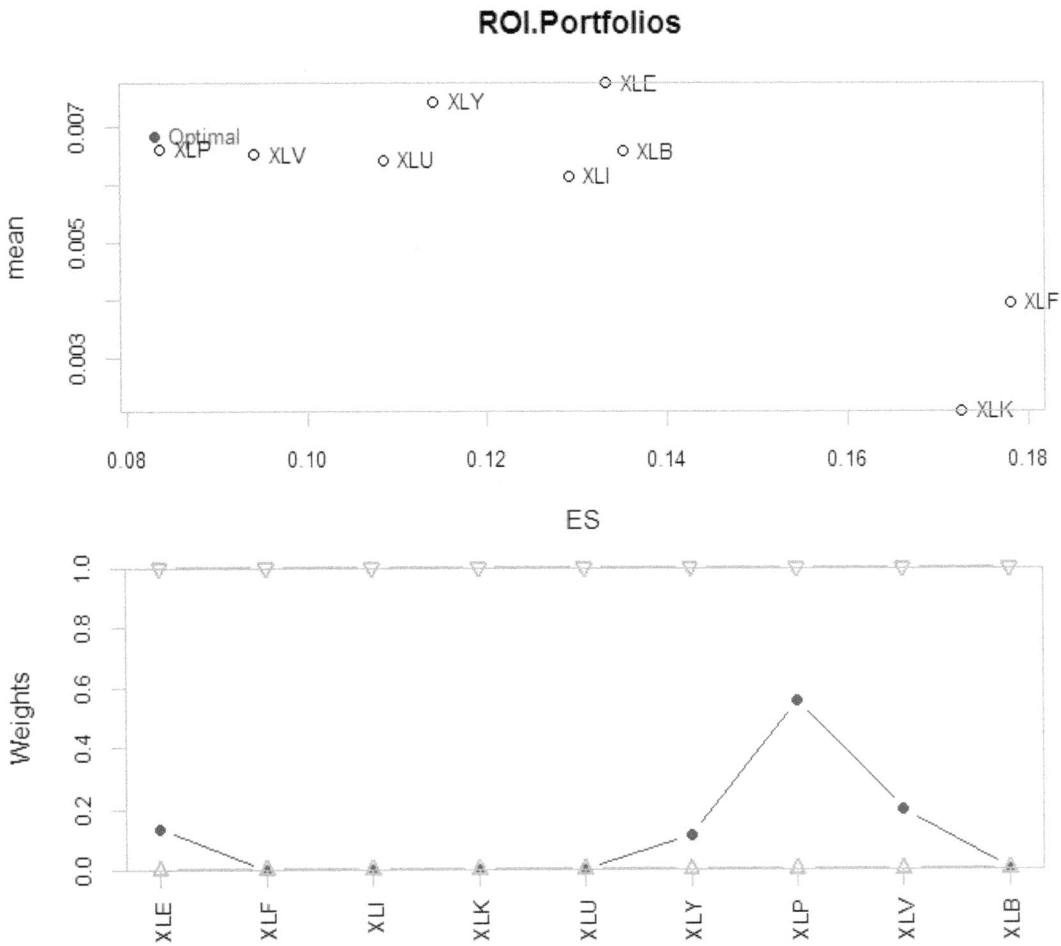


*Figure 11-5. Optimal portfolio (top) and optimal weights (bottom) for SPRD ETFs.*

Note how our optimal portfolio is selected: the asset XLP has more weight in the portfolio since it is closer to the optimal point in the risk-return space. XLF and XLK have zero weight because they are far away from the optimal point.

Now, we can examine whether or not our optimal portfolio outperforms the benchmark ETF: SPY. We already knew the weights for our optimal mean-ES portfolio (without allocation limit):

```
Optimal Weights:
   XLE    XLF    XLI    XLK    XLU    XLY    XLP    XLV    XLB
0.1347 0.0000 0.0000 0.0000 0.0000 0.1139 0.5531 0.1983 0.0000
```

We can then calculate the monthly return for our optimal portfolio:

```
> rtn.portfolio <- 0.1347*rtn$XLE + 0.1139*rtn$XLY + 0.5531*rtn$XLP + 0.1983*rtn$XLV
```

We can obtain the monthly return for SPY using the following code:

```
> getSymbols("SPY", from = "2000-01-01", to = "2016-01-01", adjust = T)
> rtn.spy <- na.omit(monthlyReturn(Cl(SPY)))
```

We can compare the cumulative returns of our optimal portfolio with SPY by plotting them on the same chart:

```
> plot(cumsum(rtn.portfolio), minor.ticks = F, col = "blue", ylim = c(-0.5, 1.4),
       main = "P&L for the optimal portfolio and SPY", ylab = "Cumulative returns")
> lines(cumsum(rtn.spy), col = "red")
> legend("topleft", c("Optimal portfolio", "SPY"), lty = c(1, 1),
         col = c("blue", "red"))
```

This produces the output shown in Figure 11-6.

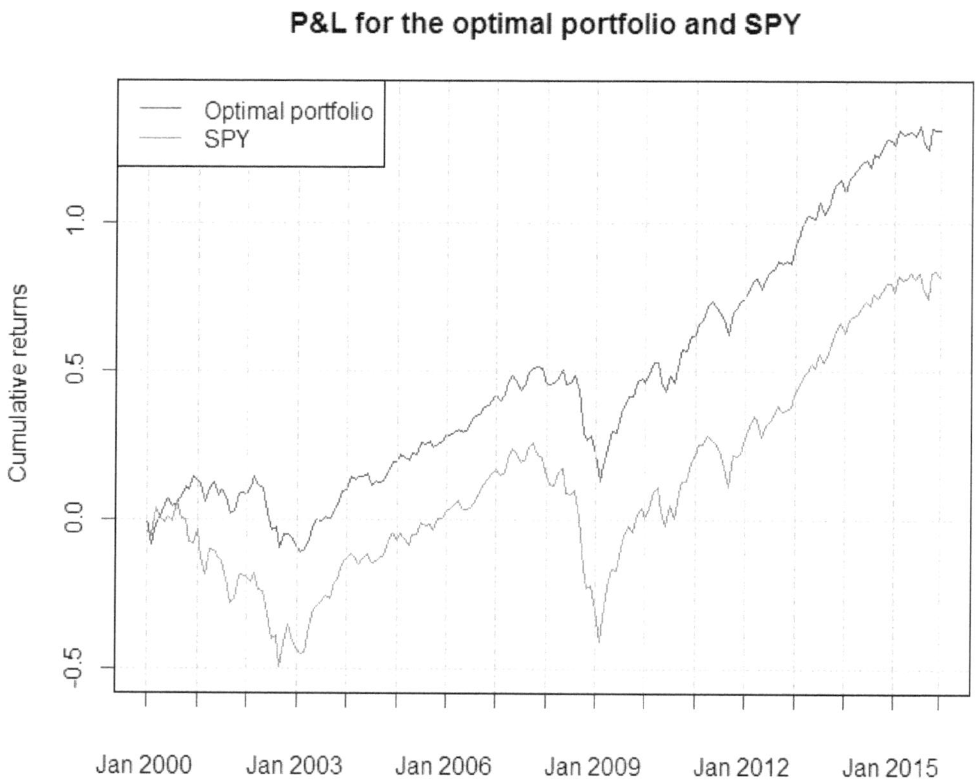


*Figure 11-6. P&L for our optimal portfolio and SPY.*

This result shows that our optimal portfolio does outperform SPY. Considering the fact that this is just a simple buy-and-hold portfolio, it is significant to have such a performance relative to SPY.

# Complex Portfolios

In the preceding sections, we discussed how to apply the QP solvers and the *PortfolioAnalytics* package to optimize portfolios that have simple constraints and simple objectives. In this section, we will demonstrate how to apply the *PortfolioAnalytics* package to some more complex portfolios. Specifically, we will consider market-neutral portfolios and portfolio rebalancing.

## Market Neutral Portfolios

Here, we consider a portfolio that contains nine SPRD ETF, which is the same as we have used in preceding examples. However, our objective is to maximize the portfolio return and minimize the portfolio standard deviation subject to market neutral (or dollar neutral) conditions. Now, our portfolio allows both the long and short positions, and the value of the long positions is offset equally by the value of the short positions. The market neutral strategy tries to make profit from both increasing or decreasing prices in the market.

First, load the monthly return data for our portfolio:

```
> tickers <- c("XLE","XLF","XLI","XLK","XLU","XLY","XLP","XLV","XLB")
> getSymbols(tickers, from = "2000-01-01", to = "2016-01-01", adjust = T)
> rtn <- na.omit(do.call(merge, lapply(tickers, FUN = function(x)
                                        monthlyReturn(Cl(get(x))))))
> colnames(rtn) <- tickers
```

We can then initialize our market-neutral portfolio:

```
> portfolio.mn <- portfolio.spec(tickers)
```

Add market neutral constraint: $\sum_{i=1}^{n} x_i = 0$. Here, we set a small range around zero for computation tolerance:

```
> portfolio.mn <- add.constraint(portfolio.mn, type = "weight_sum",
                                 min_sum = -0.01, max_sum = 0.01)
```

Add a box constraint on weights such that any single asset cannot have a weight of greater than 20% or less than $-20\%$:

```
> portfolio.mn <- add.constraint(portfolio.mn, type = "box", min = -0.2, max = 0.2)
```

Next, we specify our objectives: maximizing portfolio return with a target of 0.0015 and minimizing portfolio standard deviation (risk) with a target of 0.015:

```
> portfolio.mn.SD <- add.objective(portfolio.mn, type = "return", name = "mean",
                                   target = 0.0015)
> portfolio.mn.SD <- add.objective(portfolio.mn.SD, type="risk", name="StdDev",
                                   target=0.015)
```

We then create 10,000 random portfolios and run the optimization:

```
> set.seed(1234)
> rp <- random_portfolios(portfolio = portfolio.mn, permutations = 10000,
                          rp_method = "sample")
> optim.mn <- optimize.portfolio(rtn, portfolio.mn.SD, optimize_method = "random",
                                 rp = rp, trace = T)
```

Here, we use the "*sample*" method to generate random portfolios. This is the most flexible method that can generate portfolios to satisfy box, group, position limit, and leverage exposure constraints.

We can examine the output:

```
> optim.mn
***********************************
PortfolioAnalytics Optimization
***********************************

Call:
```

```
optimize.portfolio(R = rtn, portfolio = portfolio.mn.SD, optimize_method = "random",
    trace = TRUE, rp = rp)

Optimal Weights:
   XLE    XLF    XLI    XLK    XLU    XLY    XLP    XLV    XLB
 0.194 -0.116  0.042 -0.188 -0.152  0.156  0.170 -0.132  0.030

Objective Measures:
    mean
0.001551

StdDev
 0.015
```

These results meet our targets (mean return >= 0.0015 and *StdDev* <= 0.015). We can calculate the total weight using the following command:

```
> sum(optim.mn$weights)
[1] 0.004
```

which is almost zero, indicating that our optimal portfolio is indeed market neutral.

We can also plot the optimal portfolio and corresponding weights:

```
> plot(optim.mn, main = "Market Neutral Portfolio", risk.col = "StdDev",
       neighbors = 5)
```

This produces the output shown in Figure 11-7.

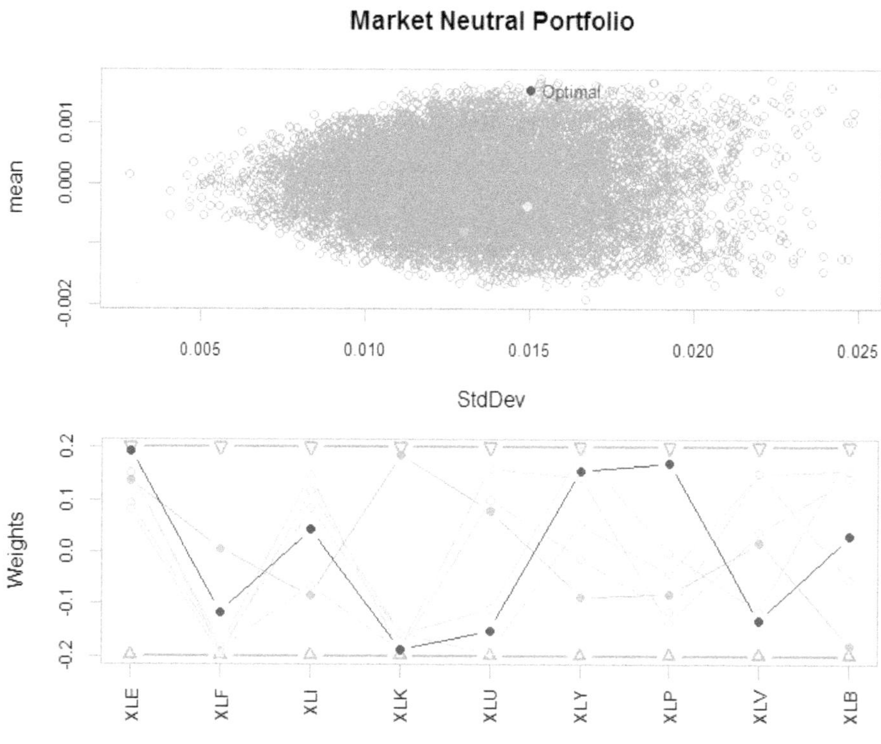


*Figure 11-7. Random portfolios (top) and optimal weights (bottom) for SPRD ETFs.*

Finally, we can calculate the returns for our optimal portfolio. Add a new helper function named *getWeightedReturn* to the *portfolioHelper.R* file. Here is the code for this function:

```
getWeightedReturn <- function(rtn, wt){
  df <- data.frame(Date = index(rtn), coredata(rtn))
  r1 <-  cbind(df[1], Map(`*`, df[-1], wt))
  r2 <- rowSums(r1[-1])
  r3 <- data.frame(Date = index(rtn), Return = r3)
  r4 <- xts(r3[,-1], order.by = r3[,1])
  colnames(r4) <- "Return"
  return(r4)
}
```

This function takes the original returns and weights as input arguments and the output is the returns for our optimal portfolio. We can then use this function to calculate the returns:

```
> source("./R/portfolioHelper.R")
> wt <- c(0.194, -0.116, 0.042, -0.188, -0.152, 0.156, 0.170, -0.132, 0.030)
> rtn.mn <- getWeightedReturn(rtn, wt)
> plot(cumsum(rtn.mn), minor.ticks = F, col = "blue",
       main = "Return for Optimal Portfolio")
```

This produces the output shown in Figure 11-8.

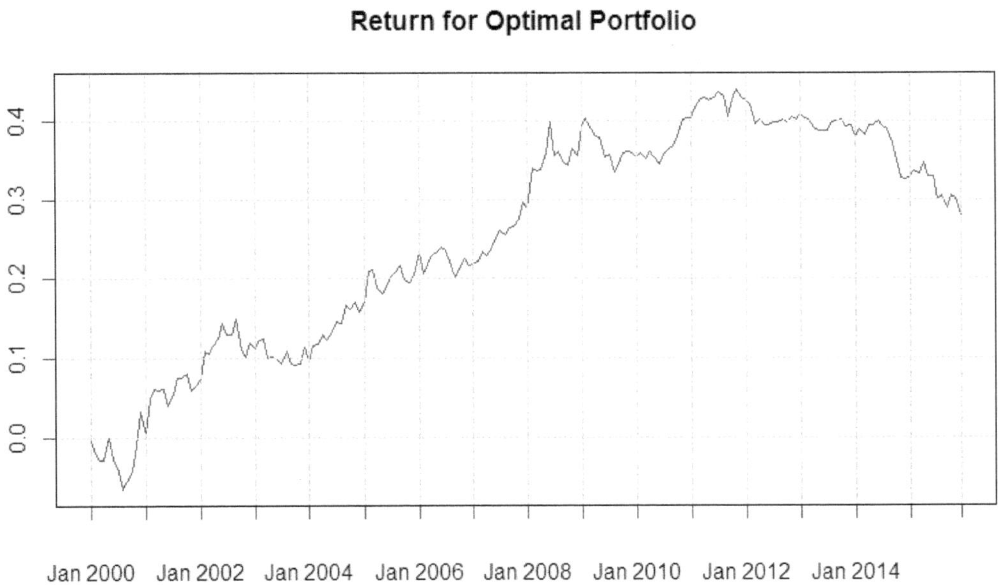


*Figure 11-8. Return for optimal market-neutral portfolio.*

## Portfolio Rebalancing

In the preceding examples, we established asset allocation with a constant weight for each asset in the portfolio. However, at the end of the year, we may find that the weight of each asset class in our portfolio has changed. This is because the fact that over the course of the year, the market value of each security within our portfolio earned a different return, resulting in a change in weights. Portfolio rebalancing is simply like a tune-up for our car: it follows individuals to keep their risk level in check and minimize risk.

Rebalancing is the process of buying and selling portions of the portfolio in order to set the weight of each asset back to its original state. In addition, if our investment strategy has changed, we can use rebalancing to readjust the weight of each security in the portfolio to fulfill a newly devised asset allocation.

We usually also require rebalancing for running portfolio optimization at specified time periods. Running the portfolio optimization with periodic rebalancing can help refine the constraints and objectives by evaluating the out of sample performance of the portfolio based on historical data. Thus, we can backtest portfolio optimization with rebalancing for each of the rolling windows using the out of sample data set.

Here, we consider a portfolio that contains nine SPRD ETF, which is the same as we have used in preceding examples. Our objective is to maximize the portfolio return and minimize the portfolio expected shortfall subject to long only condition and allocation limit to 20% for each single asset. We have discussed this portfolio optimization problem previously; we will now apply it to portfolio rebalancing.

We first create our portfolio object:

```
> init1 = portfolio.spec(assets = tickers)
> init1 <- add.constraint(portfolio = init1, type = "full_investment")
> init1 <- add.constraint(portfolio = init1, type = "box", min = 0, max = 0.2)
> meanES1 <- add.objective(portfolio = init1, type = "risk", name = "ES")
> meanES1 <- add.objective(portfolio = meanES1, type = "return", name = "mean")
```

Next, we need to set rebalancing parameter. Here, we want to perform a quarterly rebalancing with a five-year training period and a rolling window size of four years:

```
> es.reb <- optimize.portfolio.rebalancing(rtn, meanES1, optimize_method = "ROI",
     rebalance_on = "quarters", training_period = 60, rolling_window = 48)
> es.reb
**************************************************
PortfolioAnalytics Optimization with Rebalancing
**************************************************

Call:
optimize.portfolio.rebalancing(R = rtn, portfolio = meanES1,
    optimize_method = "ROI", rebalance_on = "quarters", training_period = 60,
    rolling_window = 48)

Number of rebalancing dates:  45
First rebalance date:
[1] "2004-12-31 EST"
Last rebalance date:
[1] "2015-12-31 EST"

Annualized Portfolio Rebalancing Return:
[1] 0.09918142

Annualized Portfolio Standard Deviation:
[1] 0.1271369
```

Note that our original return data starting from 1/1/2000, while the first rebalance data is 12/31/2004. This is because we use the first five-year data as the training data set. Here, we want to do portfolio rebalancing every quarter, so we need to adjust the weights quarterly. To this end, we can plot the weights over time to check how the weights change with time:

```
> chart.Weights(es.reb)
```

This produces the output shown in Figure 11-9.

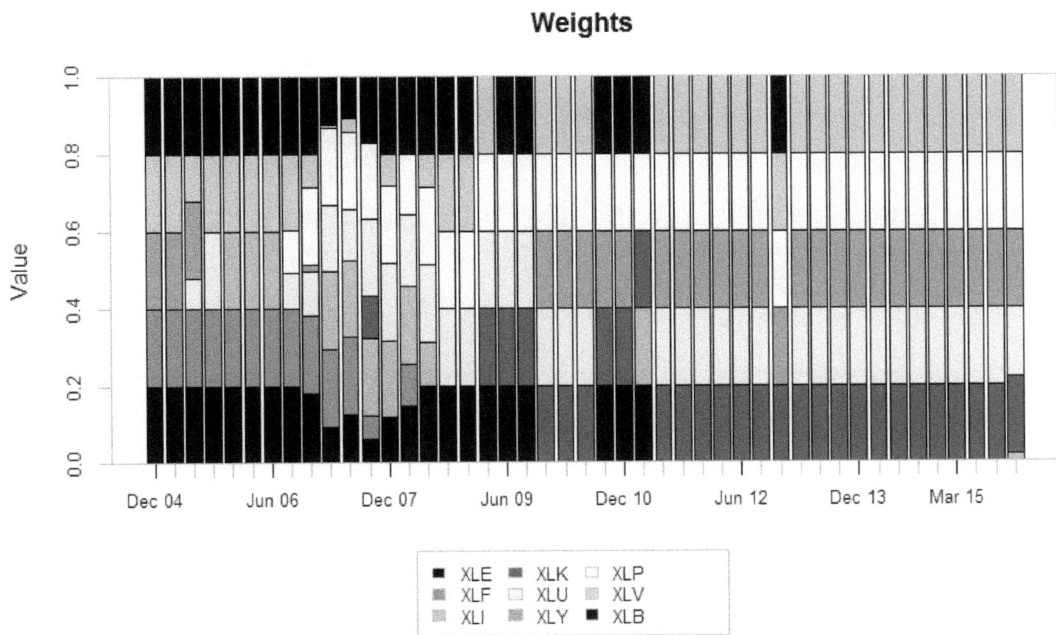


*Figure 11-9. Weights through time for portfolio rebalancing.*

Using these weights, we can easily rebalance the portfolio quarterly. More importantly, we calculate the weights for this quarter using only the historical data prior to this quarter, that is, our optimal portfolio with rebalancing is for the out of sample data set.

Now, we can compare the return of our optimal portfolio with the benchmark SPY:

```
> library(PerformanceAnalytics)
> es.rtn <- summary(es.reb)$portfolio_returns
> es.rtn$SPY <- rtn.spy["2005-01-01::"]
> colnames(es.rtn) <- c("Portfolio", "SPY")
> charts.PerformanceSummary(es.rtn, geometric = F)
```

This produces the output shown in Figure 11-10.

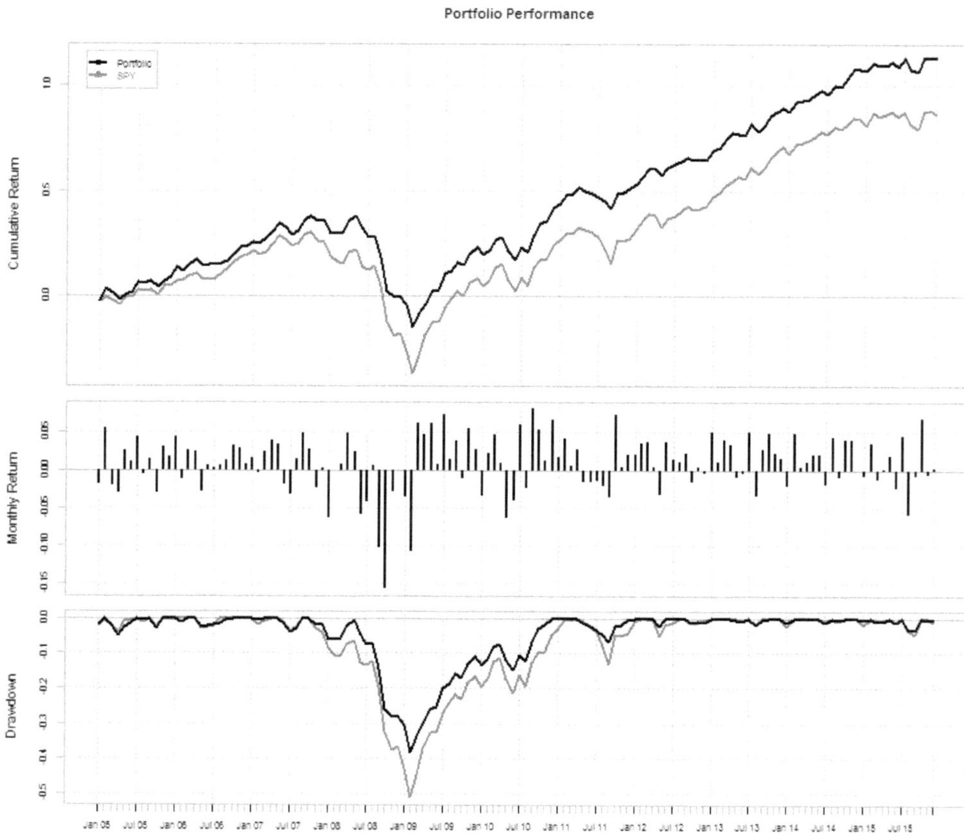


*Figure 11-10. Portfolio performance relative to the benchmark of SPY.*

Note that our optimal portfolio with rebalancing indeed outperforms SPY.

---

There are several important areas in quantitative finance that are not covered in this book, including high-frequency trading and real-time automatic order execution. I will leave these topics to my other book, *Practical C# for Real-Time Trading System*.

# Index

CPSIA information can be obtained
at www.ICGtesting.com
Printed in the USA
BVHW060936211221
624597BV00011B/301

9 780979 372575